Creative Spaces for Creative Ideas

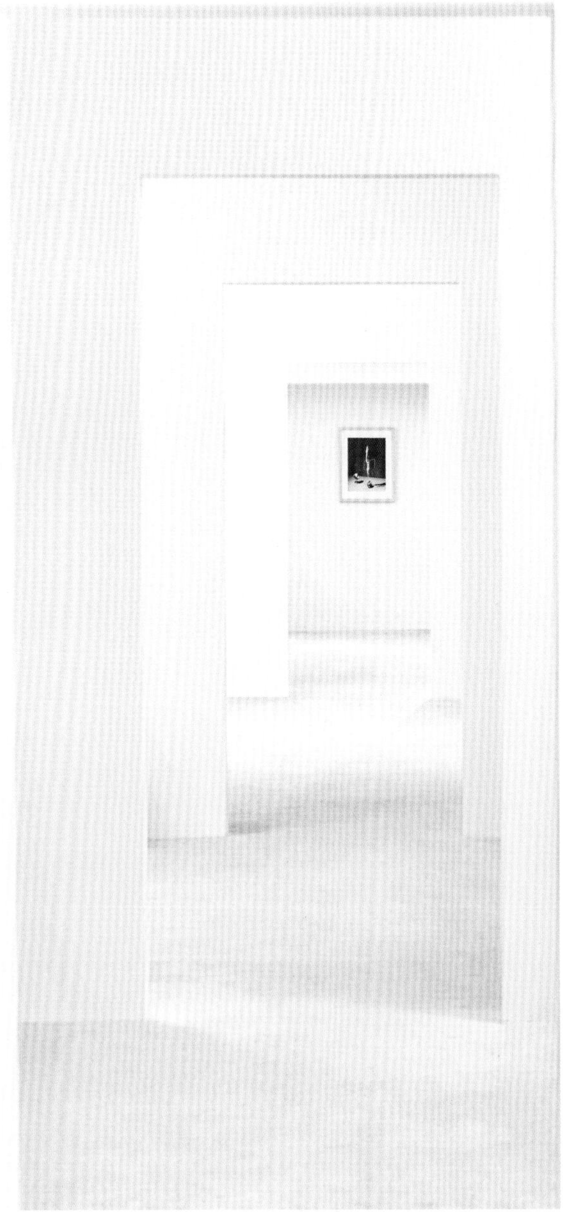

Creative Spaces for Creative Ideas

images
Publishing

CONTENTS

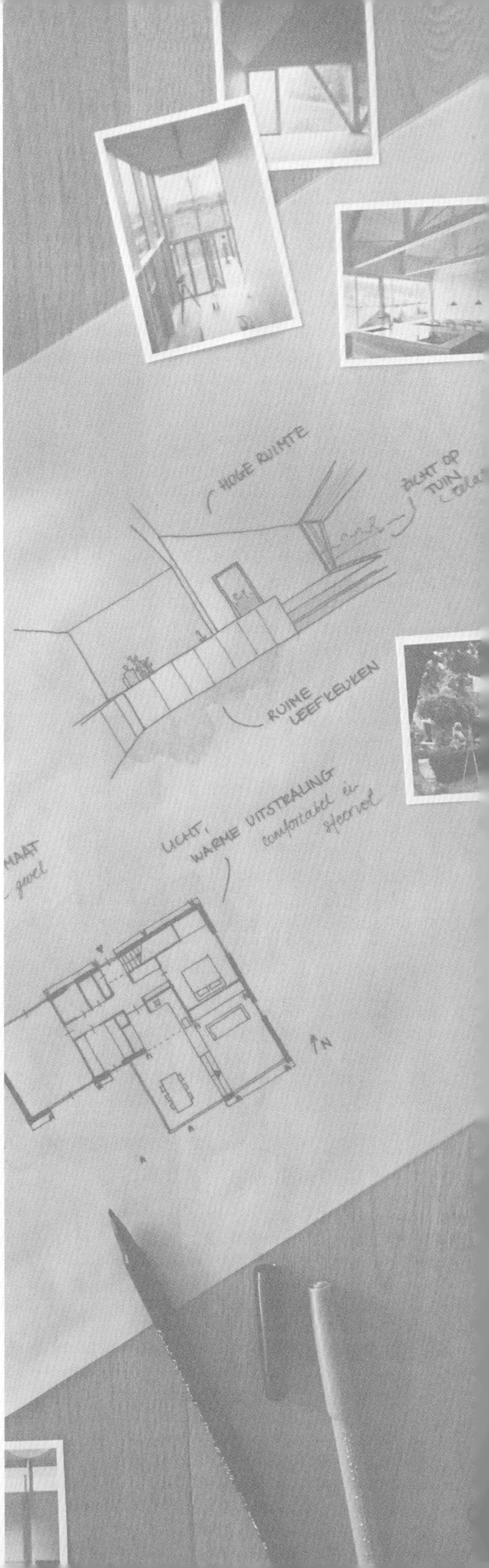

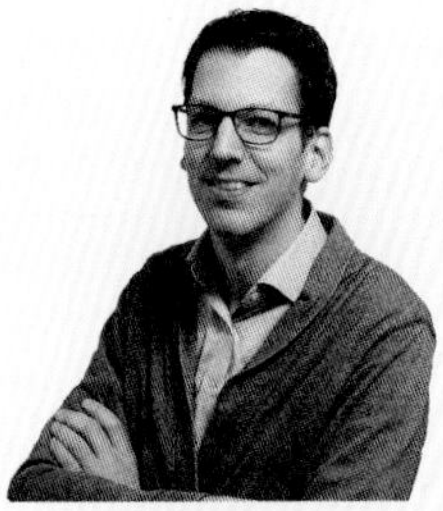

Pieter Graaff is a Dutch architect and founding partner of architectural firm and design agency Open Kaart. After studying at Delft University of Technology he started his career in research and providing solutions for assisted housing for those in need. He puts the insights he acquired there into practice in co-creating living environments. As an architect and researcher, he is committed to including the experience, inspiration, and energy of users in the process in order to achieve better planning and design solutions. He shares his findings as an author and guest lecturer at Delft University of Technology.

www.deopenkaart.nl
Photography Courtesy of the architect, Open Kaart

INTRODUCTION

Pieter Graaff MSc, Architect

People who are looking for inspiration go for a walk, search the internet, go on vacation, or buy this book. Companies that need inspiration to think about the course of their organization rent an inspiring space outside their office for a day. This helps them to come to new perspectives. And what do people with a creative profession do if they want to be creative? They go to their workplace. Day after day.

Being creative is what they do. This puts high demands on their direct working environment. And as you would expect, many of these creative people have also released creative ideas on the design and layout of these spaces. This book consists of some of the world's best examples. However, this book does not carry the title "Creative Ideas for Creative Spaces." It is the other way around: the Creative Spaces are responsible for the Creative Ideas. Creative space is therefore also mental space. And that makes the difference between a mood board and this carefully compiled book.

According to educational scientist and author Mel Rhodes, the elements of creativity are the 4 Ps: press, person, product, and process.

Press: The search for the holy grail

How can you create a place that continues to inspire? That is the million-dollar question that you as a reader of this book may be trying to answer. For your home, your studio, or for that one unfulfilled dream . . . This book offers a glimpse into the lives of creative people and is a rich collection of their creative workplaces. It also shows that inspiration and creativity come in many forms, from a serene studio to a messy workplace. What helps these creative people come up with creative ideas day after day?

The question of how a creative space stimulates the creativity of its users is an identity question. The answer is not a universal standard, but a personal perspective. How does the public influence the outcome of a football match? Do protest songs have influence over the course of history? How does the entourage influence the course of a conversation? These are questions that are academically unanswerable, but questions on which you have to develop an intuitive vision in order to act. To encourage your favorite club, to express your opinion, to get dressed for your first date, to cast your vote—or to shape a creative space. It's an act that is personal but does not have to be performed in solitude. The various examples in this book can initiate a dialogue of views and ideas in order to be able to make this personal choice.

Person: Hire a creative

In my work as an architect, the question of helping to design a space for creative ideas often comes to the fore. Our clients are not only professionals in the creative industry, but also amateurs who choose to make more time for this passion. Apparently being creative is meaningful, because the choice to follow your creative heart often comes after a major event. A creative couple wants their studio at home (inspiration sometimes comes in the evening) and wants it to be movable to a possible next home. A professional photographer has the additional ambition to make the manufacturing industry visible in his neighborhood. A company is looking for a sense of home and creativity to retain employees. A social foundation is looking for accessibility and informality.

They all ask to think creatively and to make this touch of creativity tangible in the end result. That question is not limited to creative functions. Even when removing sidewalk tiles for a more water-sensitive outdoor area or setting up a mobility-scooter garage in a

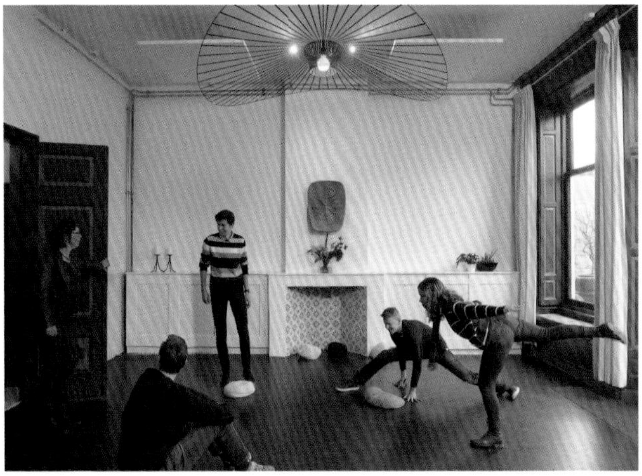

care home, a creative approach can make the difference. So, the question of what creative spaces give rise to creative ideas is not only driven by curiosity about the lives of creative people. How wonderful would it be if not only the people in this book, but all of us, could work and live in environments that inspire us?

Product: Do new ideas need old buildings?

If you look for inspiring environments in architectural magazines, you will often come across new uses of older buildings. In recent years, in the Dutch city of Rotterdam where I have my office, the majority of completed homes came about through the transformation of offices, schools, or shops. During the same period, restaurants in former factories opened. A subtropical swimming paradise became a hotbed for entrepreneurs, churches became bookshops, and an office became a swimming pool. Re-use seems to be the norm rather than the exception and really appeals to the imagination. The unusual aspects of these projects create a certain tension that attracts people and can lead to creativity. The autopilot is turned off and makes room for wonder, attention, and interest—exactly what design and architecture prefer to achieve.

A wide variety of creative crafts is included in this book. And of course you can ask yourself which activity requires what kind of space. When can we see an unusual detail, when do we want to feel that anything can and may still happen, and when do we prefer to surround ourselves with a serene rest? The examples in this book will help you with this. For example, a painting studio may be more messy than a photo studio, while a design agency can combine its sleekly designed computers and furniture with unfinished walls. Yet the question of which activity requires which space is the wrong question for this book. This "form follows function" approach does not do justice to the question. This introduction is not about unraveling the formula; it is about how a space can breathe creativity. The popularity of re-uses suggests that an inspiring space may not be a tailored suit.

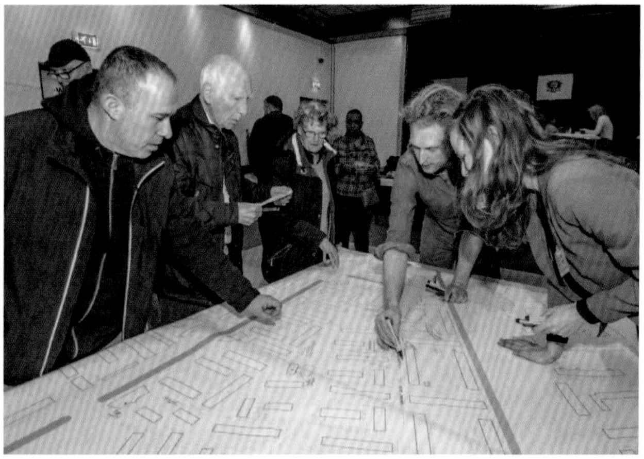

Process: Where the magic happens

I am convinced that the creativity of the process in which a space itself is designed matters. Just as you feel at home with photos of family or vacation and your own things that carry a history, your creativity can be stimulated by a place that has been designed and decorated with great joy and attention. Sometimes that process of conceiving and making is still visible. I personally find it strong when that process is visible. If you see that things have been hung, added, made to measure, or have not been consciously finished—if there are references to how it used to be, to personal anecdotes, or to examples from which inspiration has been drawn. You see: attention has been paid to this, something has been set in motion here, or anything can happen here.

Another challenge is the balance between visibility and emptiness. Often the place where something is made is also the place that serves to receive people who want to see what you do—customers, students, colleagues. It's a workplace and exhibition space at the same time. The fact that you temporarily withdraw from daily life, that you detach yourself from the "normal" living environment, may be visible and tangible in those spaces. They may be rougher, stranger or—on the contrary—more refined and calmer. In that environment you can receive people who focus their attention on this work. To do this, you need to show what happens and what has been created earlier, while the creative process itself requires more emptiness or, alternatively, more junk. It is the enlarged version of the problem of anyone who wants everything within reach in a tidy house. The creative process that takes place in people's minds must be visible in space. There must be emptiness for new ideas, while the energy and the result of previous creative processes must be felt.

Inspired by you

But creative spaces are not just for creative people. Because what is creativity anyway? In which places do you need creative ideas? In the kitchen, the carpentry workshop, on the sports field, when waiting for the bus, in the sewing workshop, or in the play corner? In short, creative spaces are important for everyone. In fact, perhaps a touch of creativity in the places where we do our shopping and do our work is more vital than for the people in this book who are already creative of themselves. How beautiful would it be if we were all surrounded by inspiration and attention instead

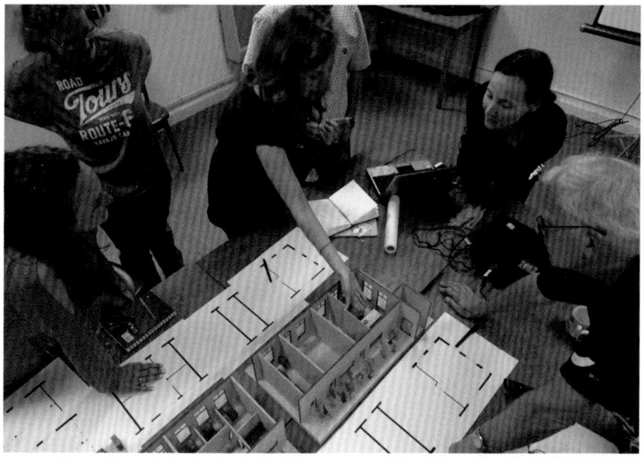

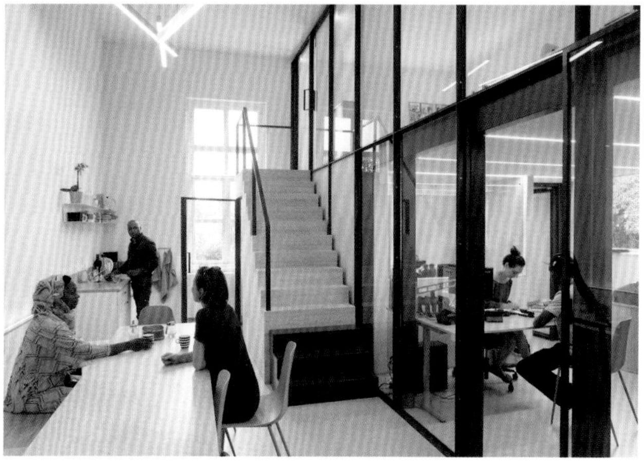

of a sometimes depressing lack of fantasy? Perhaps the notion of place is the starting point for our search for inspiration.

This book is full of places. Dedicated, carefully designed spaces that are the result of a creative process. Because no matter how obvious a solution sometimes seems, it is often a creative process that precedes this and that determines the ultimate quality of the result. It is in the process that implicit wishes and unexpected opportunities can come to something that turns out to be a joy forever. This is often a bumpy road in which directions can be found, reversed, and released again in order to arrive at surprising perspectives.

Co-creating creative spaces

A creative place starts with the question: what else could the place where I am now be? Just as art allows you to look at the world with different eyes, design allows you to look at your everyday environment with different eyes. At our Open Kaart office we often ask this question to those with whom we collaborate, be they residents, students, churchgoers, volunteers, or employees. The answers and the responses to those answers often lead to insights about use and experience that you would not get if you only asked directly about use and experience. What seems solid becomes fluid and small things can become very important.

The paradox of this introduction is that for us as creative professionals it is precisely the everyday and sometimes dull environment of our clients that can release a stream of creative ideas. For example, we spent a day at the kitchen table of private individuals who wanted to renovate their house. While the children crawled under the table and their parent walked to the washing machine in the back of the garden, we came up with the idea of drastically changing the relationship between home and garden. By keeping a temporary office in an old building we got exactly enough insight to solve three problems in one go, while some lost pieces of furniture gave rise to the idea of restoring an old meeting area.

We are trained as architects to see unexpected possibilities in something ordinary. The art of co-creation is to let users nourish those ideas consciously and unconsciously and to take them into the possibilities that you see. The point is then to create a metaphorical creative space that releases creative ideas in interaction. That space is not physical, but mental.

Creating imaginative space for an alternative reality is an important task for those who want to work with creative spaces. This mental space often benefits from physical space. Models and test setups help with this. Draw out the contours of the space you have in mind with a ribbon or tape and walk through it. Or pre-enact this new reality during an afternoon with your friends or colleagues. It provides a lot of fun, connectedness, and new creative ideas.

Get inspired

Creative Spaces for Creative Ideas shows that it is not only the factual circumstances but also the connection with the place that can provide inspiration. As Einstein is said to have remarked: "Logic will get you from A to B. Imagination will take you everywhere."

Let's allow ourselves more creative space for creative ideas in our schools, work environments, hospitals, and homes. Let the studios of artists, photographers, and designers gathered here inspire us to look differently at our own daily environment. With this book in your hand, look around you and ask yourself: have I already given my own twist to this?

THE HOME STUDIO

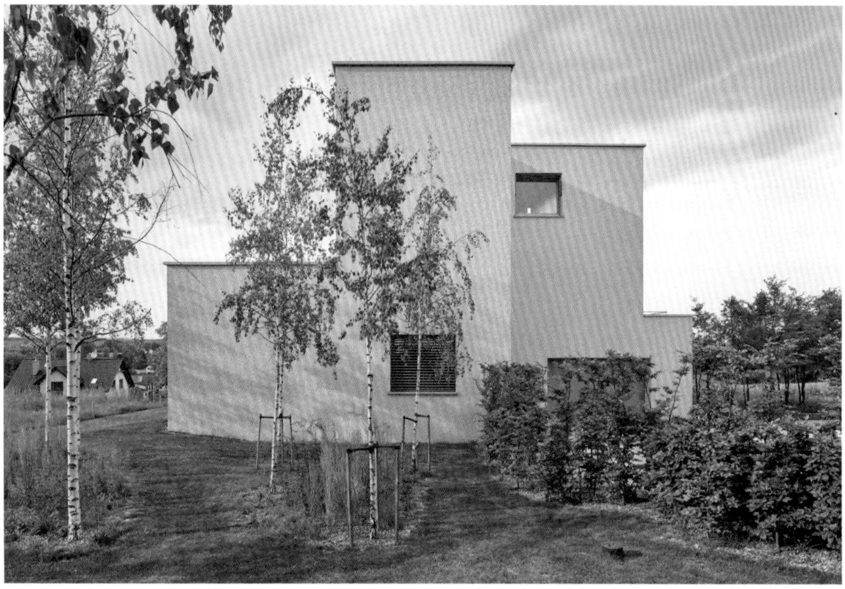

Area:
9,418 square feet (875 square meters)

Completion:
2017

Design:
Piotr Brzoza Architekten GmbH

Photography:
Jakub Certowicz

Kraków, Poland

Artists' Home and Studio in Kraków

Two buildings—a residence and a studio—for an artist couple and their children were built on two adjacent plots in an old residential district on the outskirts of Kraków. One of them is a transformed house started by somebody else and left unfinished; the other was built from scratch. The rear side of the site opens to the hilly landscape and fields behind the back fence.

Separate yet united

Each building was designed as an autonomous volume in its geometry and materials. Nevertheless, their cohesive formal language and detailing make them belong together as a precise spatial composition—both in their relation to each other and in defining a small square at the end of a quiet street.

Views that could be paintings

The views onto the beautiful surrounding landscape, and the presence of the views in the interiors, were the leading issue when the floor plans and the layout of the façades were being designed. As they provide the best prospect, the main rooms were located on the upper floor and enhanced by generous terraces. Every window opening is as precisely directed and positioned in the space as a wood-framed landscape painting.

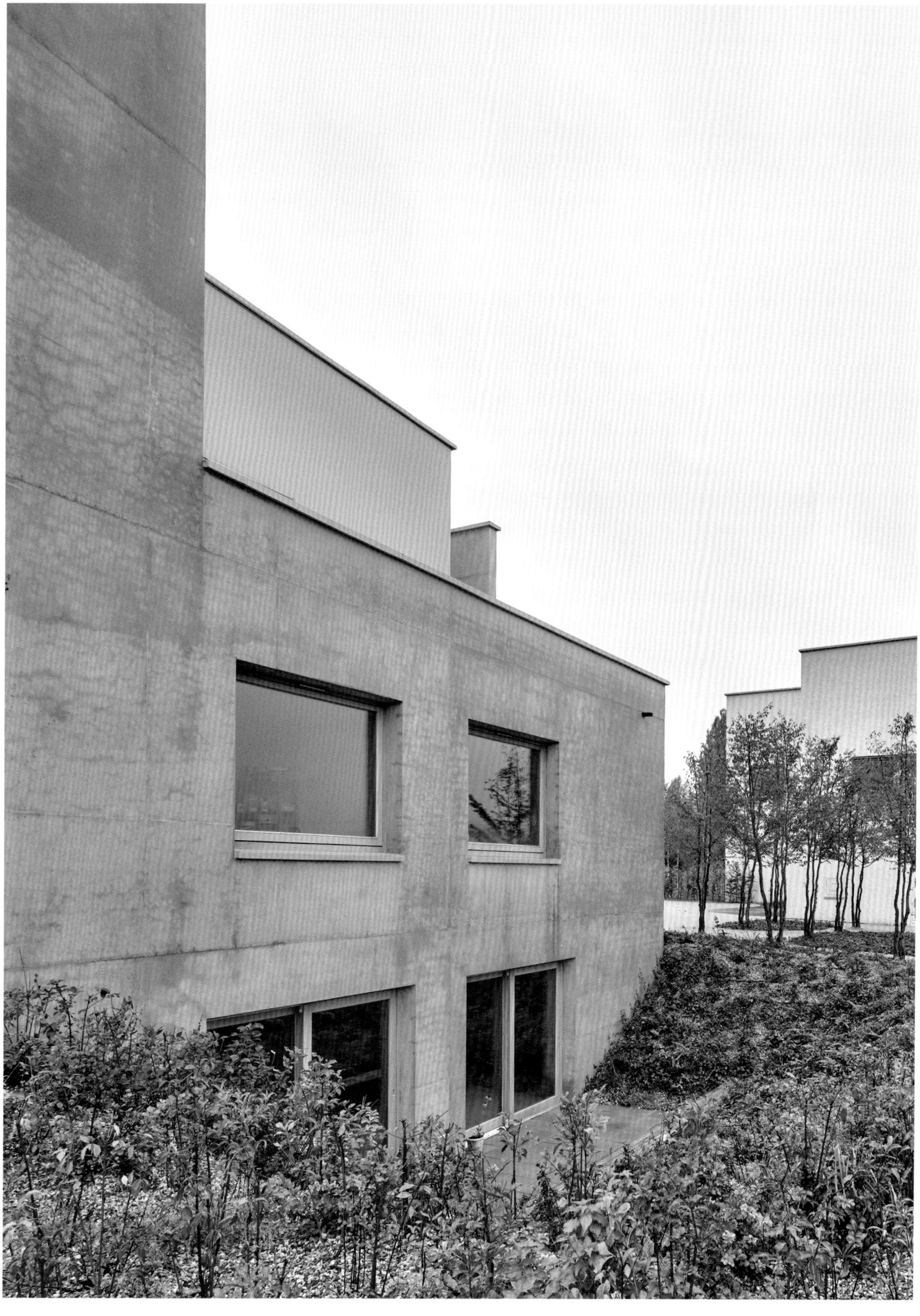

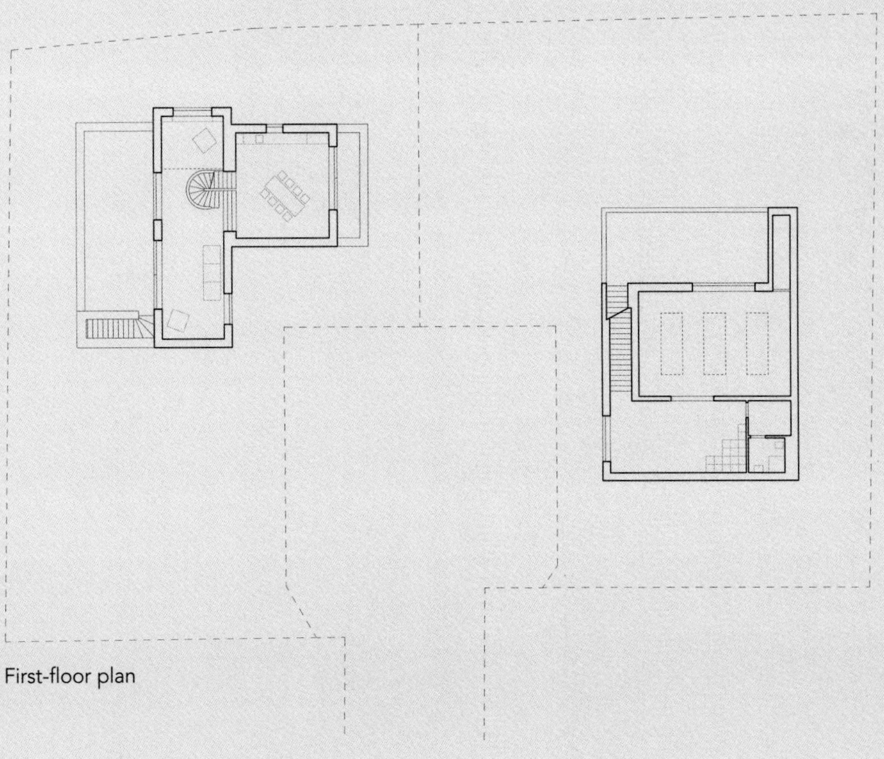
First-floor plan

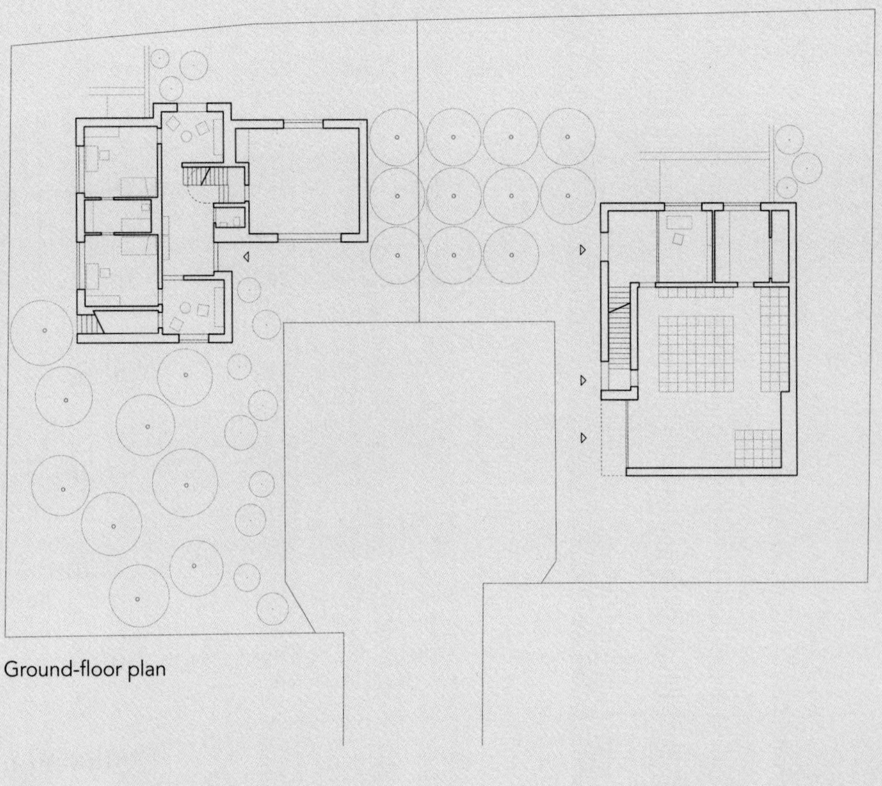
Ground-floor plan

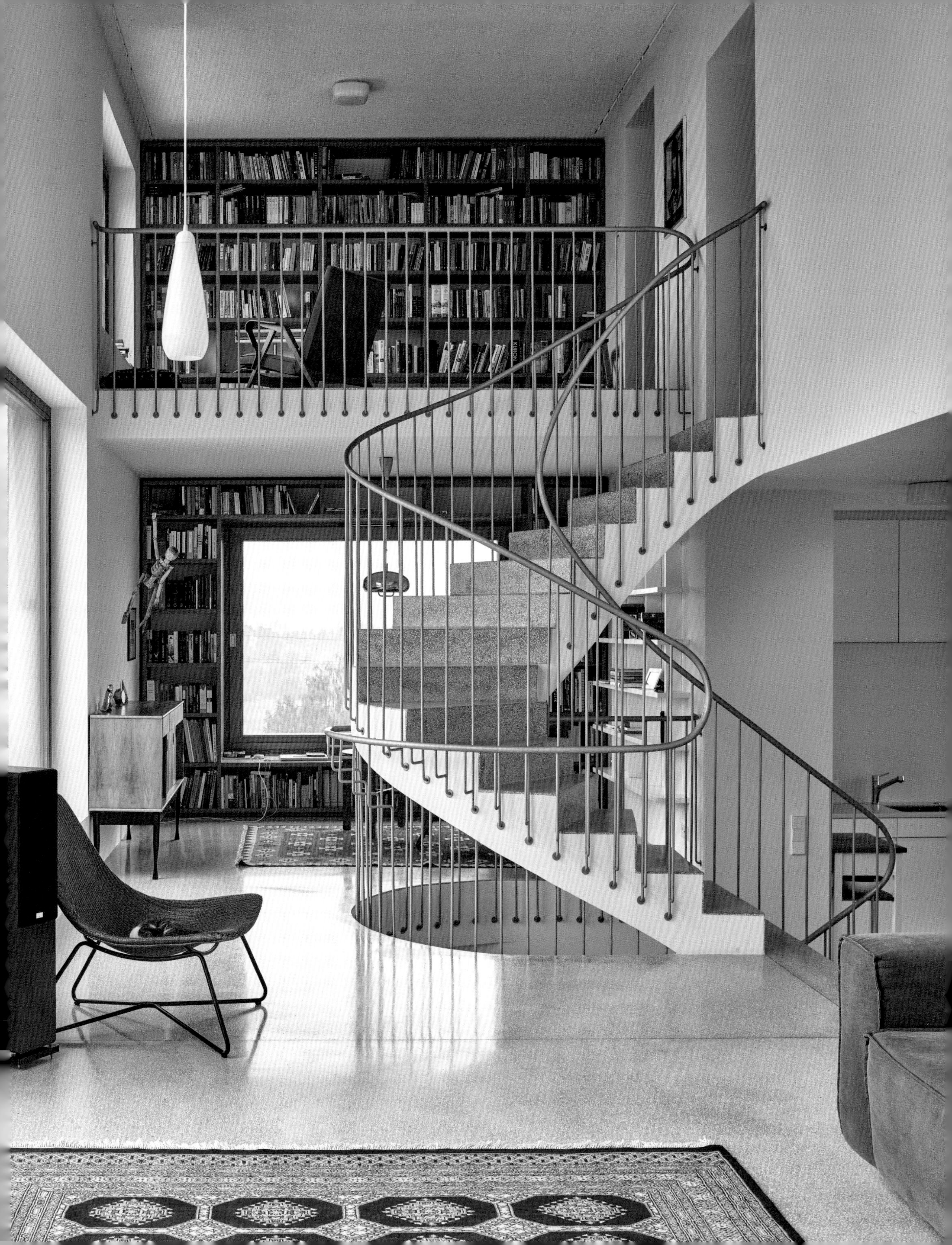

Light and space

The studio building houses a painting atelier on the upper floor—gaining both the best view and the optimal light conditions of the generous skylights above the main central workspace. The areas with the most intense external communication—assistants' office and storage—are located on the street level, while the basement with an intimate half-sunken patio gives space to a film studio, with a small cinema room behind.

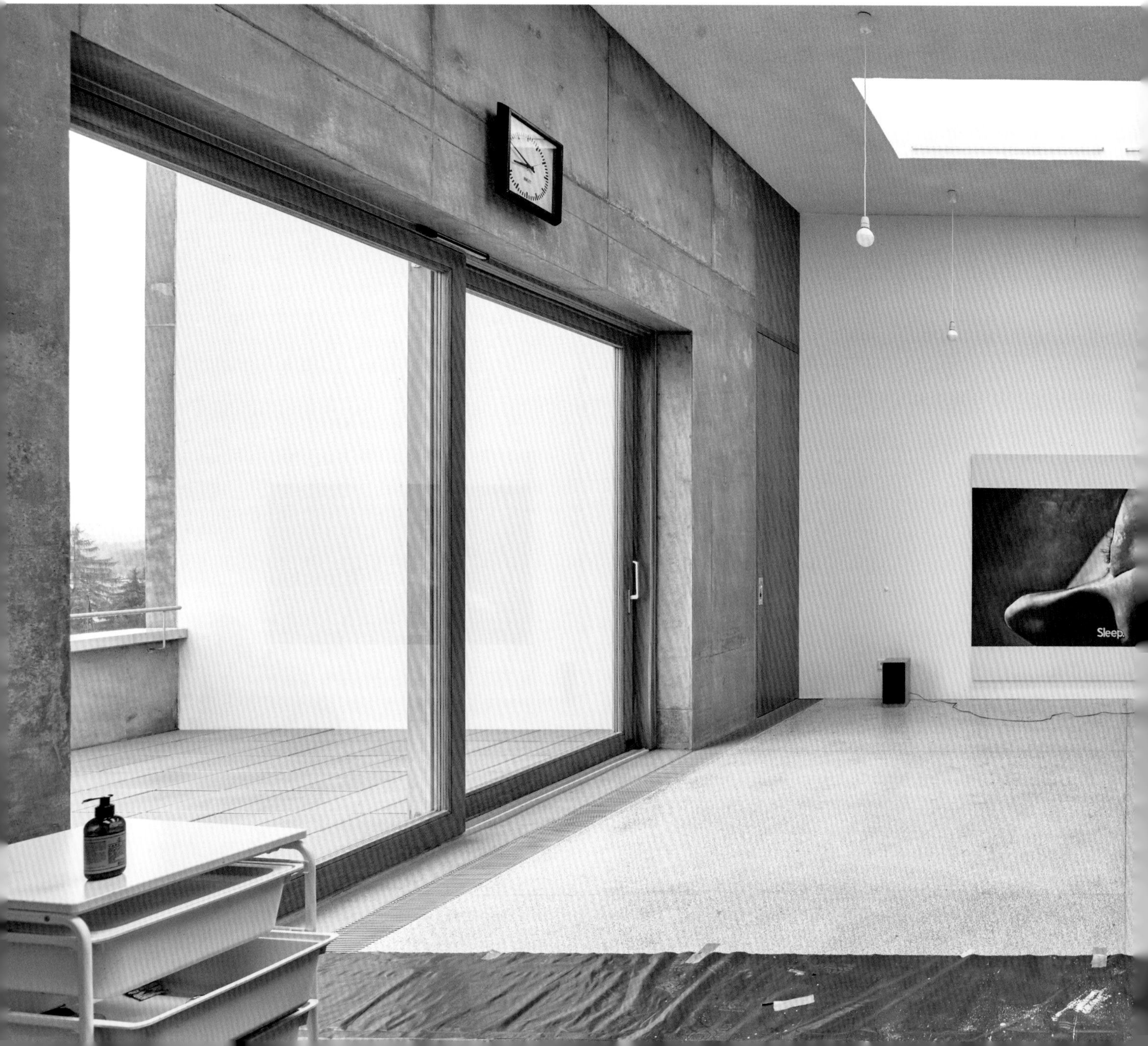

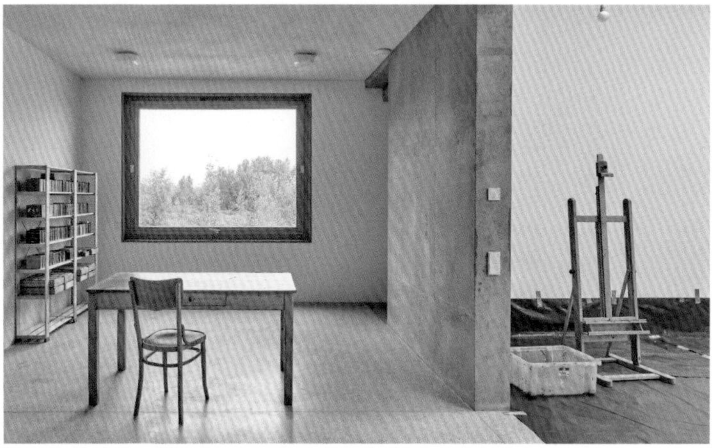

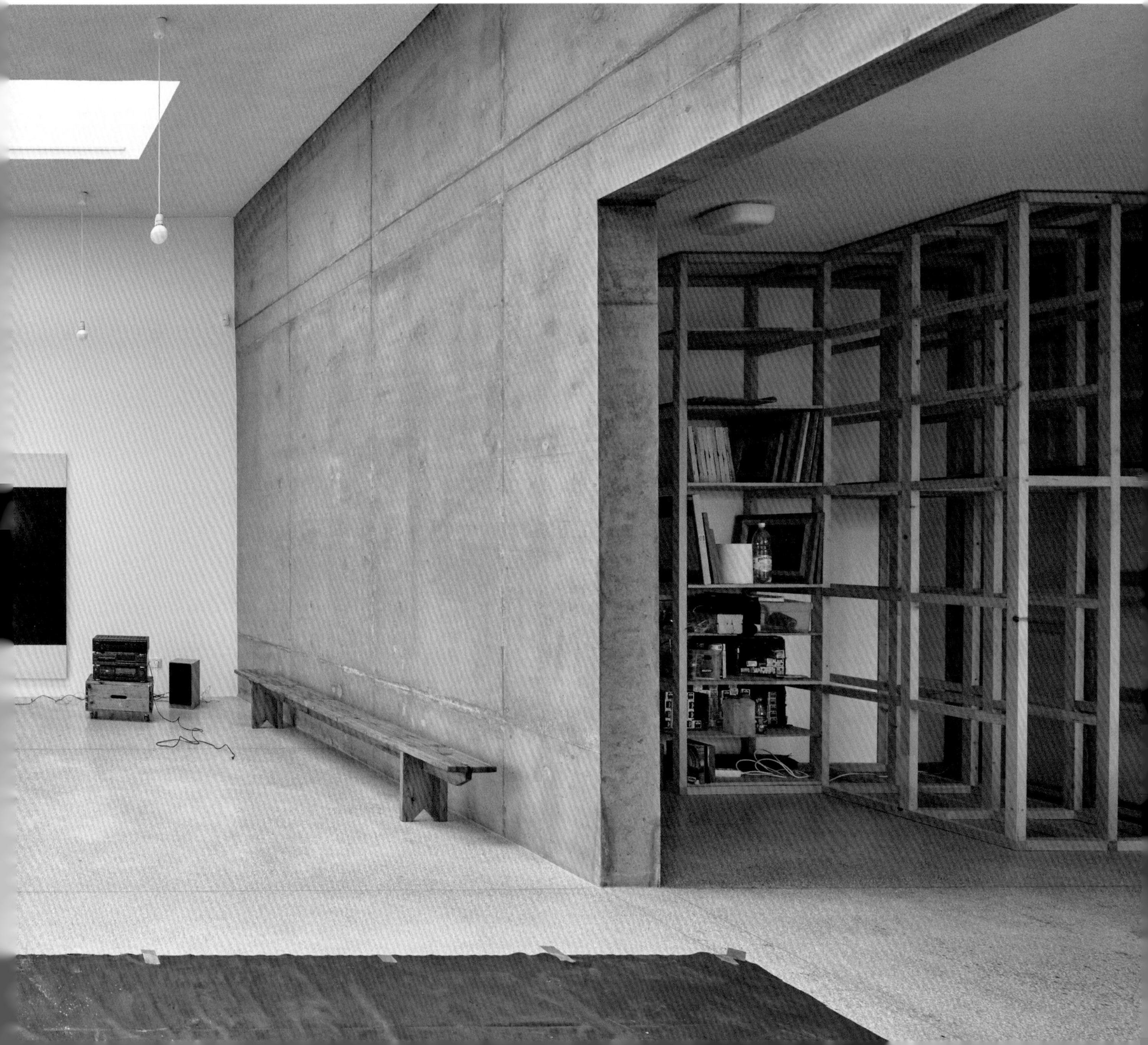

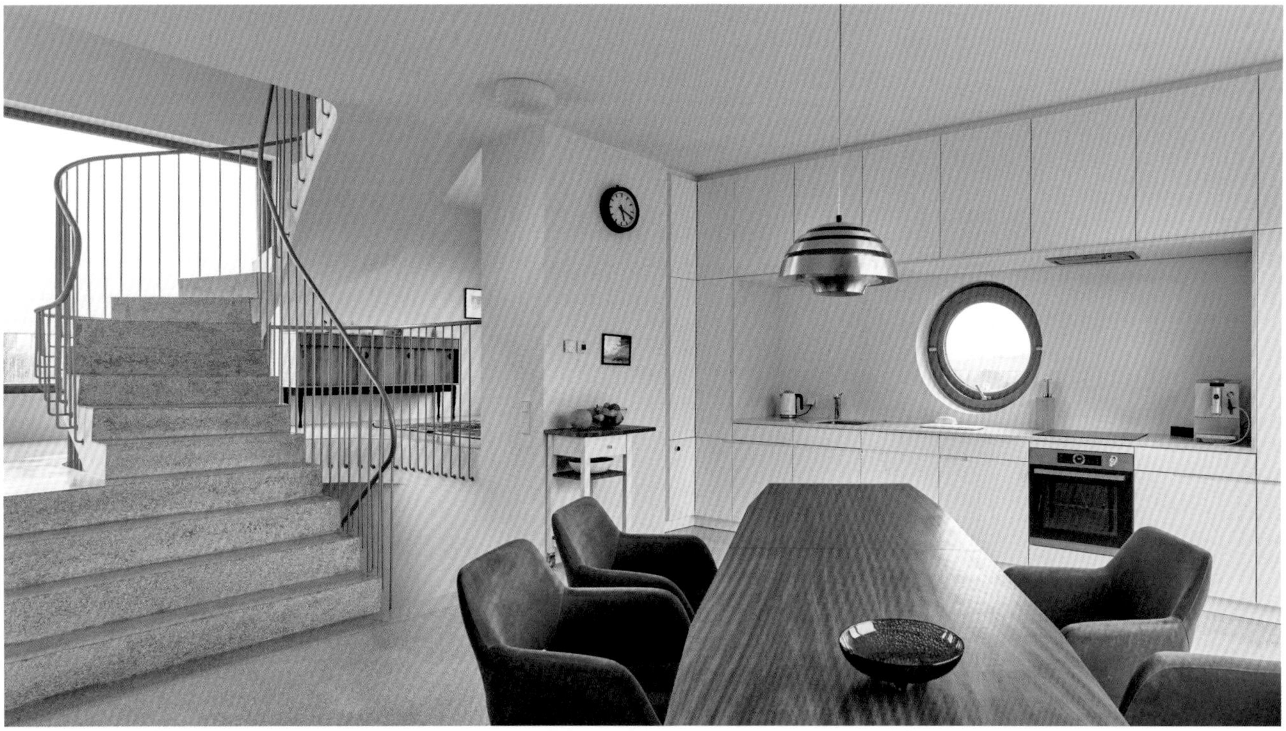

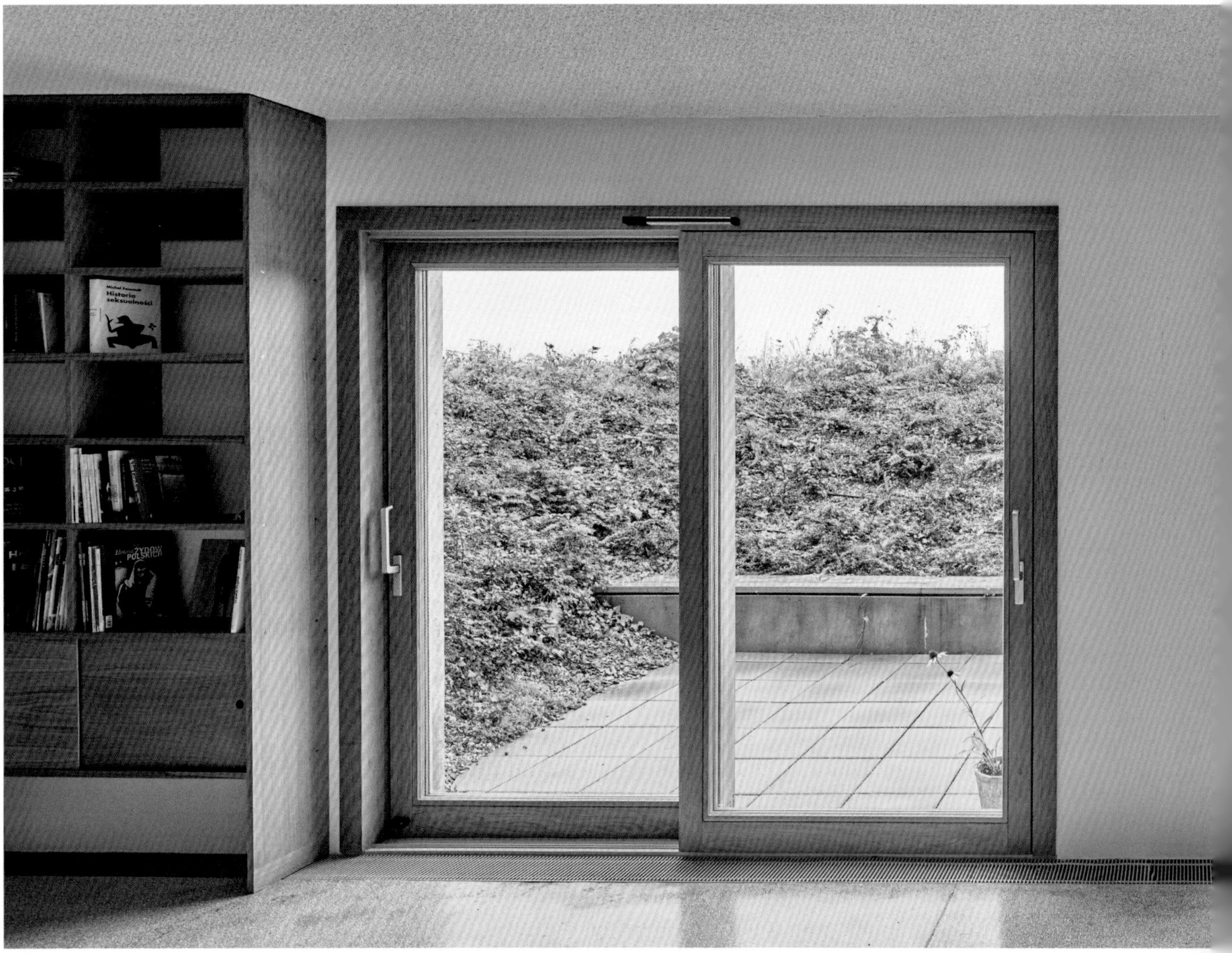
Historia
seksualności

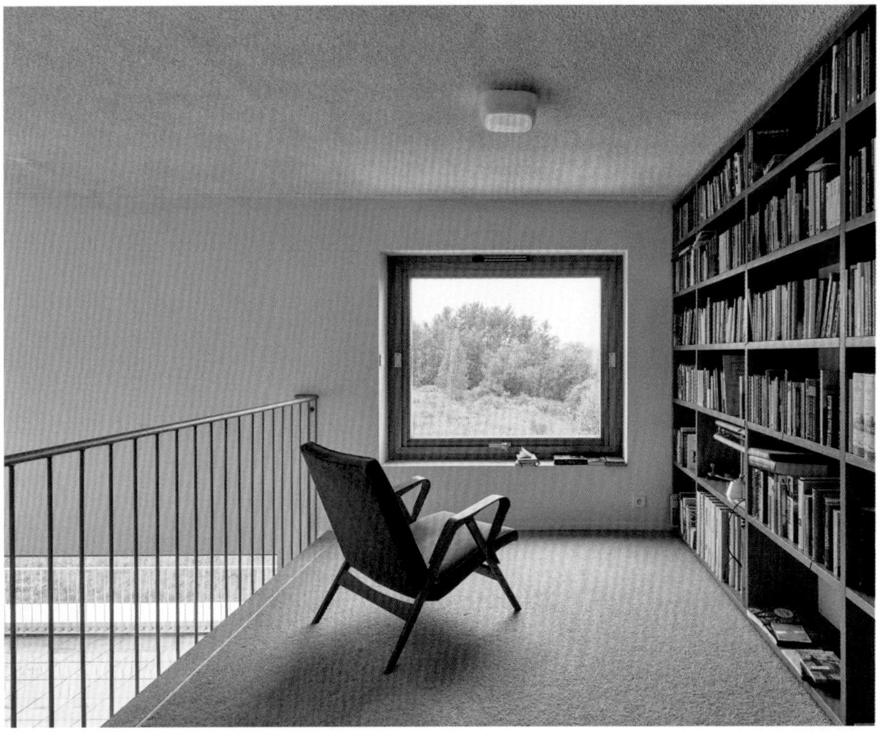

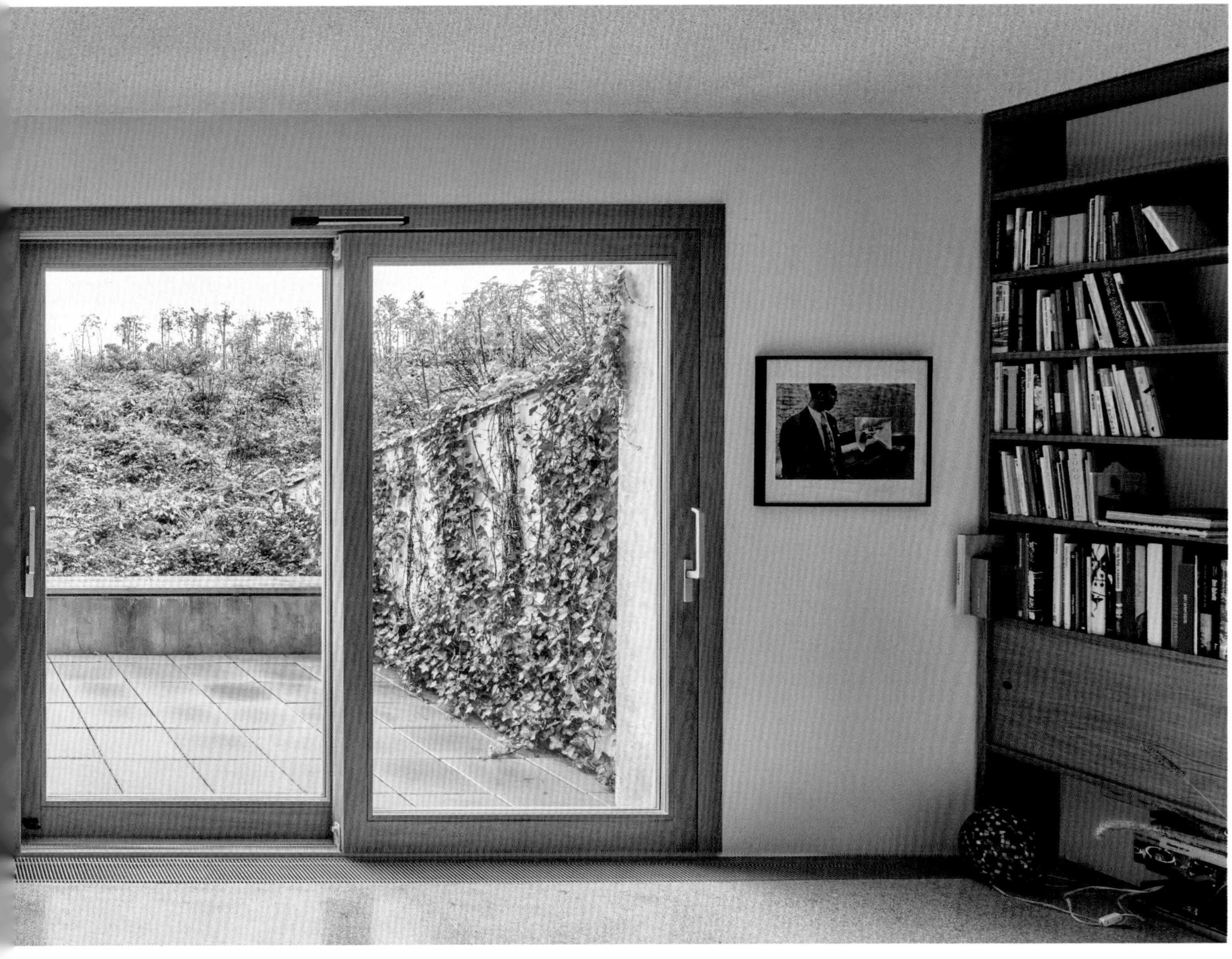

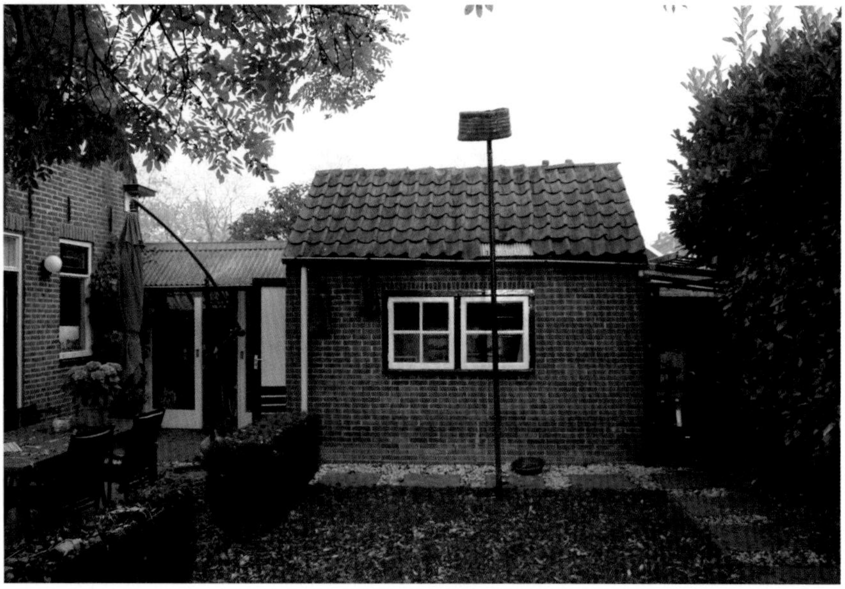

Area:
205 square feet (19 square meters)

Completion:
2017

Design:
Open Kaart

Photography:
Rufus de Vries

Woerden, The Netherlands

Backyard Painting Studio

The long-cherished wish of the artist for a private painting studio became a reality in their back yard, where an unsightly shed became a light-filled studio with attic, retaining the side walls of the old barn.

The old and the new

After the house and garden were renovated a simple shed remained, waiting for a purpose. At first glance it offered few possibilities: it was small, did not have any insulation or foundation, and had a leaking roof. In addition, its function as a storage space had to be retained. But by replacing the roof and one of the façades, enough space was created to carry out the owner's business—giving painting workshops—at home. Designers found that by building on the existing shed, a studio with attic could be realized within a limited budget. Sophisticated detailing, in line with conservative local building requirements, made the new construction an elegant building that stands out in a cluttered sea of sheds.

Creation by community

The clients worked intensively with the designers on the project, with many design sessions taking place at the kitchen table. The youngest son of the client made a model of the preliminary draft, and a brother-in-law made a new stained-glass window. Neighbors were consulted early and were positive about the quality and possibilities of the plan.

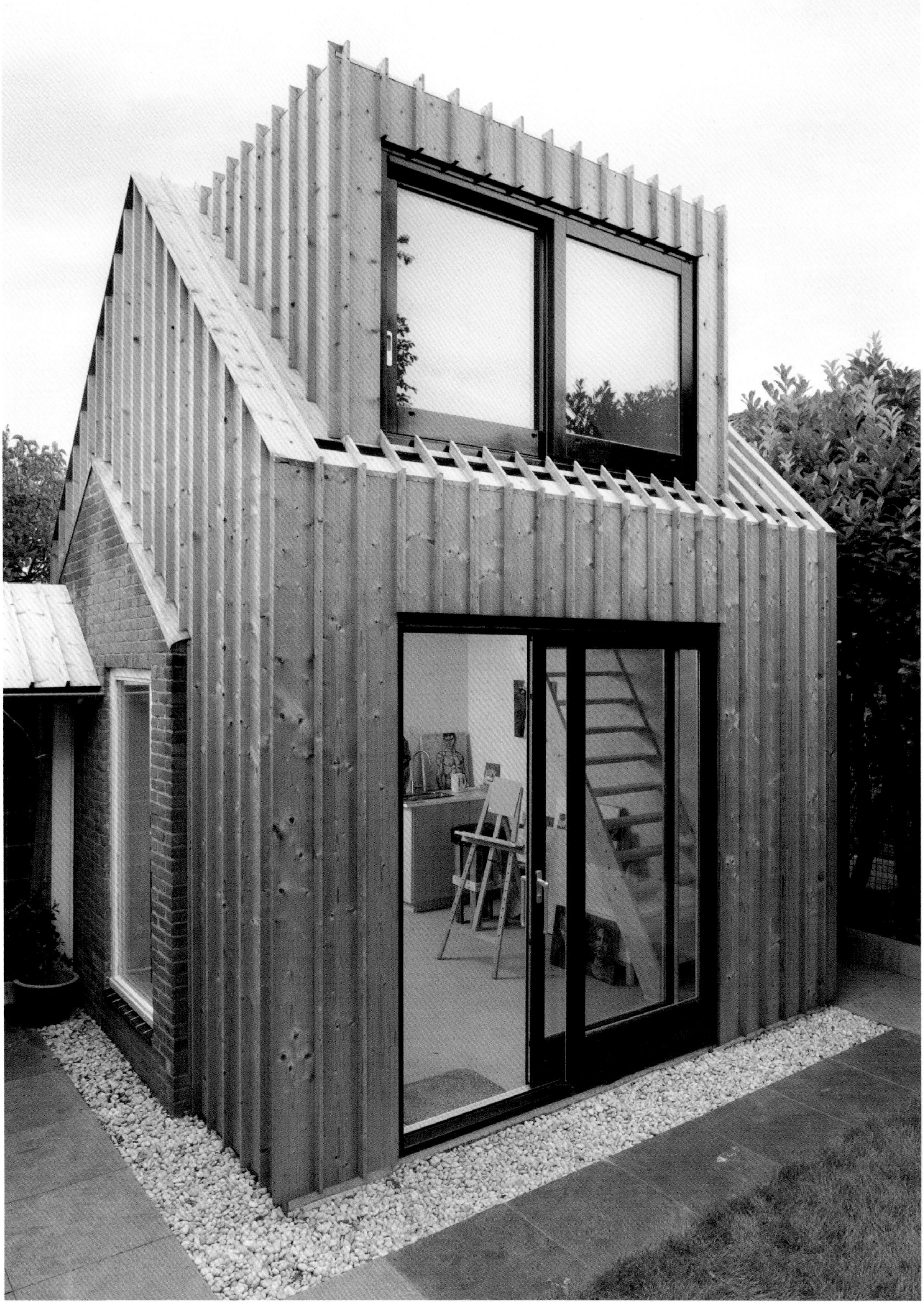

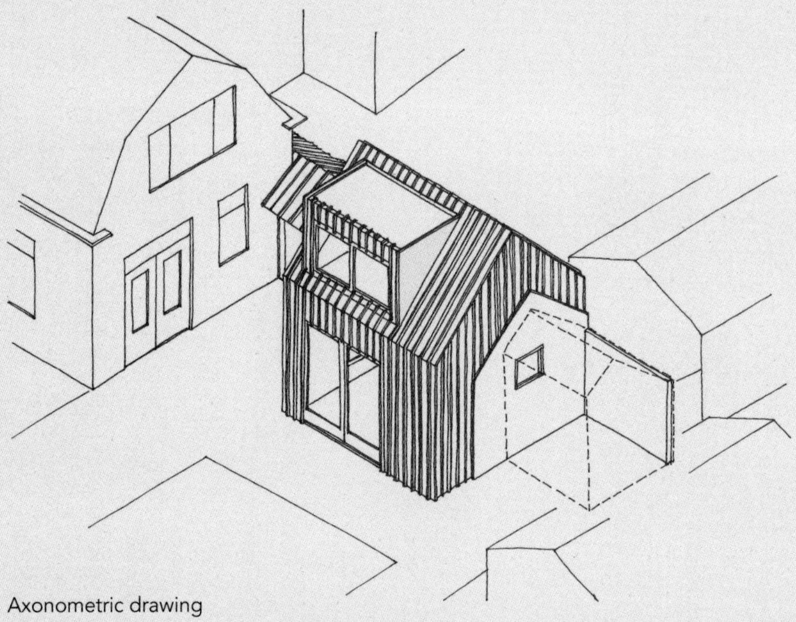

Axonometric drawing

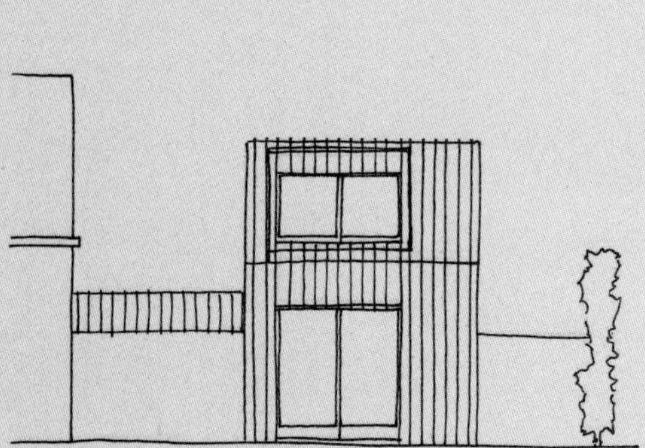

Front view

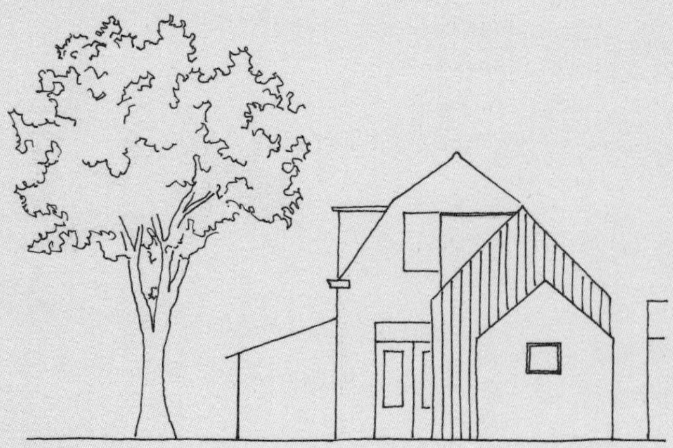

Side view

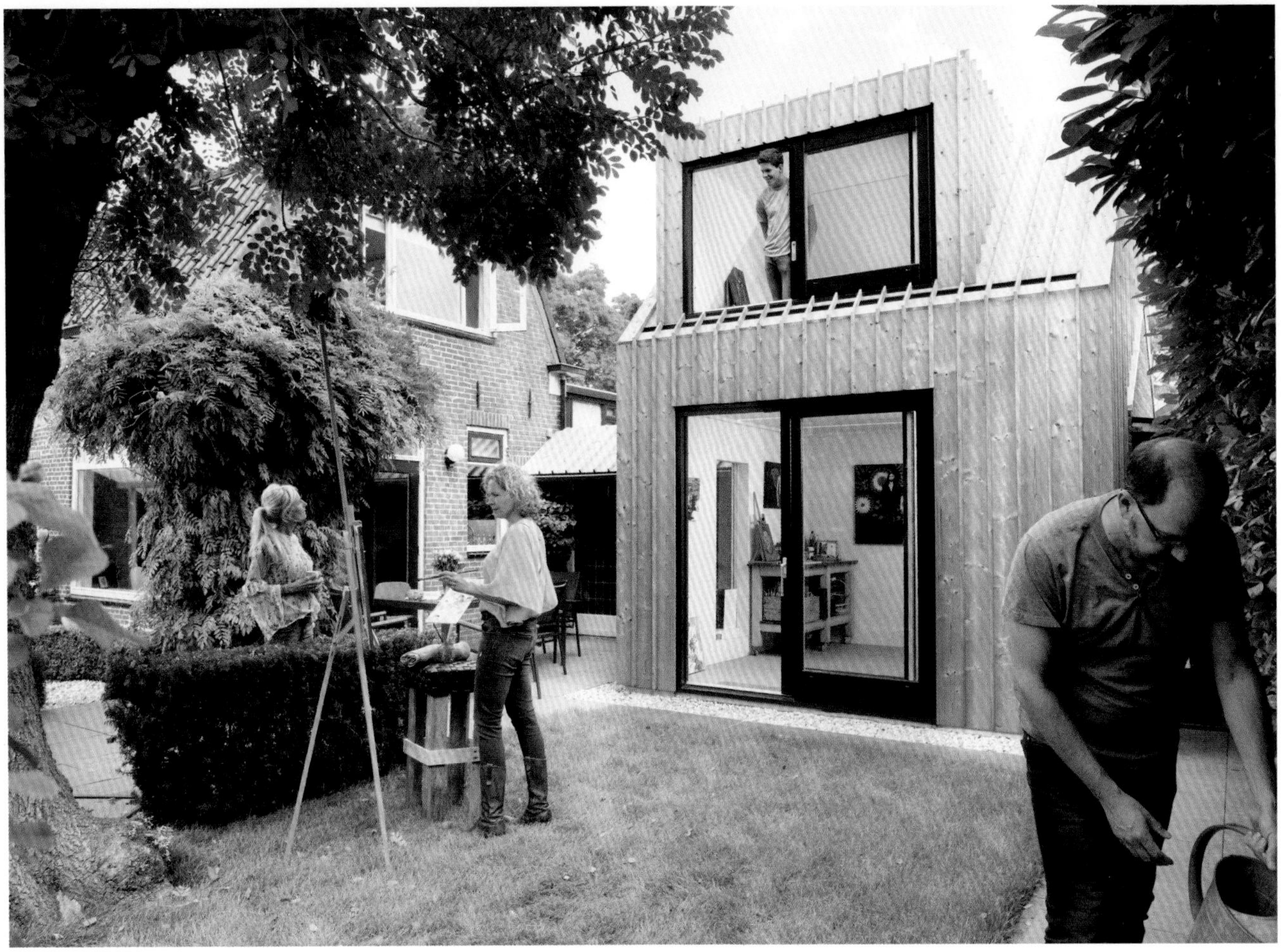

Transformation

Designers chose to leave three of the four existing walls of the shed. Within these limits a new wooden volume was raised. The half-stone masonry was maintained, which helped express the relationship between old and new. The planks and slats of preserved wood give depth and rhythm to the simple volume.

The interior is finished with multiplex plates in which LED lights, rails for paintings, and an infrared radiation panel are embedded. The floor is equipped with electric under-floor heating and the tap water is heated with an electric boiler. The studio is all-electric and energy efficient.

Designing for the future

The attic is spacious enough to function as storage space and retreat at the same time. A tree in the garden offers privacy and a pleasant view through the dormer window. The design took into account the option of expanding the studio later on with a bathroom, with the potential for it to serve as a tiny house for one of the sons or a future owner.

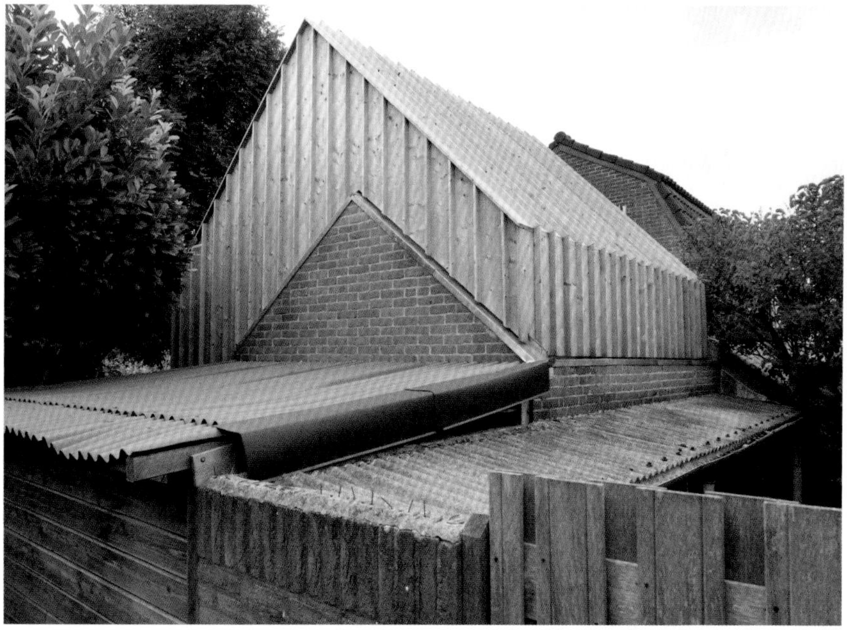

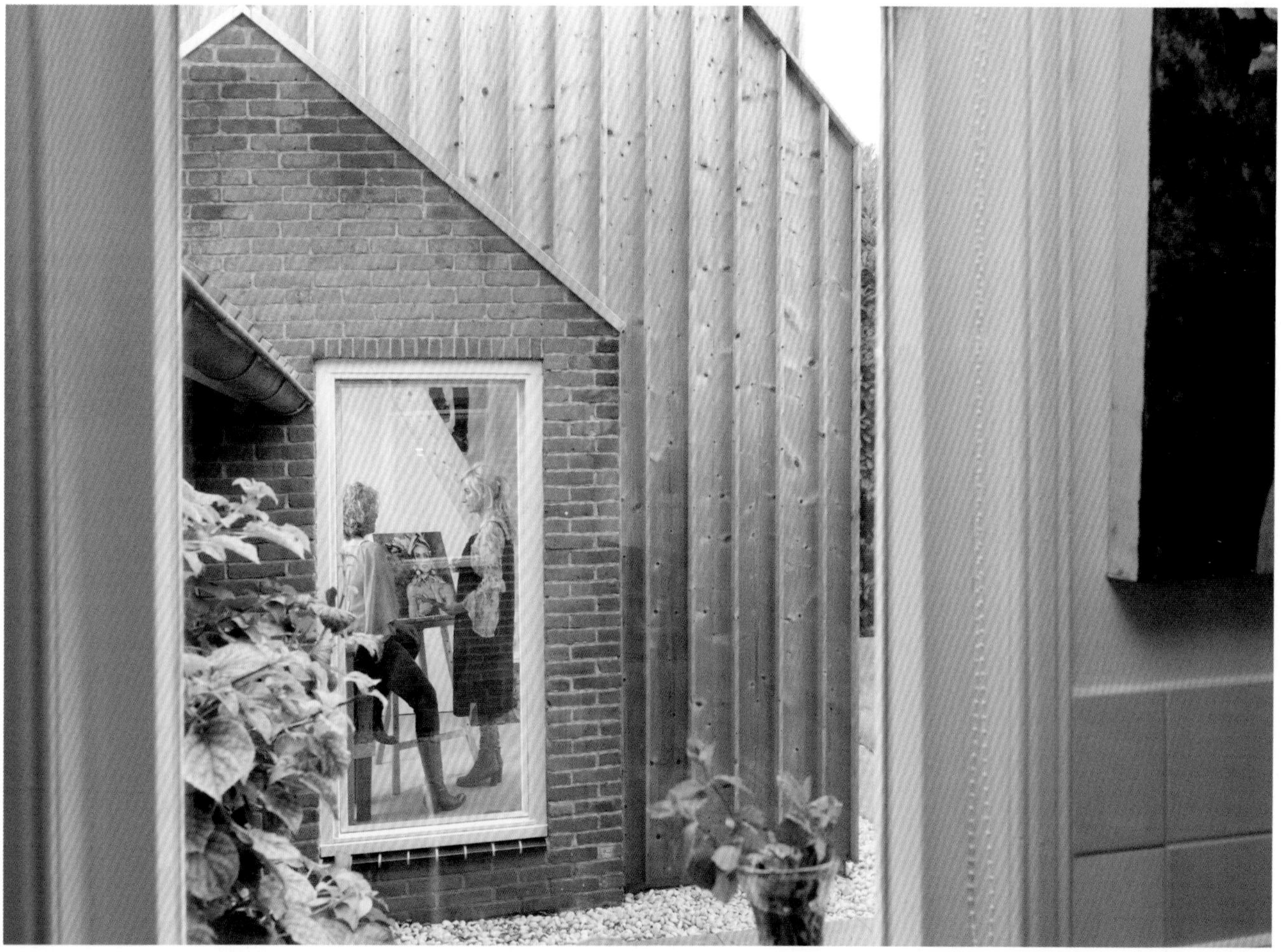

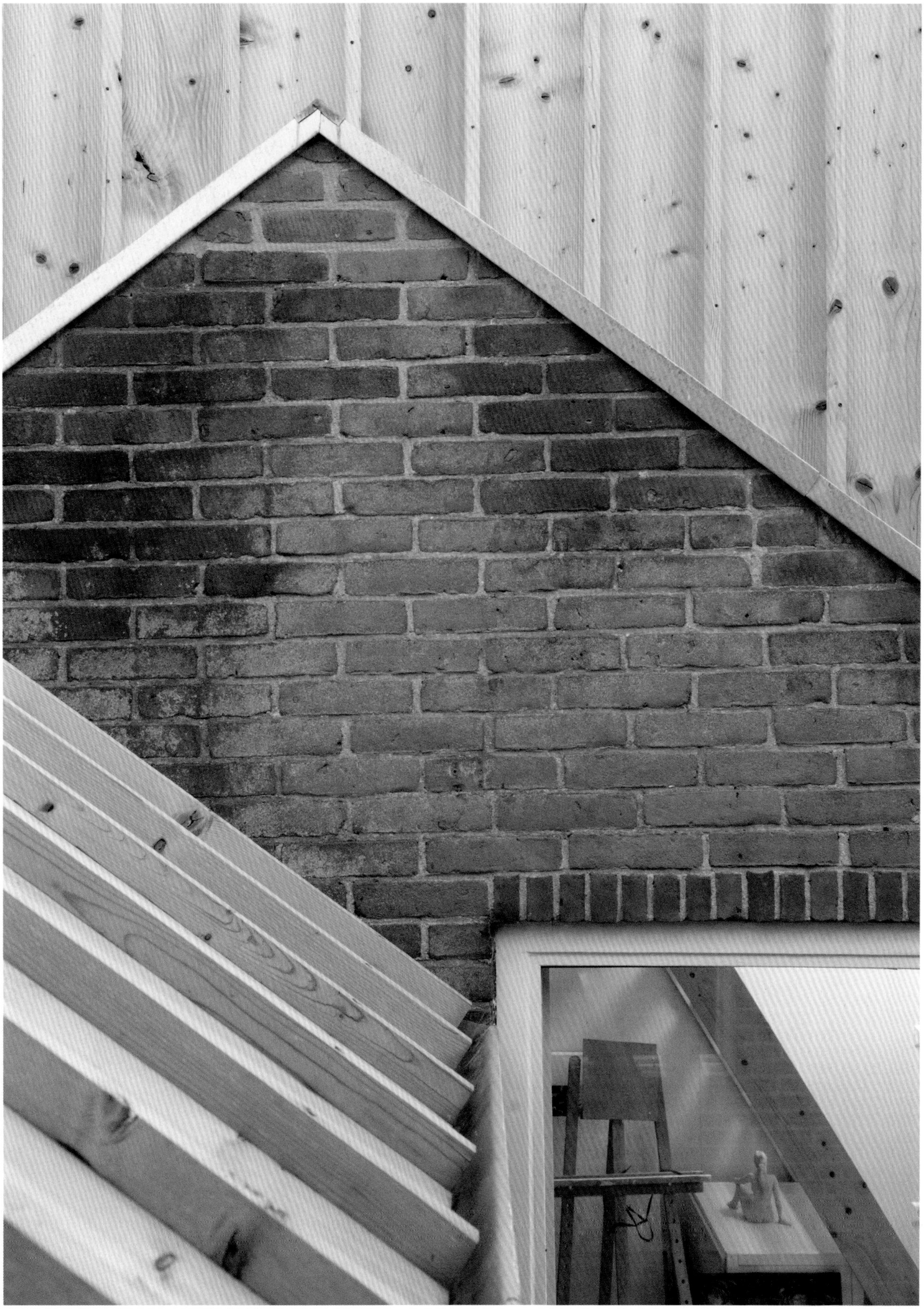

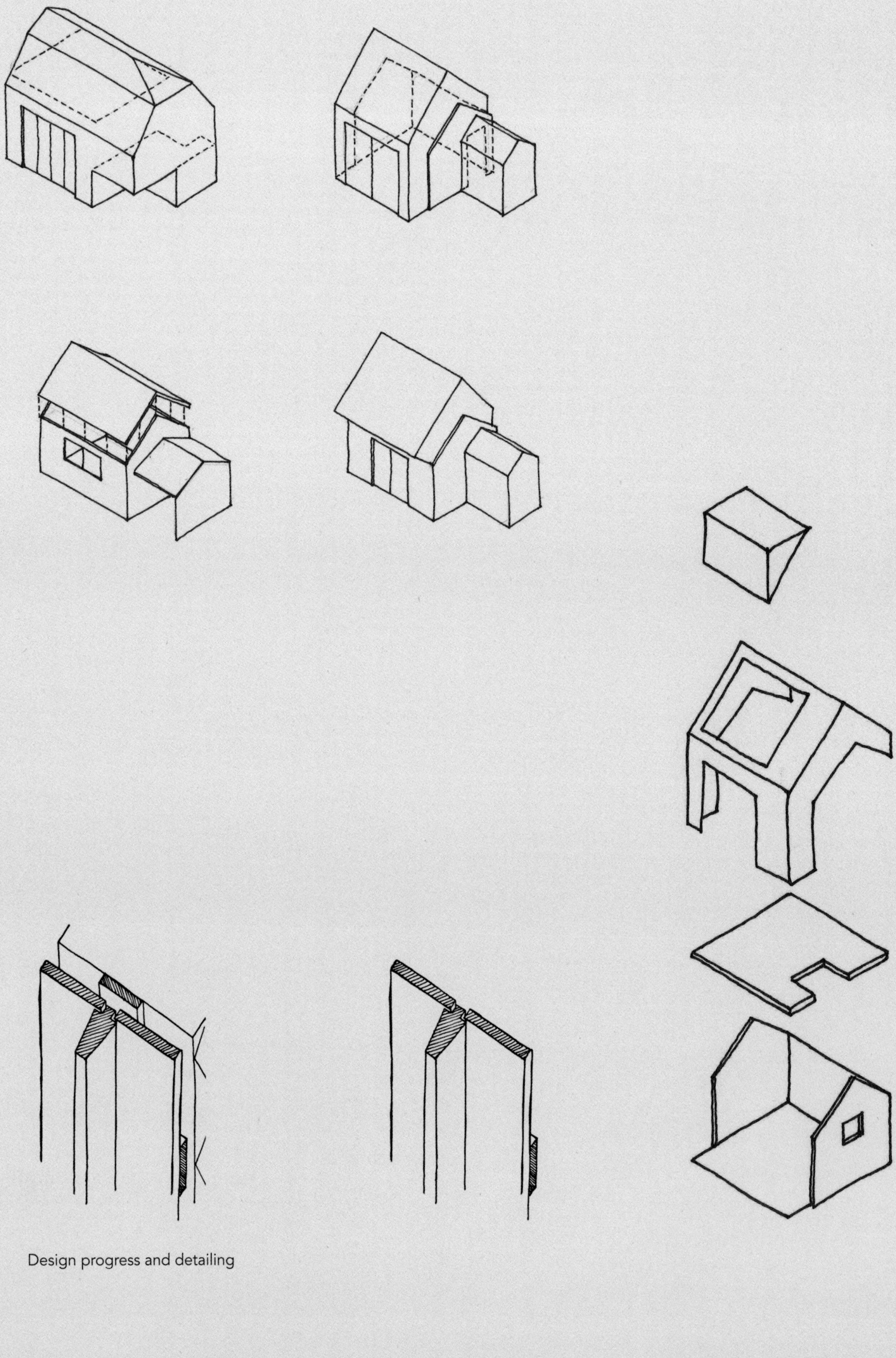

Design progress and detailing

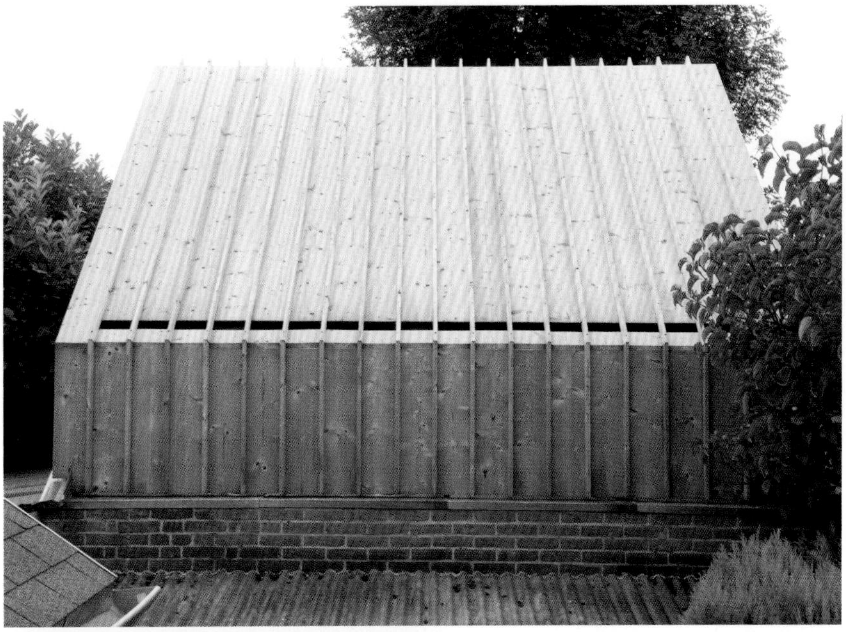

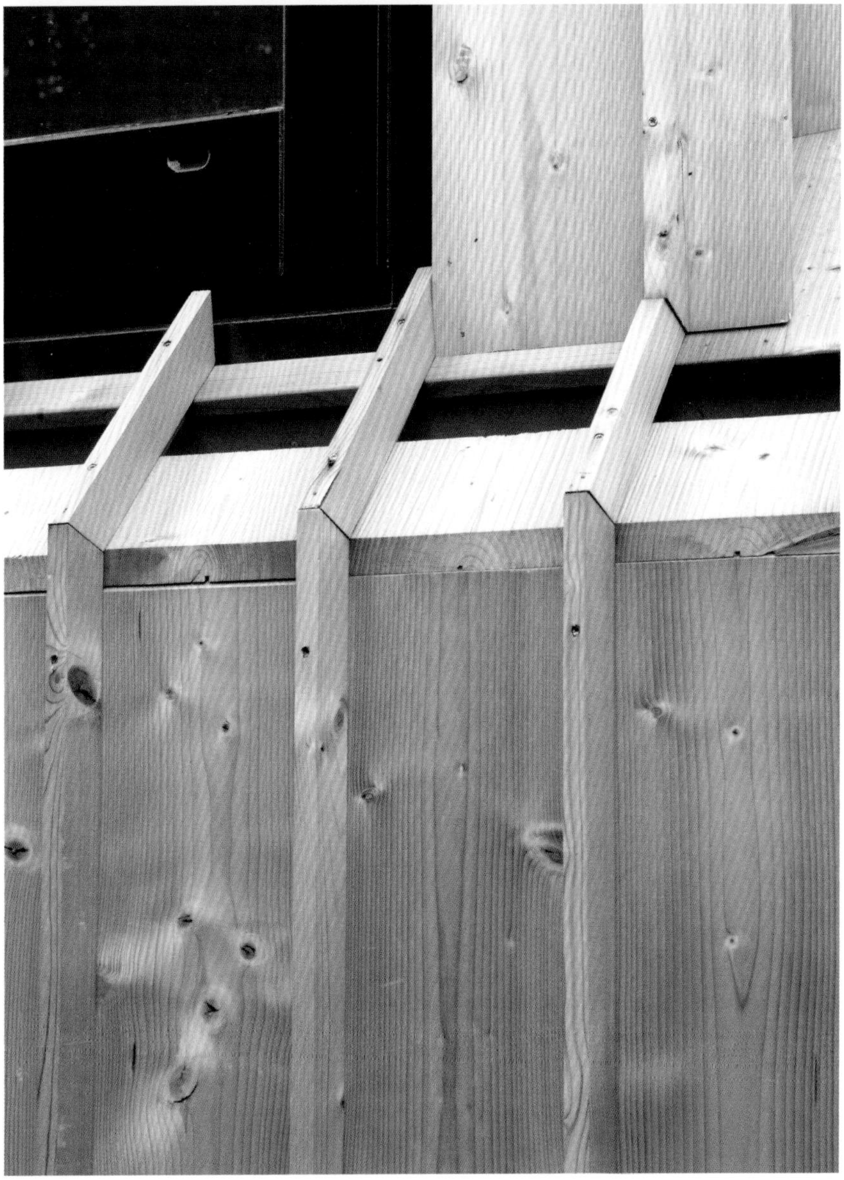

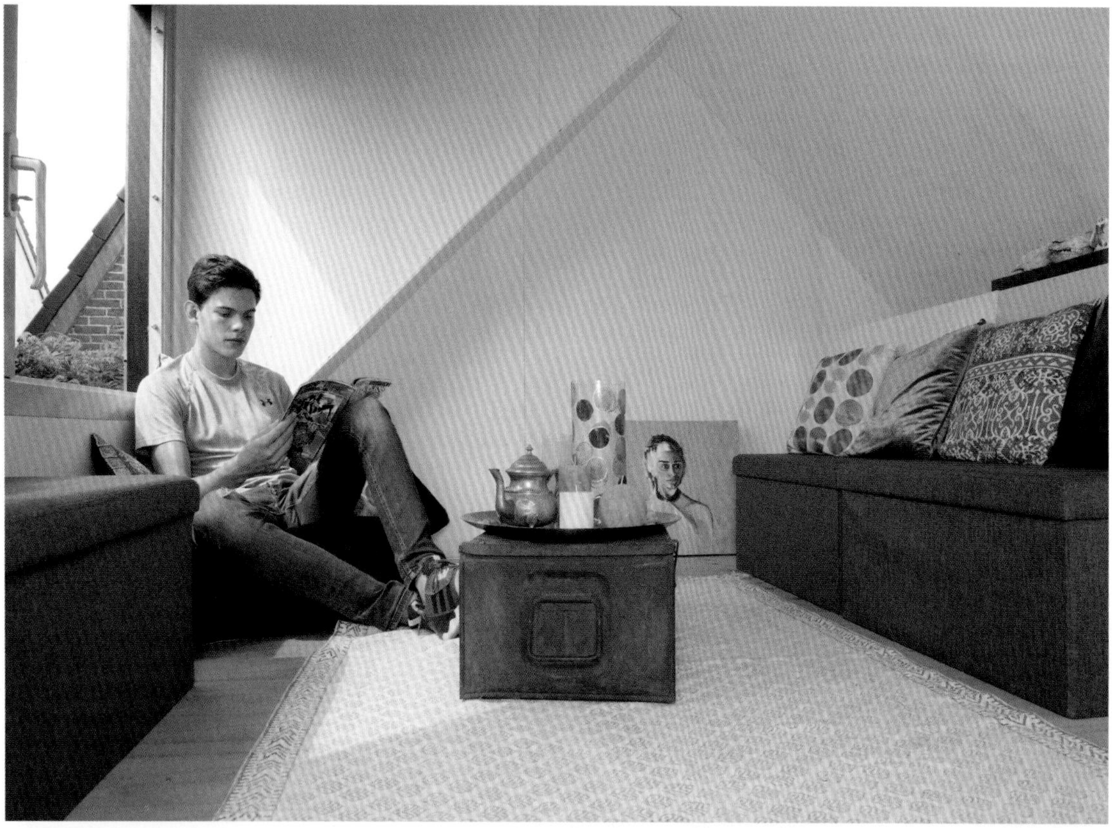

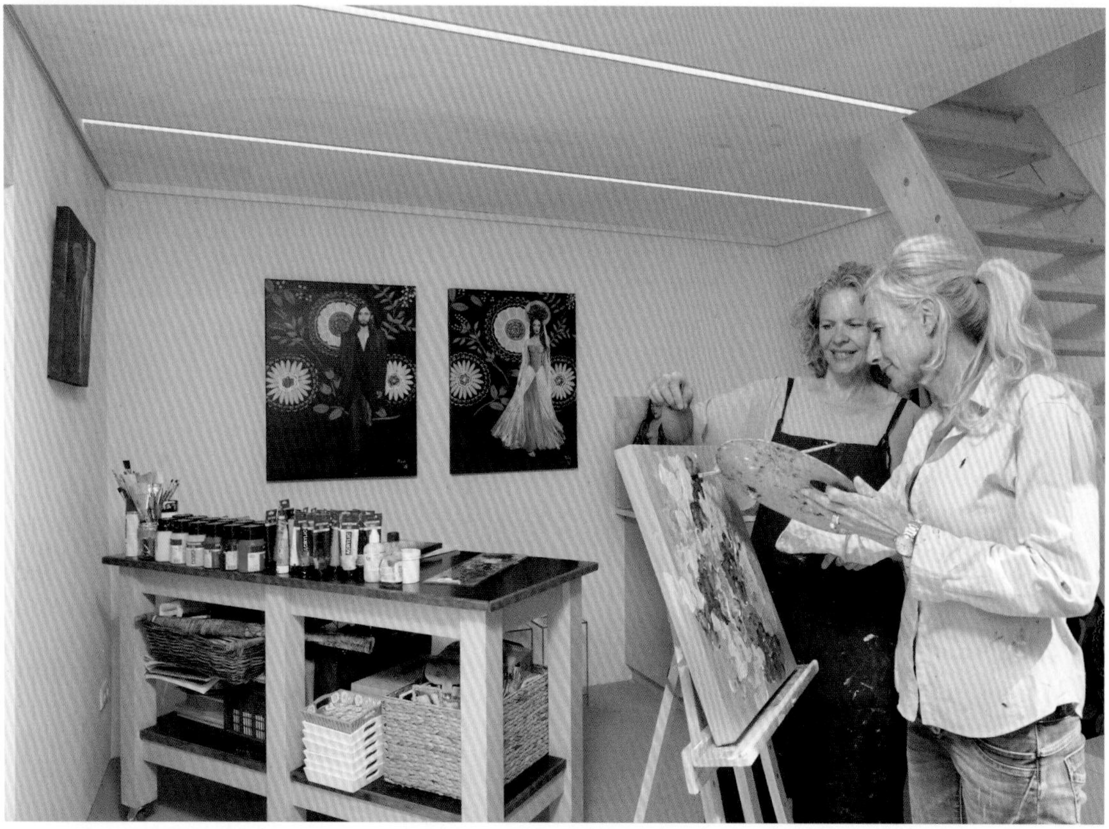

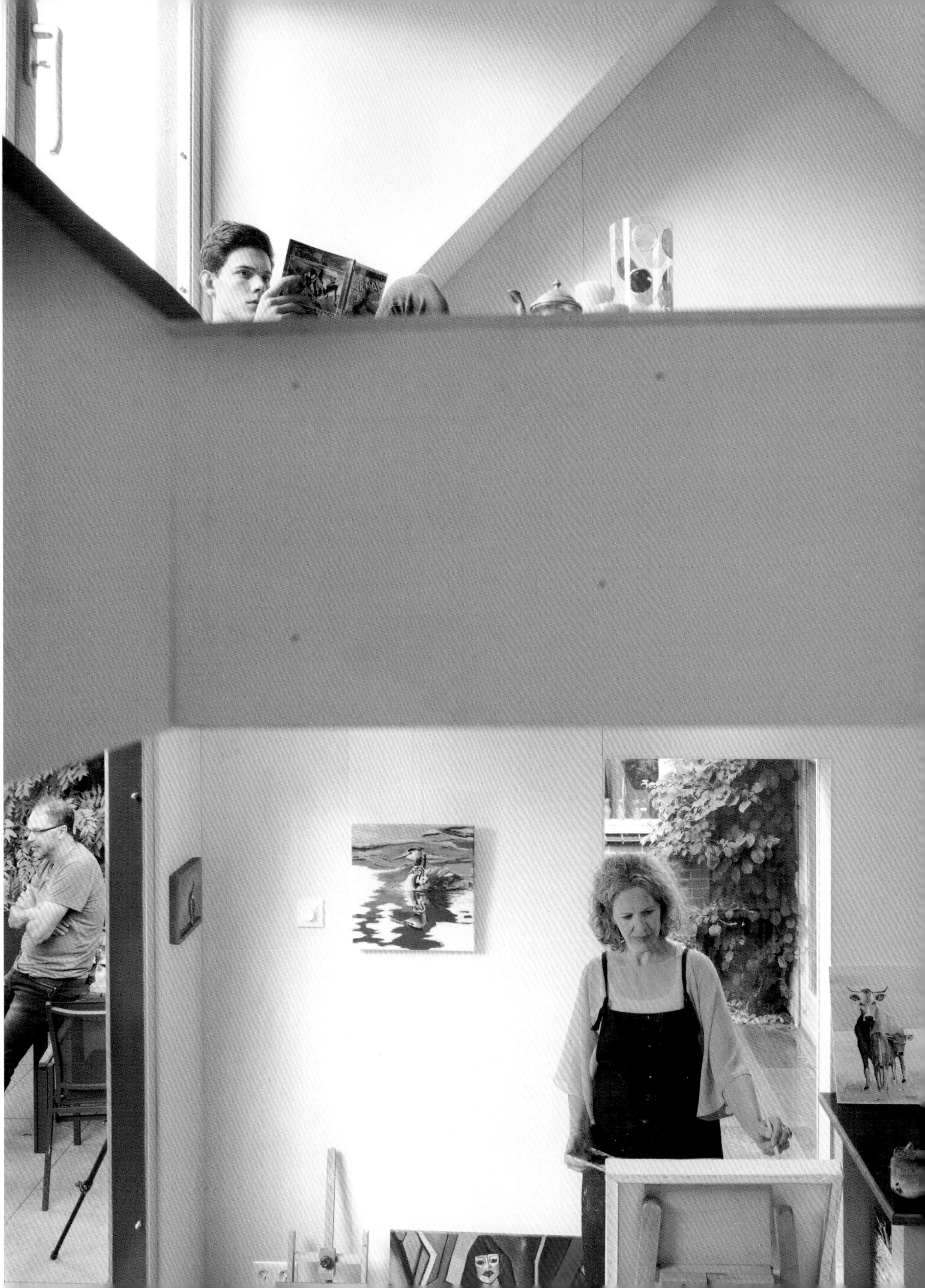

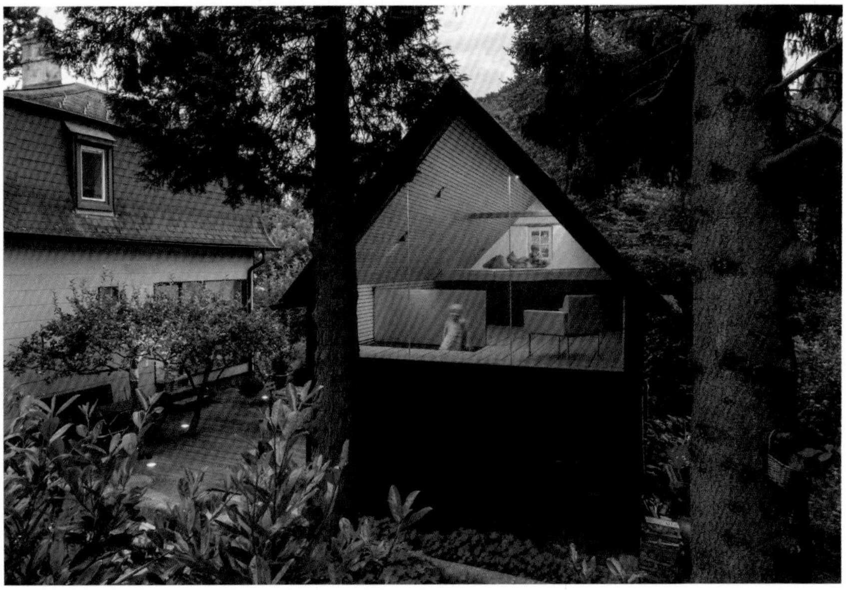

Area:
1,399 square feet (130 square meters)

Completion:
2015

Design:
Franz&Sue

Photography:
Andreas Buchberger, Veronika Hofinger

Eichgraben, Austria

The Enchanted Shed

An old outbuilding has been transformed into a writer's workshop, a garden room for guests, and a children's paradise.

A radical and respectful renovation

The workmen from the village wanted to tear down the black shed from 1934: they said it was draughty, weather-beaten, and worm-eaten. But the designers liked this black outbuilding of the mansard-roof house in the Vienna Woods and were keen to renovate it in a radical yet respectful manner. The history of the building gave it a special appeal; back in the 1930s, few people could afford a basement, let alone a garage, and so they built their own sheds to store wood, raise rabbits, or boil laundry in, which was then hung up to dry in the attic.

A magical place of retreat

Over the past few decades these structures have lost their original purpose, and many are falling apart. But when converted into small, cozy hideaways, they become affordable, magical retreats for families and their guests.

The designers inserted a large pane of glass into the front wall of the attic floor and carefully insulated the trusses. The walls were paneled with varnished gray fir, and an elevated section at the rear was upholstered so that the attic can also be used as an out-of-the-ordinary guest room.

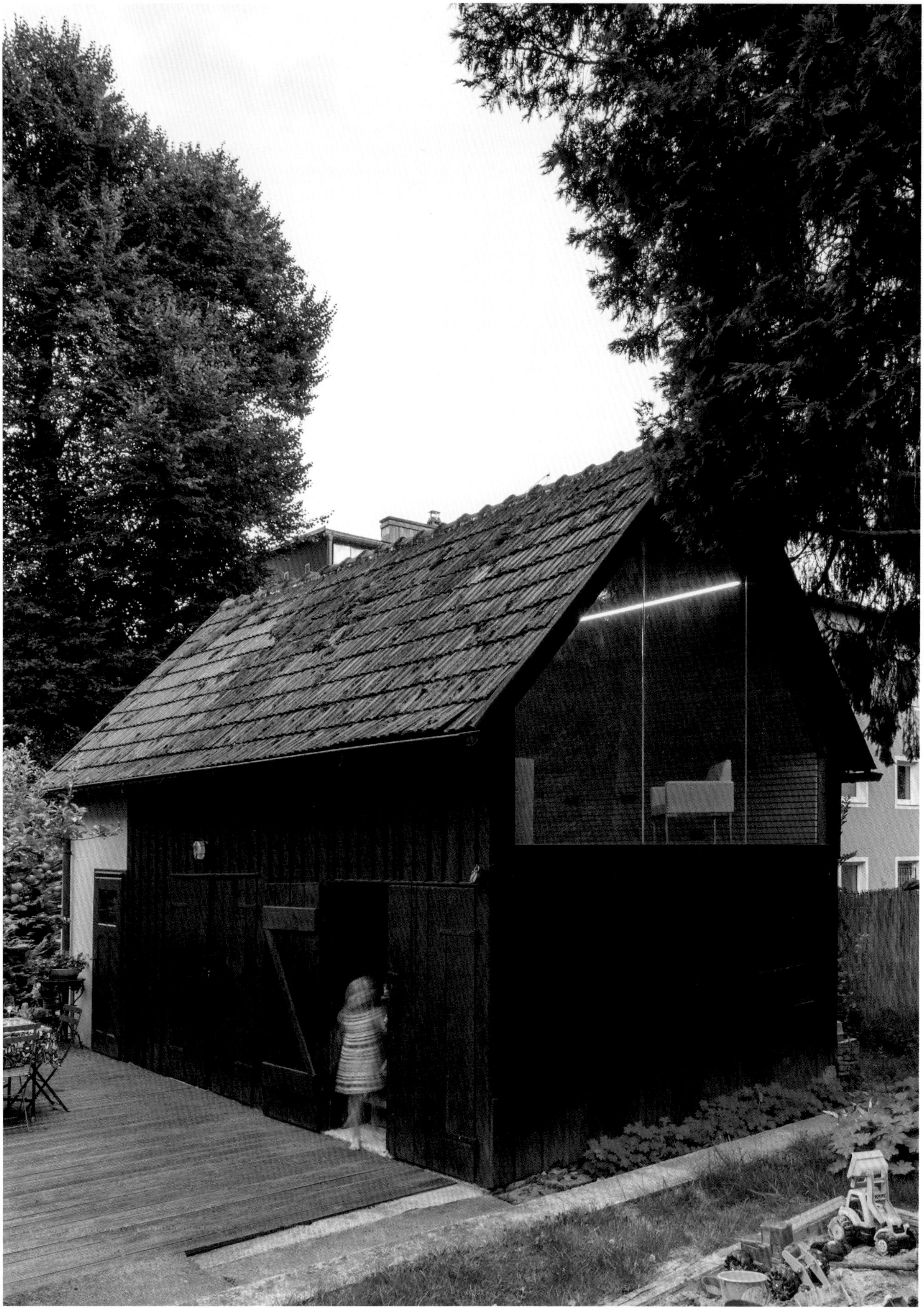

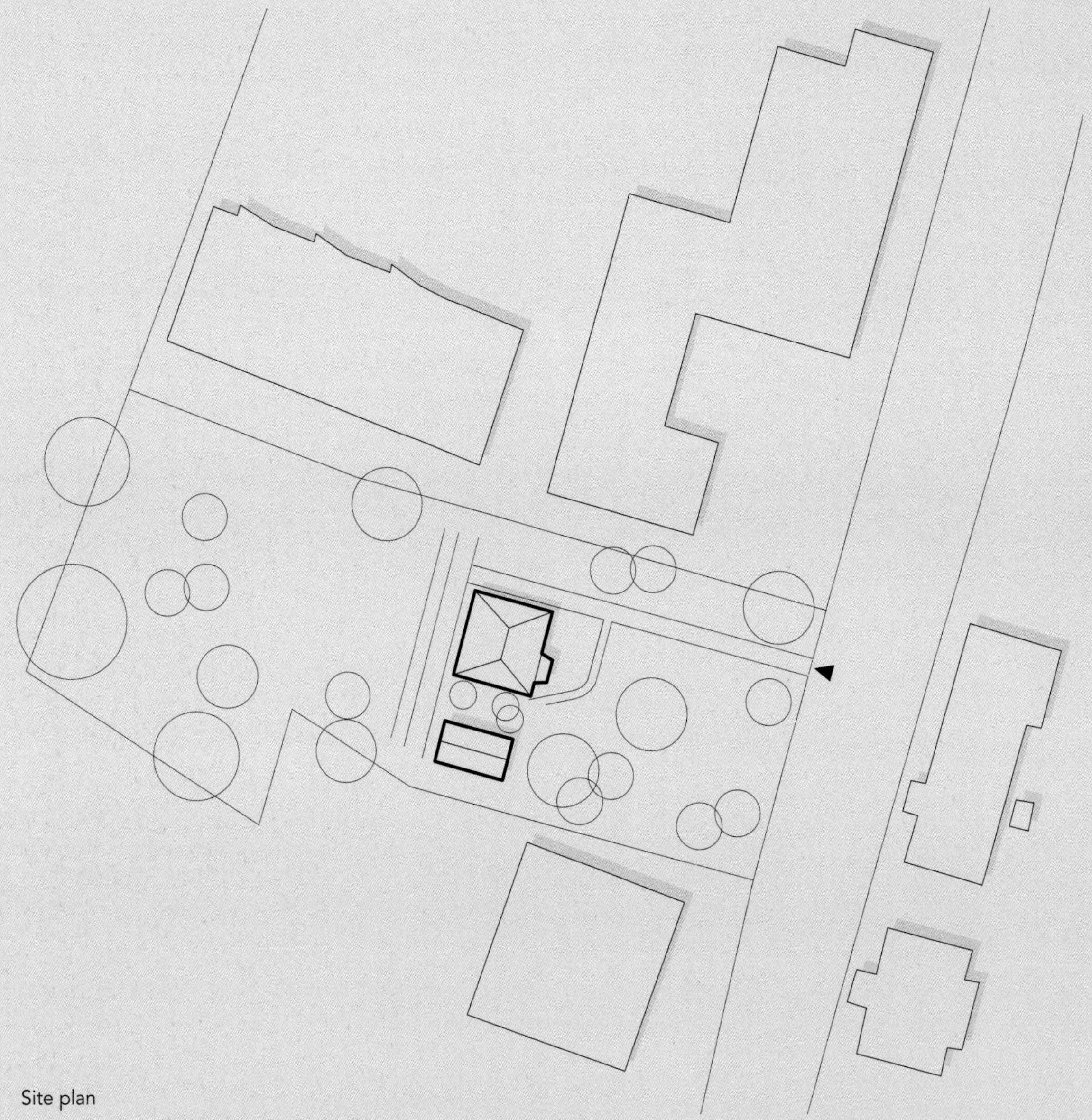

Site plan

Watching the squirrels

An elegant brass trapdoor closes off this enchanted place, from which people can watch the squirrels play in the treetops. The ground floor is still used for storing garden tools, the lawn mower, and fruit crates, while upstairs it is snug and comfortable. Spotlights illuminate the brass in the evening, creating a warm light even in freezing winter when the unheated room is used for cooling down after a sauna session.

The attic is ventilated via an already existing window and small air vents installed along the sides. The designers didn't touch the roof, though, as it is covered in moss, which they liked.

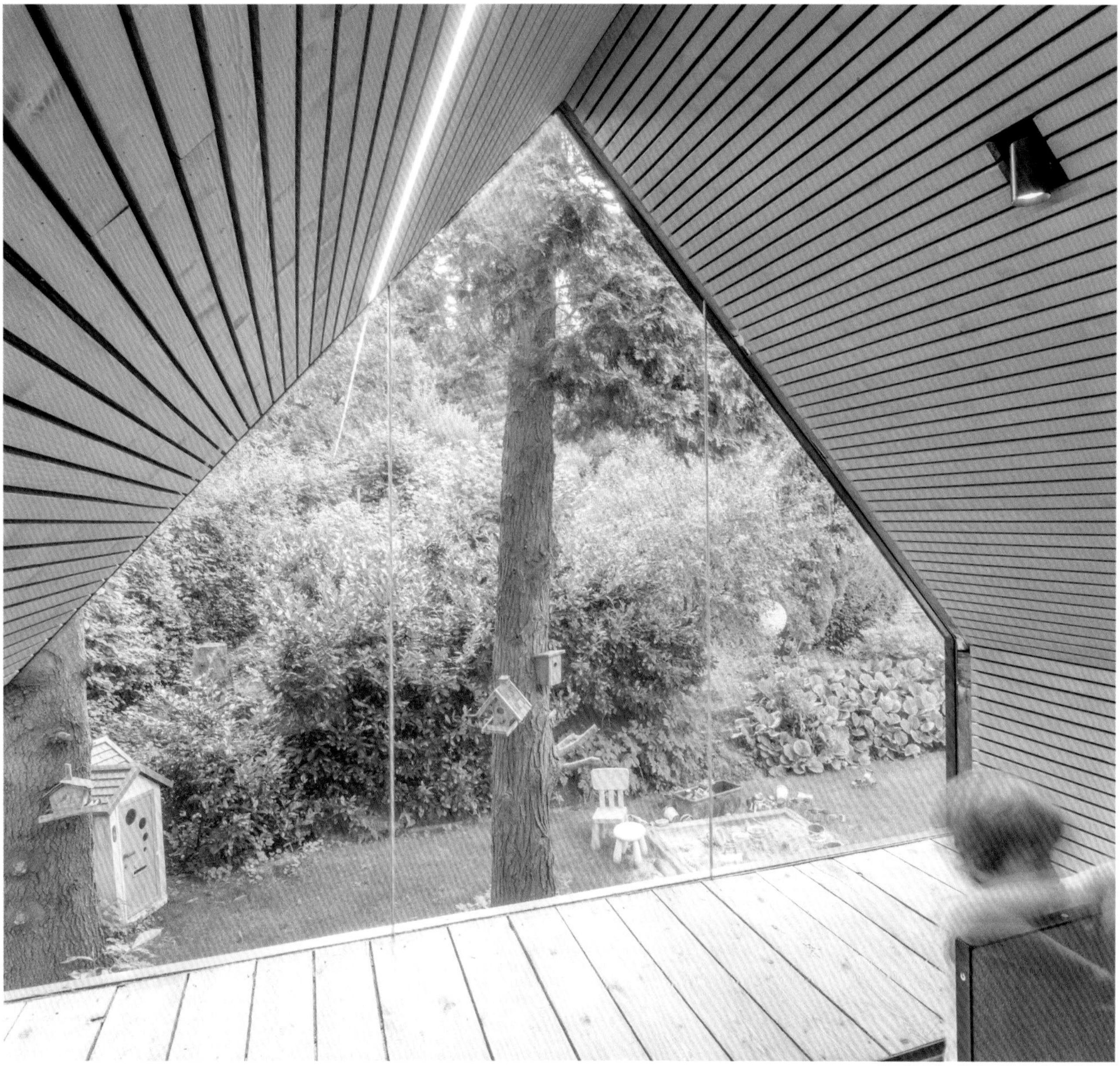

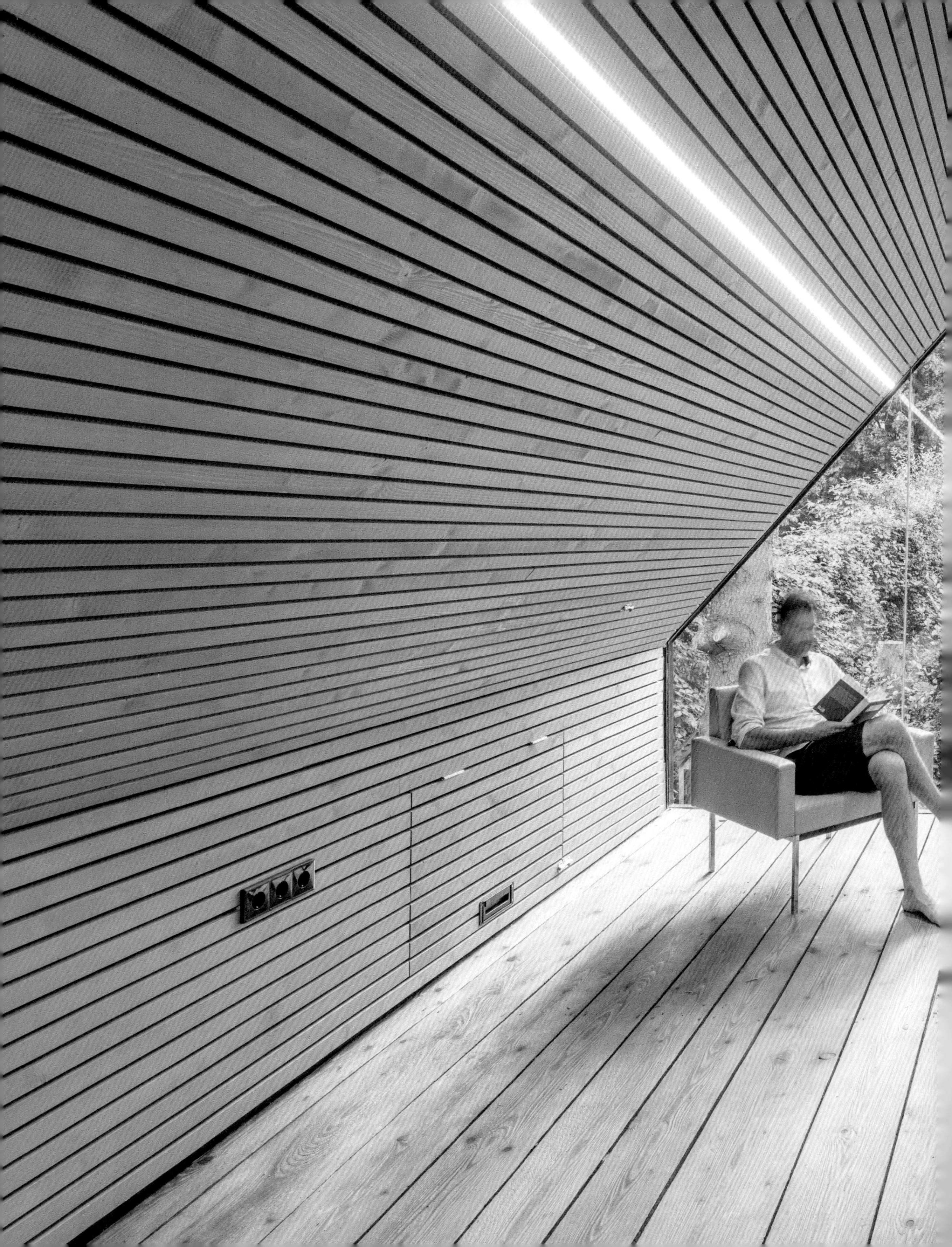

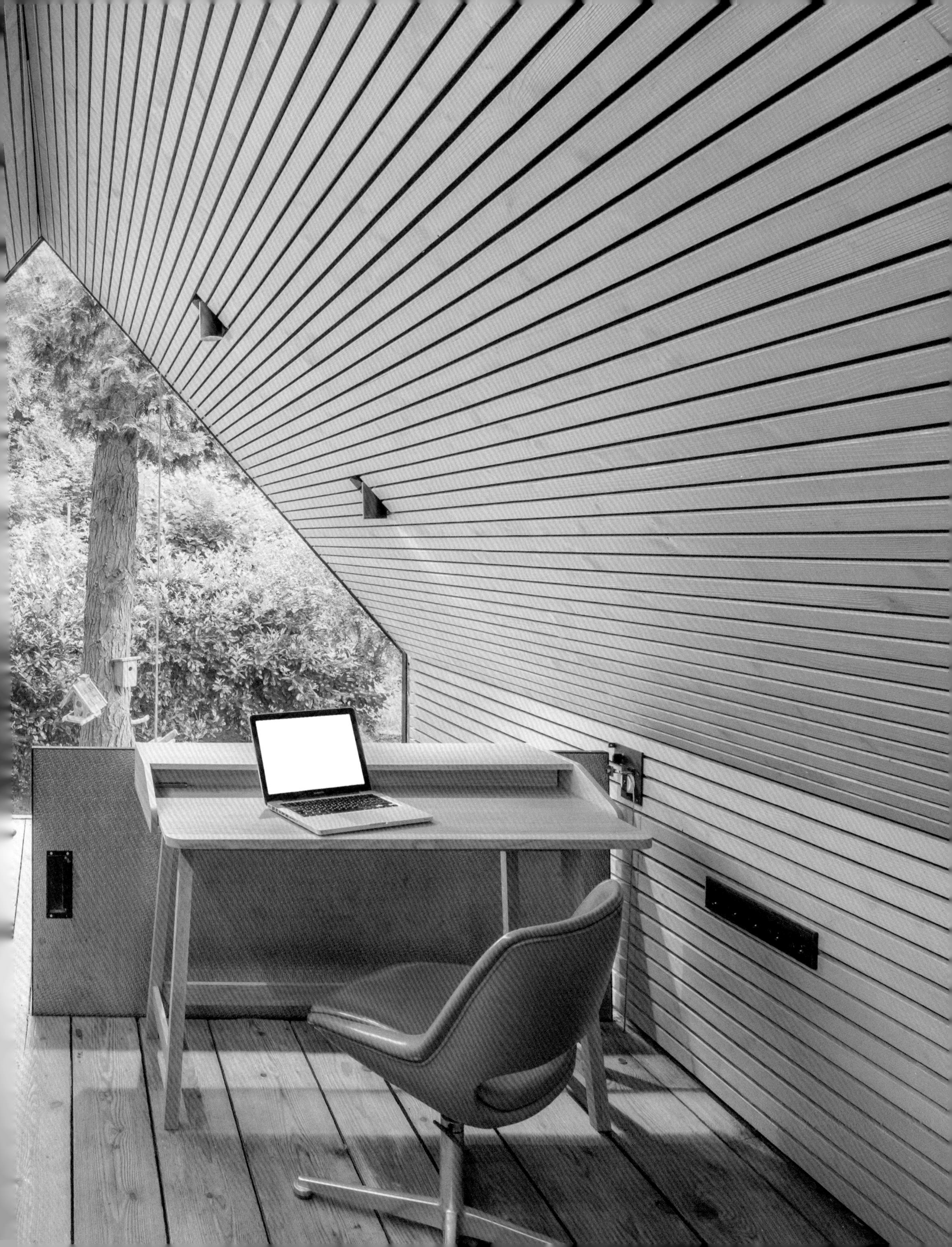

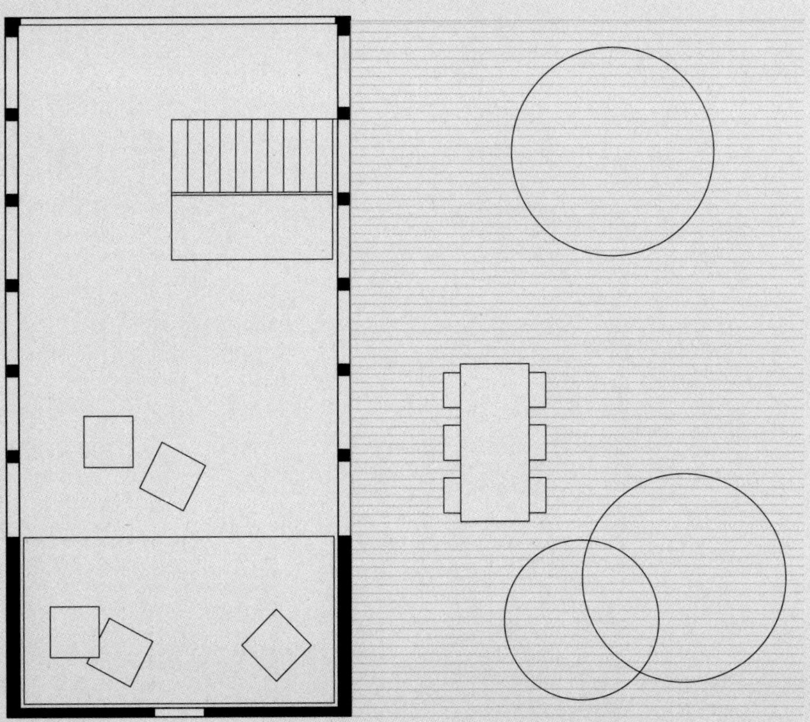

Floor plan

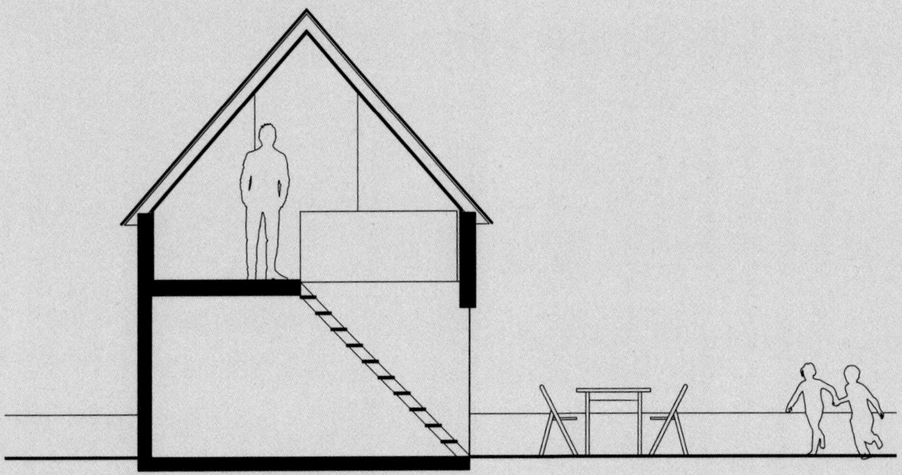

Section

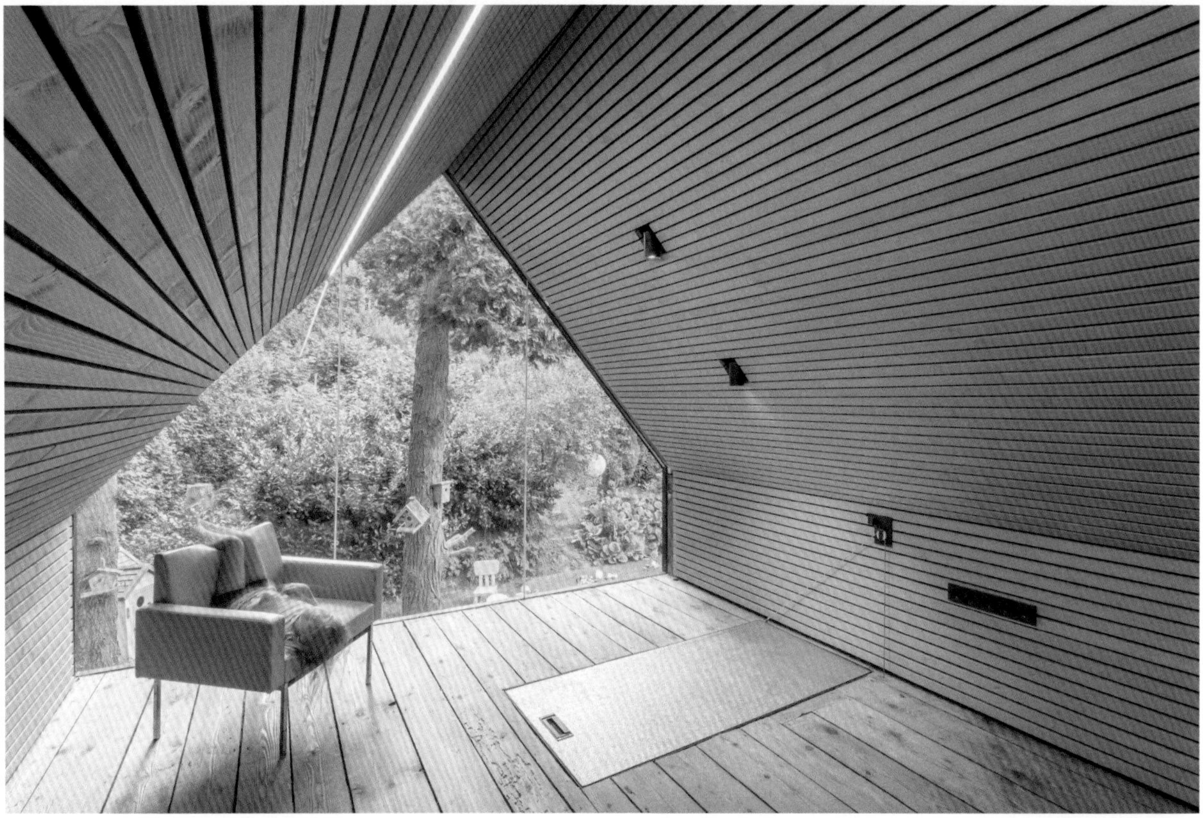

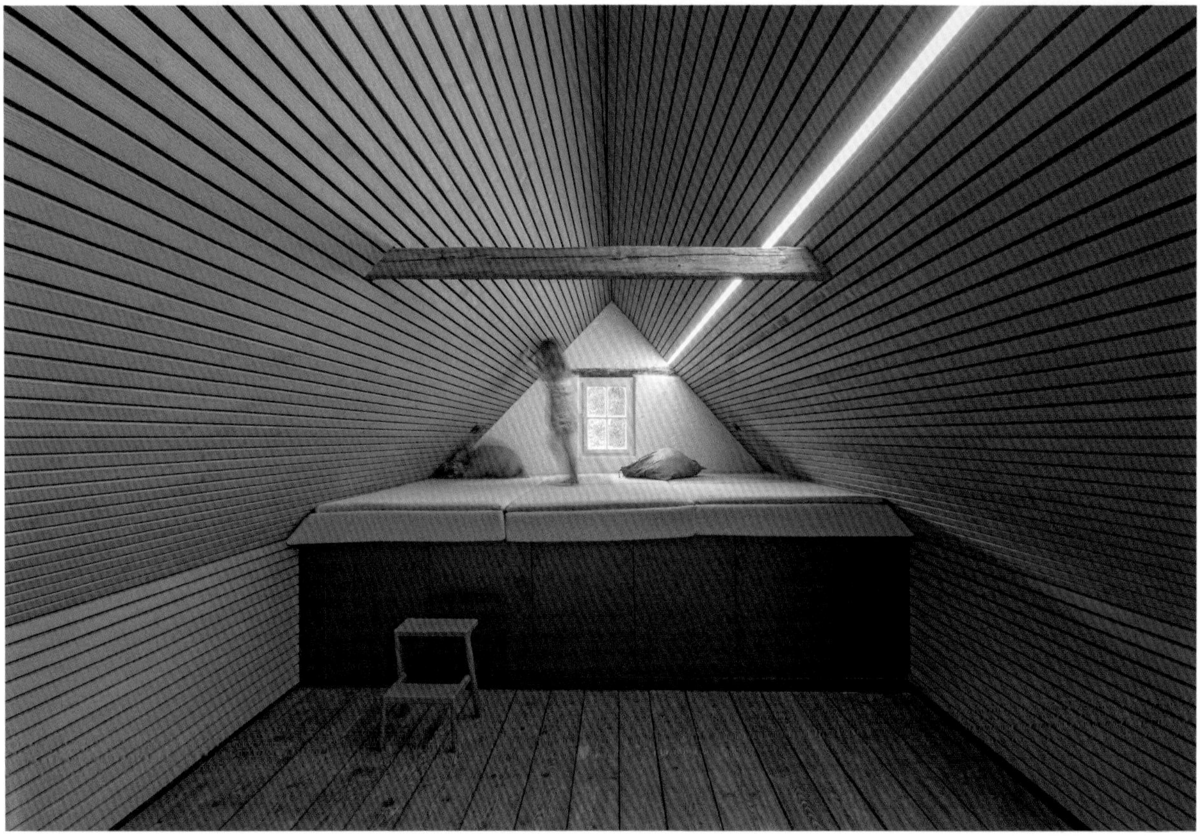

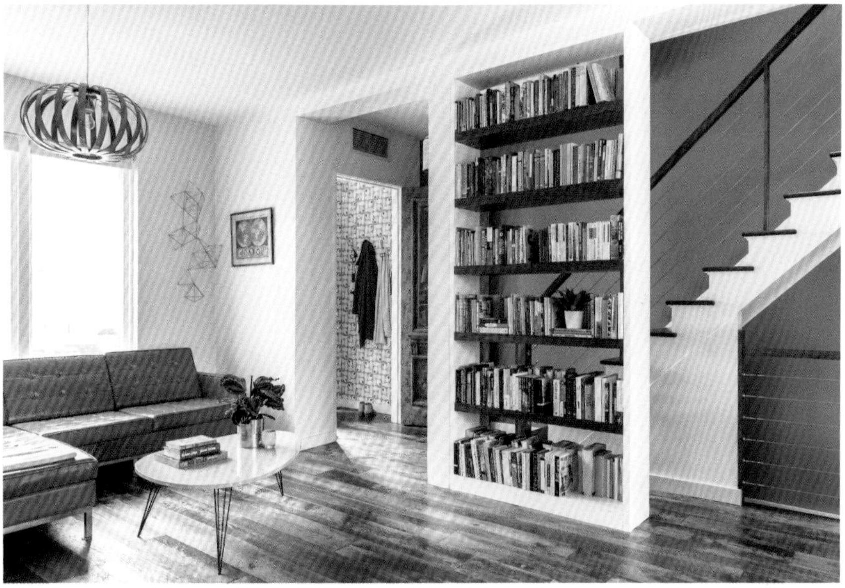

Area:
1,785 square feet (164 square meters)

Completion:
2016

Design:
Barker Associates Architecture Office (BAAO Architects)

Photography:
Lesley Unruh

Brooklyn, United States

House for a Writer and Musician

Gayle Forman, a Brooklyn-based author of young-adult titles such as *If I Stay* and *Where She Went*, and Nick Tucker, her musician-librarian husband, approached the architects with a request to overhaul the living spaces of their semi-attached wood-framed row house.

Books and music

The couple's love of books and music inspired the open layout of the house. Instead of completely eliminating intermediate supports for the 20-foot (6-meter) span of the first floor, the columns were incorporated into open bookshelves between the stairs and the living space, reminiscent of stacks that might be found in the recesses of a library. In the living room on the opposite wall, a gas fireplace is flanked by deep shelves proportioned specifically to house Nick's vinyl record collection.

Family spaces

The kitchen occupies the L-shaped back of the house and provides space for food preparation and cooking with the family. Full-height glazing and corner-wrapping windows allow ample light into the space. Semi-handmade cabinet doors of reclaimed pine match the reclaimed floorboards in the dining and living space. Full-height flush-mounted doors conceal the extensive storage capacity of the pantry.

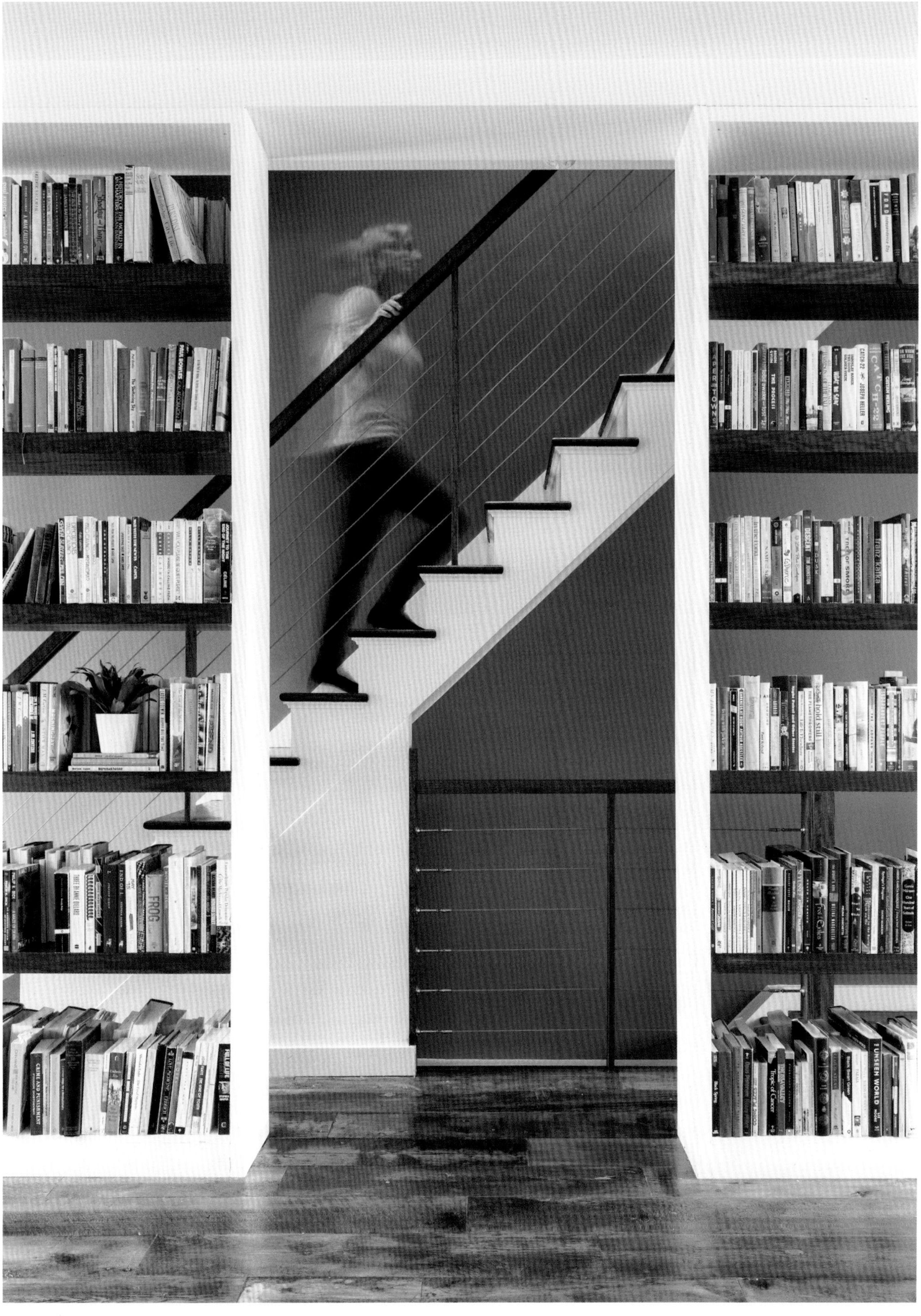

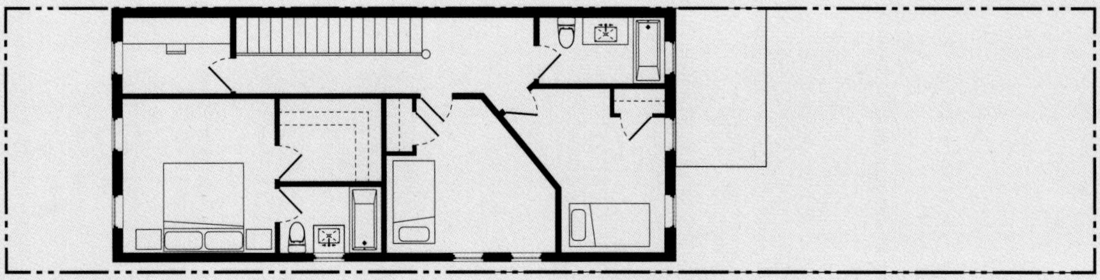

First-floor plan

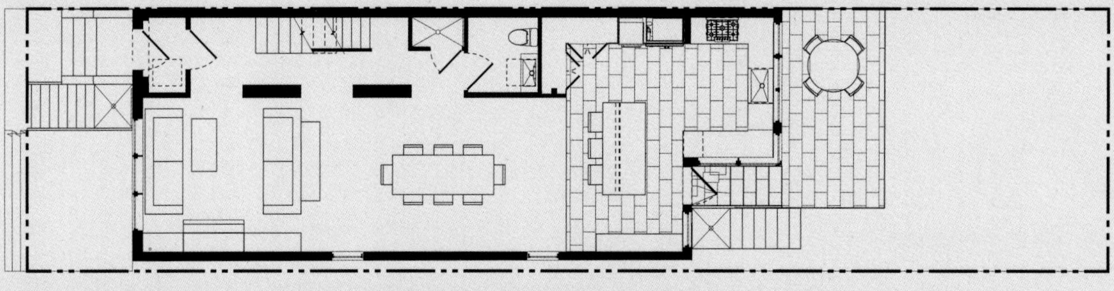

Ground-floor plan

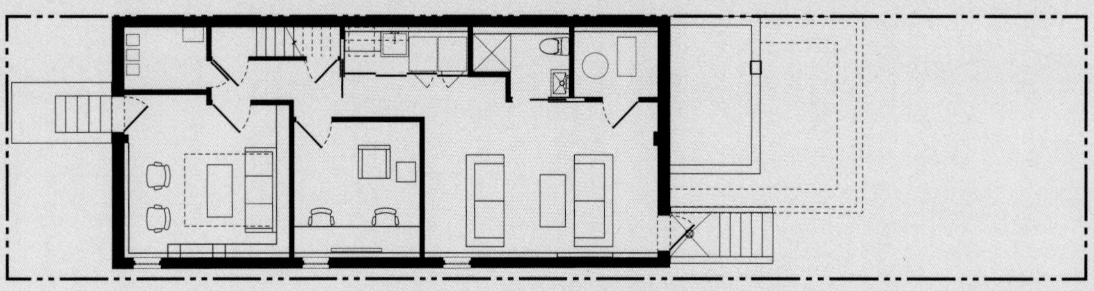

Basement floor plan

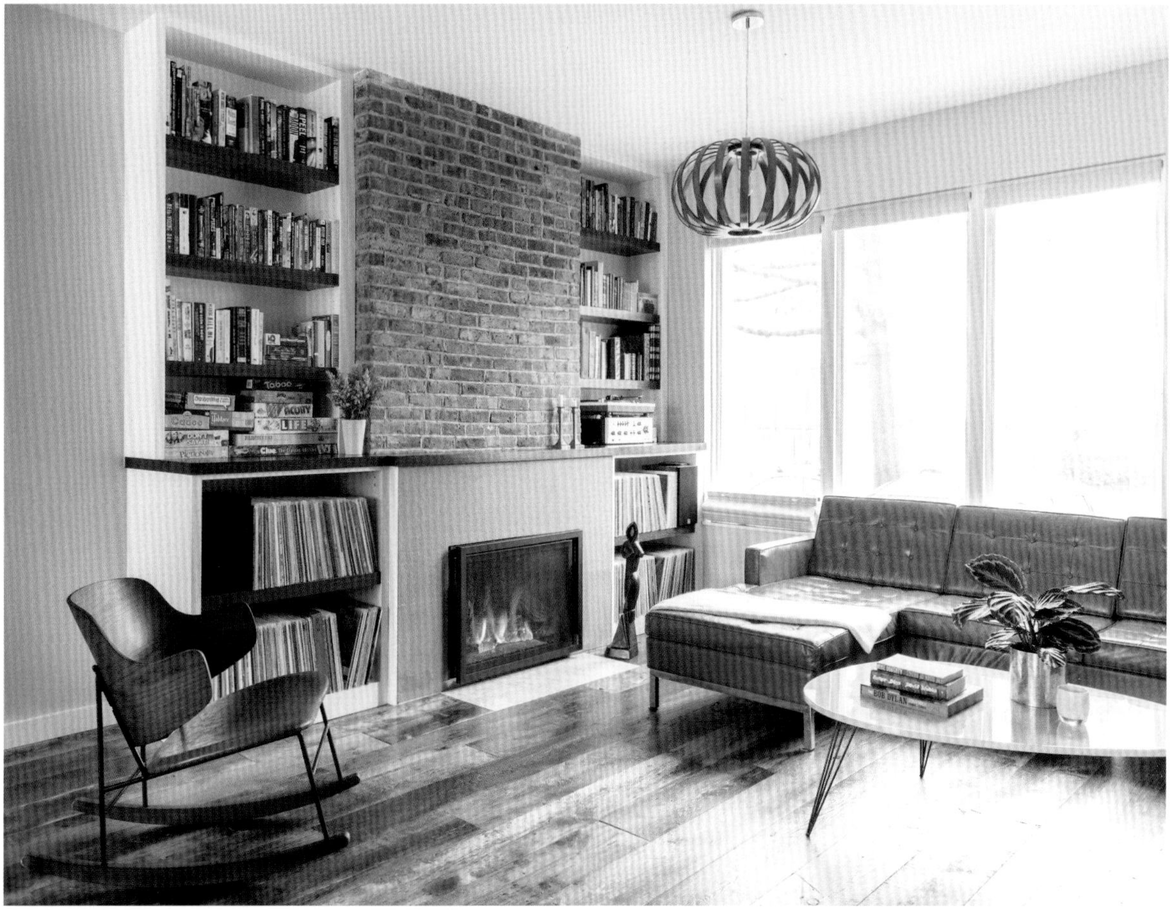
BOB DYLAN

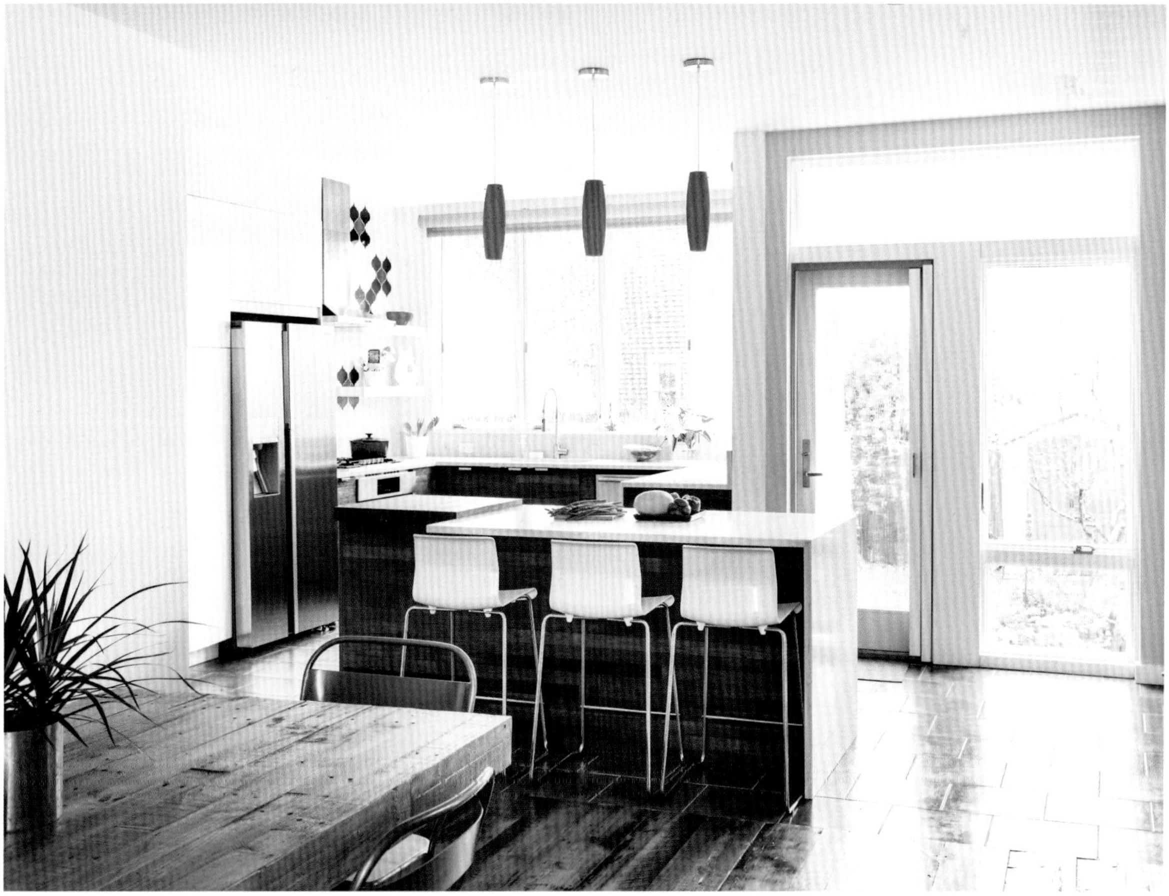

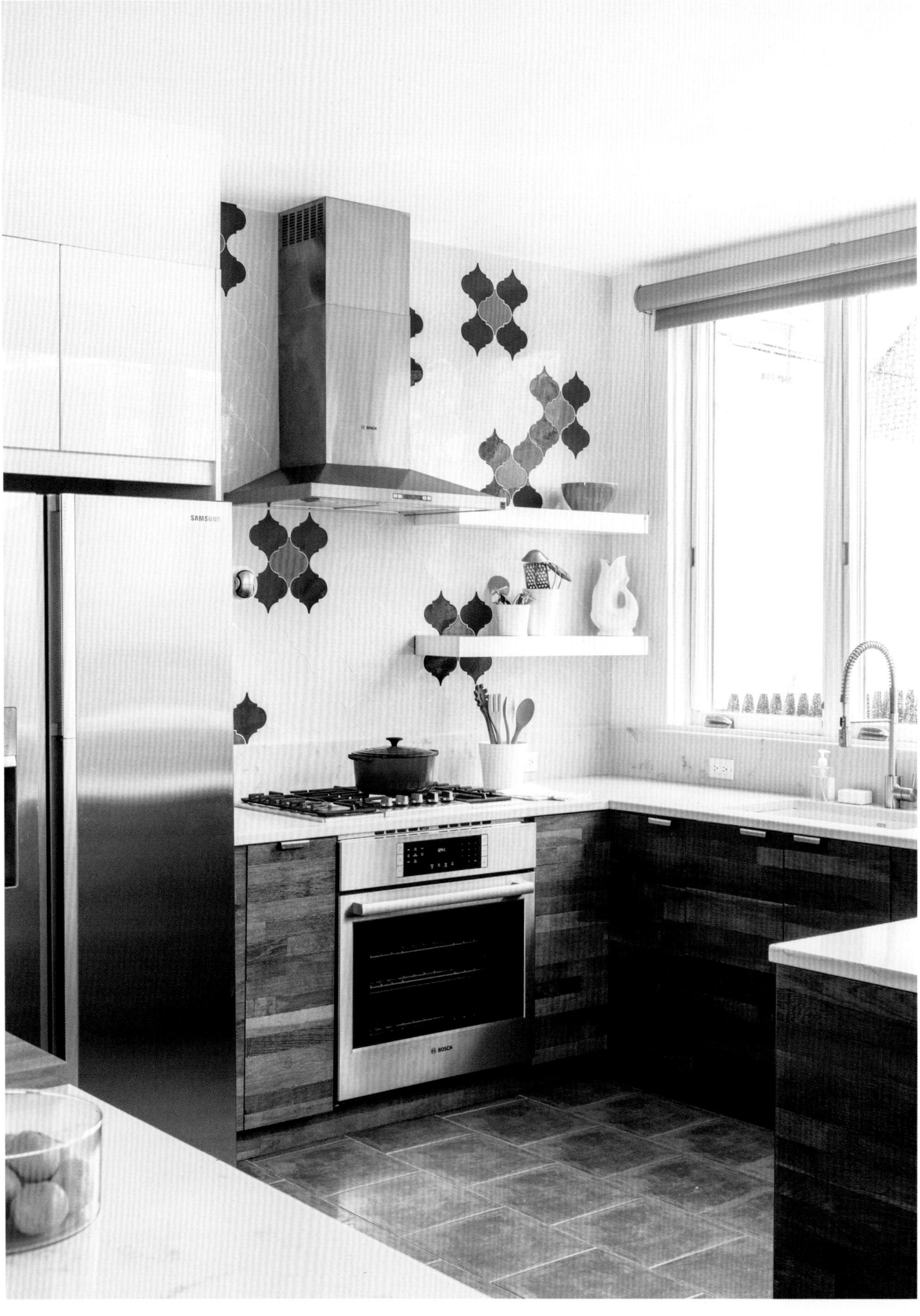
SAMSUNG
BOSCH

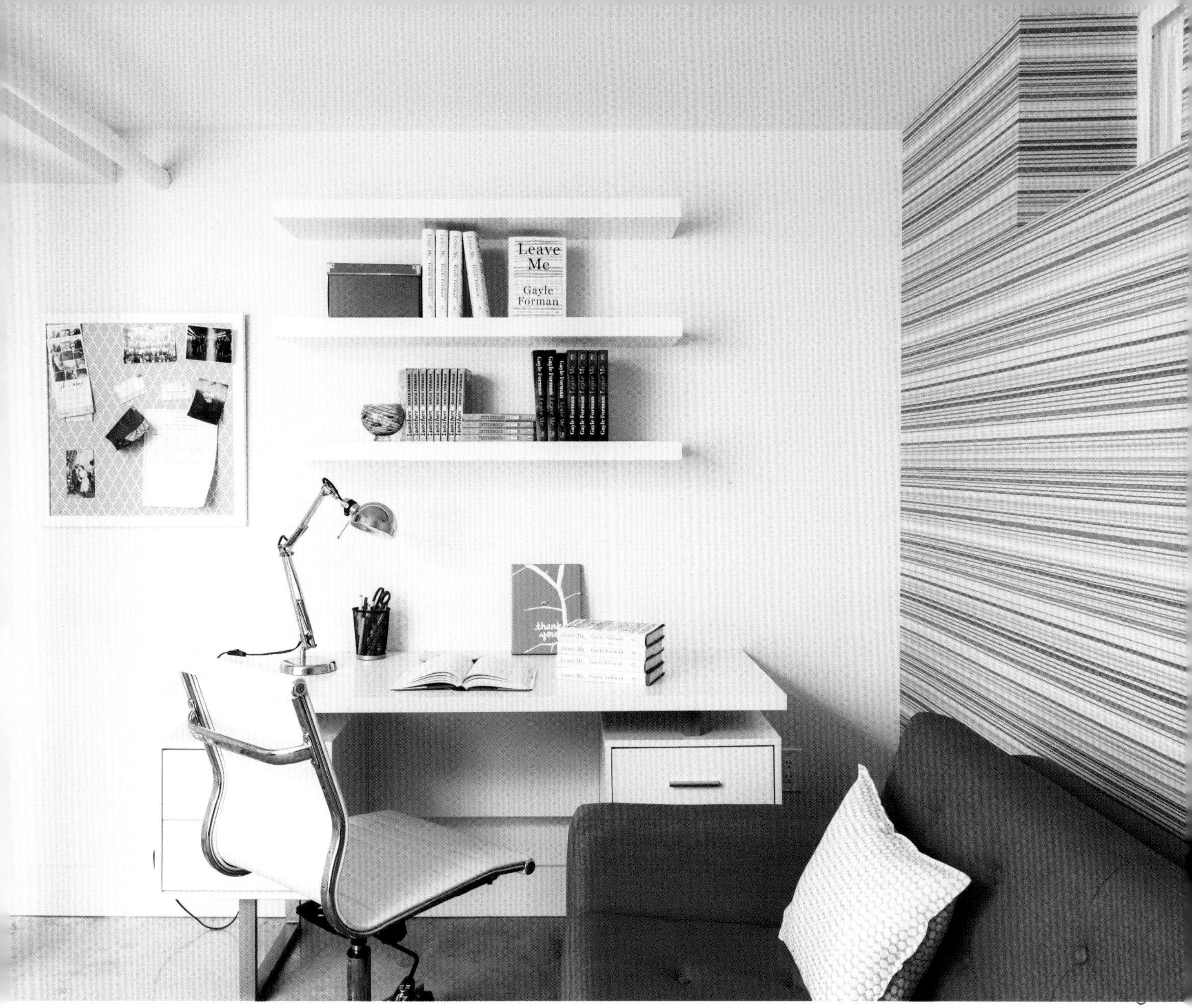

The island is positioned in direct view of the living spaces and provides the visual and functional focal point for food preparation. Color accents of blue and orange backsplash tile, entry-hall wallpaper, and light fixtures tie the living spaces together.

The basement is divided into private spaces. Gayle's candy-striped writing studio and Nick's blue-hued music studio are located at the bottom of the stairs.

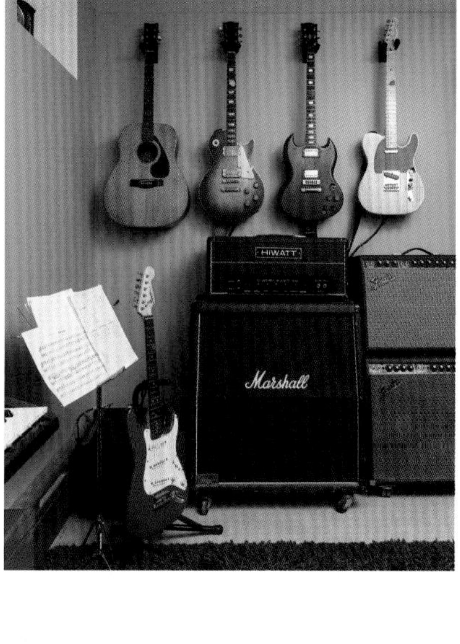

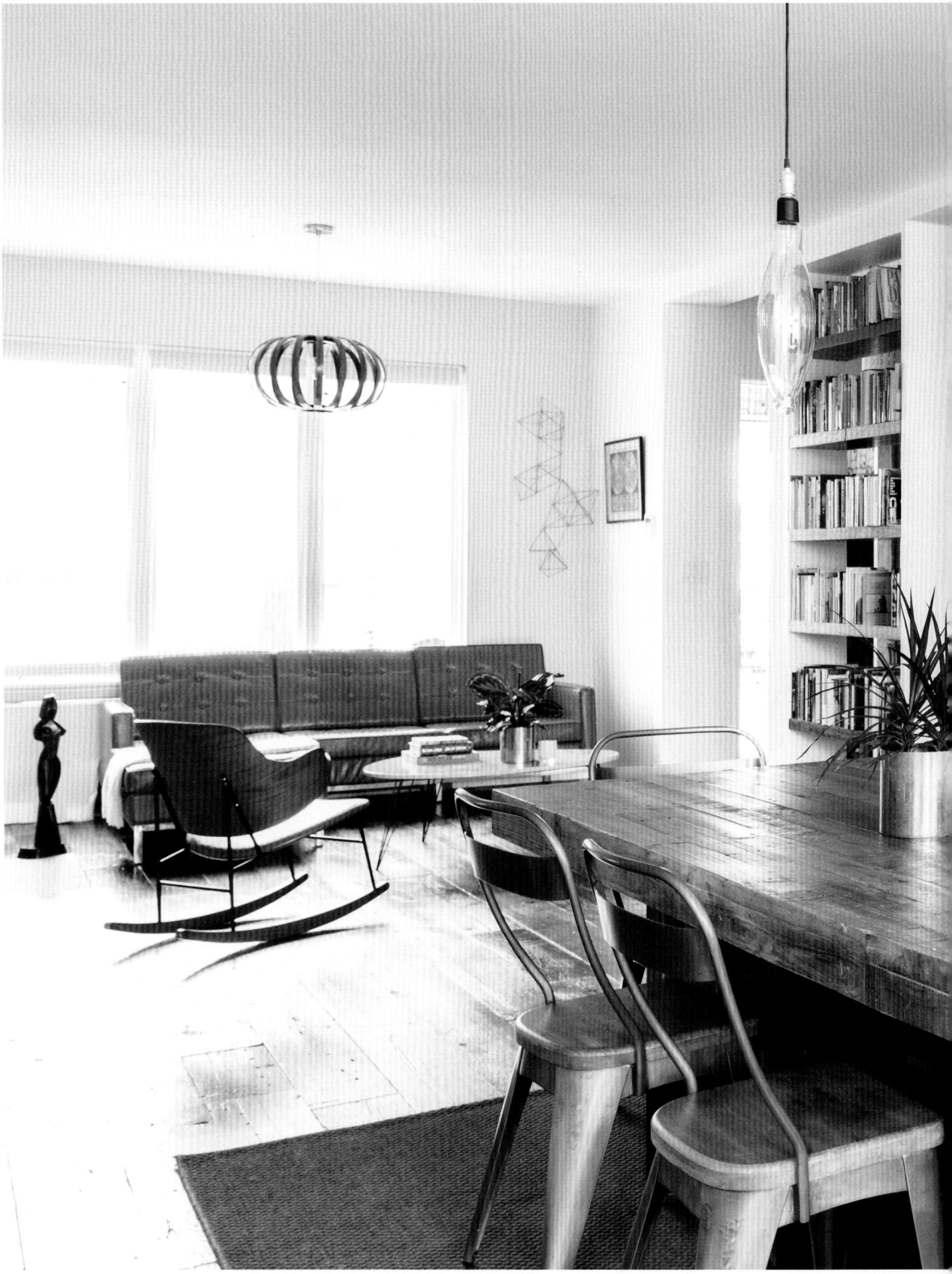

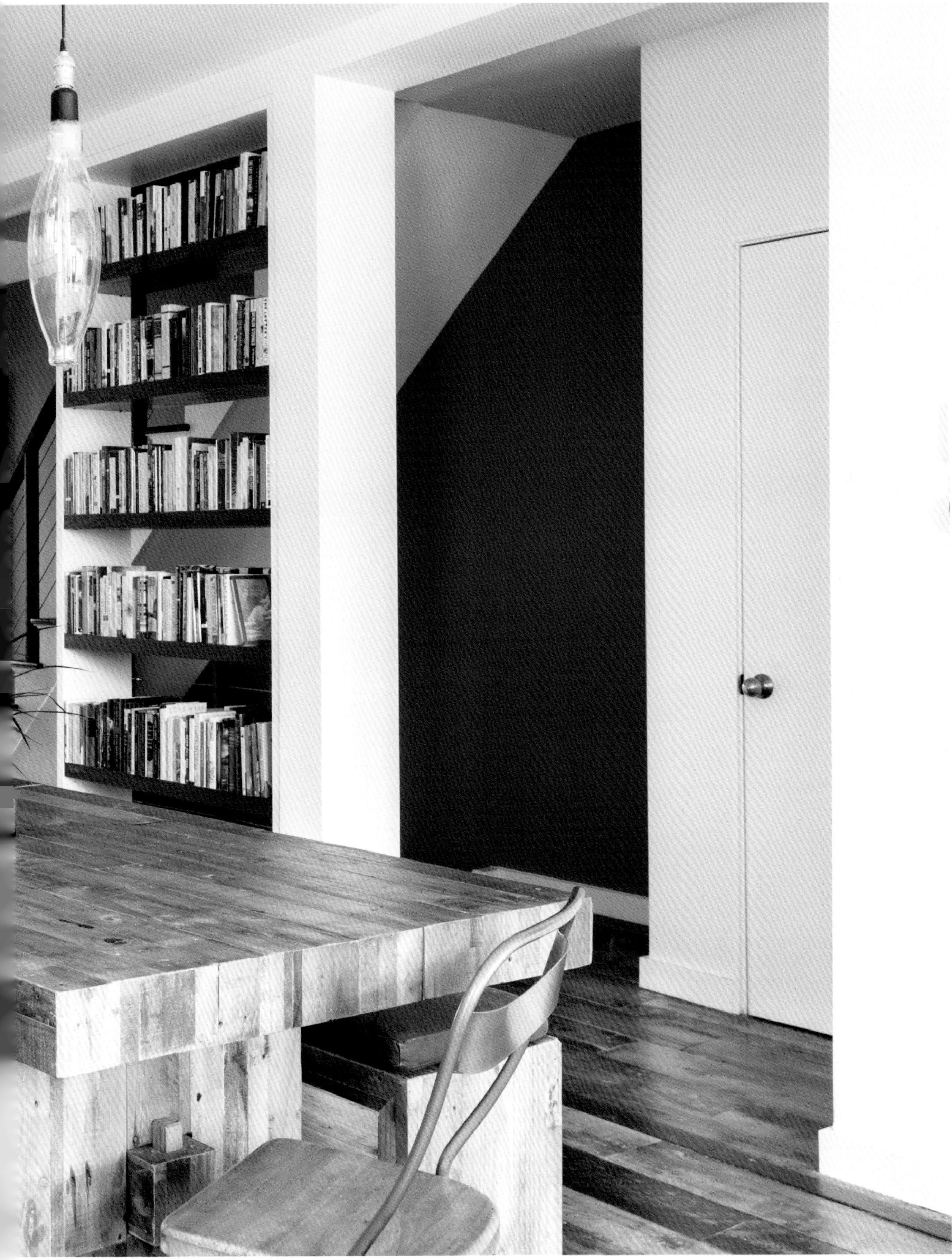

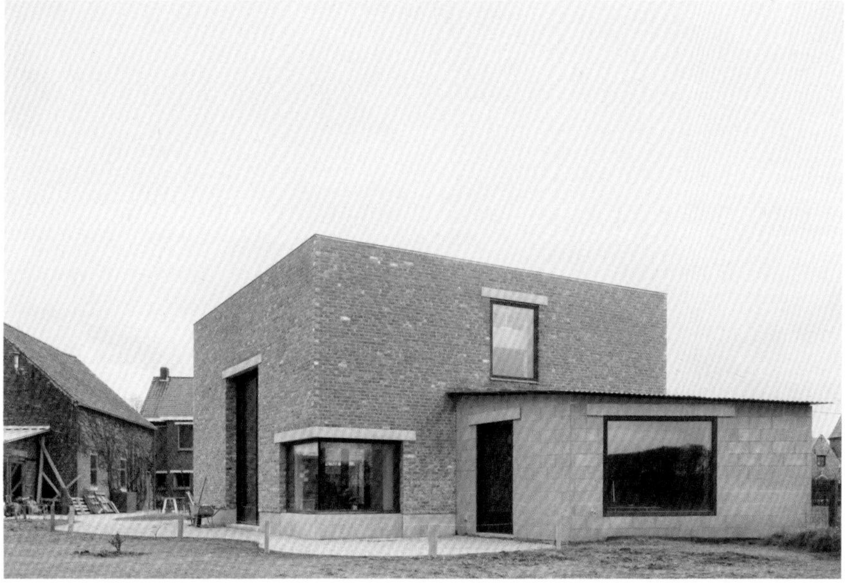

Area:
1,400 square feet (130 square meters)

Completion:
2018

Design:
Graux & Baeyens Architects

Photography:
Jeroen Verrecht

Deinze, Belgium

Studio SDS

The project involved the renovation of Belgian artist Stief Desmet's painting and sculpting studio, which adjoins the family home. The studio was no longer meeting the needs of the artist, who has been creating ever-larger sculptures. The new atelier consists of a primarily double-height brick volume, partly embraced by lower secondary buildings.

Peace and serenity

The new studio has a symmetrical floor plan that aspires towards peace and serenity. The sober but brutal materialization supports the function that it includes. Both narrow vertical gate doors vary in width and give the opportunity to create large sculptures. The corner window forms a resting point within the large space. The study area is located at the back with a view of the vast landscape.

Connections

Together with the other buildings, a story has been told in which the whole has a reinforcing effect on the components. The use of materials seeks connection to the main house and the adjacent stables, without falling into copying. The sloping location allows an inner court to be formed without closing off from the natural garden behind it.

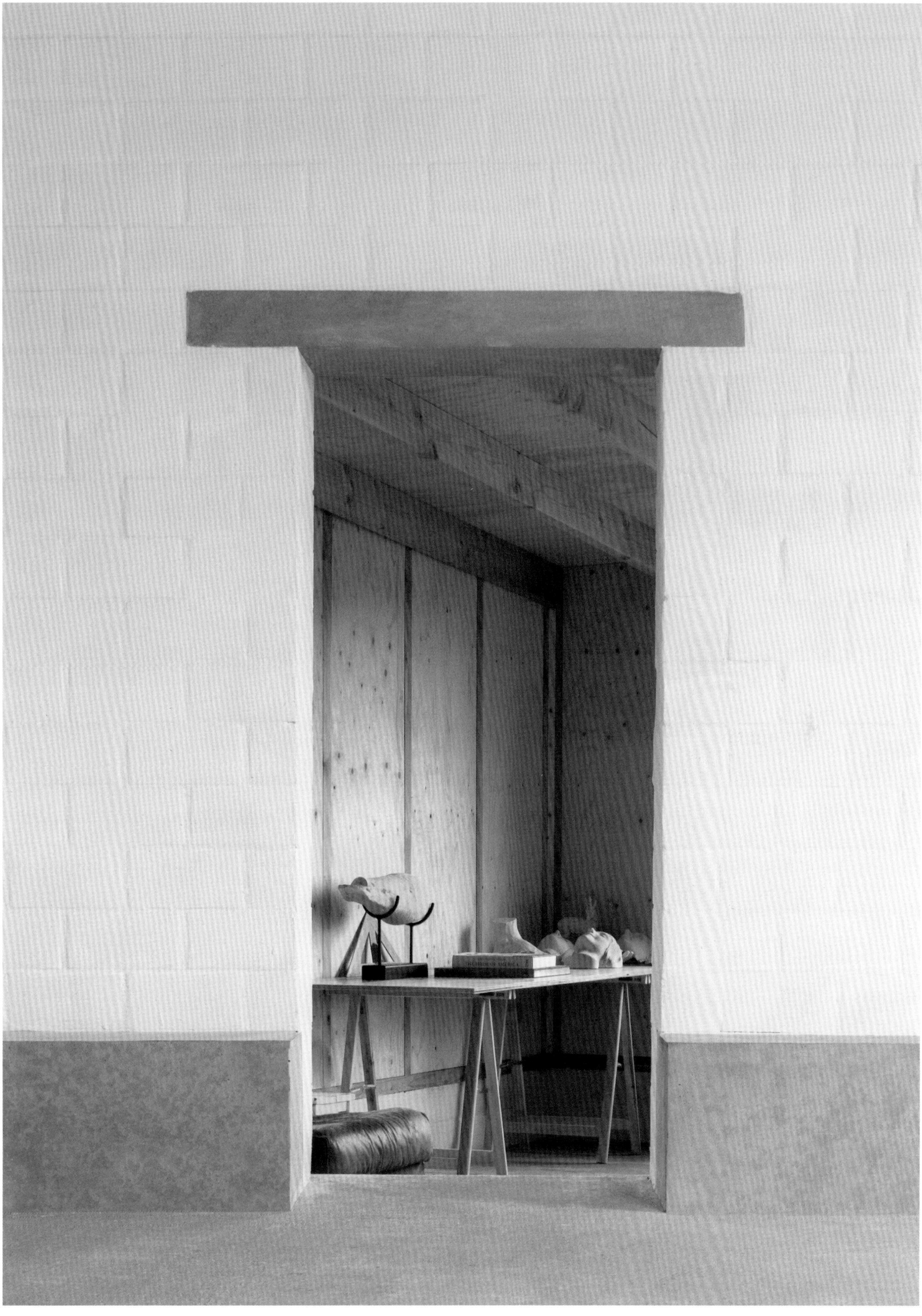

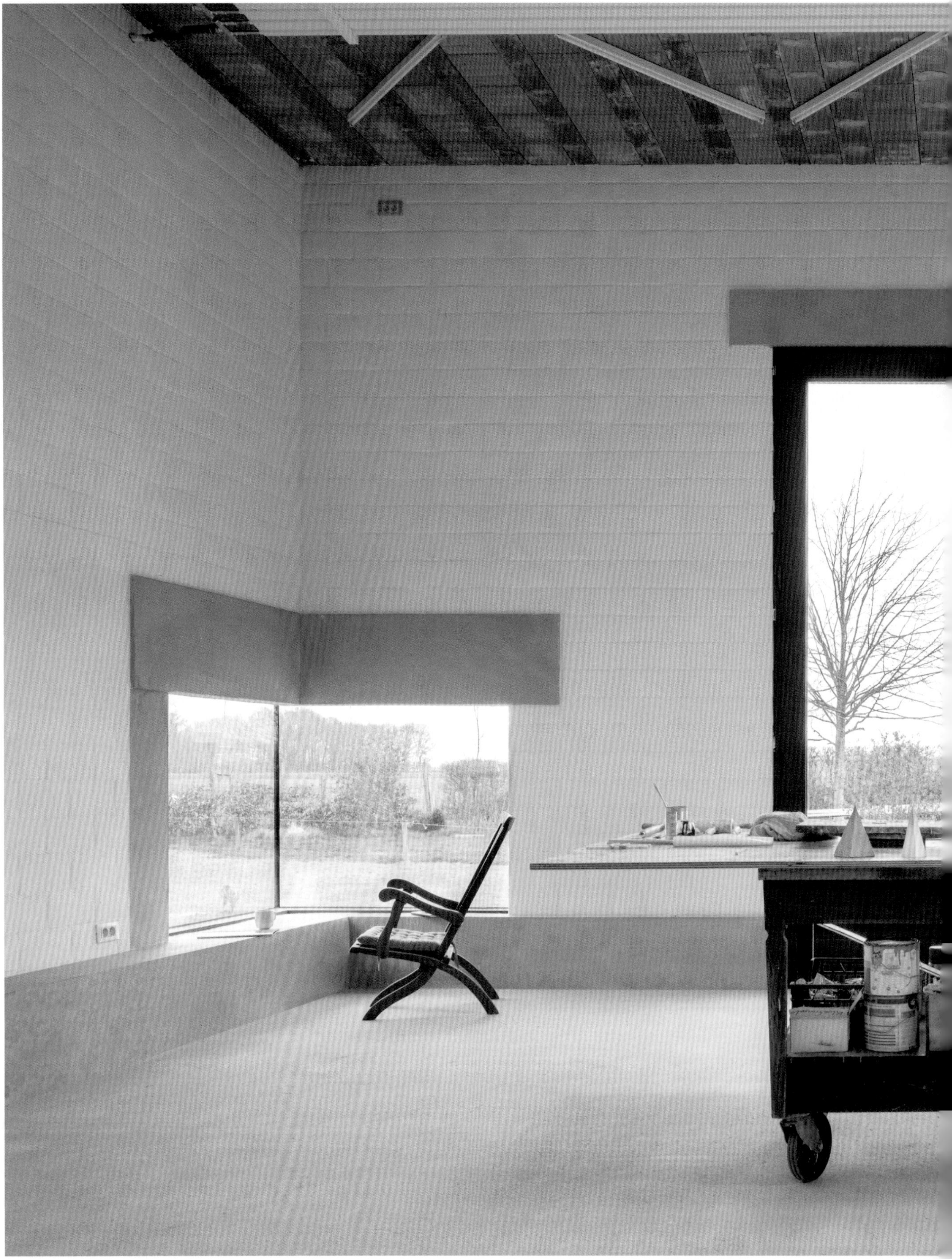

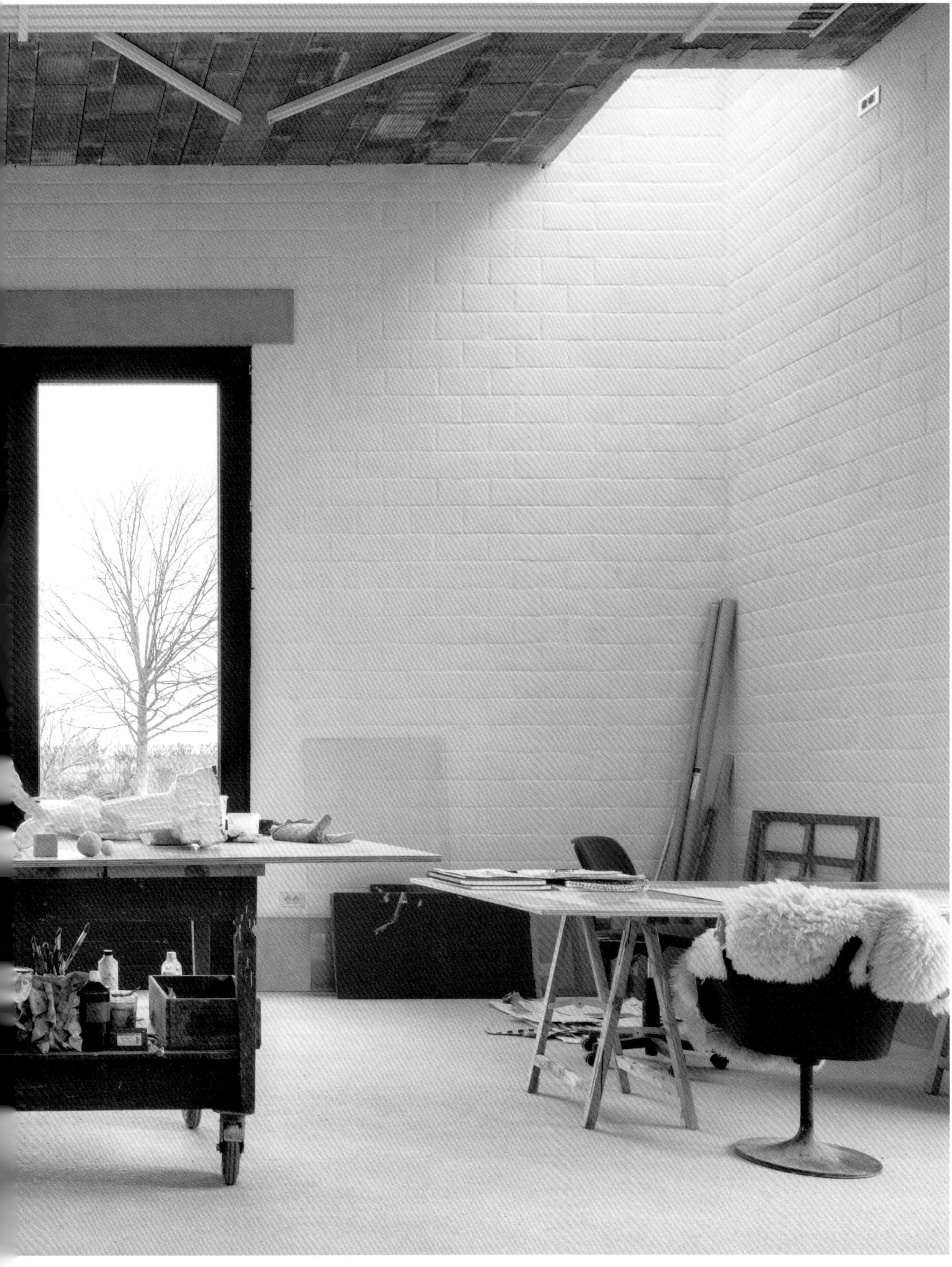

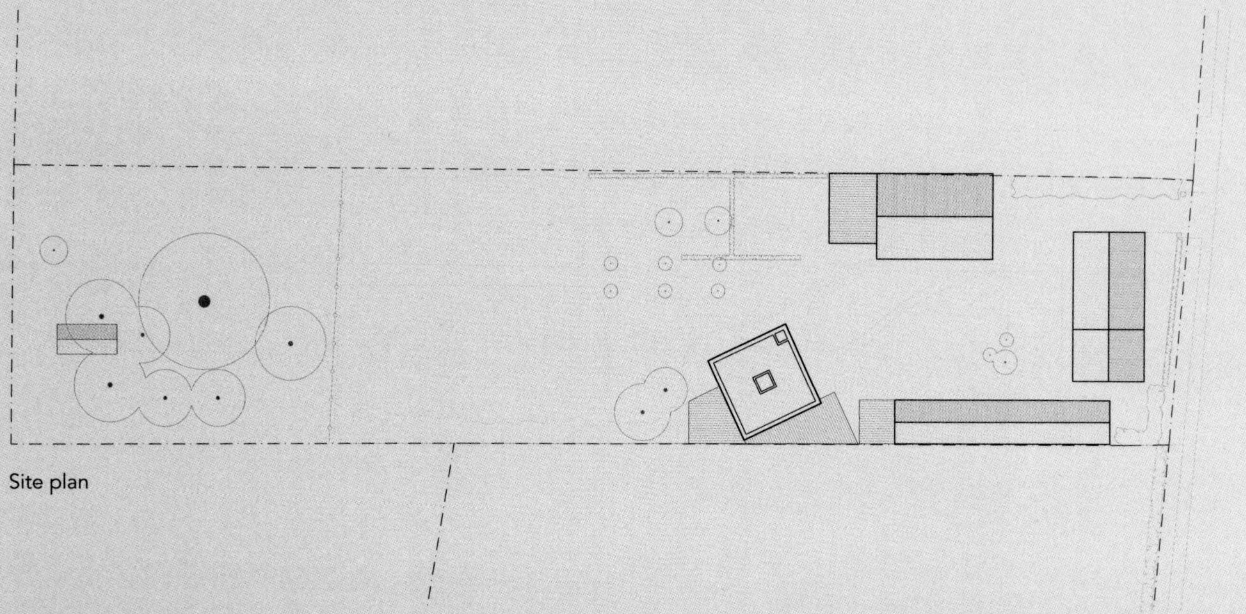

Site plan

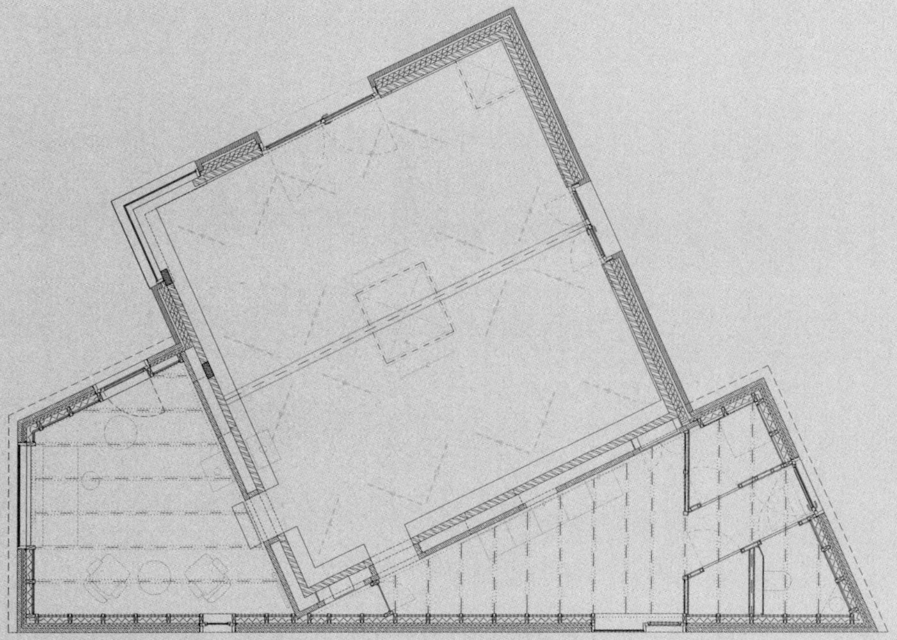

Floor plan

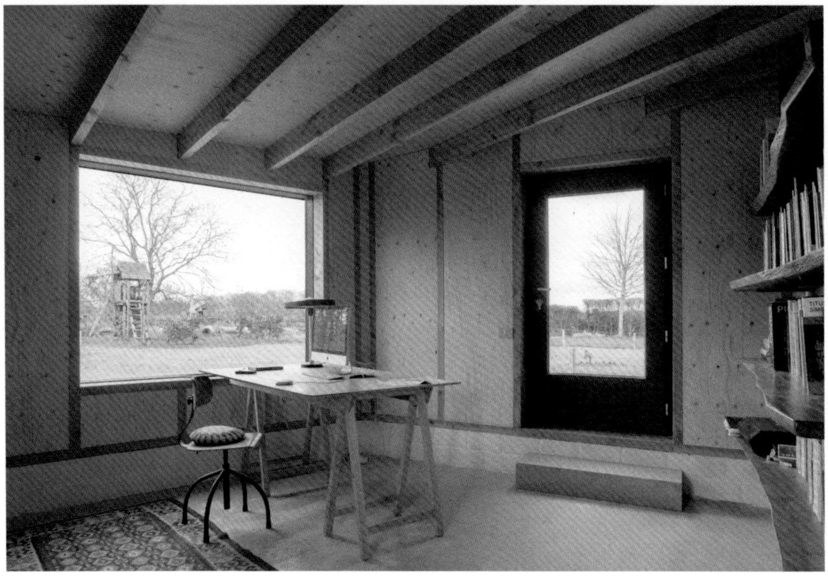

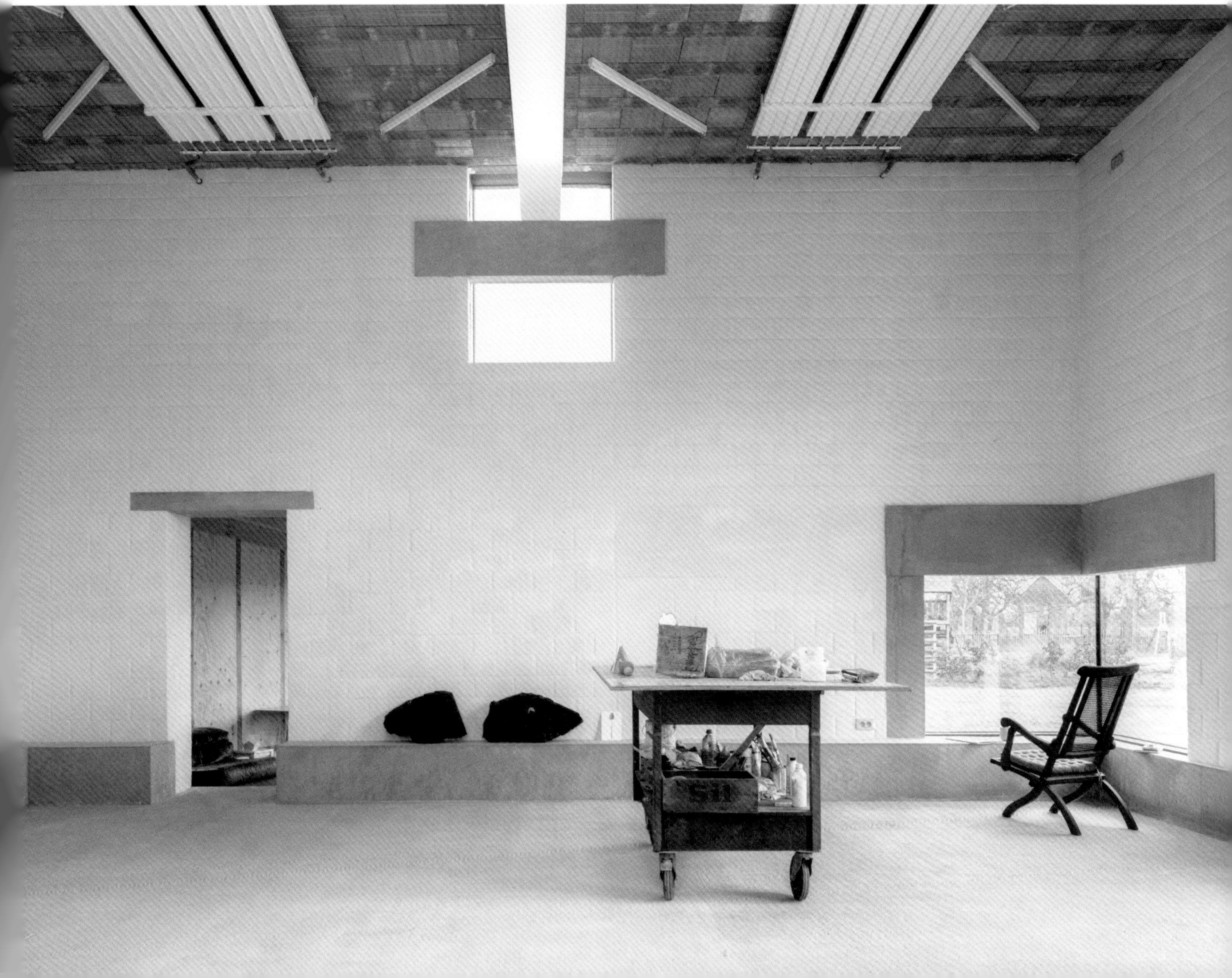

AT ONE WITH NATURE: GARDEN AND LANDSCAPE SETTINGS

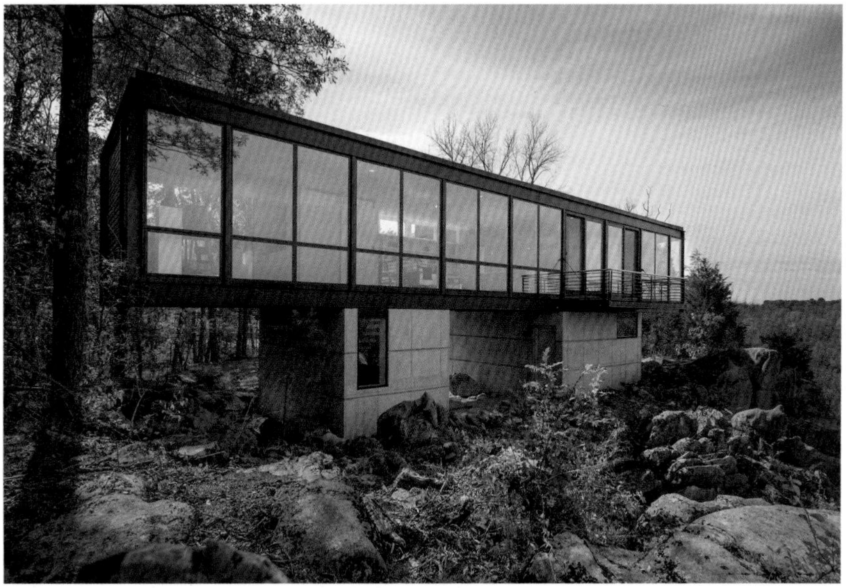

Area:
2,100 square feet (195 square meters)

Completion:
2015

Design:
Wiedemann Architects

Photography:
Anice Hoachlander

Falling Waters, United States

Hawk's Nest

Hawk's Nest is a studio and home for a sculptor from Paris who was drawn to the site, the former Nestle limestone quarry in Falling Waters, West Virginia. The house is perched close to the edge of a 90-foot (27-meter) nearly vertical cliff that overlooks the Potomac River.

Inside and outside

The goal was to create a simple form that was simultaneously separate from and intertwined with nature. Two simple cast concrete volumes rise seamlessly from the limestone, framing views of the river and providing a perch for the steel and glass structure above. The grid of steel columns modulates the space and creates framed views of the ever-changing play of nature, blurring the line between inside and outside. Ipe wood, allowed to weather naturally, provides a material counterpoint to the steel and was used on rain-screen walls, on balconies that extend the interior space, and on bridges that leave the site otherwise untouched.

The residence is designed to enhance the experience of nature and inspire the client's work in her ceramic and metal studios. The atelier is of the place and, at the same time, provides a greater appreciation of the natural beauty of the landscape.

Respecting the site

The cliff-side site presented a major challenge, with fissured limestone with subterranean karst formations and an uneven surface littered with boulders discarded from when the quarry was active. With the assistance of a local geologist, the foundation design had to contend with subsurface caves, active springs, and fractures. The site was disturbed as little as possible, while the concrete volumes span between the pilings that sit directly on bedrock. Boulders that were scattered about the site were left in place and the native vegetation was allowed to grow and return the surrounding landscape to its natural setting.

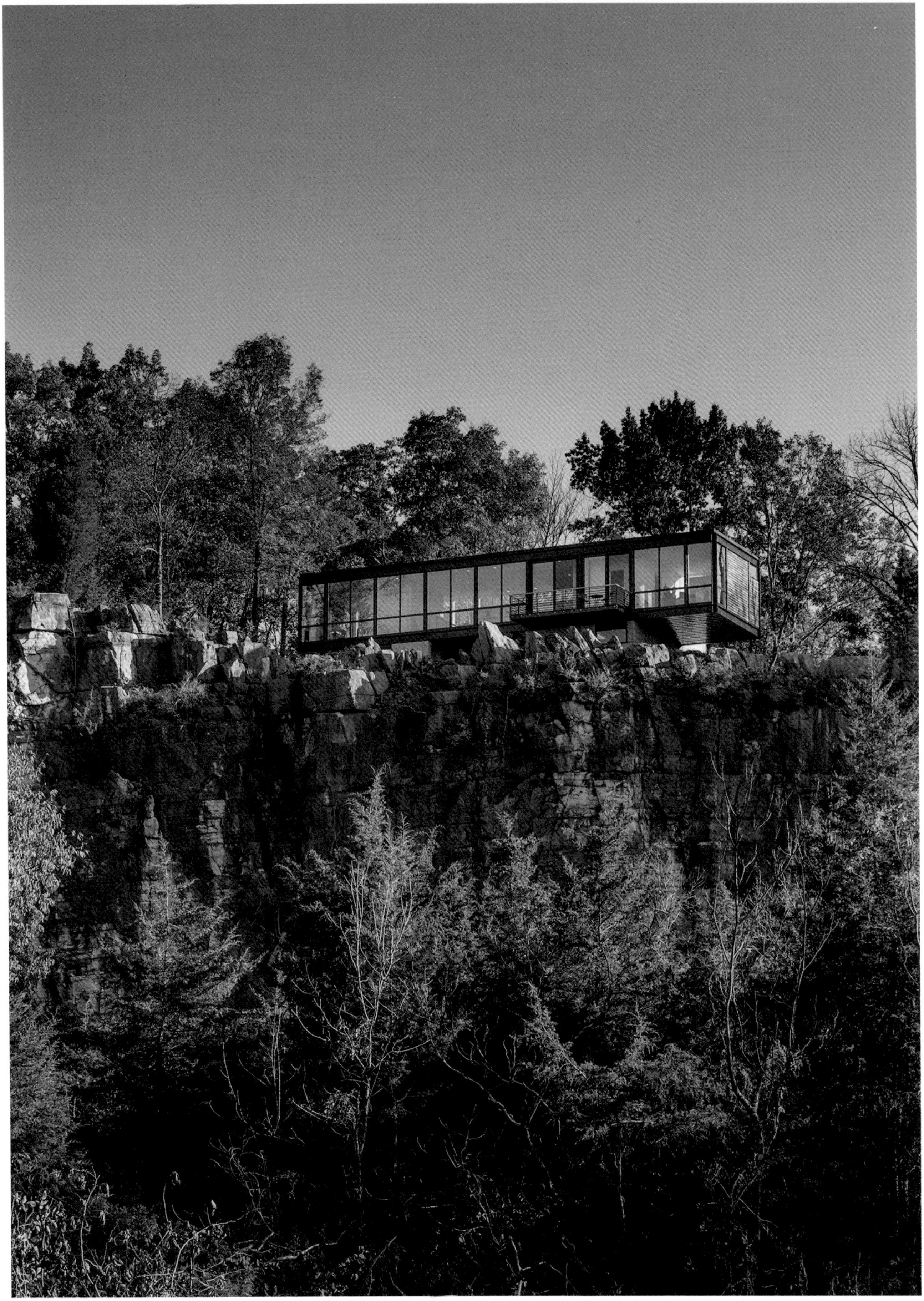

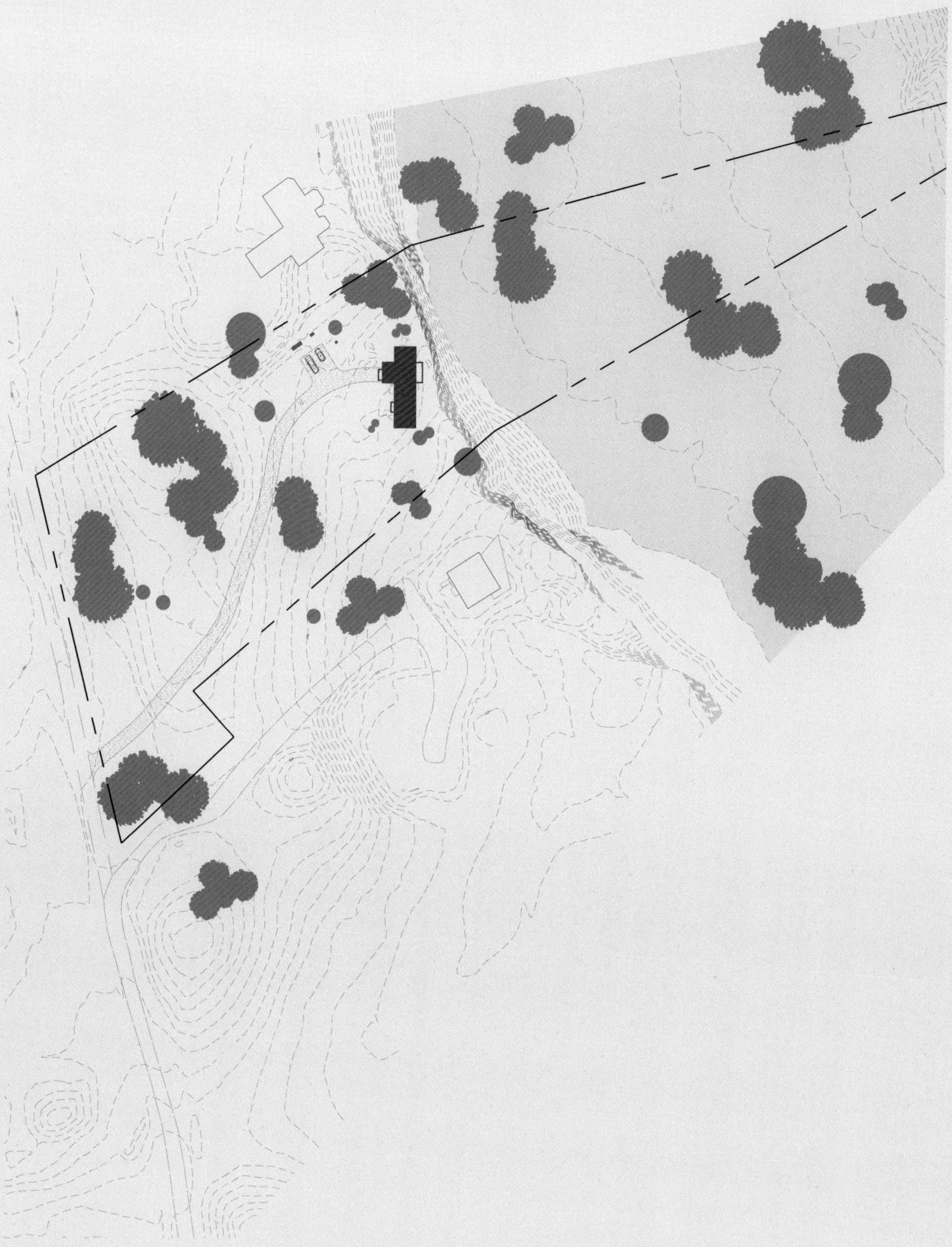

Site plan

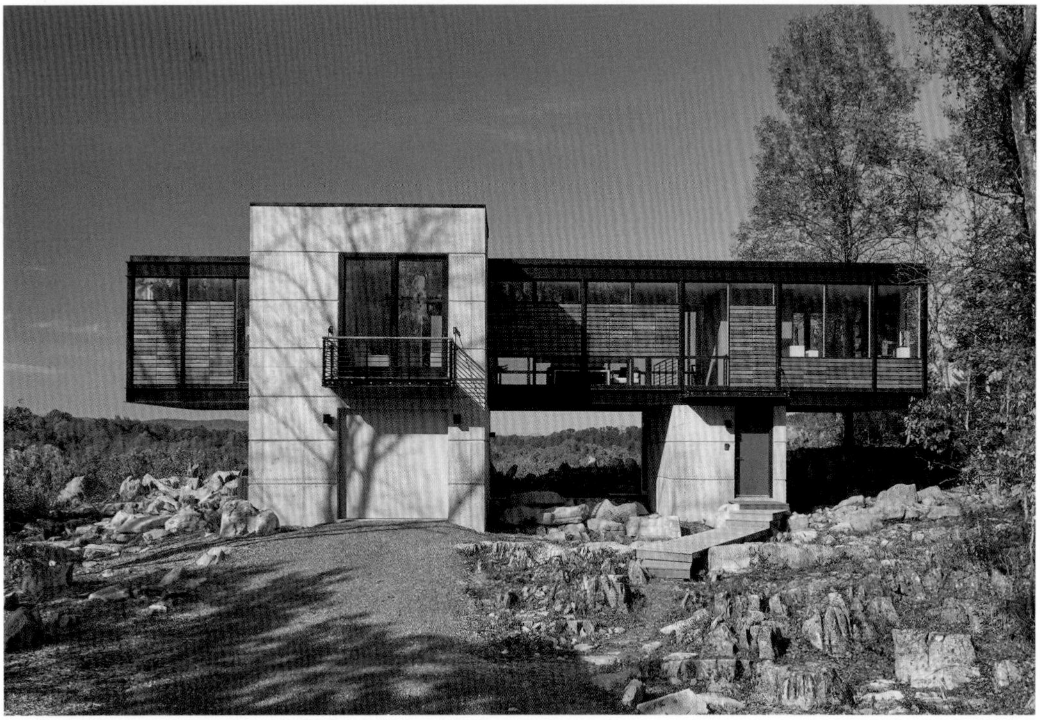

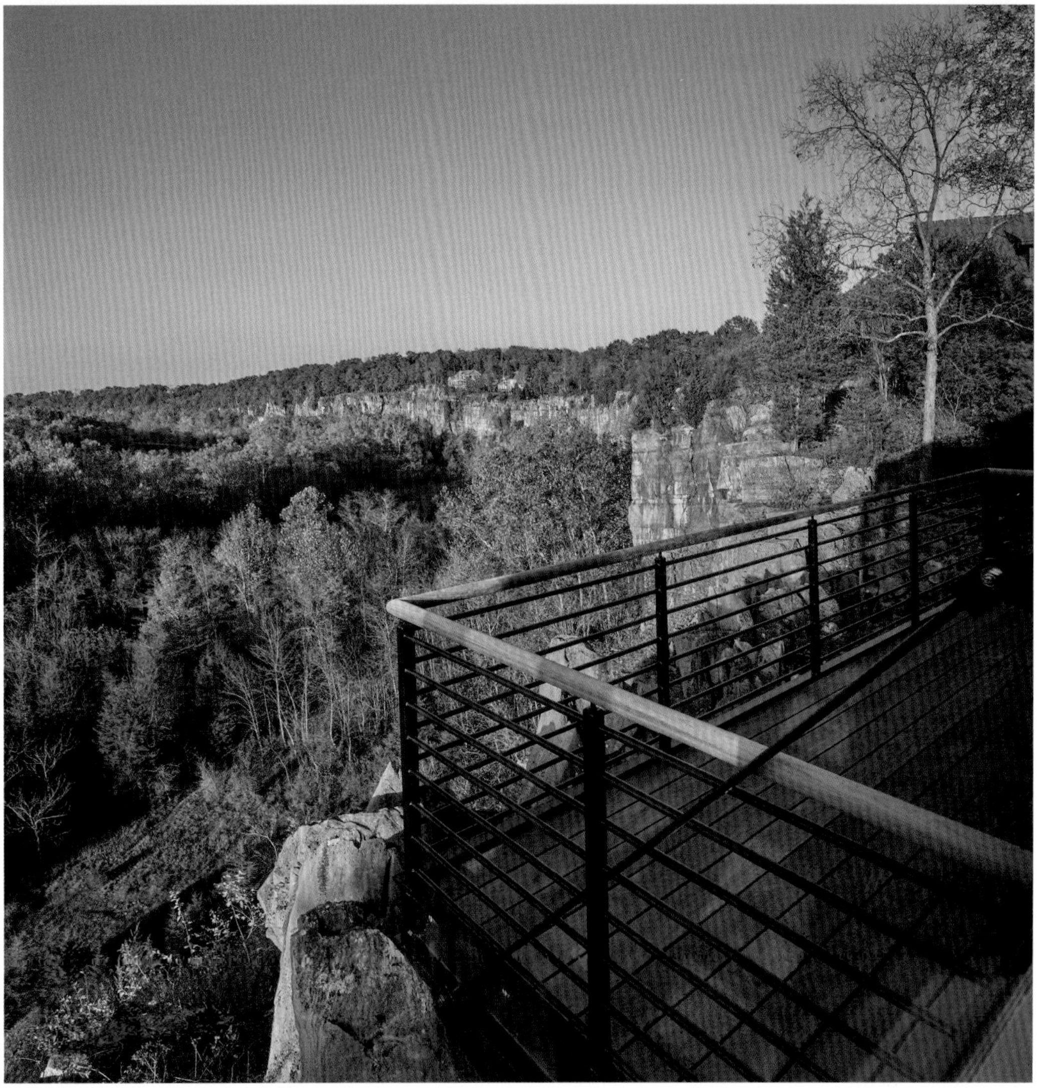

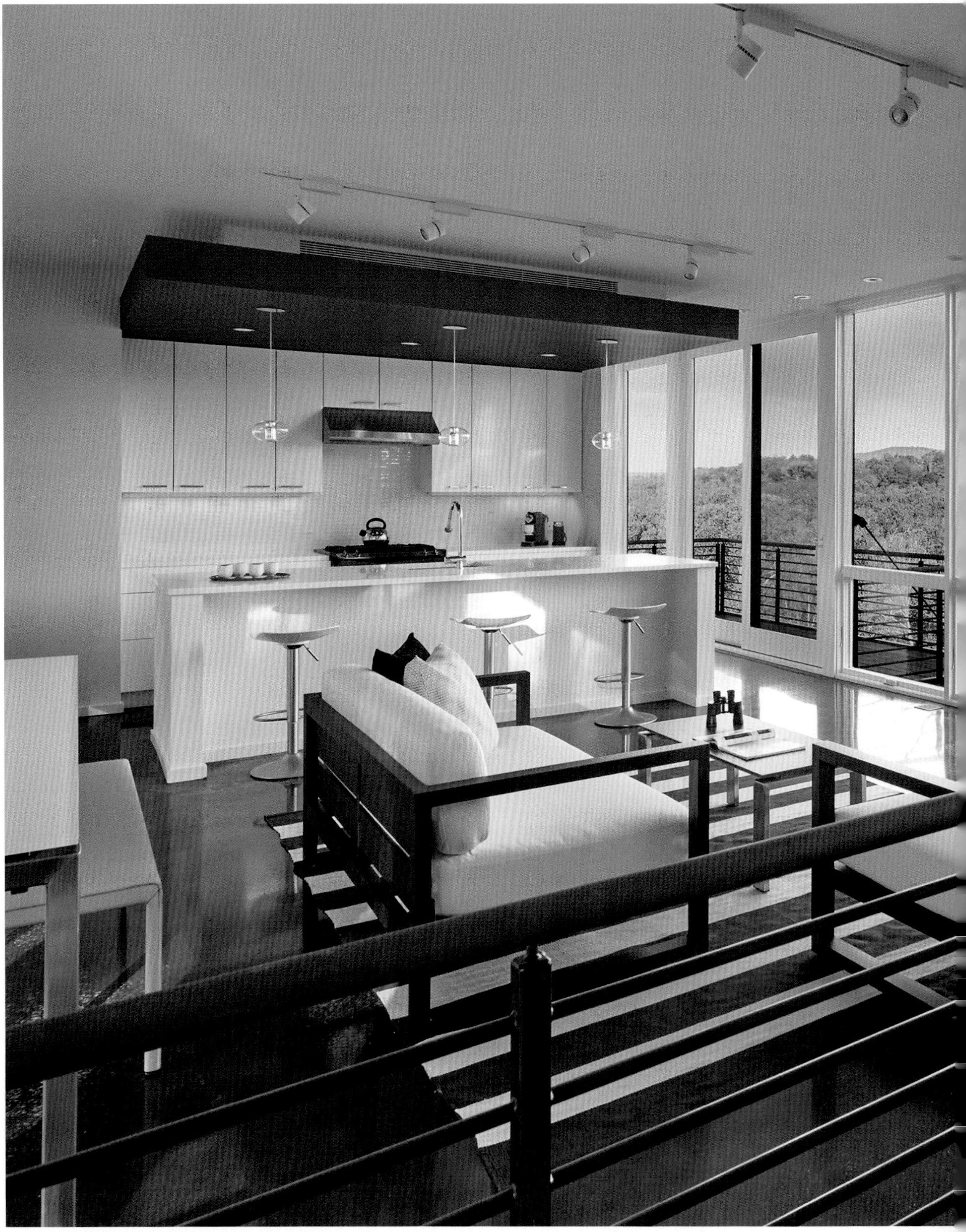

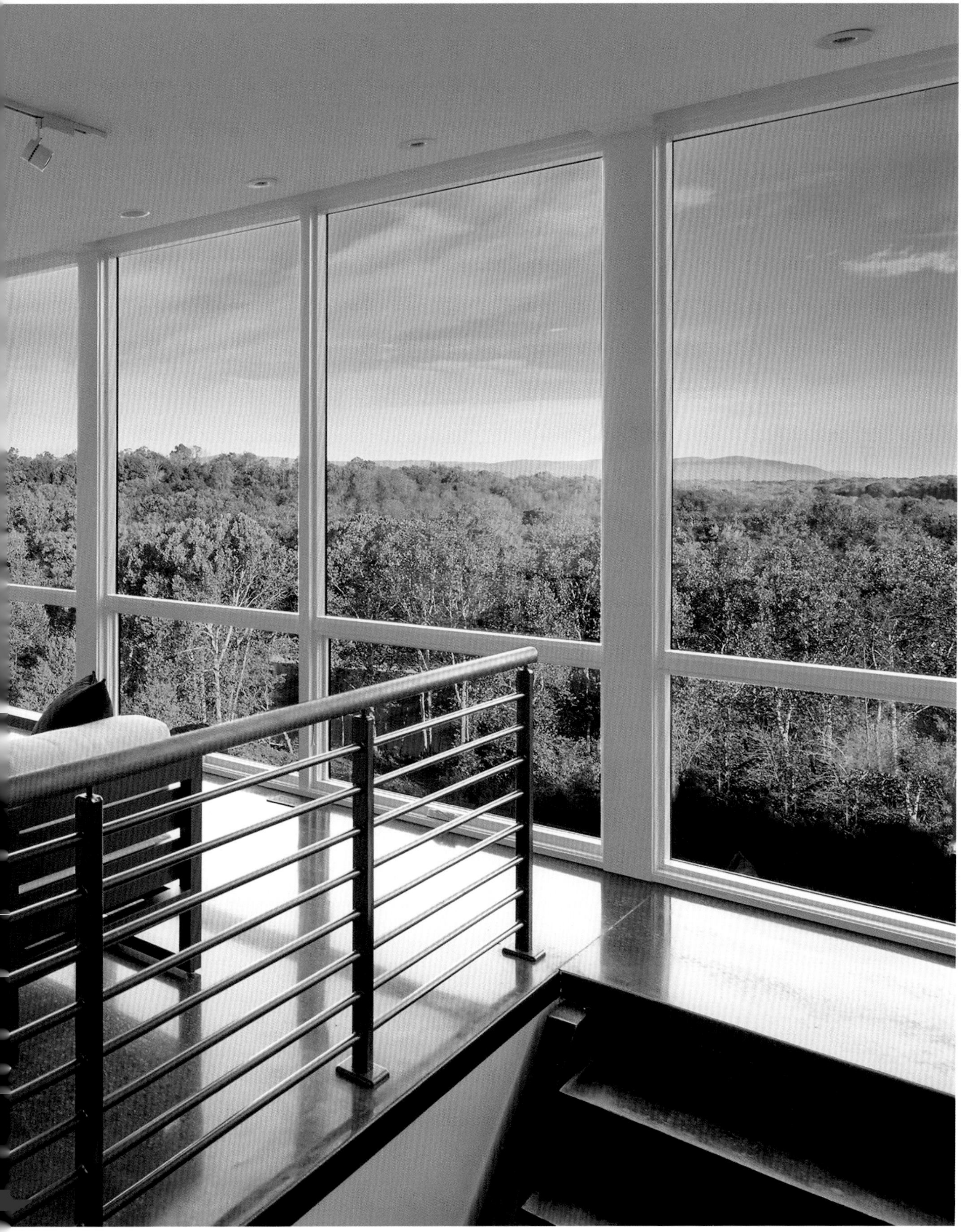

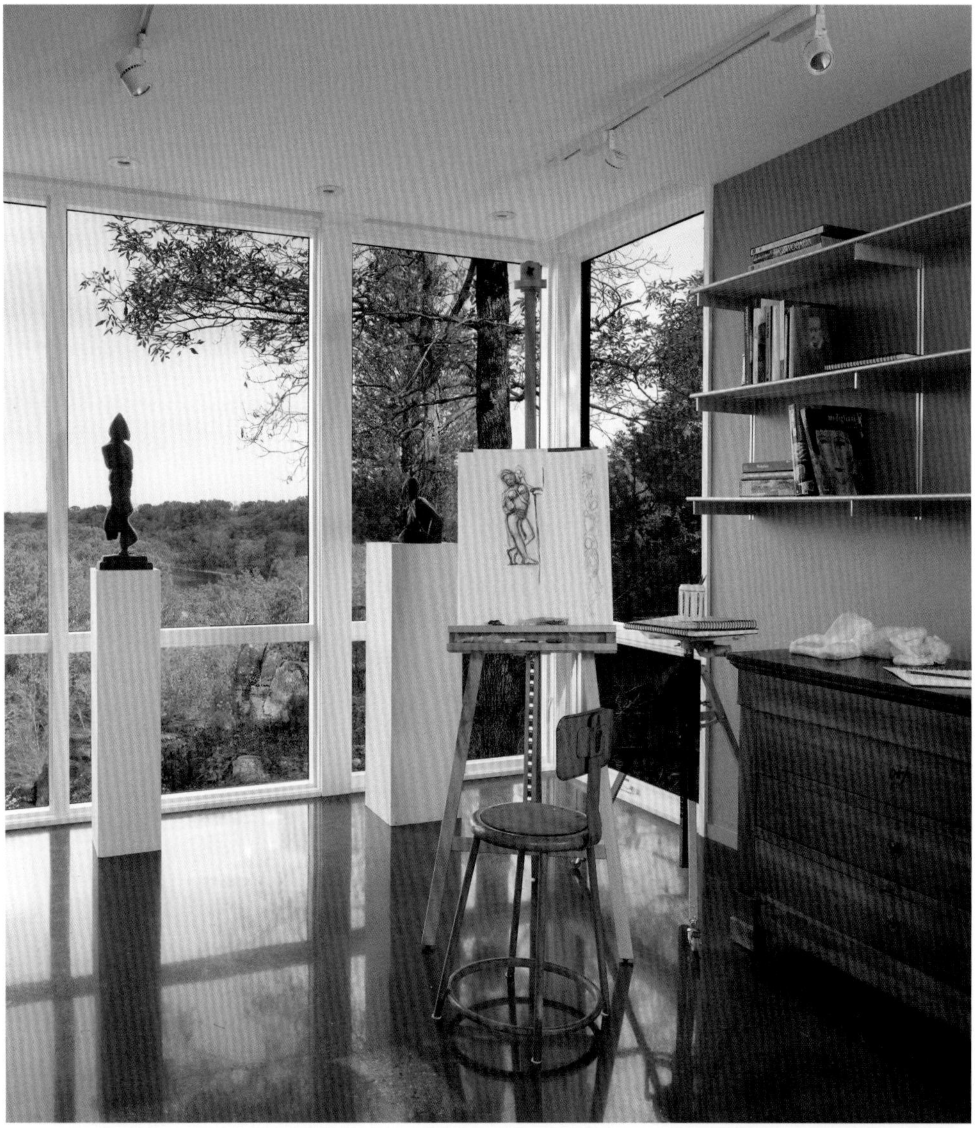

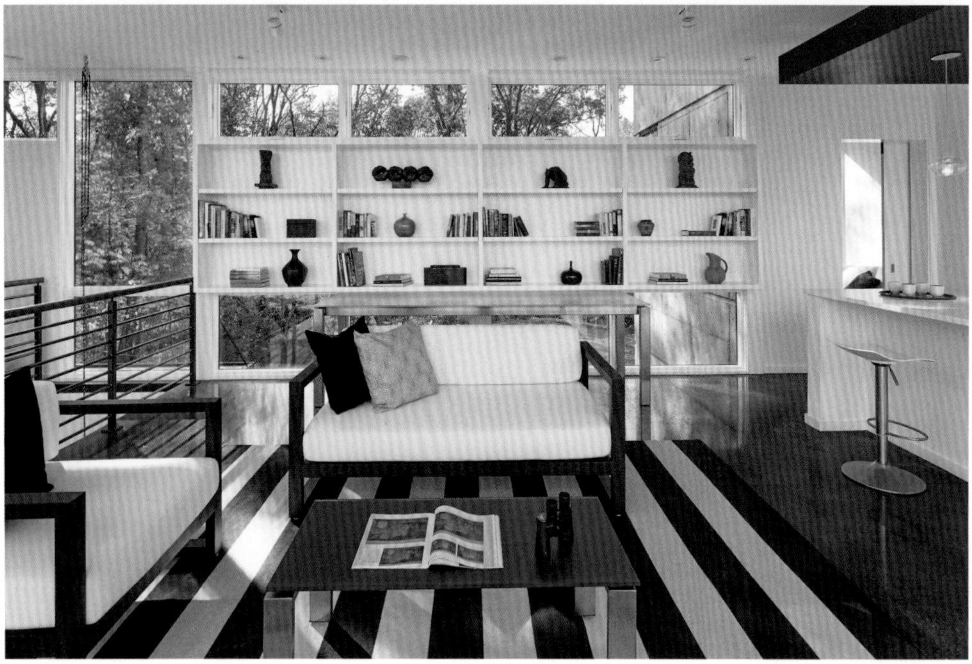

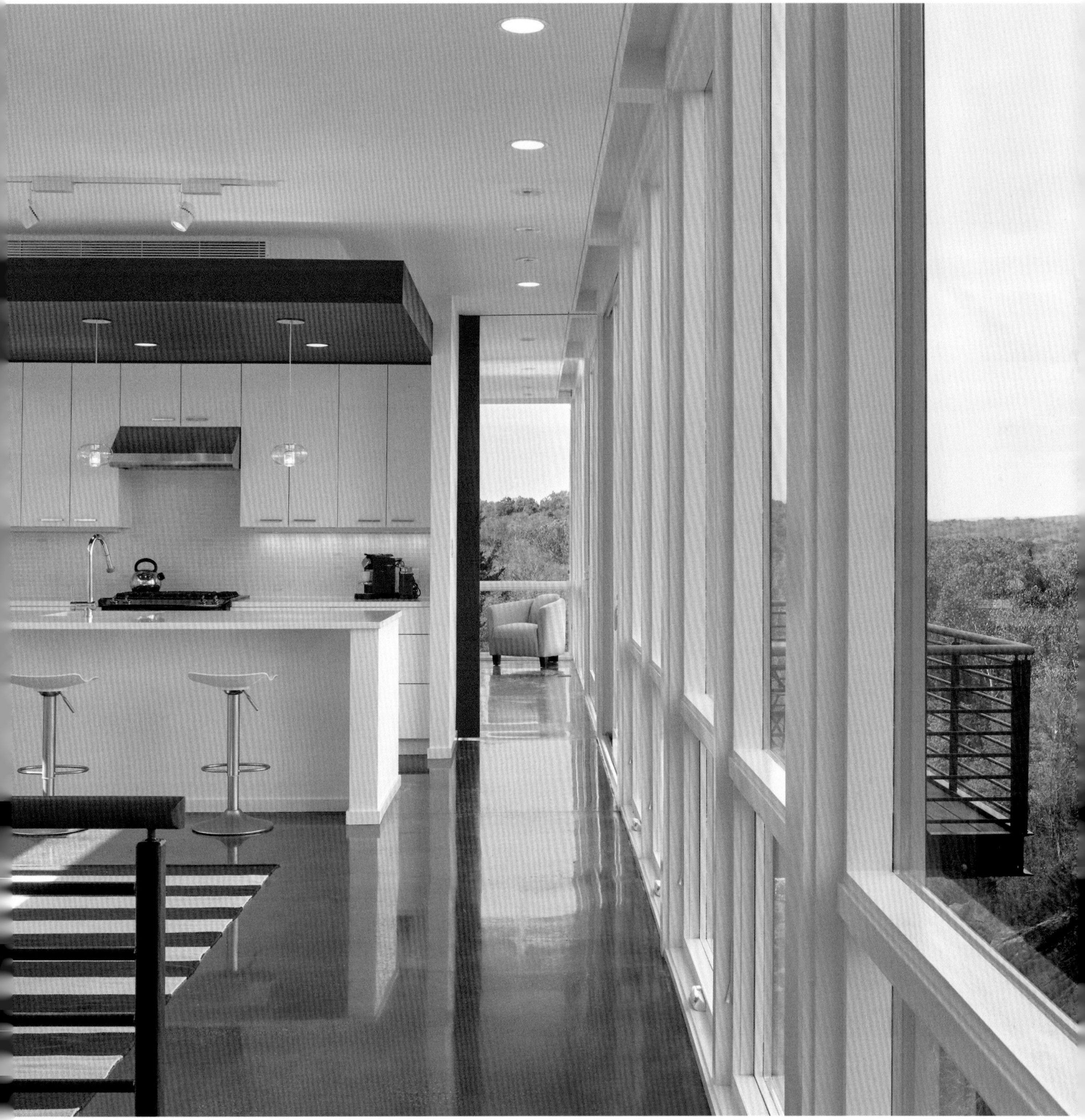

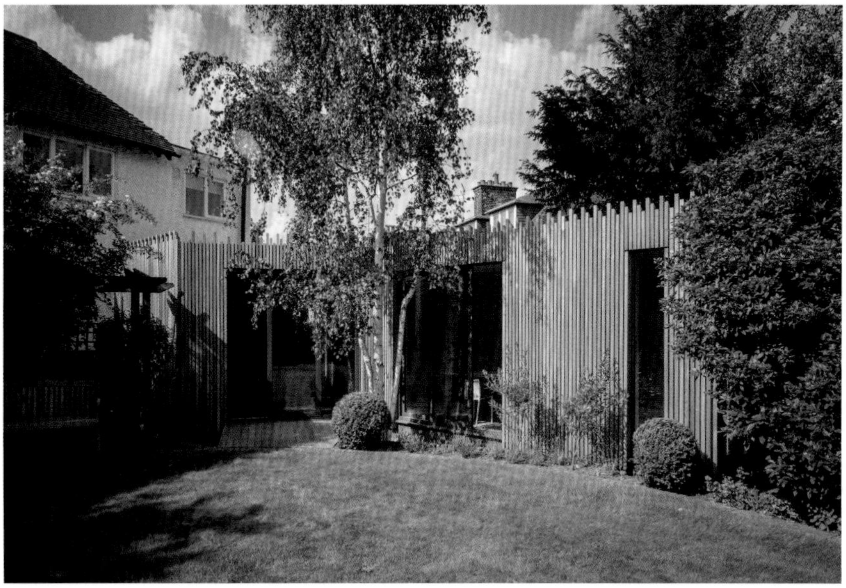

Area:
388 square feet (36 square meters)

Completion:
2015

Design:
Mustard Architects

Photography:
Tim Crocker

London, United Kingdom

Nestle Studio

The studio is nestled into the corner of a once overgrown and neglected area of a suburban garden containing a prominent silver birch tree. With an expanding family the client wanted to create a functional painting studio within the garden that retained, formed part of, and enhanced the existing landscape.

Building around the silver birch

The silver birch tree was a key focal point of the garden, and the studio was designed to wrap around it while allowing light to penetrate deep into the studio. To ensure the tree survived the construction process and would grow to full maturity, the studio was built on piles to avoid the weight of the studio crushing the tree's roots. The tree also acts as an important sunshade for the studio in summer, creating a dappled light within the space through the main windows on either side. The studio is clad in western red cedar vertical cladding and has been left untreated so that the timber cladding will gray and weather over time, allowing the studio to blend into the garden. Inside, the birch-faced plywood and concrete floor offer natural warmth with industrial robustness.

Sunshine and views

The windows were positioned to split views out of and into the studio, giving occupants views across the garden or back to the house and creating strong landscape connections. The glazed door to the rear allows light from the summer setting sun to penetrate though the studio, making the inside glow as sunset approaches.

The main emphasis of the project was to create a new art studio that would weather and blend in with the garden, and to protect the silver birch tree that the studio is nestled around. The client was delighted with the success of the studio, which is used on a regular basis and has reinvigorated their appreciation and use of the garden.

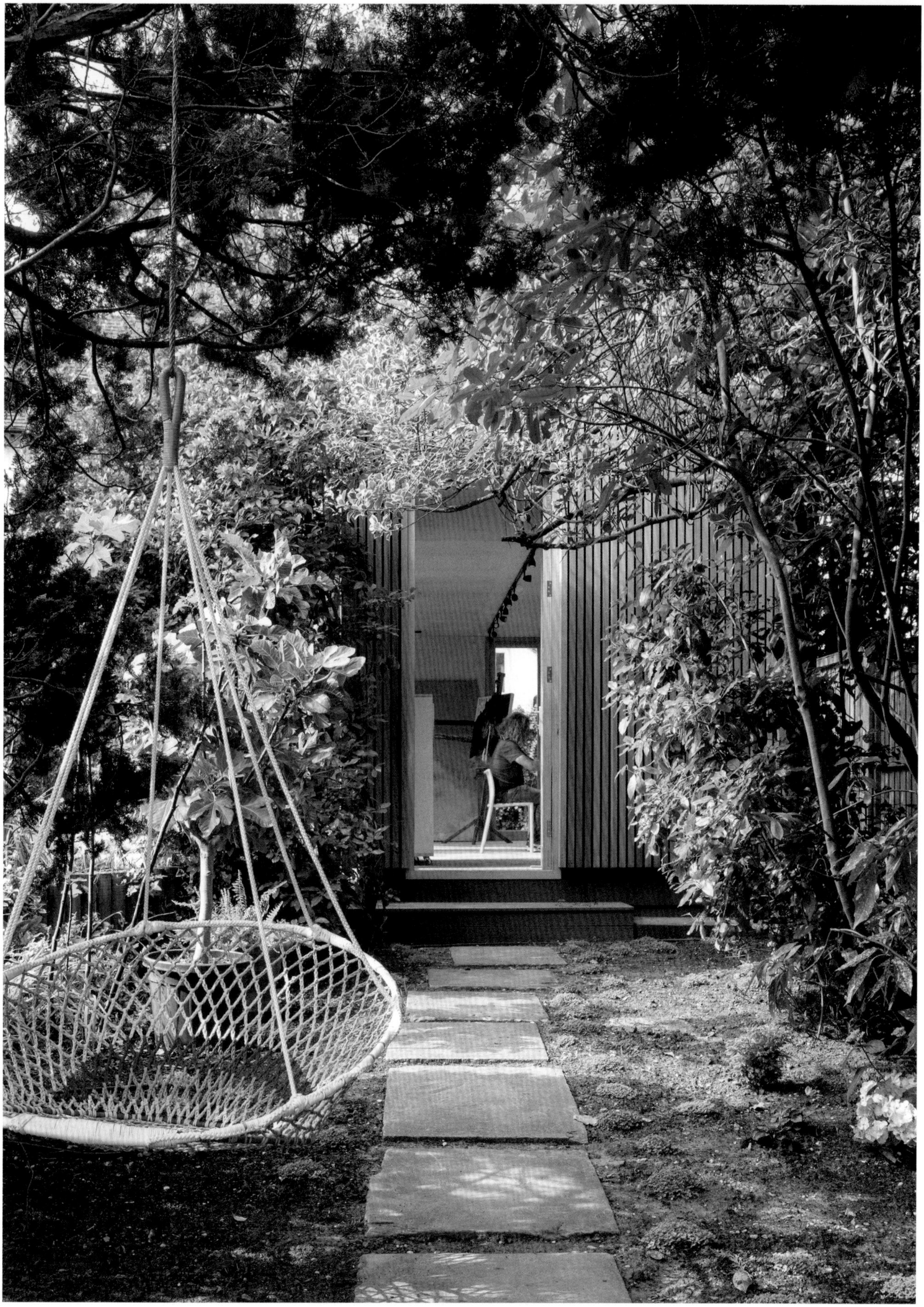

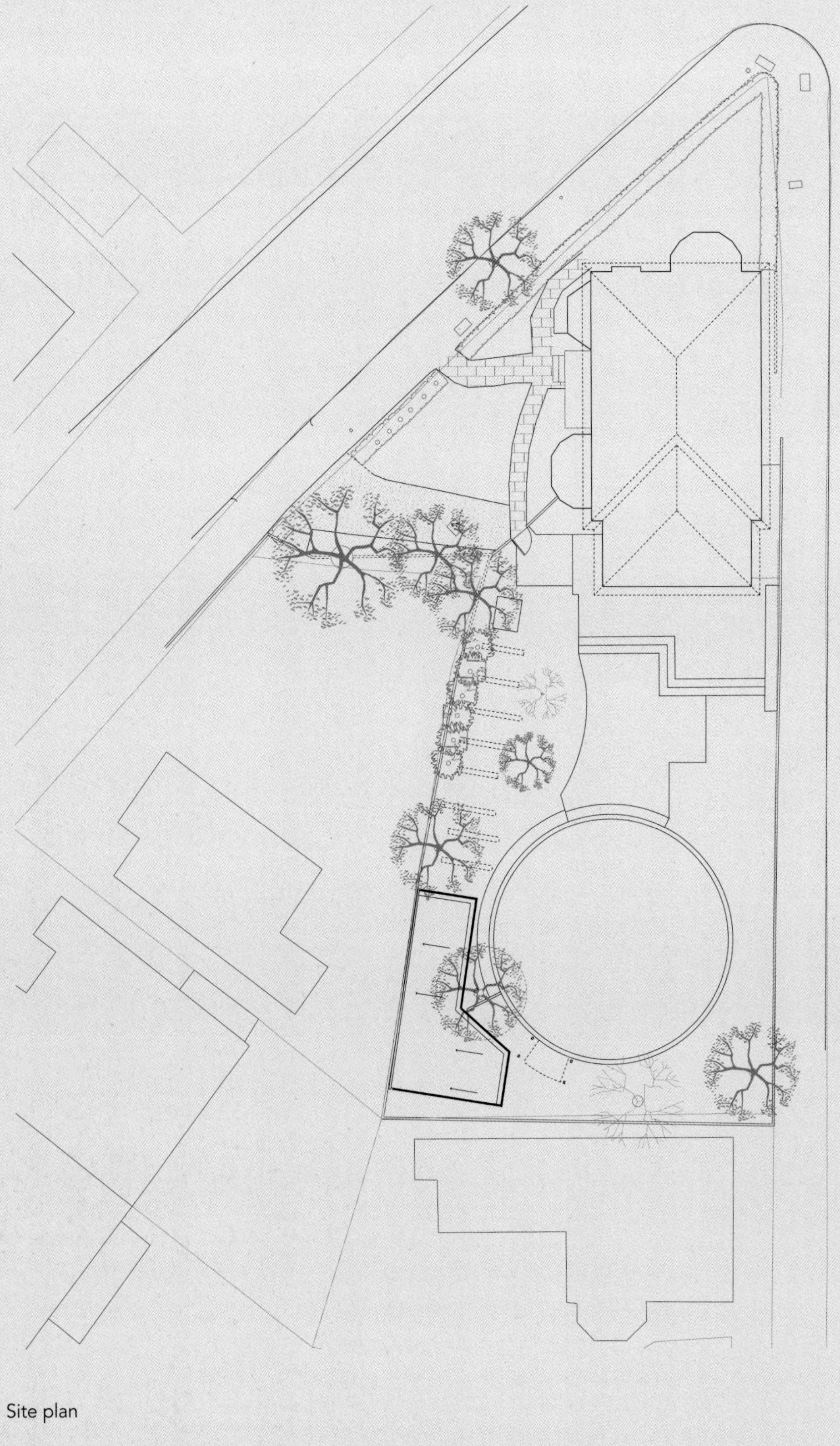

Site plan

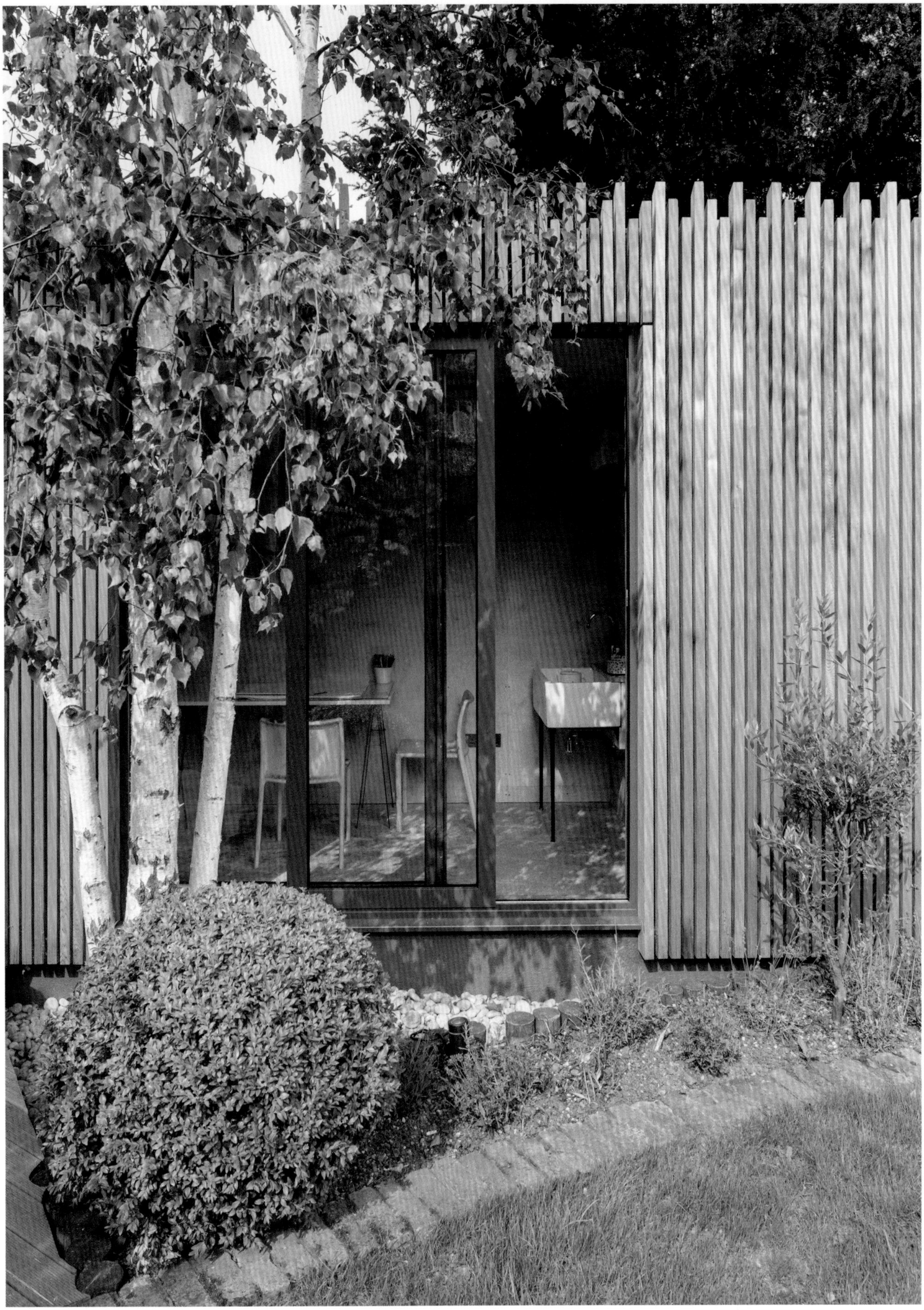

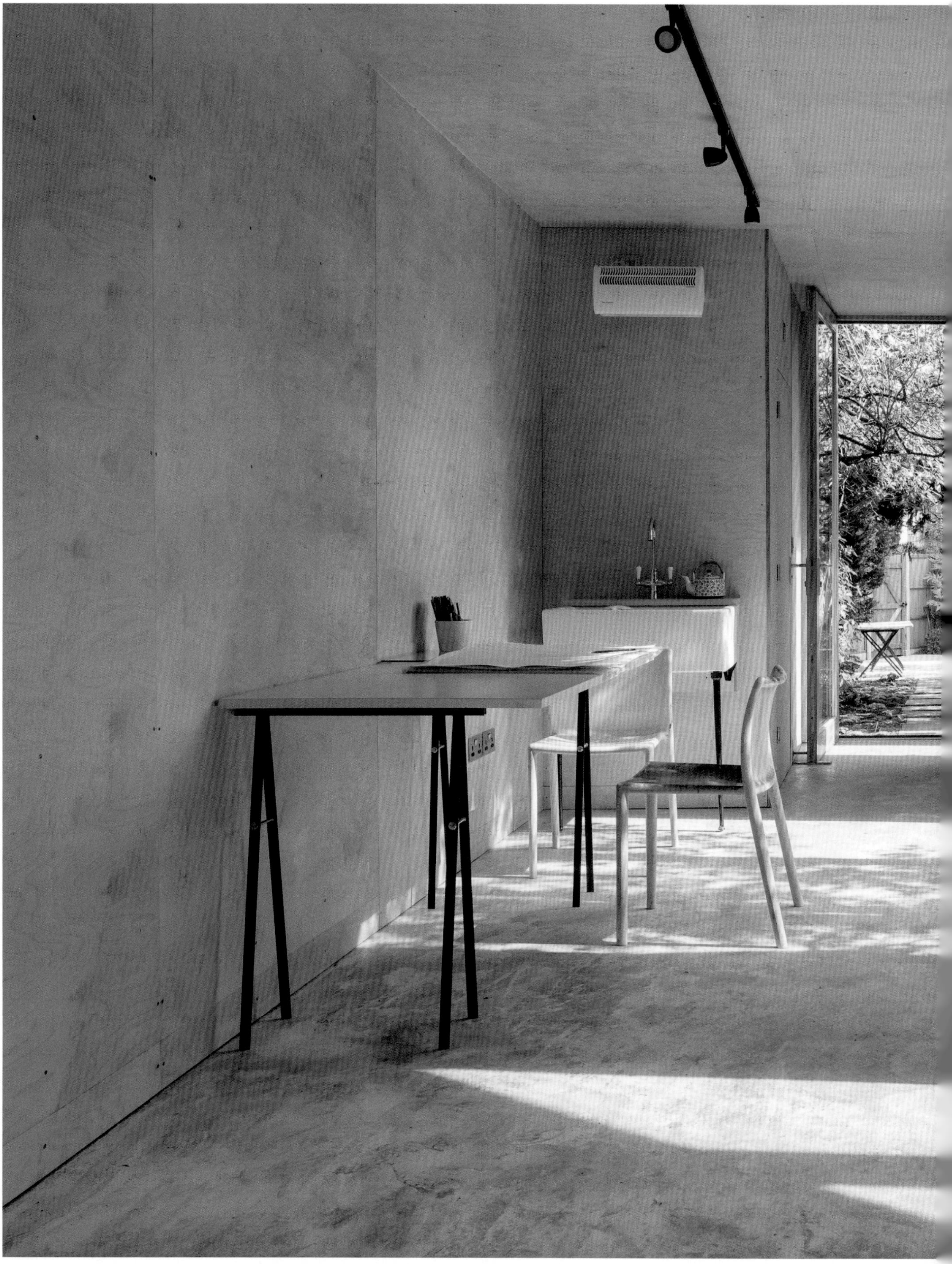

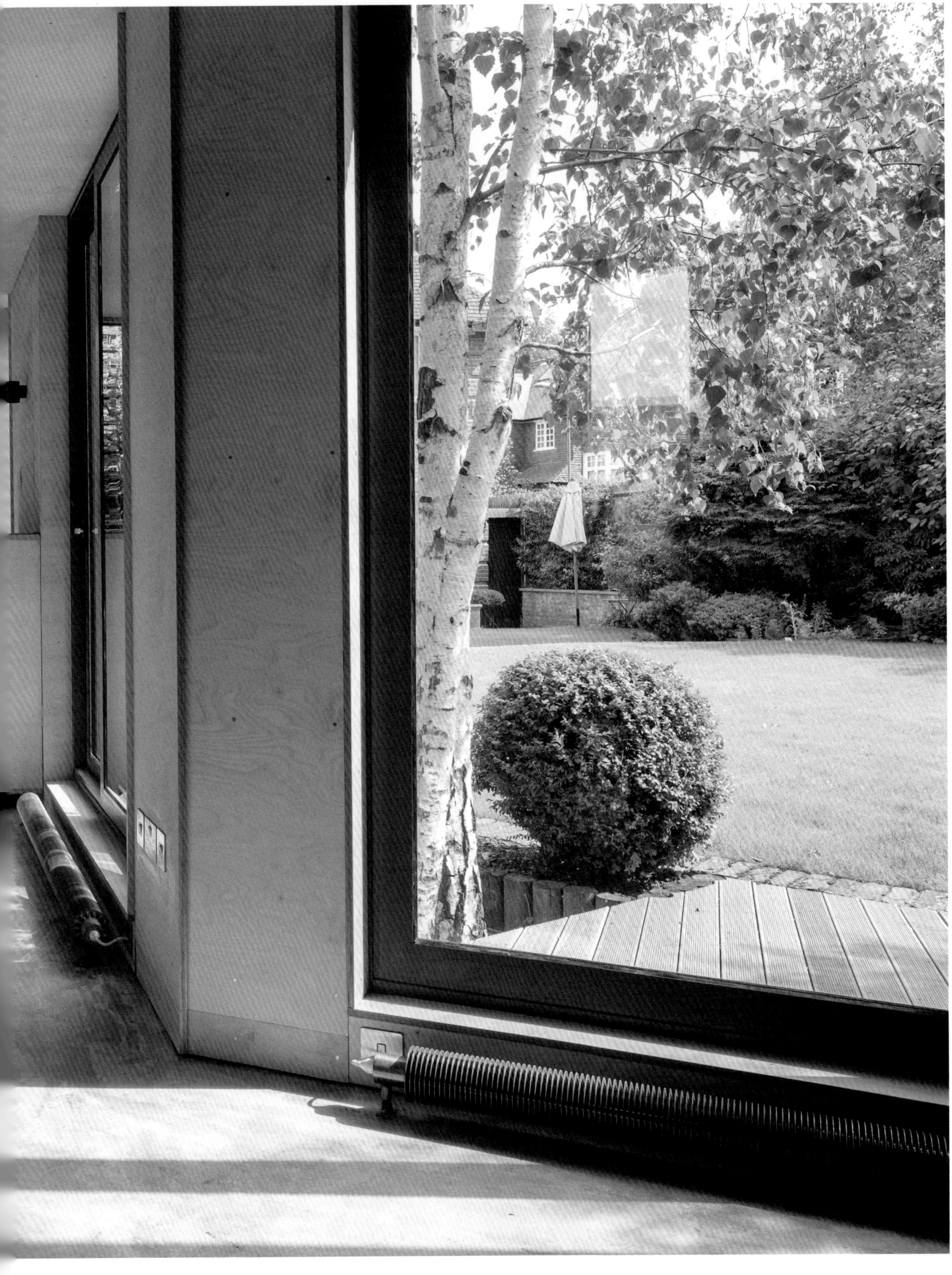

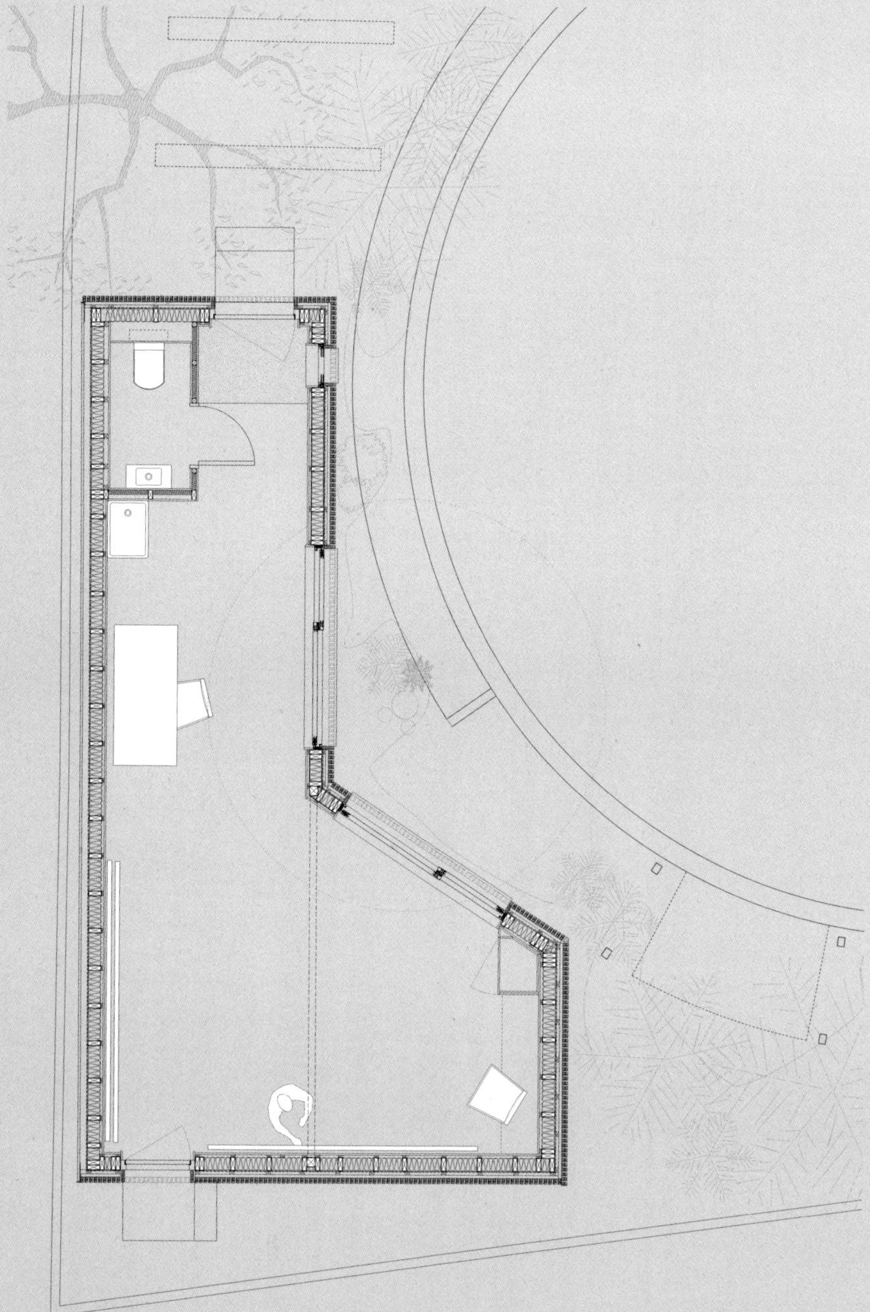

Floor plan

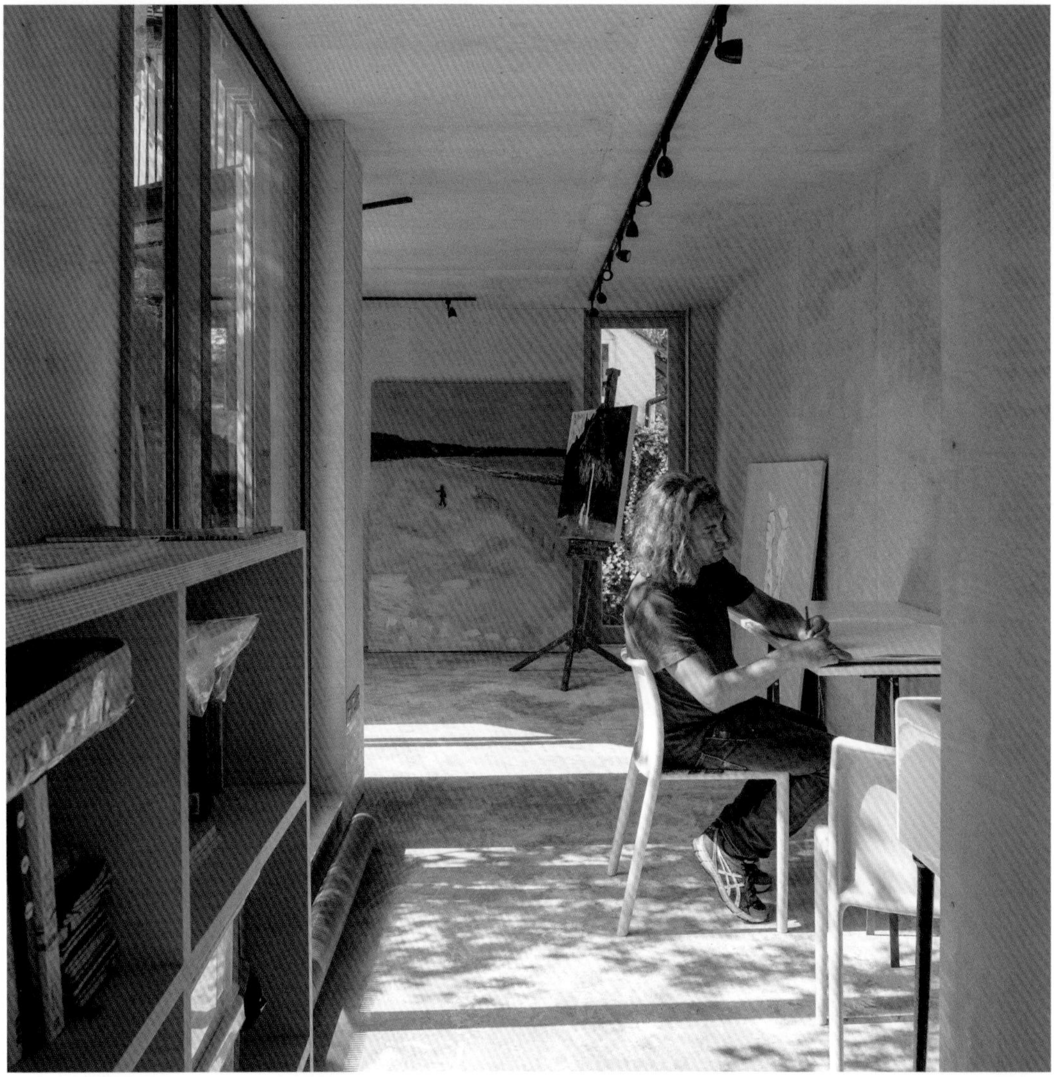

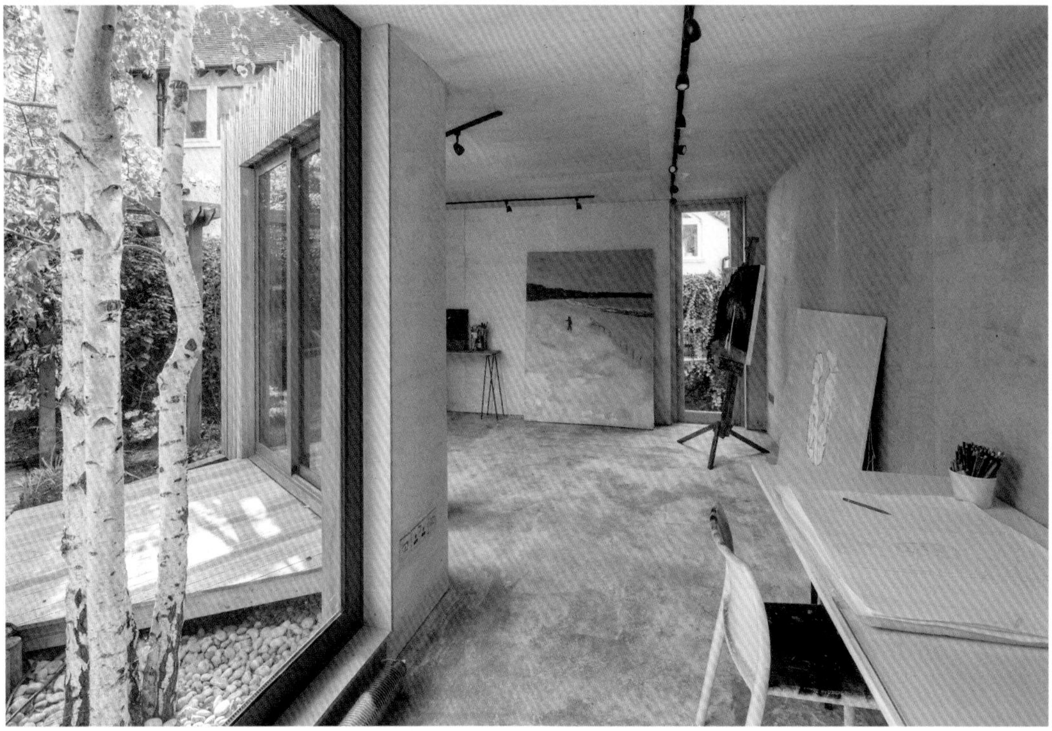

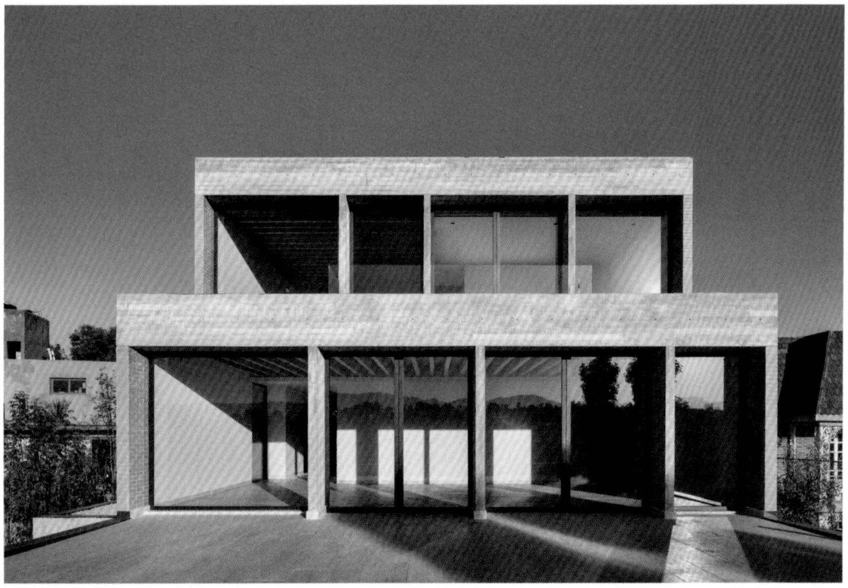

Area:
4,844 square feet (450 square meters)

Completion:
2017

Design:
Mariloly Rodríguez
(Manuel Cervantes Estudio)

Photography:
Rafael Gamo

Mexico City, Mexico

Two Houses and Studio Amatepec

This project was designed by the Mexican architect Manuel Cervantes as his personal home and studio. It is a set of two dwellings built in an area of Mexico City that adjoins a ravine; from a site length of 410 feet (125 meters), only 230 feet (70 meters) were used due to the natural reserve in which the property is set. The design included a series of terraces that, at each level, are the extension of the interior space. This staggered design allows the whole project to be integrated with the topography of the property.

Common spaces and green places

The program consists of two dwellings whose main access is in the common space for both; this is located half a level below the bench level, and serves a parking and common gathering area. The penthouse has a lobby that gives access to a garden located half a level above the bench level; this space serves as an extension of the social gathering area, which leads onto a terrace overlooking the ravine. This property has two levels: in the upper level the several bedrooms are distributed and in the lower level are the common areas and services.

An exterior lobby gives way to the upper level of this house where the bedrooms and family room are located and to an exterior staircase that descends to another level where the common areas and services are located; this exterior lobby also serves as a private access to the studio, located two levels below. The

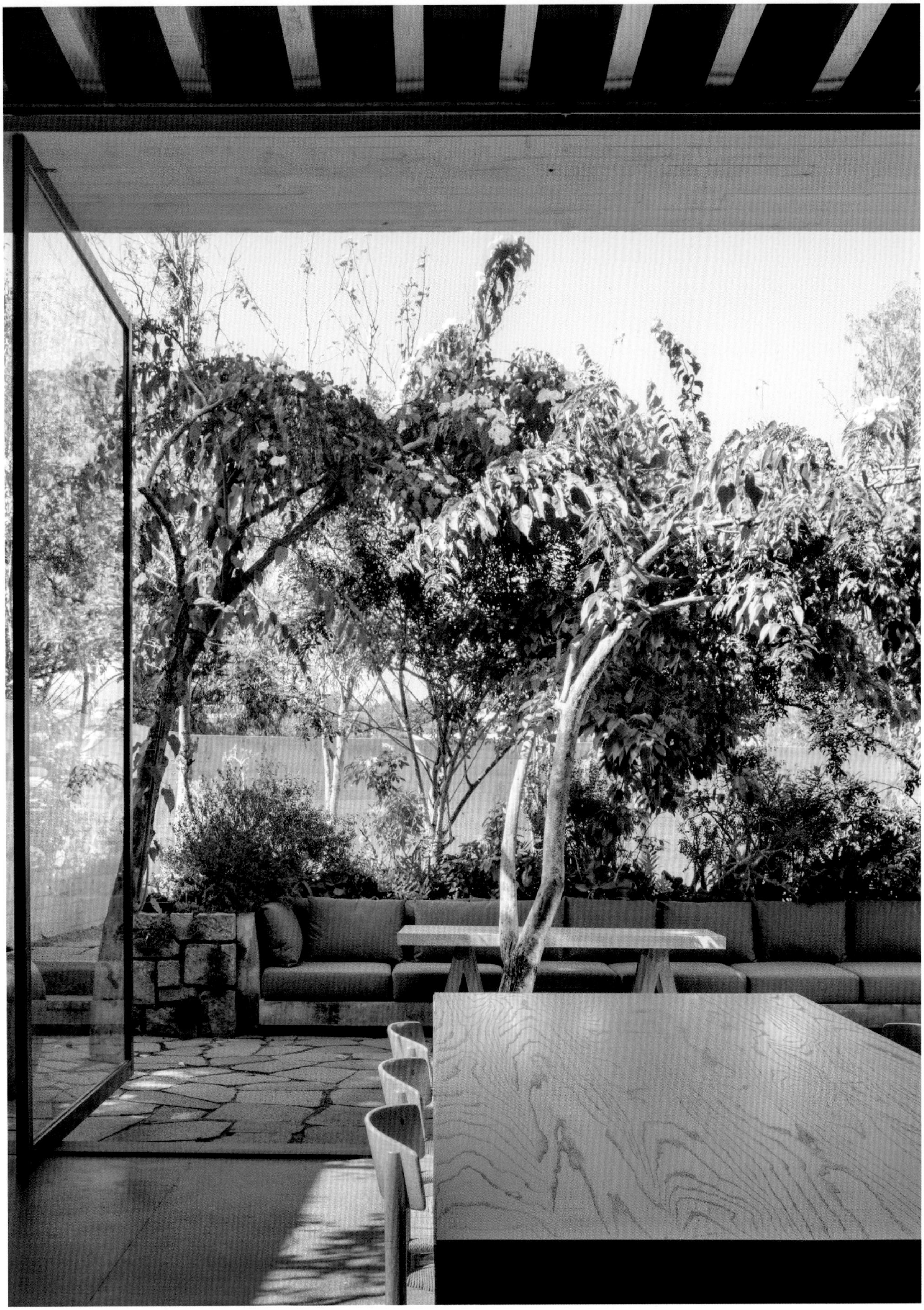

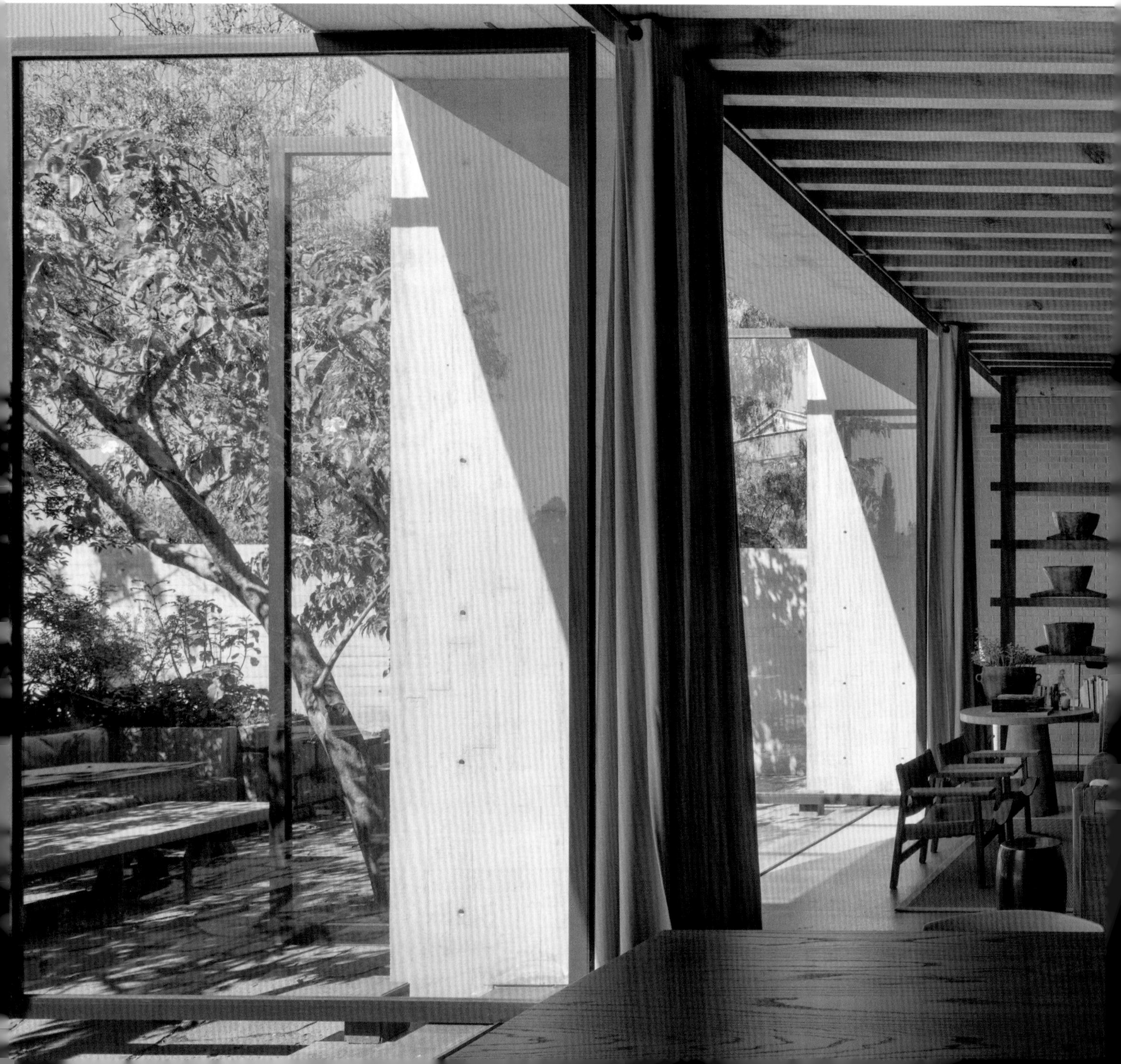

common gathering area is placed toward an interior garden with an apparent concrete wall that follows the language of the architecture of the house, with the idea of creating a space that is more intimate, instead of another one looking toward the ravine.

The studio located two levels below is an apparent concrete box that looks completely toward the view of the ravine with a free height of 16 feet (4.8 meters), which is segmented by a mezzanine that creates two different environments.

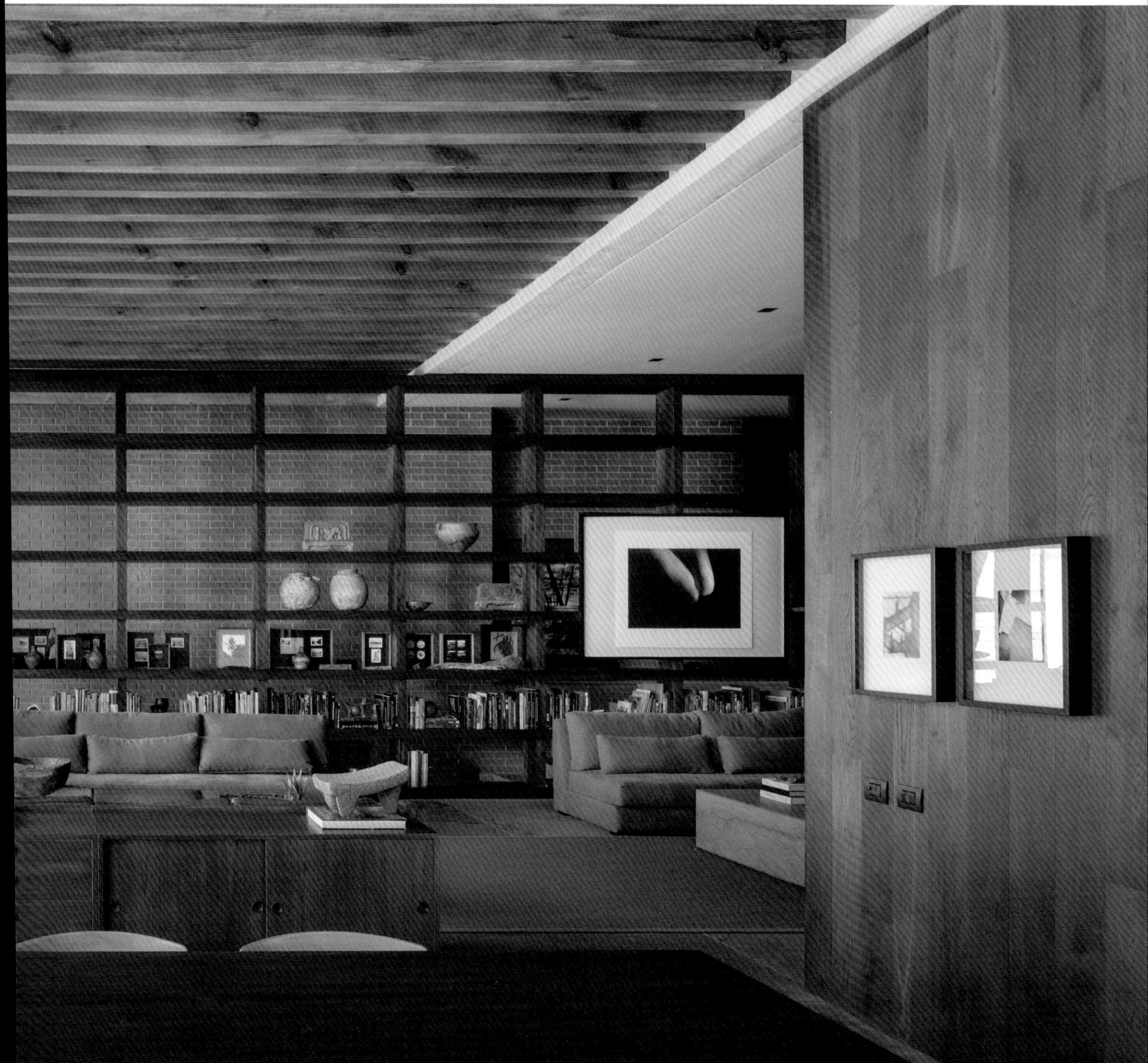

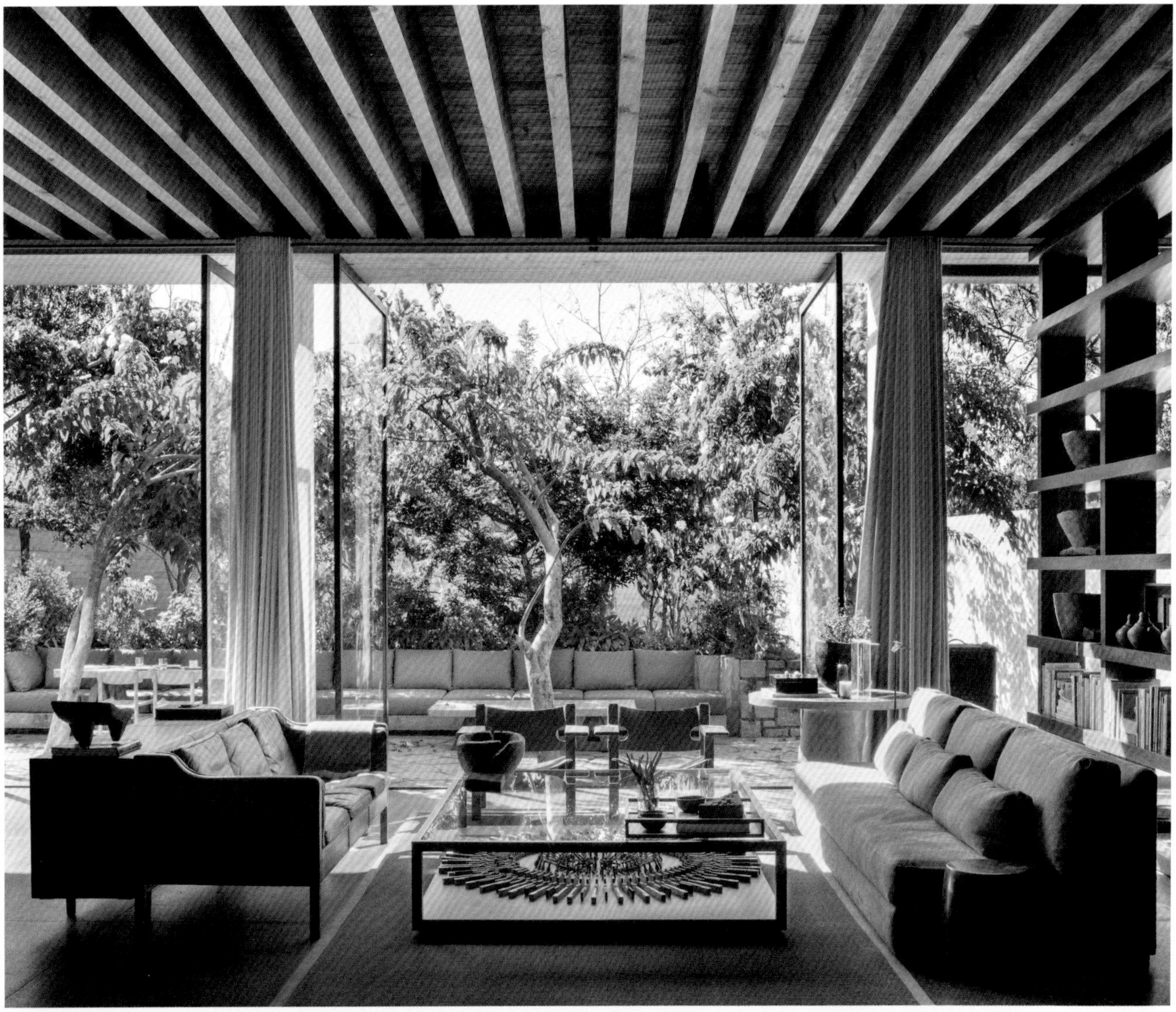

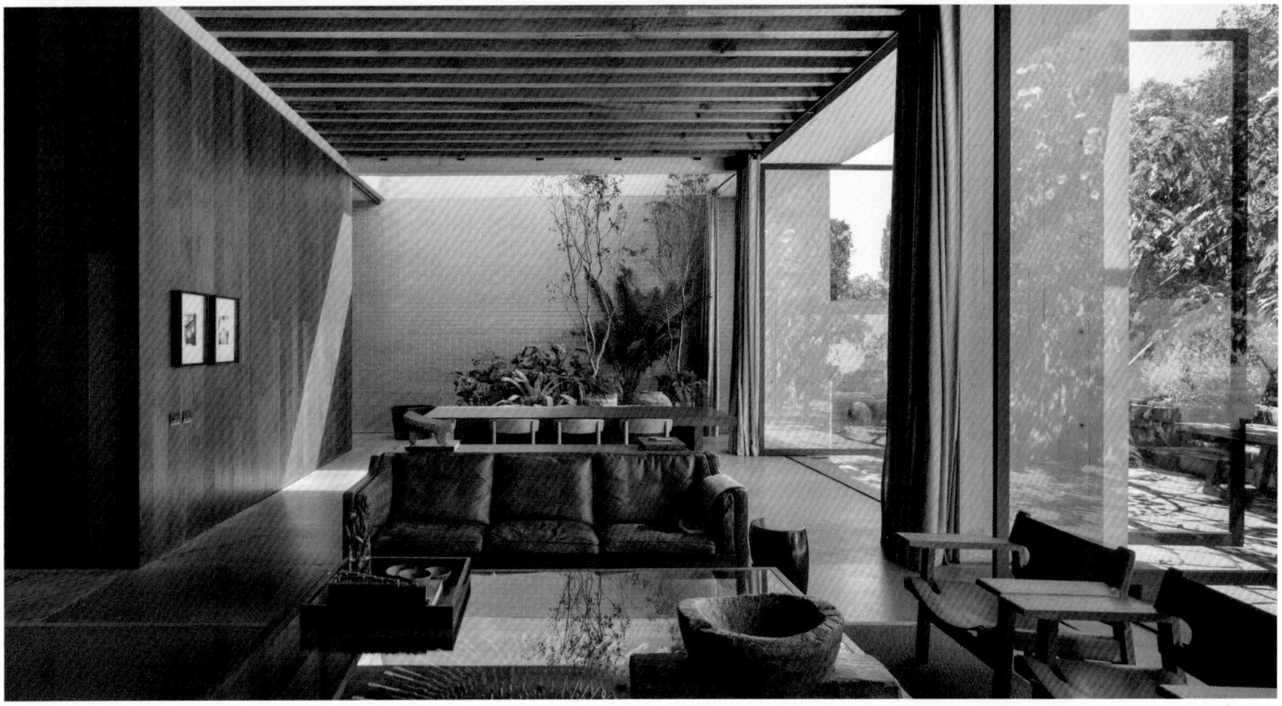

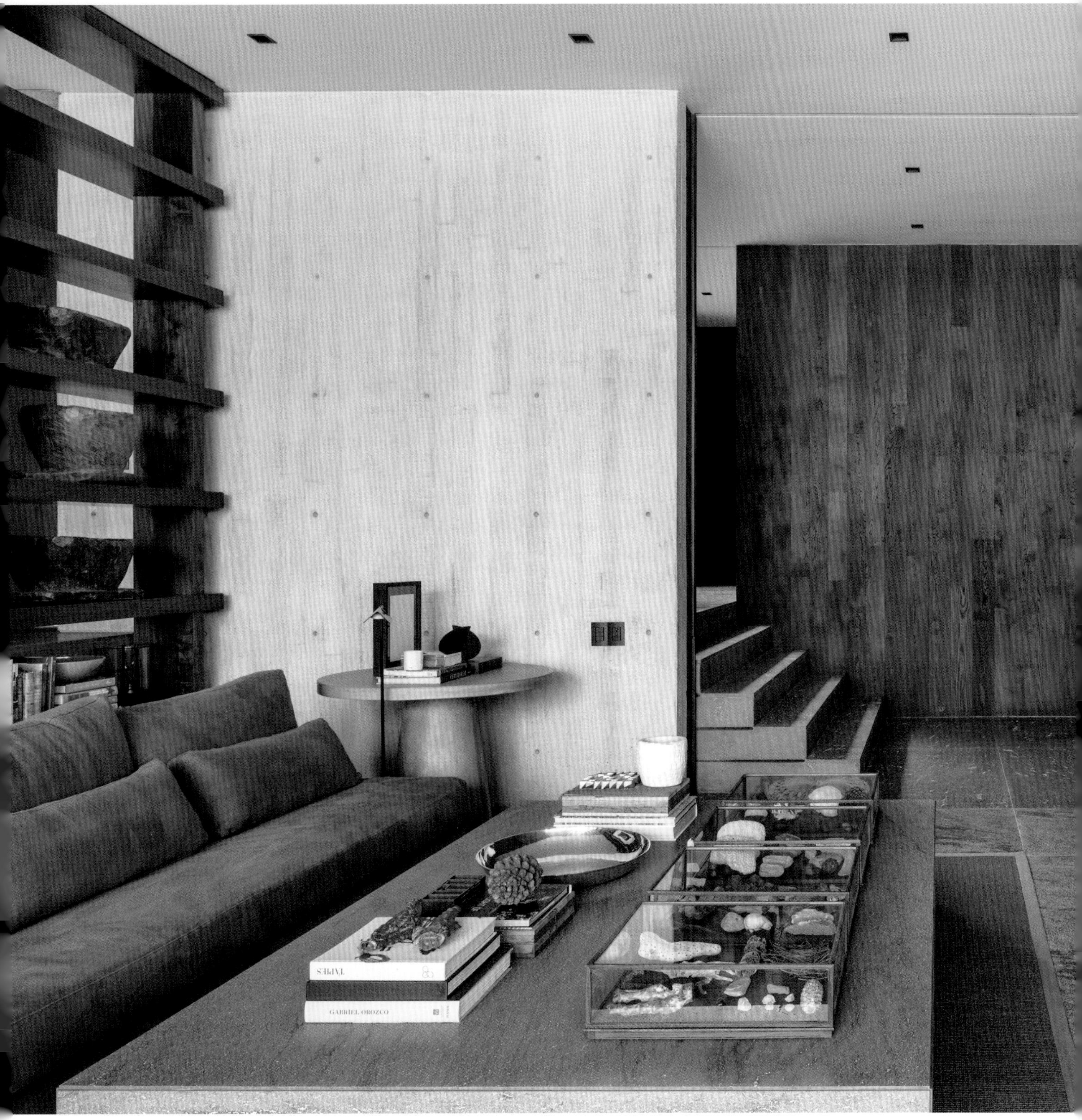
TÀPIES
GABRIEL OROZCO

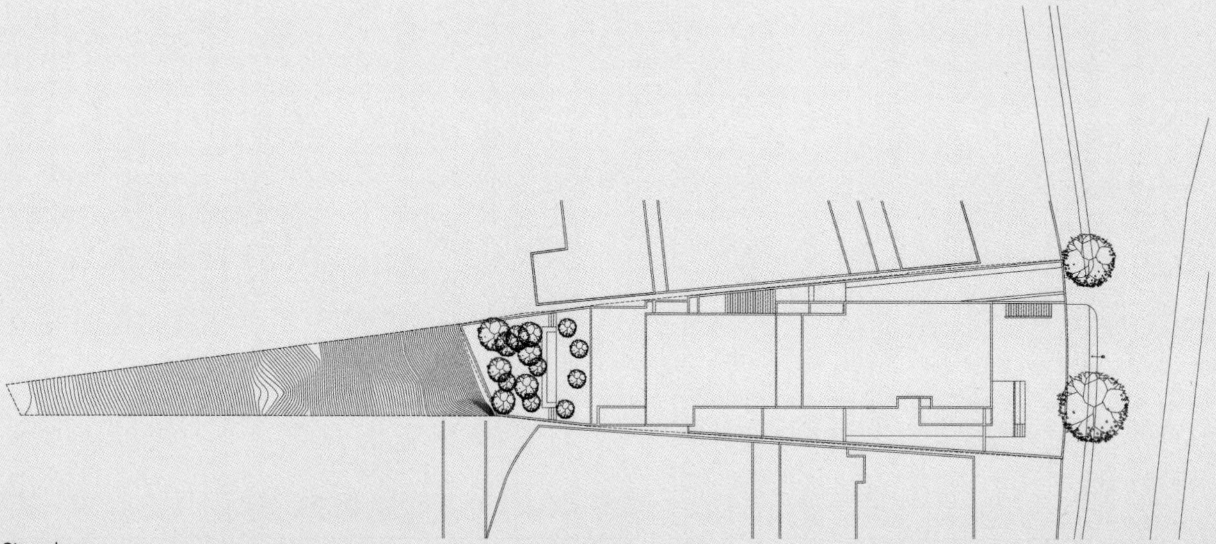

Site plan

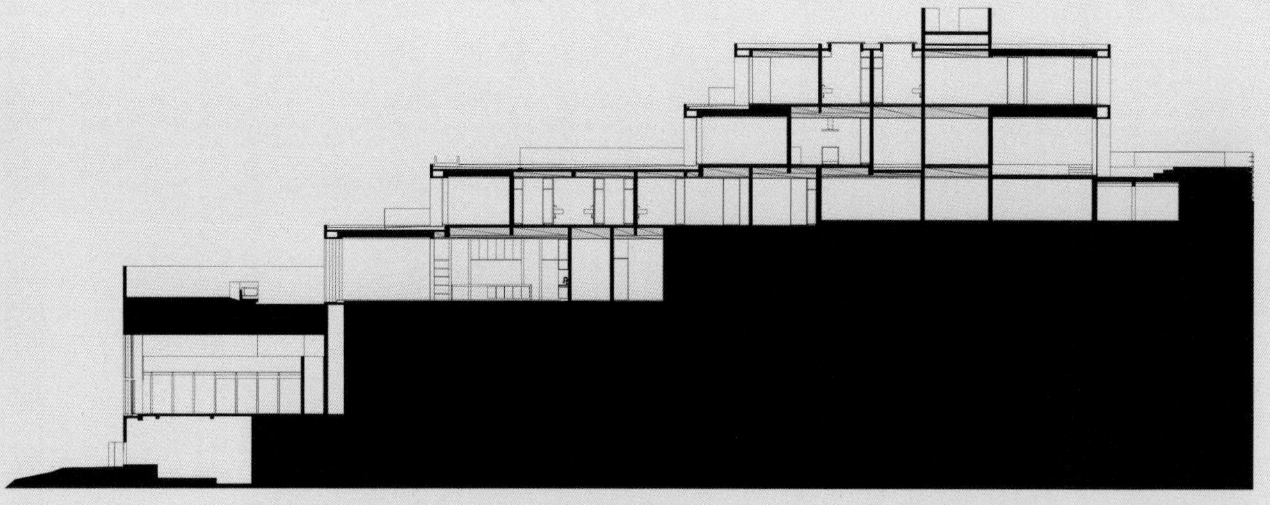

Section

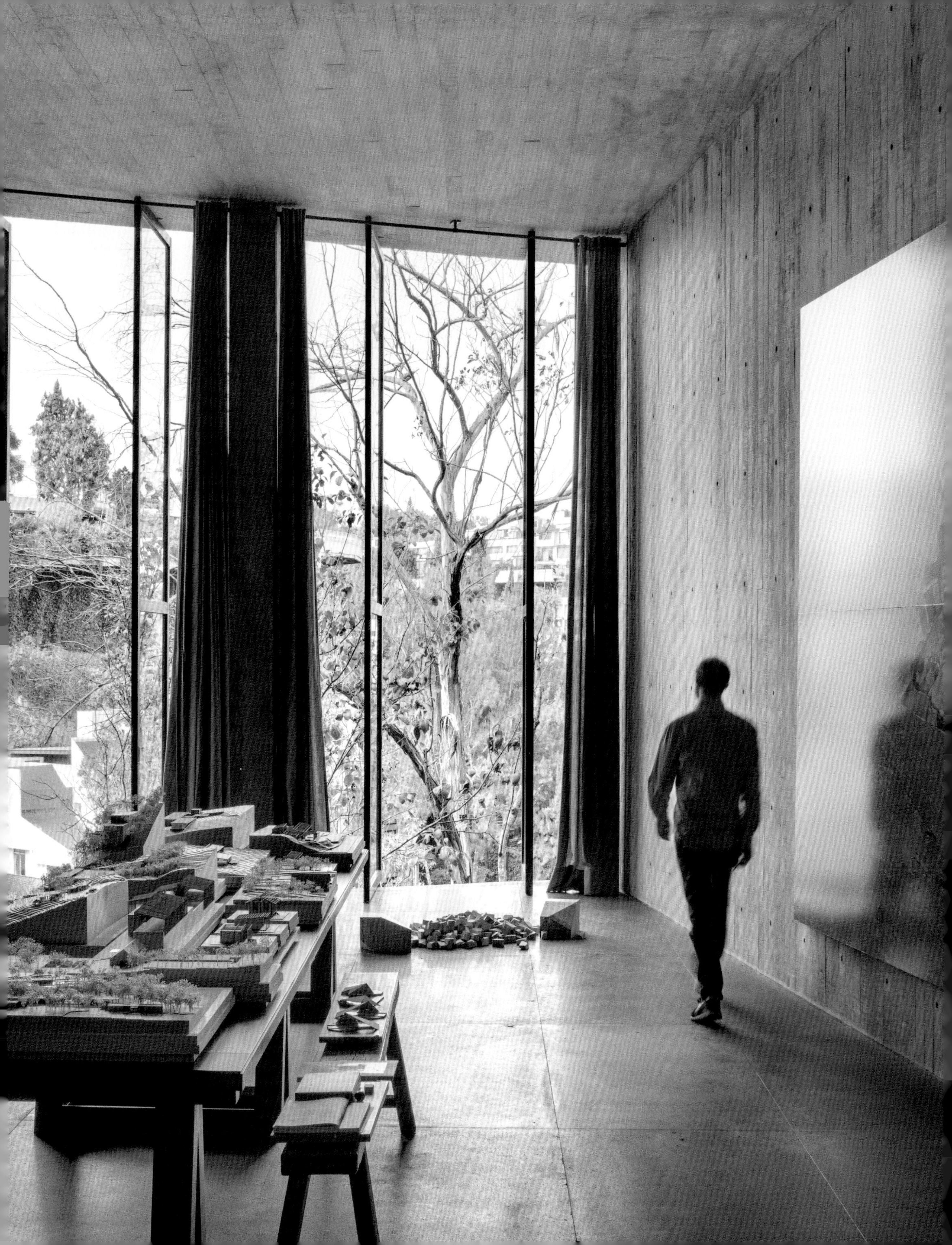

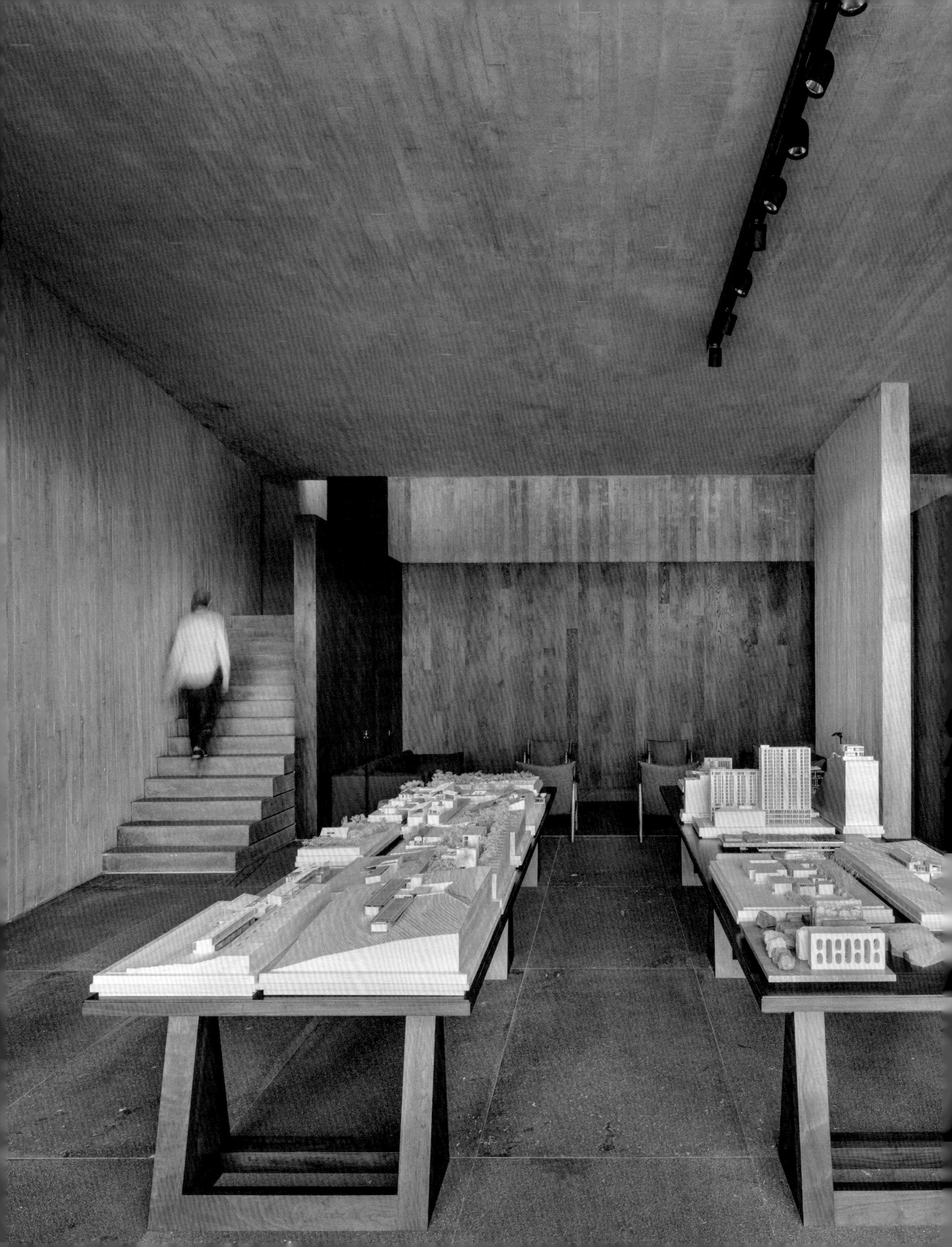

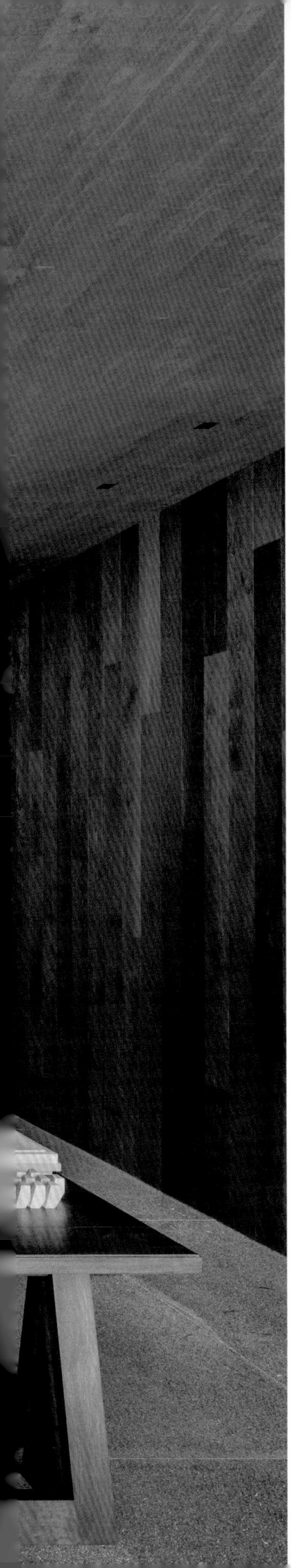

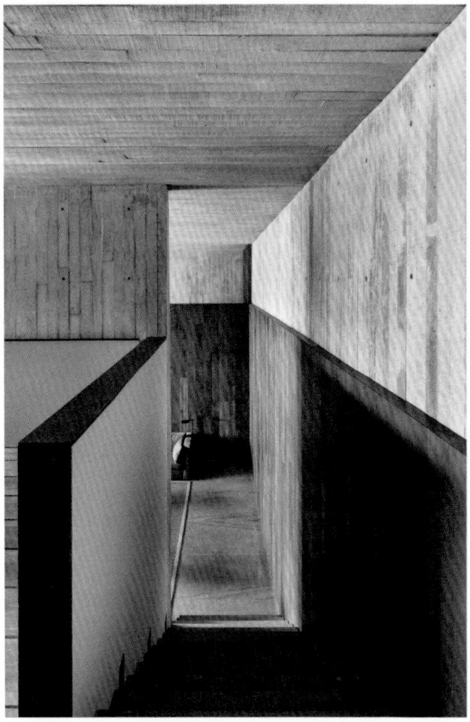

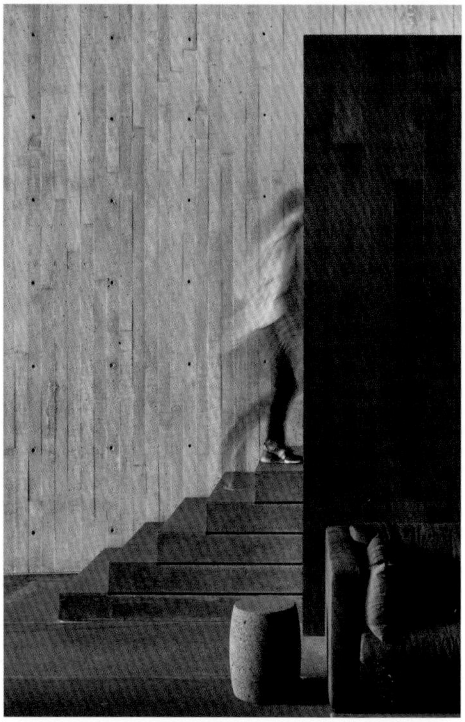

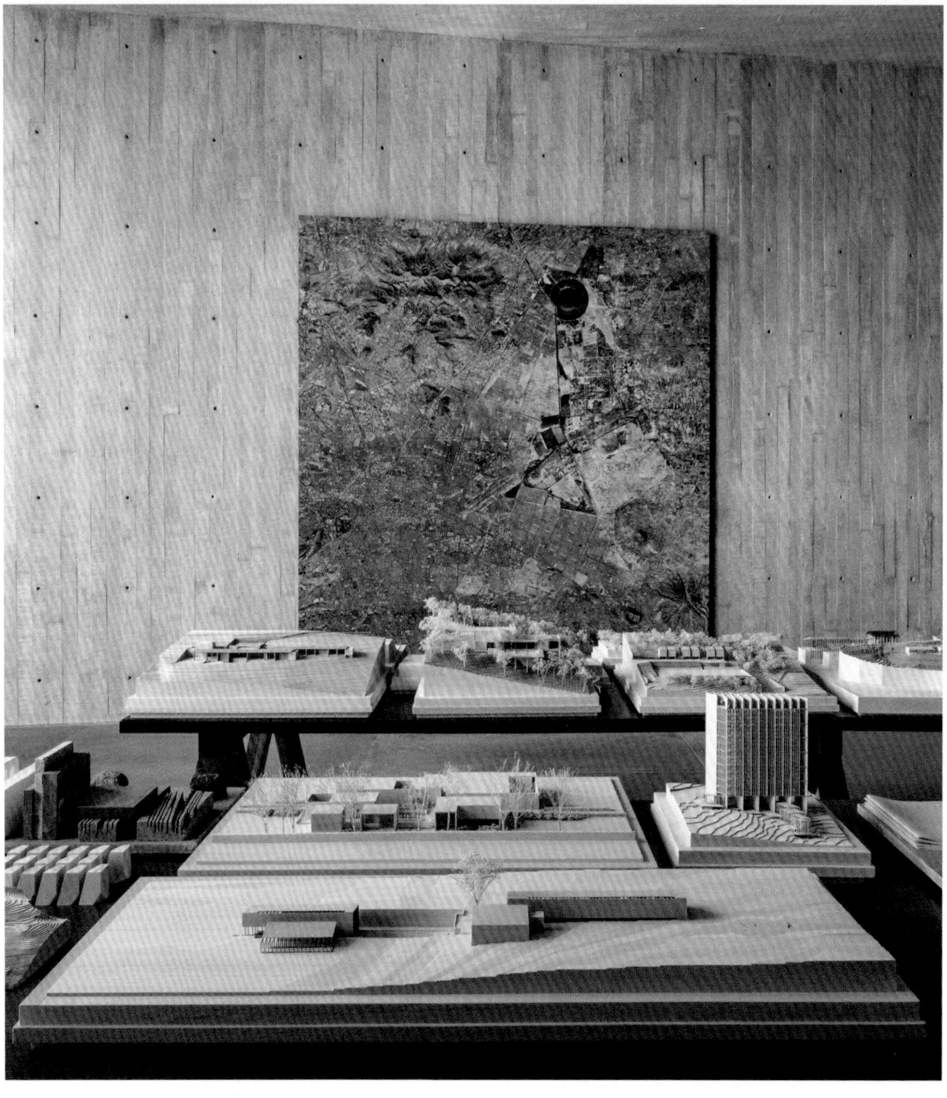

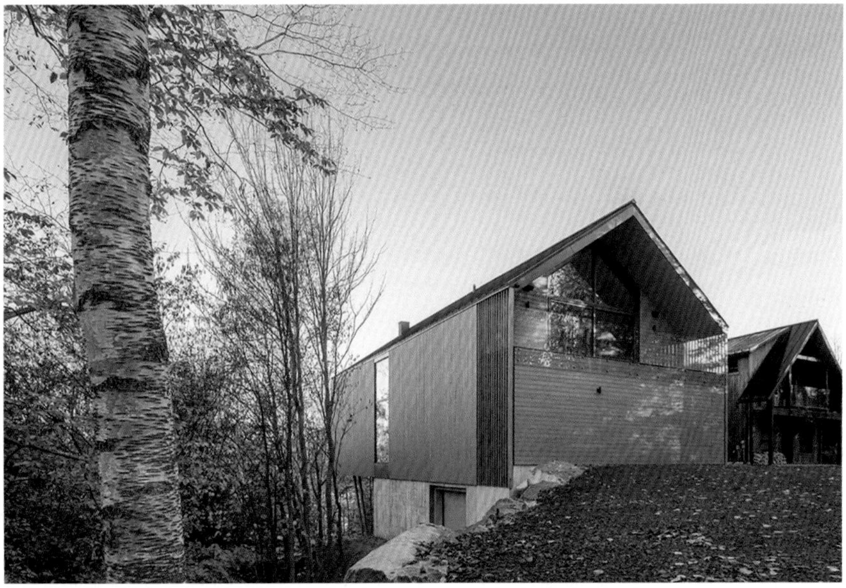

Area:
5,000 square feet (465 square meters)

Completion:
2017

Design:
MU Architecture

Photography:
Ulysse Lemerise Bouchard

Sainte-Adèle, Canada

Workshop on a Cliff

Located in the countryside of the Laurentian Mountains, in the province of Quebec, this modern addition is not a typical garage. Over the peaceful Deauville Lake, this minimalist wood workshop stands out from the surrounding green mountains. Reminiscent of the typical barn, this vast modern addition projects over the cliffs of the lake and houses two garages, a workshop, a large creative room, and a mezzanine.

A forest of columns

Connected to the main residence by a cantilevered bridge, the workshop is a powerful space for reflection and creation. Its structure, entirely free, rests on a set of inclined columns evoking the forest, suspending it above the tree line.

Northern light and dizzying height

Pierced with light, the workshop is oriented toward the north and has views onto the lake. Spacious but intimate, the interior volume accommodates large-formats paintings. The minimalist design creates a setting for the artist's work.

The mezzanine offers a relaxation and play area under a large uninterrupted ceiling. A smaller area in its center shelters a bathroom and another smaller mezzanine set even higher, a perfect

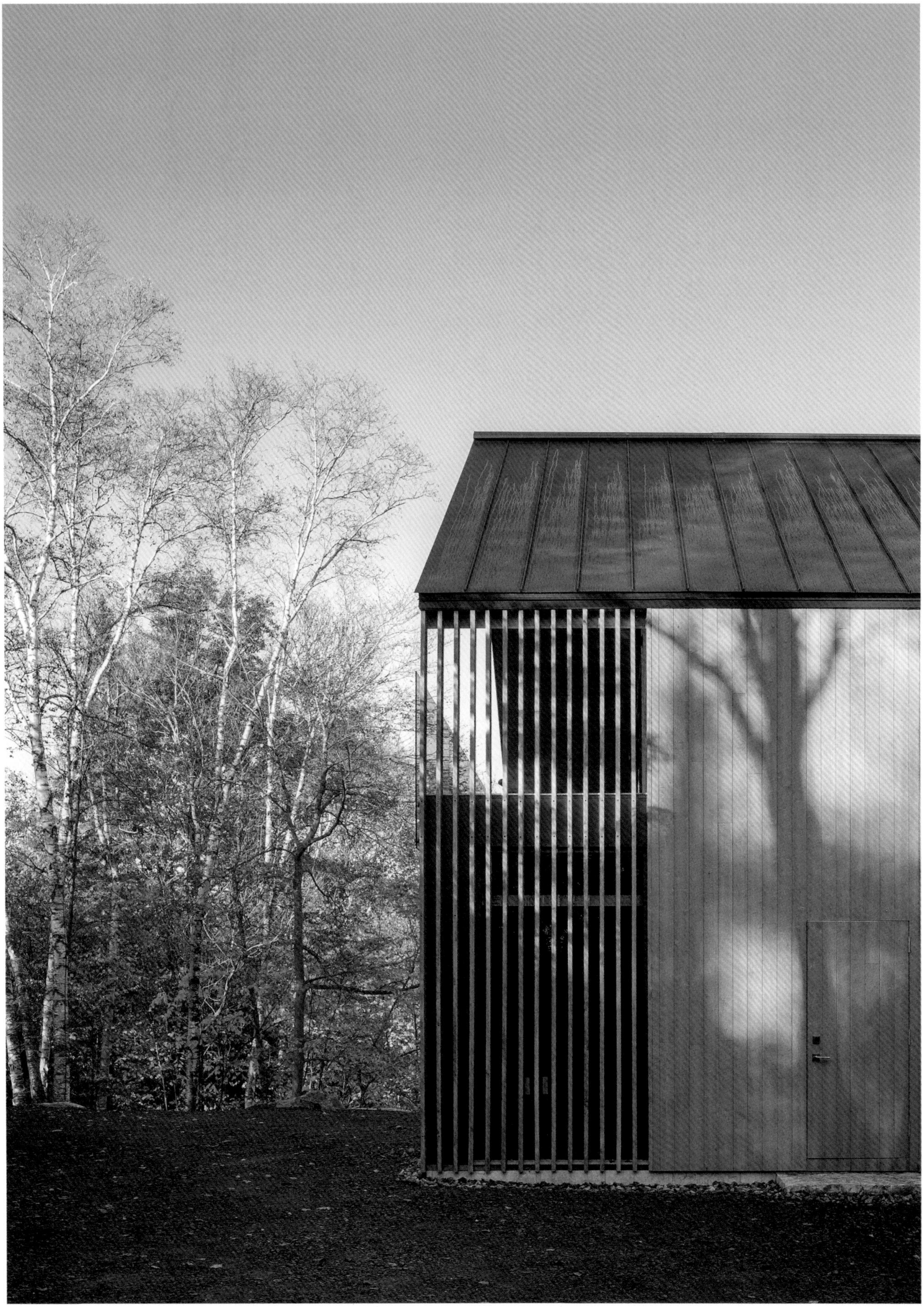

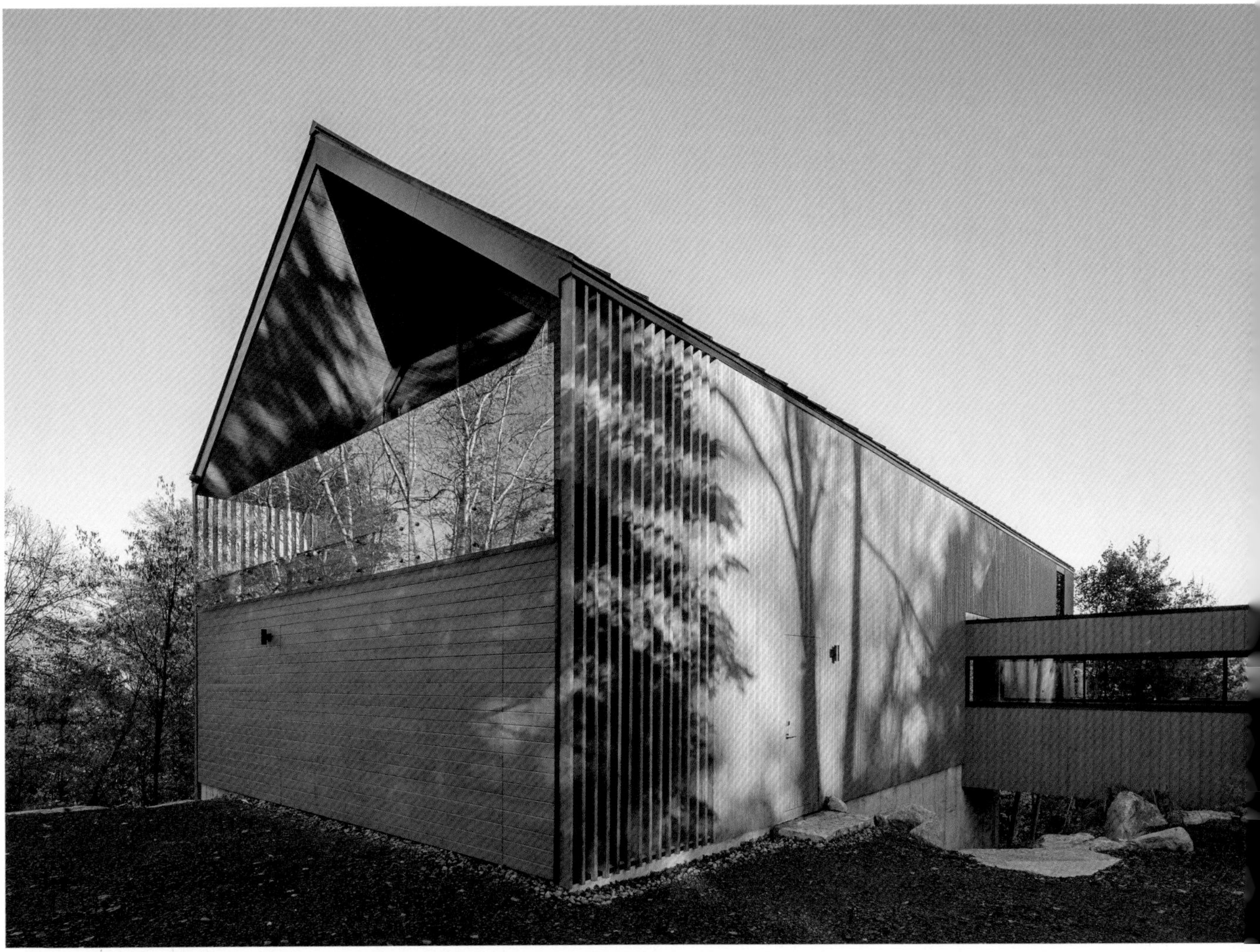

hideout for kids. On this aerial platform, the polished concrete floor reflects light as well as views and increases the feeling of vertigo. It is accessed by an open staircase that acts as a connector between the bridge and the mezzanine. Consisting of a series of large plates of cold-rolled steel, it represents the gesture of the artist sketching away their first brushstrokes on the canvas.

Sophisticated simplicity

The workshop is presented as a simple volume covered with a pre-aged gray wood. Its thick exterior walls are built to the energy efficiency standards of the "passive house" movement. Sophisticated details were developed to ventilate the building between the walls and the roof and to completely conceal the garage door while responding to insulation needs that are necessary in the harsh climate of Quebec.

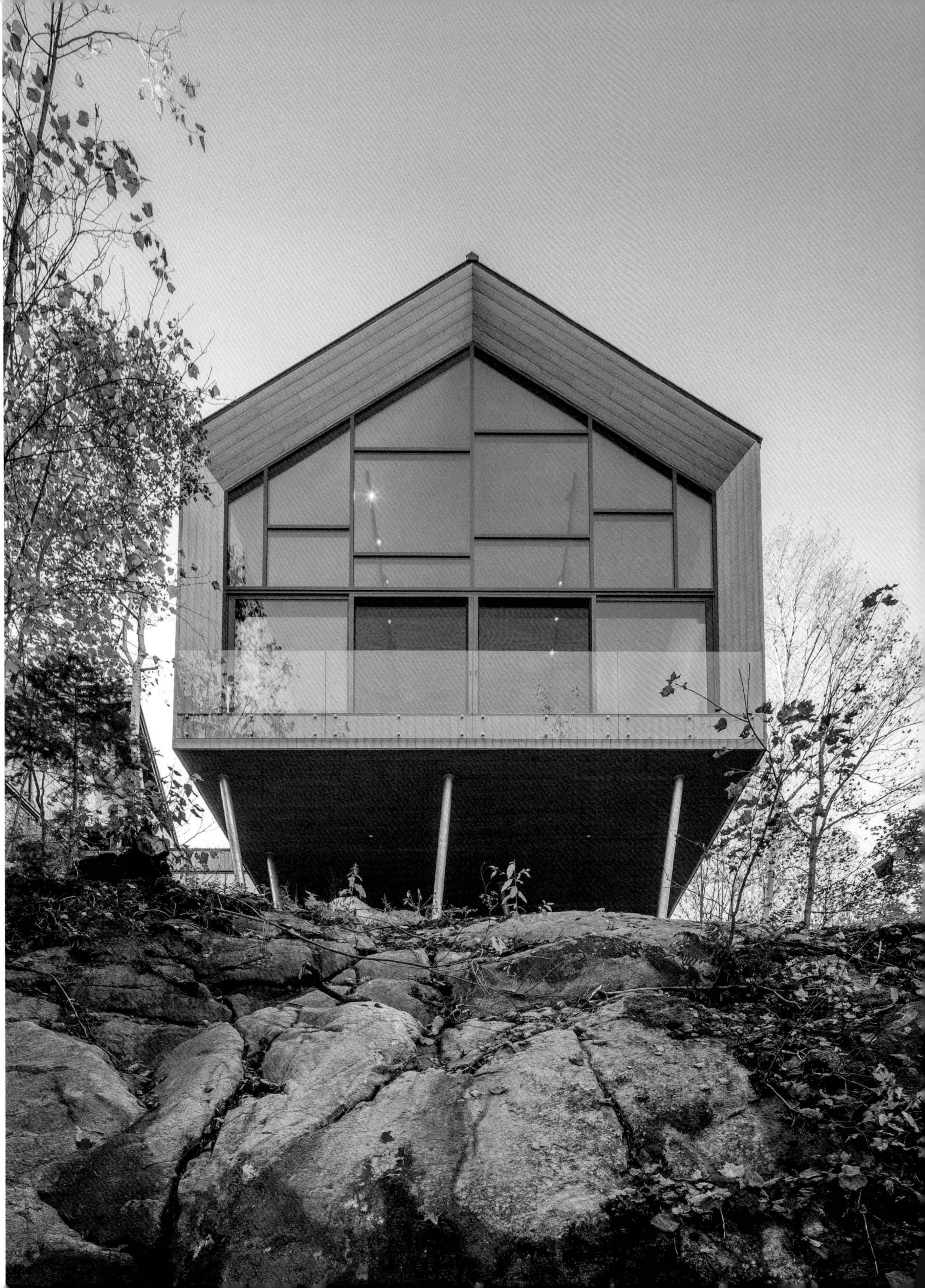

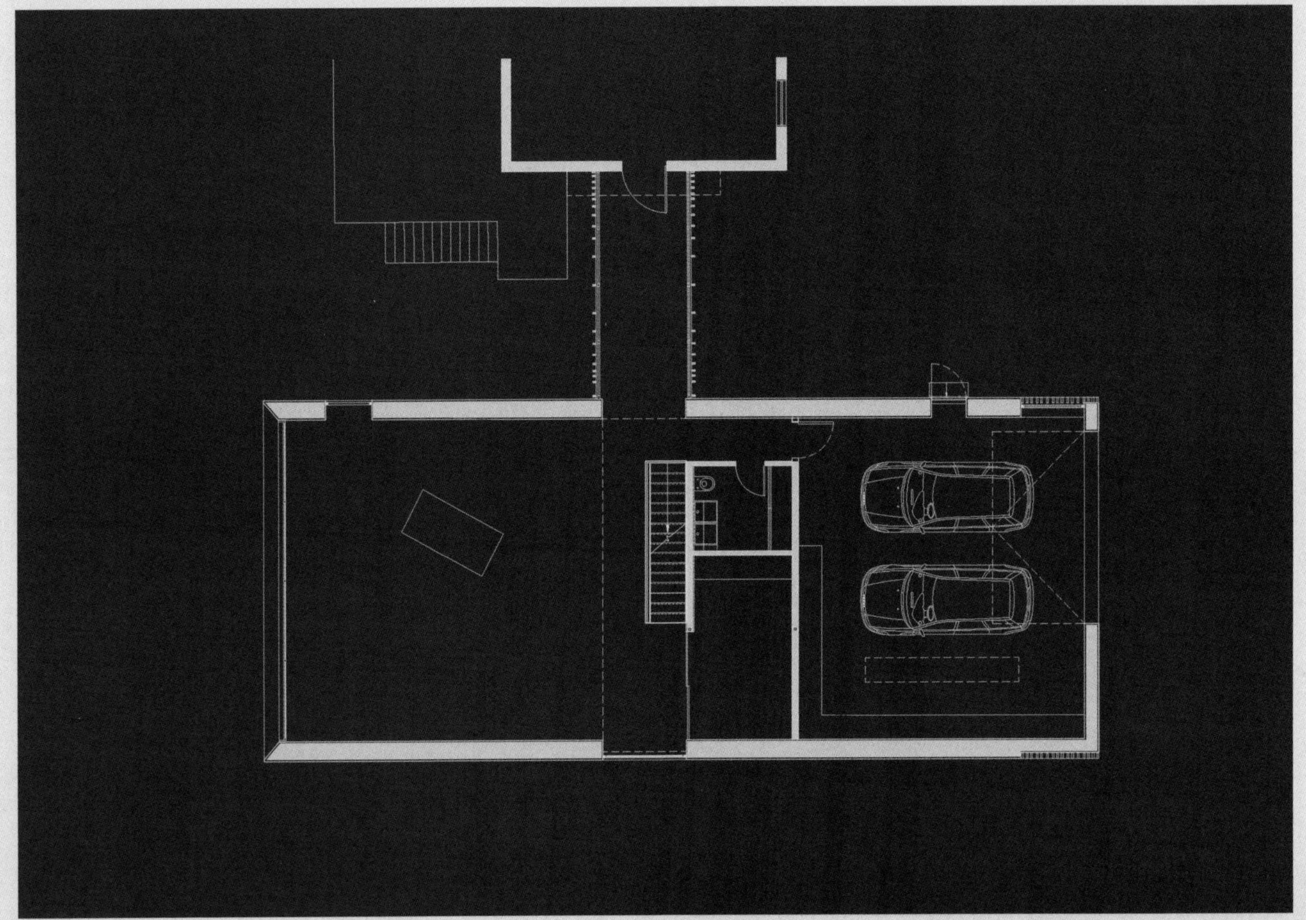

Floor plan

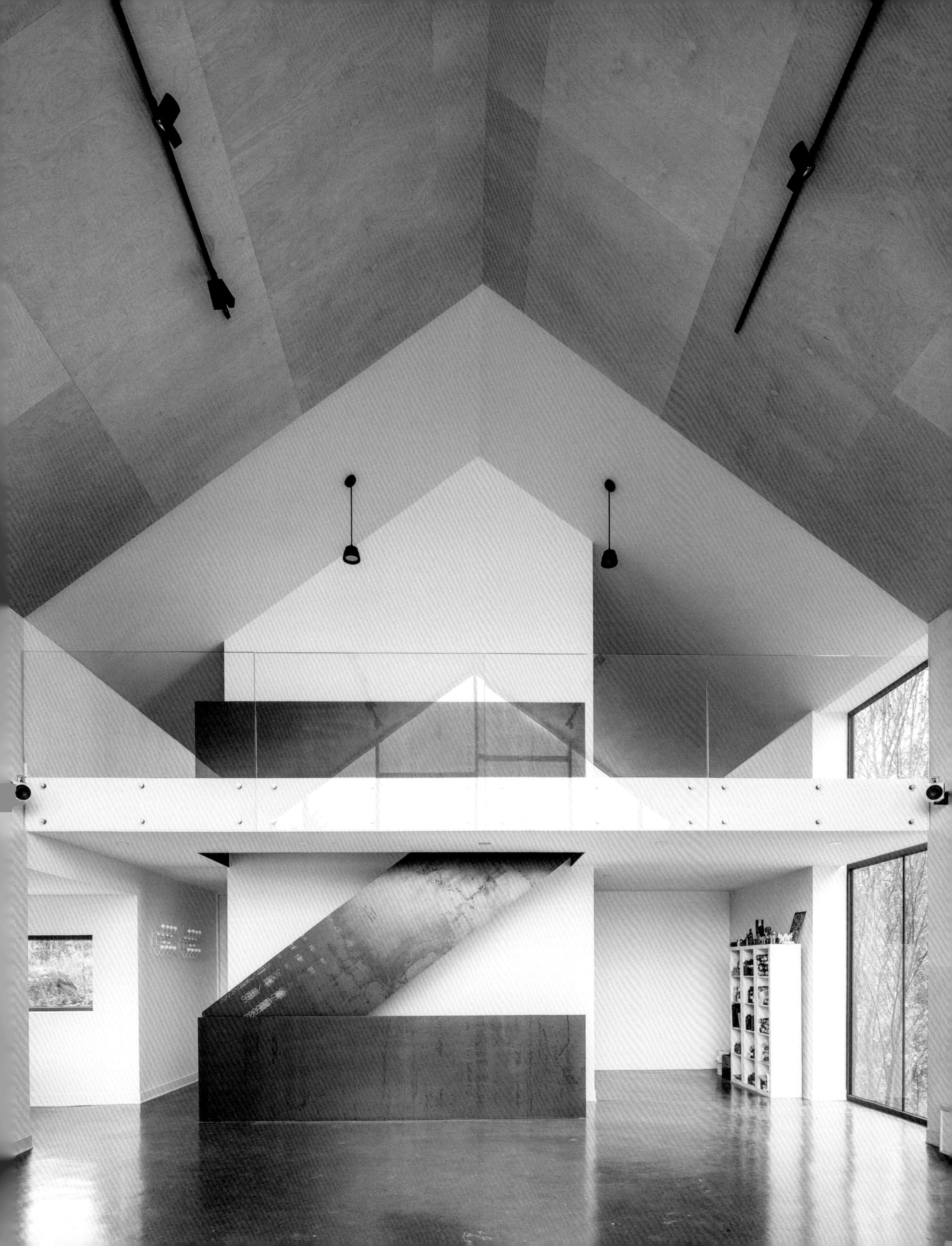

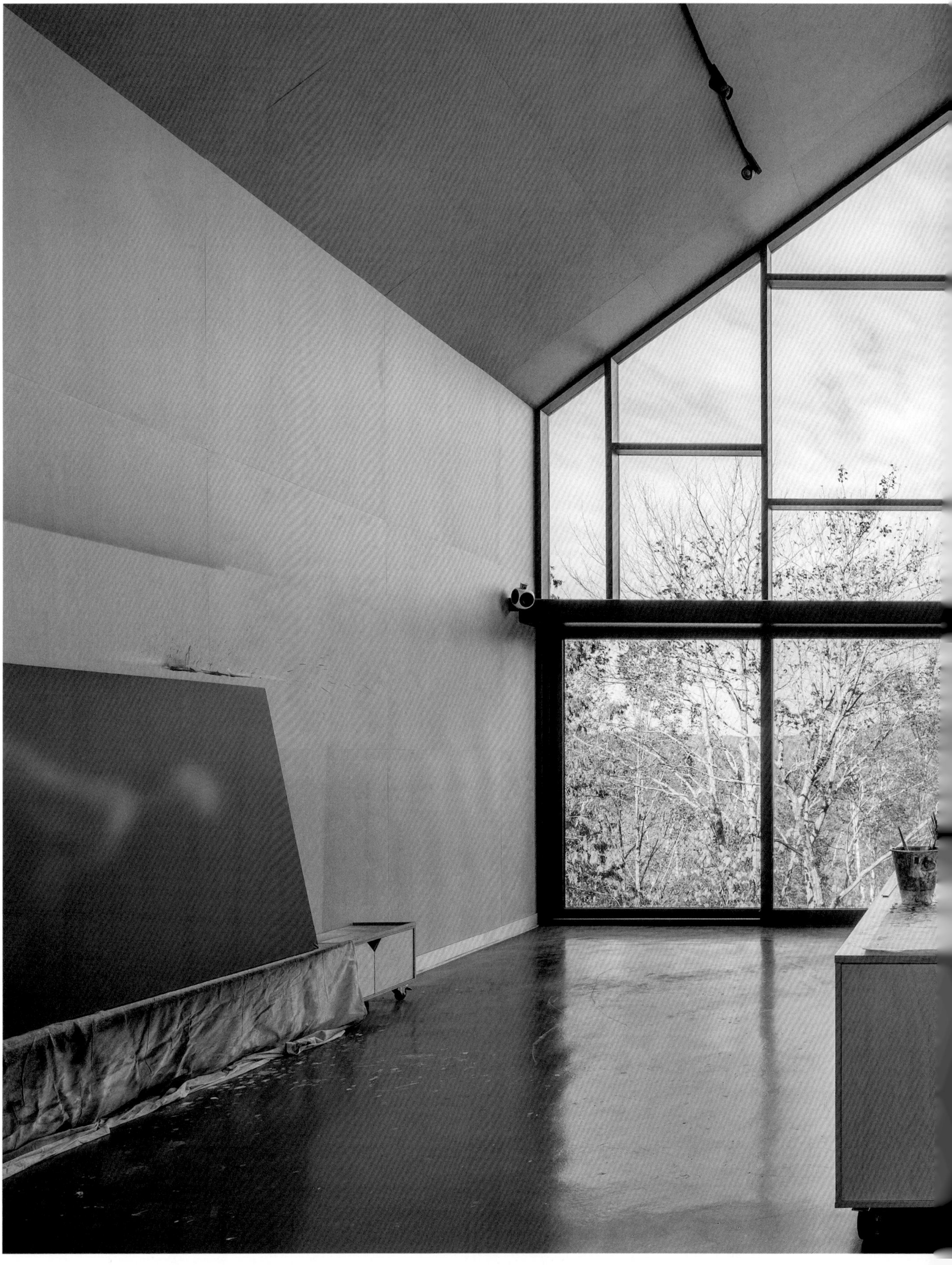

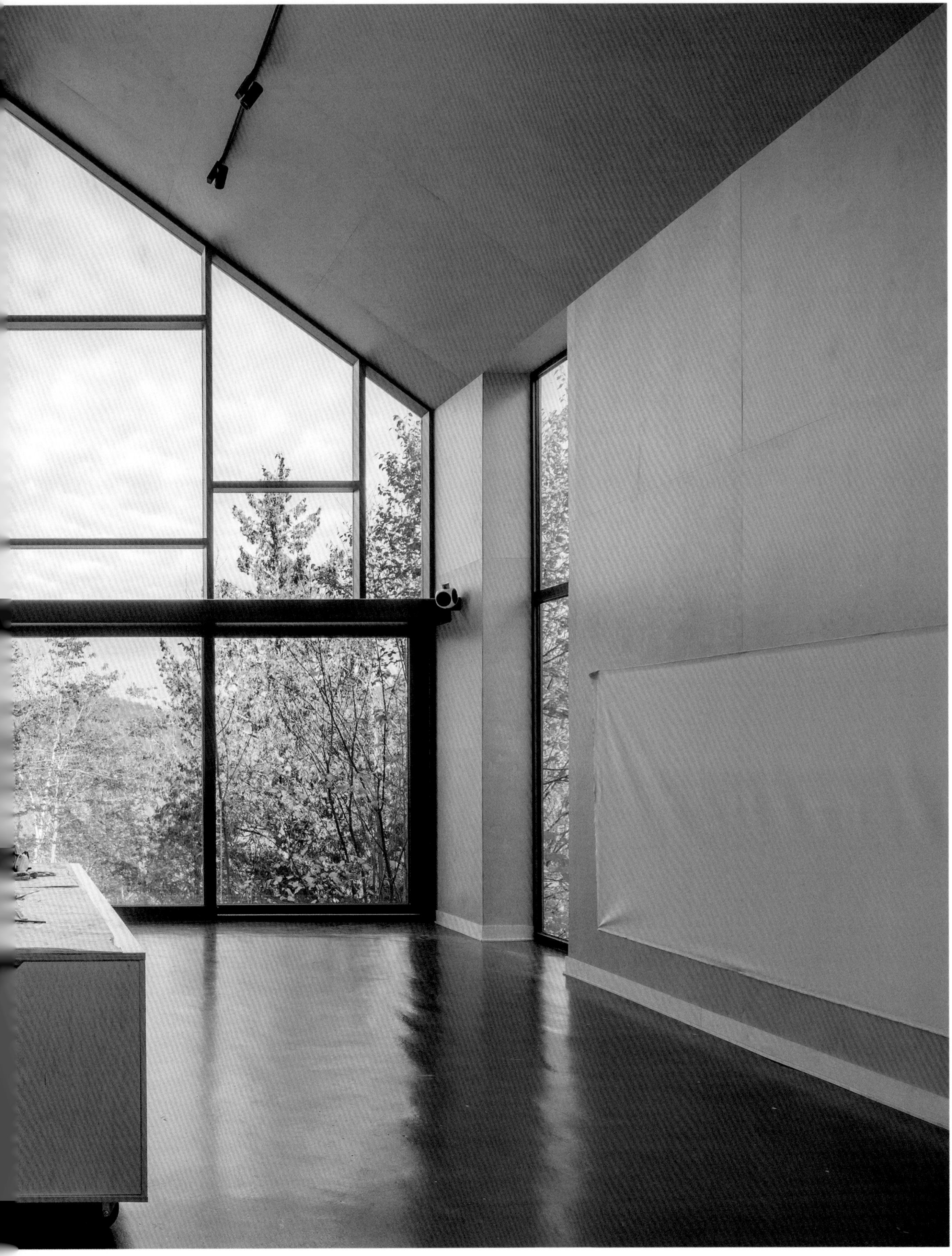

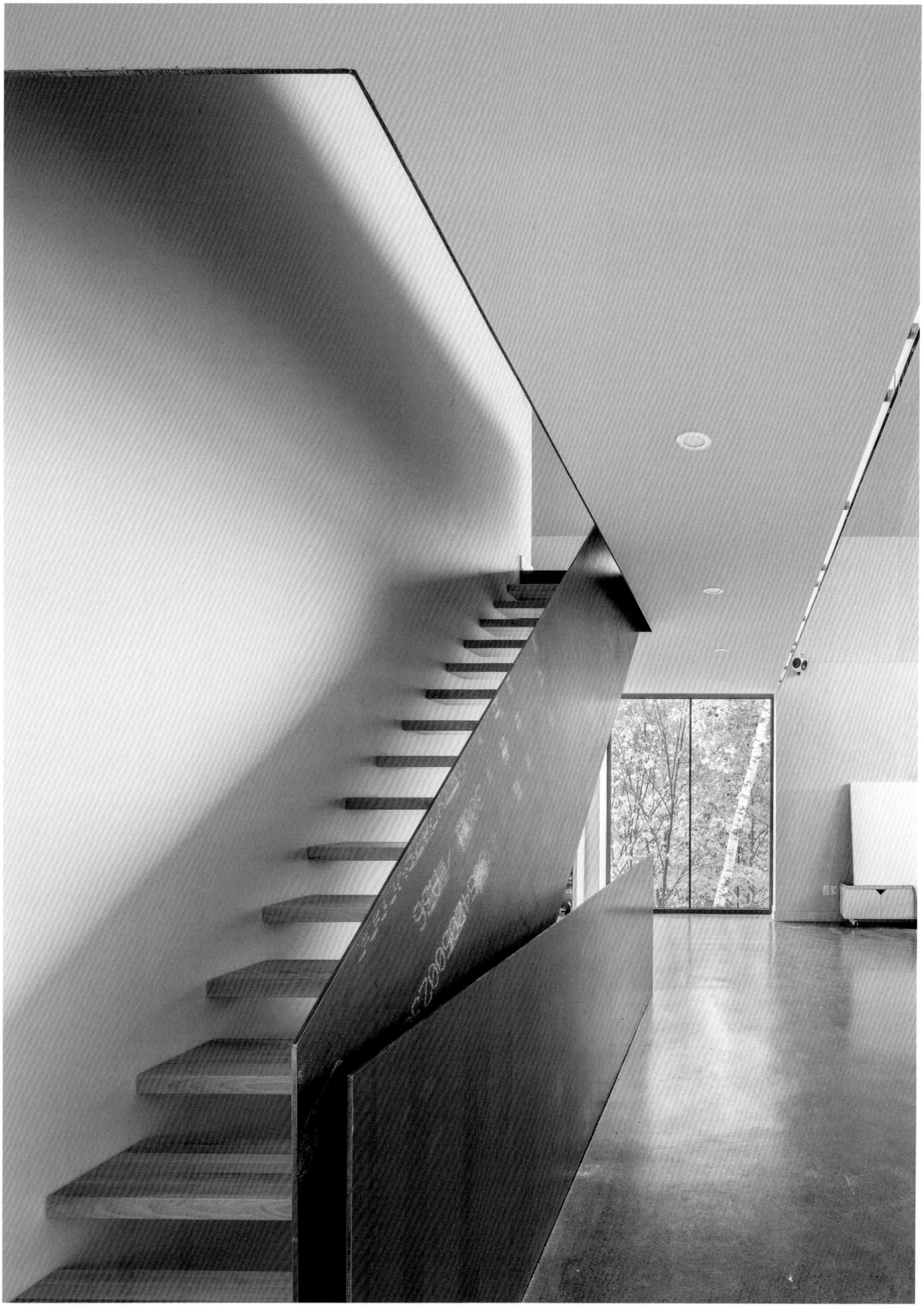

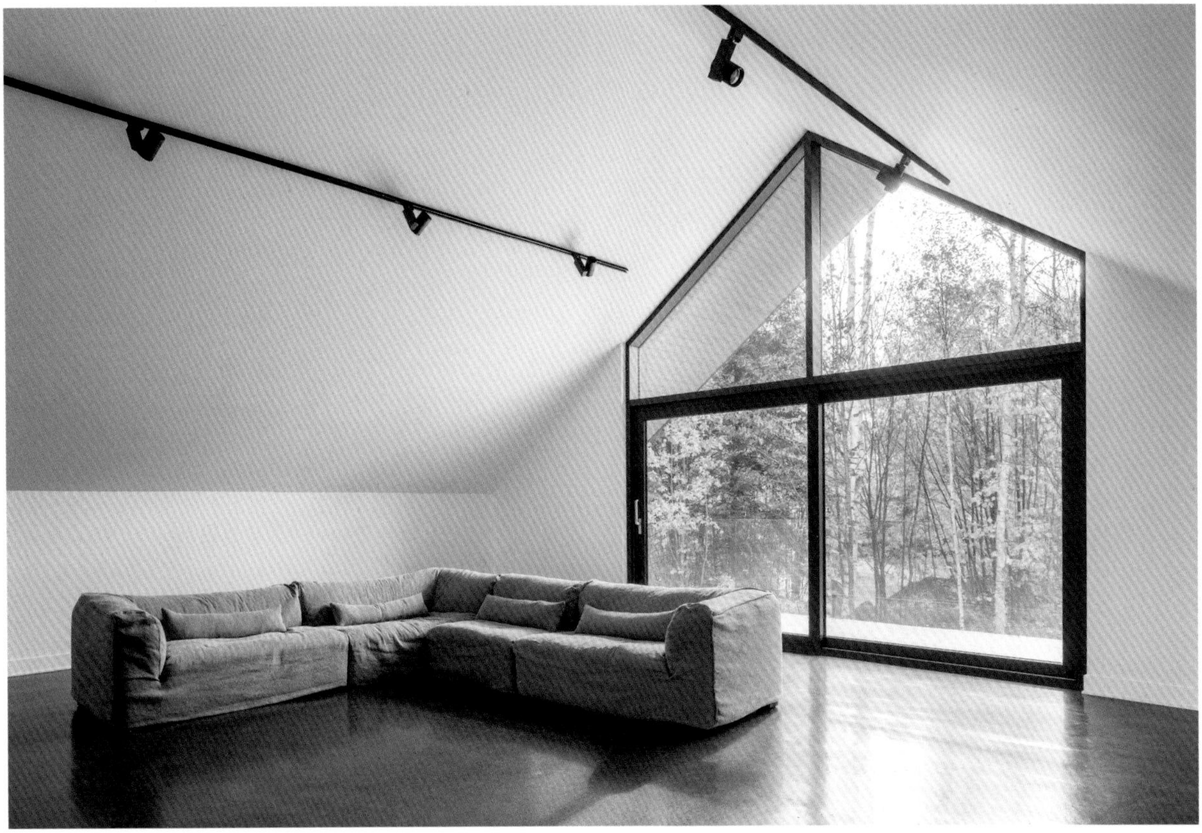

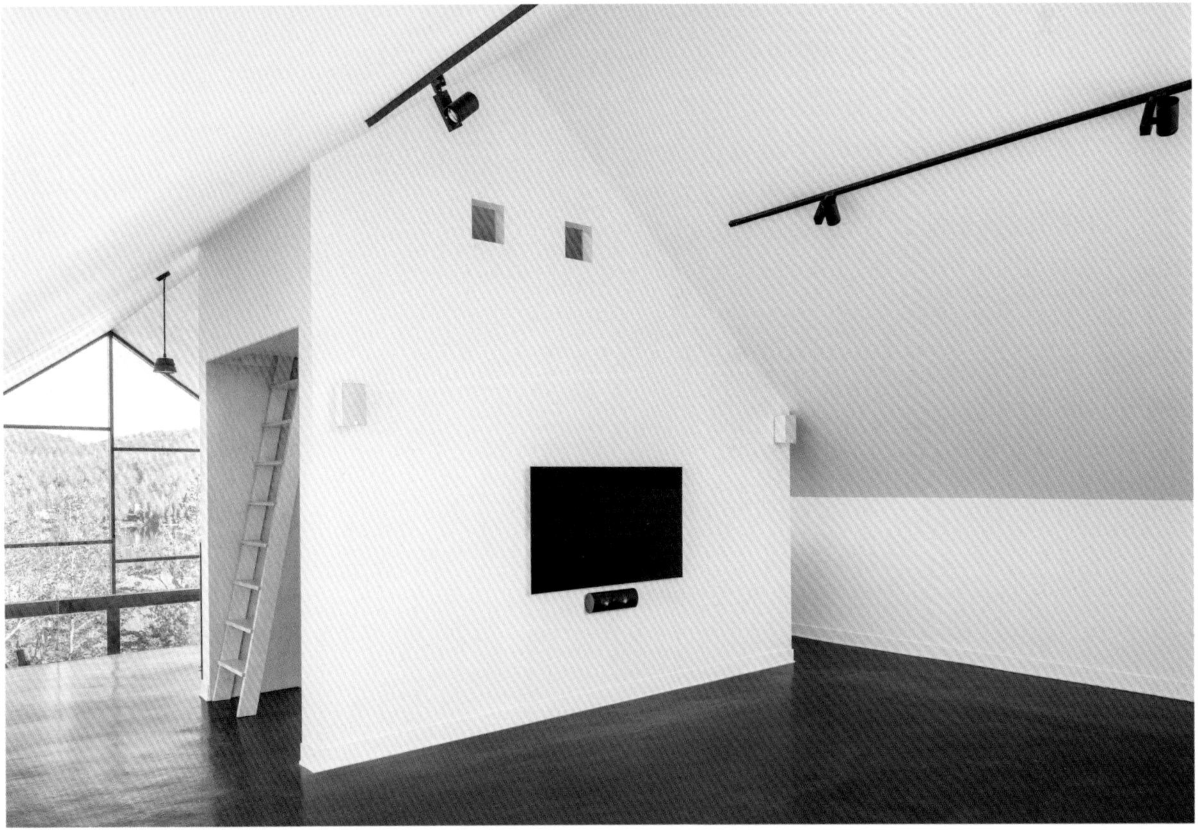

LIVING, WORKING, AND EXHIBITING TOGETHER

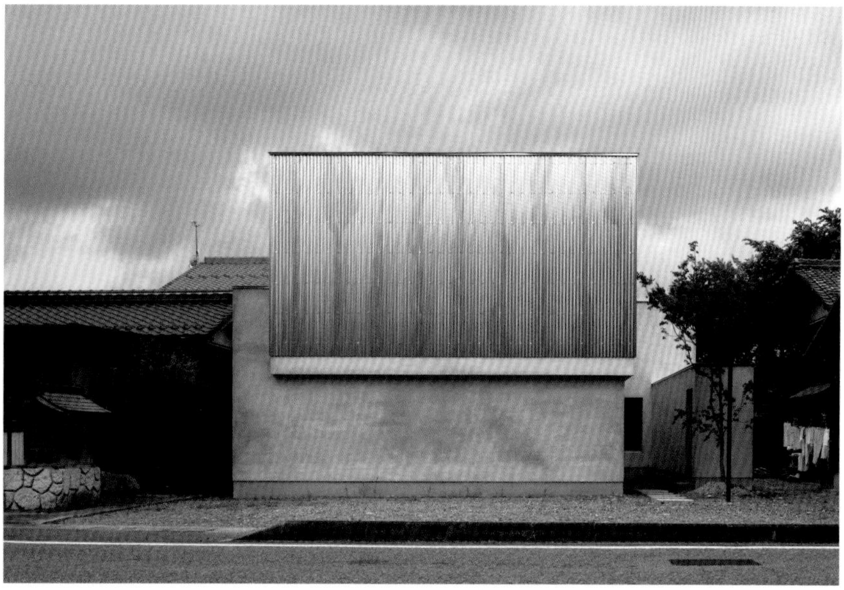

Area:
1,819 square feet (169 square meters)
Completion:
2017
Design:
FORM/Kouichi Kimura Architects
Photography:
Yoshihiro Asada, Norihito Yamauchi

Shiga, Japan

House for a Photographer

On an arterial road that runs through countryside in a neighborhood of private residences, reached via a passage through a temple grove and standing across from the village shrine, one finds this photographer's combined residence, studio, and gallery. The building is made of mortar and galvanized steel, which reflects dull light, making it look massive.

A place to live and work

The client asked the designer to unite the studio where he produces works with his living space and the designer came up with a plan by clarifying how the resident wants to live instead of simply segmenting the space by function.

The dim passage from the entrance approach invites visitors into the inner space while guiding them with light thrown from the ceiling of the connected gallery. Contrasting scales and natural light resonate with each other. The space is also a photogenic shooting location.

The long thin passage serving as a route around the gallery has functions other than a mere pathway; it is also used as a space to post artworks and photos on the wall. It makes use of different ceiling heights, and shade and shadow created by natural light.

The hall in the center of the building with different floor levels plays the role of a hub that connects with each space. It also

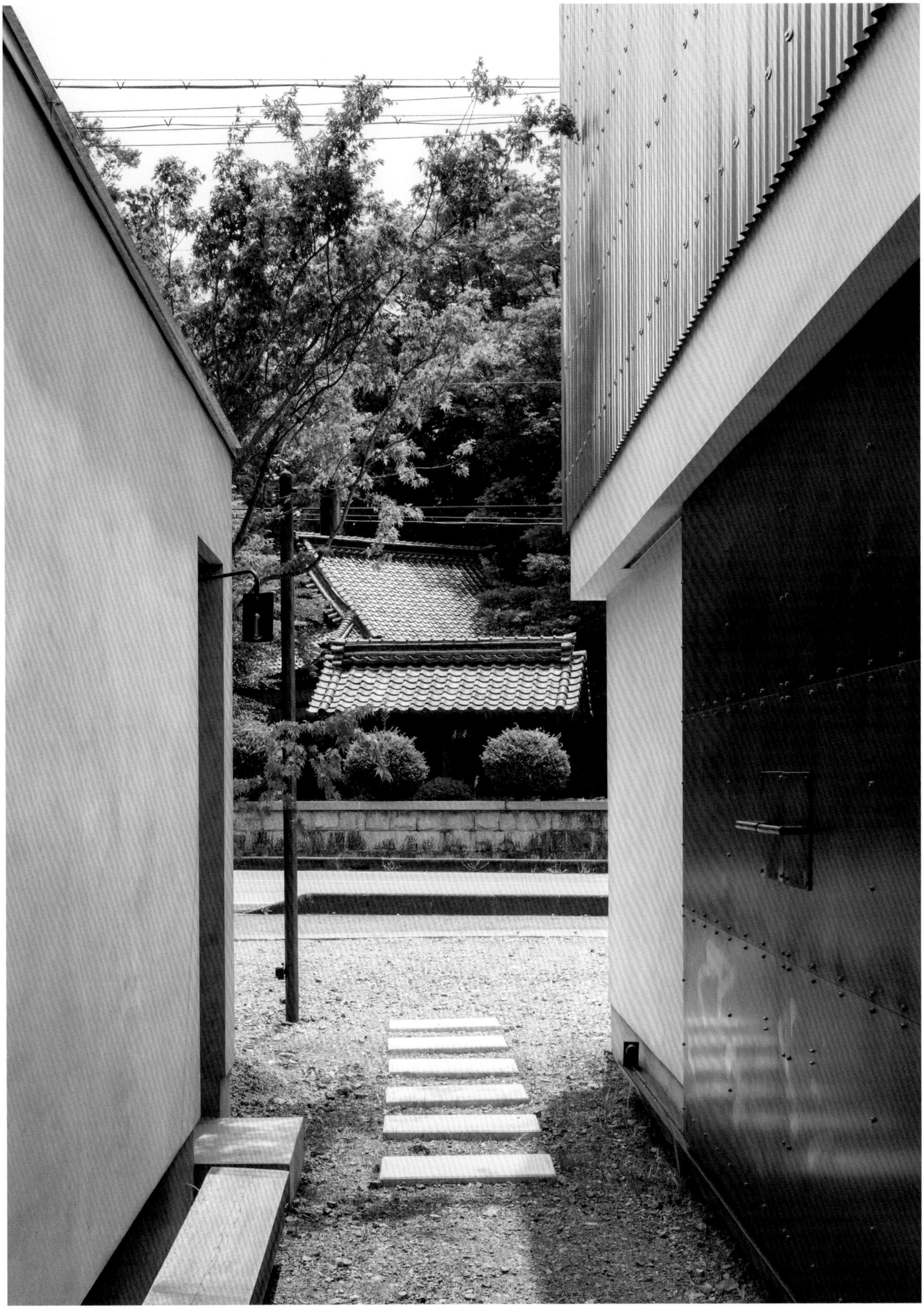

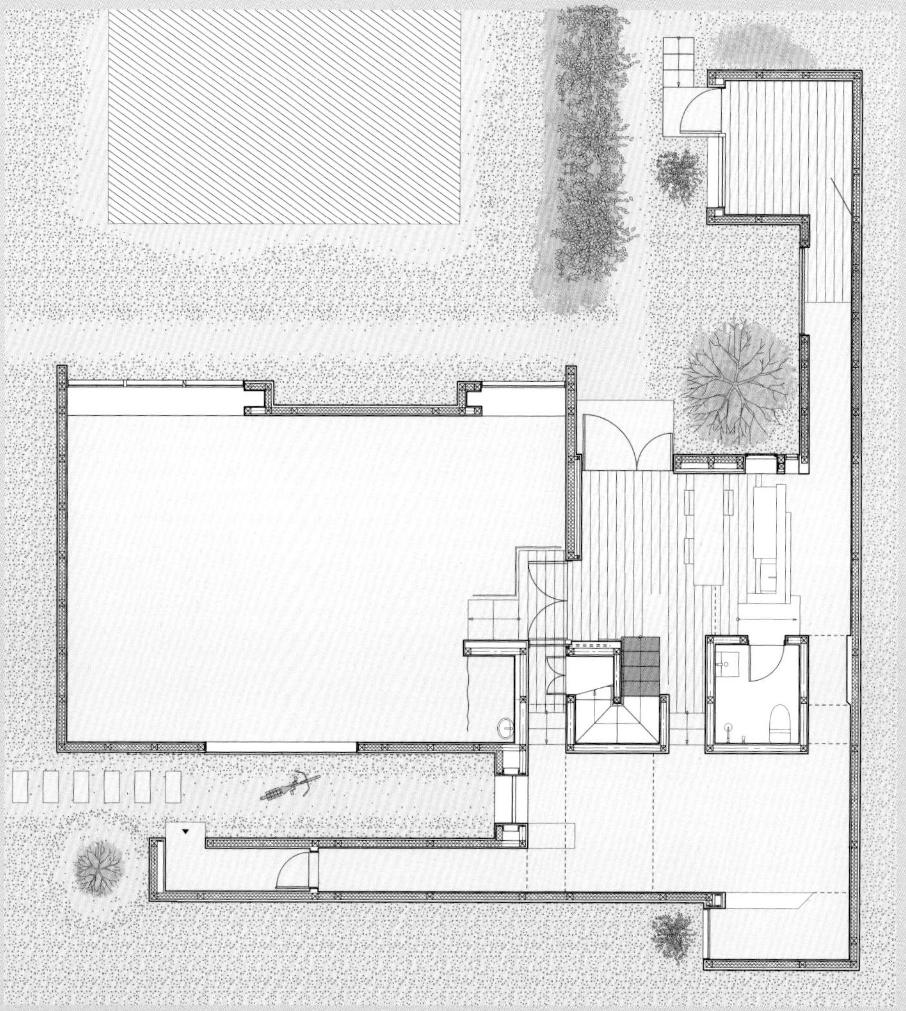

Ground-floor plan

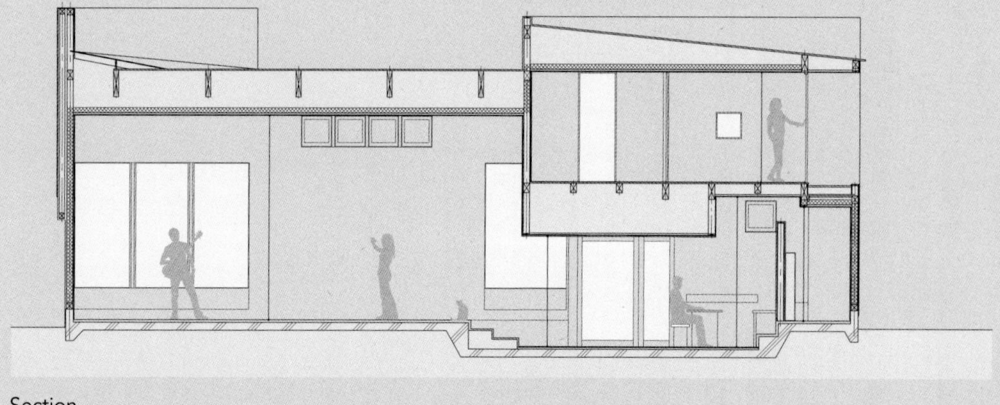

Section

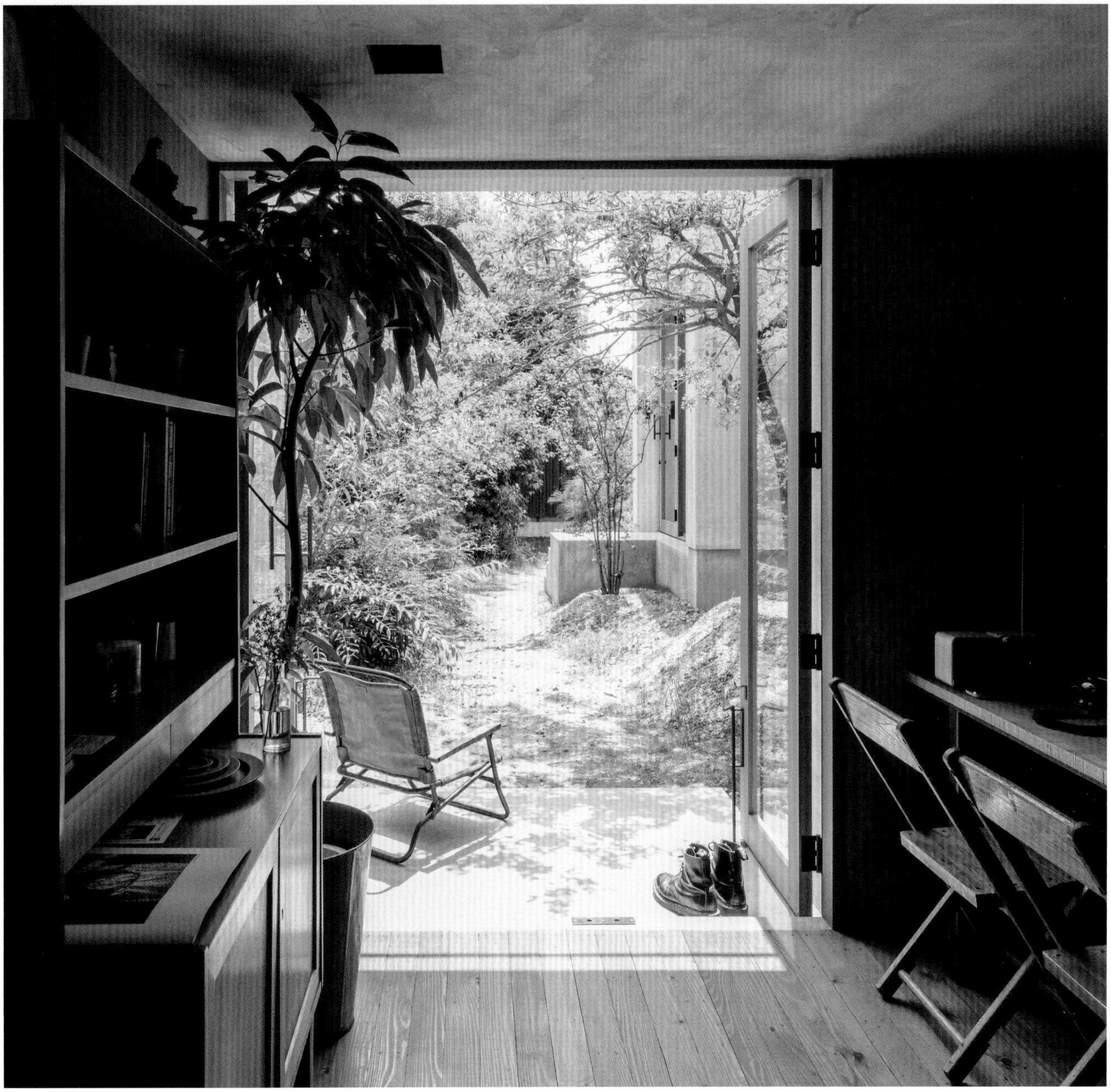

incorporates plumbing equipment, a counter, and a staircase, and is connected to an approach from the courtyard, providing functional comfort as well as displaying scenic beauty.

The building used as a living space also offers a dynamic space with proportion and scale that allows it to serve as a photo studio that enables shooting with natural light.

Photography equipment, vintage furniture, musical instruments, and artworks are placed around the space, reflecting the photographer's aesthetic.

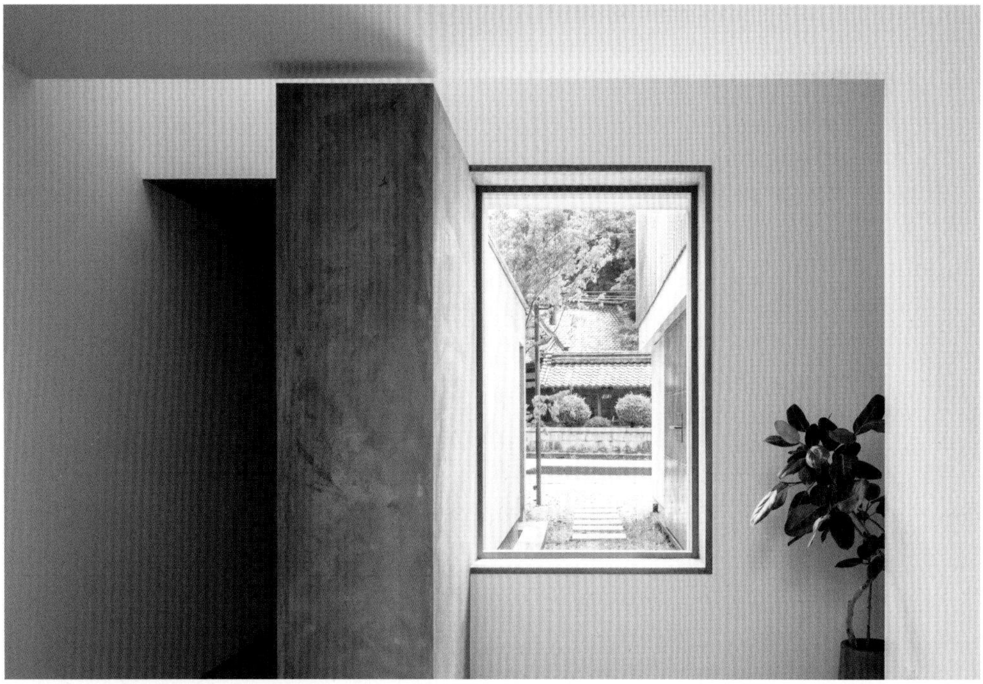

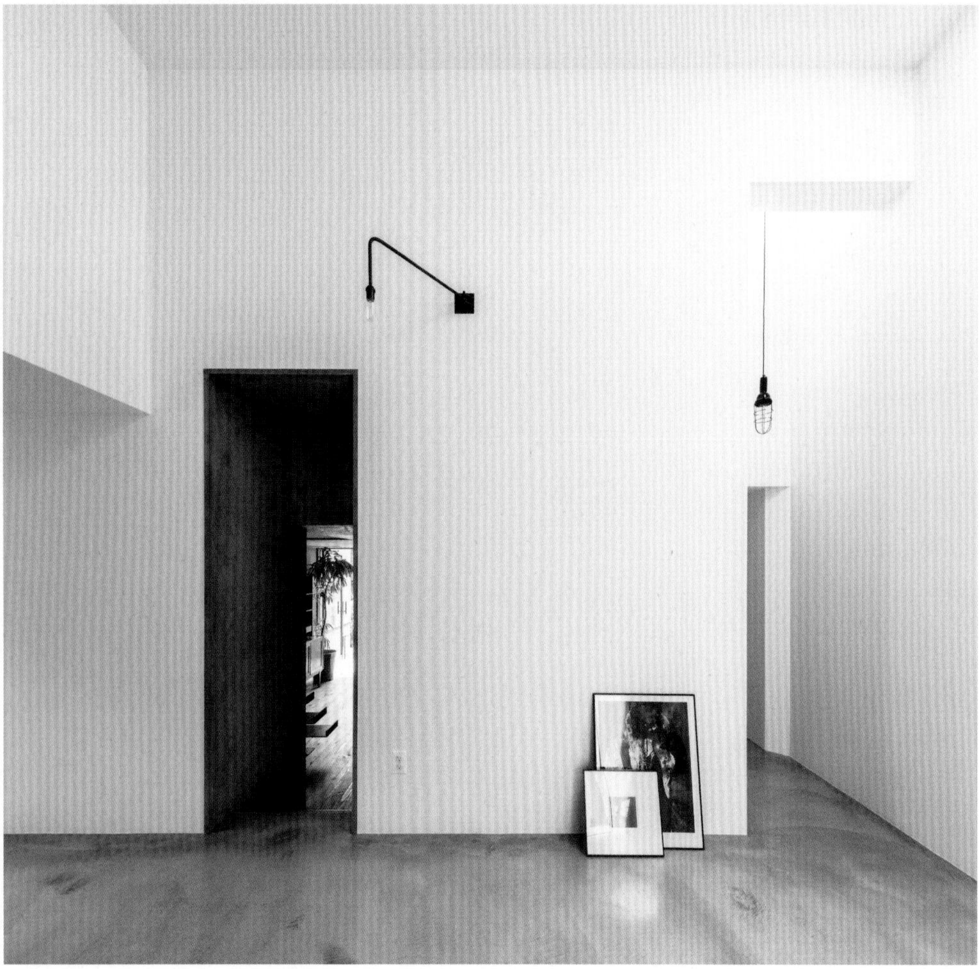

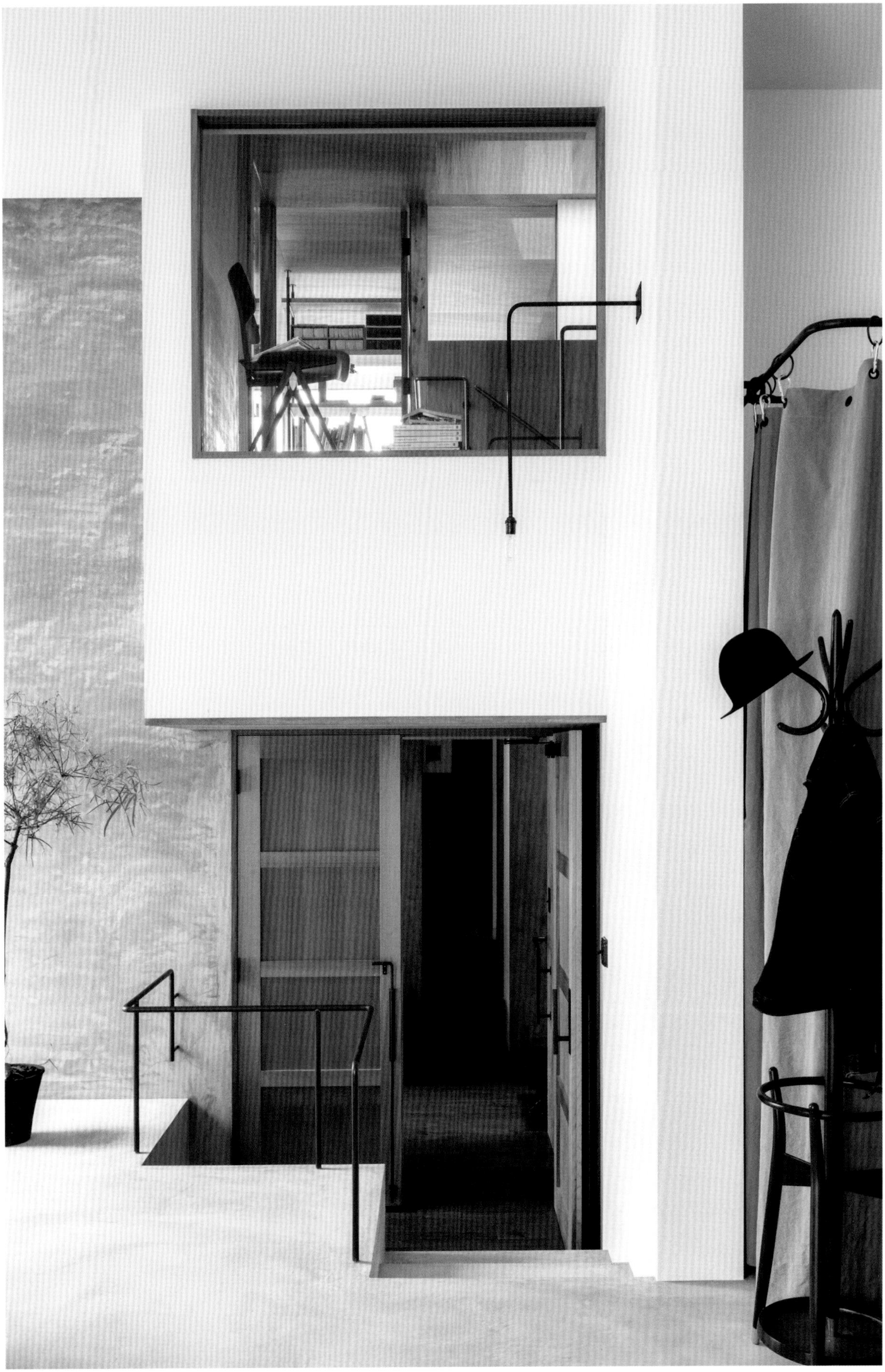

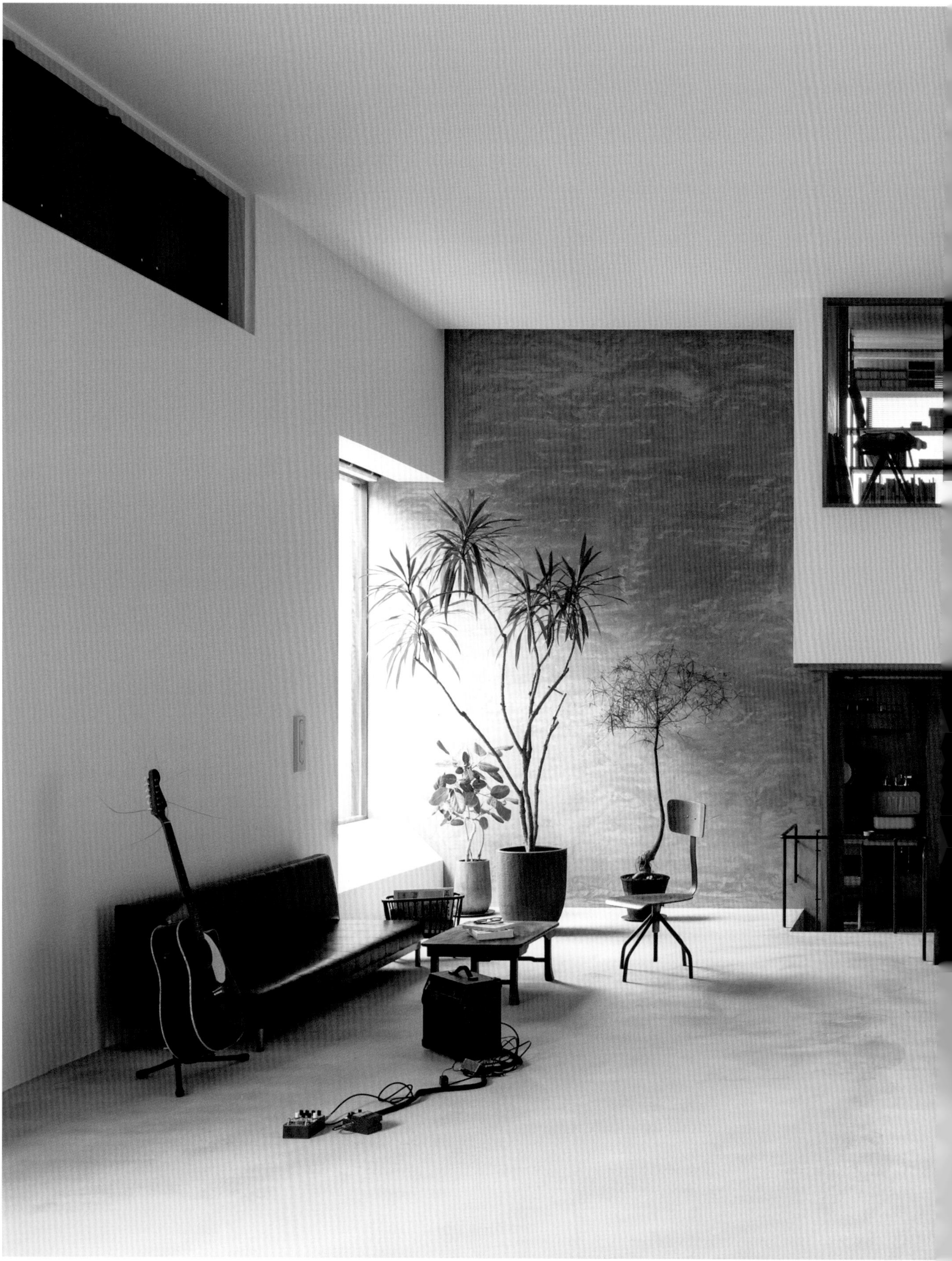

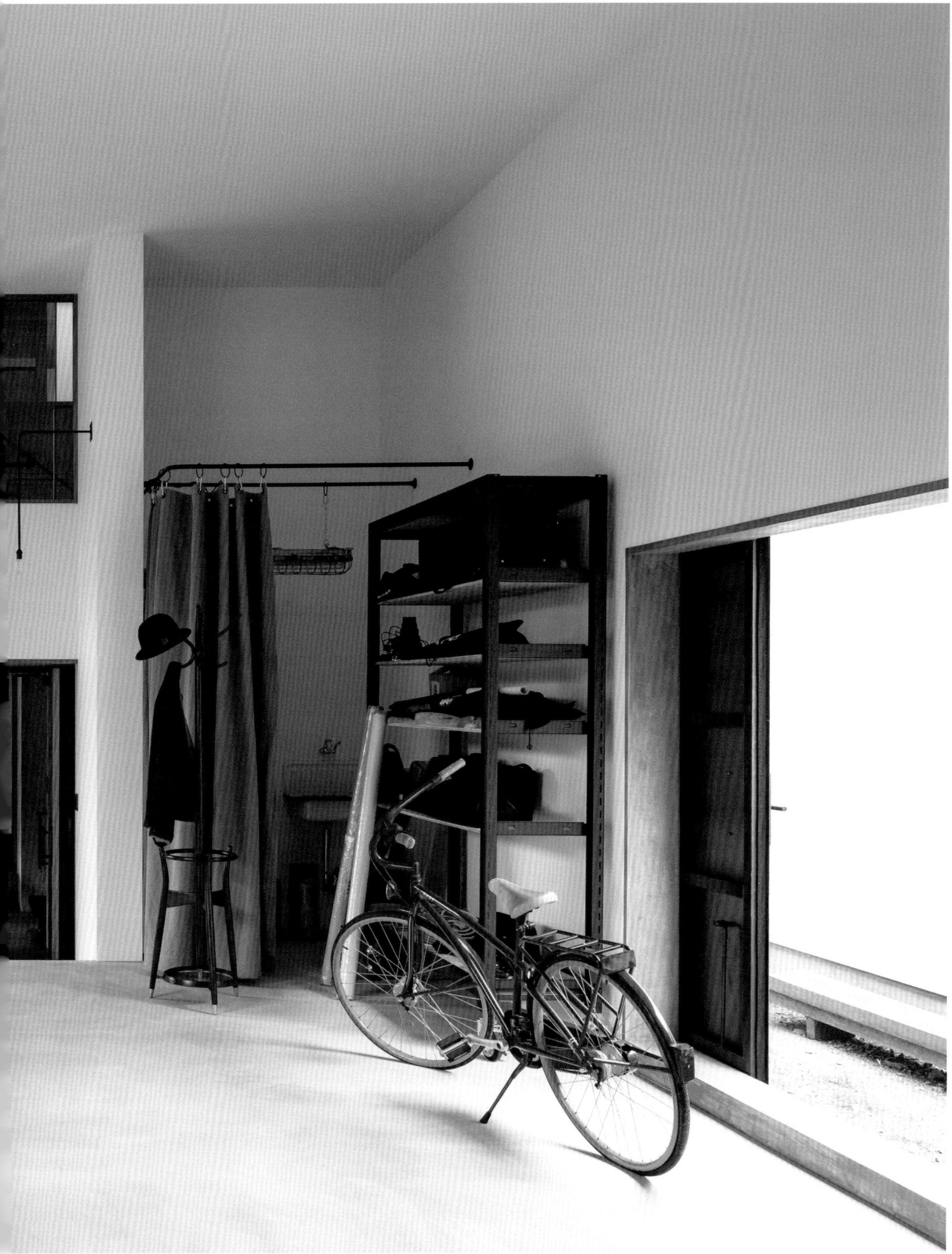

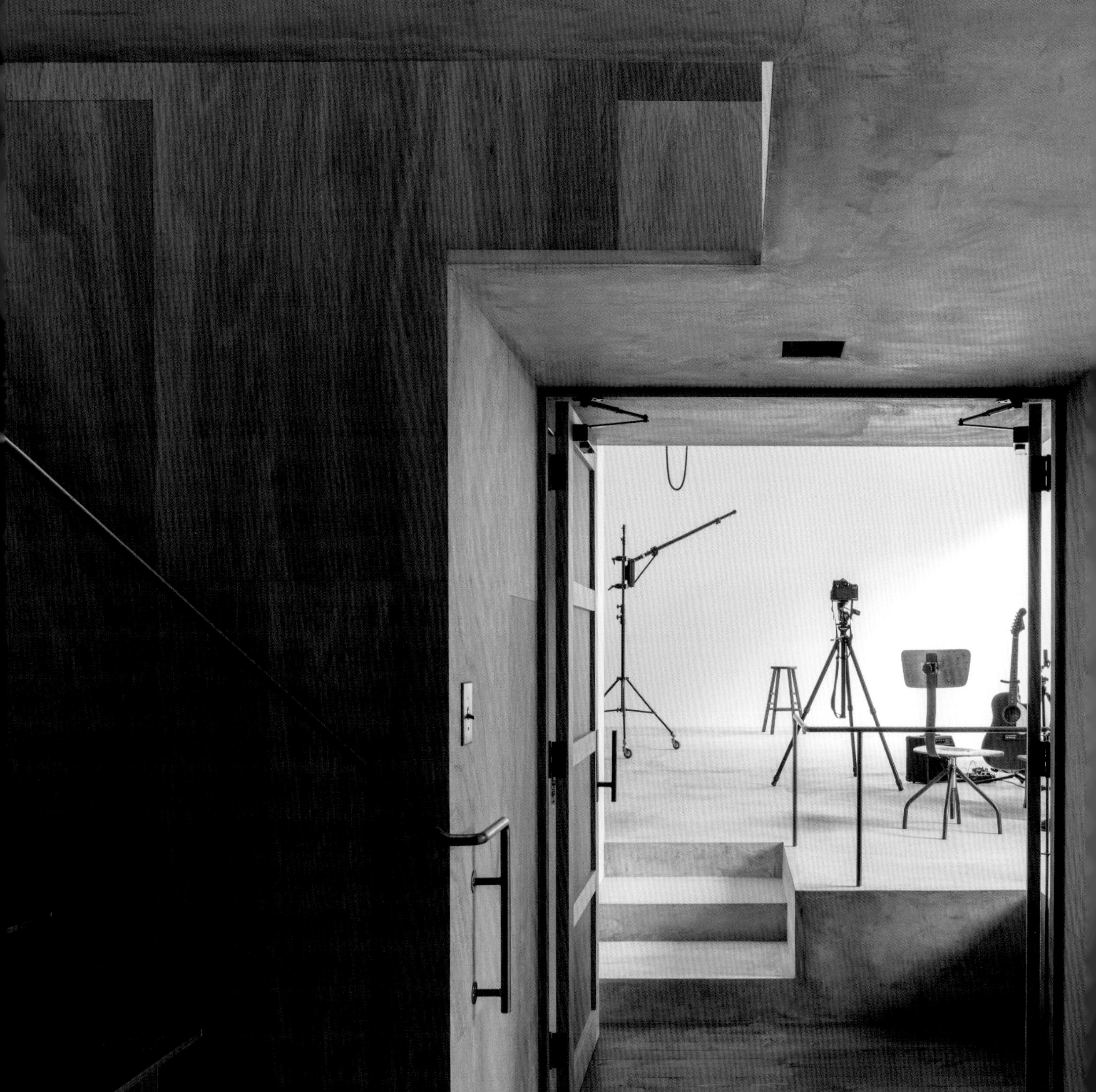

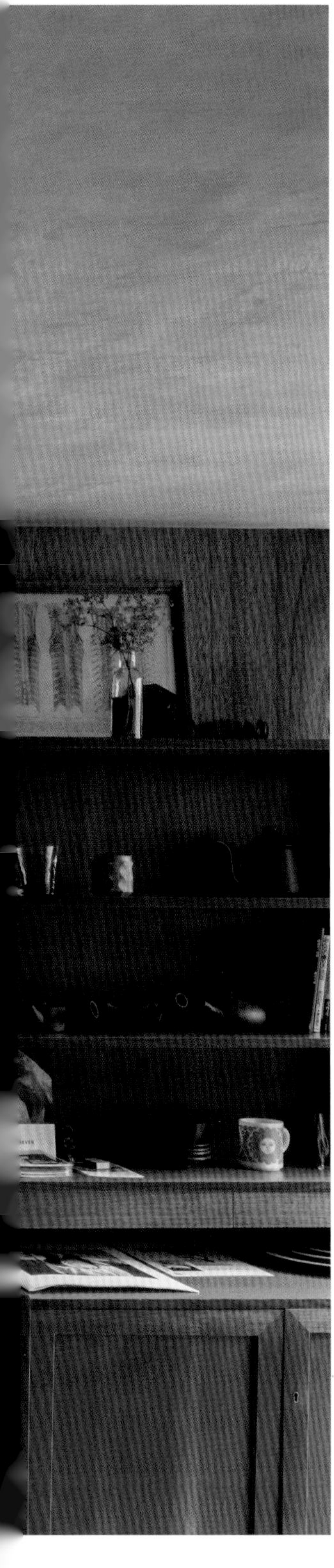

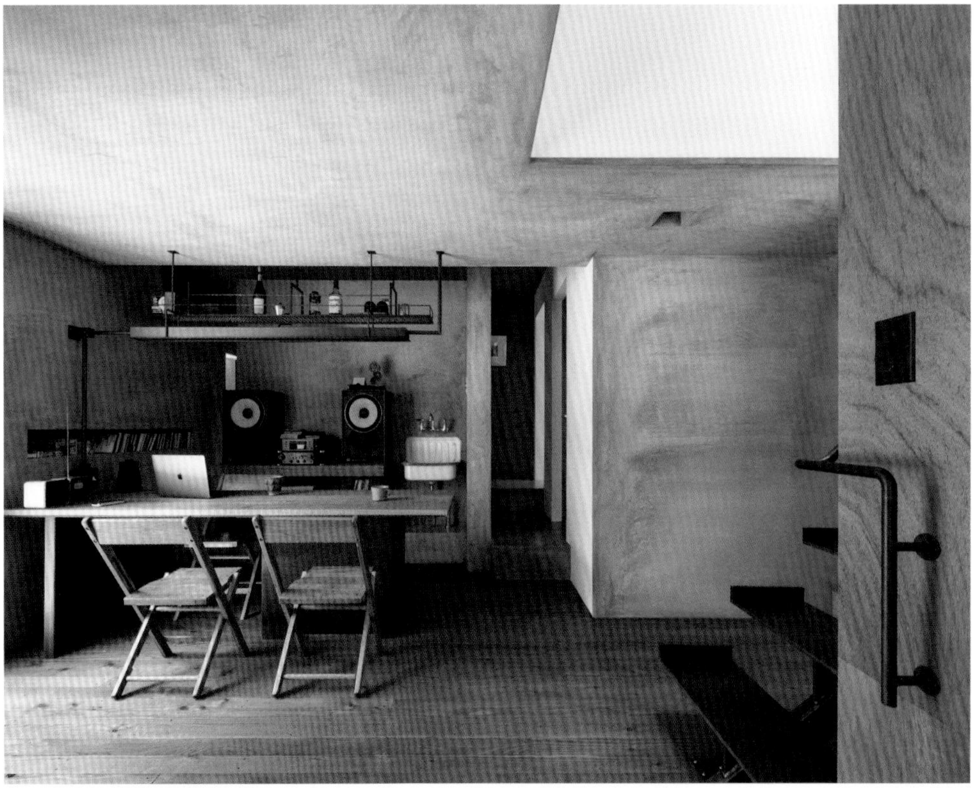

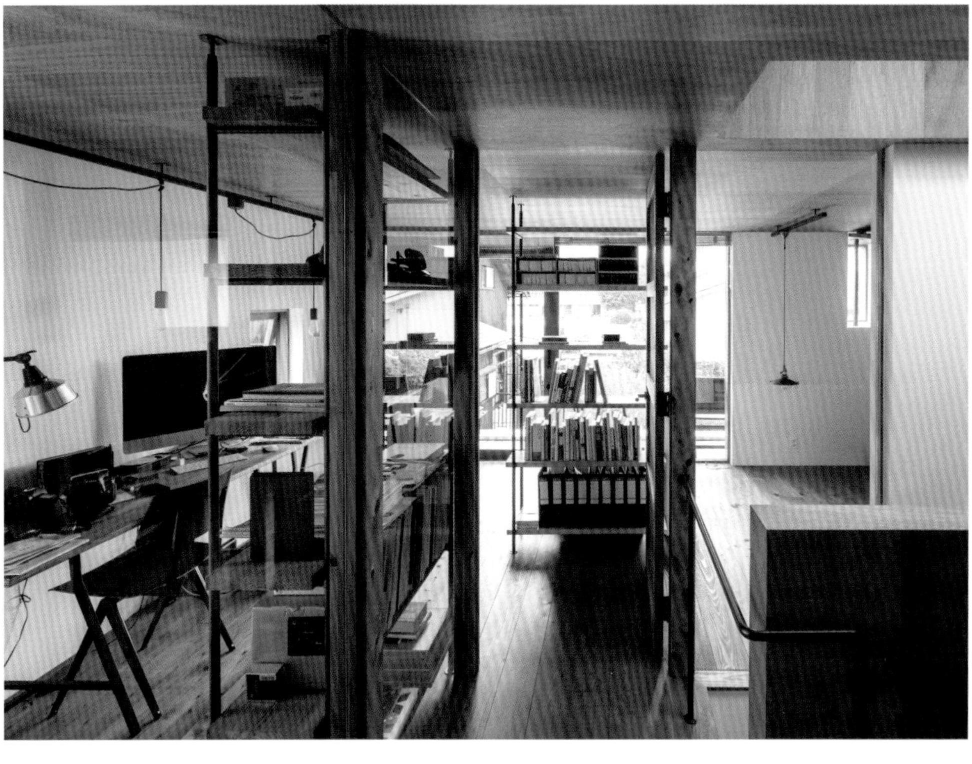

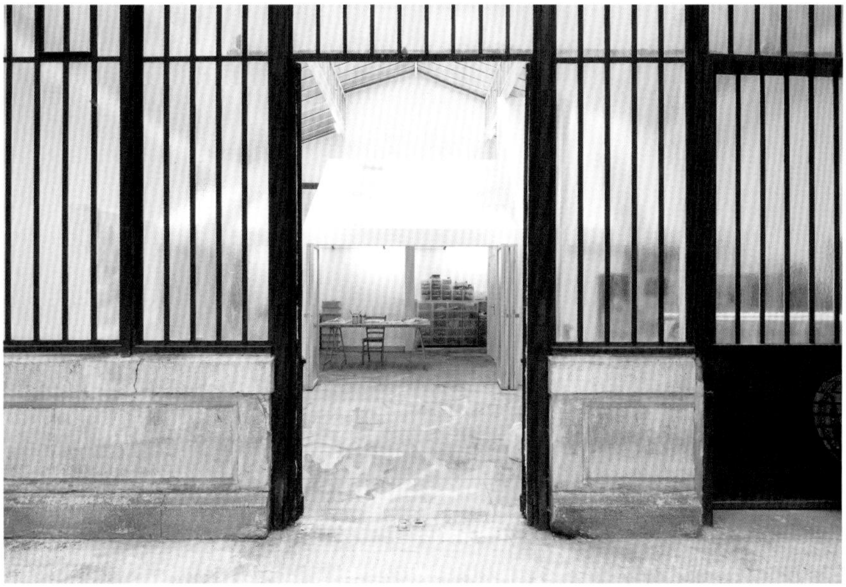

Area:
753 square feet (70 square meters)

Completion:
2016

Design:
WY-TO architects

Photography:
Svend Andersen

Paris, France

Light Folds

In the heart of a paved courtyard situated in the 10th arrondissement of Paris, this artists' studio occupies a space covered by a magnificent 1900s glass canopy. This neighborhood has an industrial past and flourished with arts and crafts activities. When the owner was looking to move from her suburban house to the heart of the capital, this building offered the perfect backdrop for her professional artistic practice, with the creation of a new studio space.

The architectural vocabulary of this contemporary addition echoes the geometry of the original glass roof by introducing a variety of geometric lines in the roof and façade composition, the design of the railings, and the choice of light fittings.

The artist creates artworks that transform recycled paper into impressive paintings and sculptures; she saw that unobstructed open space, flexibility, and natural light were the key requirements for her to enjoy a place of solitude and grow in her artistic practice. The studio has become a peaceful and functional environment, away from the hustle and bustle of Paris.

A workshop within a workshop

Mindful to support a sustainable lifestyle, the project improves space and energy efficiency by providing flexible solutions adapted to the seasons. The generous and spacious main volume can be subdivided, creating the concept of a "workshop within the workshop." The additional workshop space can be used at all times: in winter time its small volume reduces the load on the heating system, while during warmer seasons it can be connected to the main space by opening the system of bi-fold polycarbonate-glazed panels. The fan-shaped geometry of the new structure brings natural lighting into all newly created volumes and provides an ideal visual environment for the artist.

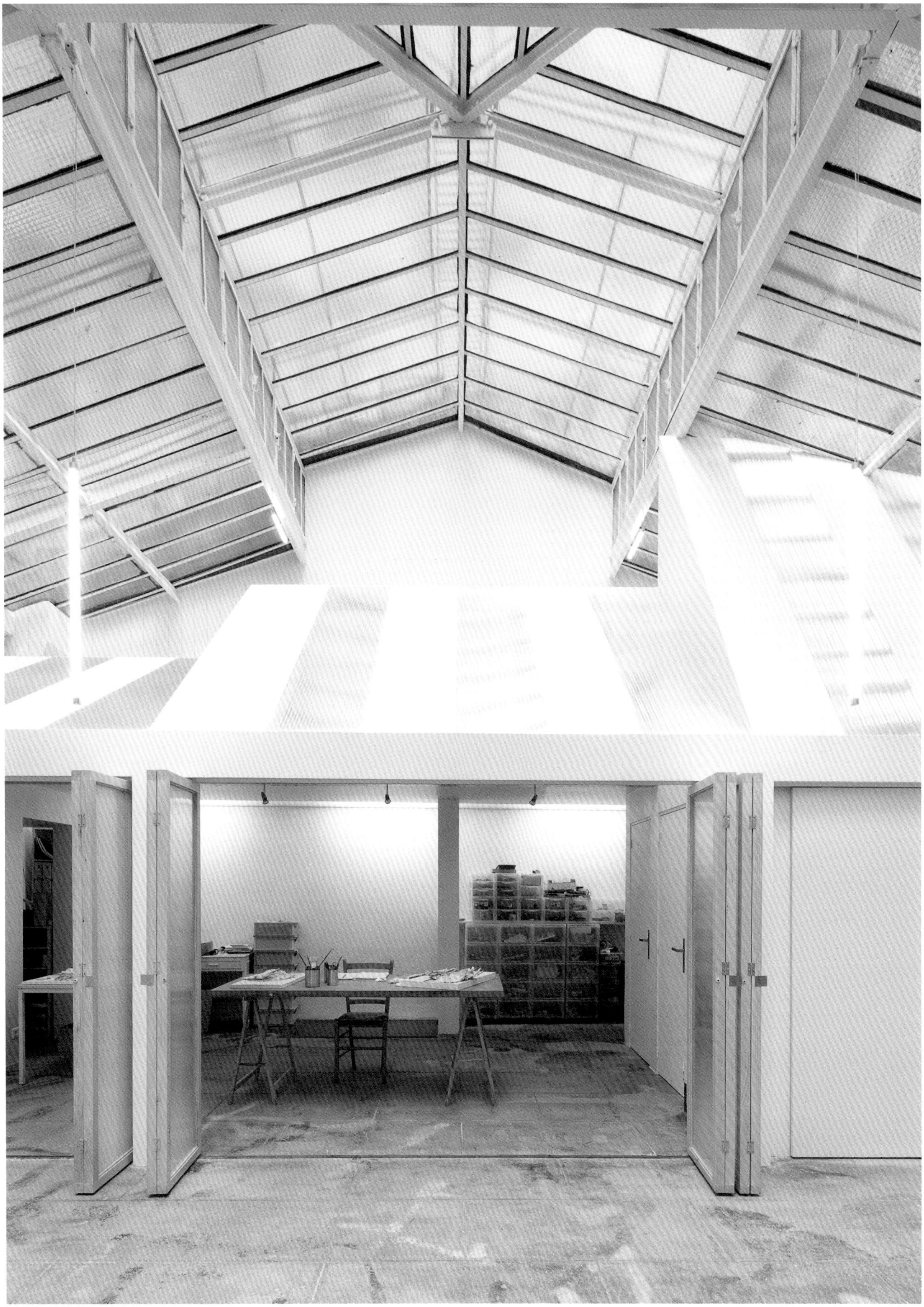

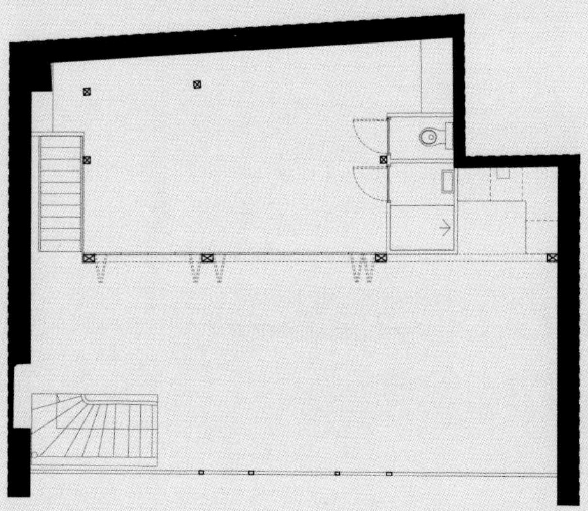

Floor plan

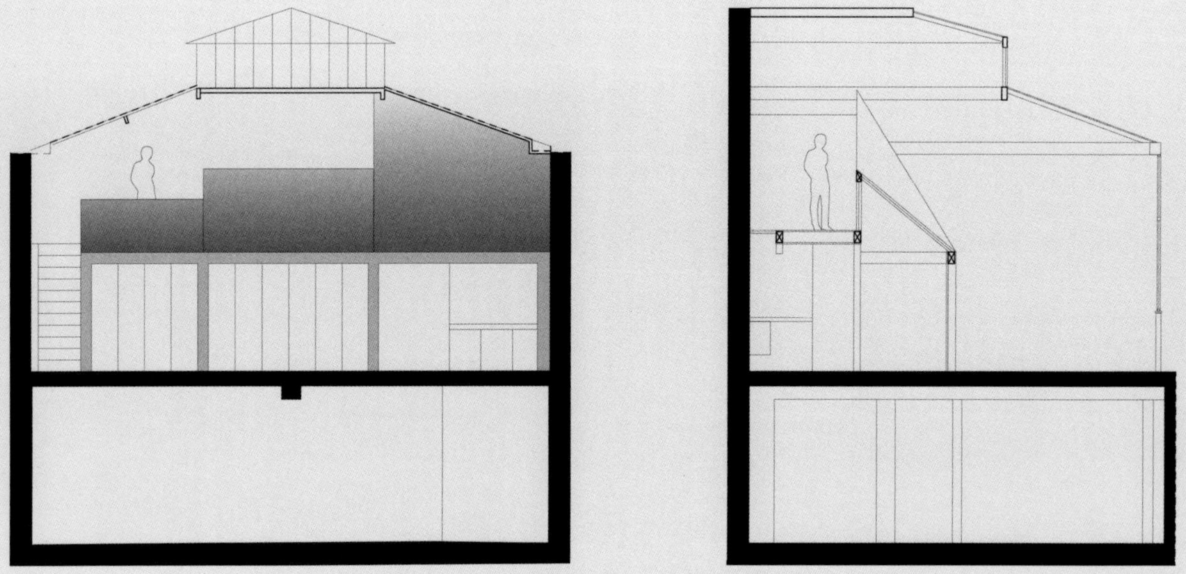

Section

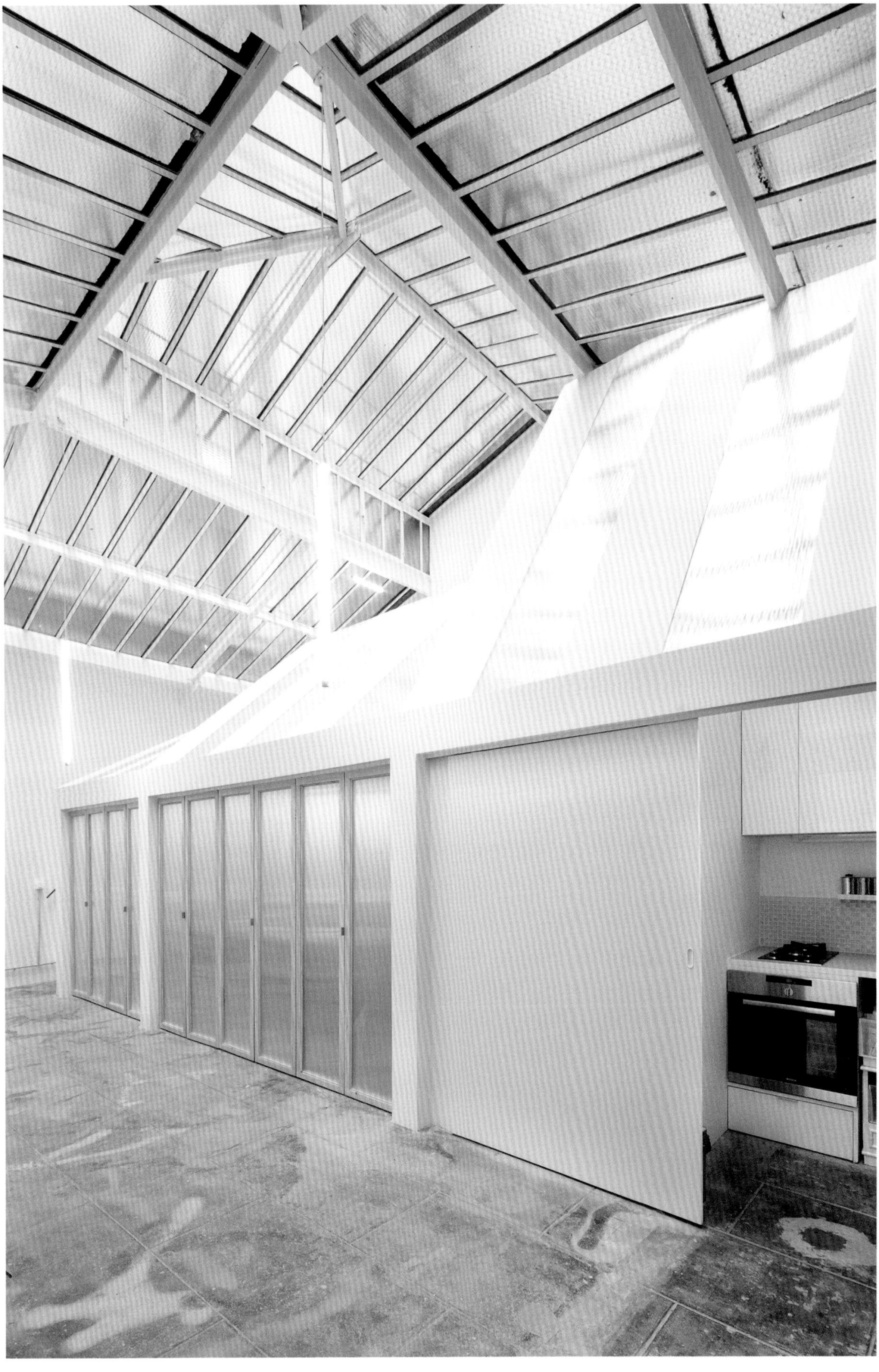

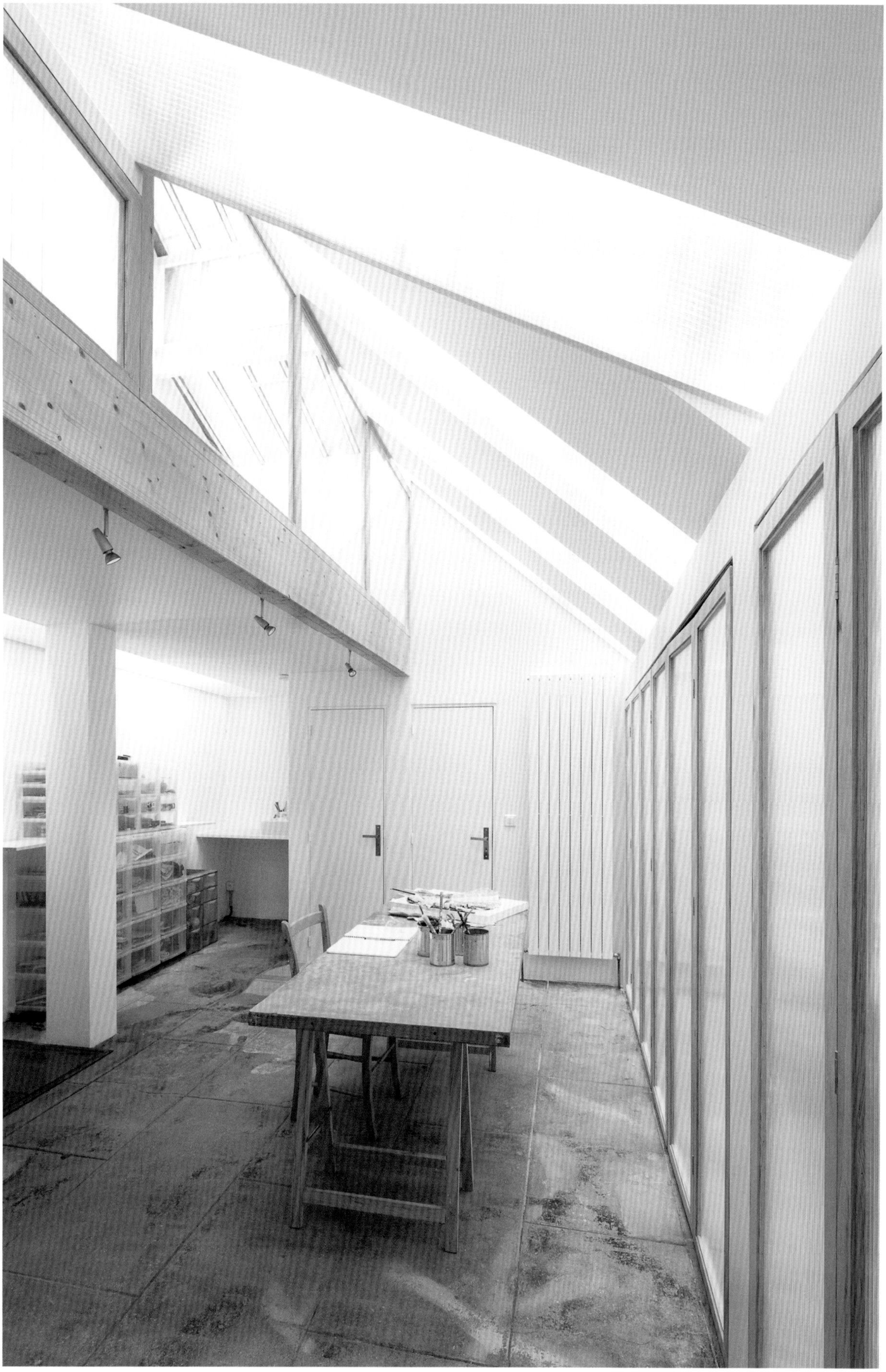

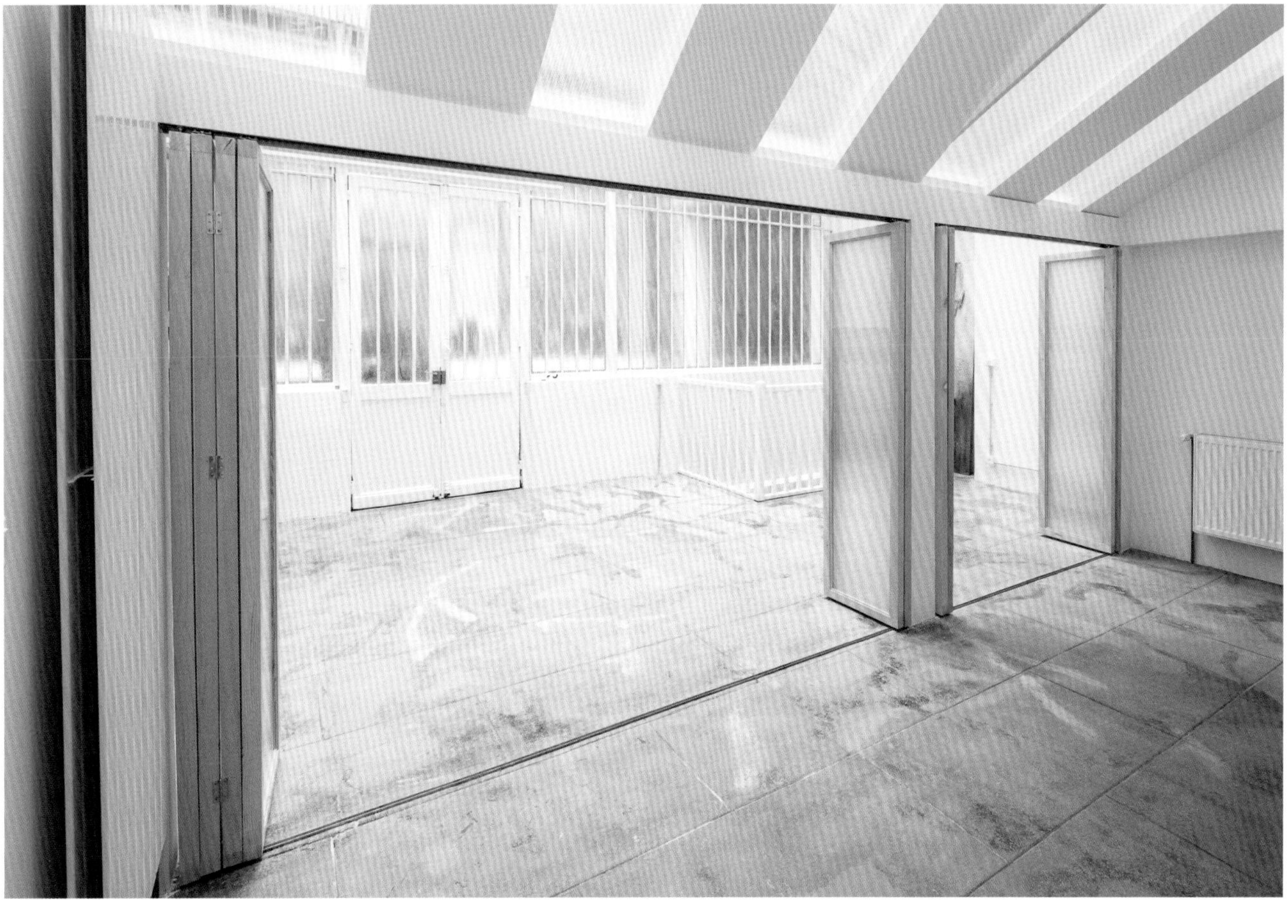

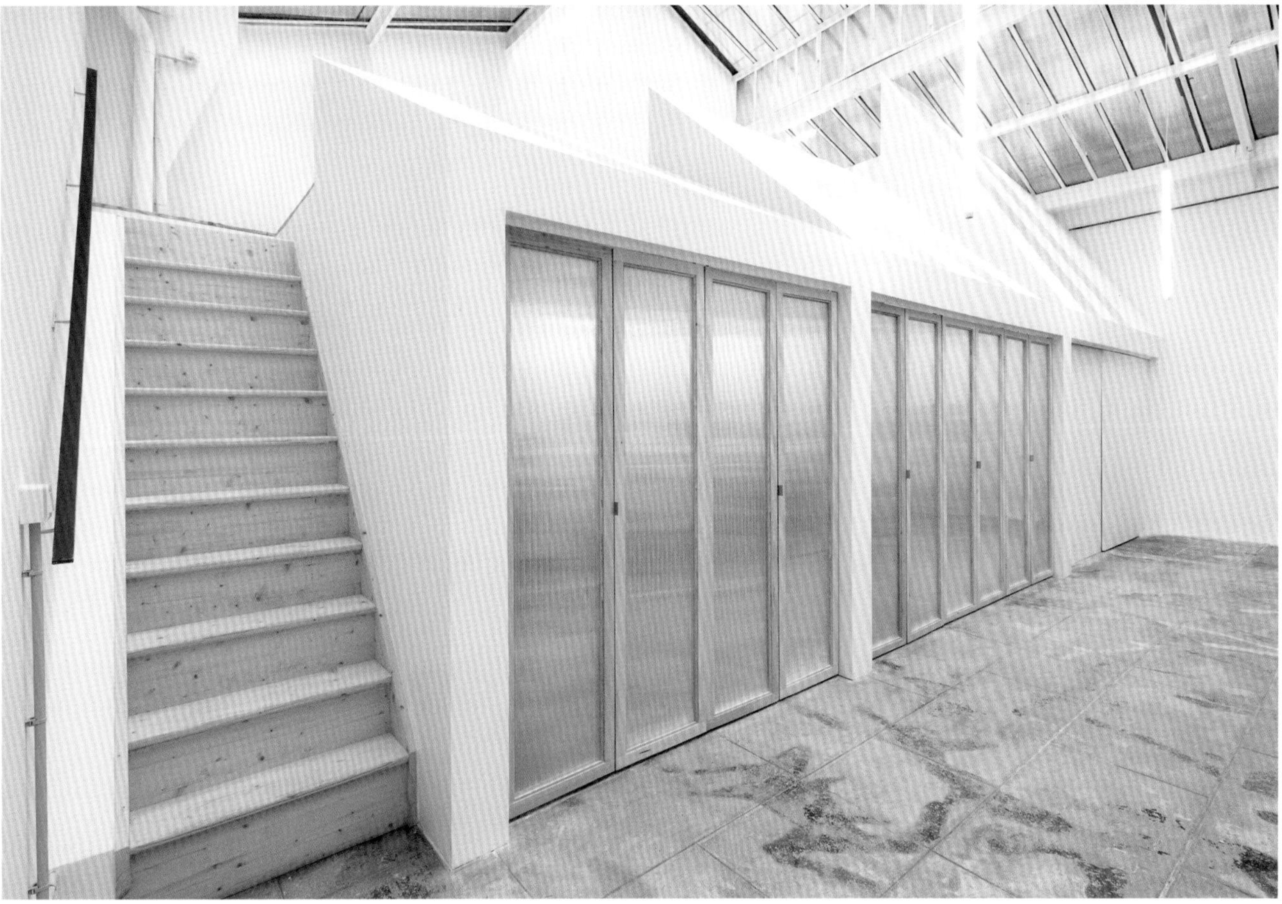

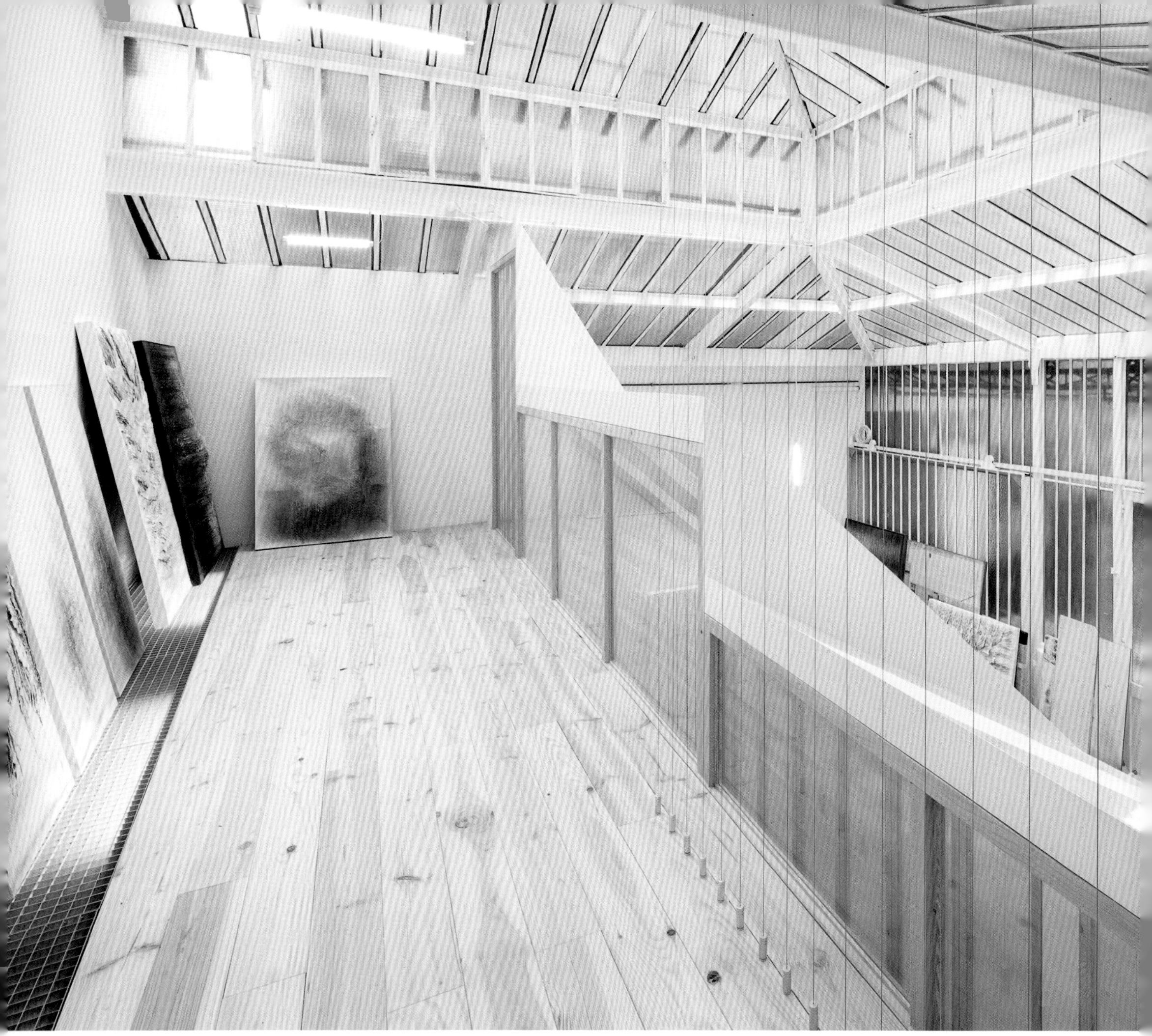

Versatile spaces

A mezzanine space on top of the studio can be used for relaxation and plays an important role in stimulating the artistic process, as the artist overlooks and contemplates the main workshop full of artworks from above. The versatility of the space has been designed to cater to the artist's lifestyle and can be transformed for public openings or exhibition events. The kitchen not only supports the needs of public gatherings, but can also be used on a daily basis. The owner can convert the space to a temporary guestroom that has all the required facilities, including a bathroom.

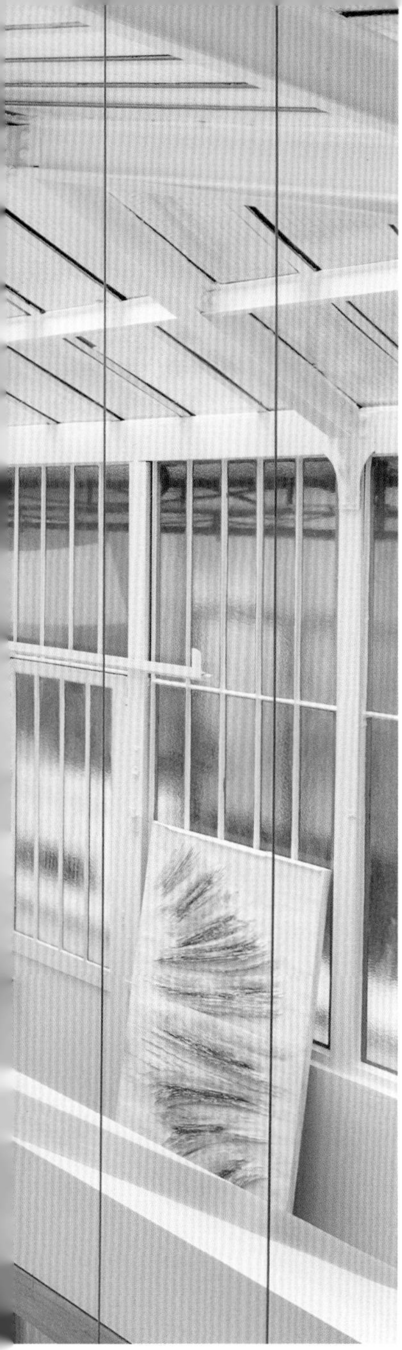

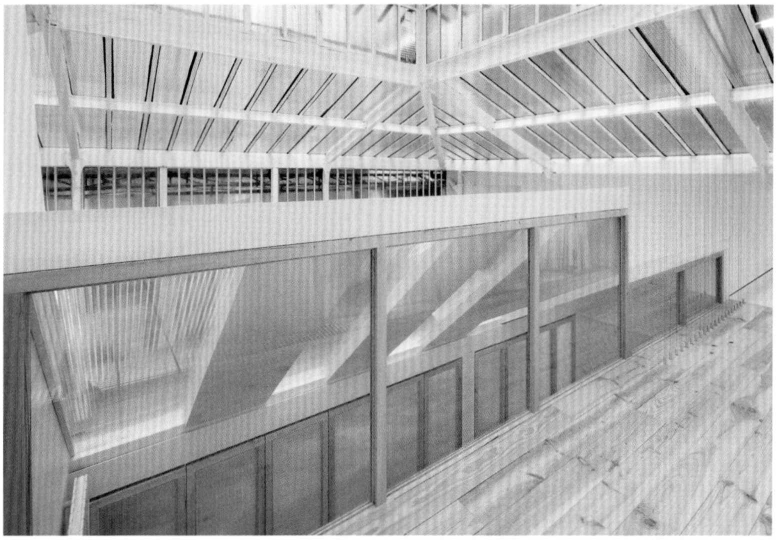

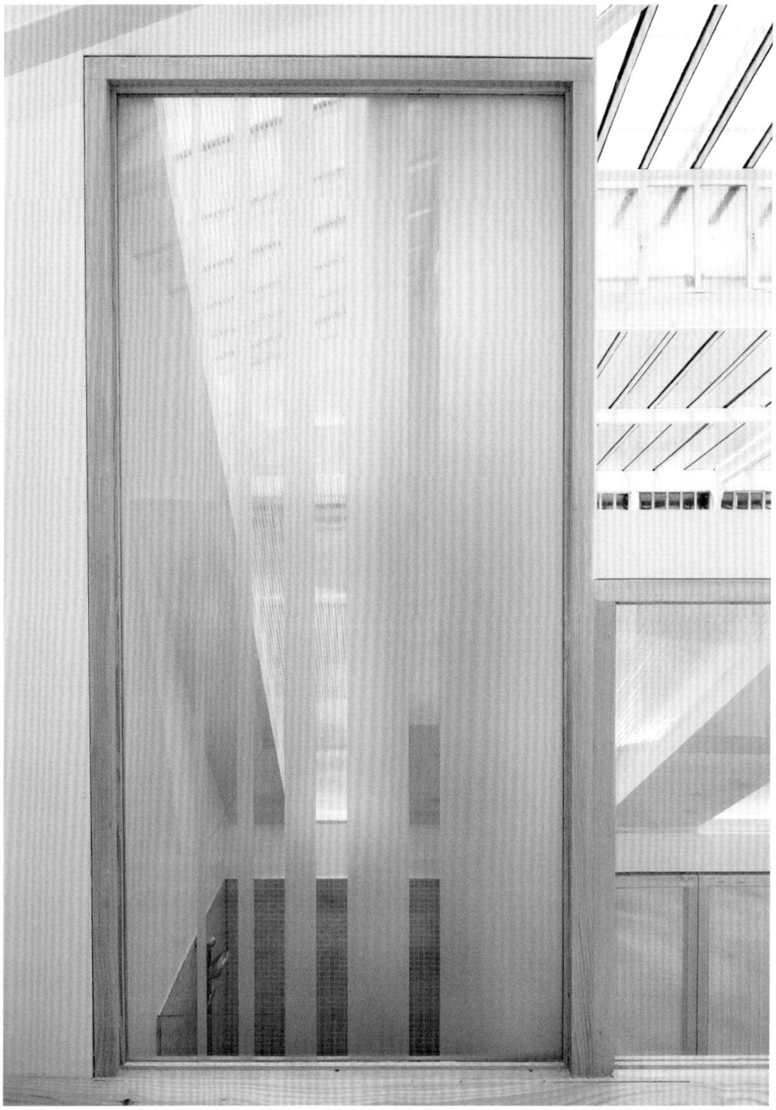

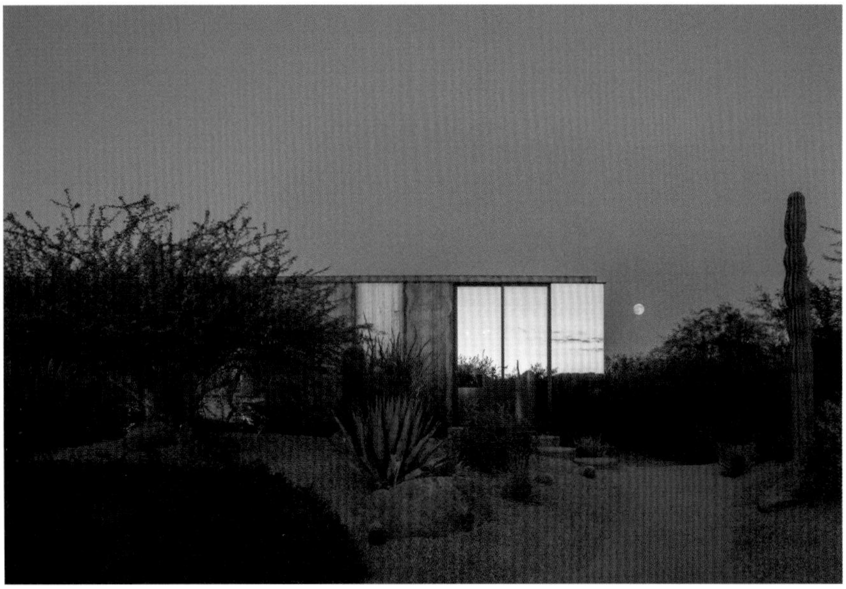

Area:
1,400 square feet (130 square meters)

Completion:
2017

Design:
Chen + Suchart Studio

Photography:
Matt Winquist, Winquist Photography

Paradise Valley, United States

The Little Art Studio

The Little Art Studio is a 1,400-square-foot (130-square-meter) addition to an existing contemporary stucco-and-glass residence. The addition of this project to the site provided a backdrop and bookend to an existing desert courtyard and a gathering area surrounding a fire pit. The design for the studio deliberately established its own language that was a clear departure from the language of the existing main residence while maintaining respect for the site's desert landscape.

A floating studio

In order to distinguish the studio from the existing residence, the design allowed the studio to establish its own identity, and the way in which the addition meets the ground plane was designed to minimize the disturbance to the existing desert landscape. The steel-beam floor structure and composite concrete deck is supported by six 36-inch-diameter concrete caissons that allow the studio to "float" over an existing wash by touching the ground in only these six locations. This design further distinguishes the construction of the new addition from the conventional slab-on-grade construction of the existing main residence.

Building for the desert climate

The cladding of the studio is largely comprised of standard weathering steel panels. Reflective insulated glazing is used throughout, and is configured with the reflective surfaces to allow for maximum heat rejection while offering the most reflection.

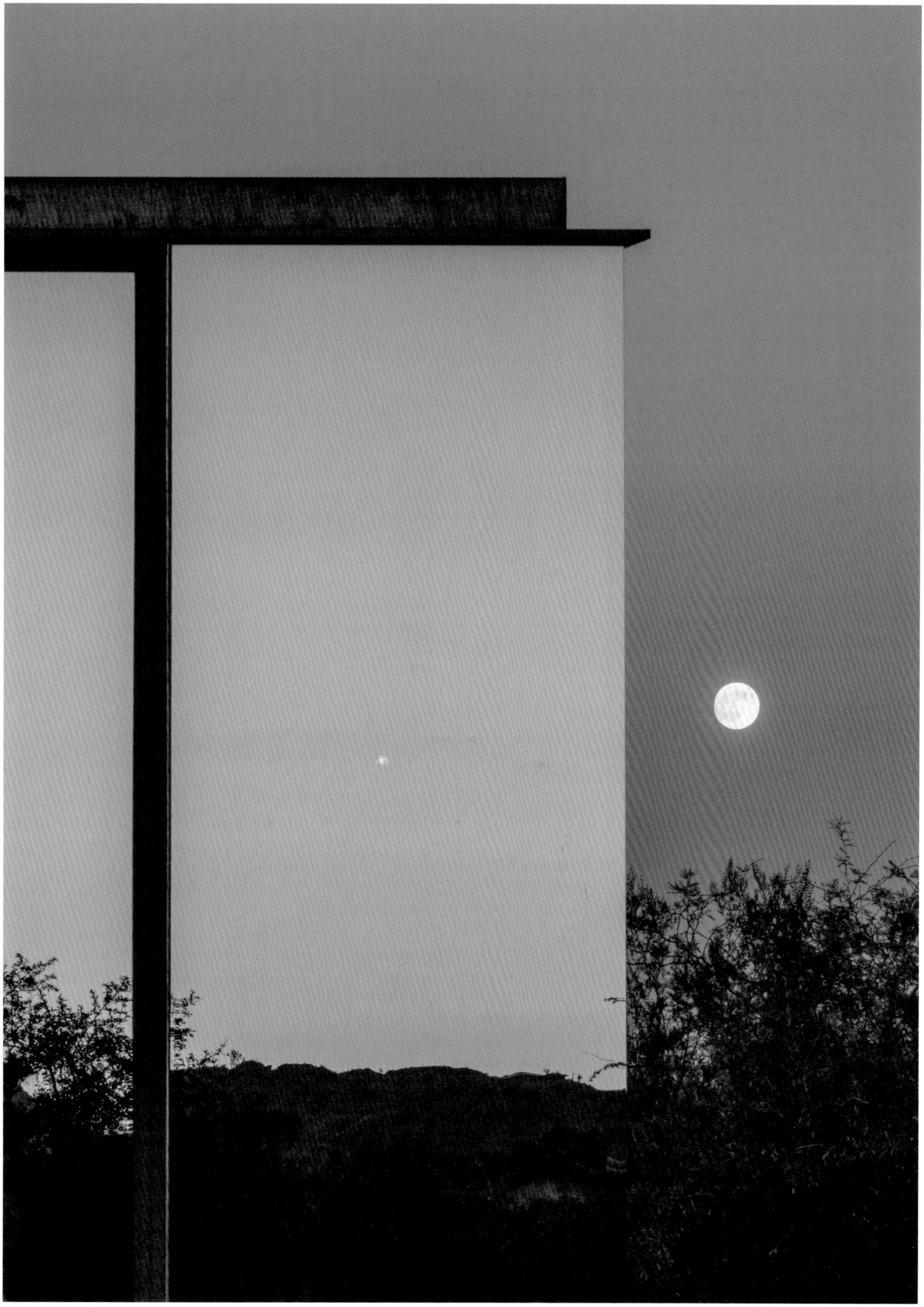

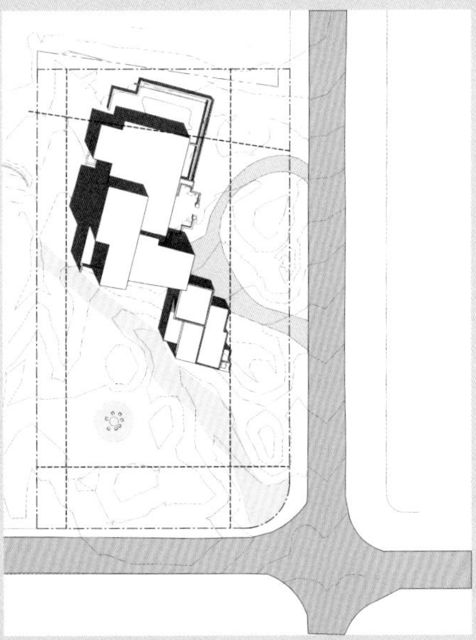

Existing site plan

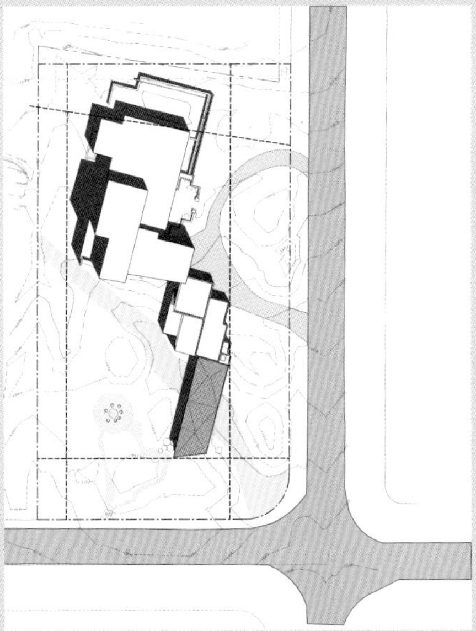

New site plan

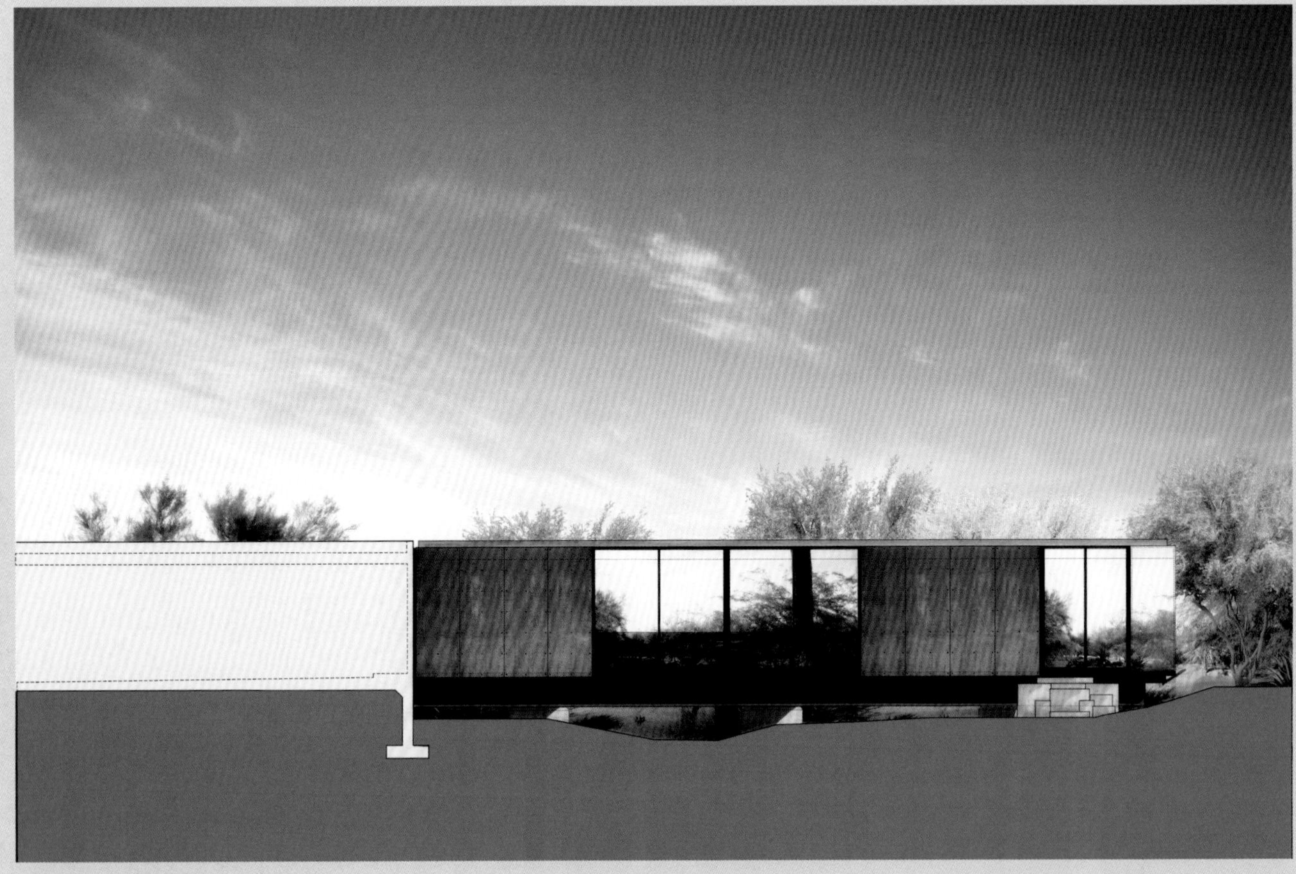

West elevation

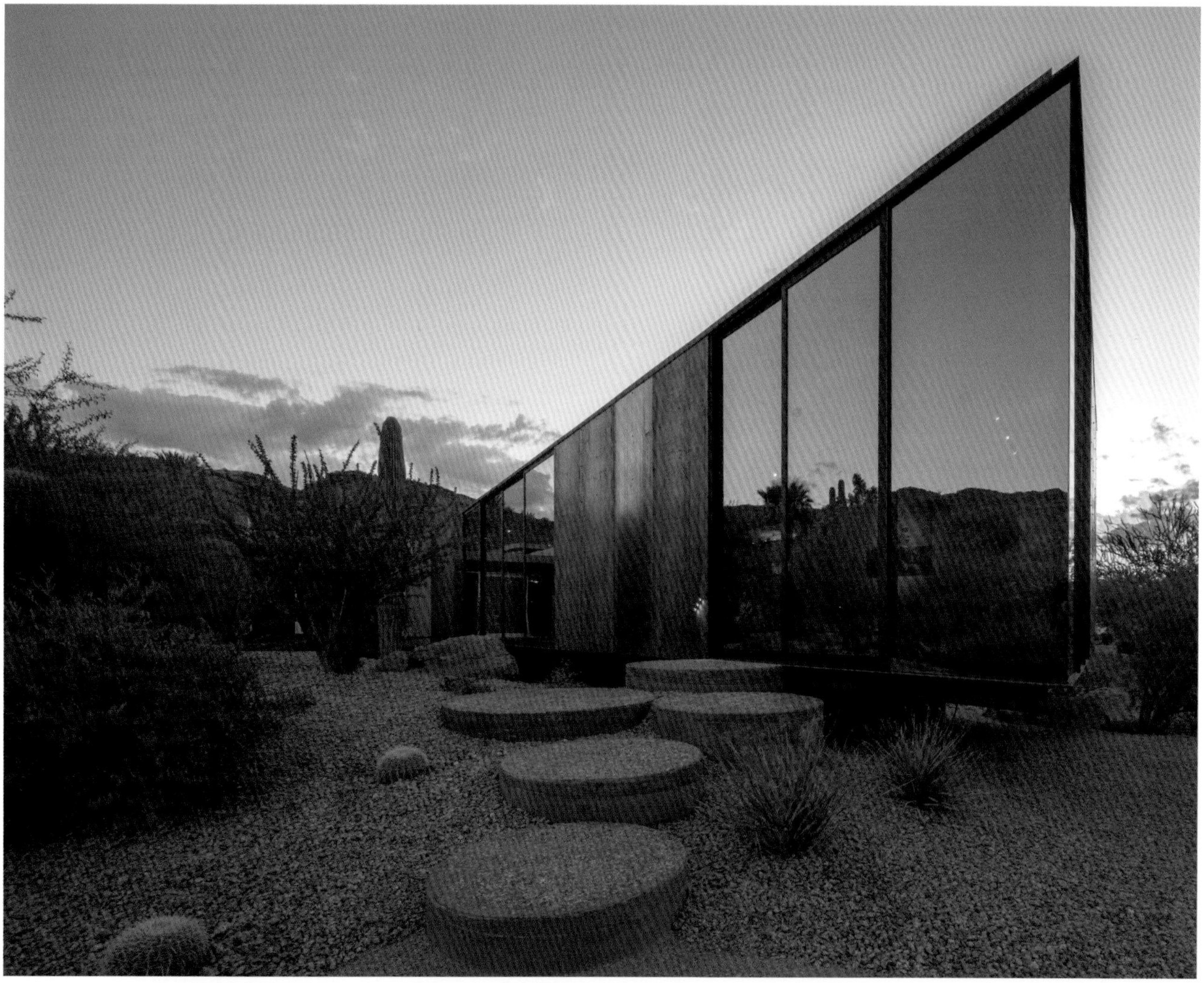

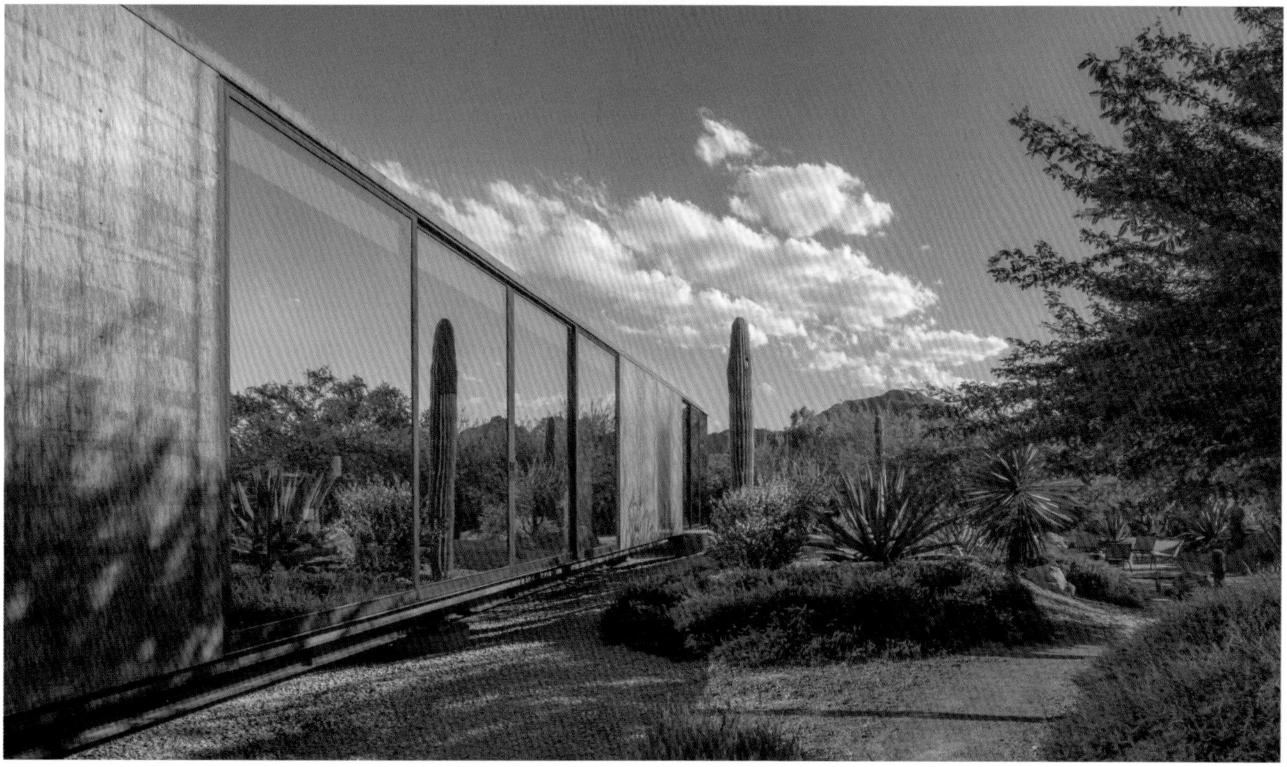

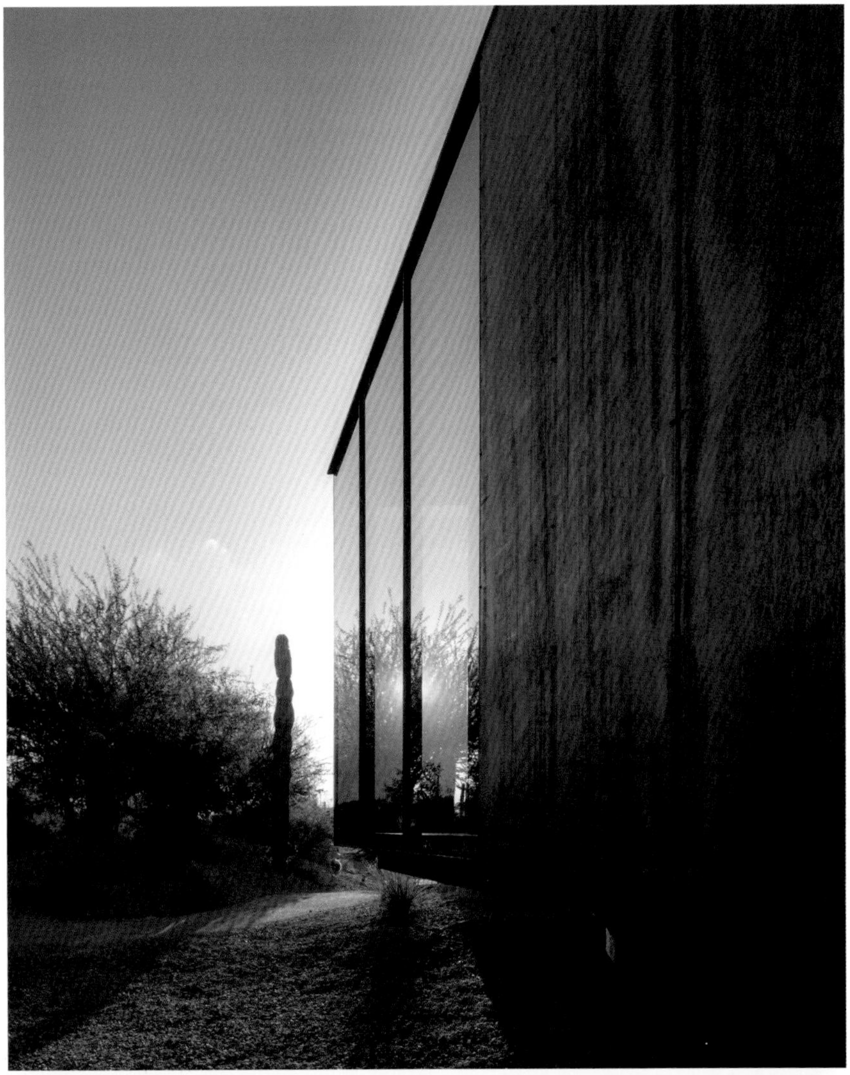

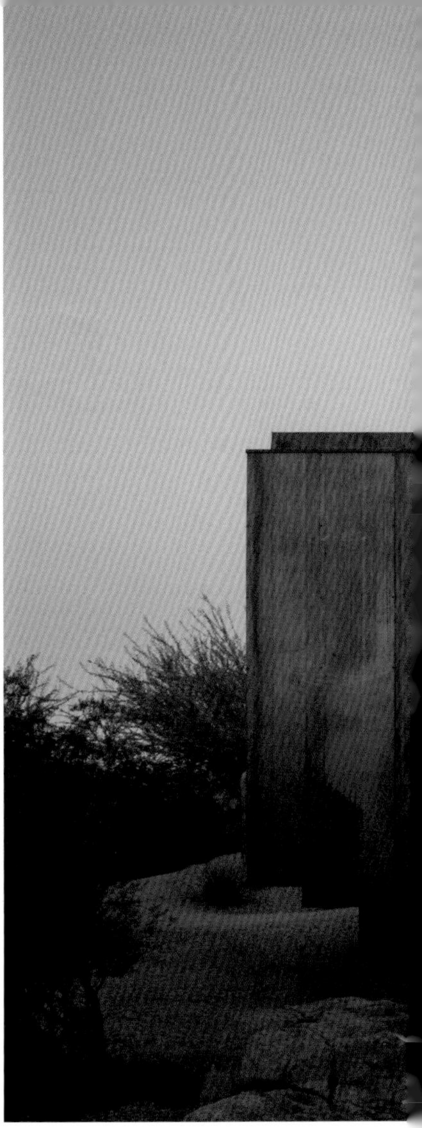

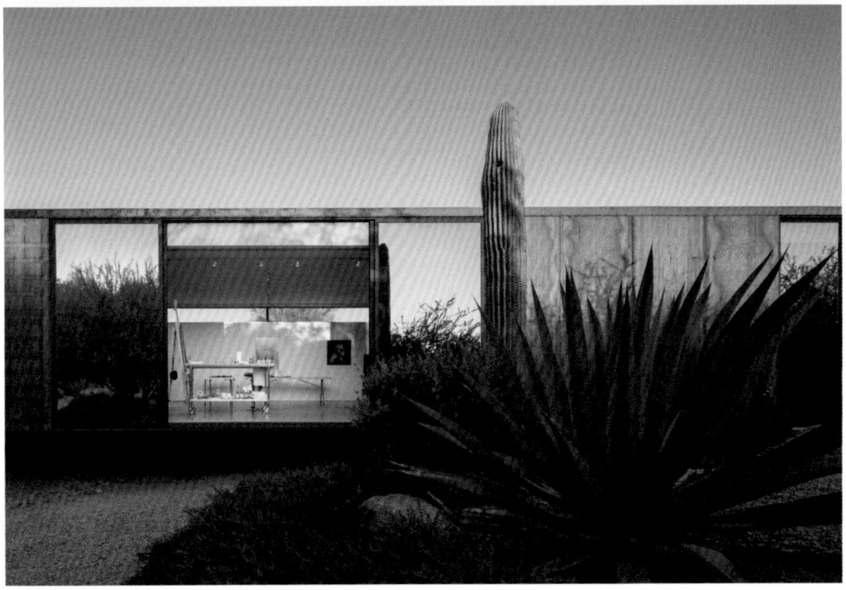

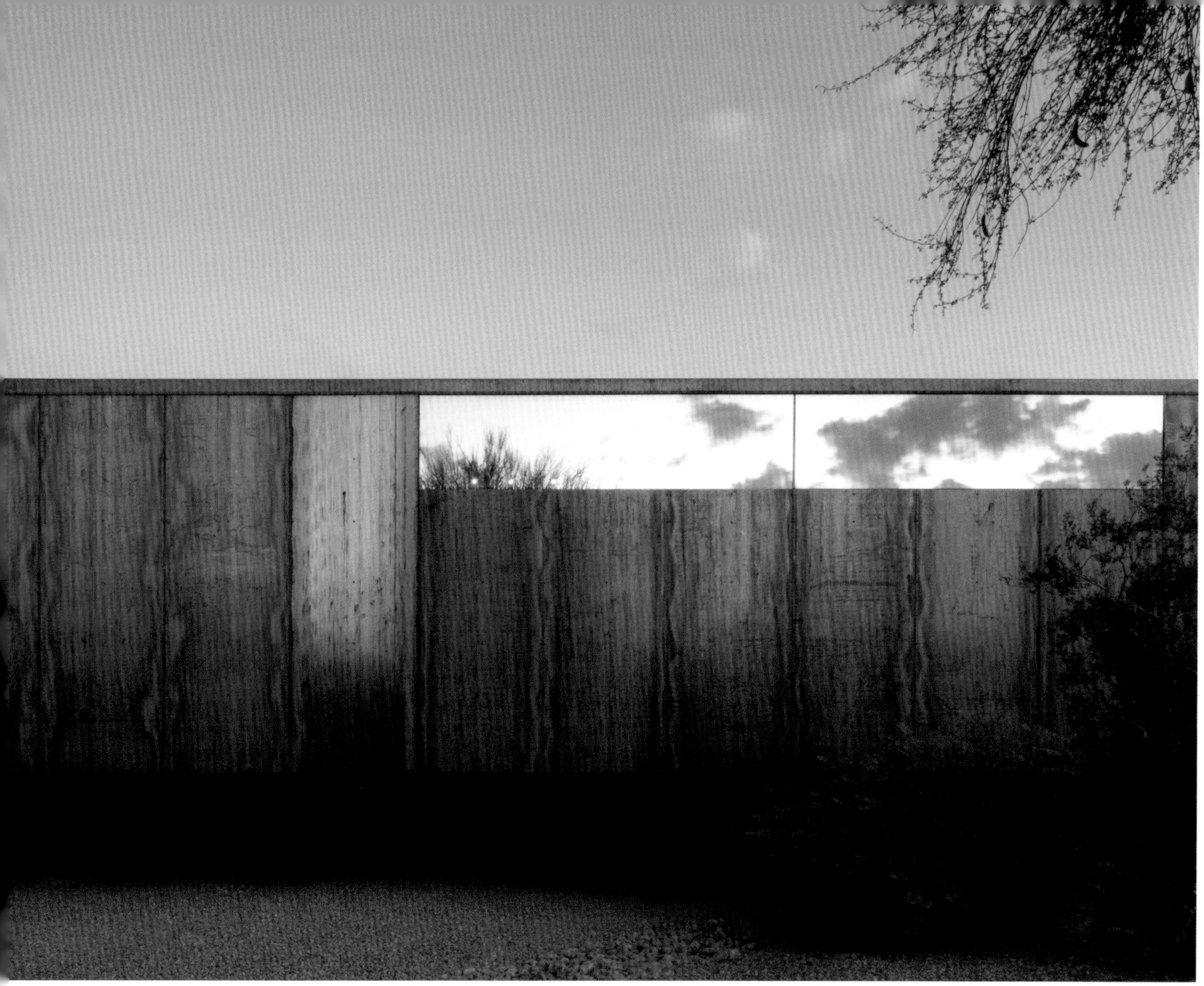

The combination of these two materials for the cladding is intended to complement, absorb, and reflect the existing residence's landscape, and further distinguishes the addition from the existing residence.

Spaces for artwork

The interior space is configured as an open plan to allow the studio to be used as a working artist's studio or gallery space. Three large movable partitions can be configured in various ways to allow for spatial diversity and increased surface area for hanging the artist's work. An integrated artwork hanging system is embedded with the drywall to establish a place for hanging artwork for review and display. Bi-parting sliding glass doors are located directly over the wash in order to celebrate a specific moment in the desert landscape. The configuration of the windows allows views of the existing courtyard and Camelback Mountain.

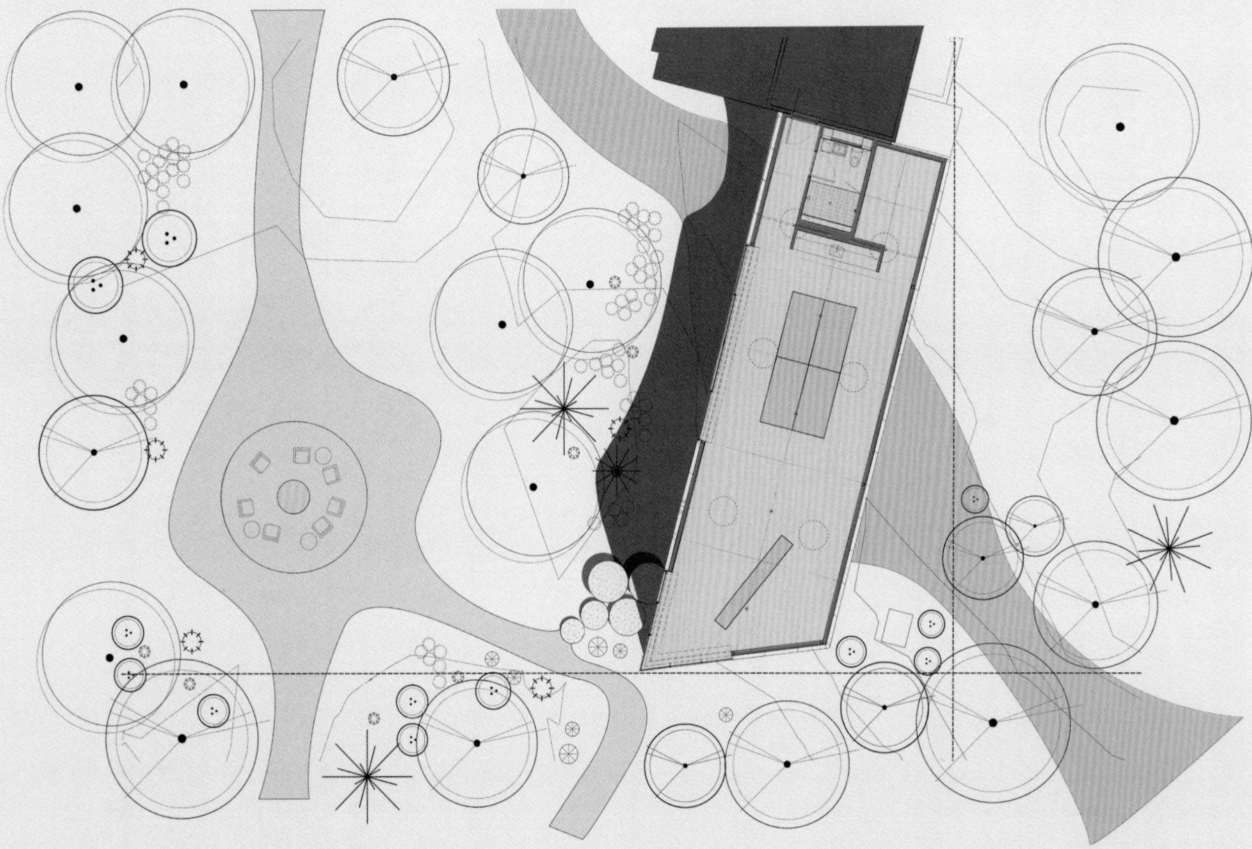

Floor plan

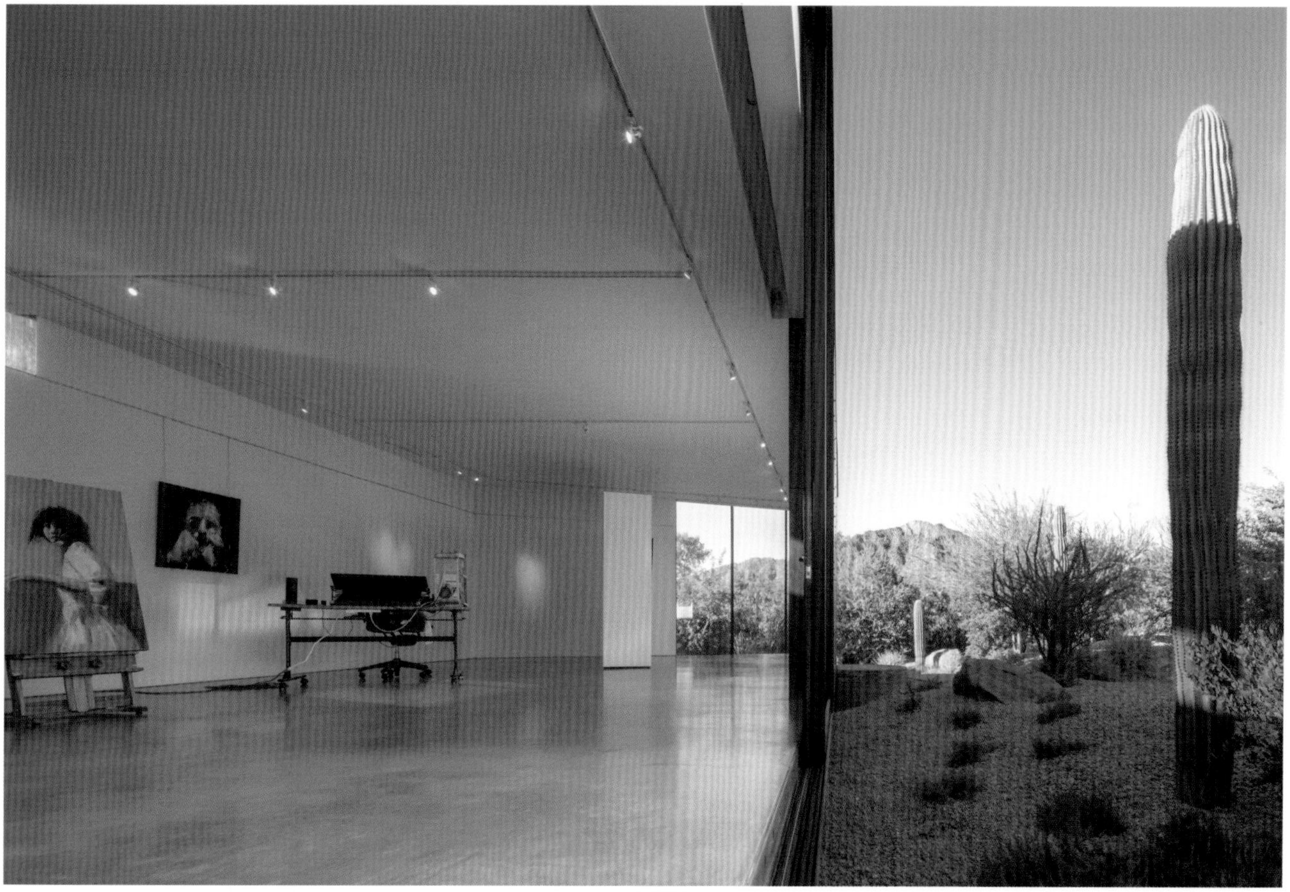

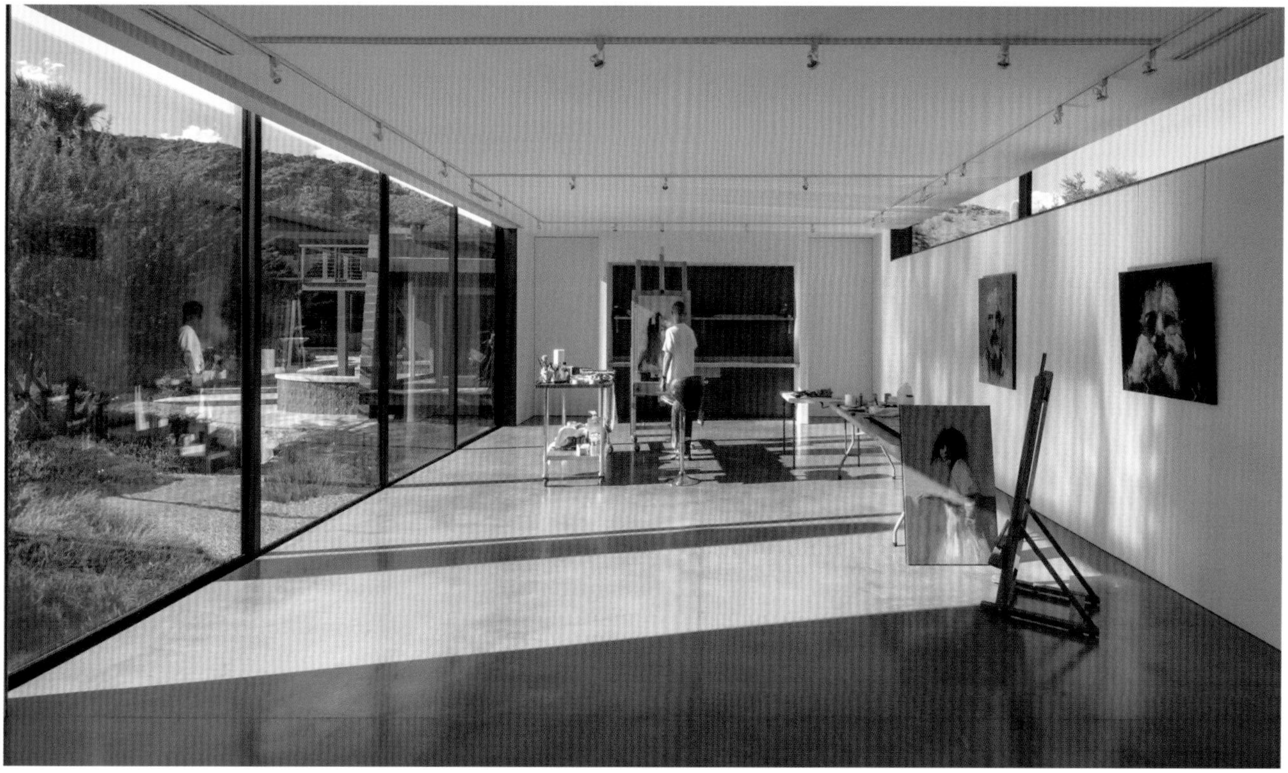

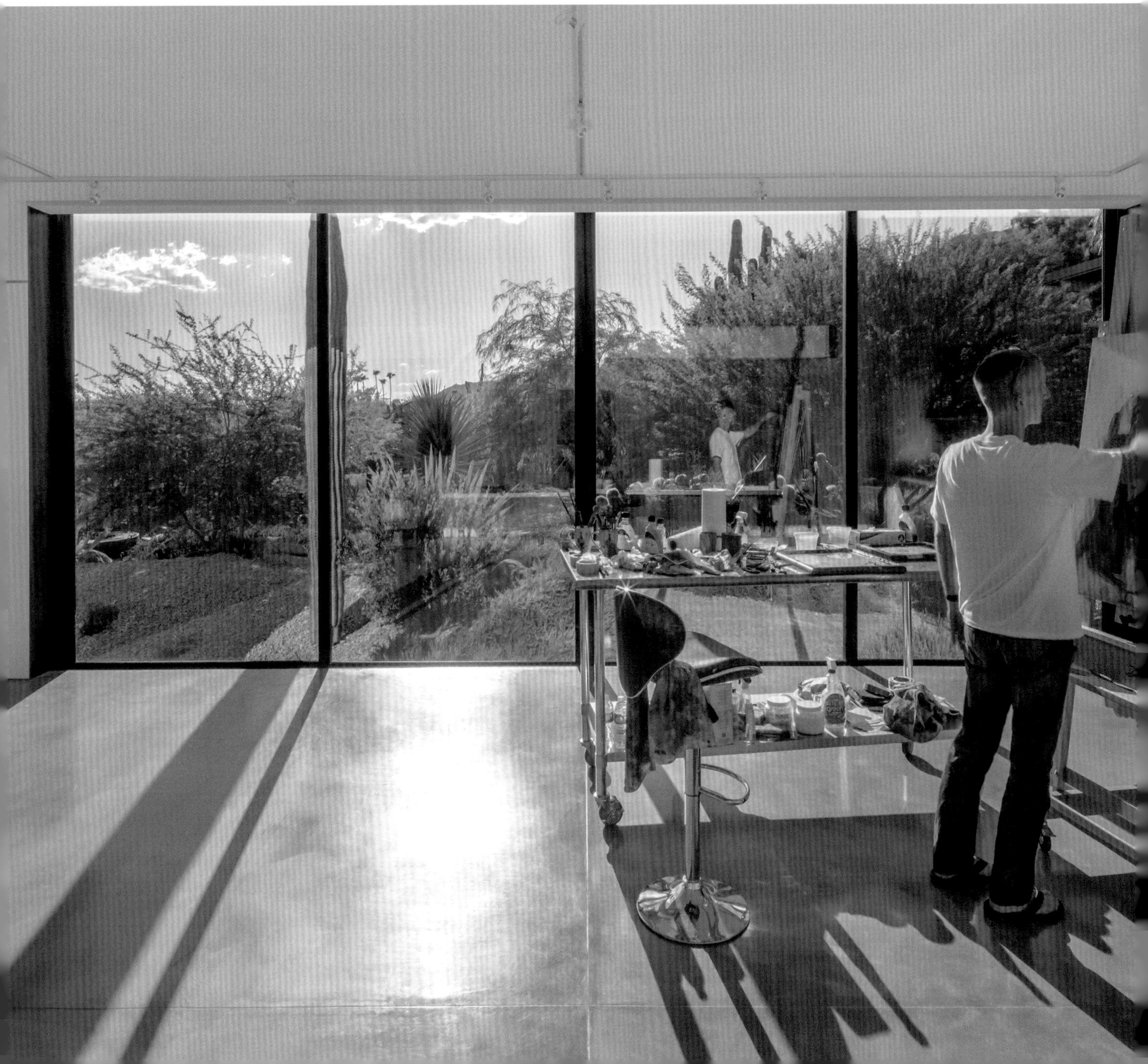

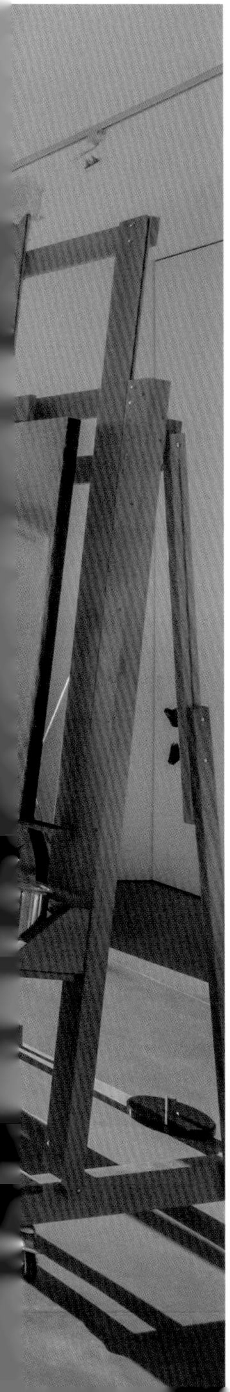

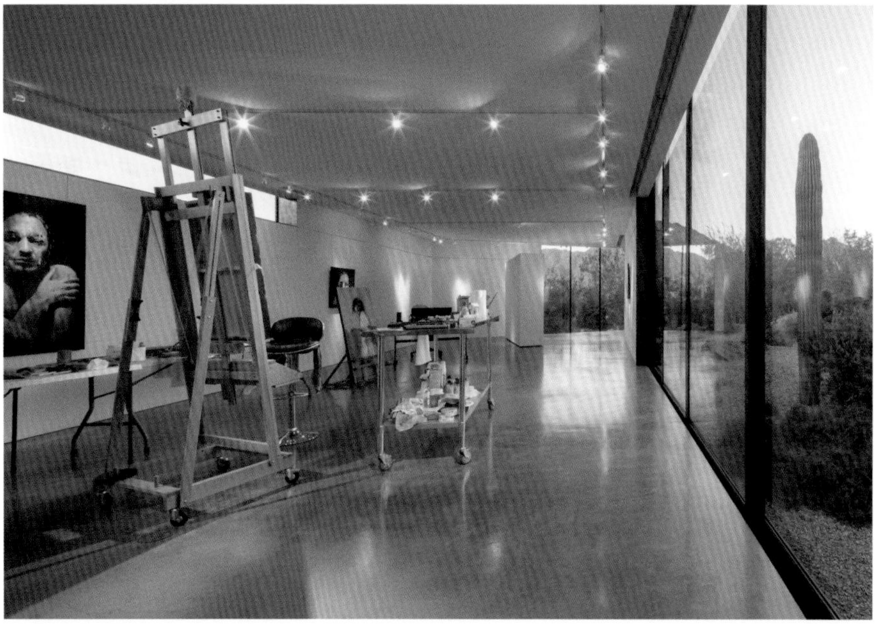

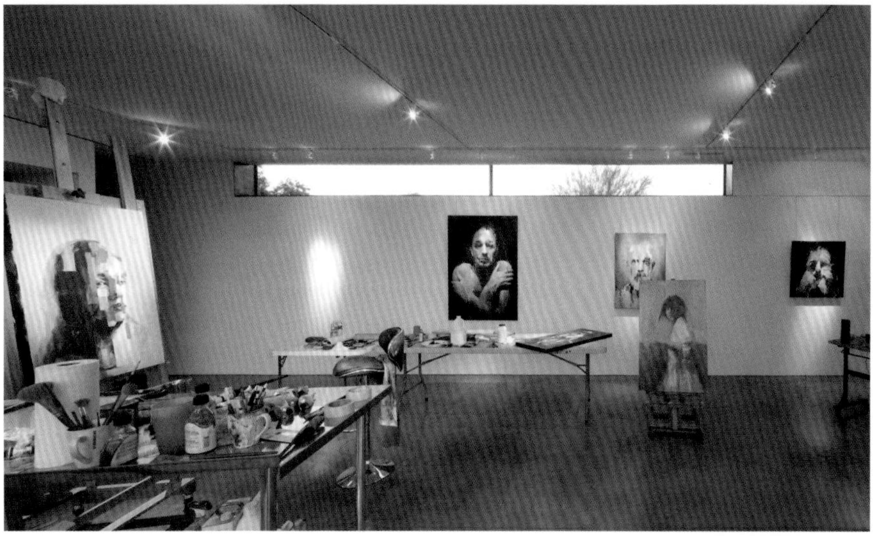

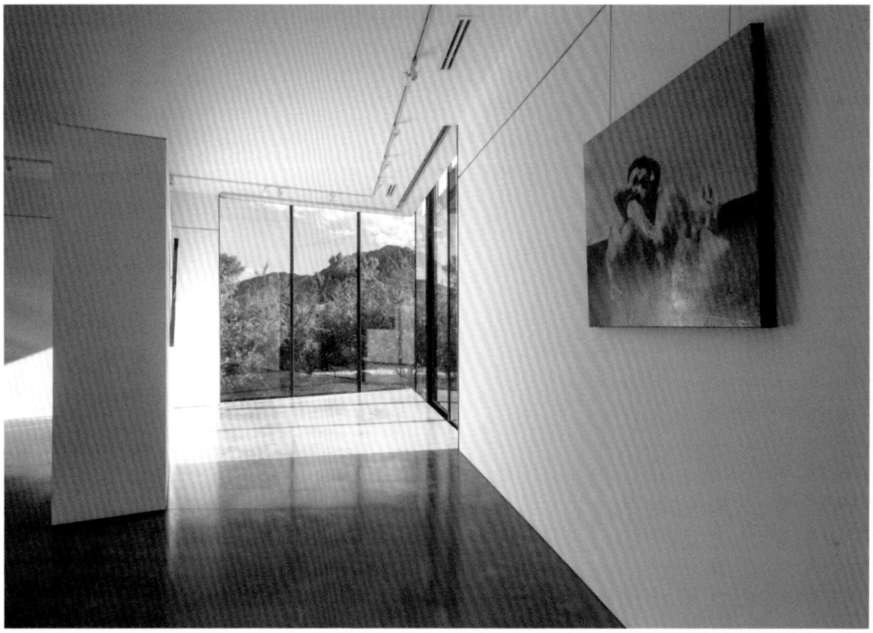

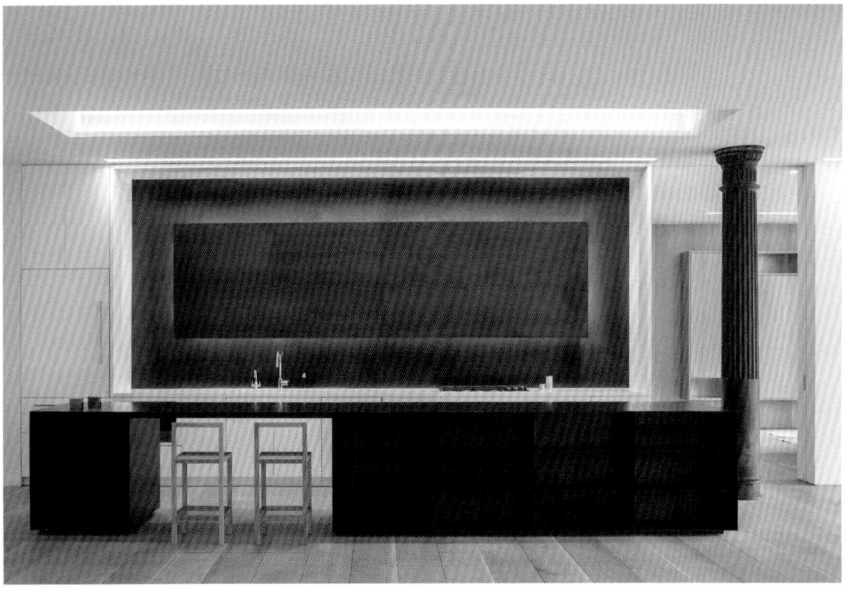

Area:
5,000 square feet (465 square meters)

Completion:
2015

Design:
Katherine Chia, Arjun Desai
(Desai Chia Architecture)

Photography:
Paul Warchol

New York City, United States

Photographer's Loft

Desai Chia Architecture designed this loft for a photographer who was looking for a serene living and working environment. The industrial space was fully renovated to include a library/reception area, living and dining areas, a kitchen, a photo studio, two bedrooms, two bathrooms, a powder room, and ample storage space.

An open flow

The existing industrial building had a cast-iron column structure. Designers created an open flow throughout the home, taking advantage of long axial views through the space and drawing light through. The wall planes act more like sculptural screening elements while letting light and space flow around them. Concealed pocket doors provide privacy when needed.

Home, work space, and gallery

The owner wanted a home that would serve as a work space and gallery for her photography while also providing spaces for entertaining with friends. A library/reception area immediately off the entry vestibule allows her to meet with clients, present her work, and have her collection of research materials on hand for discussion. The reception area serves as a hinge for two distinct zones in the loft: the east zone flows directly into the "private" domain of her photography studio and back to her private bedroom, while the south zone flows into the "public" domain of her kitchen, dining, and living areas. A new wide-plank oak-wood floor connects all of these areas. The oak planks are used on the wall paneling and cabinetry, unifying the rooms with a warm texture.

Entertaining

The living area, kitchen, and dining area create an ensemble that is cohesive and very adaptable for a range of entertaining. Windows on two sides of the room bathe it with light. Additional folded and

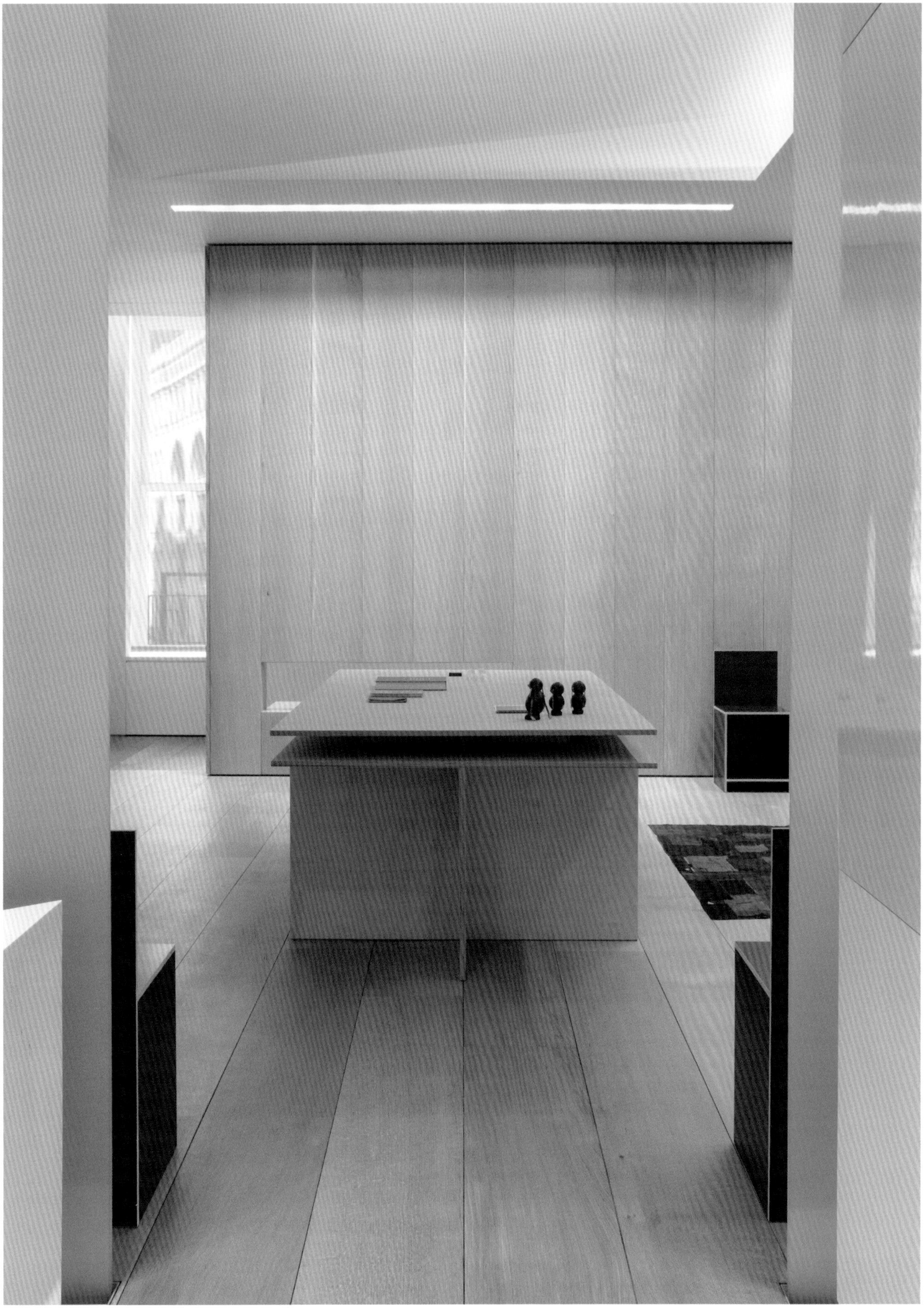

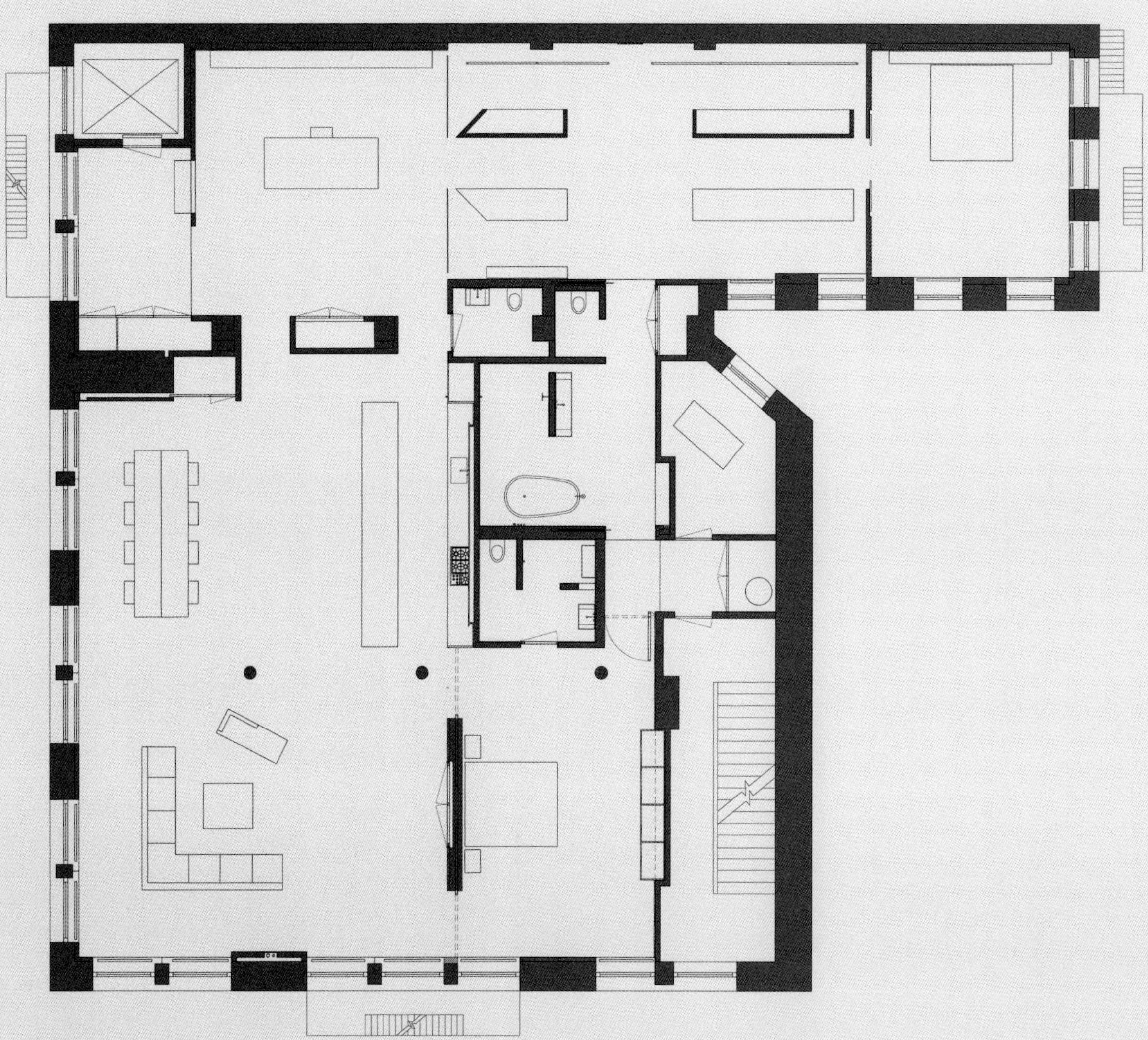

Floor plan

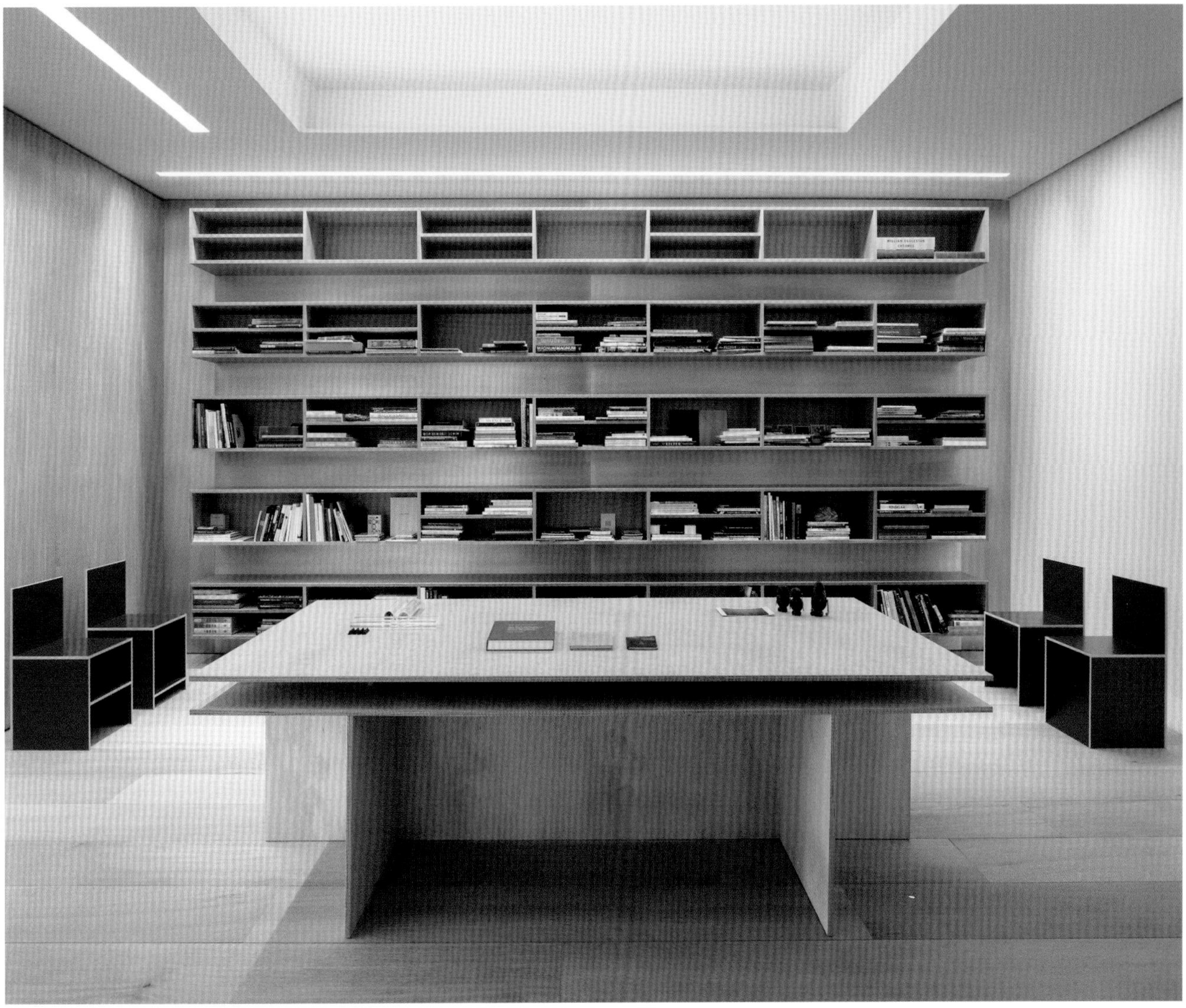

recessed lighting coves on the ceiling anchor the seating areas and wash them with a warm glow at night.

Interiors with form and function

Designers crafted raw steel, satin aluminum, solid oak, and white resin design features throughout the loft. They are designed as minimal art moments as much as they are functional elements for storage, dining, and work areas. For example, the steel kitchen island has ample storage and seating areas, while maintaining a sculptural presence in the room—it serves to frame the kitchen in an artful way. The white resin work tables in the photography studio have a similar presence: they are functional for work, yet also visually compelling. The wall planes in the photography studio are cleverly sheathed in white magnetic panels to allow the client to easily display and reposition her work.

The bathrooms were designed as an immersive chamber of light and striated stone, a soothing respite from the intensity of the city. The walls of the bathrooms are finished in waterproof resin, which provide a surface that is both luminous and very easy to maintain. Custom resin sinks, shower areas, and niches for toiletries were fused into the bathrooms to create a seamless and fully integrated concept.

Lighting up

Inspired by the art of James Turrell, Desai Chia designed several lighting strategies to enhance the architecture while giving form to the light. By cutting and folding the ceiling planes, they were able to gently bounce light into the living areas, kitchen, bathrooms, and library. Even rooms that do not have windows feel airy and luminous. The extensive use of LED lighting reduces energy costs while providing strong architectural lighting throughout the home.

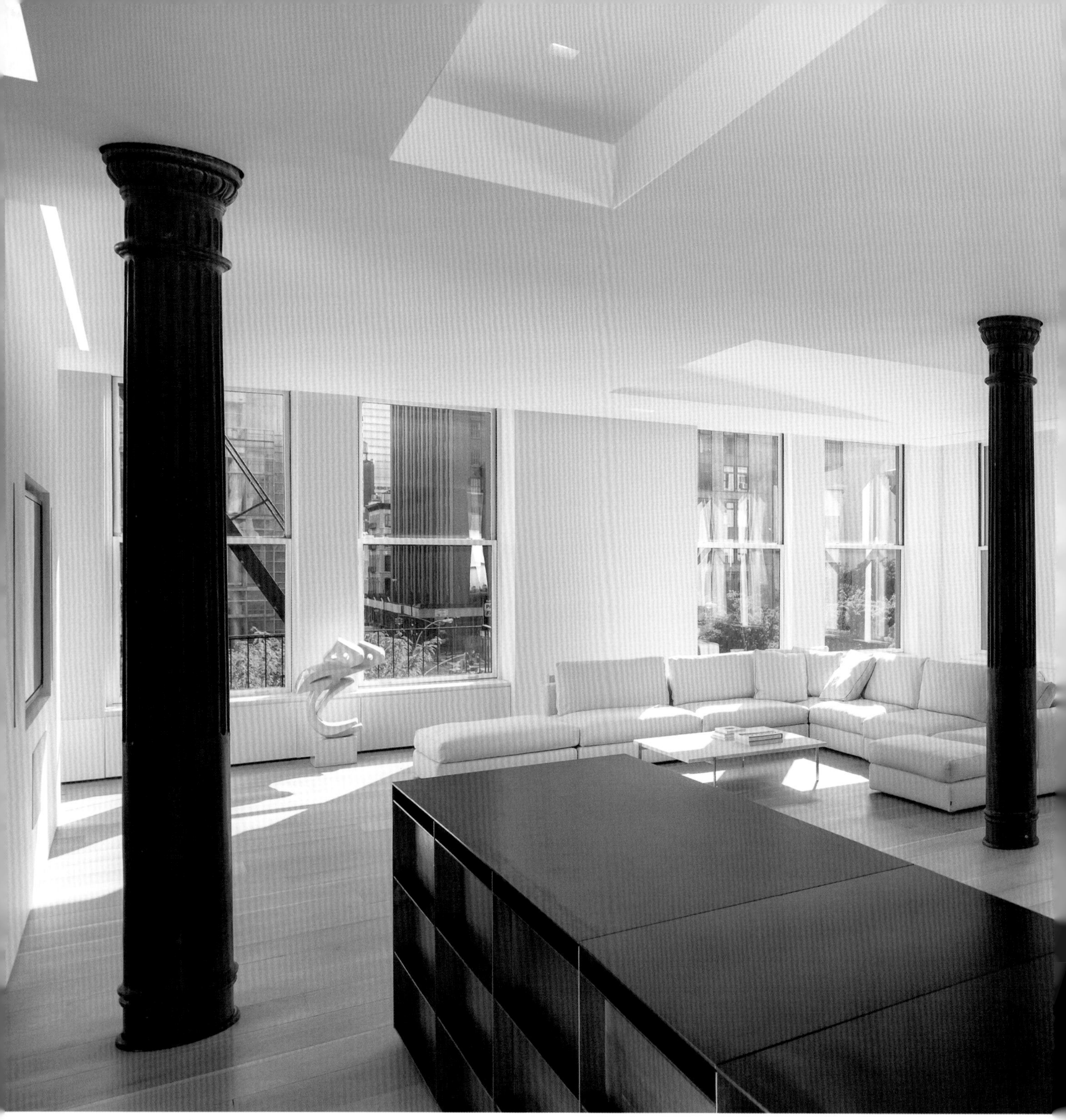

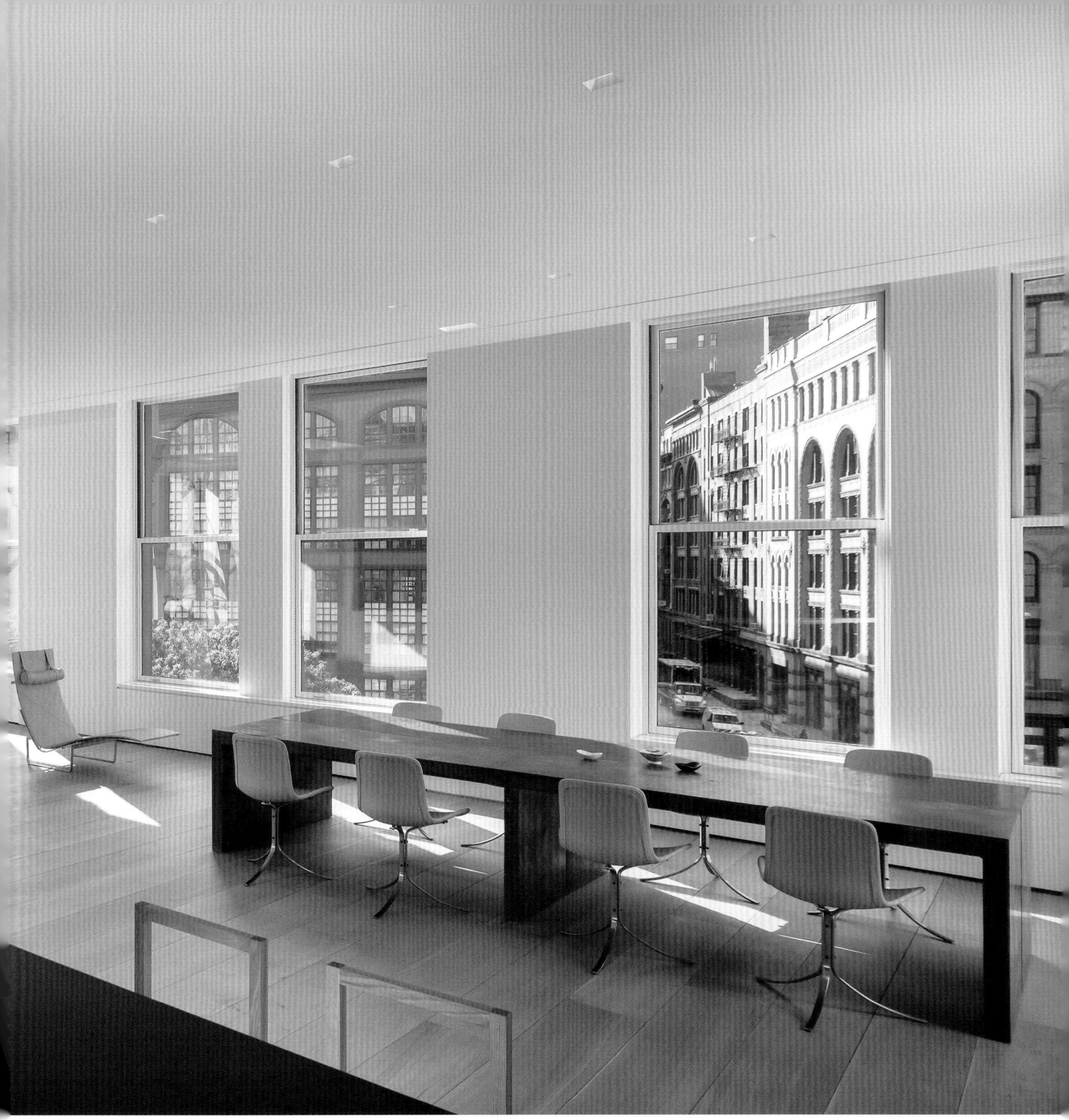

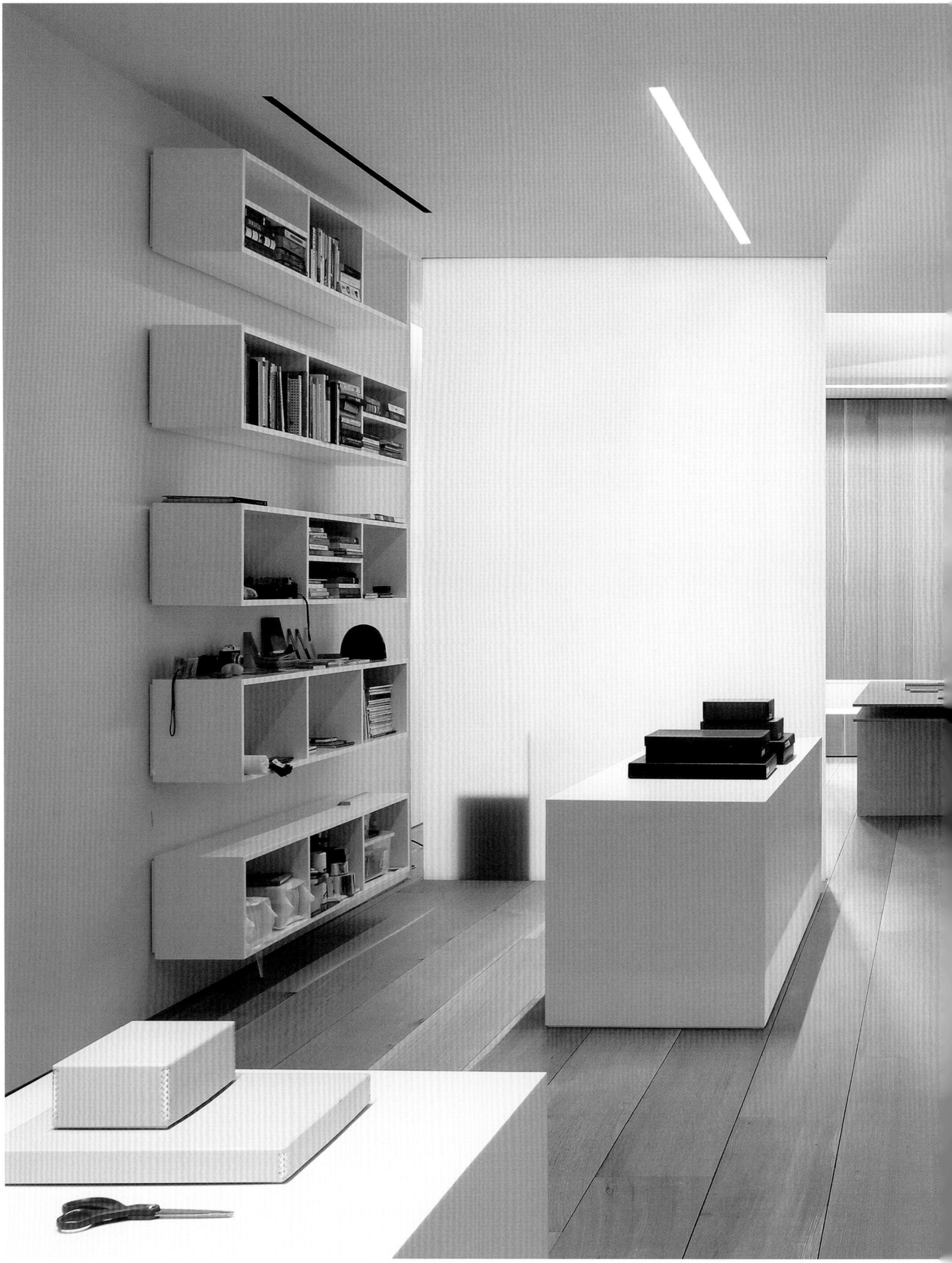

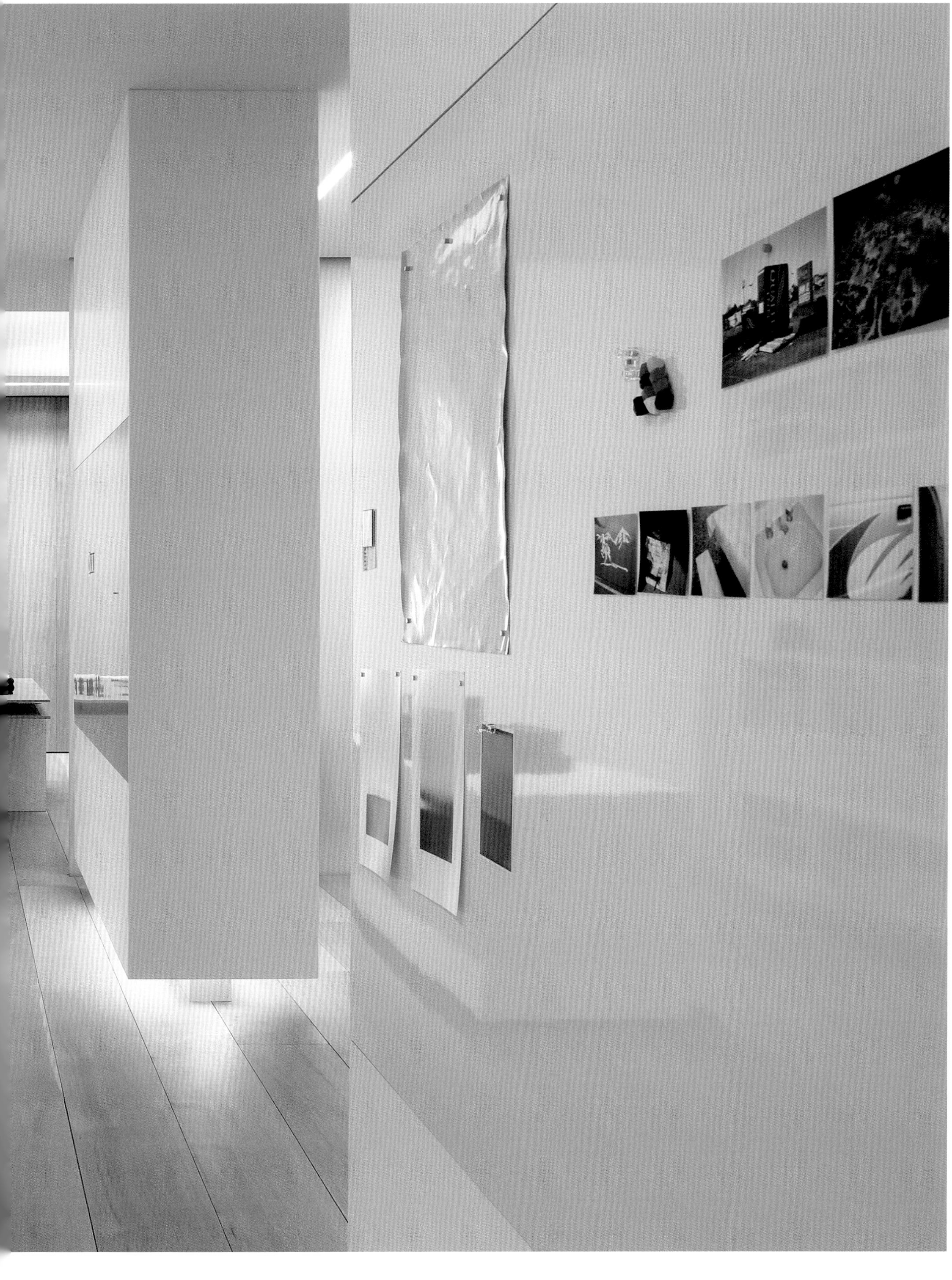

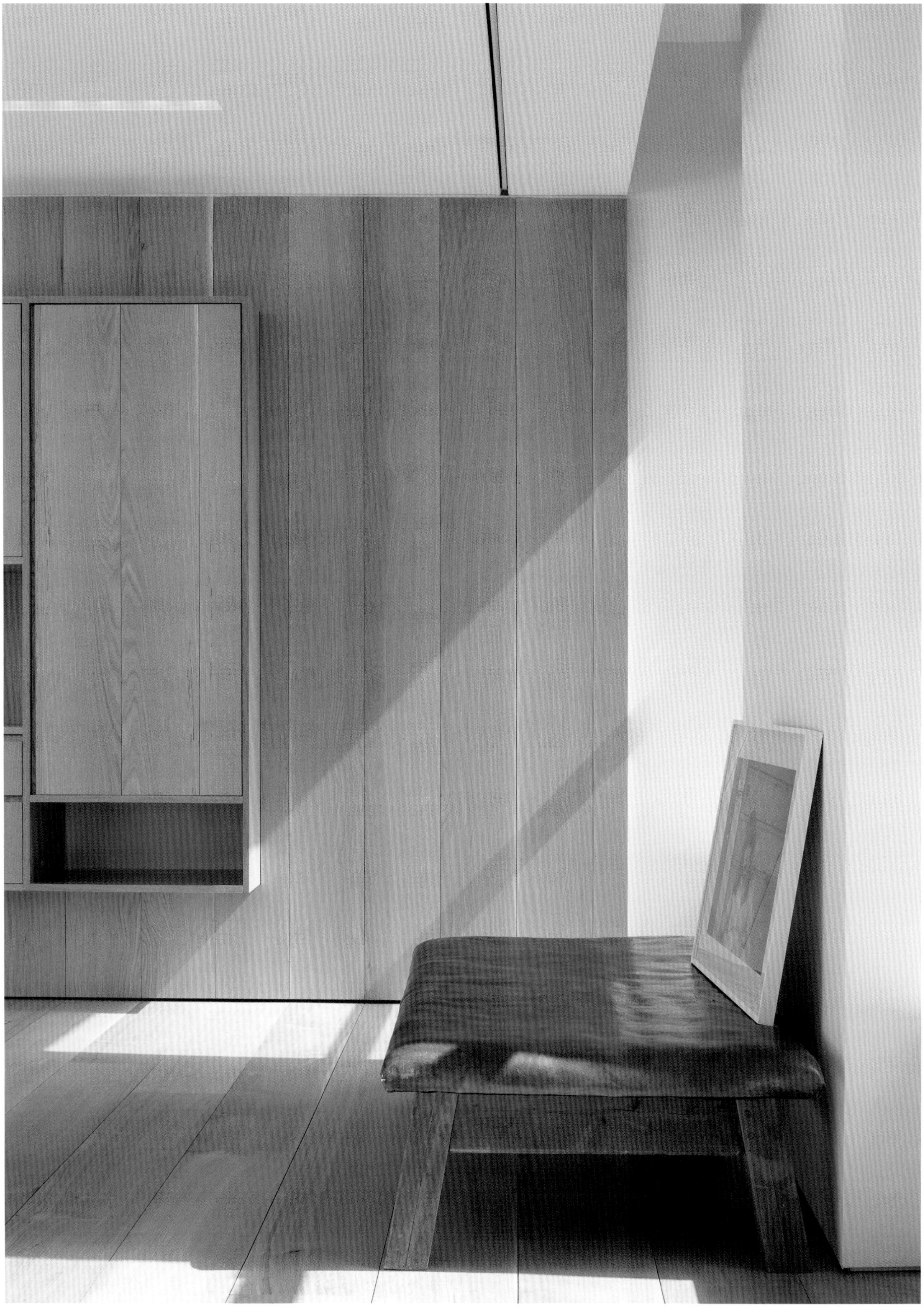

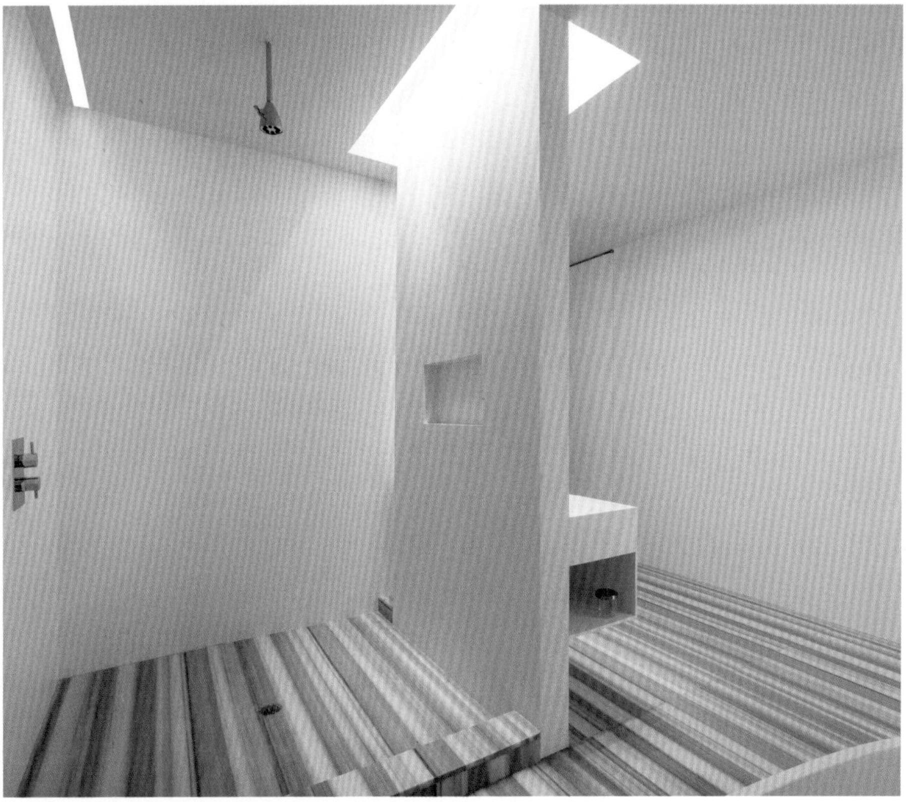

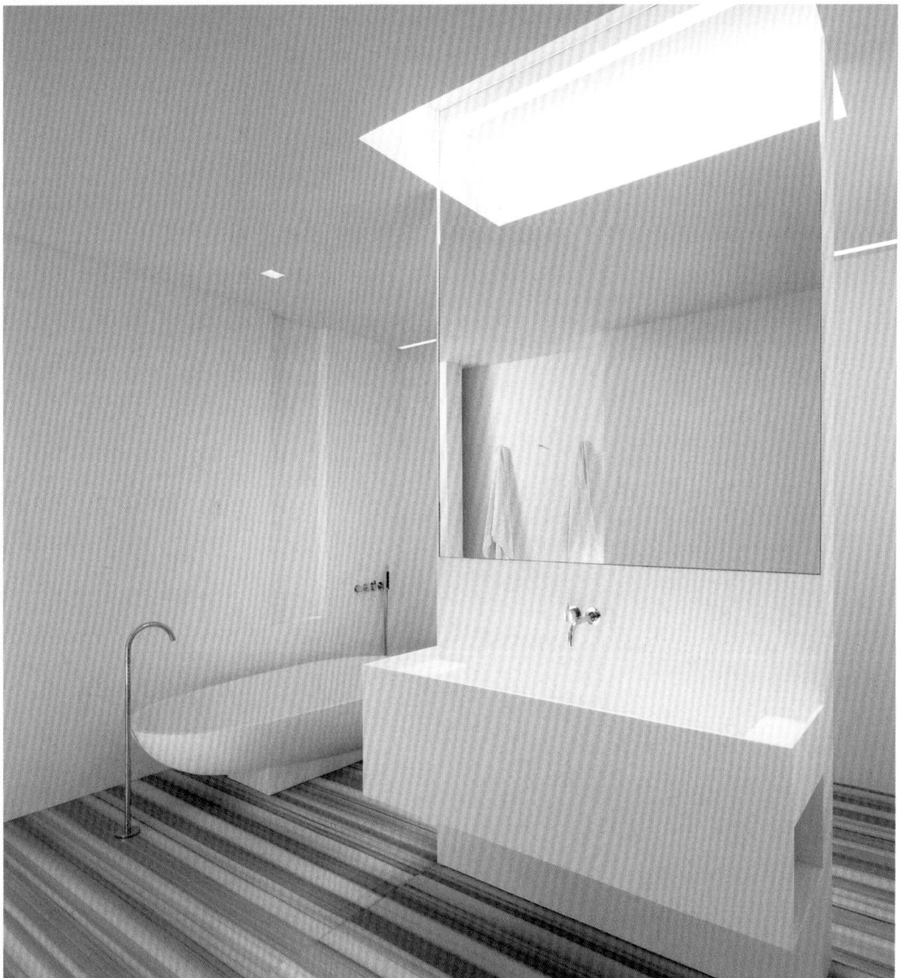

OLD RESIDENCES, NEW STUDIOS

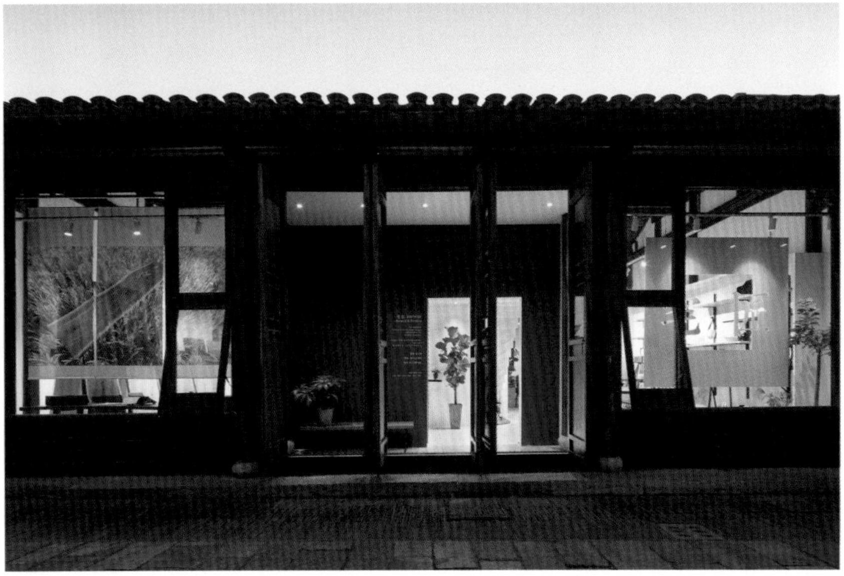

Area:
2,239 square feet (208 square meters)

Completion:
2017

Design:
Turing Design

Photography:
EMMA, LIGAN

Nanjing, China

Curtilage Artisan

This project is an old traditional house with an inner courtyard, located in the East Zhonghua Gate historic district in Nanjing. Artisans working in the studio produce and display wooden flooring, tables and other types of wooden furniture.

The old and the new

The aim of the project was to keep the original structures of the old house, repair the ground in the original courtyard space, and retain the architectural features of the old residential buildings, while injecting new vitality and possibility into the space.

On the outer façade the original small and complicated doors and windows were replaced with large-scale windows and open folding doors, effectively improving the natural light in the indoor area. The designers set up a suspended transparent glass box at the interior wall of the courtyard, which stretches into the courtyard and provides a seating area with natural lighting.

The new center of the space is a white building inside the original buildings, creating a "house in house" concept with a bar and VIP area.

Blue is the main color of the studio, with blue walls in the entrance and bar. The designers also used lots of white, with white terrazzo to make the walls and ground, white sheet iron and white paint, which created a strong contrast with the original wood structures, doors and windows.

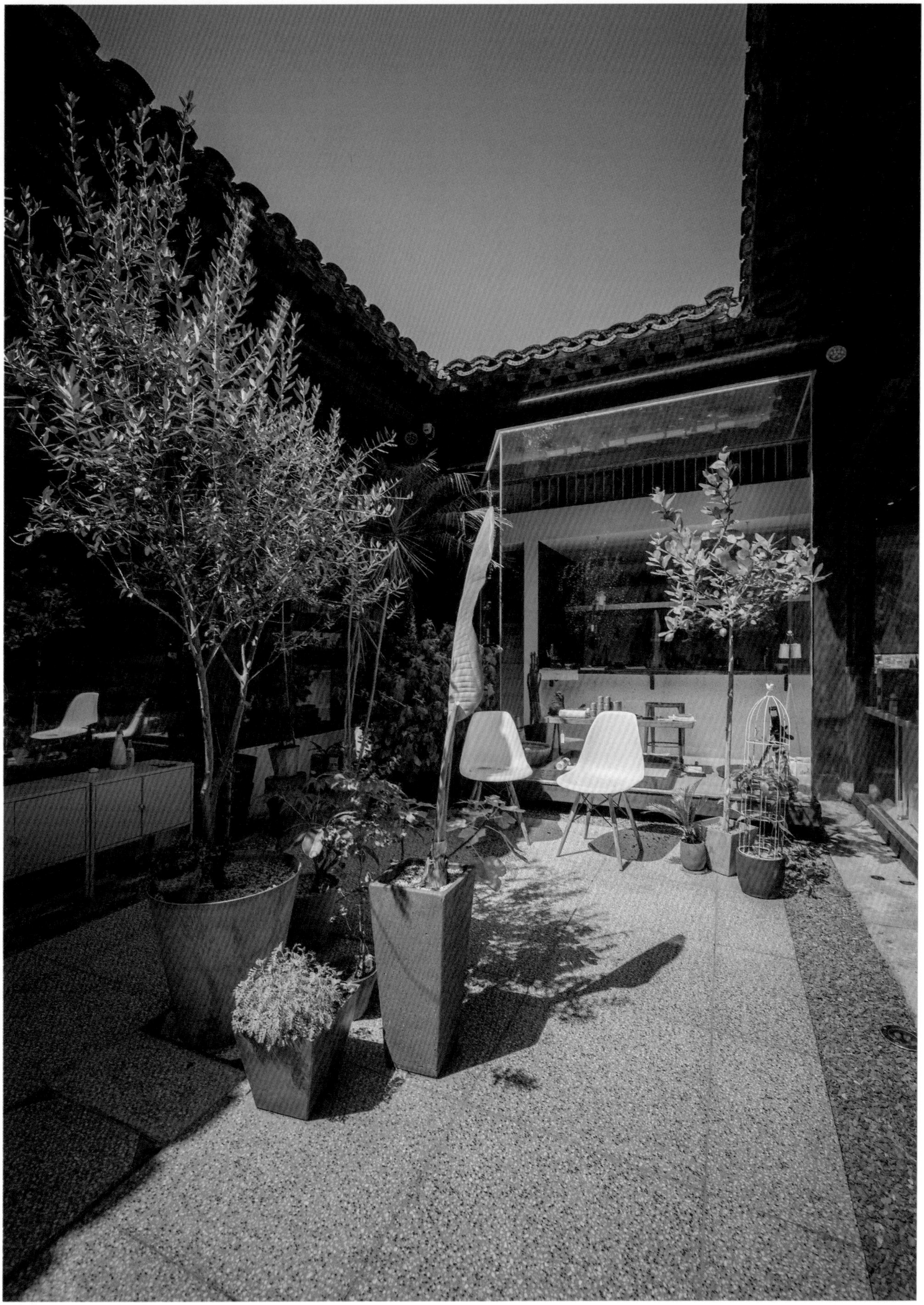

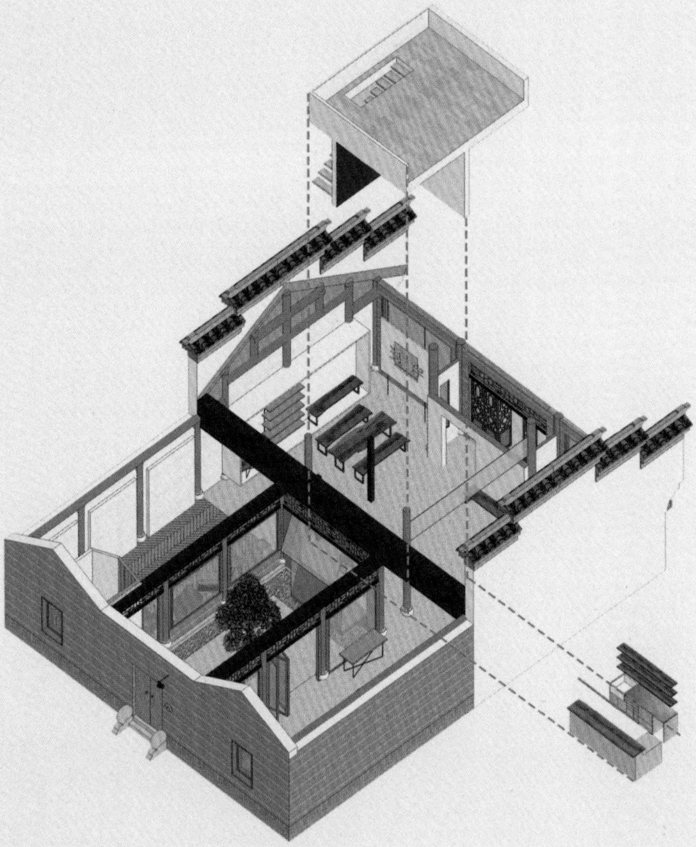

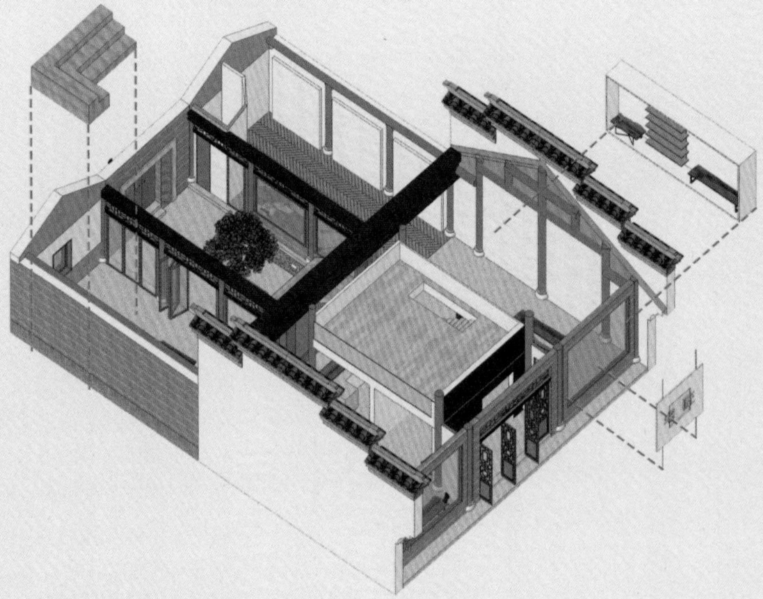

Axonometric drawings

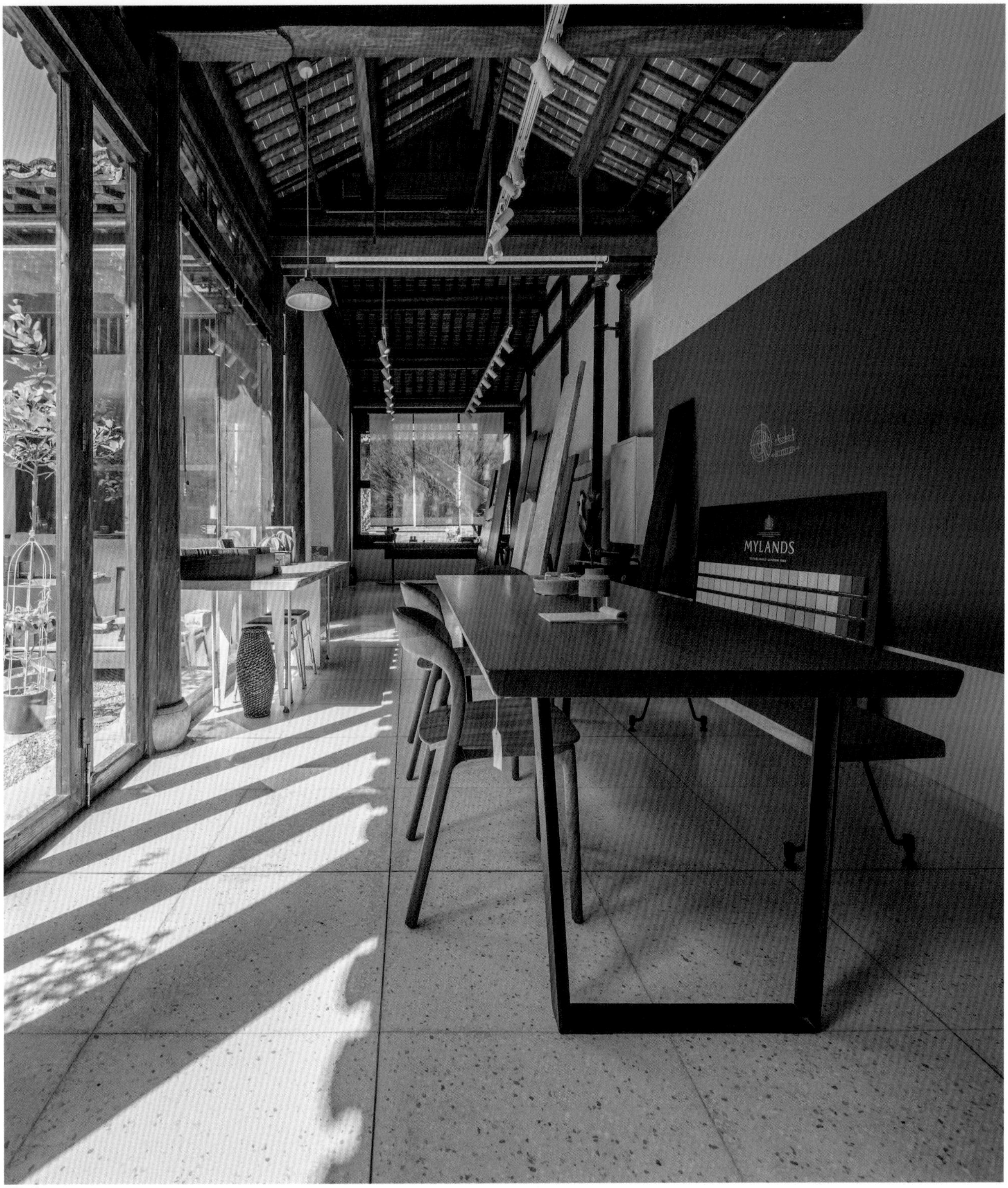
MYLANDS

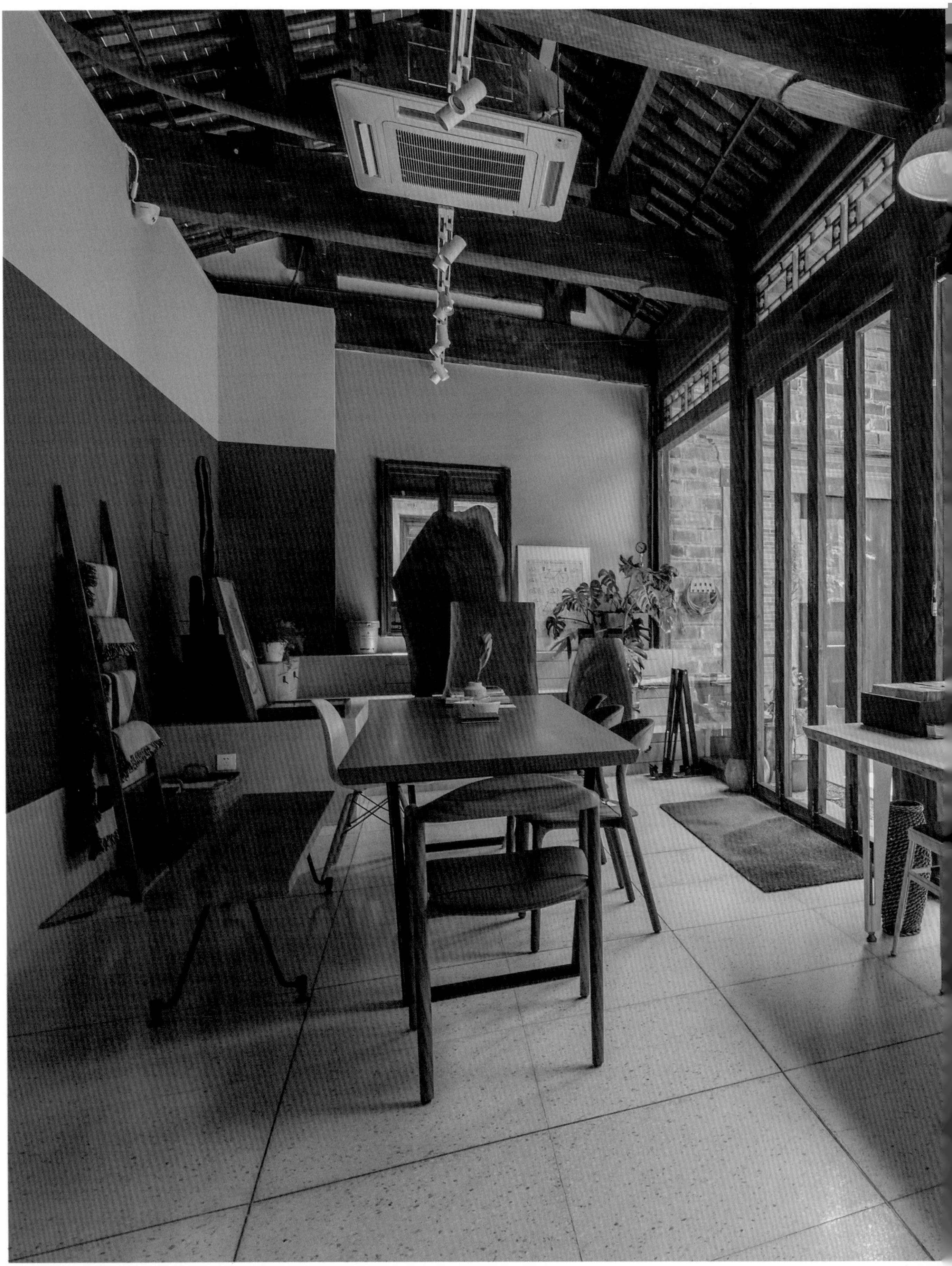

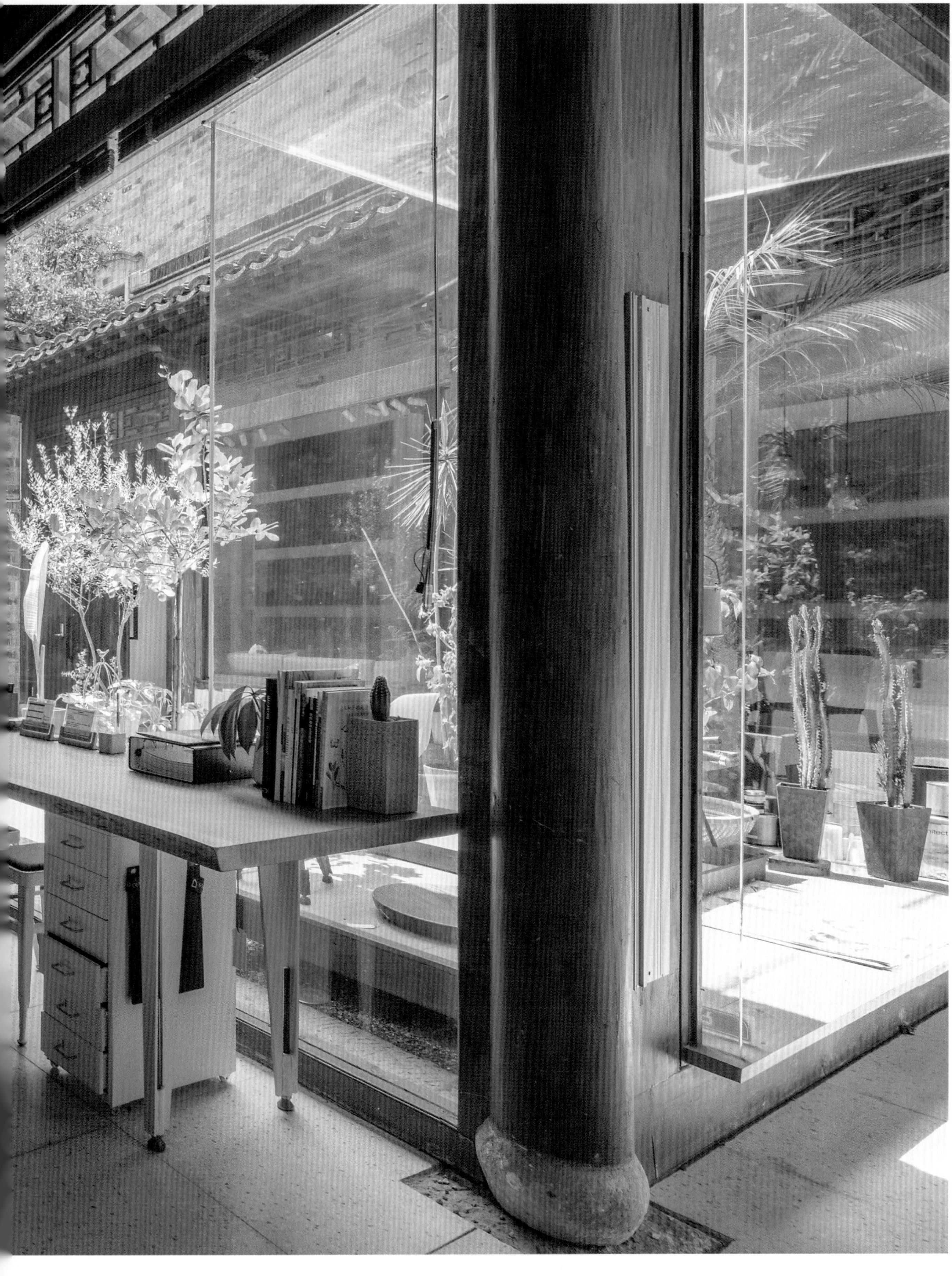

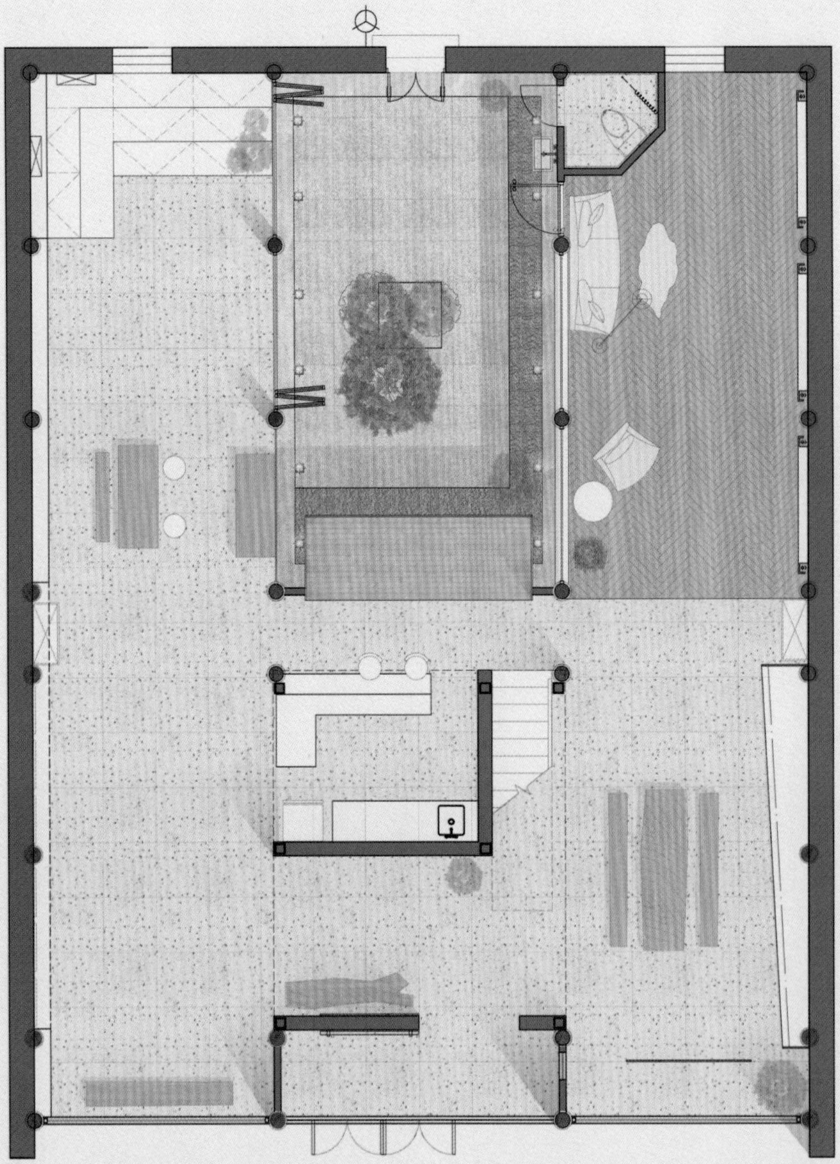

Floor plan

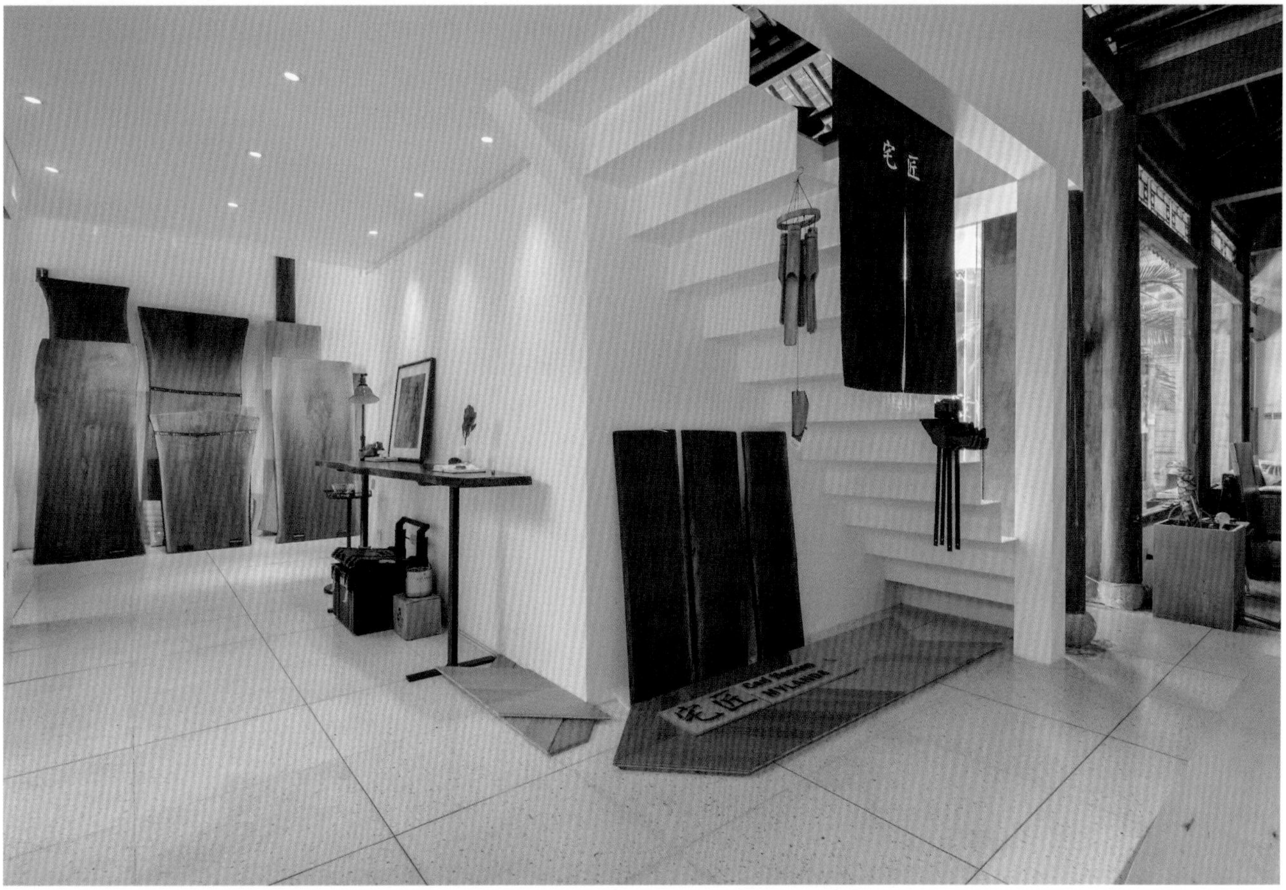
宅匠

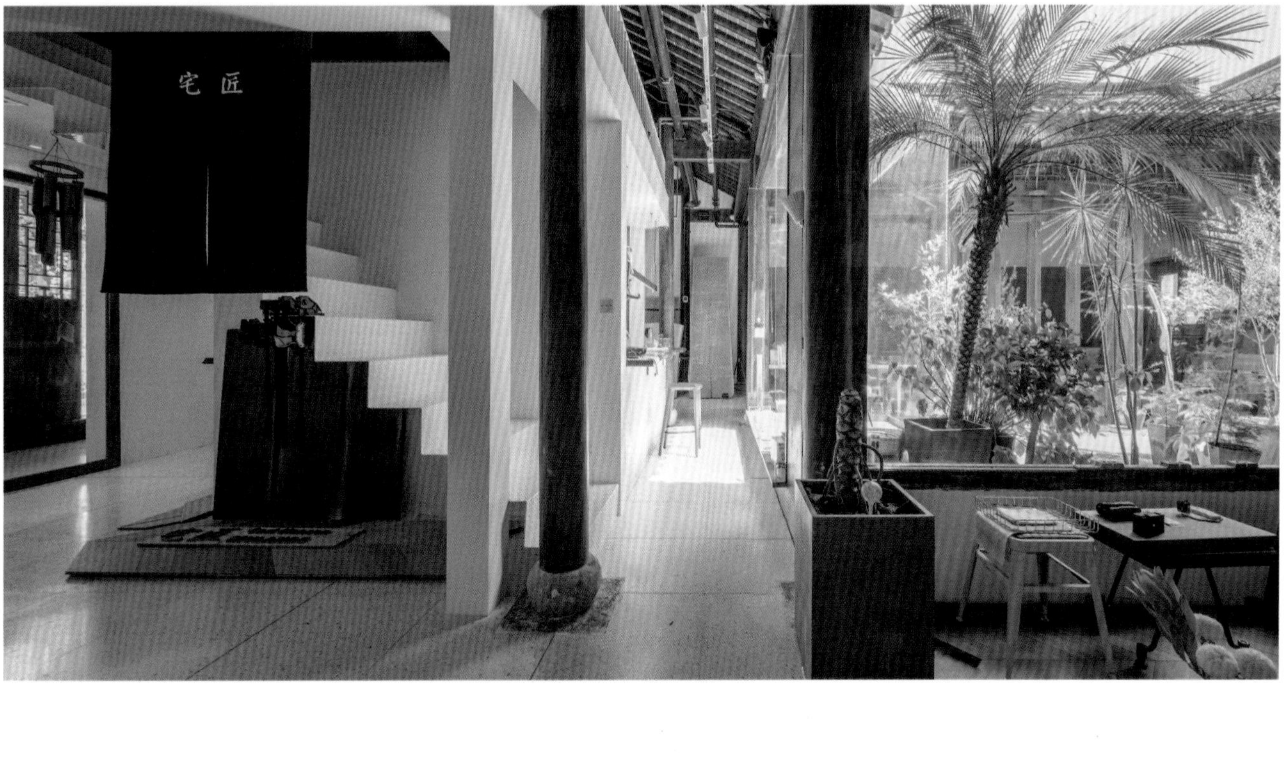
宅 匠

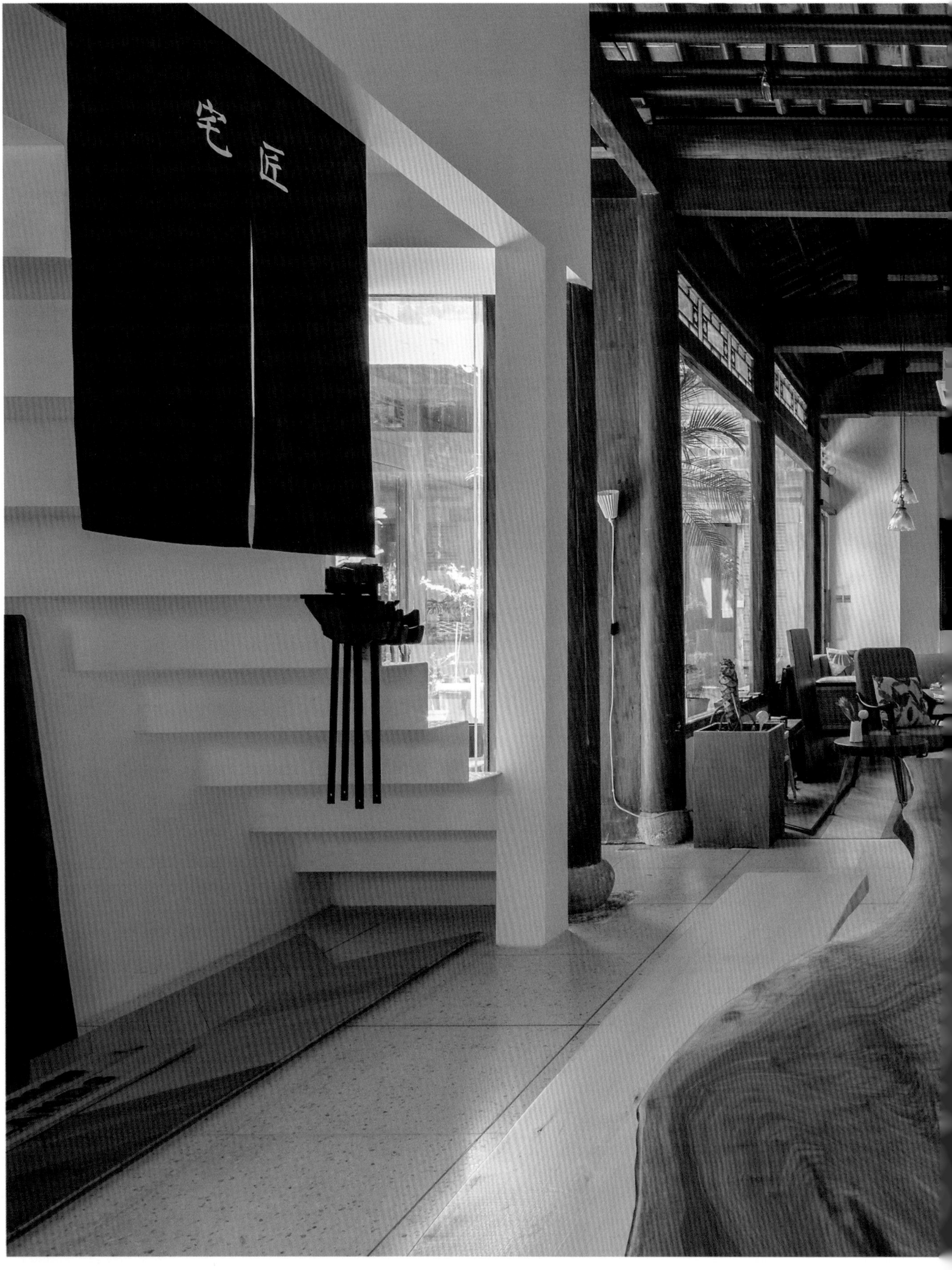
宅匠

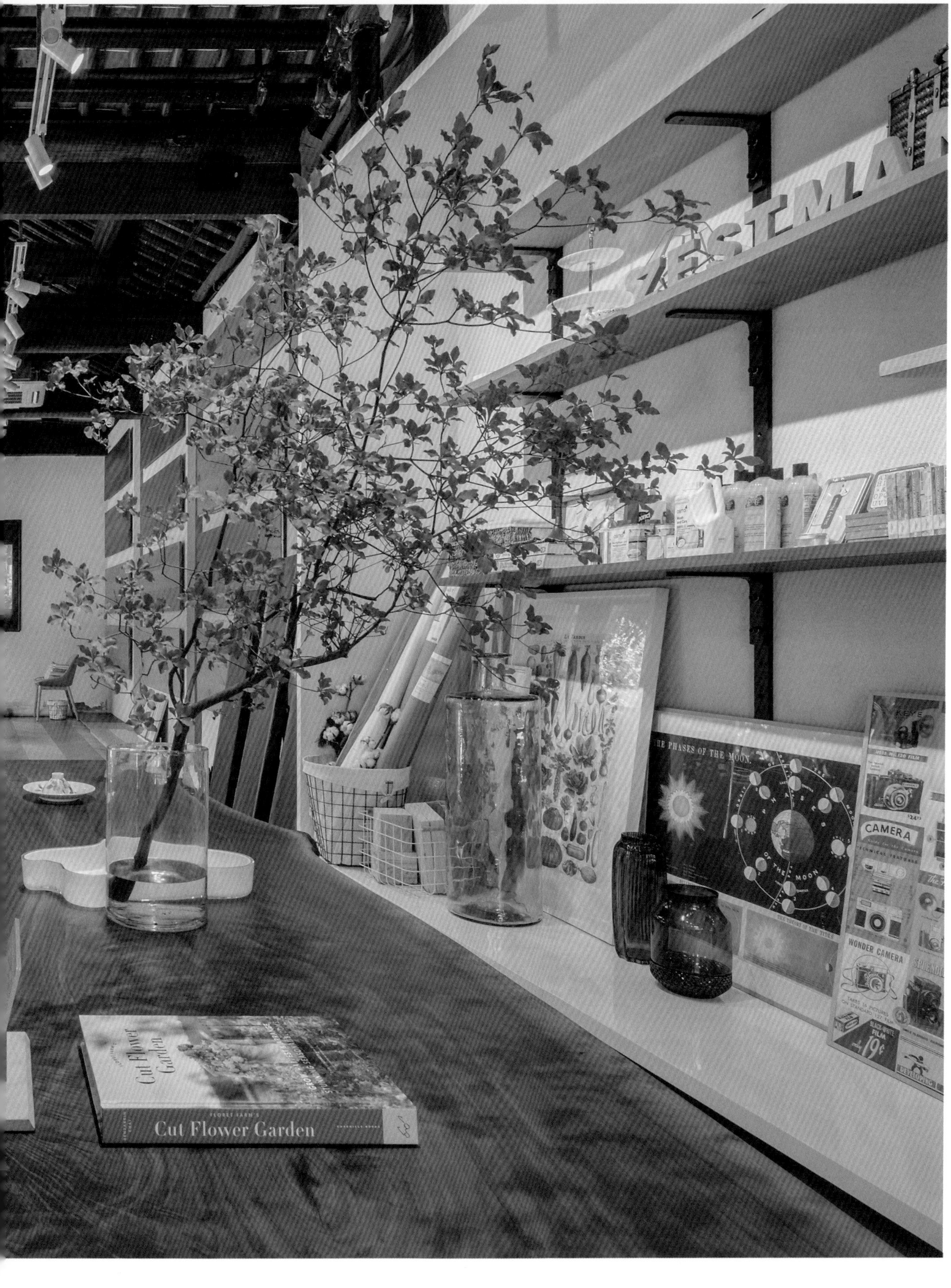

Cut Flower Garden
Cut Flower Garden
THE PHASES OF THE MOON
CAMERA
WONDER CAMERA

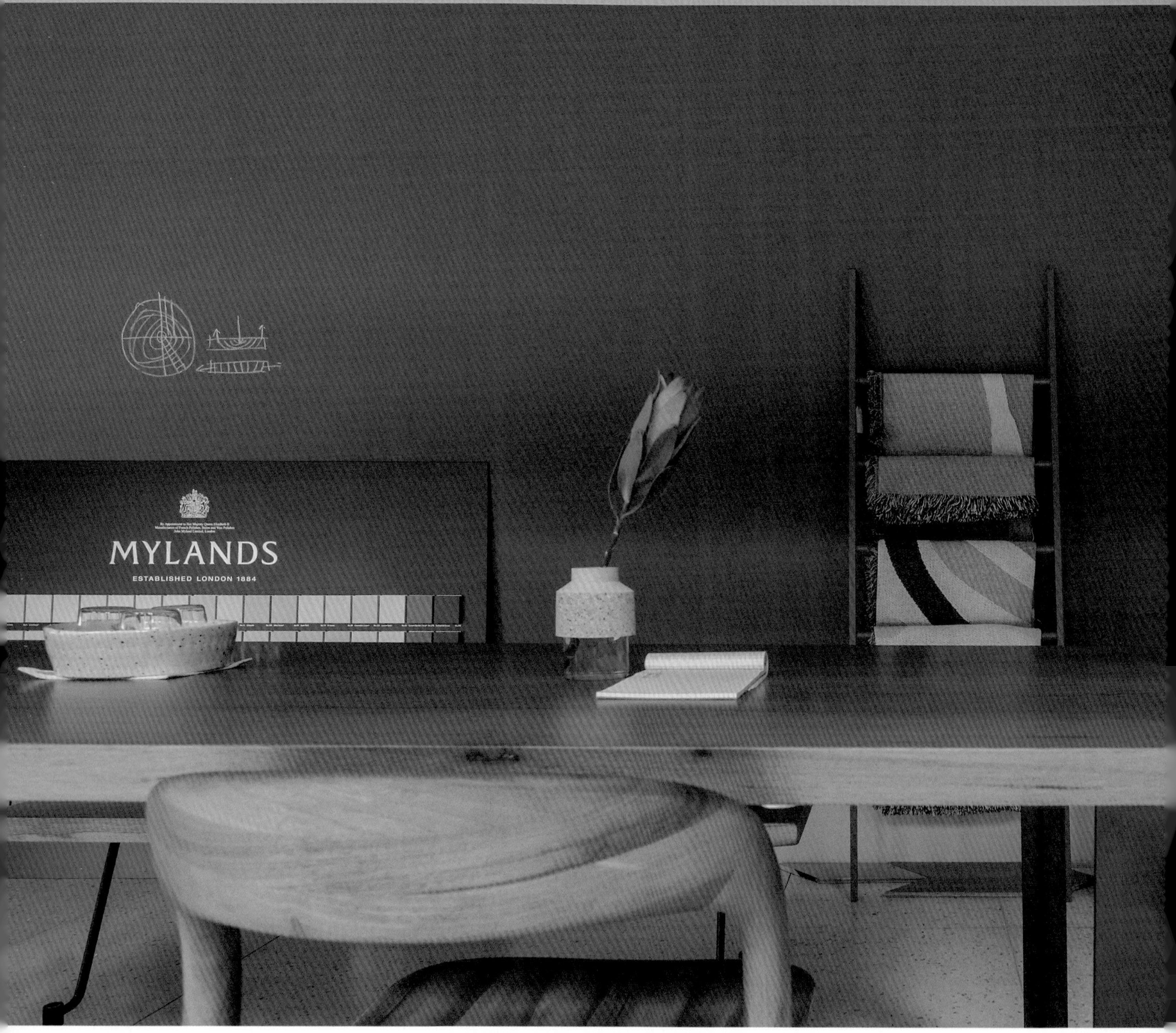
MYLANDS
ESTABLISHED LONDON 1884

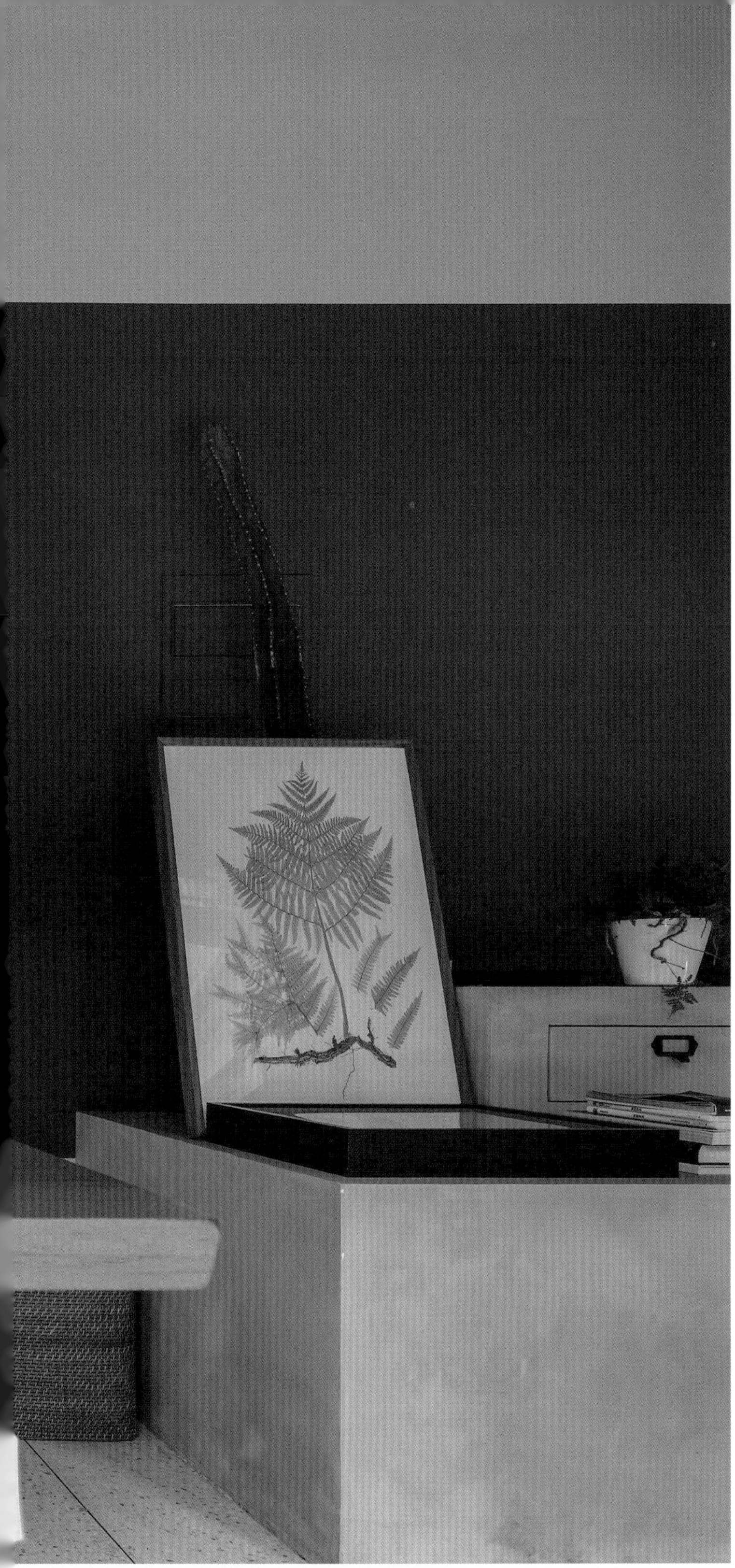

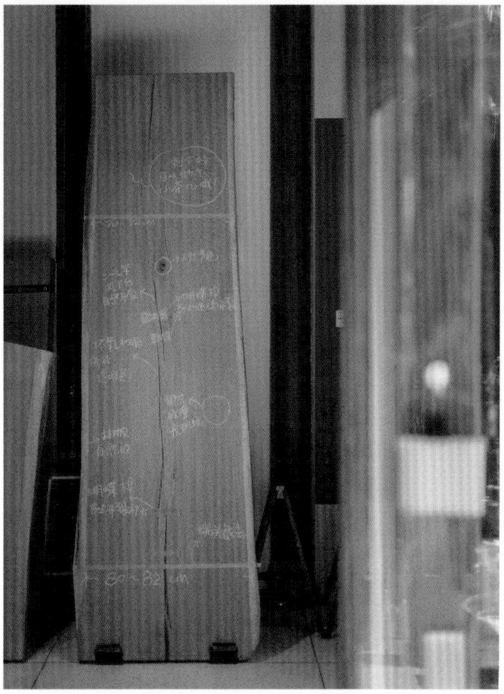

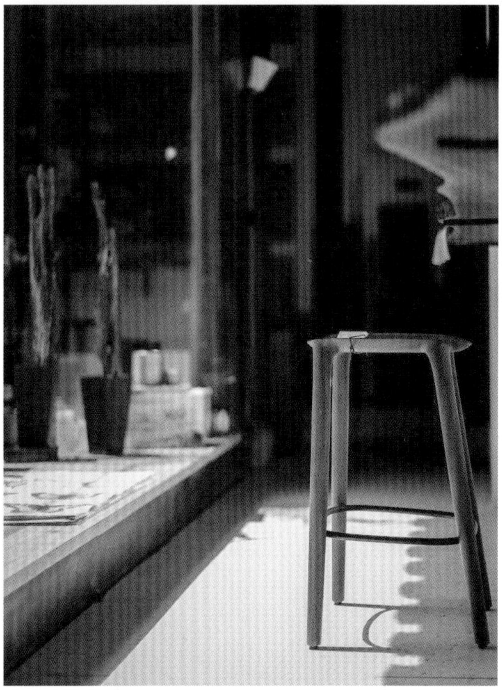

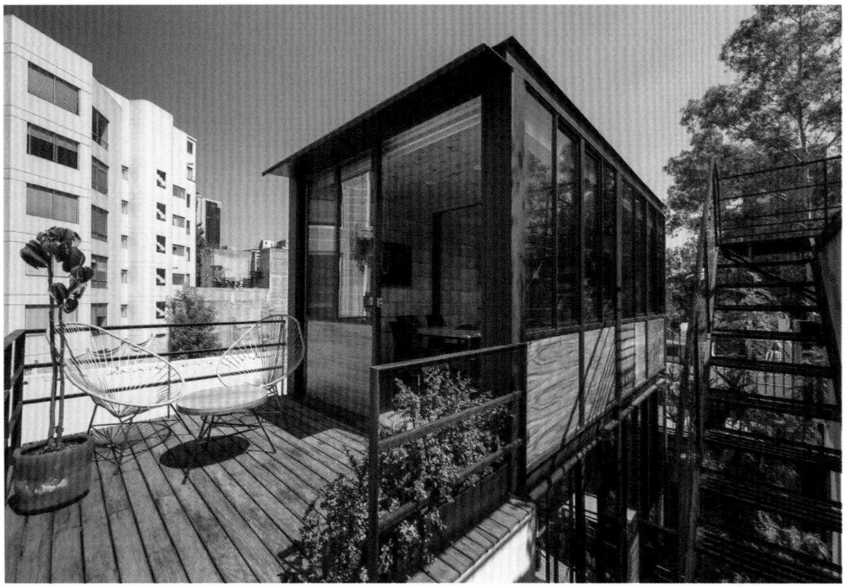

Area:
1,281 square feet (119 square meters)
Completion:
2017
Design:
Estudio Atemporal
Photography:
Luis Gallardo LGM Studio

Mexico City, Mexico

Grupo Sicario

This project arose from the need to increase the amount of work space in the headquarters of Grupo Sicario, located in an old building of the Colonia Roma, a distinctive midcentury neighborhood in Mexico City. The group functions as a meeting point for young creatives around the products and activities that transformed the millennial generation: social networks, live entertainment, and the movement toward entrepreneurship. It is divided into three branches—architecture, hospitality, and entertainment—with more than 24 projects, among which are the Limantour liquor store, the Ceremonial Festival, and the Campobaja restaurant.

The old and the new

In order to deal with a building that had an important historical value within its context, the decision was made to respect the original structure on the side and create an independent space that didn't put at risk the existing house but could integrate the historical traces with the new experiences. In order to achieve the functional adaptation, the flooring levels and height were aligned and respected; that way the new structure would work as an extension of spaces of the existing house.

The courtyard of the house was used to contain the new building, which consists of a four-level steel structure, in which the first floor is dedicated to a common space and the rest to office spaces.

Contrasting elements

The new structure rises in striking contrast with the old building, finding its own identity by the use of a contemporary language than can be seen in its materials such as gray blocks, wooden floors and ceilings, steel window frames, and raw carpentry furniture. Despite its minimal plan, the choice of elements transforms these functional spaces into wide and comfortable ones.

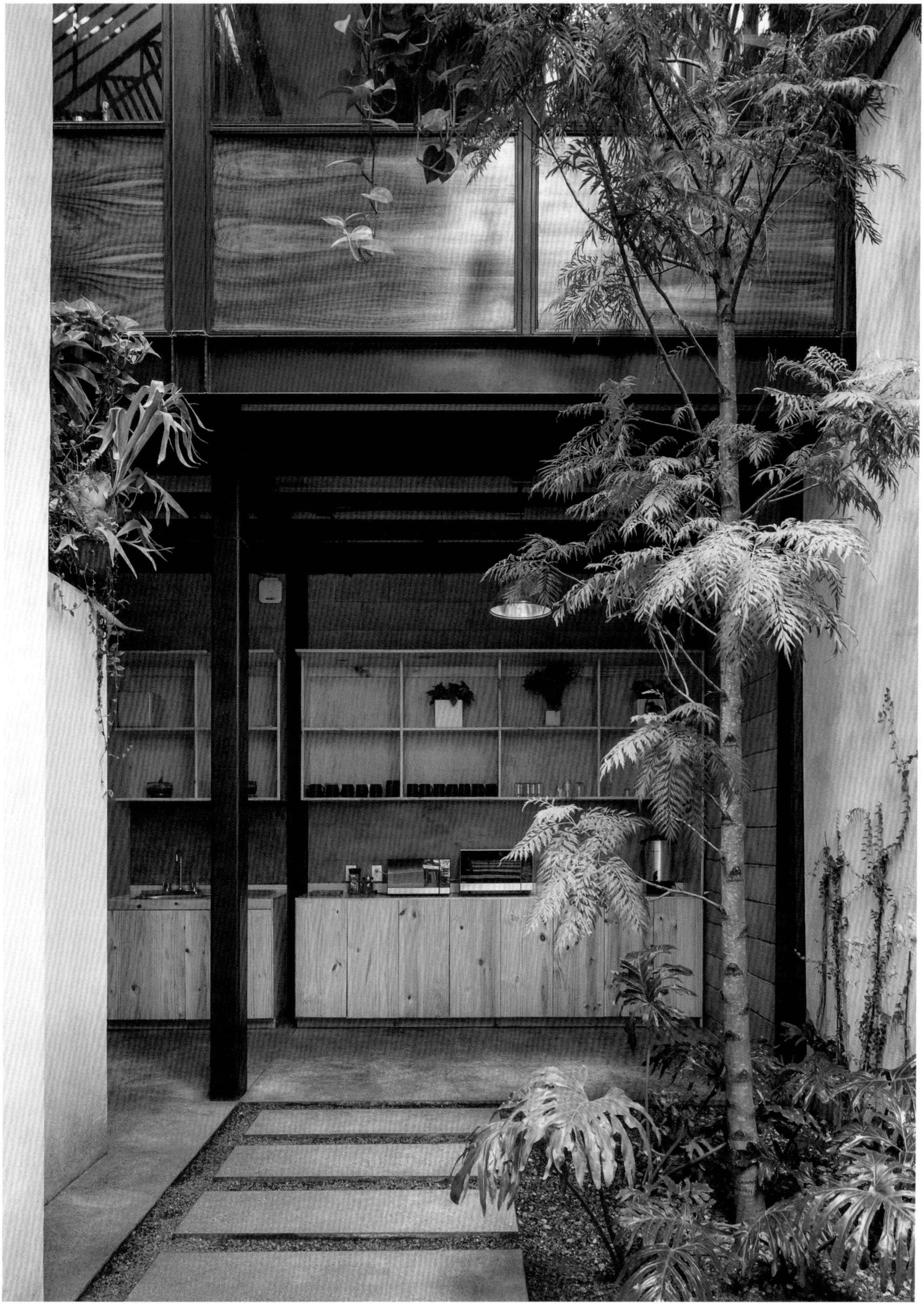

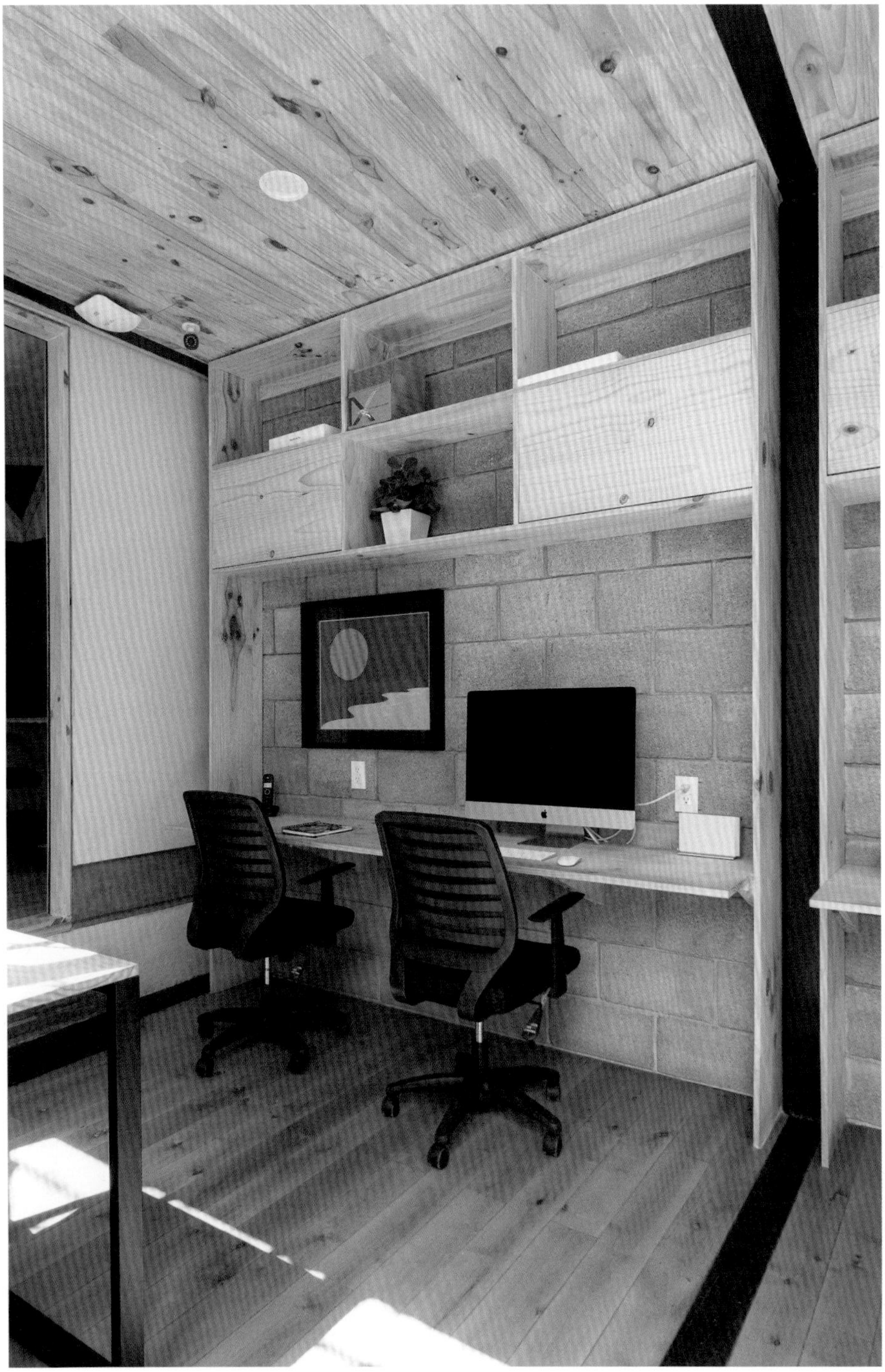

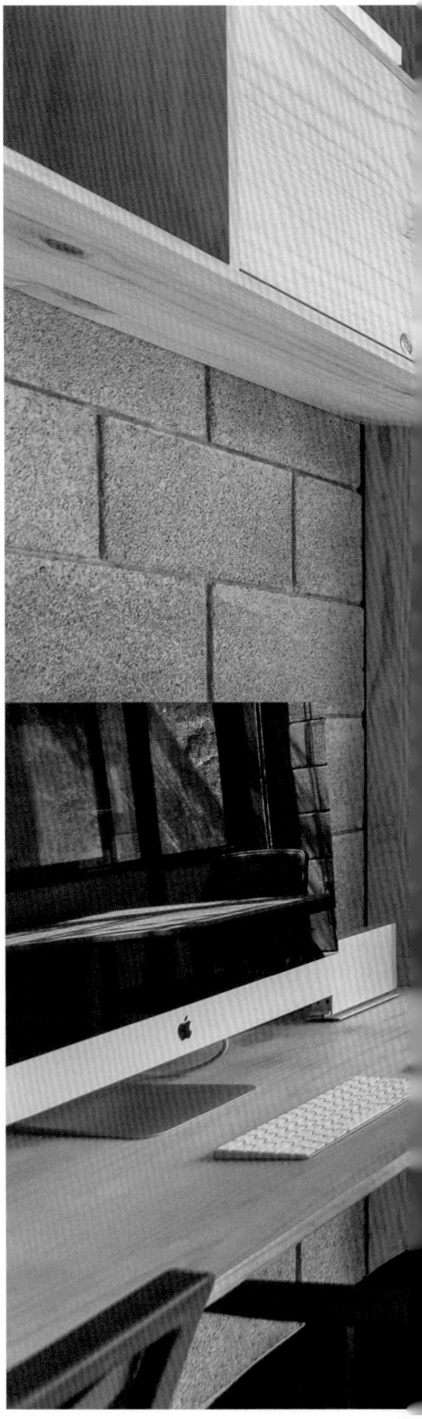

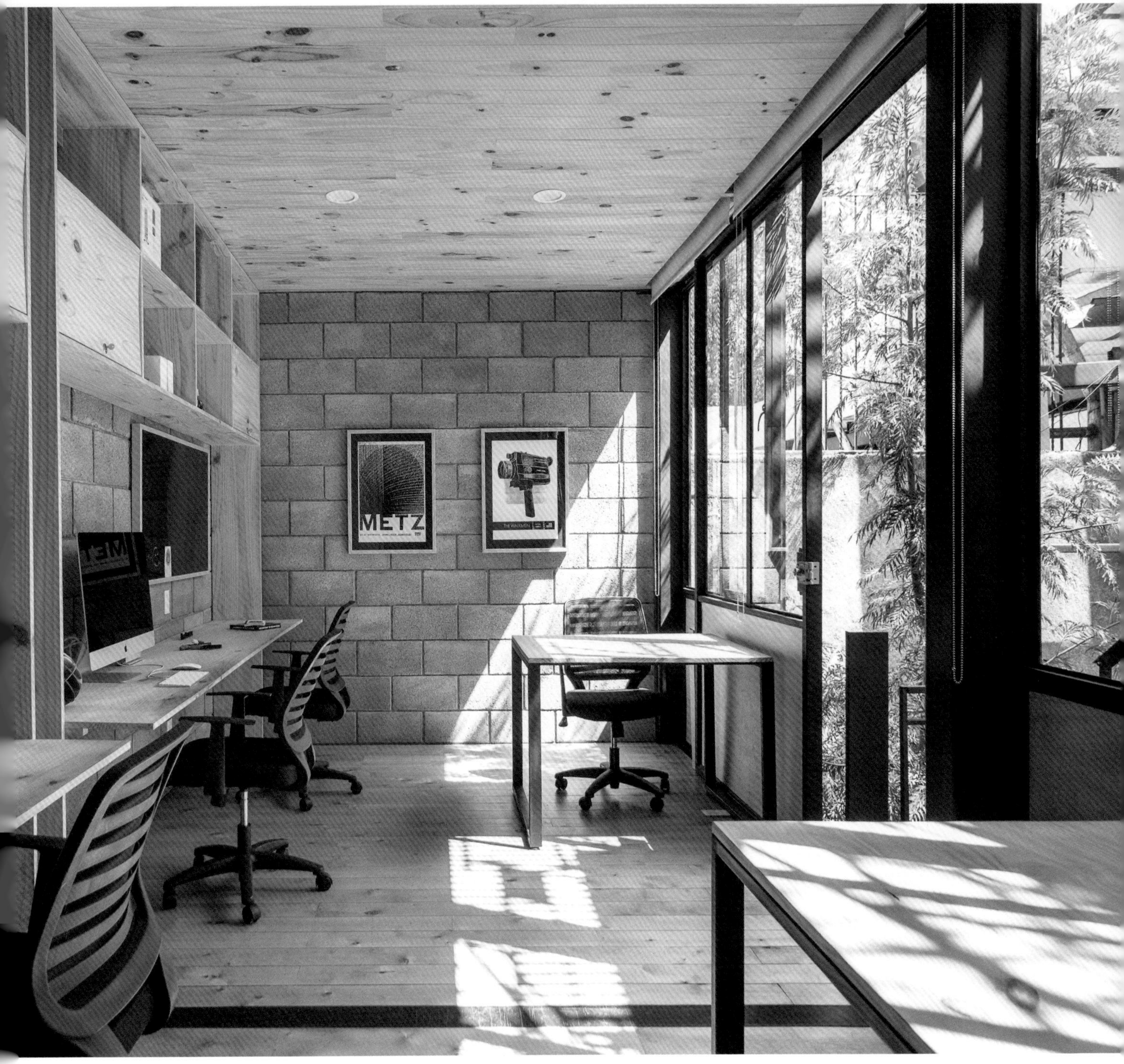
METZ

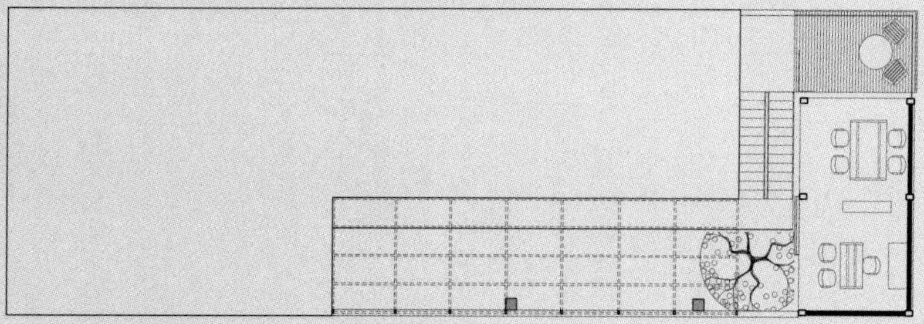

Second-floor plan

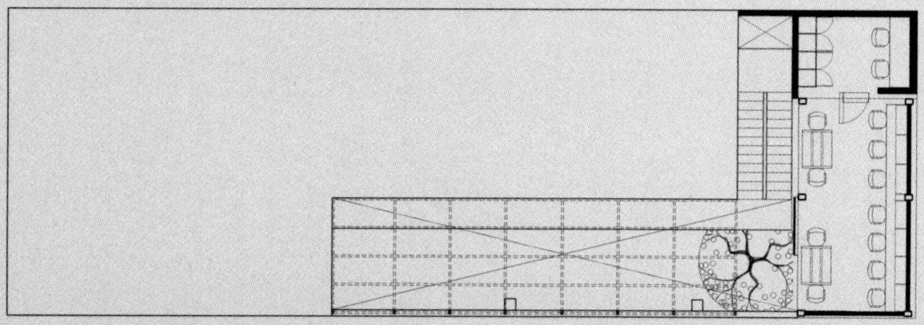

First-floor plan

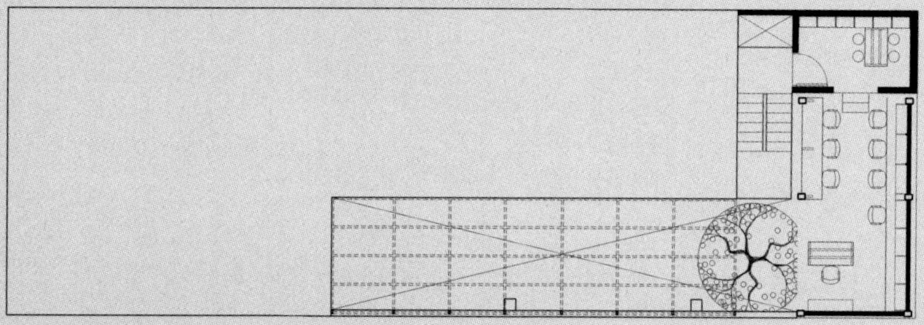

Ground-floor plan

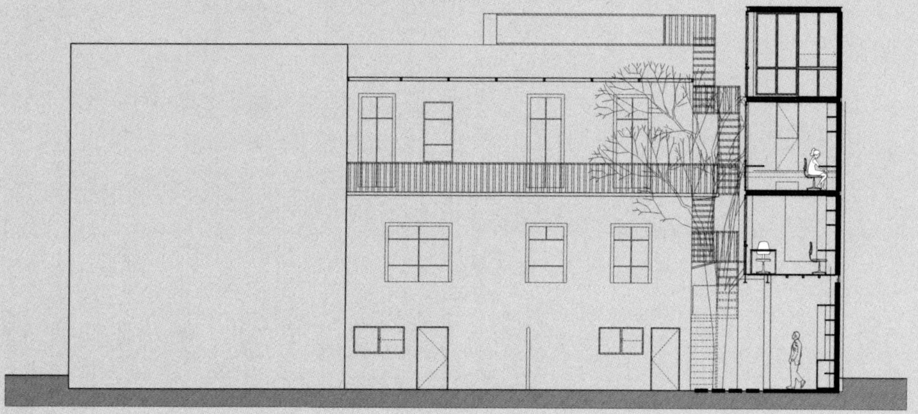

Section

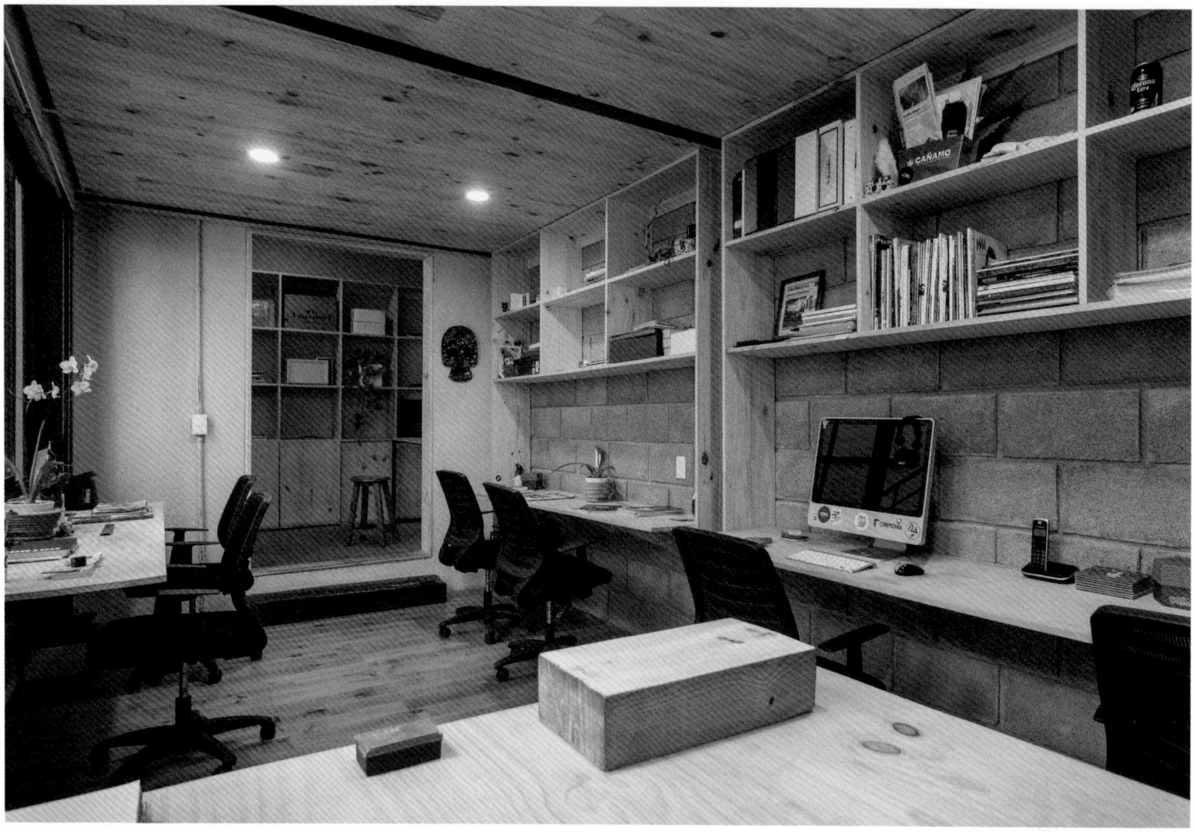
CAÑAMO

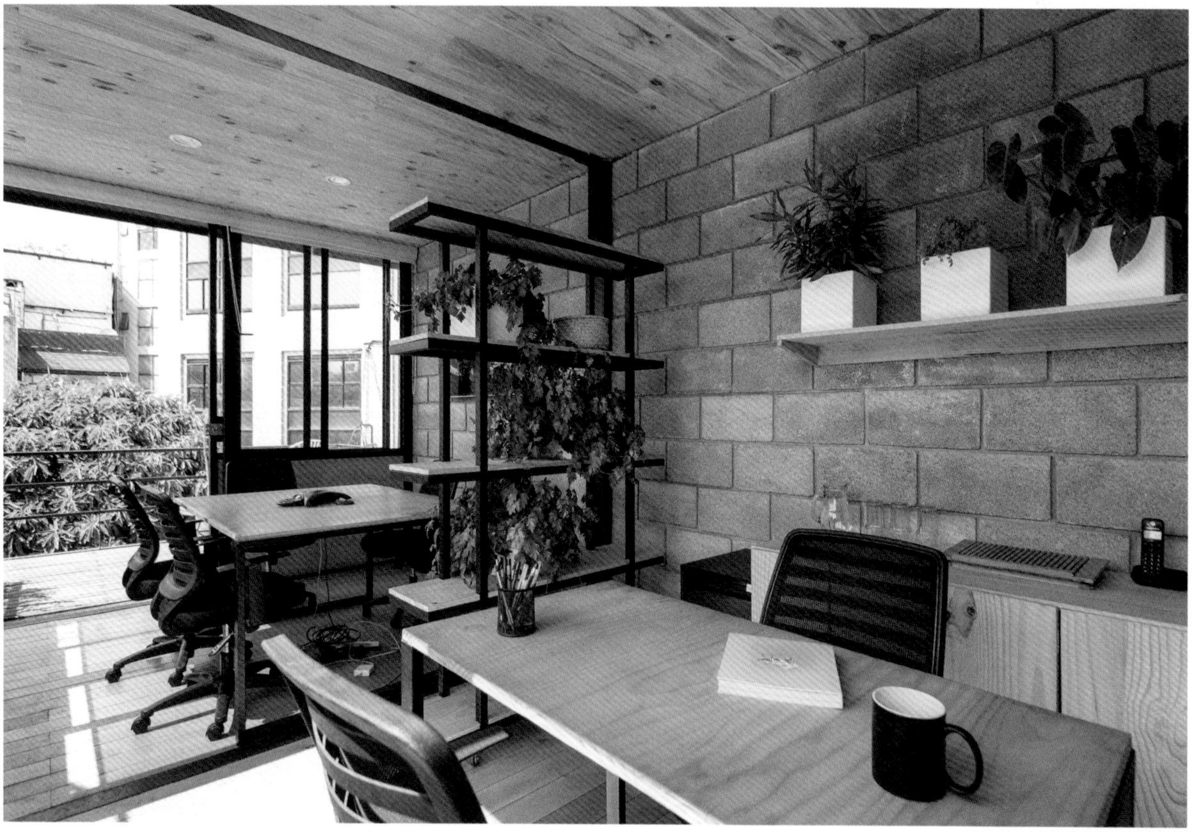

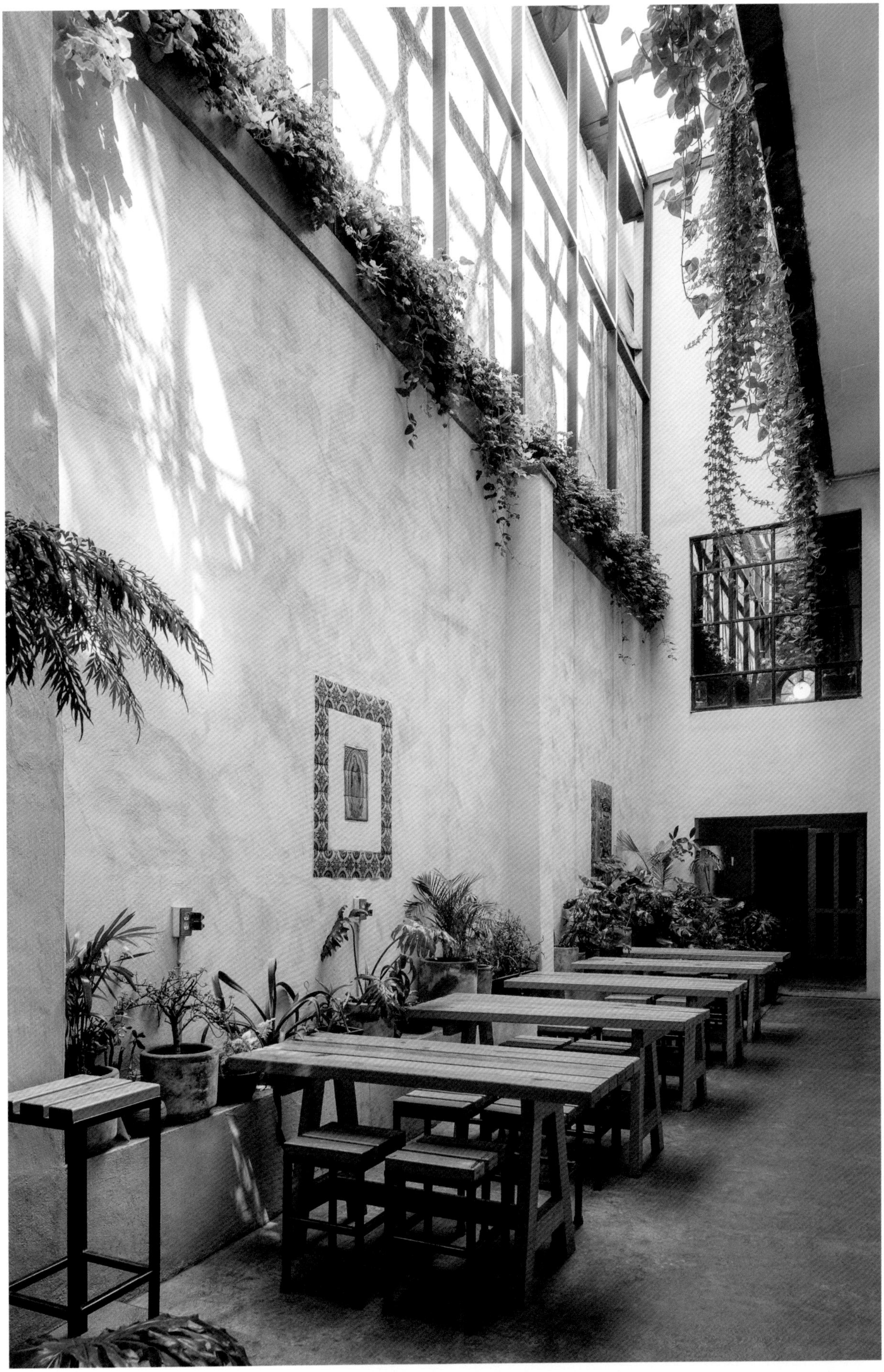

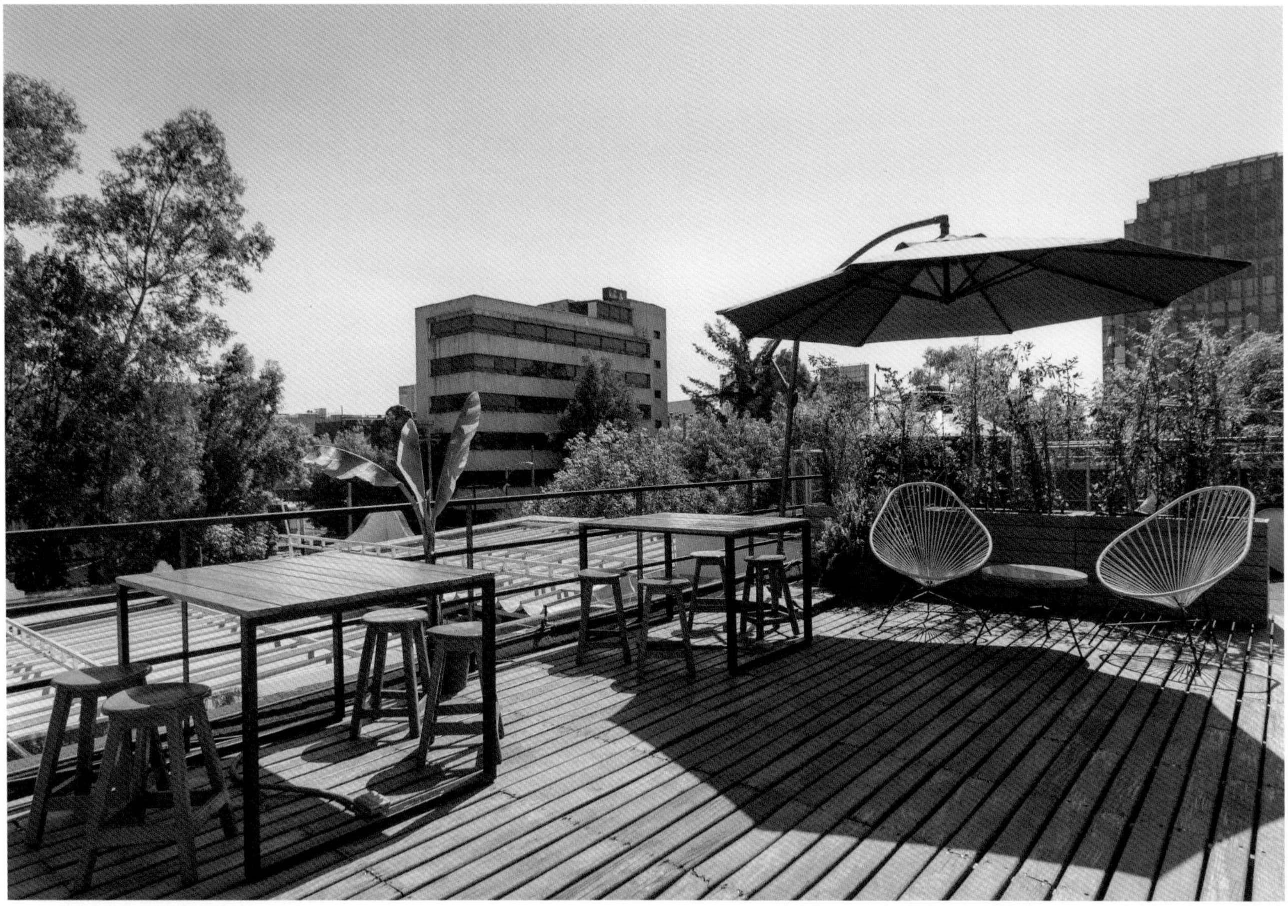

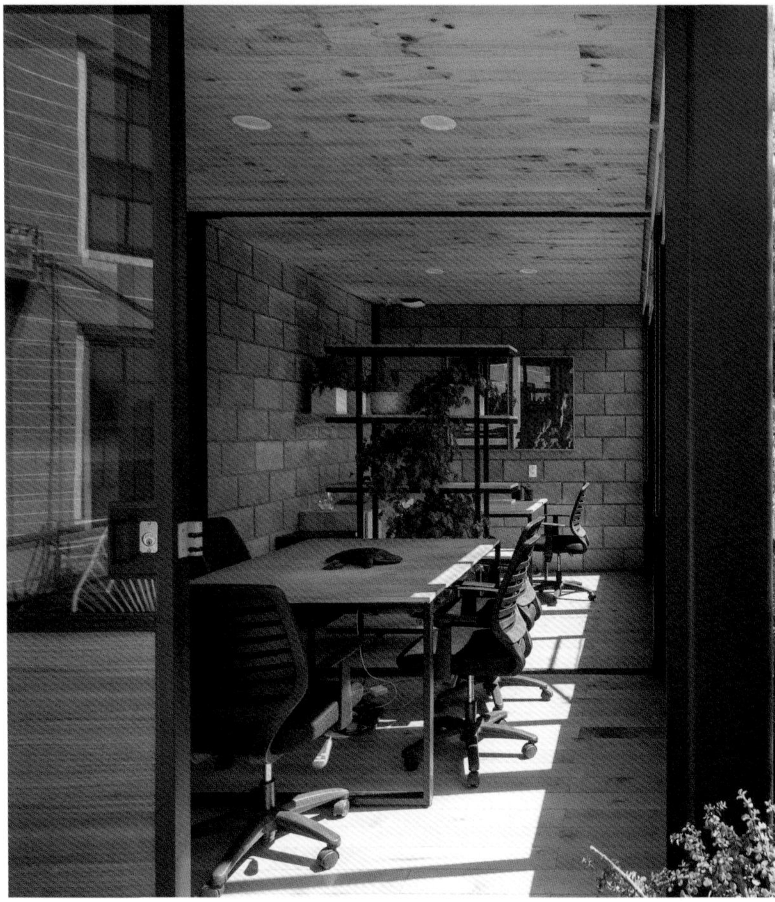

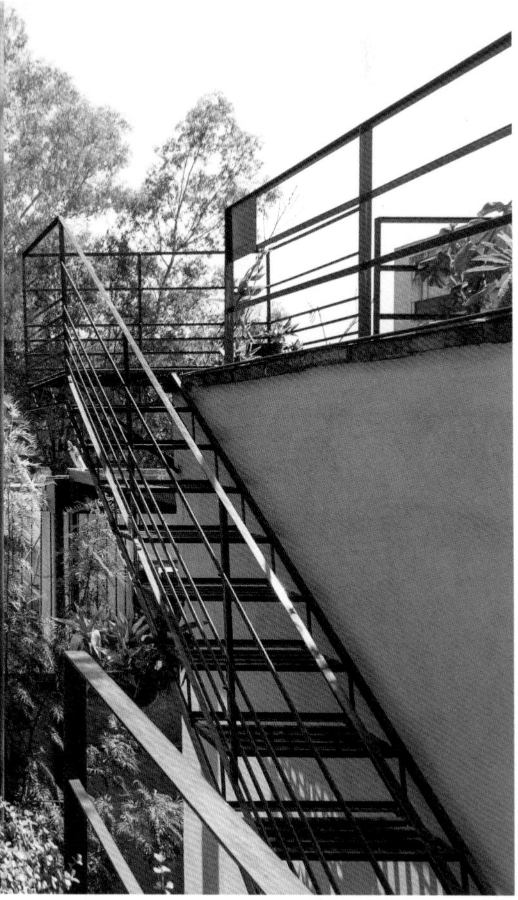

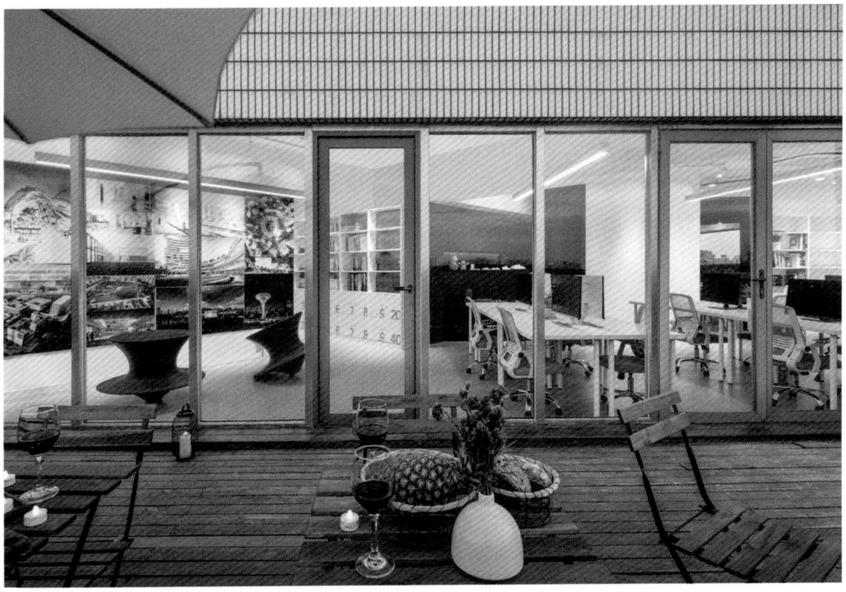

Area:
5,382 square feet (500 square meters)

Completion:
2019

Design:
L&M Design Lab

Photography:
Hu Yijie

Shanghai, China

L&M Design Lab

L&M's new office is located in an apartment in a 1990s residential neighborhood. With only two rooms and a dark patio, as well as poor lighting and ventilation, it was difficult to imagine it as a contemporary studio space.

Time tunnel

The solution to the dark, narrow layout was the introduction of a long, silver-colored space that brought lightness and vitality into the flat, invoking a feeling of dream and fantasy.

The mirrored vortex, designed to appear both modern and magical, connects the north and south of the flat, solving the lighting, ventilation, and scale problems in a single step.

The twisted stainless-steel surface allowed the light to be reflected multiple times indoors, increasing the illumination as well as creating a magical "time tunnel" experience. Meanwhile, introducing an open work area allowed for air flow through windows on both sides, which improved the indoor environment significantly.

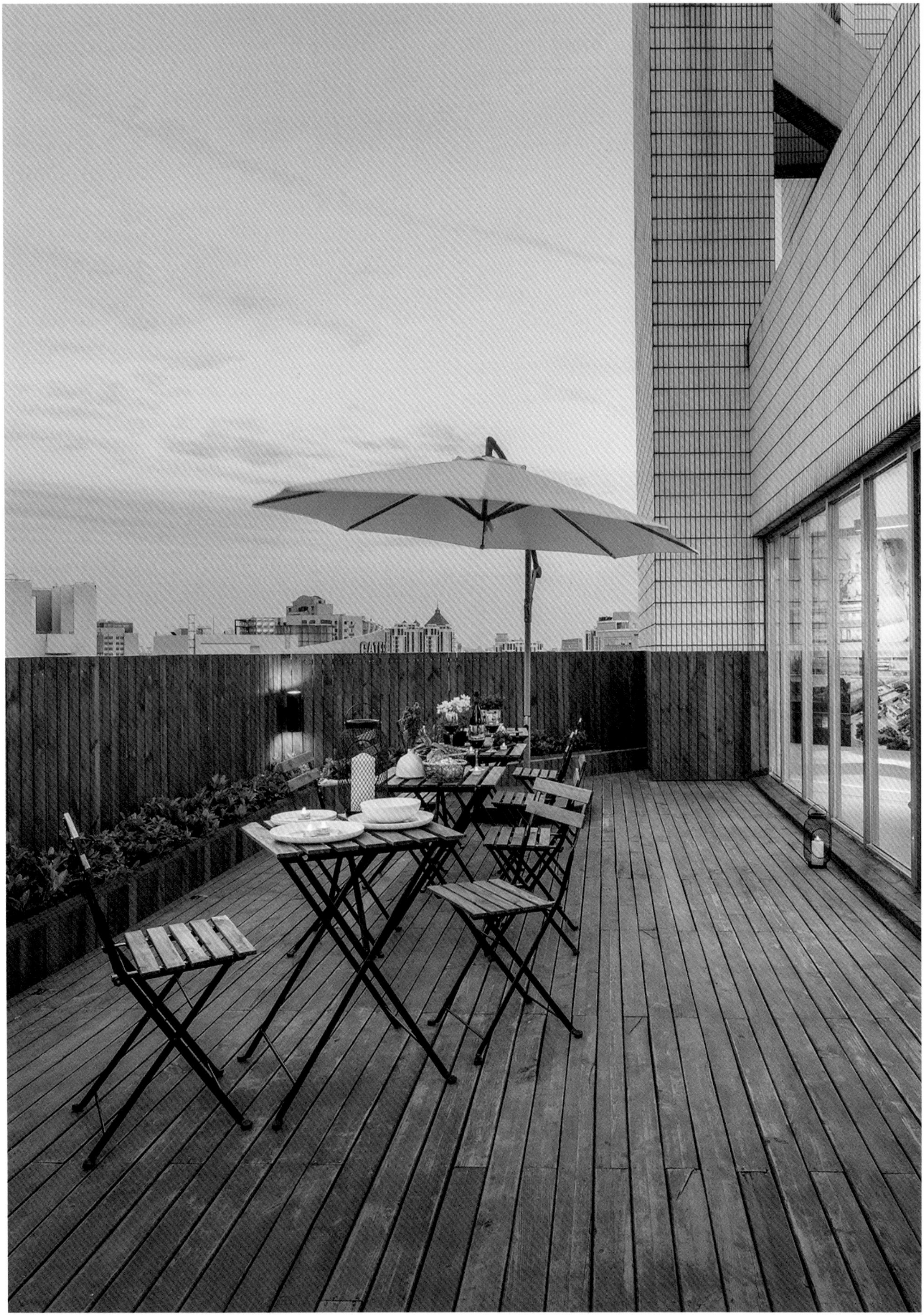

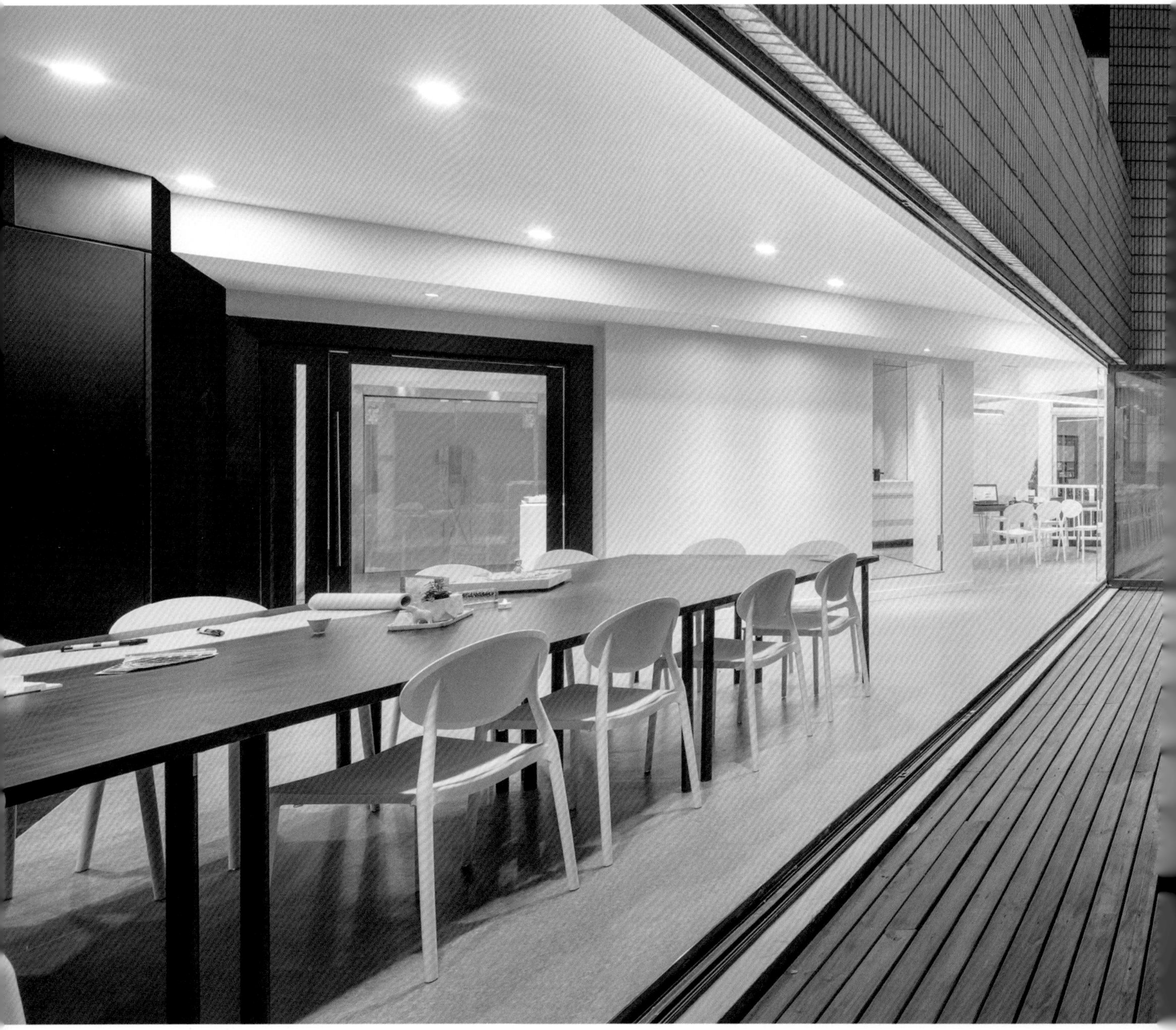

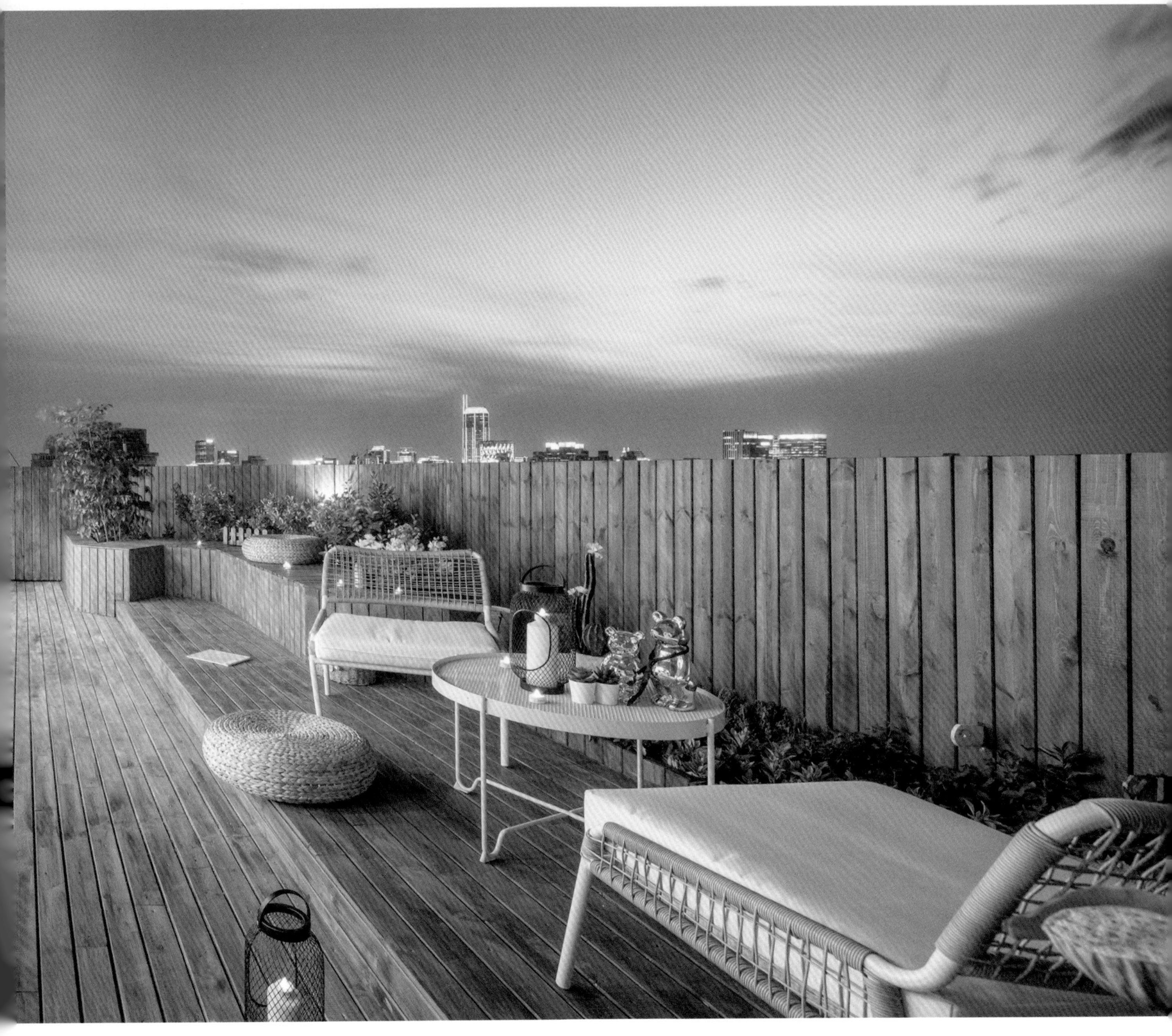

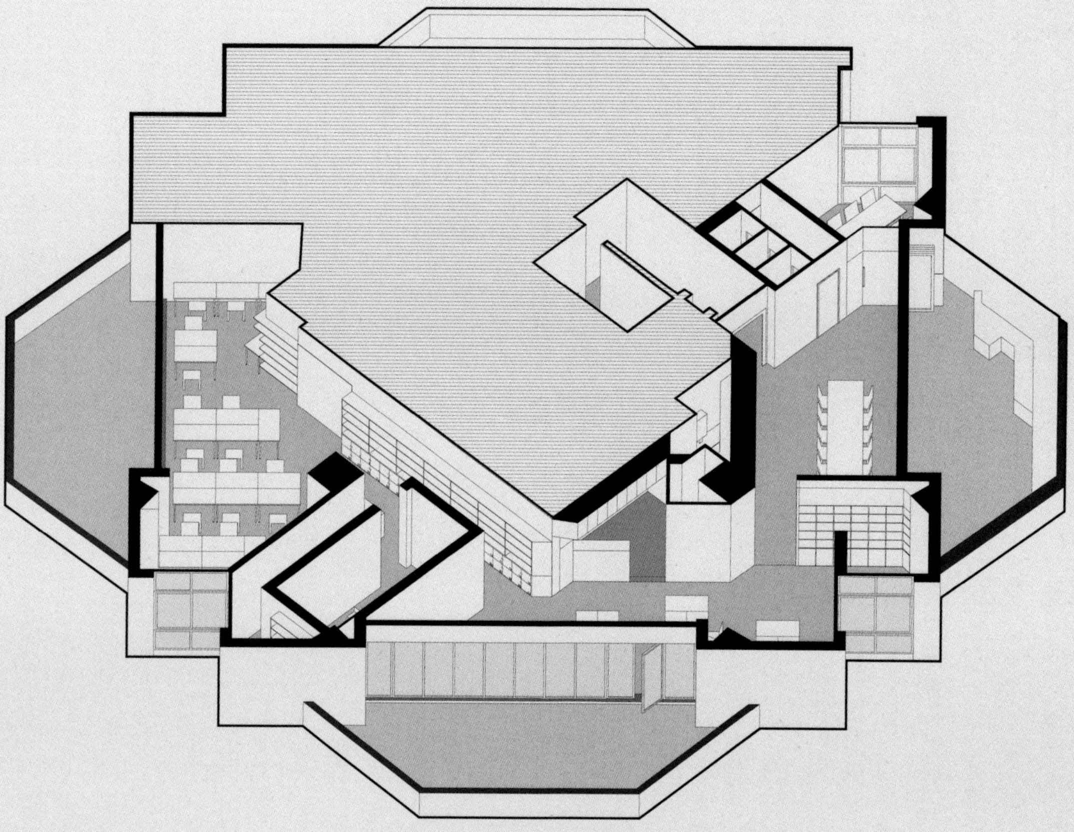

Axonometric drawing

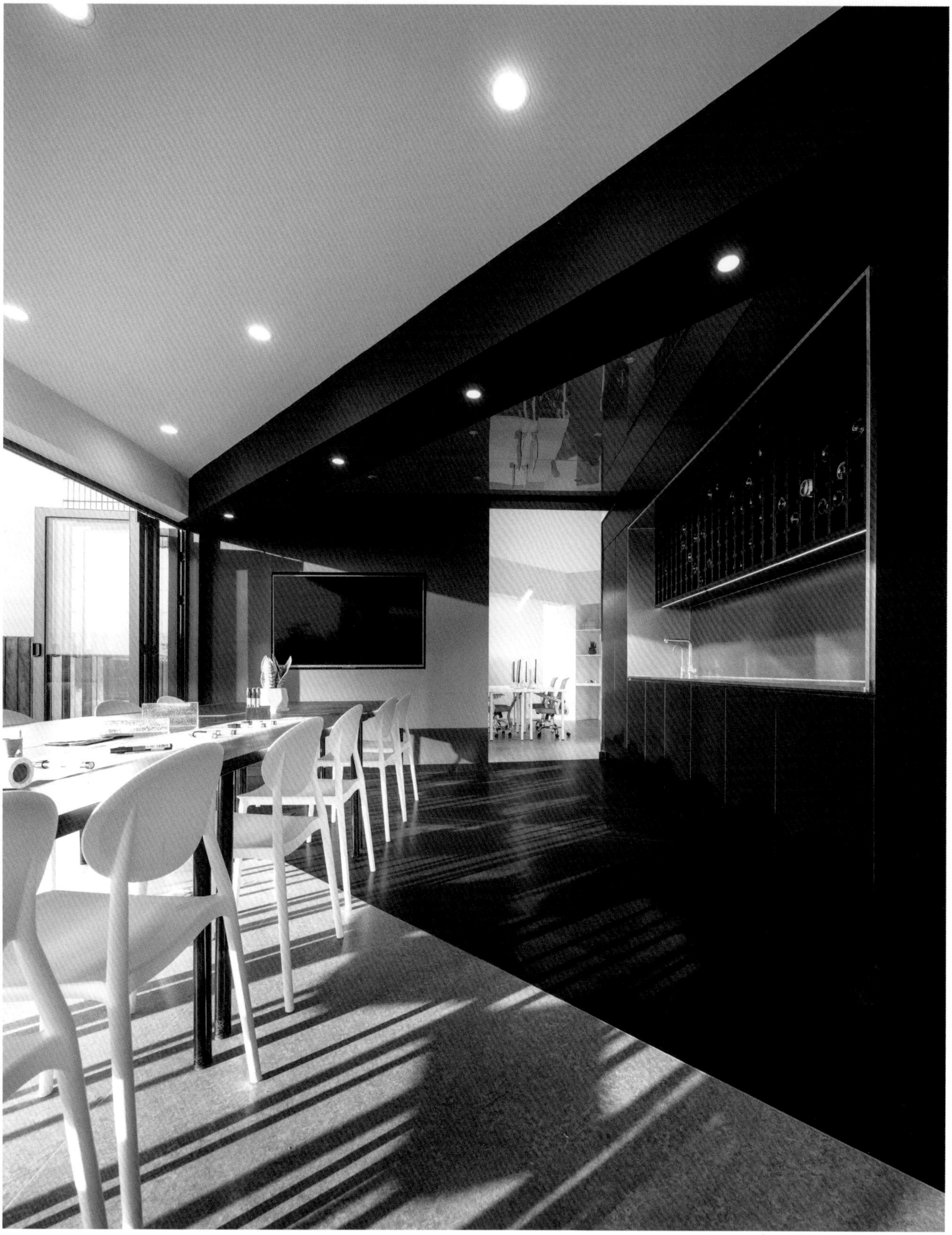

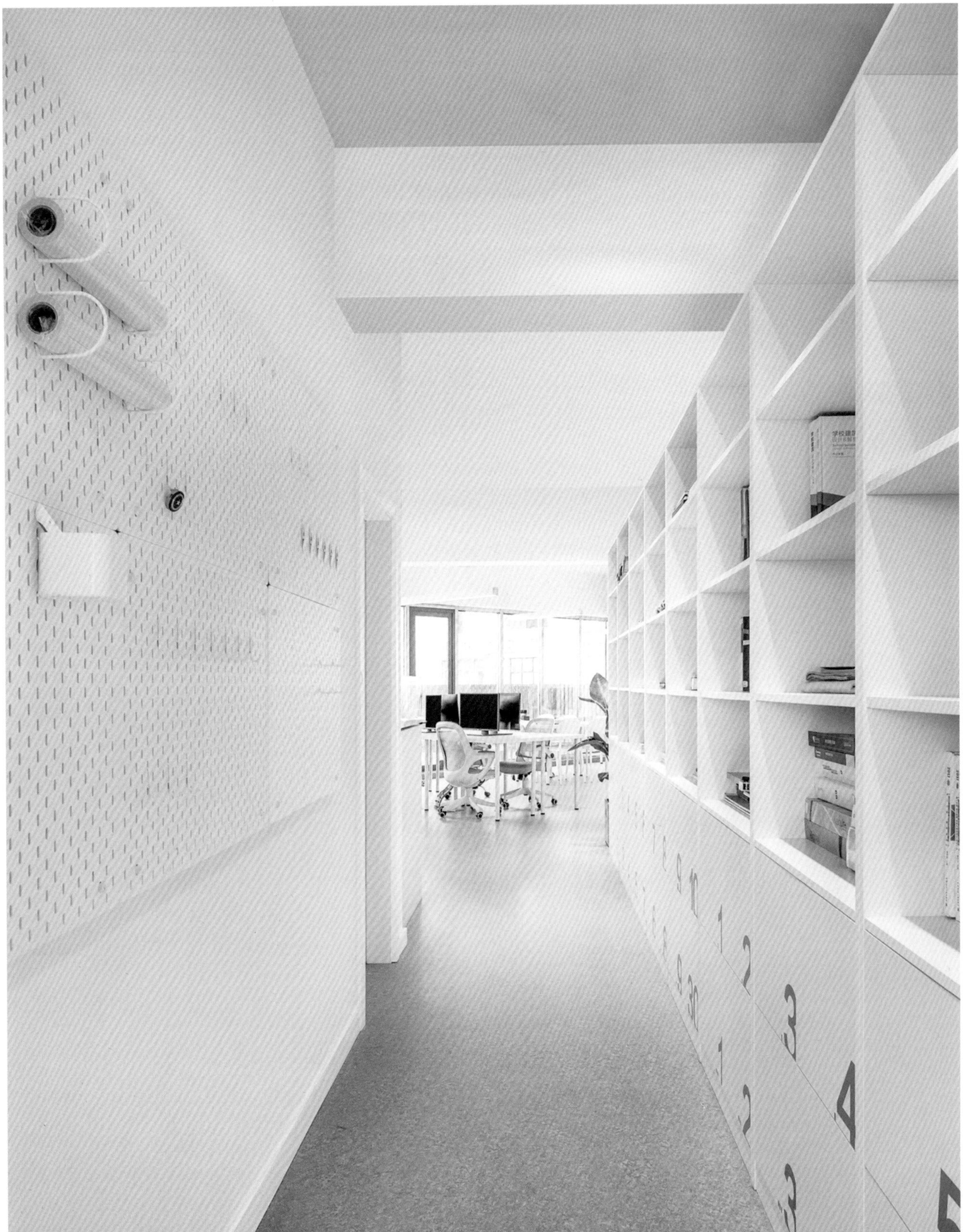

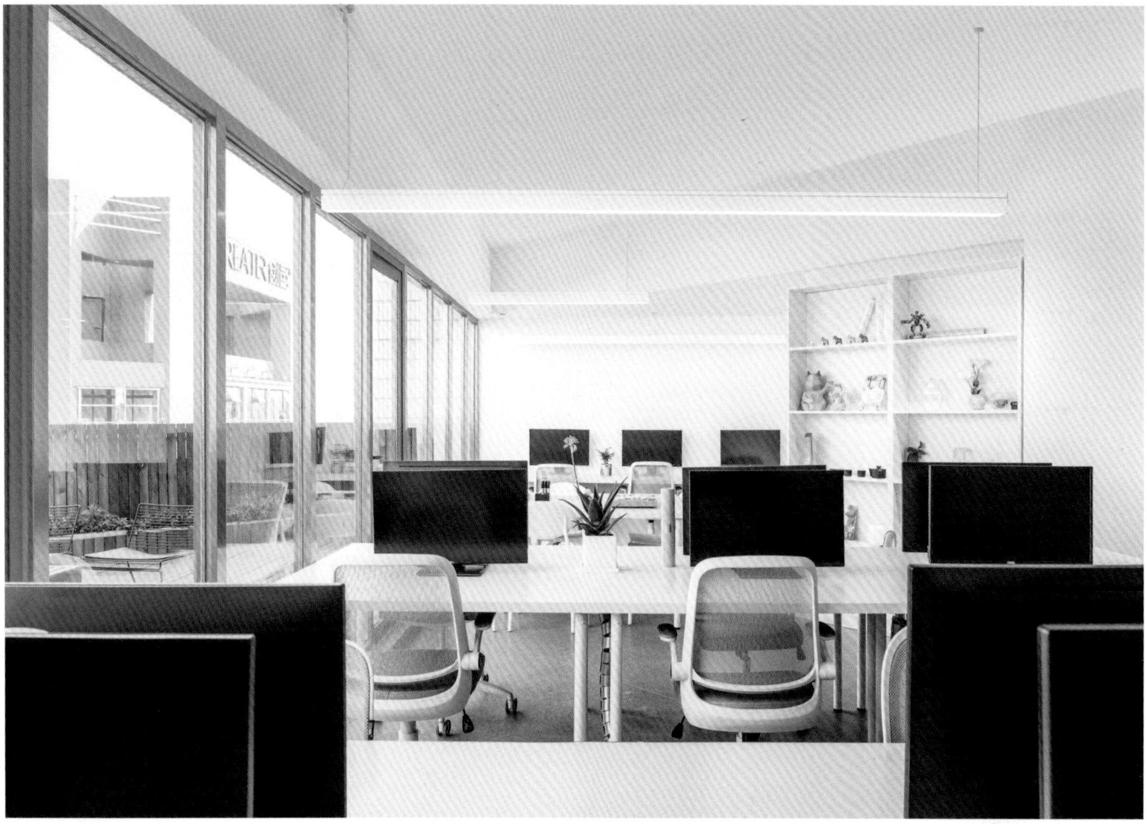

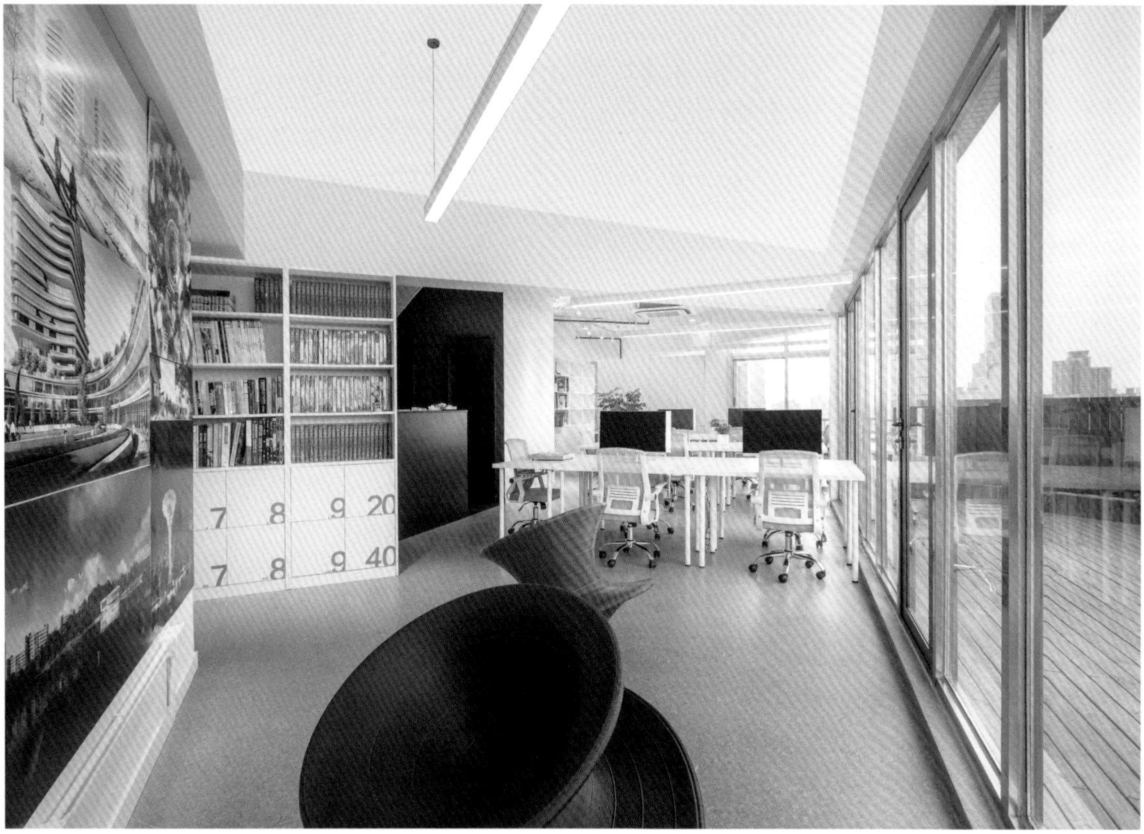

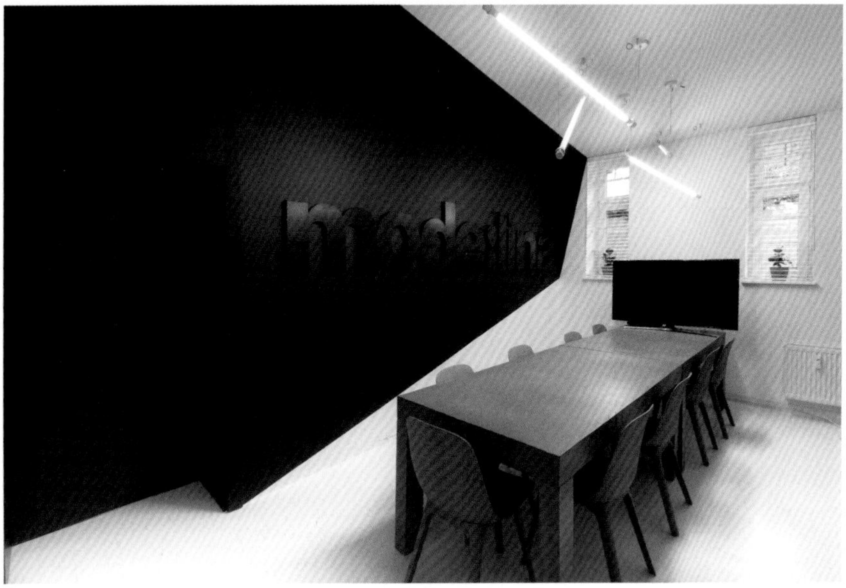

Area:
967 square feet (90 square meters)

Completion:
2017

Design:
mode:lina

Photography:
Patryk Lewiński

Poznań, Poland

mode:lina

With the growth of the studio and the arrival of new staff, mode:lina needed to increase its office space. The new premises were set up in a renovated townhouse situated in the trendy and fast-developing Poznań neighborhood.

Minimalism and dynamic lines

The new studio has a simple, minimalistic form with a monochrome palette, consistent with the visual identity system of mode:lina. The design of the workspace is based on two contrasting black and white areas.

The bright space is where the creative work takes place, with work areas for designers. Custom-designed large shared desks allow for an easy transition from individual to team work. It was important to find a way to hide electrical cords, which were placed inside the desks.

Dynamic diagonal lines separate the white part of the office from the black one. This is where the kitchen area and spacious storage units are. The units run along the length of the office and have enough room to hold all necessary equipment. Behind one of the doors lies a hidden bathroom with a shower, which is not noticeable at first glance.

Visual identity

To link the arrangement of the new office with the studio's visual identity system, the designers introduced large logotypes made of acoustic foam, which further increase the acoustic comfort of the space. In the conference room and entrance hall, awards and copies of publications on mode:lina's work have been displayed.

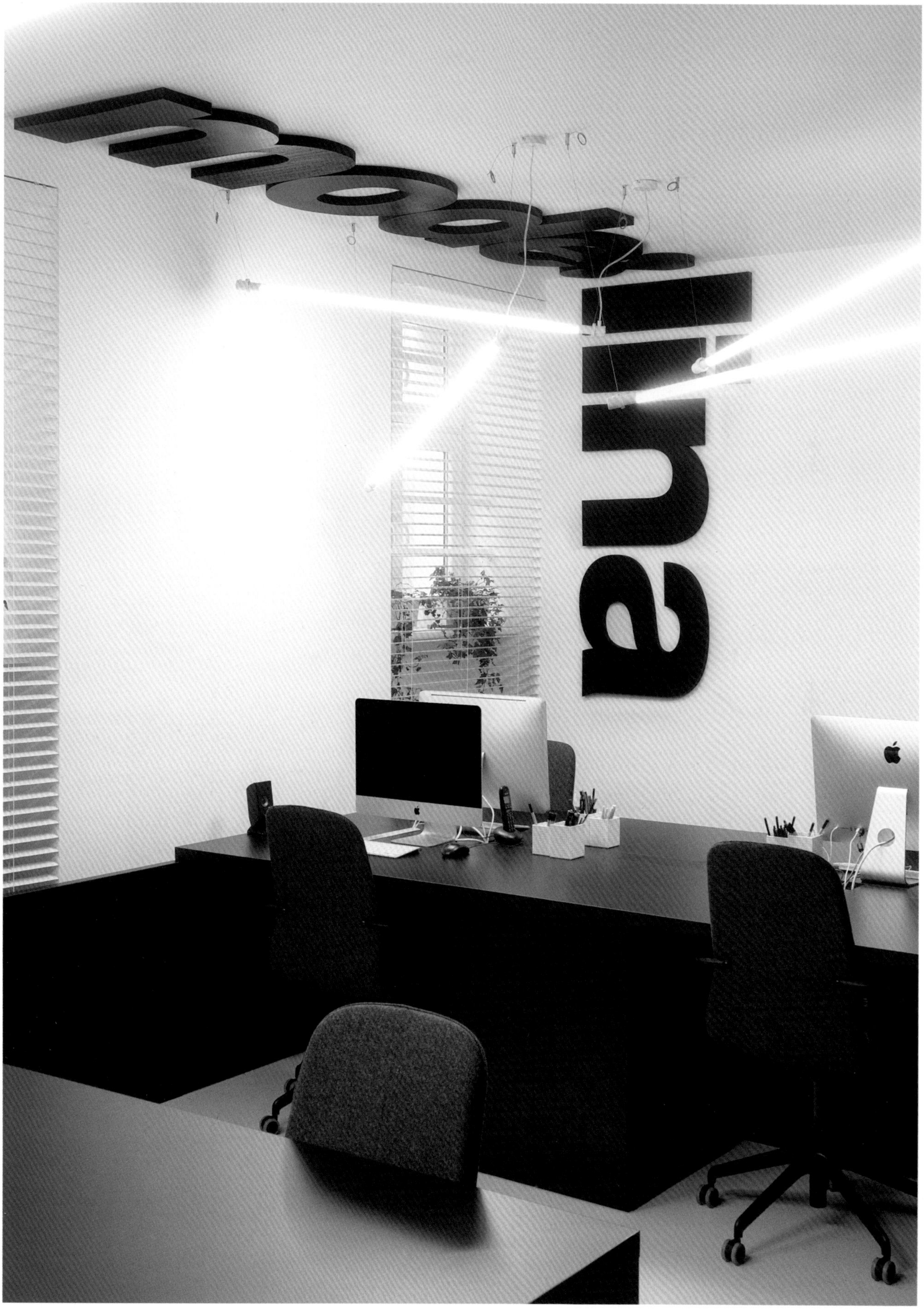

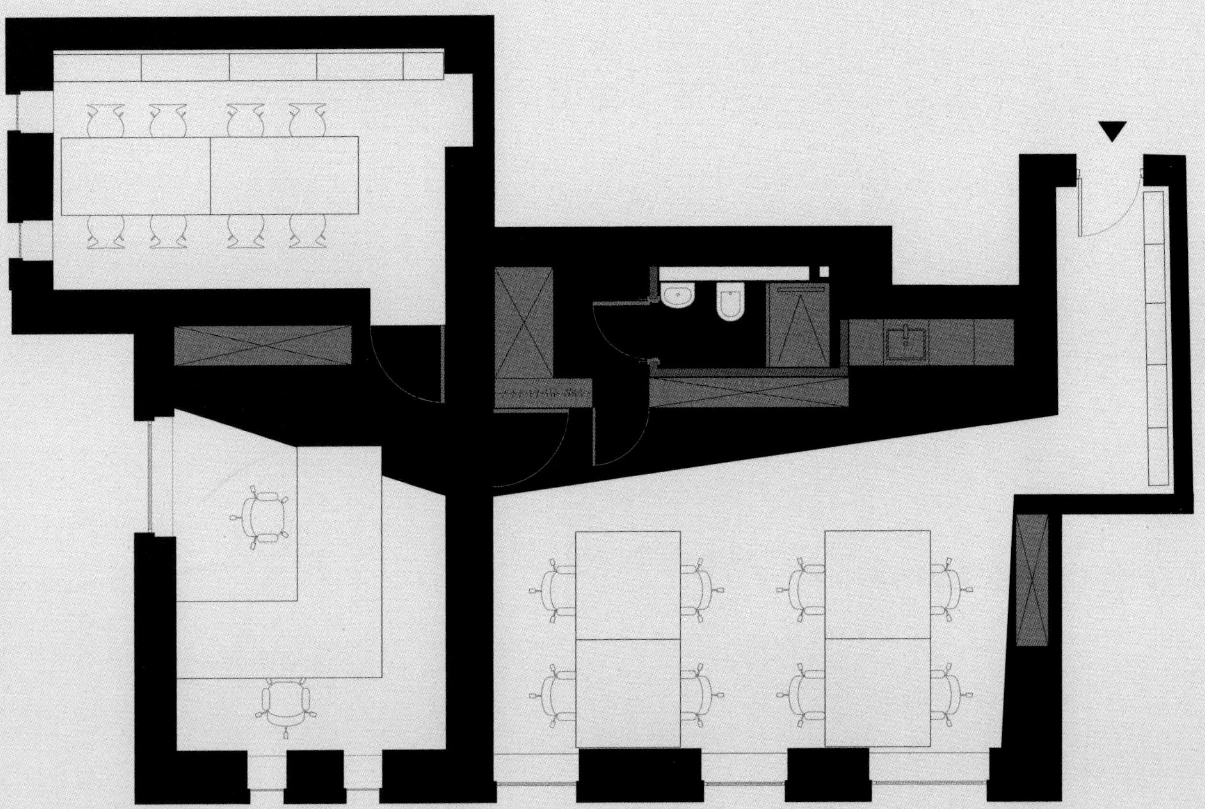

Floor plan

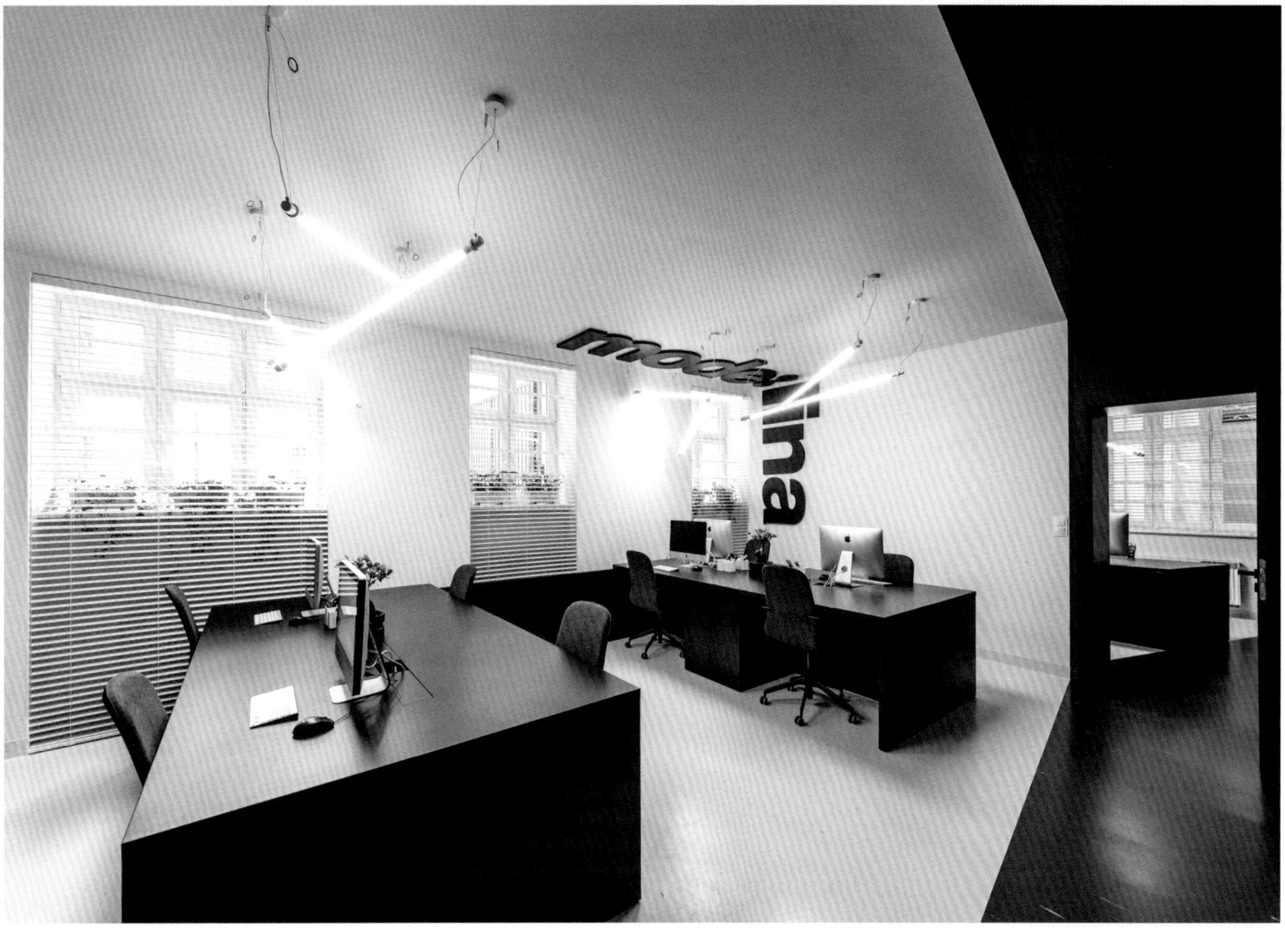

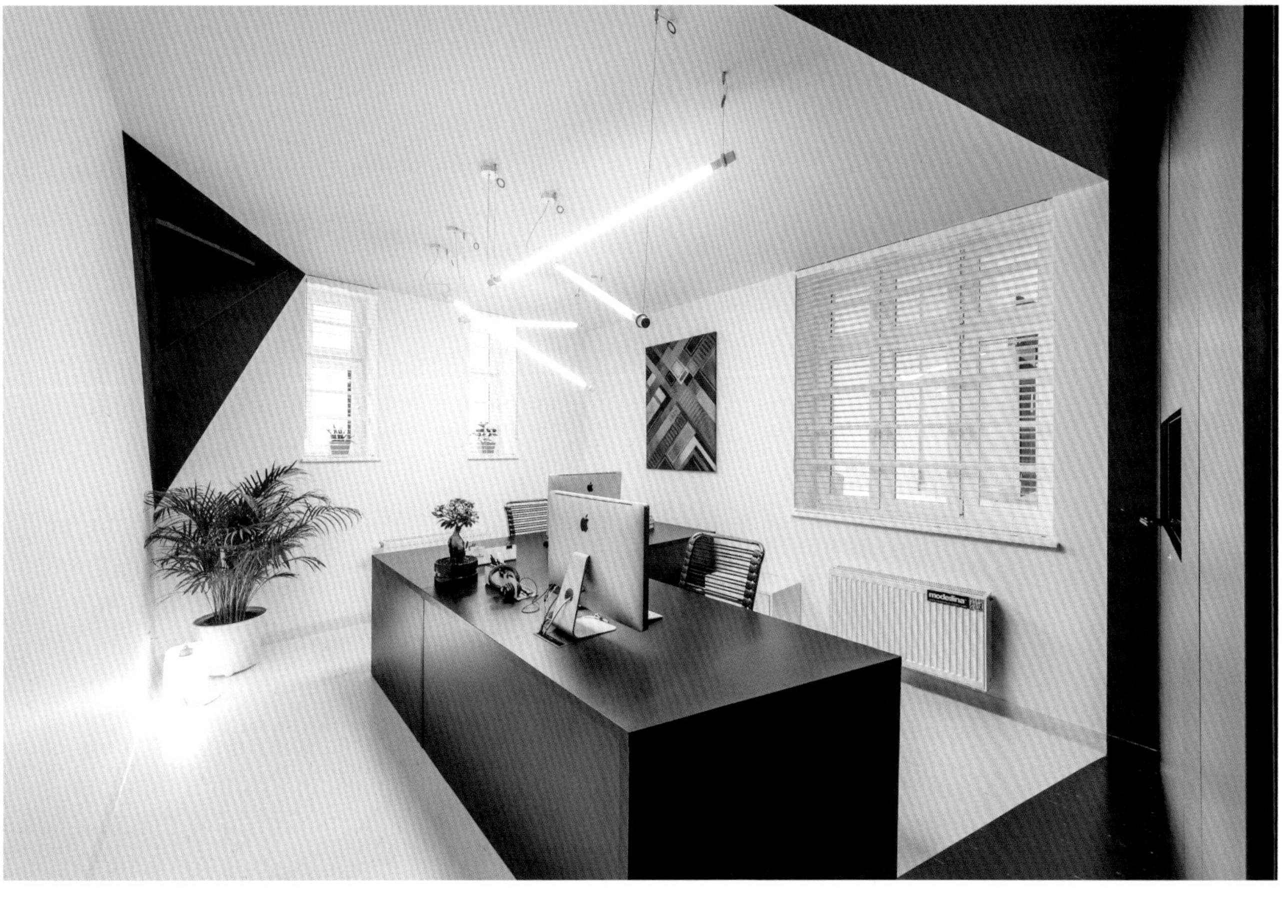
modelina

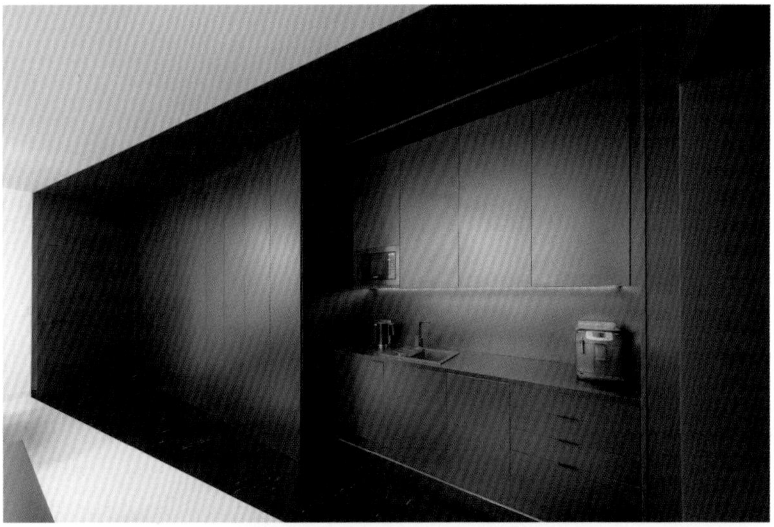

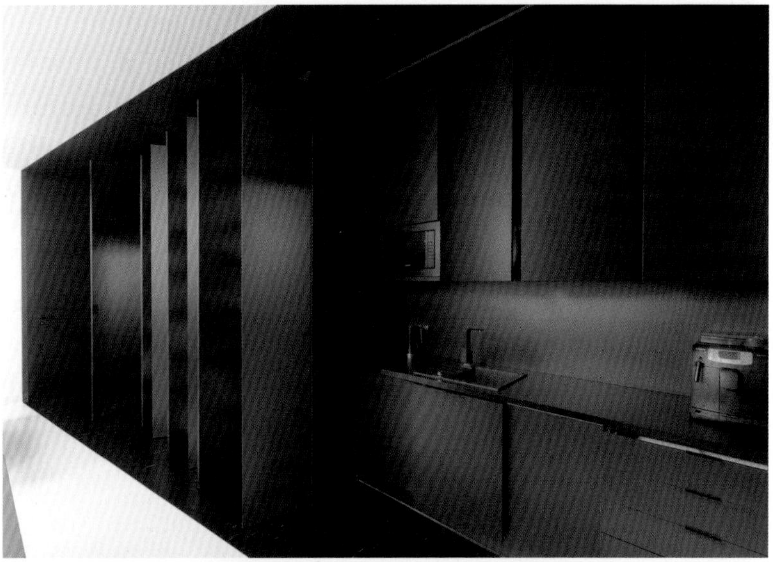

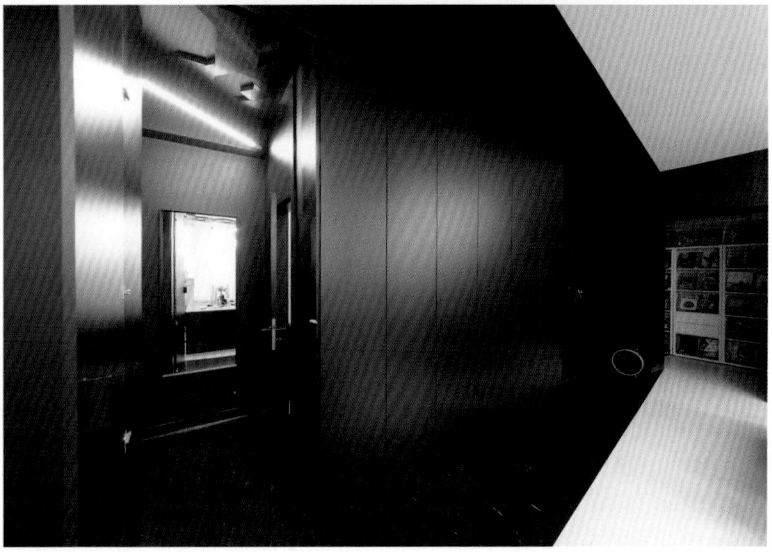

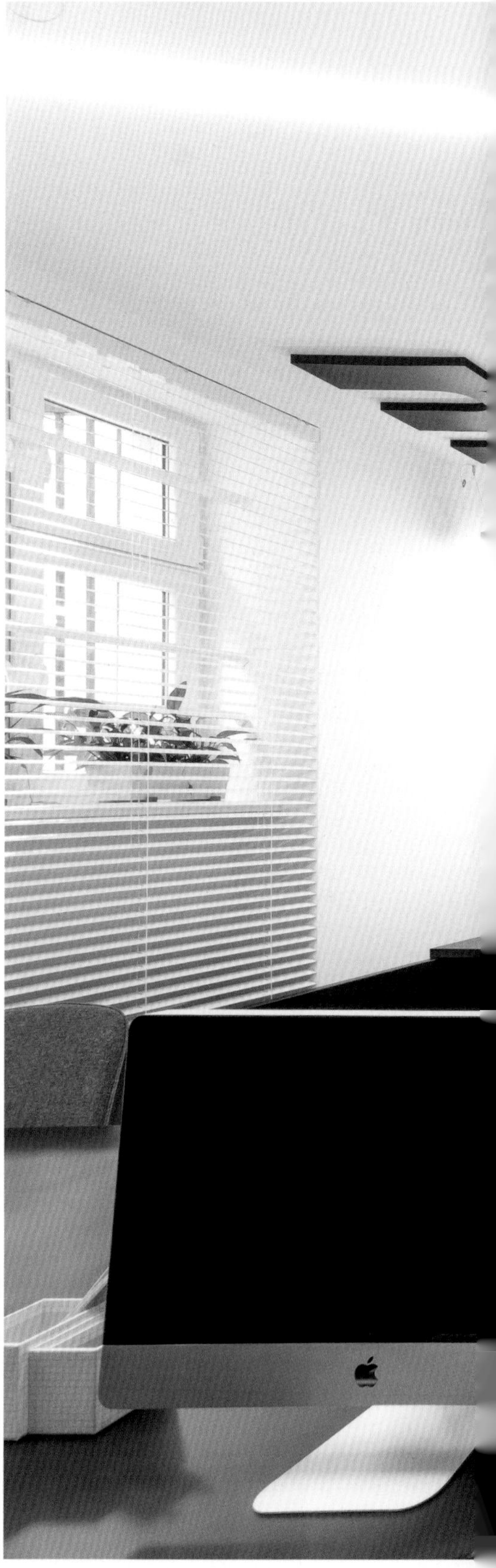

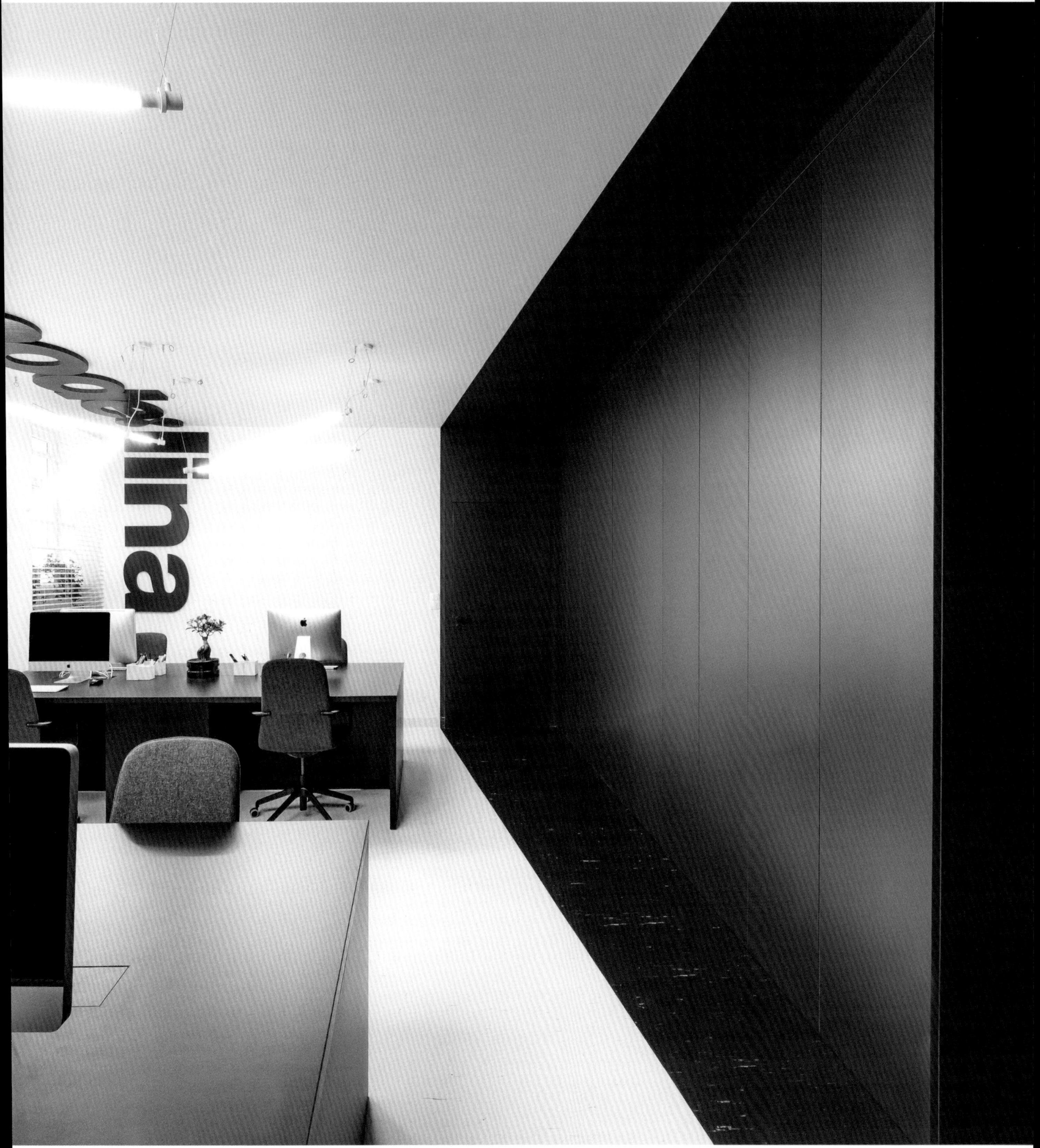

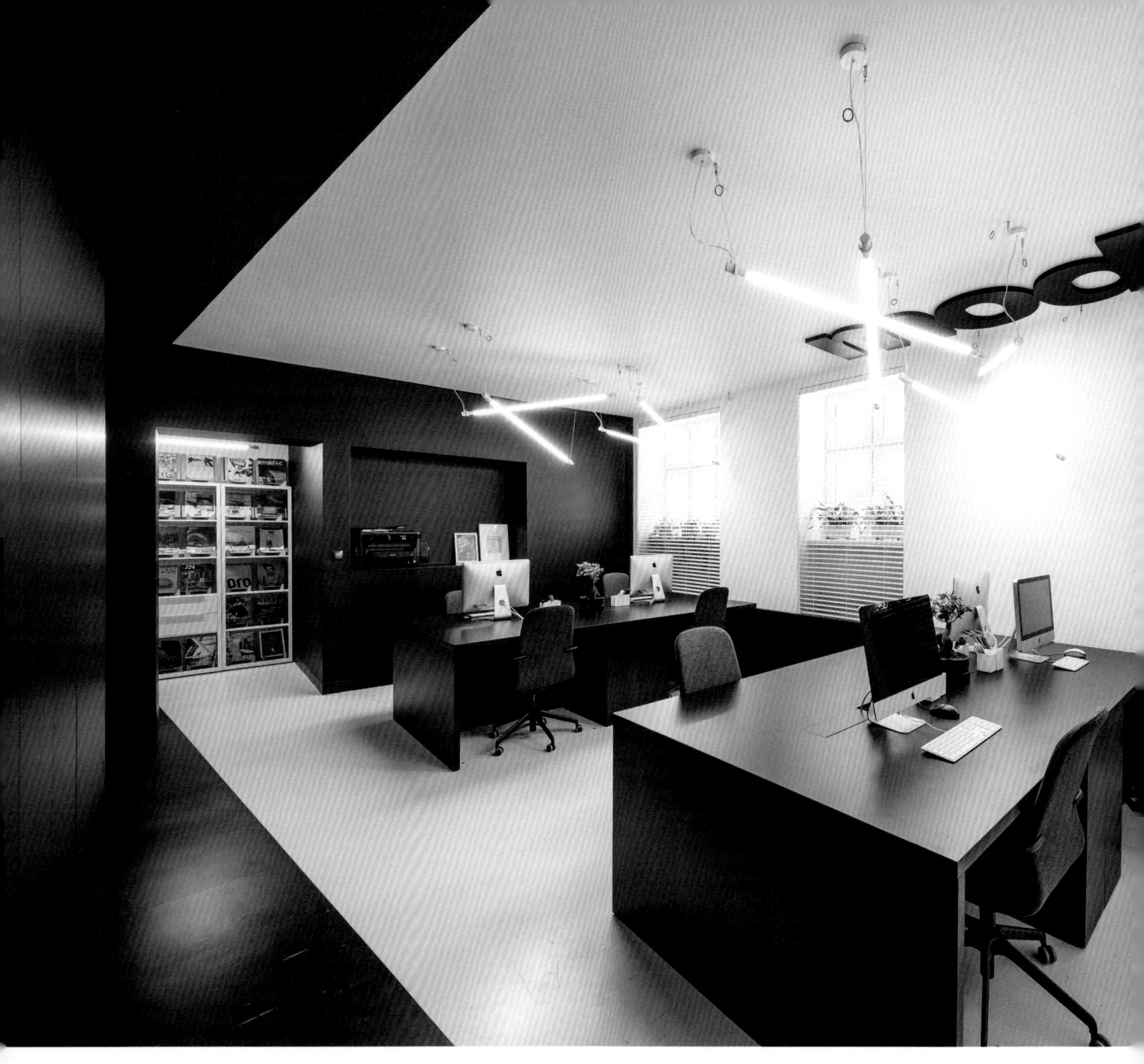

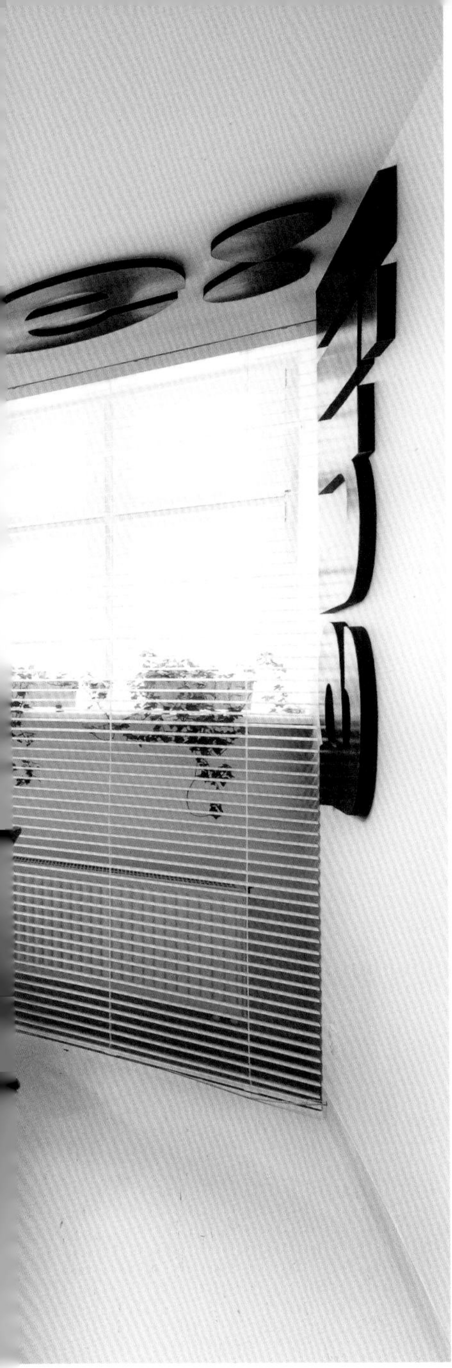

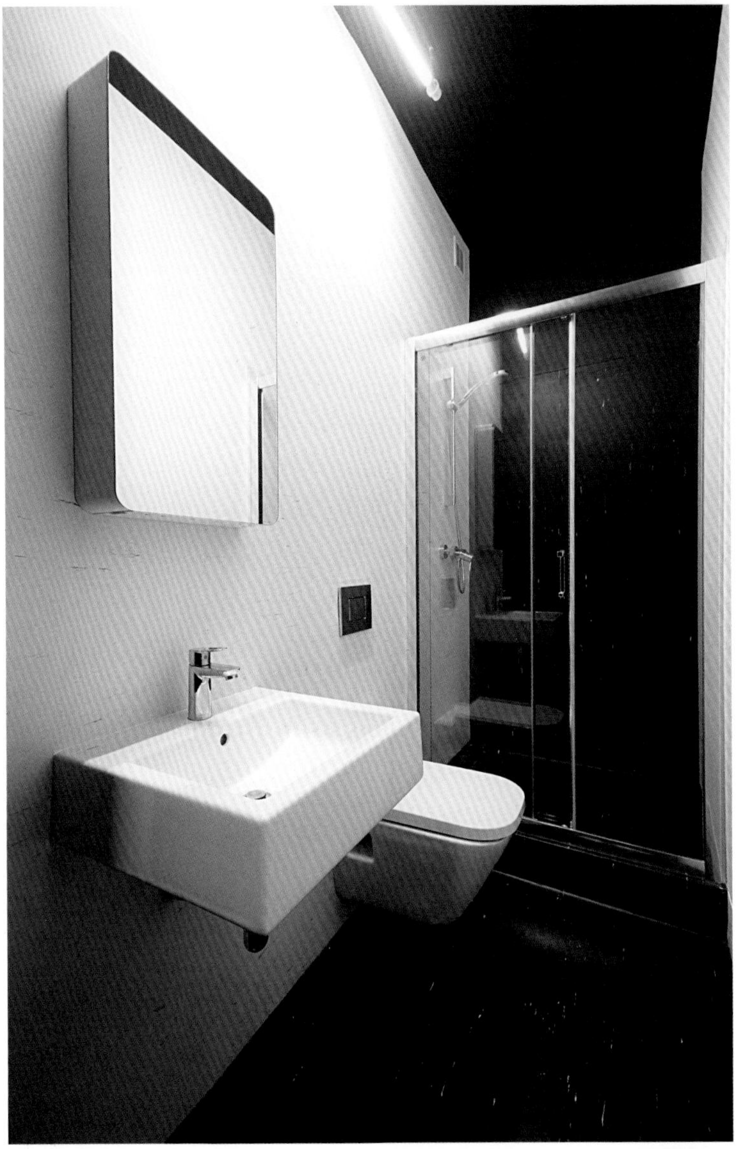

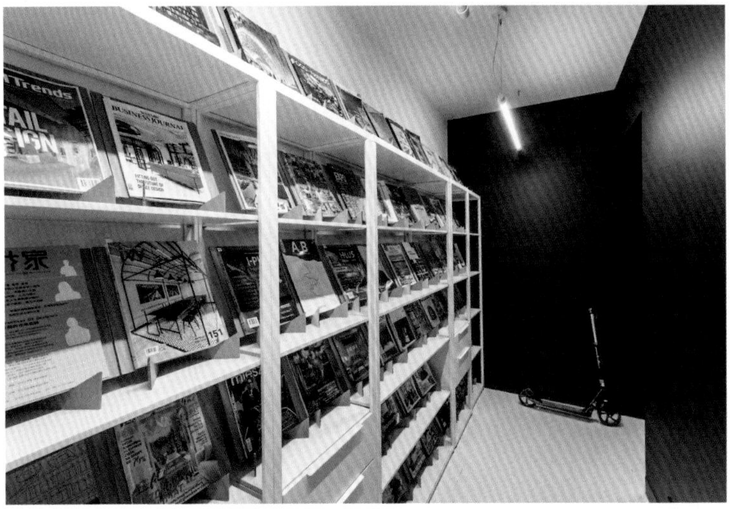

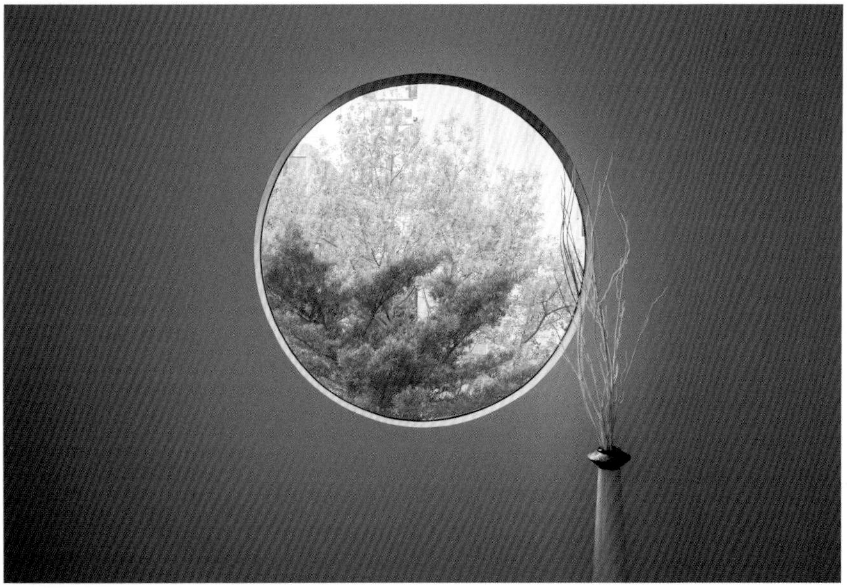

Area:
89 square meters (960 square feet)

Completion:
2017

Design:
Studio In2

Photography:
Jackal Liu

Taiwan, China

Studio In2

The goal for this design was to construct the best space for creative work. Starting with the notion that two thirds of our time is spent working, while one third is spent resting and generating inspiration and creativity for further work, the designers transferred these ratios to the space itself, designing two thirds of the space as a work area, with the other third of the space serving as a place of inspiration.

A blank canvas

The creative space resembles a blank white canvas, where any color can be freely expressed; its simple white elements provide flexibility for change. In addition, designers took advantage of the conditions of the site itself, emphasizing links to outdoor scenery and natural sunlight.

Hints of the past

In order to reveal the original appearance of the forty-year-old traditional wooden windows, their paintwork was dissolved, and their surfaces were smoothed, adding an element of the unique original style of the space's location and preserving its heritage. In changing the layout of the space, a portion of the original wall was deliberately retained to prevent wasting building materials. By whitewashing the old wall, the mottled ceramic tiles and red brick walls were given a fresh face, a reminder of the relationship between the studio and the old building.

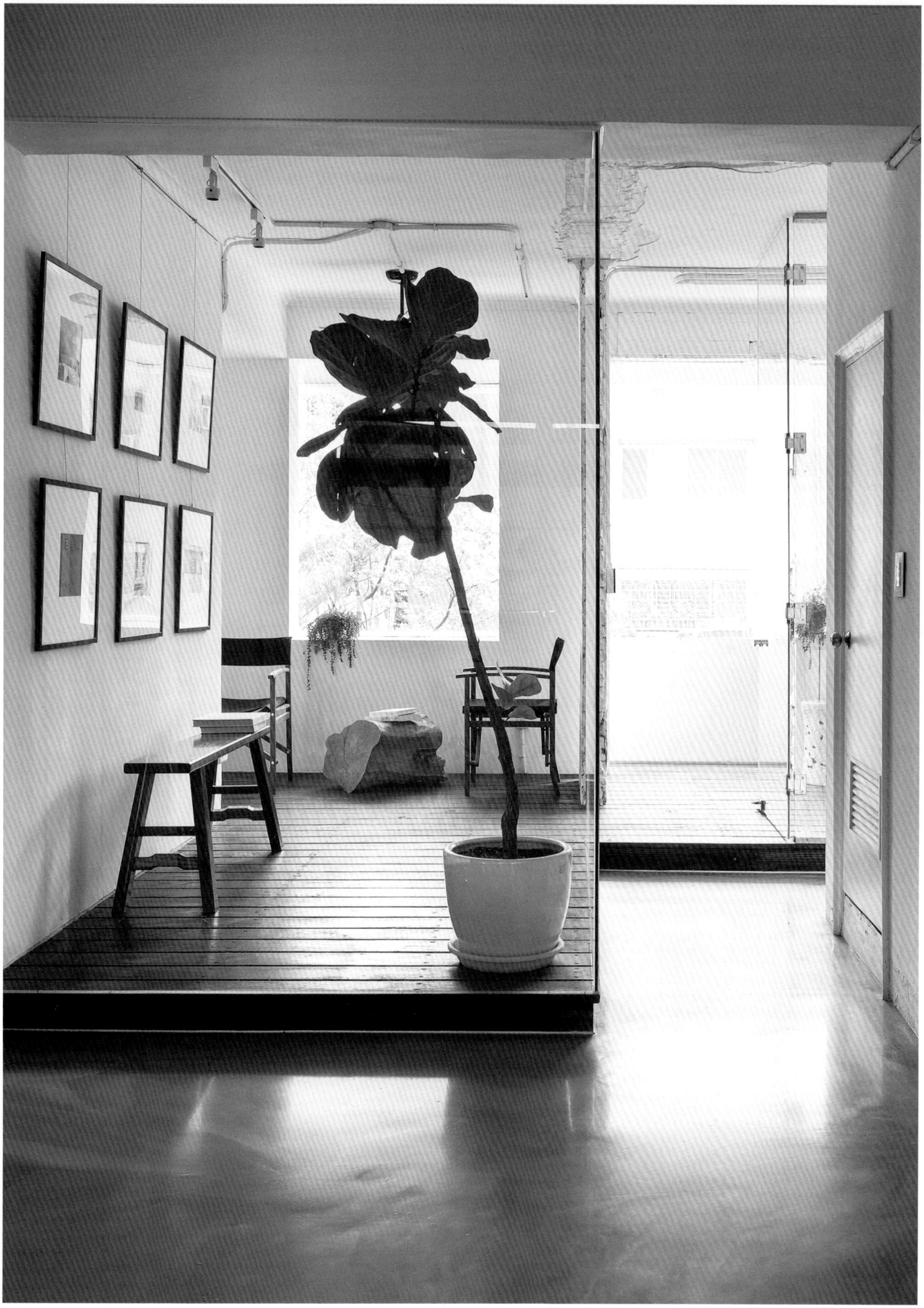

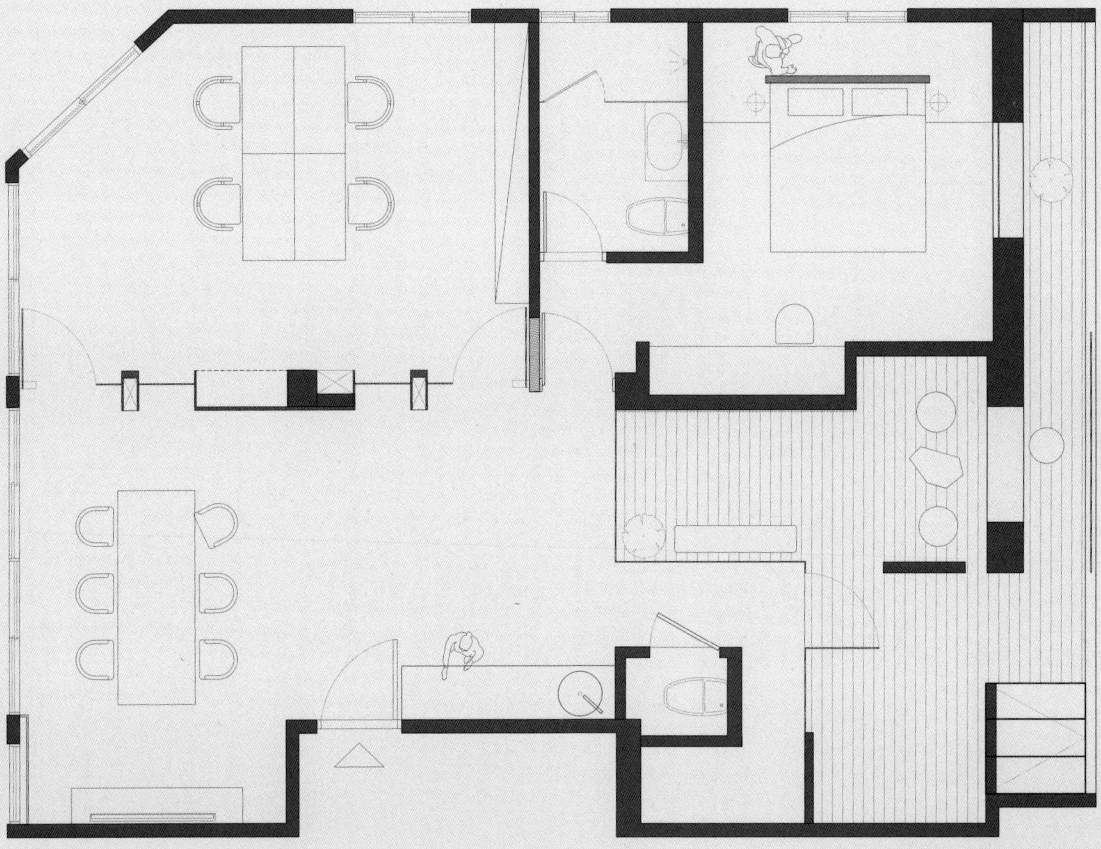

Floor plan

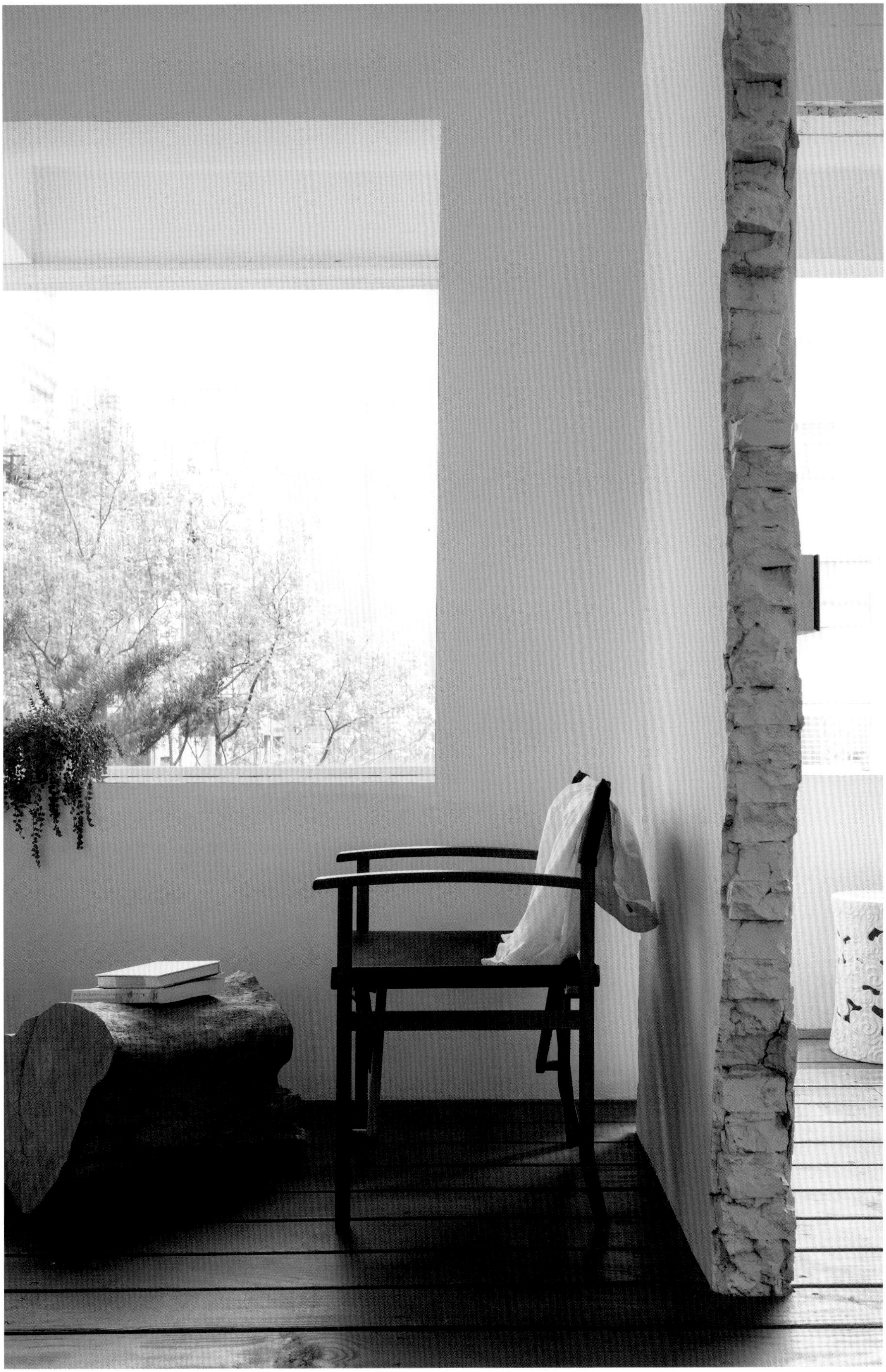

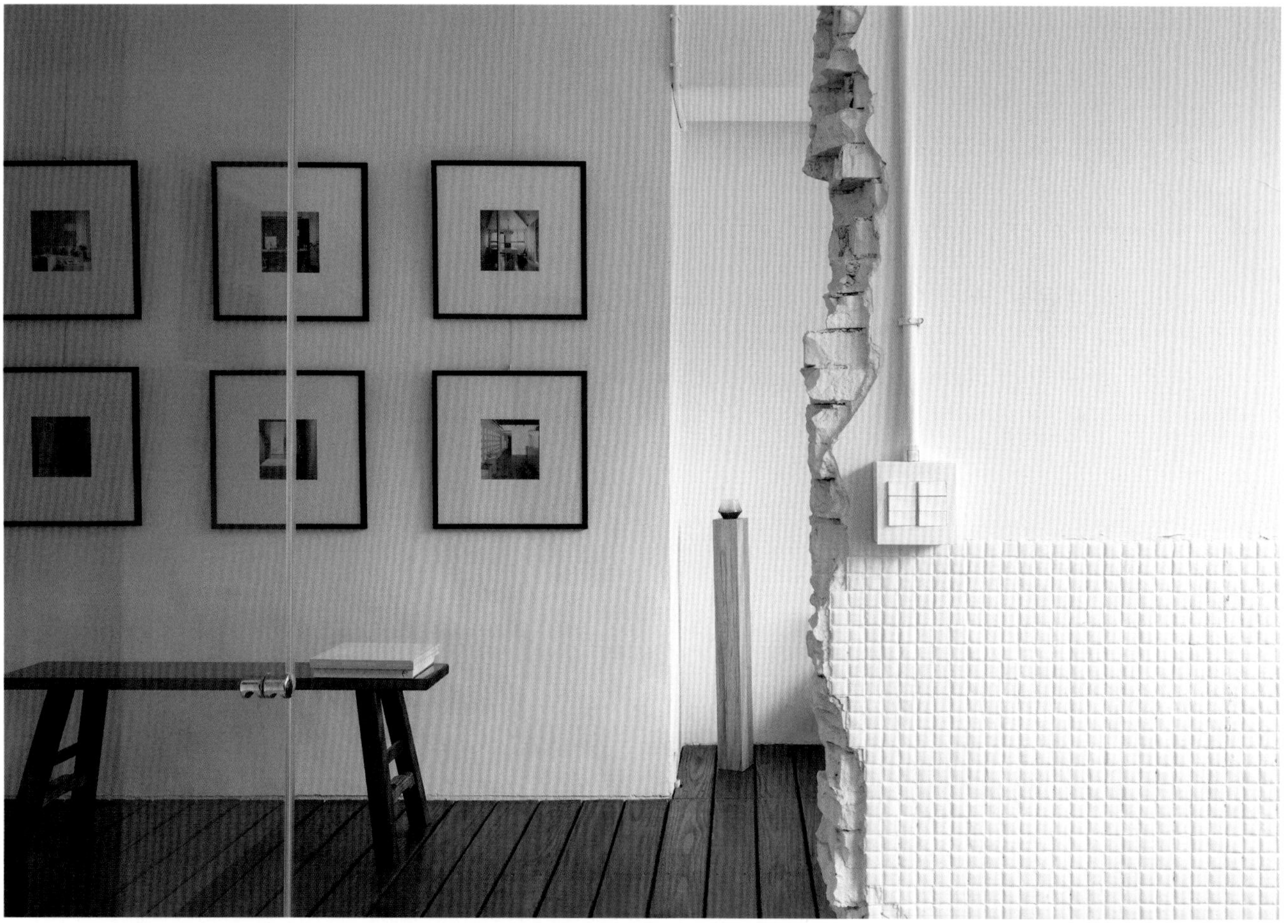

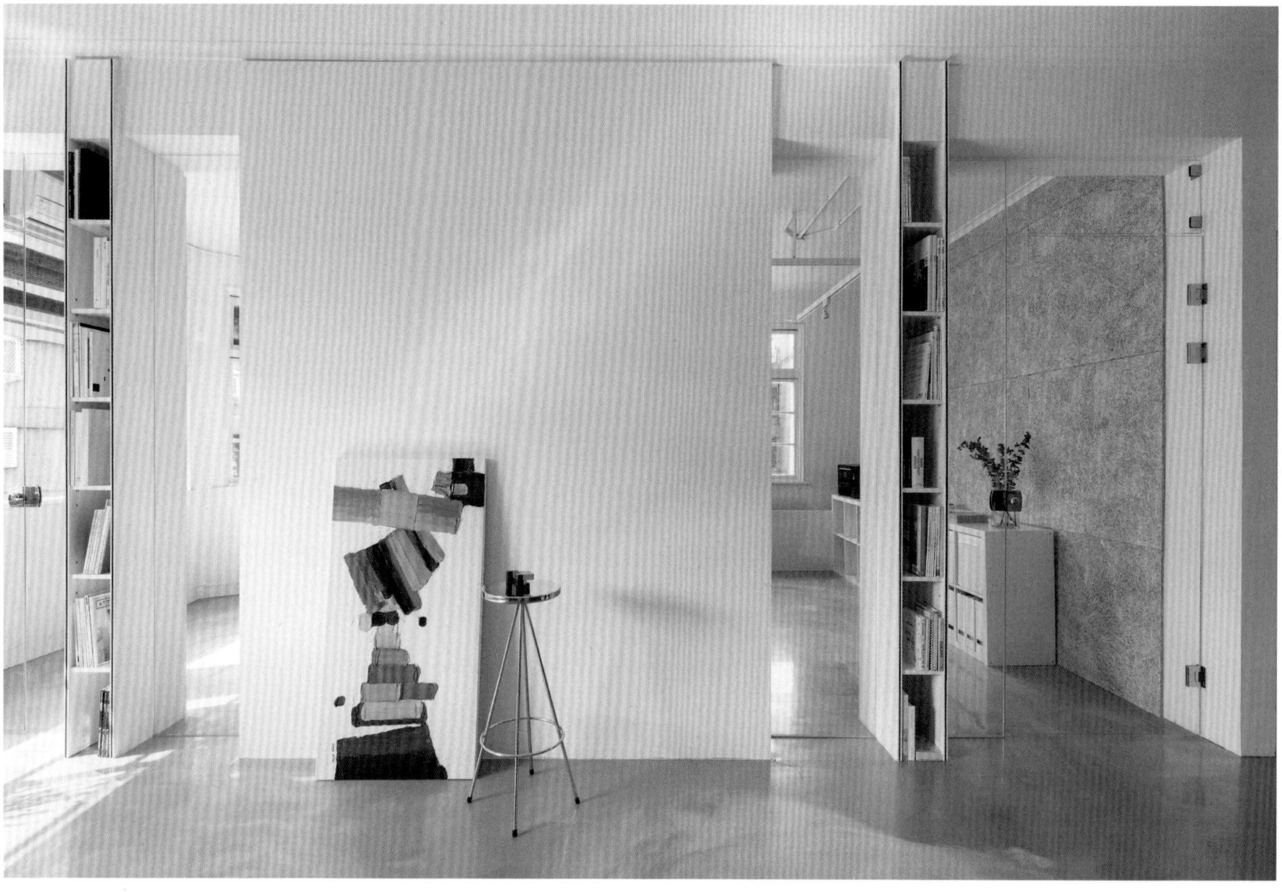

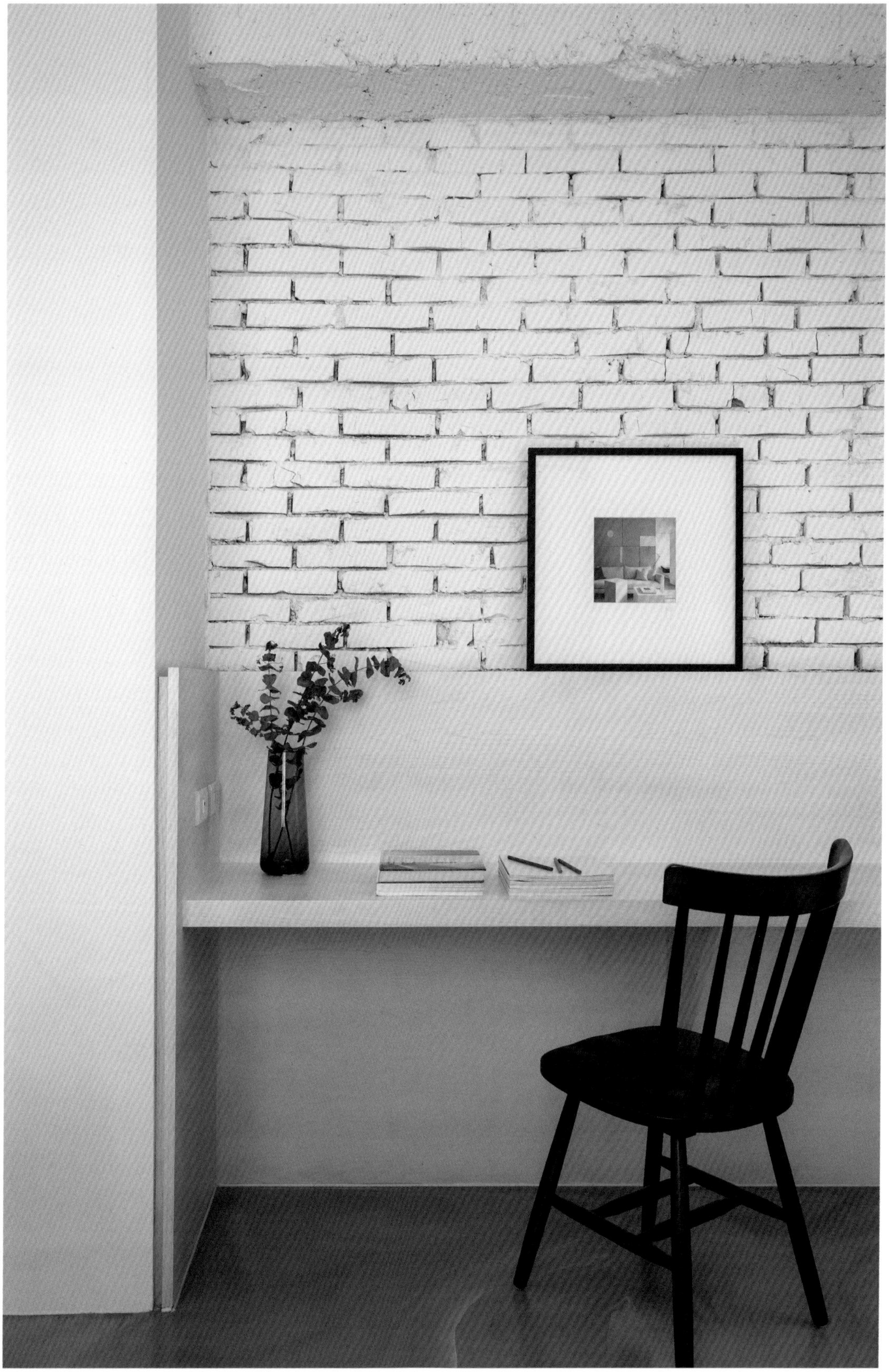

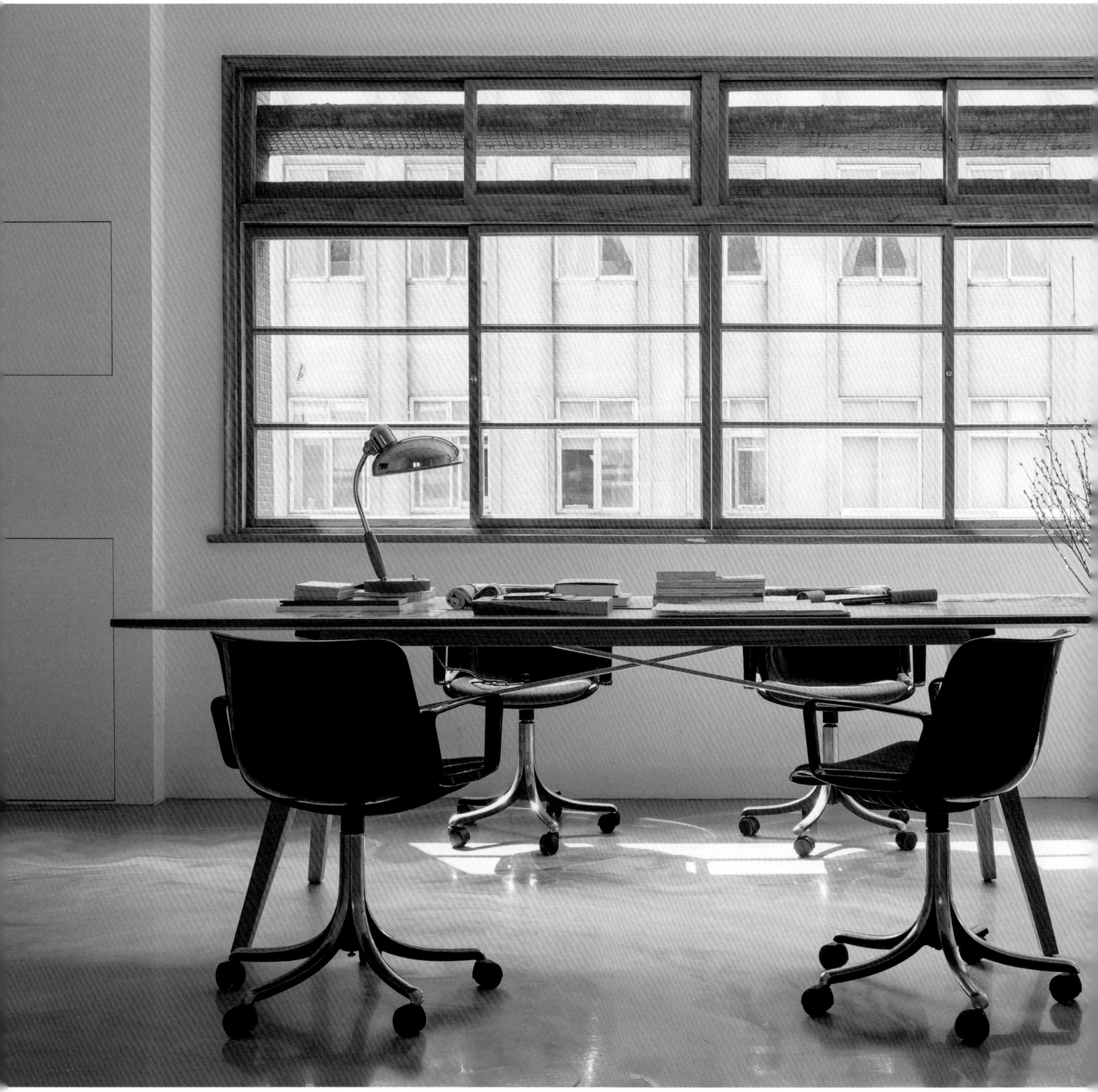

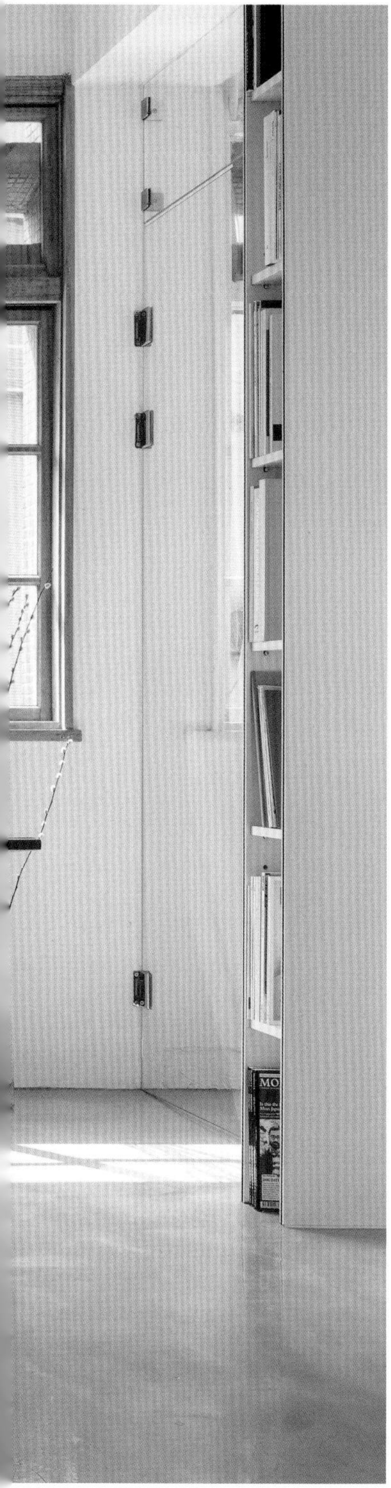

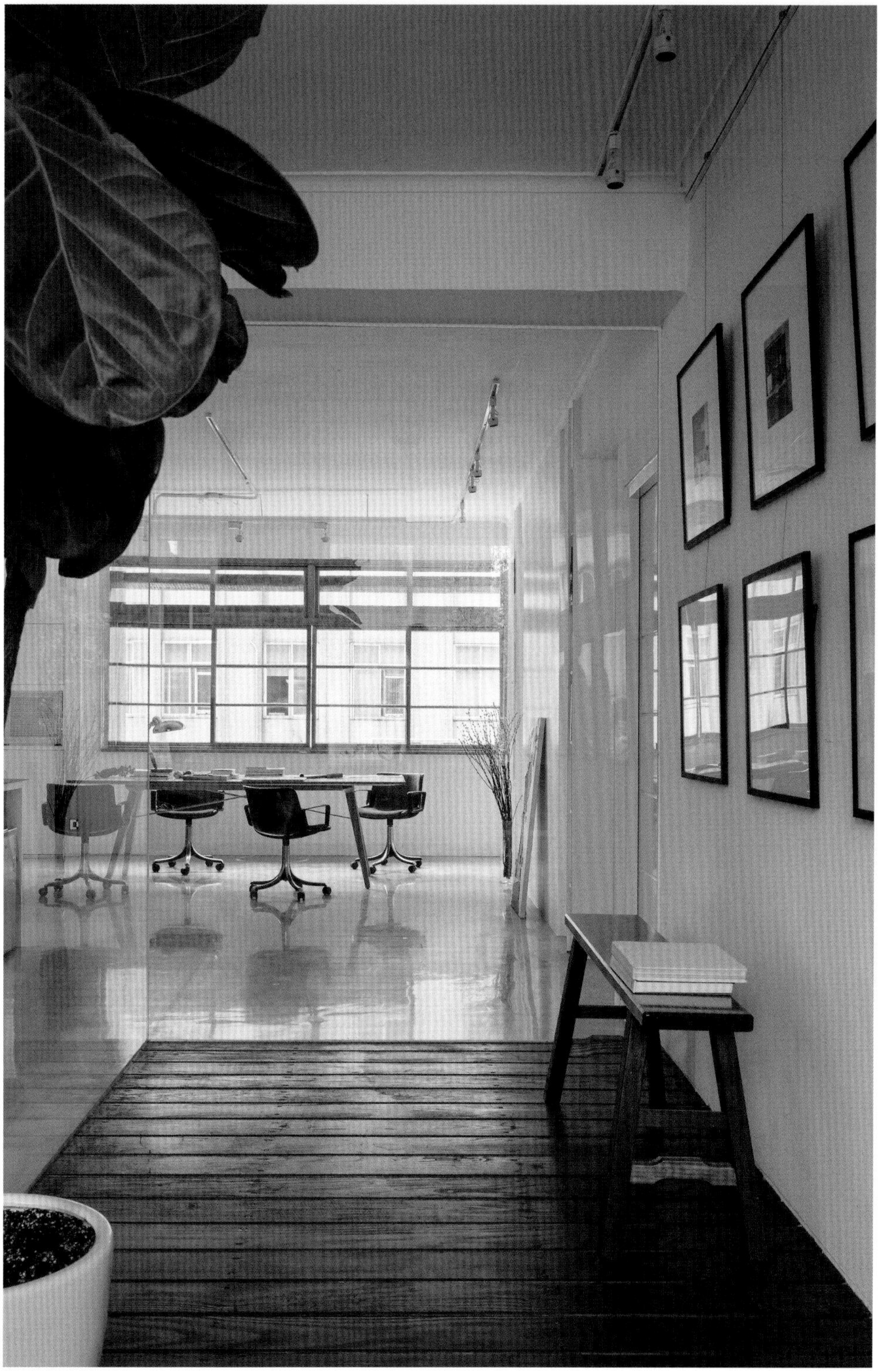

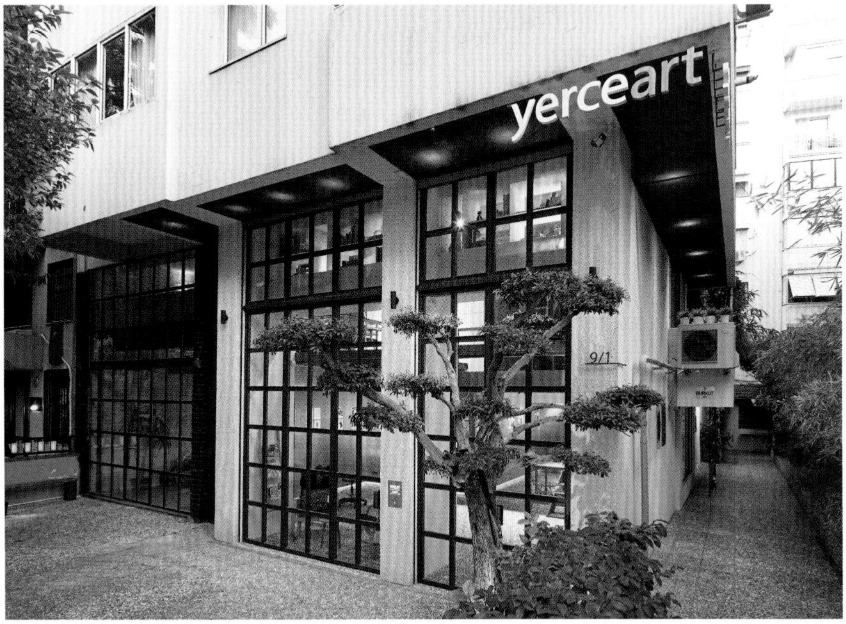

Area:
2,691 square feet (250 square meters)

Completion:
2016

Design:
Yerce Architecture & ZAAS

Photography:
Emin Emrah Yerce, Yerce Art Photography

İzmir, Turkey

Studio Loft

This is the story of the conversion of a regular, standard flat into a photography studio, private house, and art gallery. The apartment is located on a quiet street parallel to a busy boulevard in Alsancak, one of the most densely populated neighborhoods in İzmir.

Working, living and exhibiting

The brief was to design the ground floor and the upper floor of the apartment, part of a five-story housing block on a calm and green street, to be used as a photographic studio. During the design process, together with the client it was agreed upon that the space could go beyond being just a photographic studio. The client, a well-known photographer in İzmir, had initially wanted a place of his own where he could live and work, but the idea of integrating an exhibition area into this space was quickly embraced. While enabling his studio to exhibit and share the photographic work that it produces, this space would also host other photography exhibitions and become an alternative art exhibition spot in the city.

Maximizing the creative space

The plan was for the ground floor to be used as a photographic studio and exhibition space, while the upper floor was designed to have the office space, kitchen area, sleeping area, and private resting zones. However, one of the important targets of the project was to maximize the creative space for the photographic studio, and so during the design process the upper floor and mezzanine were designed to serve as spaces for photo shoots if needed. In this way, the project turned into a "loft" space where working, living, and exhibiting functions intertwined with each other under the roof of a photographic studio.

The designers grappled with questions such as how to transform a space that was constructed and used initially as a standard apartment into a multifunctional area, how permeability within these functions could be established, and how the flow of life and space could be carried out in such a place.

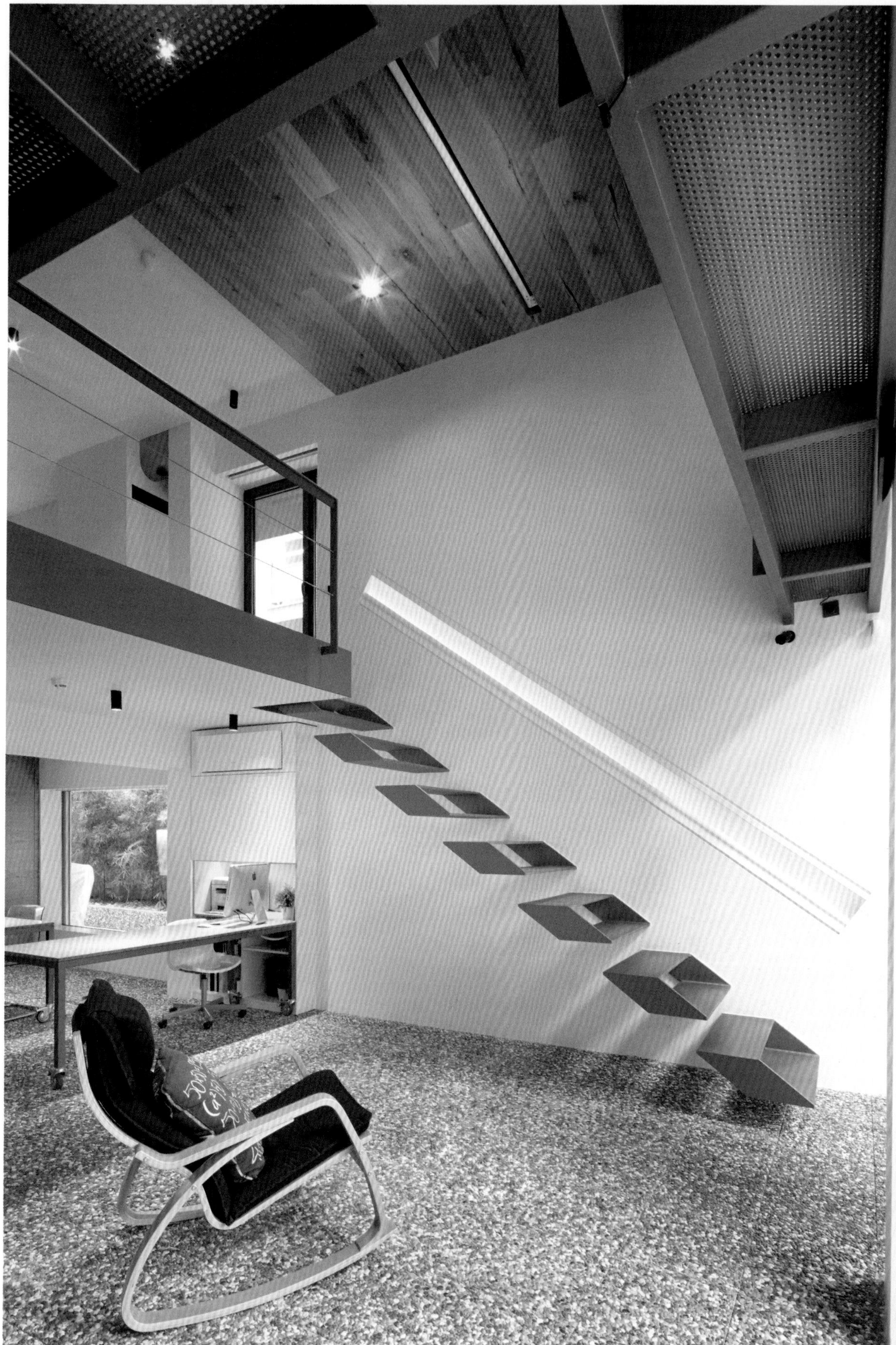

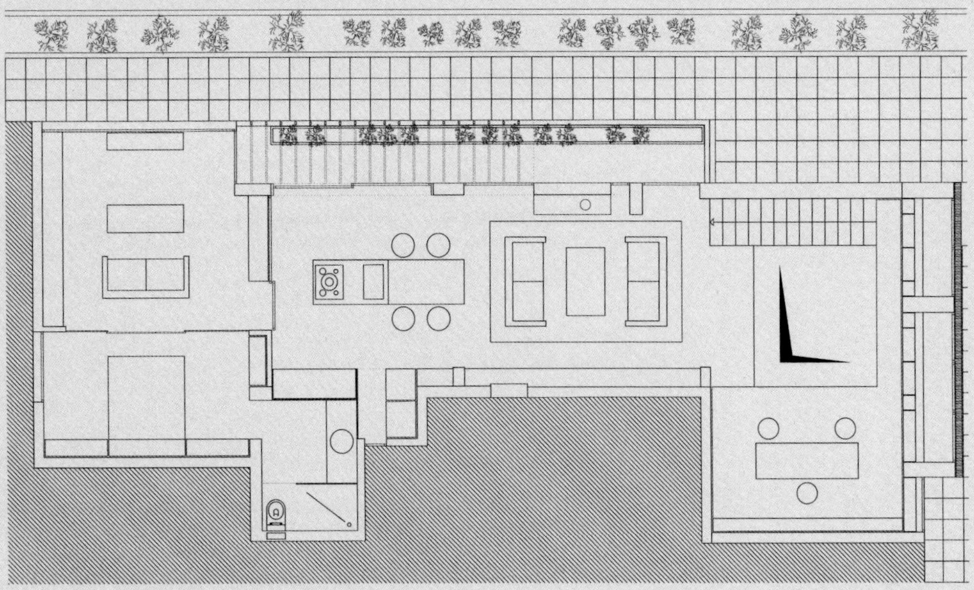

First-floor plan

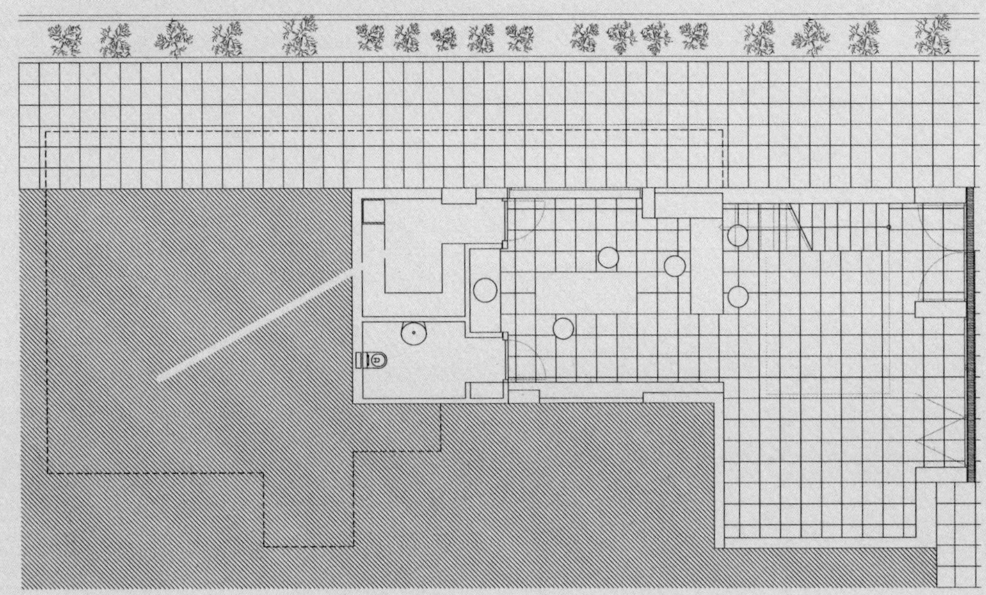

Ground-floor plan

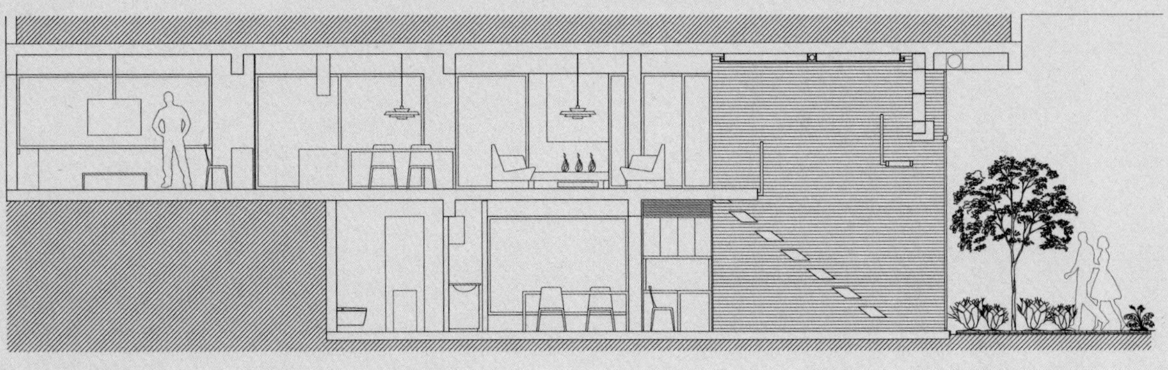

Section

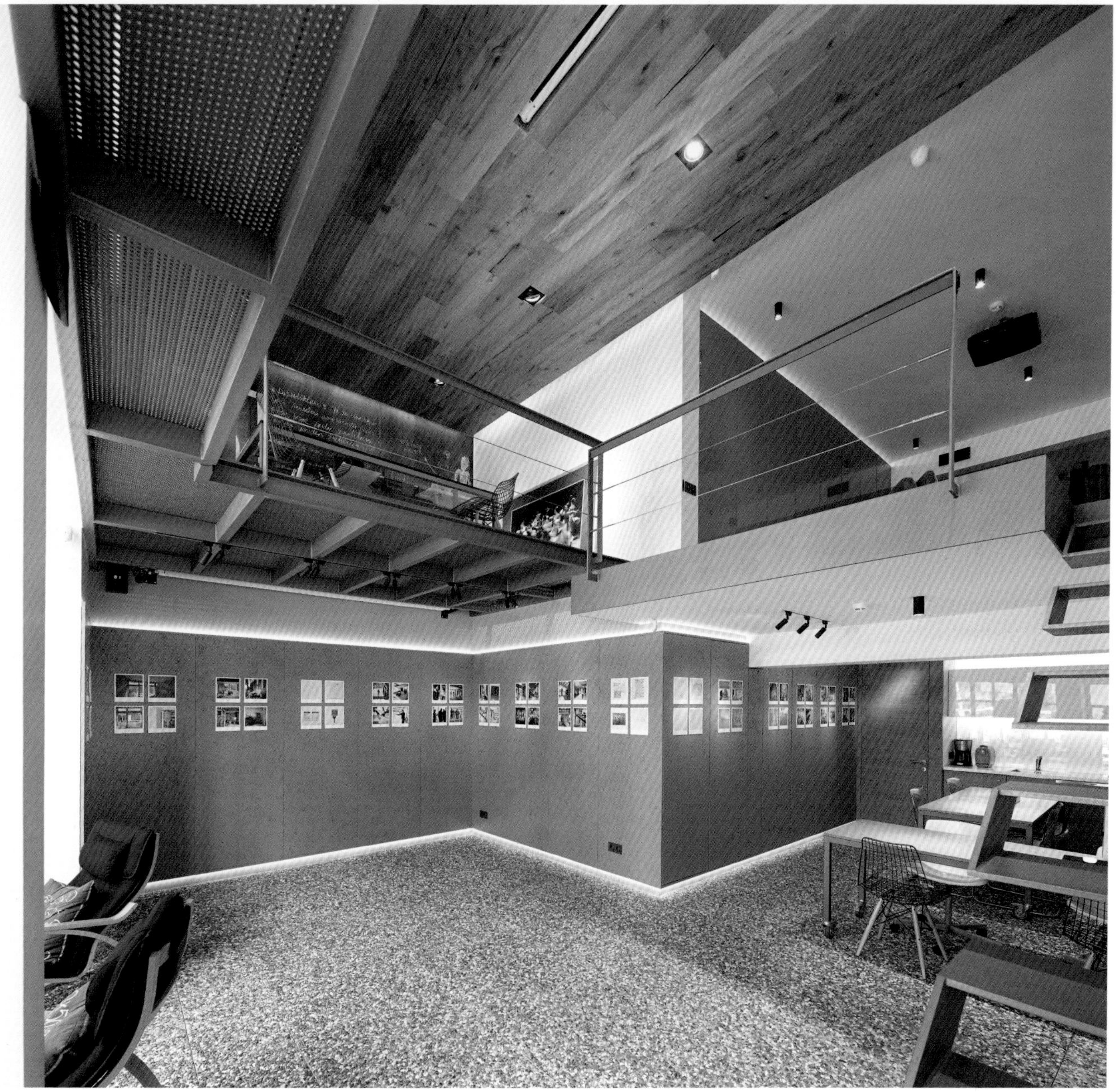

Public and private spaces

The project became more open to the public thanks to the exhibition space that it had gained, so integration with the wide sidewalk in front of the apartment was essential. The space between the apartment and the street became included in the design. The folding glass doors forming the façade could open completely on either side and contribute to the fusion of the inner space with the urban space during exhibition events, with the street flowing into the inner space and vice versa. This wide sidewalk that belongs to the city, together with the apartment, could become a social area on an exhibition opening night where people could move between the street and the enclosed gallery space.

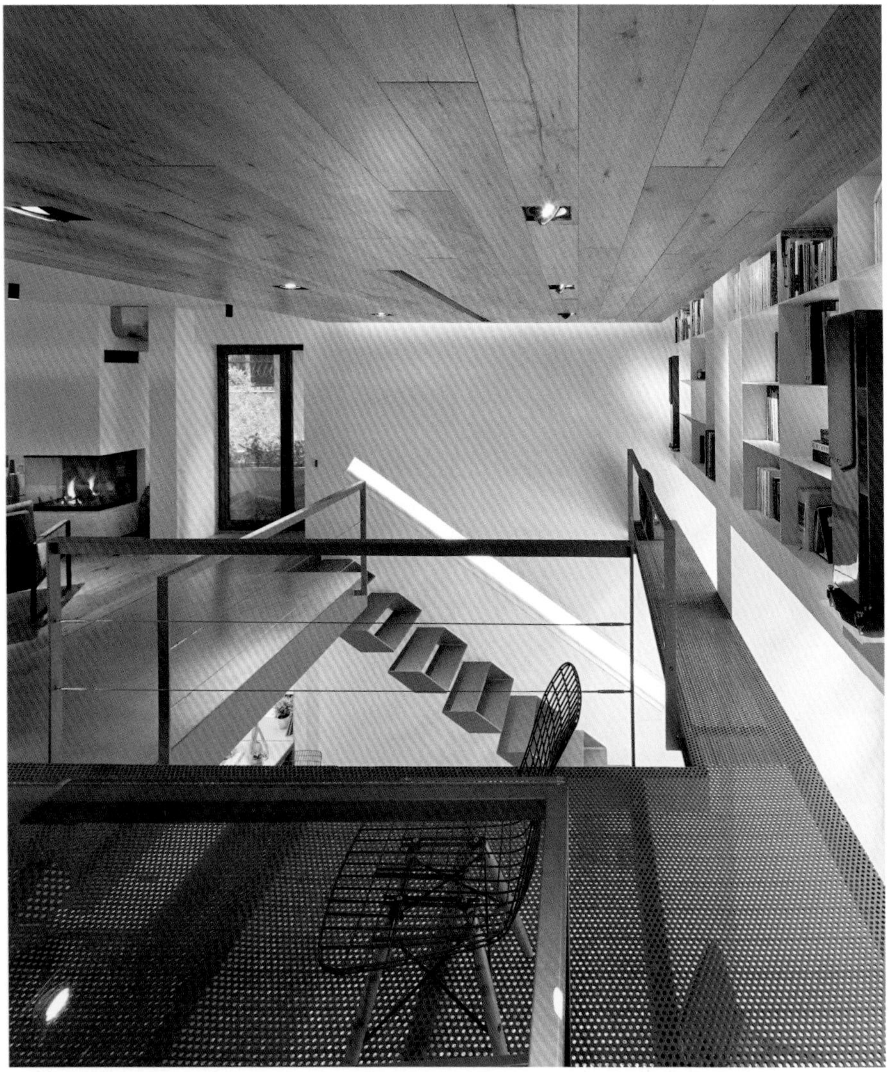

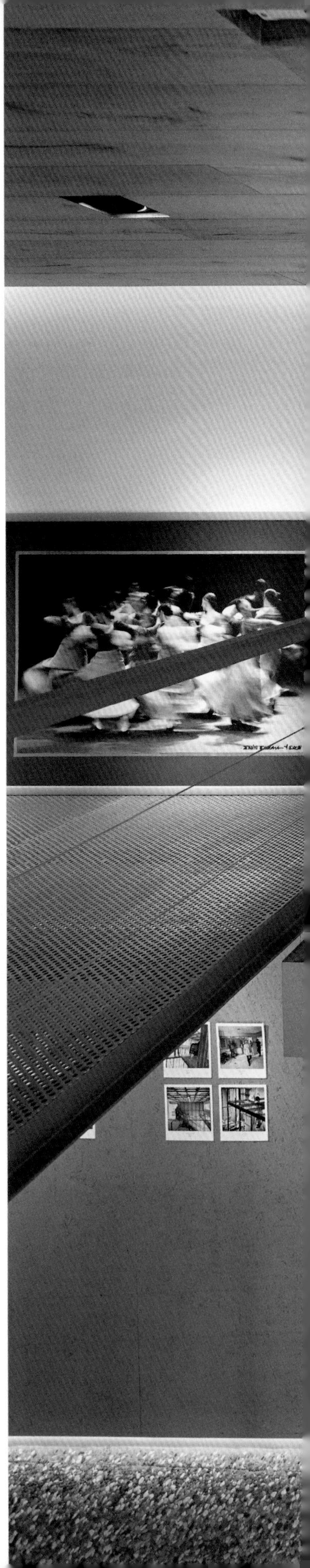

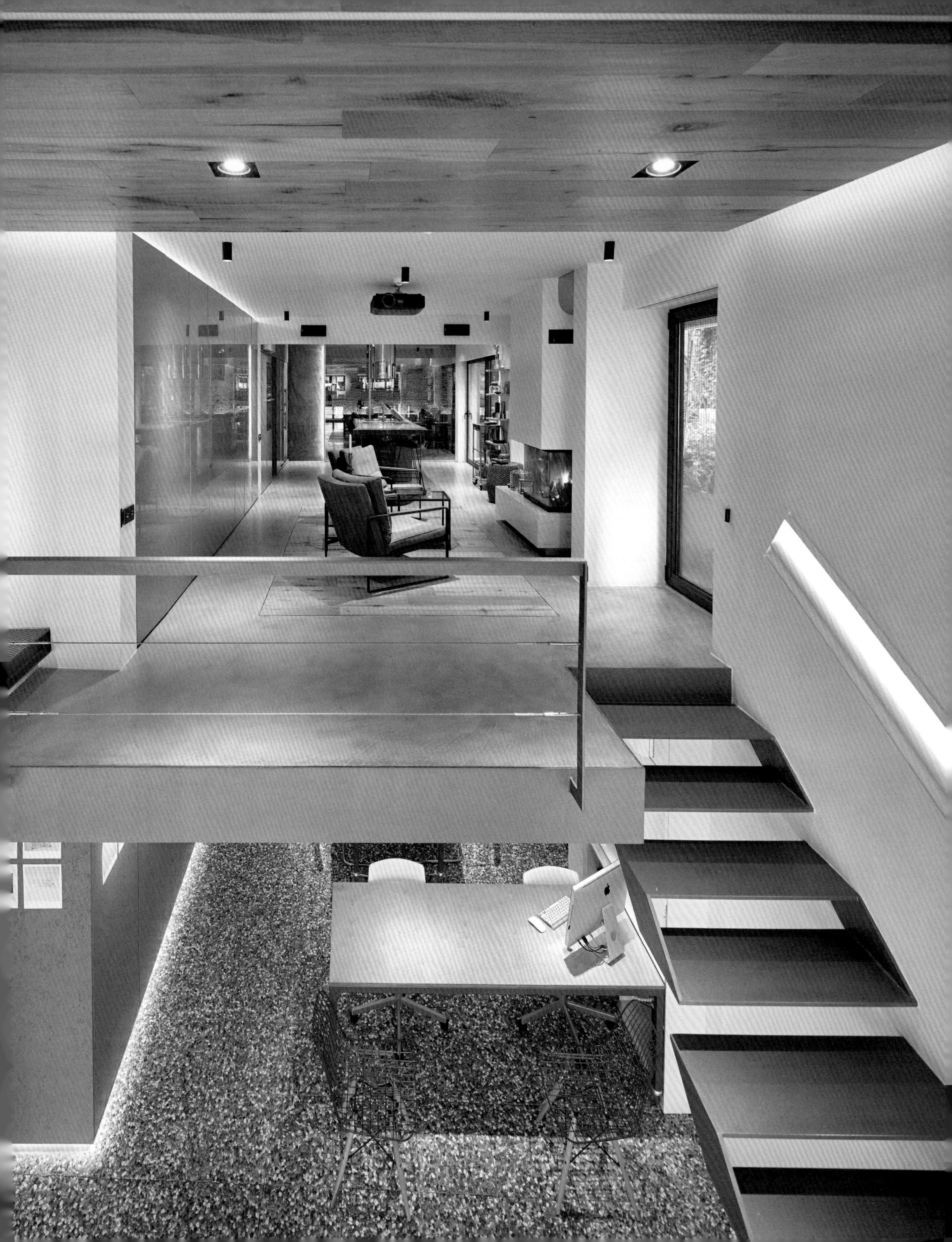

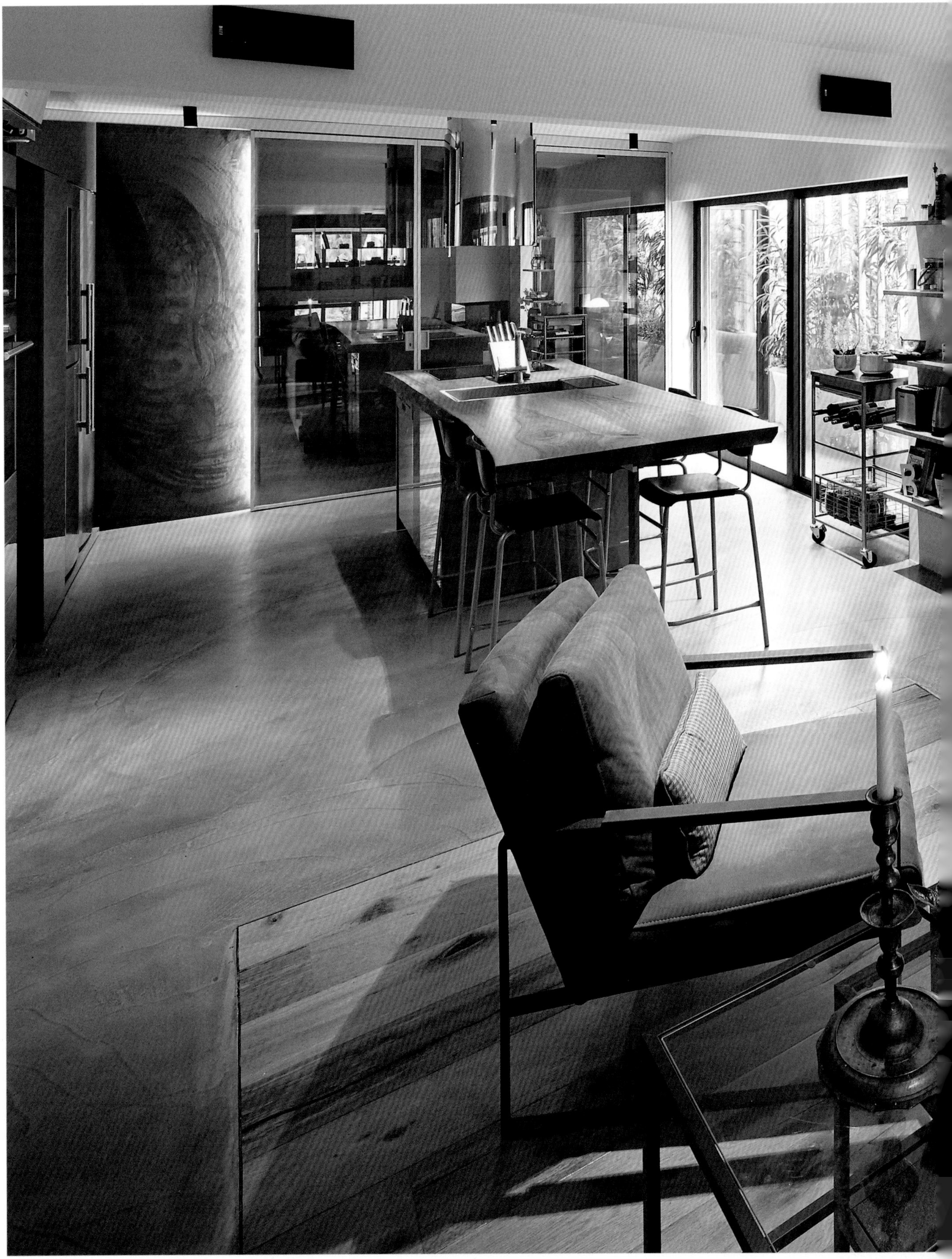

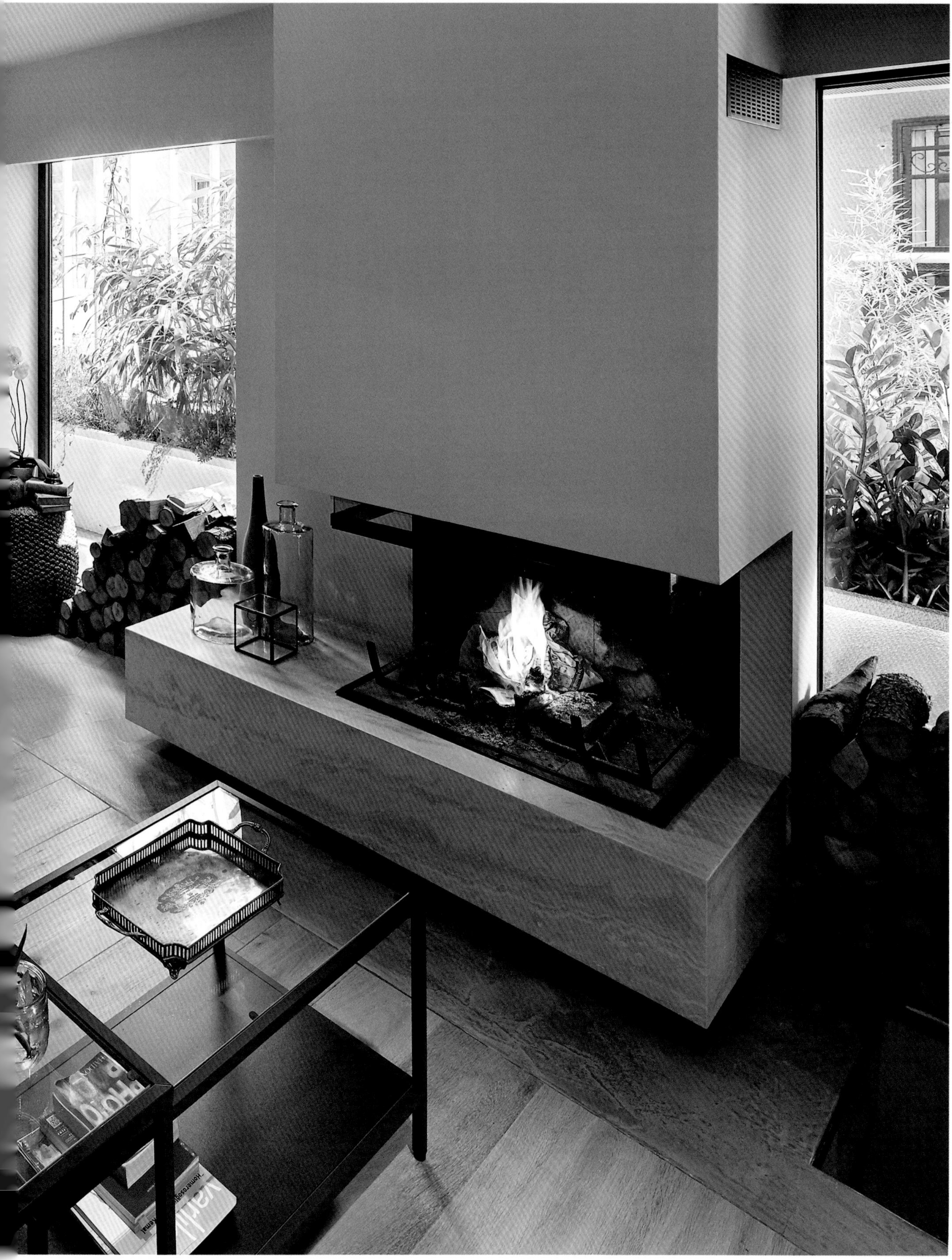

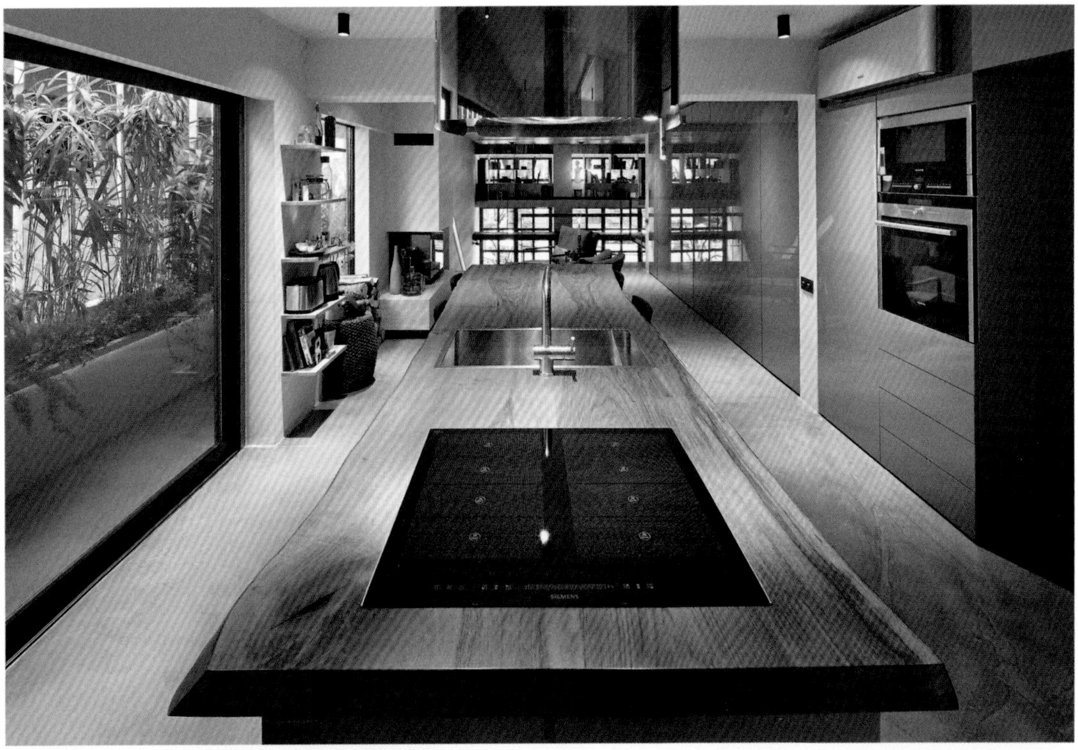

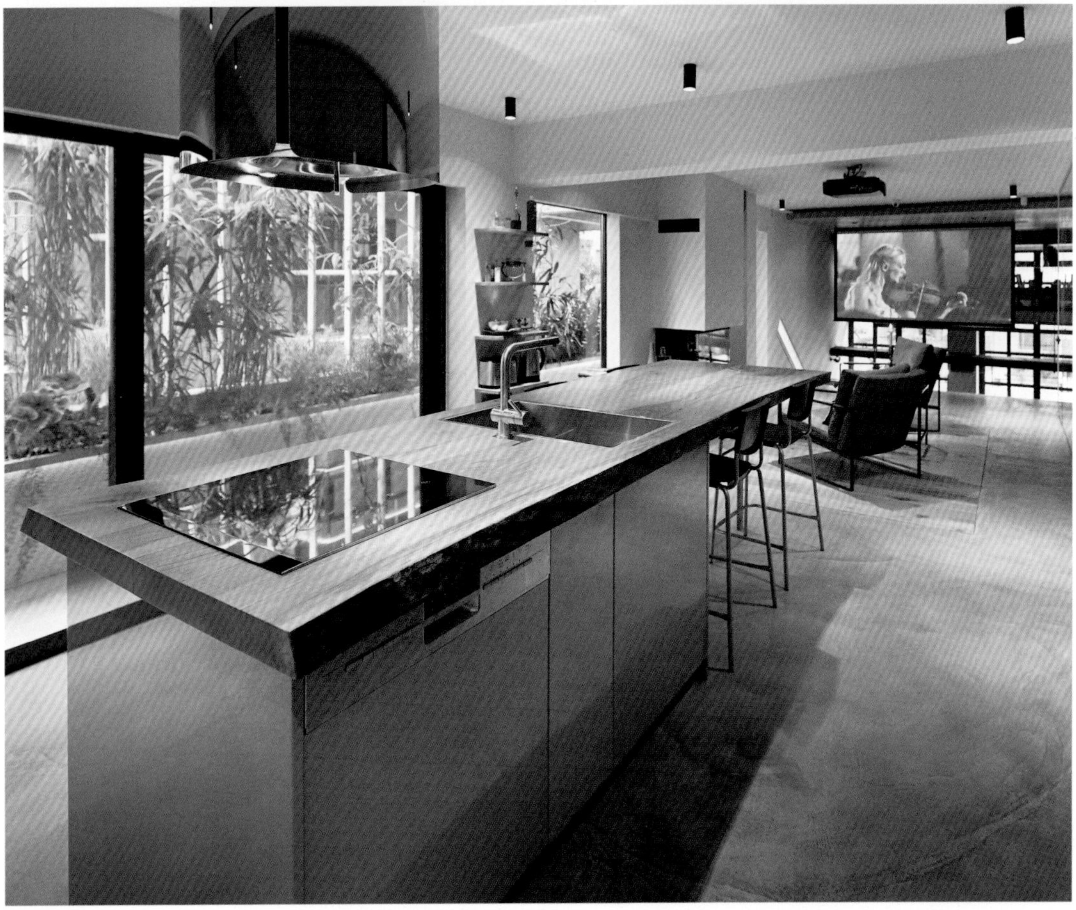

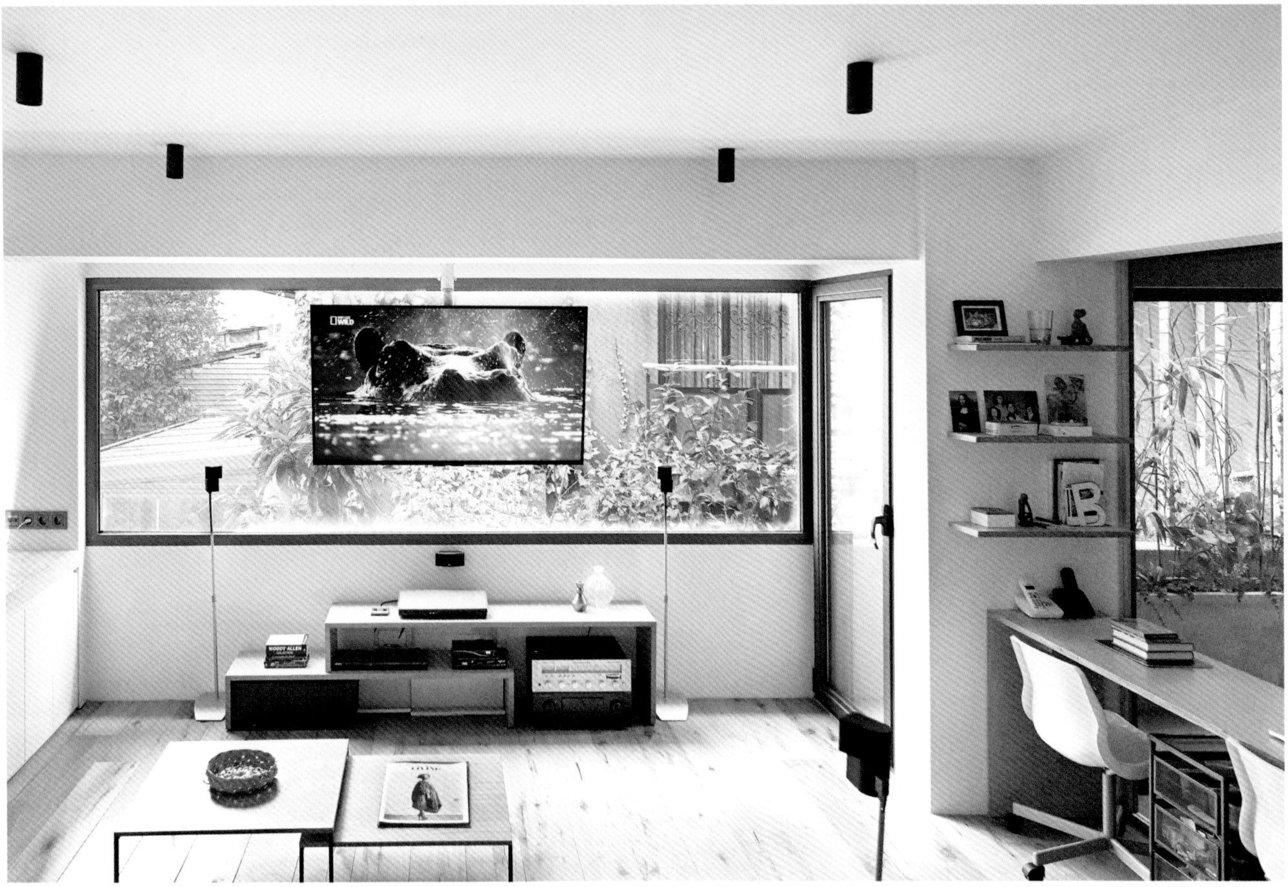
WOODY ALLEN
LIVING

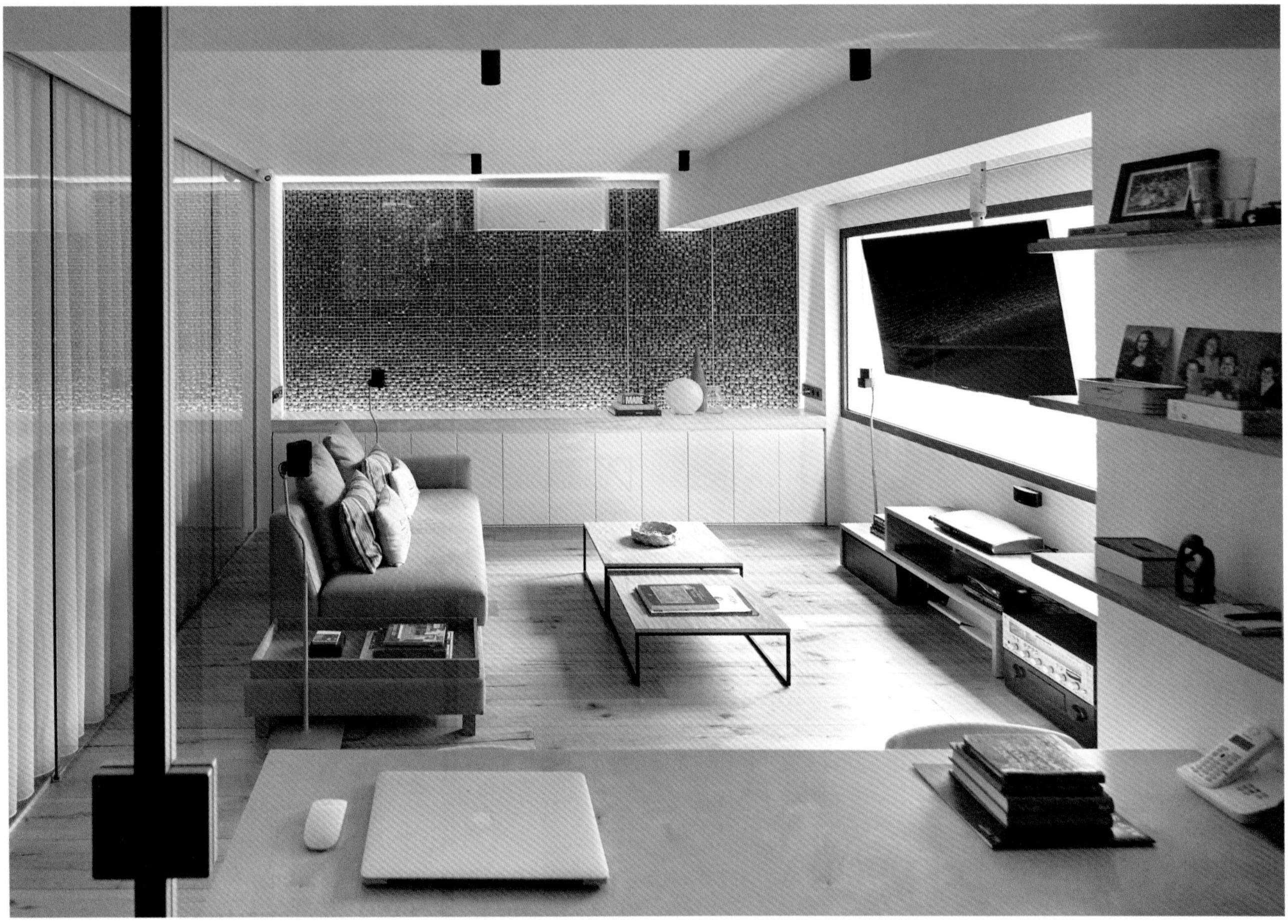

INDUSTRIAL AND OFFICE SPACES—NOW CREATIVE PLACES

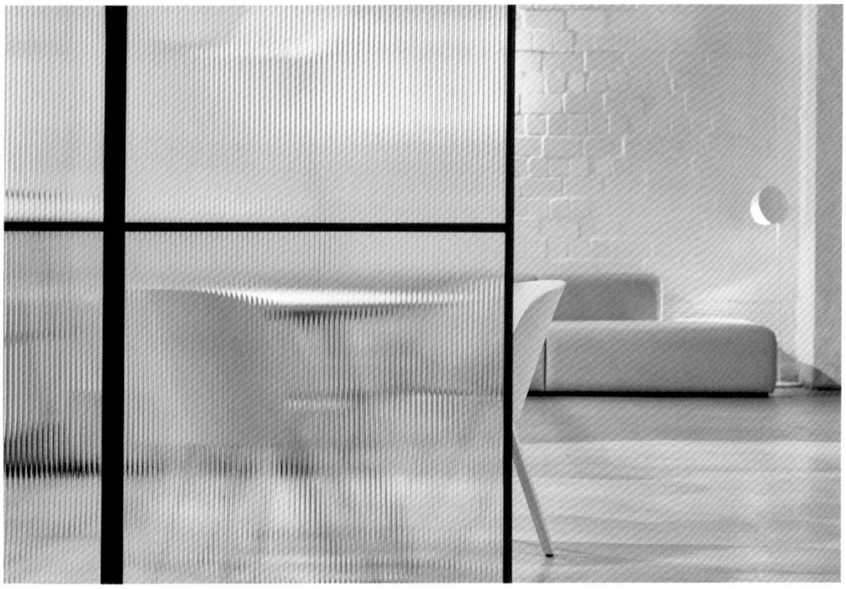

Area:
9,795 square feet (910 square meters)

Completion:
2017

Design:
Studio Besau-Marguerre

Photography:
Silke Zander

Hamburg, Germany

About You

For the young online fashion label About You, the German design-duo Studio Besau-Marguerre transformed an old industrial building in Hamburg into a vibrant and inspiring photo studio.

A collage of colors, forms, and textures

The interior concept and furnishing for the label's in-house photo studio, About Shots, reflects the assets of the aspiring fashion brand while taking advantage of the architectural characteristics of the old industrial factory. The interior was designed to contain a dynamic, collage-like mix of striking colors, textures, and forms.

Reflecting the brand

About You is all about fashion, great textiles, well-tailored clothes, strong colors, and the perfect staging of all of these elements. The design brief was to to reflect the unique character of the fashion brand as well as offering staff a space for relaxing and taking their minds off work.

Colors and spaces

The designers responded to this brief by conceptualizing a lounge area as a central square, signifying it with a rose-colored circle on the floor, annexed by partly cordoned off and private islands where people could relax, exchange ideas, recharge, and even sleep.

To break up the industrial character, Studio Besau-Marguerre added a palette of three strong colors that simultaneously relate to the surroundings of the old factory and the building itself, as well as the façade. Large panels of structured glass with bold black metal frames were installed as room dividers, separating the different areas into semi-private spaces. The glass panels act as a pleasant diffusor, letting the surroundings fade into the background. In addition to the glass walls, designers specified heavy curtains from high-end upholstery fabrics, acting as flexible, bold room dividers that had a positive effect on the acoustics in

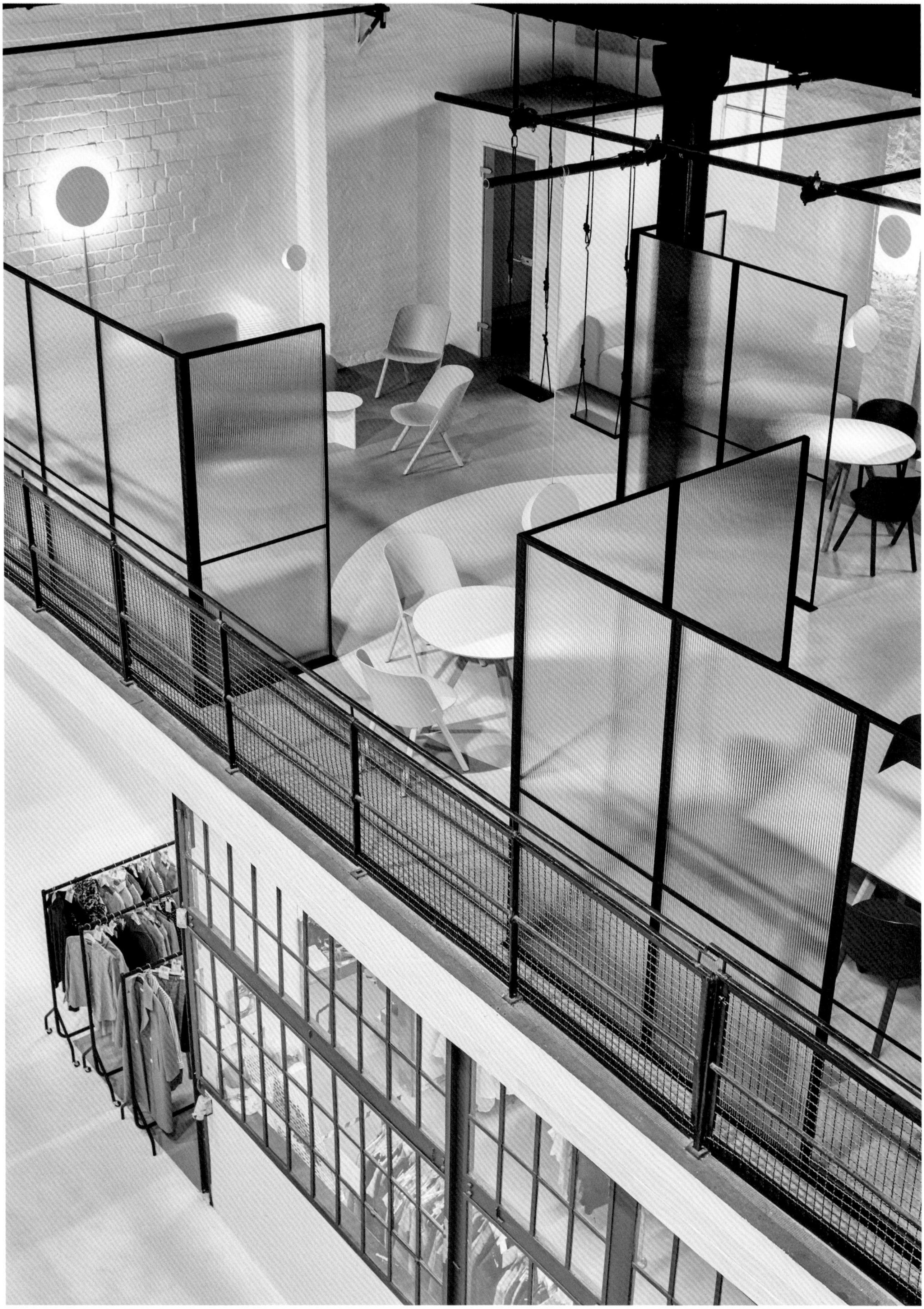

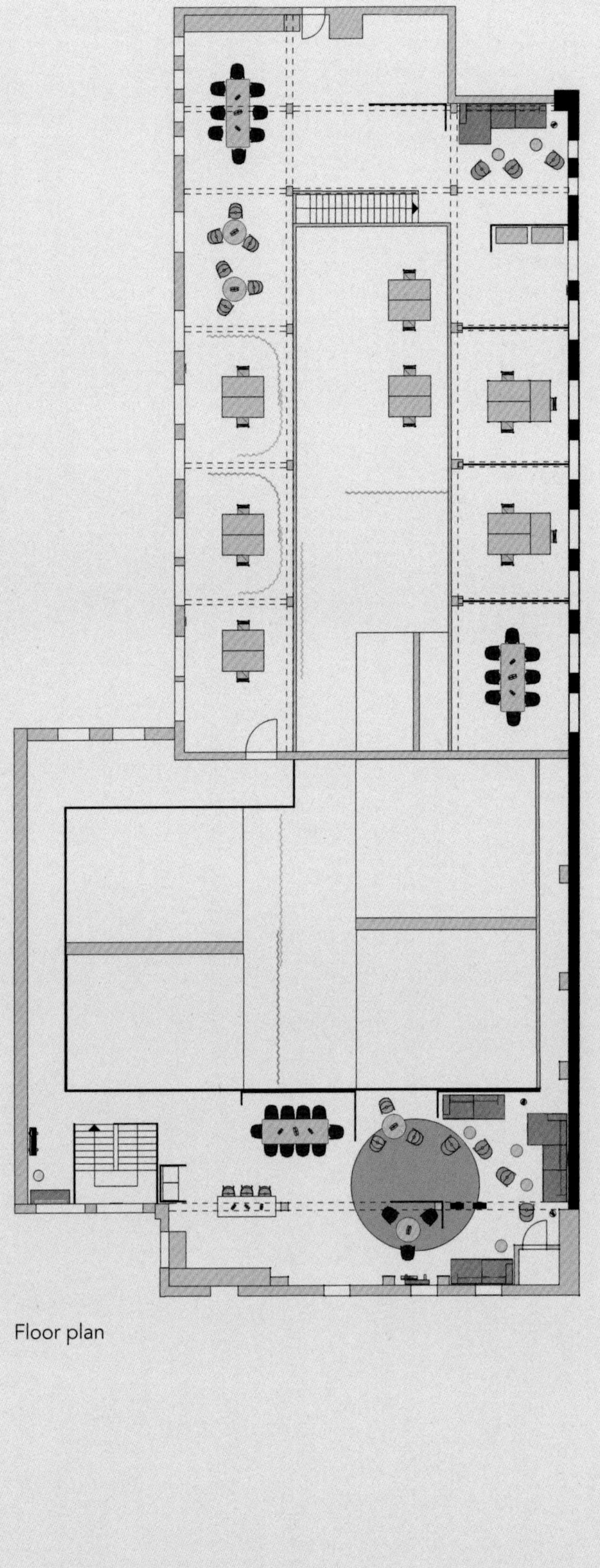

Floor plan

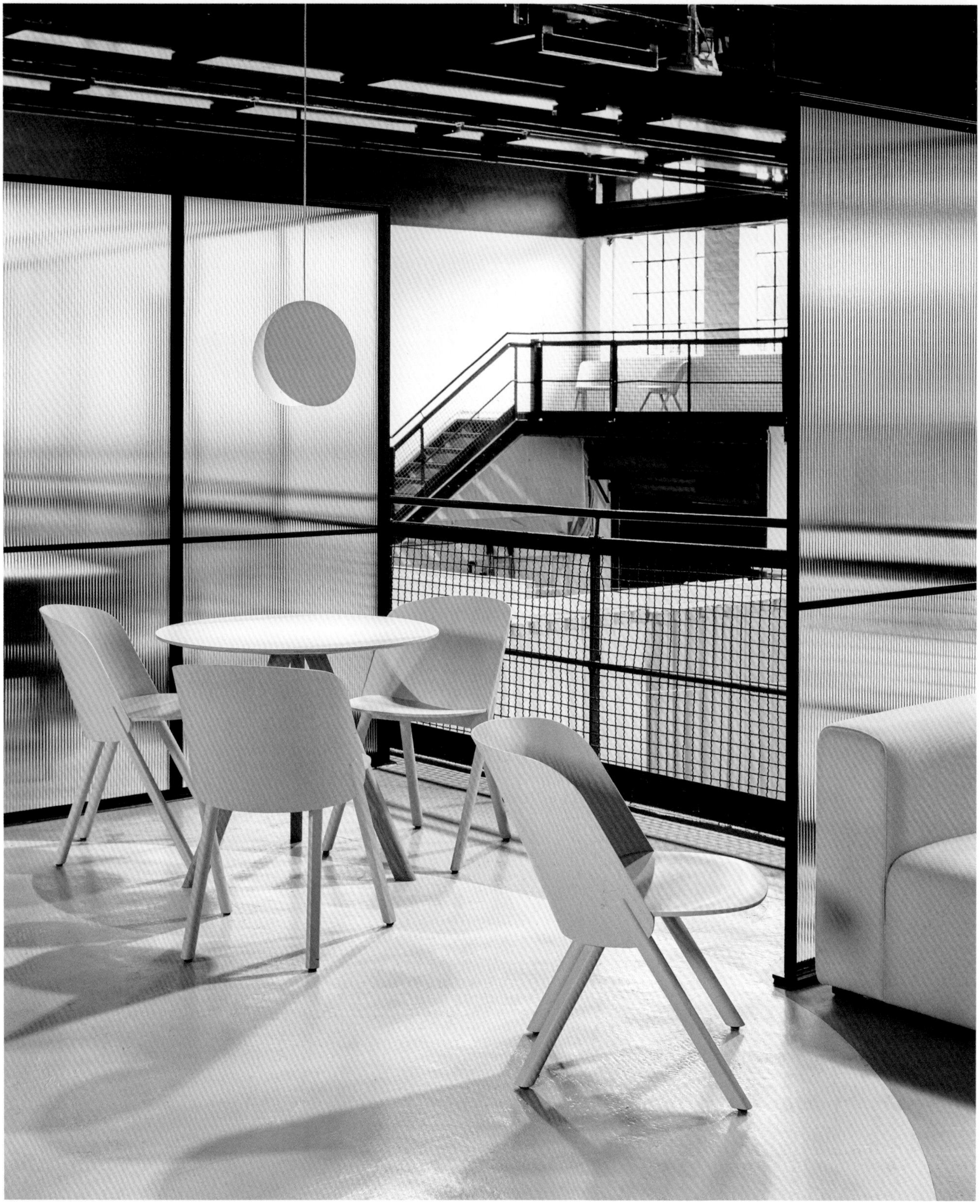

the busy photo studio. Large textile panels and About You fashion prints provide additional focal points, casually leaning on the wall as if someone had just set them briefly aside.

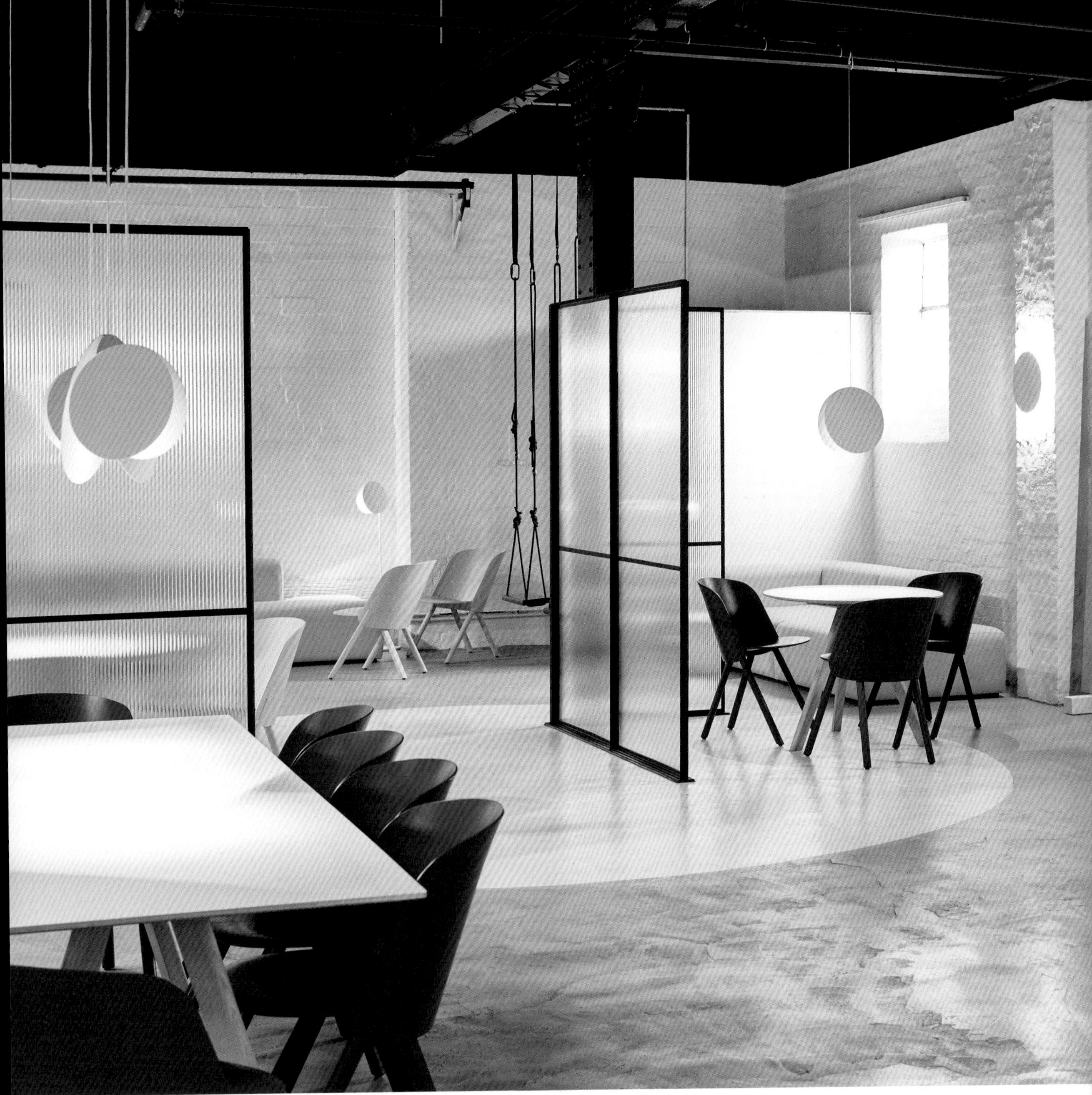

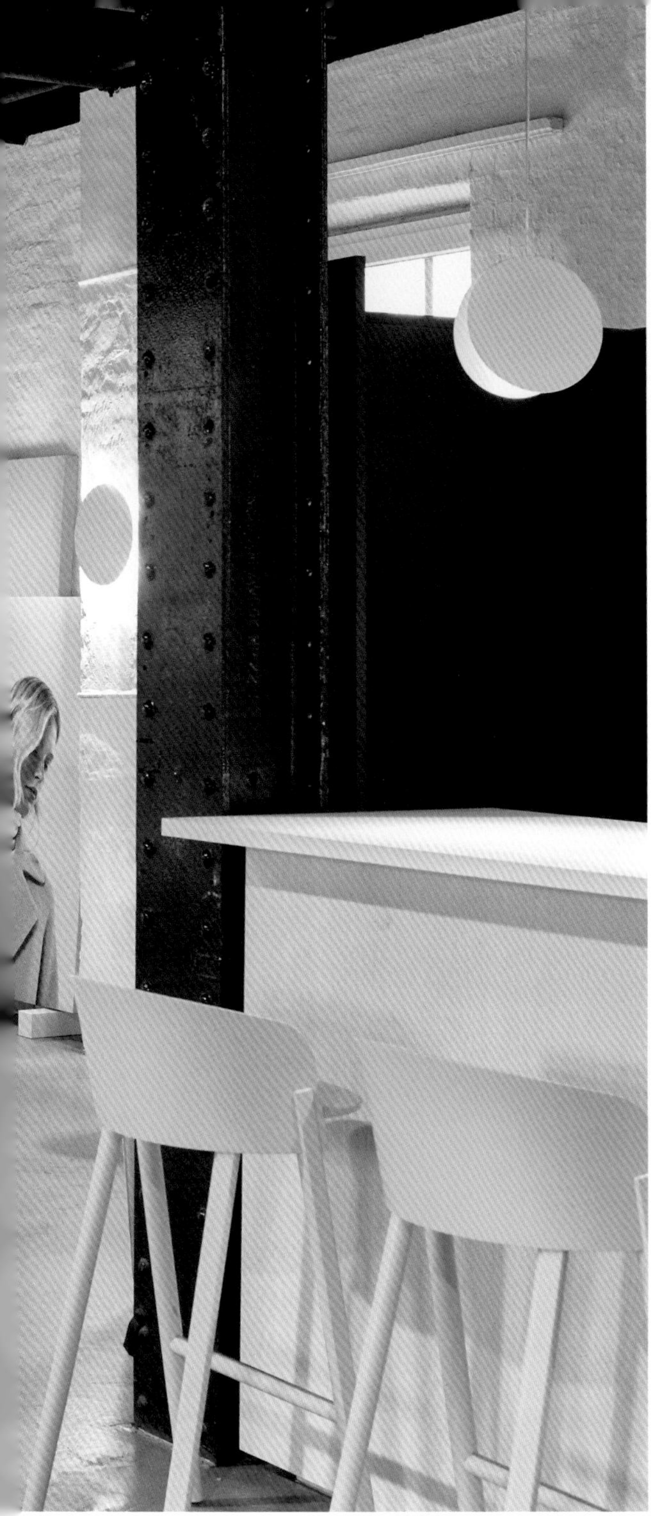

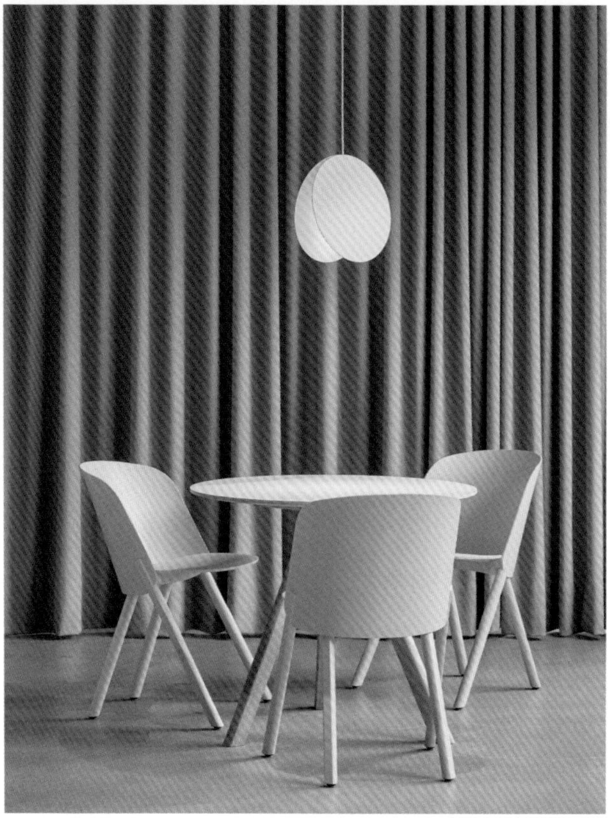

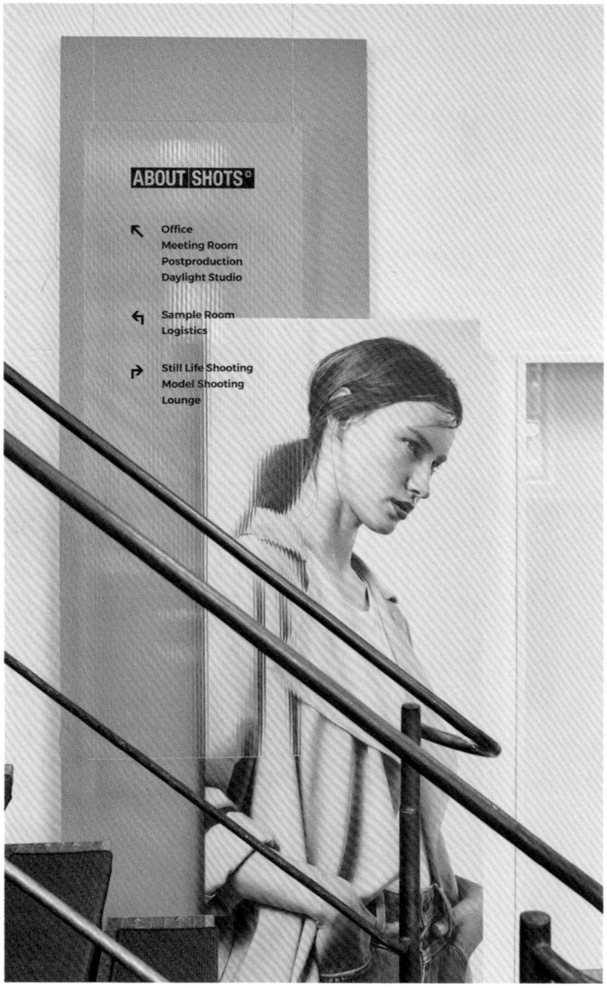
ABOUT SHOTS
Office
Meeting Room
Postproduction
Daylight Studio
Sample Room
Logistics
Still Life Shooting
Model Shooting
Lounge

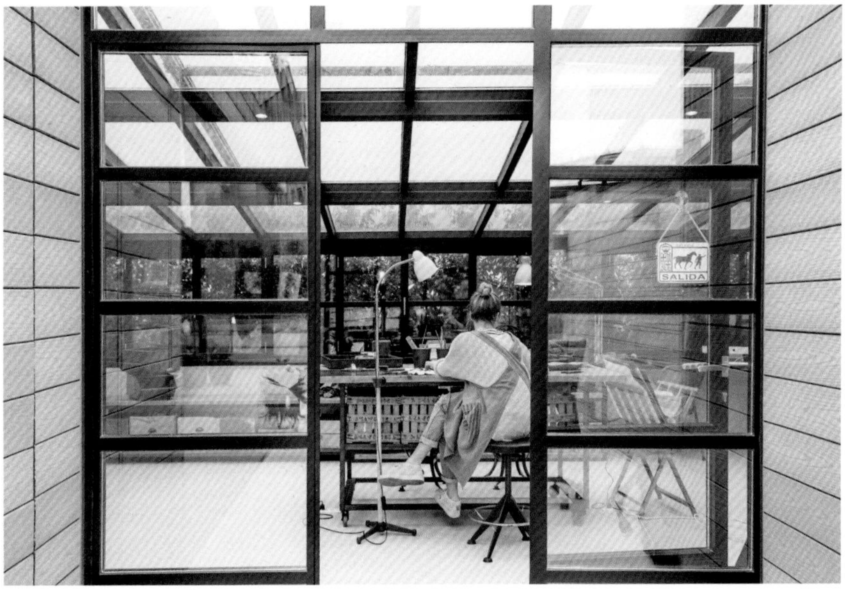

Area:
1,507 square feet (140 square meters)

Completion:
2015

Design:
Miriam Barrio

Photography:
María Pujol

Barcelona, Spain

Atelier

This project saw the conversion of a small soccer field into an atelier, or art studio; a place to unleash the imagination and make art; a place created to create; an inspiring space.

Flooded with light

The fully glazed structure, supported by a super-light black steel, allows light to flood the studio space. Ceiling and walls allow streams of light to enter the interior of the studio, while the level of light can be controlled by the use of automatic rolling screens.

The interior is wrapped in light-colored microcement on the floor and walls, which allowed the designers to introduce colorful pieces without complicating the vision of the whole. The microcement is continuous and has no joints, and is practical for cleaning. For the flooring designers used a finishing that is more resistant to wear.Microcement in another color was also used for the terrace, creating volumes that allowed for planters, benches, and a large chill-out space.

Keeping the artist in mind

The industrial-style and recovered furniture combines wood and iron, creating completely customized pieces to meet the needs of artists. Mobile tables contain space for storage, boxes, brushes, and all kinds of items that need to be ordered in a functional way. Some of the furniture was created to be customized by artists, such as doors that are now large collages.

Cool and comfortable

The great challenge of the project was the insulation and interior fittings. In order to ensure sufficient comfort inside the atelier—a space with lots of glass exposed to sunlight, where the temperature inside could become very high in hot weather—it was important to fit reliable air-conditioning. The climate installation and solar screens were automated by connecting them to a weather sensor. Screens were designed to filter the heat and retain privacy.

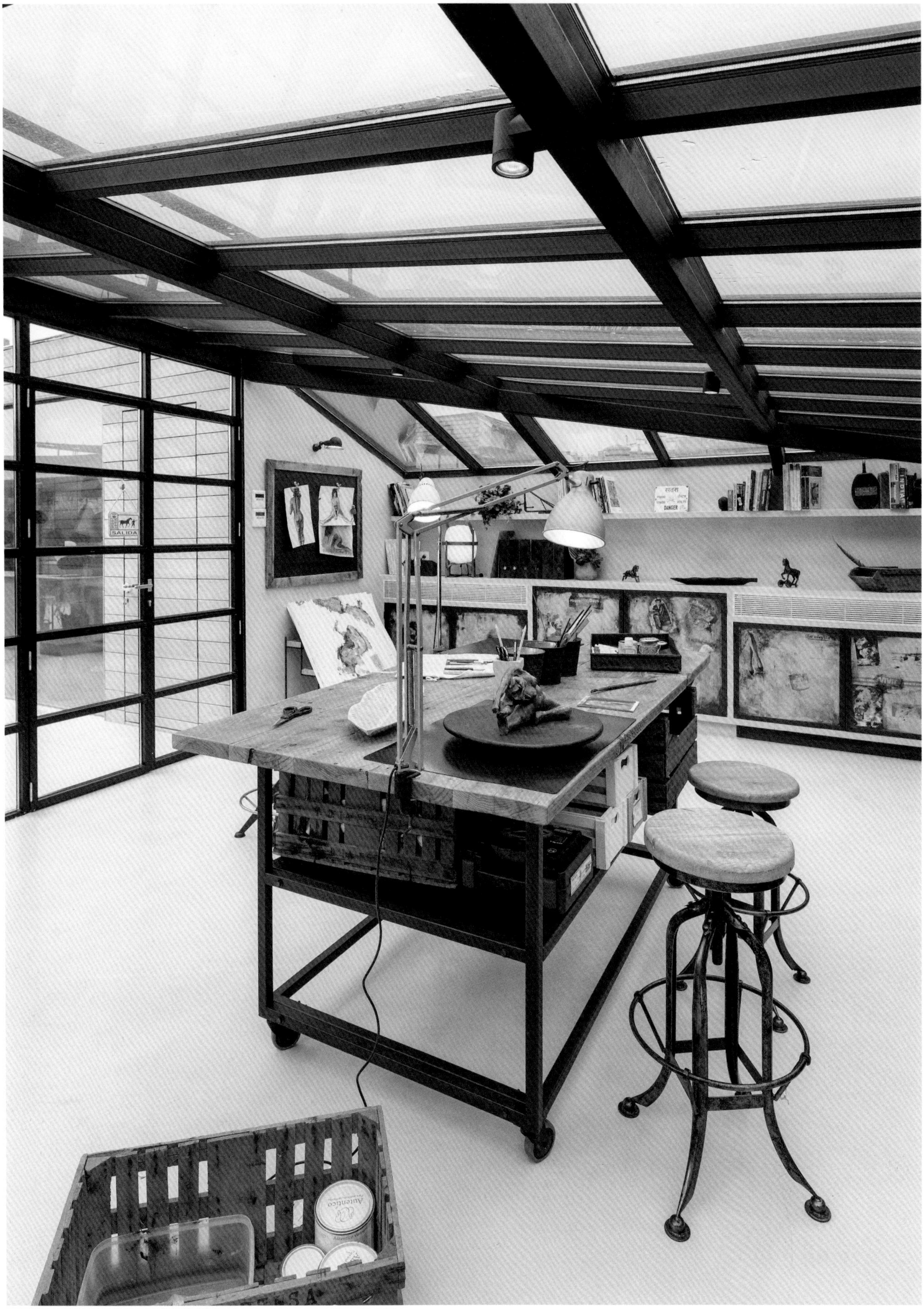
SALIDA
DANGER

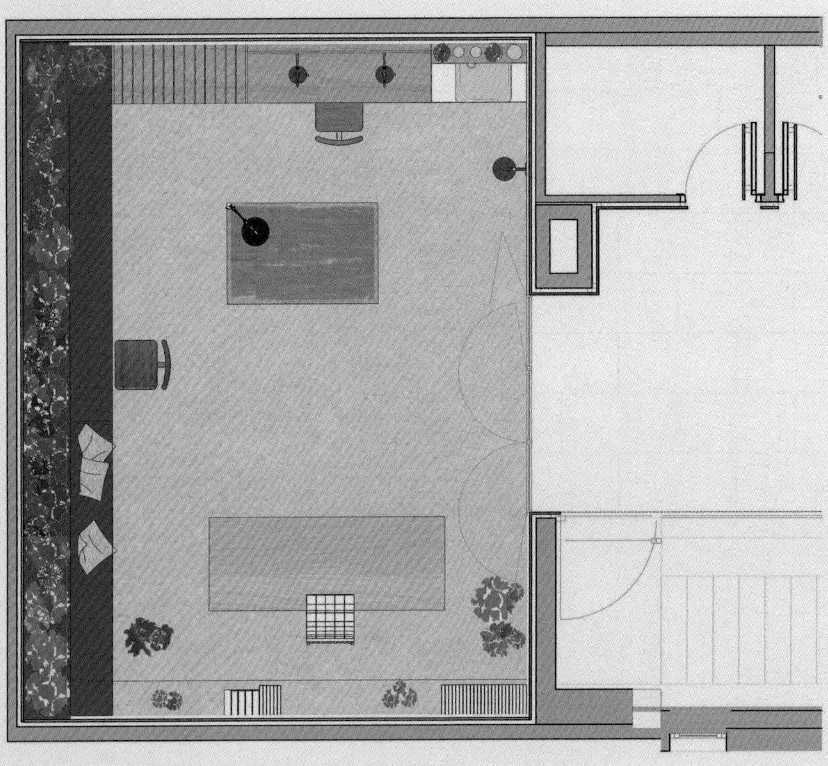
Floor plan

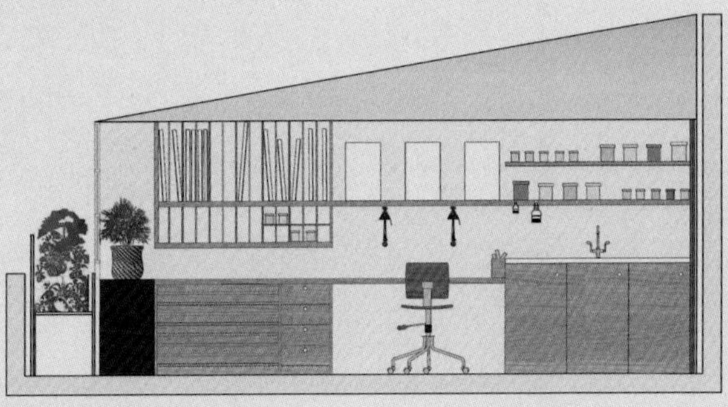
Section

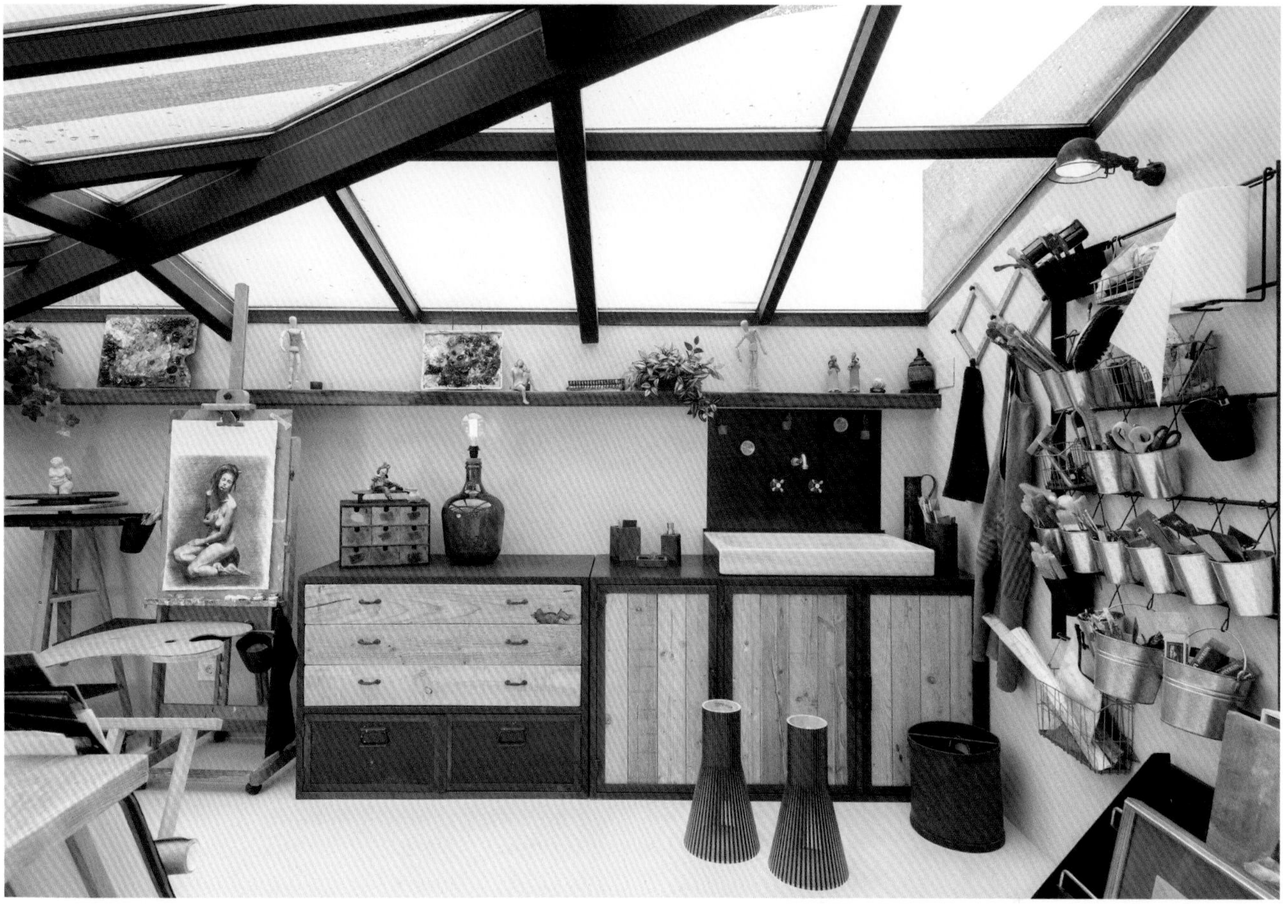

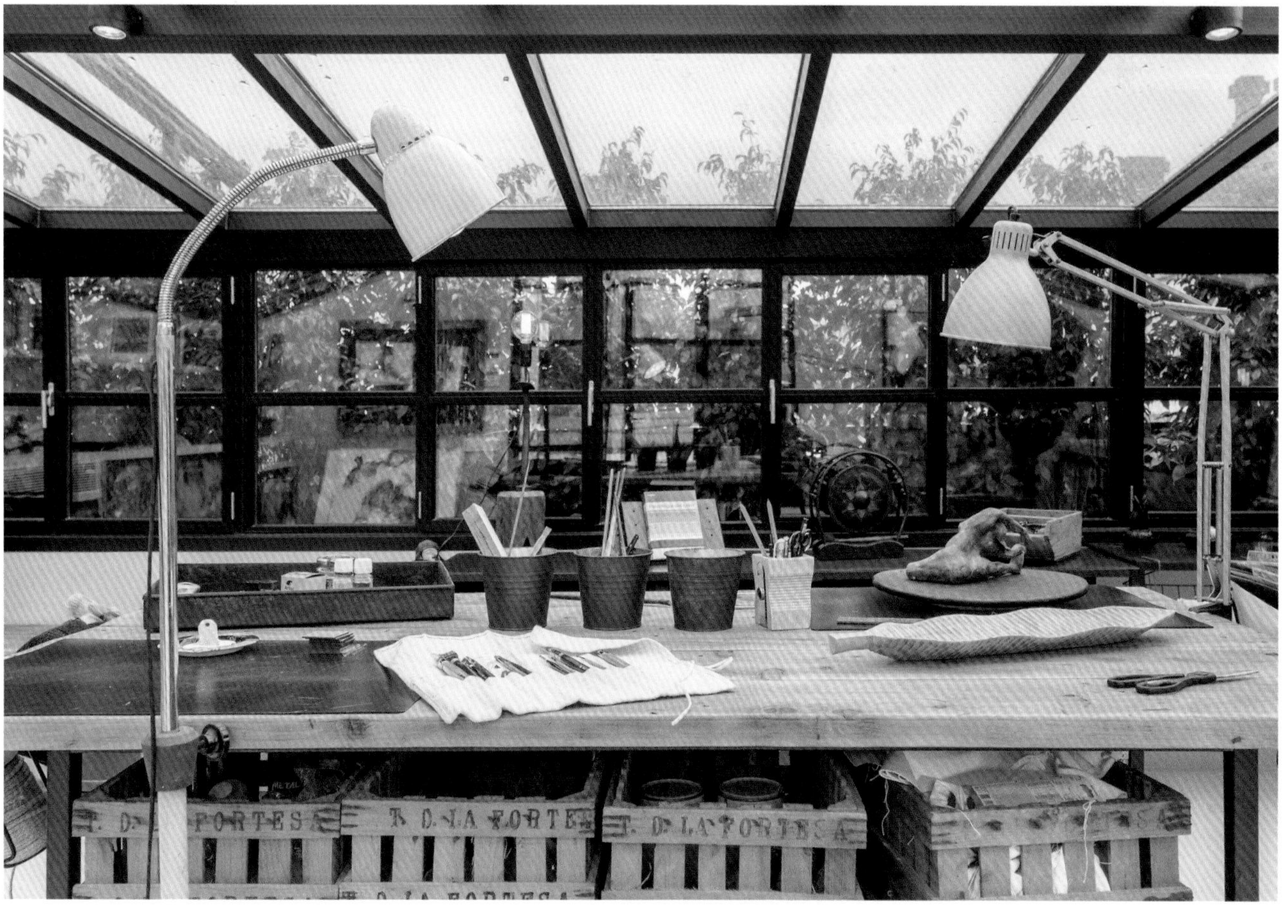

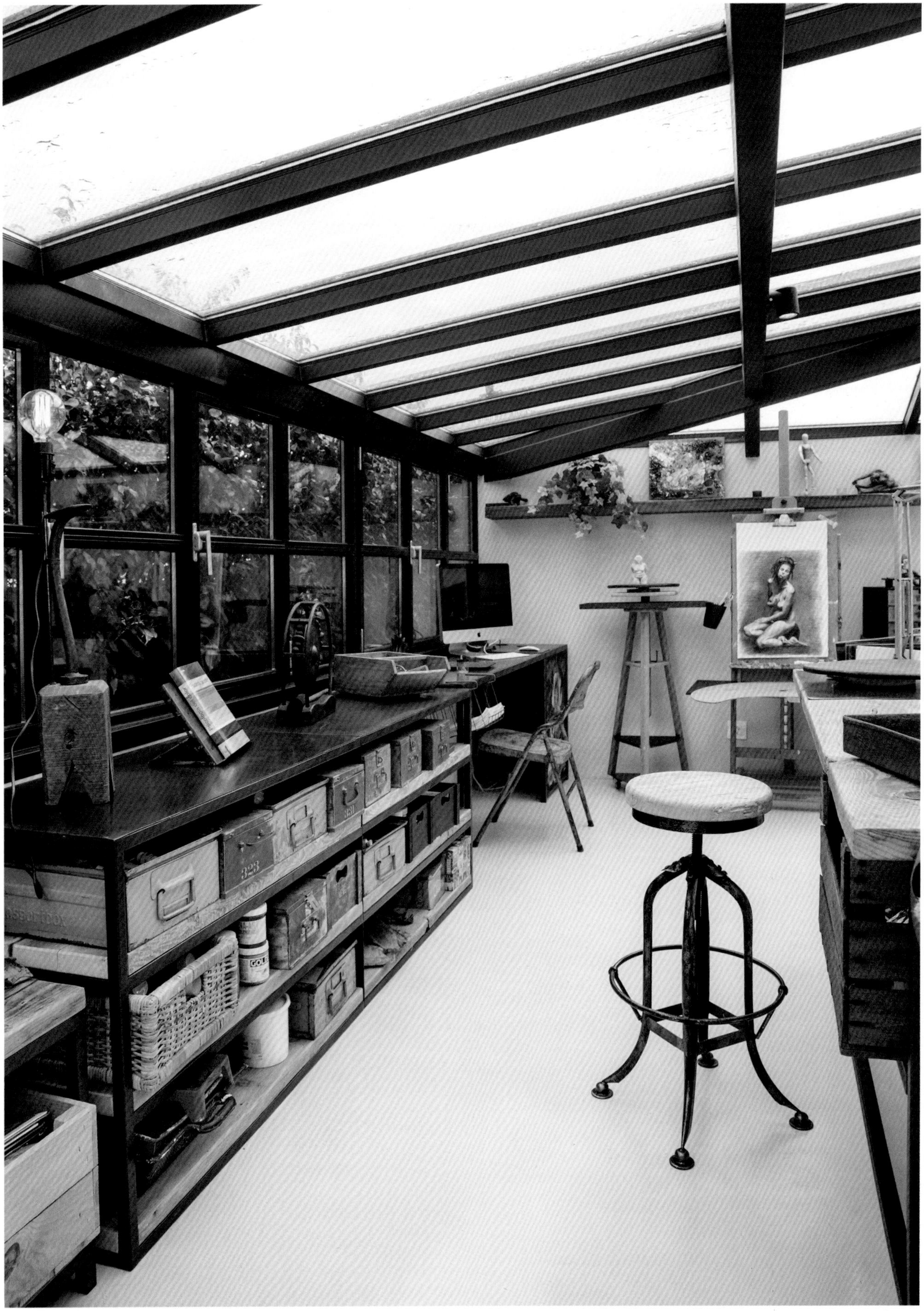
323

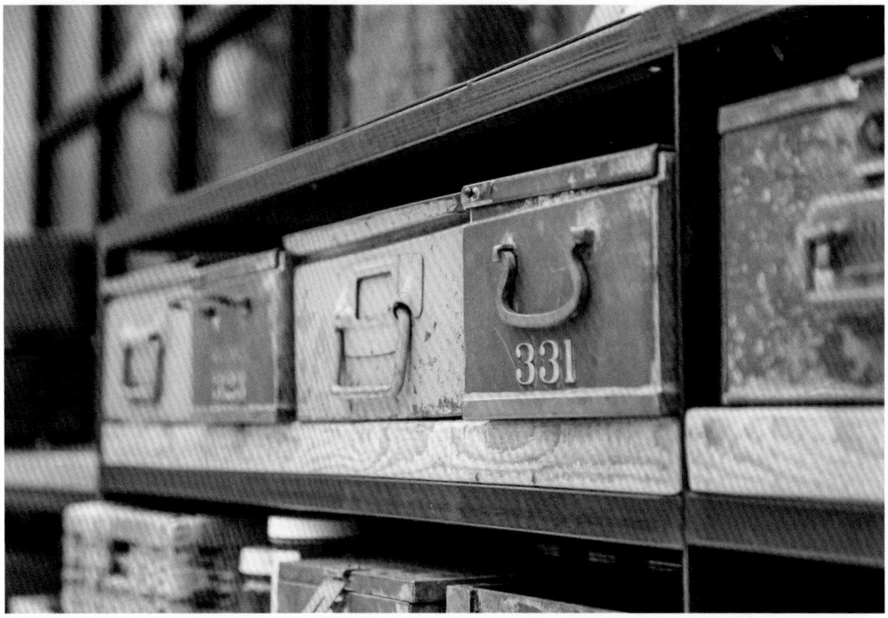
331

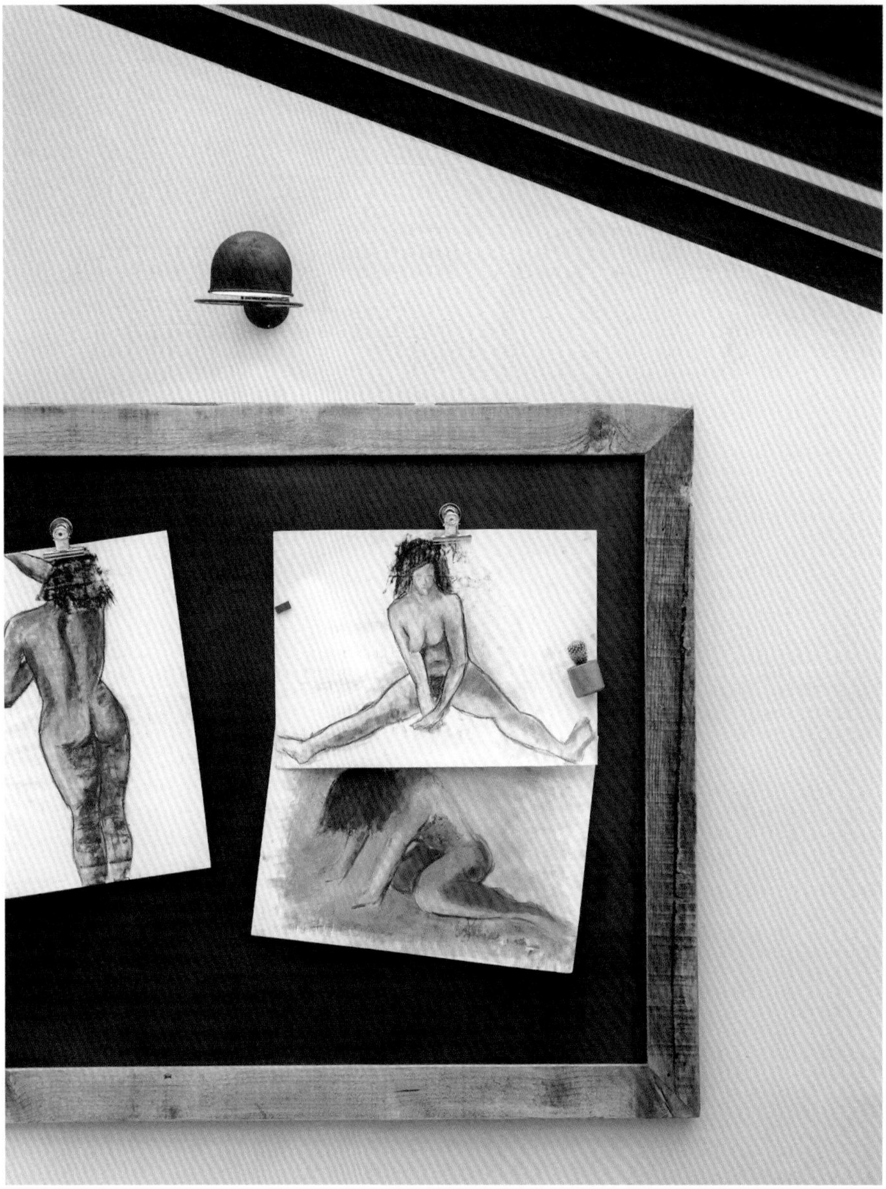

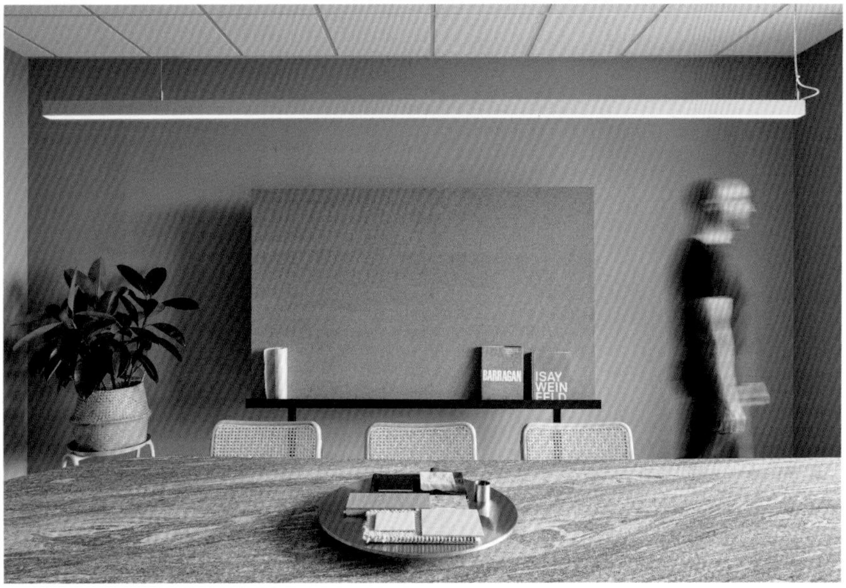

Area:
1,087 square feet (101 square meters)

Completion:
2018

Design:
Davidov Architects

Photography:
Jack Lovel

Melbourne, Australia

Davidov Architects Studio

This new studio fit-out was the first purpose-designed space for the architectural practice. The designers were determined to design a series of spaces that conveyed many of the architectural devices and the general approach to space that is evolving in their built work.

The interior is divided into two core spaces with a third minor space for services and "back of house" spaces. The commercial shell of the office runs north to south, providing natural light and views through large windows toward the south. This helps orientate the two linear spaces; the first is a meeting room, the second the workroom.

The design of the studio is innovative for its versatility and the range of options for working and interacting.

From formal to casual

The meeting room has three tables: one large (six to eight people), one medium (two to four people), and one small (one to two people). Each allows for meetings of different scales and intents to be conducted in different ways, either more formally or casually depending on the appropriate dynamic and type of discussion or work to take place.

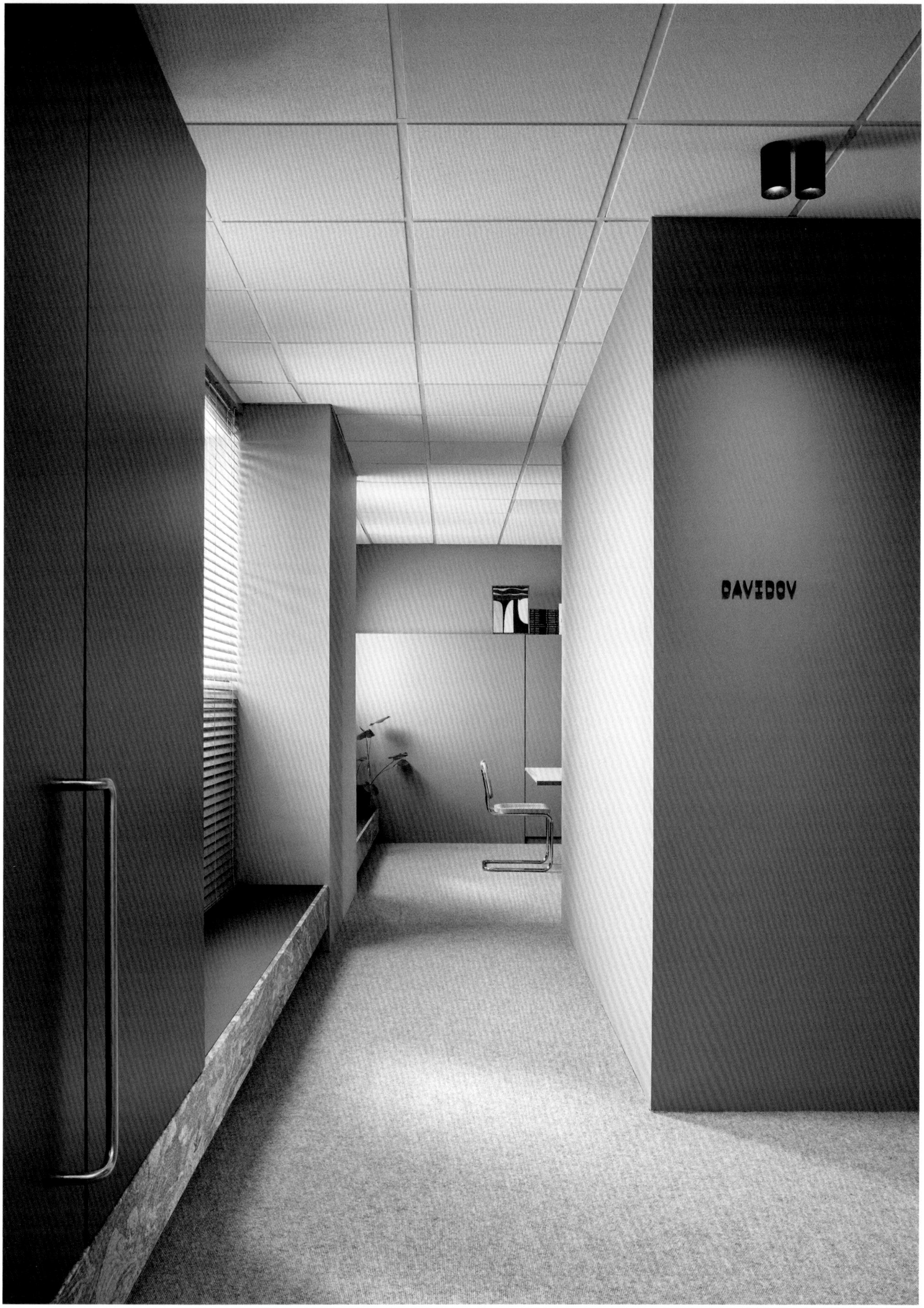
DAVIDOV

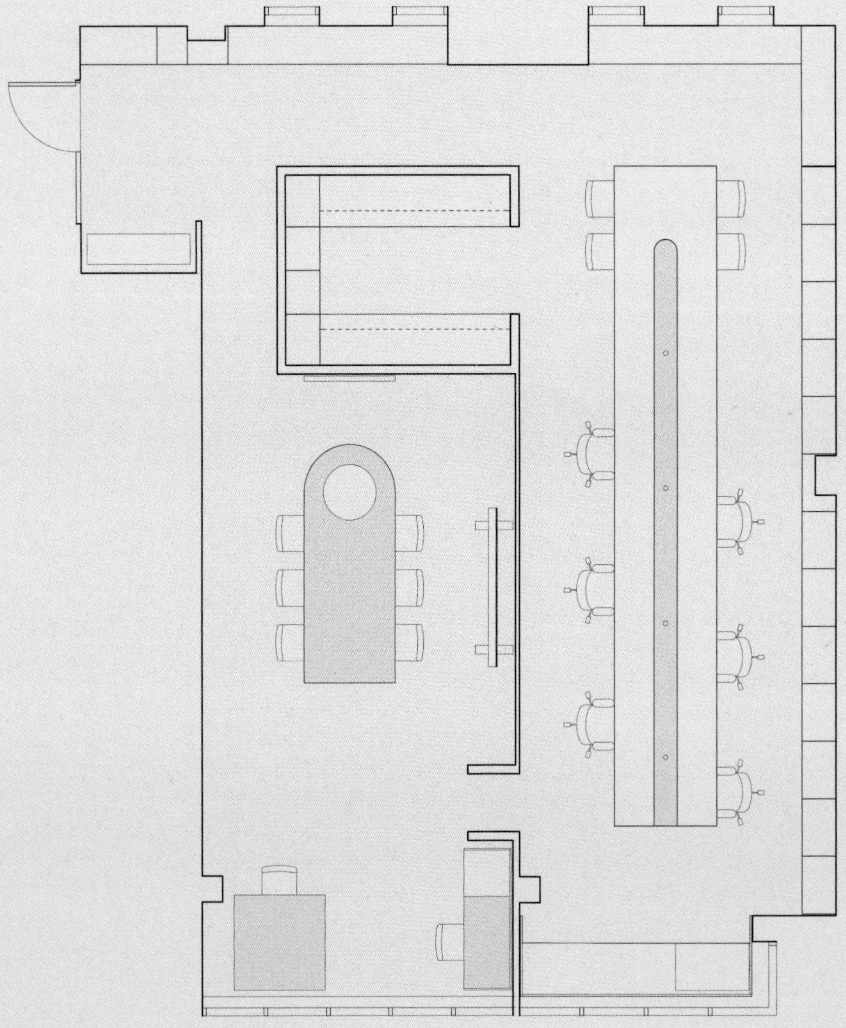

Floor plan

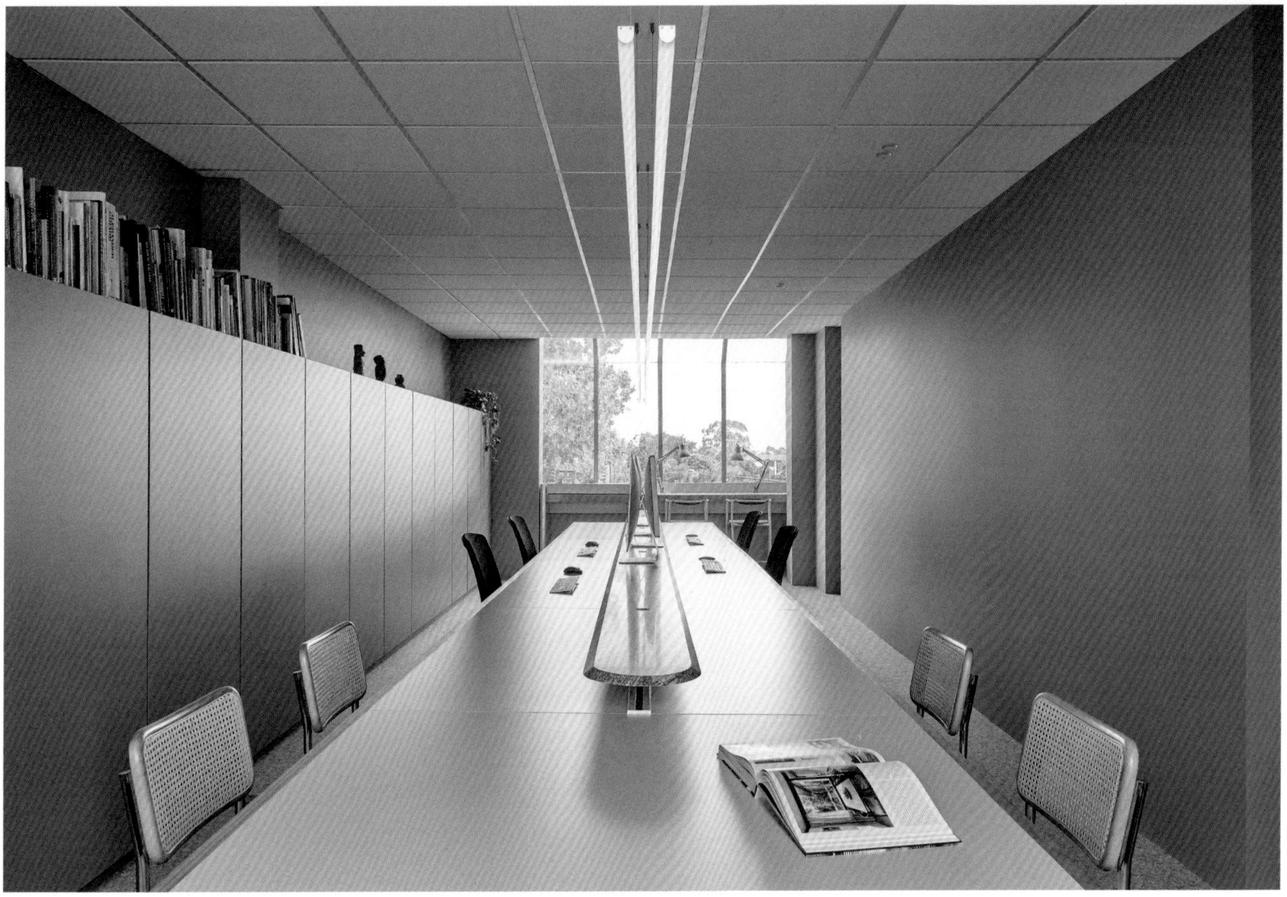

Room for growth

As the firm is young and growing slowly, it was important to create an environment that allowed for growth while maintaining a close-knit studio environment. As such the common table model was adopted, which allows for natural growth along the spine. The length of the table is also divided into two zones—work and talk—that allow for other areas to have informal or in-house conversations.

The studio space creates an interior that is free flowing and unexpected, while the circulation between the two main spaces adds interest and scale.

The small studio also allows for multiple environments and scenarios for individual and group work, either along the different zones of the common table or at the raised bar, and conversations and meetings at different scales at the various meeting-room tables.

Meetings can be held with two people by a window or a group around a large table, likewise the way in which work is carried out can be varied between different spaces, environments, and dynamics.

Designing for the scale

Joinery is executed in a more residential approach, complemented by the use of natural stone, hardwood, and indoor plants. Familiar domestic furniture, art, and sculpture has been brought into the studio to reinforce this setting and scale.

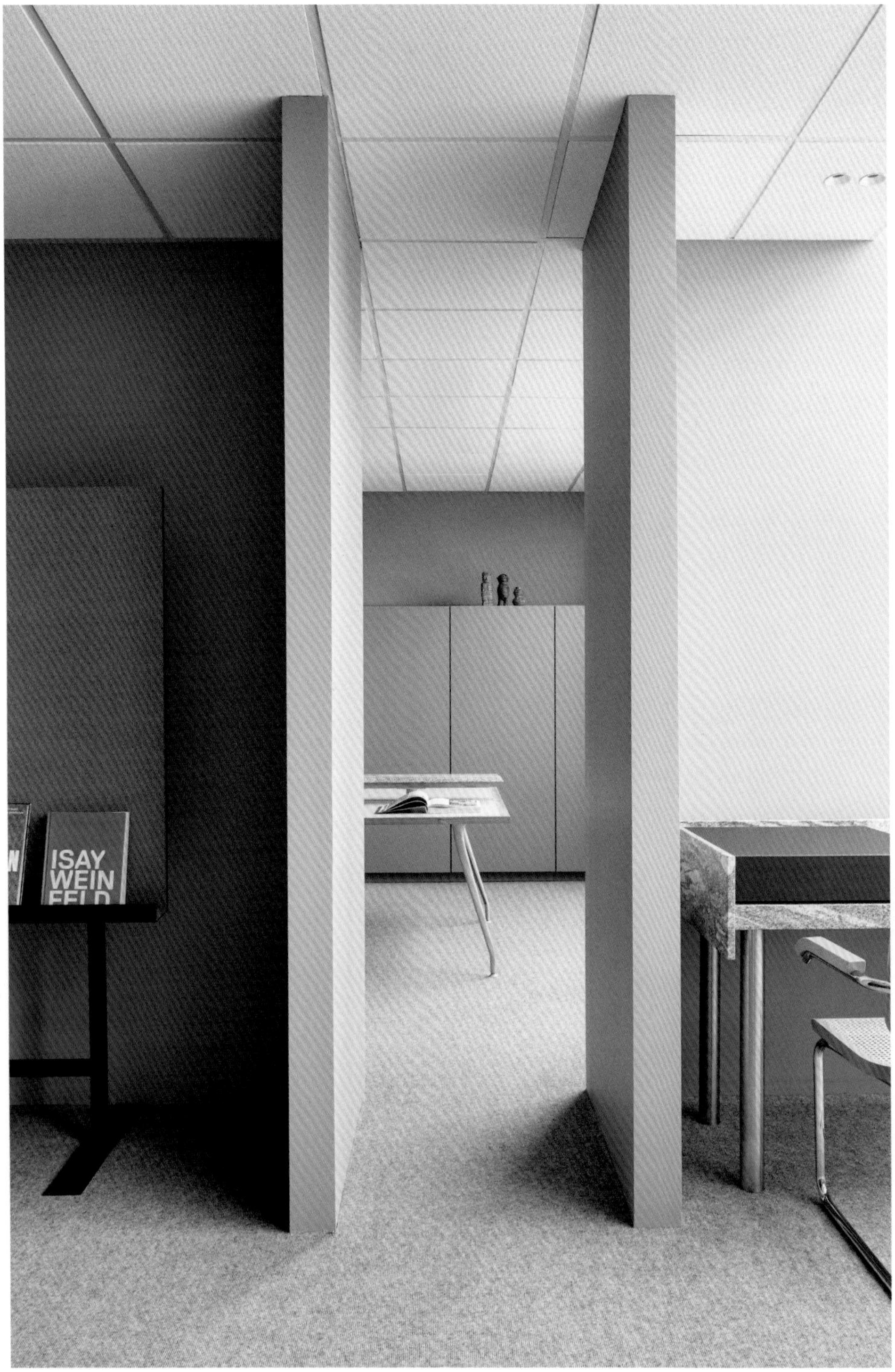
ISAY
WEIN

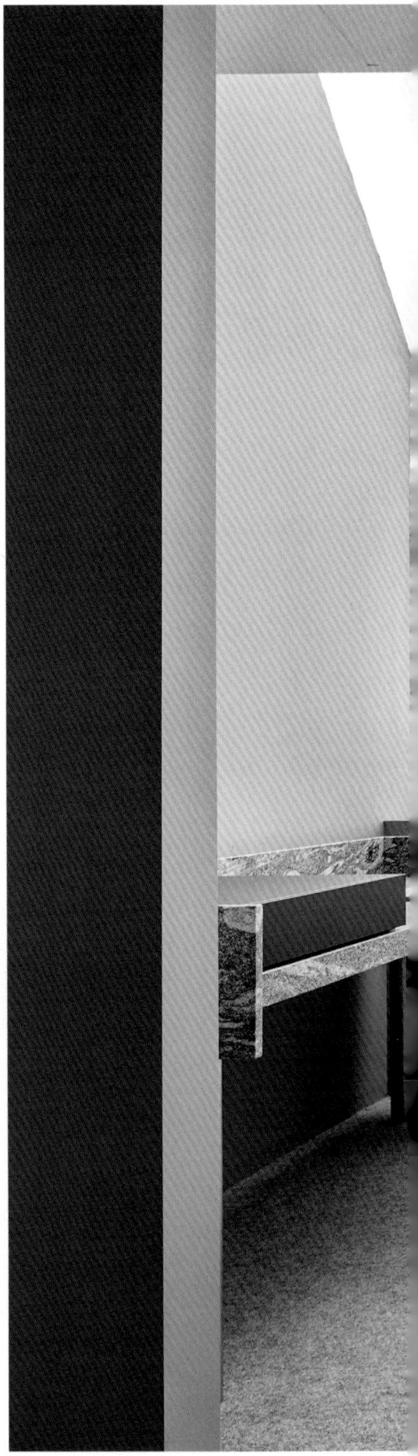

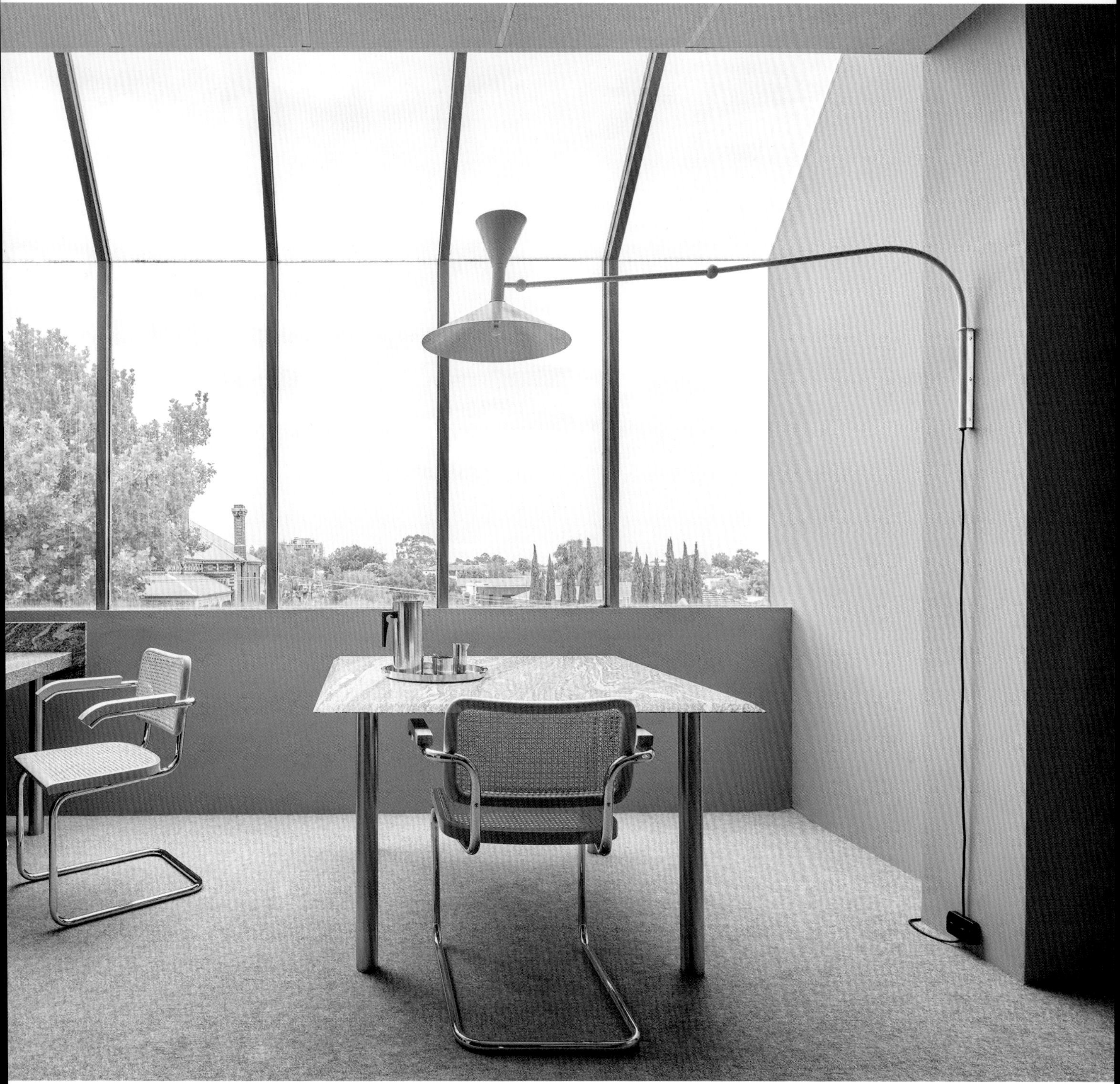

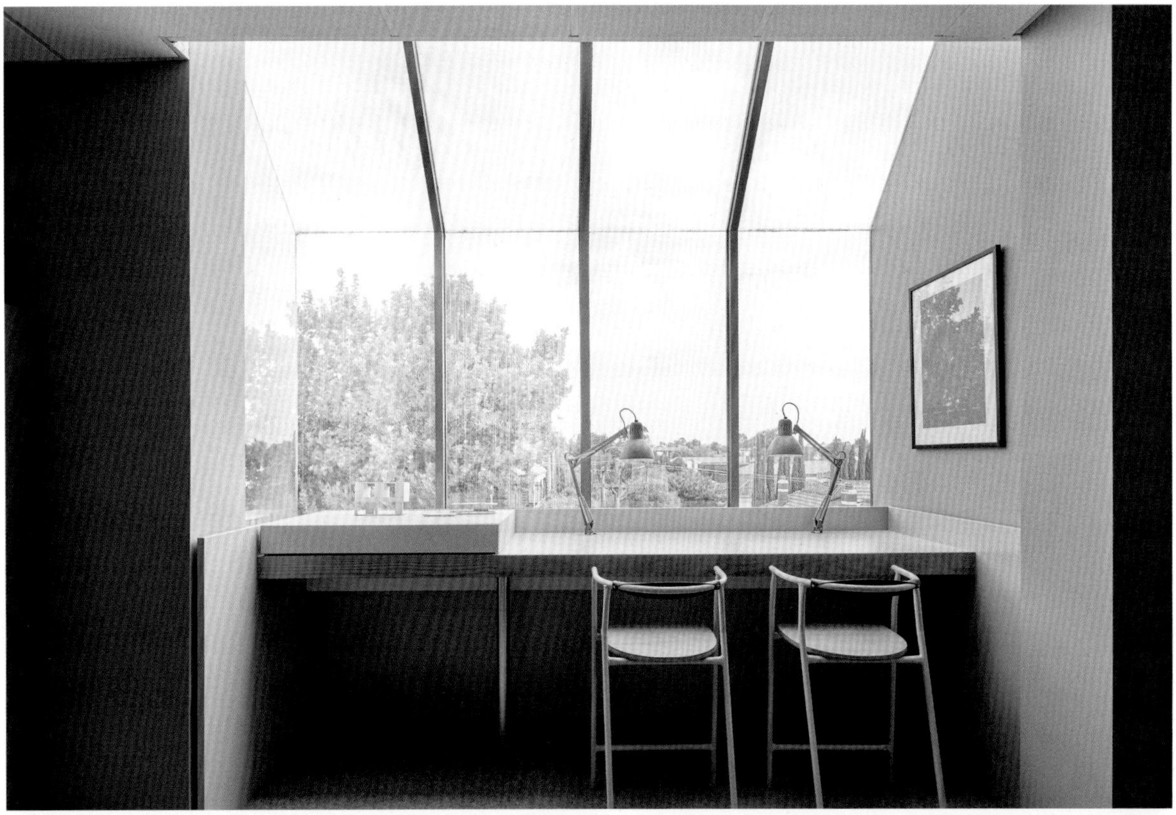

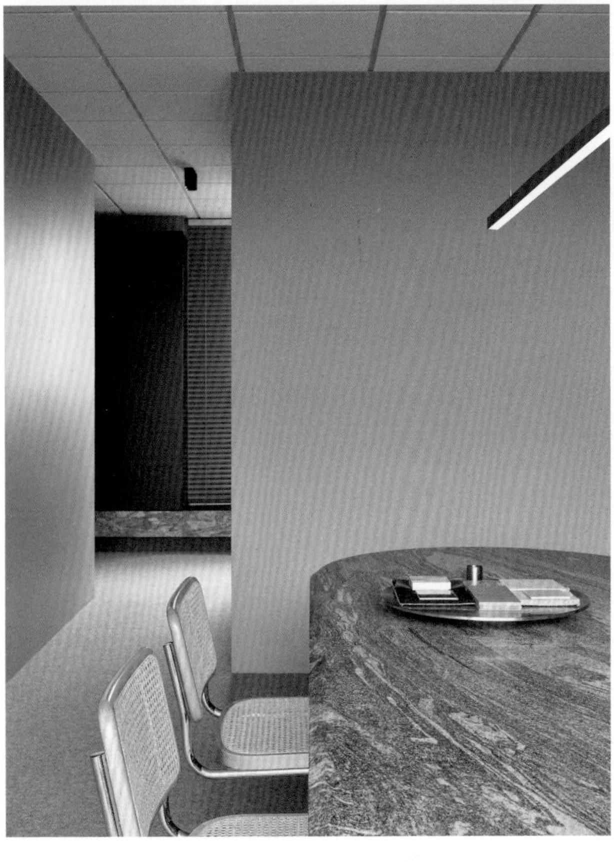

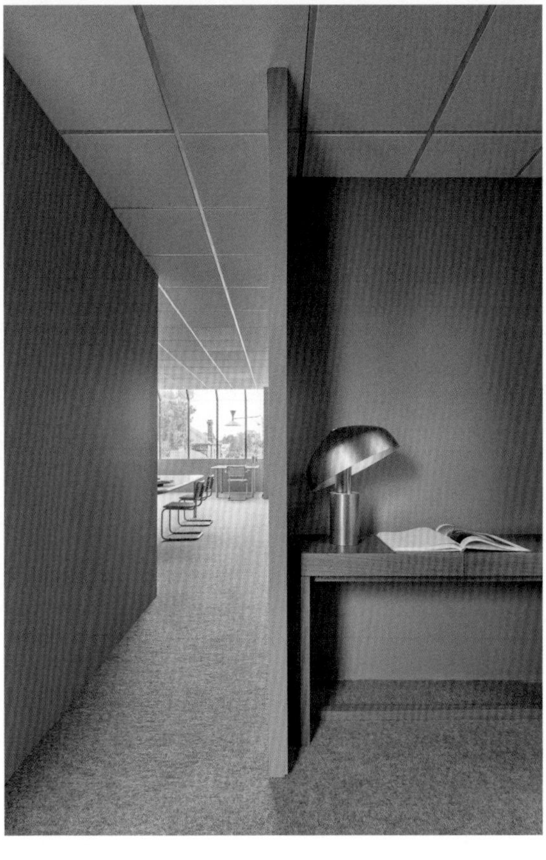

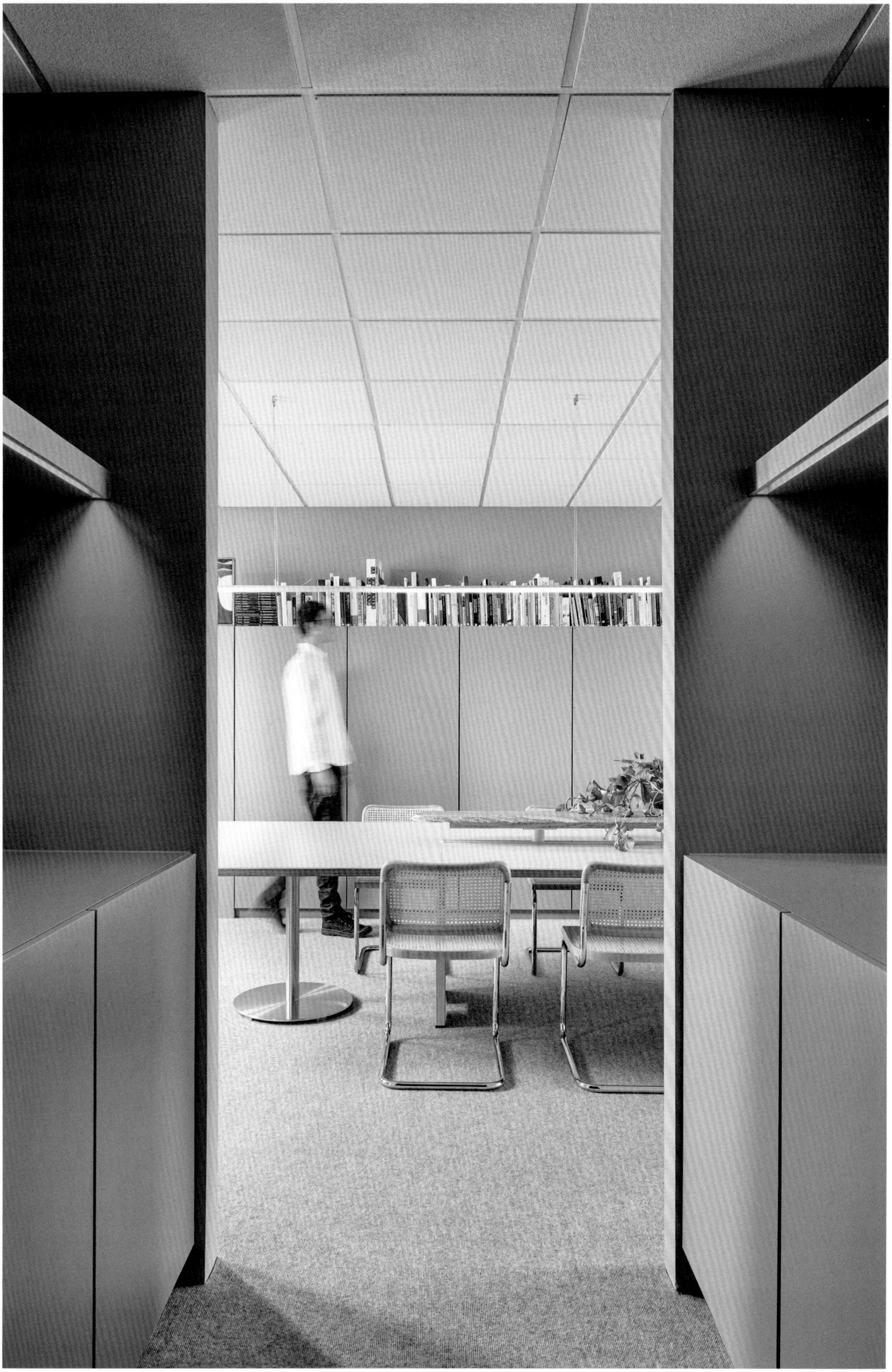

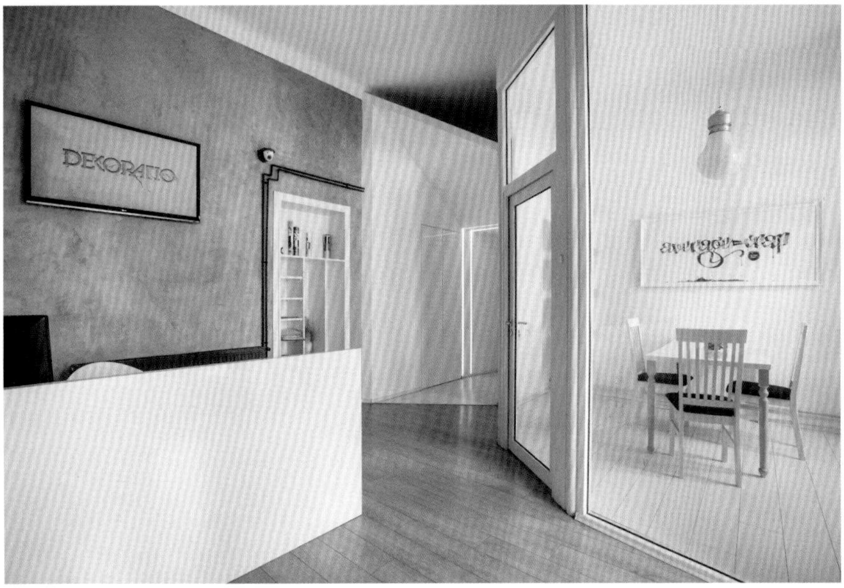

Area:
1,076 square feet (100 square meters)

Completion:
2015

Design:
kissmiklos

Photography:
Bálint Jaksa

Budapest, Hungary

Dekoratio Branding and Design Studio

With its new studio, Dekoratio Branding and Design wanted to create an experience that inspired ambitious companies to use better design and to demonstrate how design can have a positive effect on their business. Its number-one goal was to design a space that offers a creative experience and serves as a showroom for interior design and decoration.

A clear white office and an industrial space

In the interior a line cuts through the space in the angle of the "K" from the Dekoratio logo. It divides the rooms between a clear white office space and an industrial space. This separation expresses the studio's main characteristics: its capacity to do both brand strategy and design, as well as the actual production of signs and prints.

A corridor was built in the same angle to connect the reception with the rest of the studio and also to separate out a space for the account manager team. Its special shape in the reception is designed to create a visual image that draws the visitor into the studio.

Several references to branding and the design profession appear around the studio: the Lorem Ipsum sign on the wall, and the round meeting table that is designed as a big Pantone Palette. The symbols of world-famous superhero characters are also a tribute to the extraordinary branding achievement of Disney, Marvel, and DC.

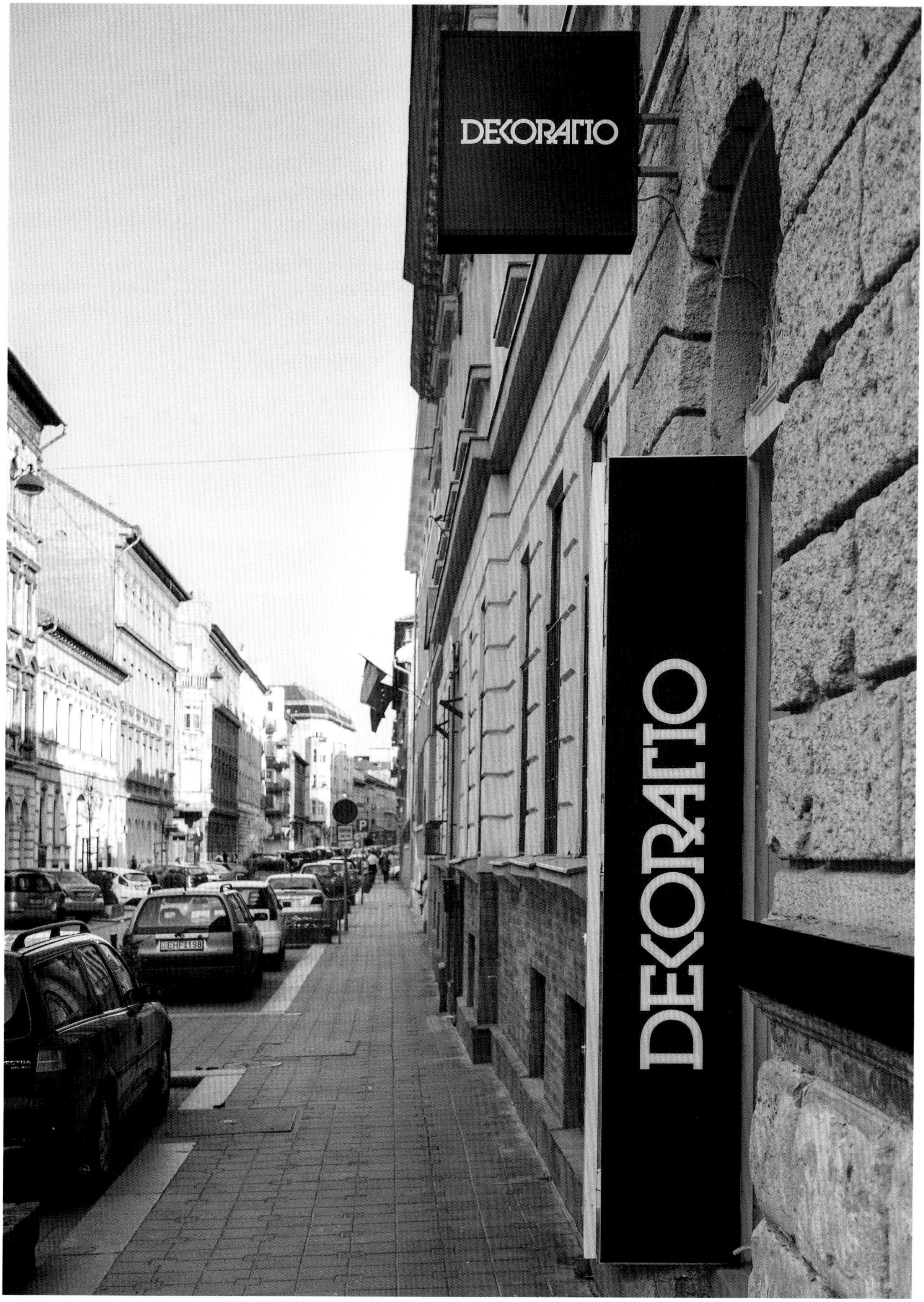
DEKORATIO
DEKORATIO

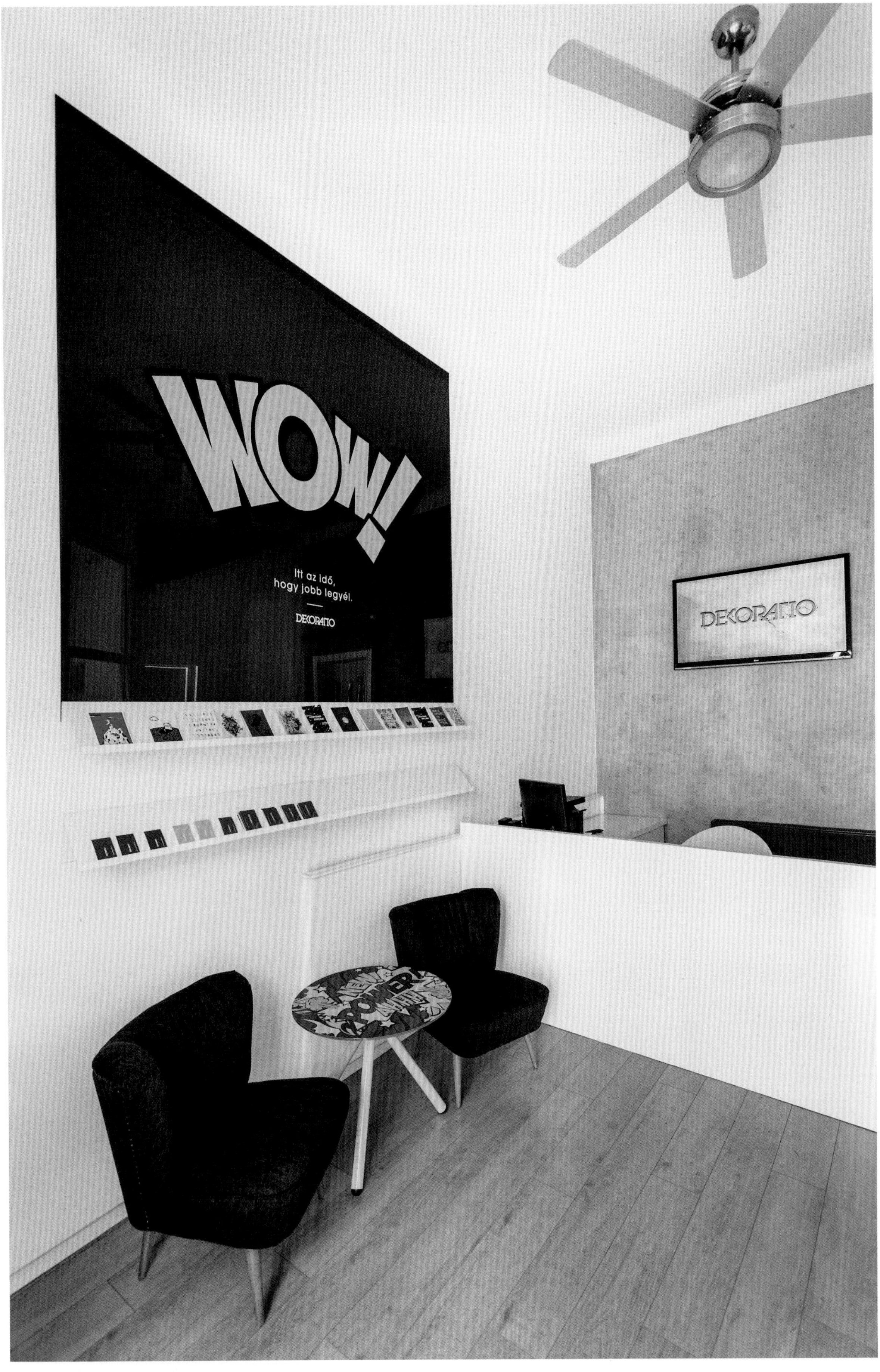
WOW!
Itt az idő,
hogy jobb legyél.
DEKORATIO
DEKORATIO

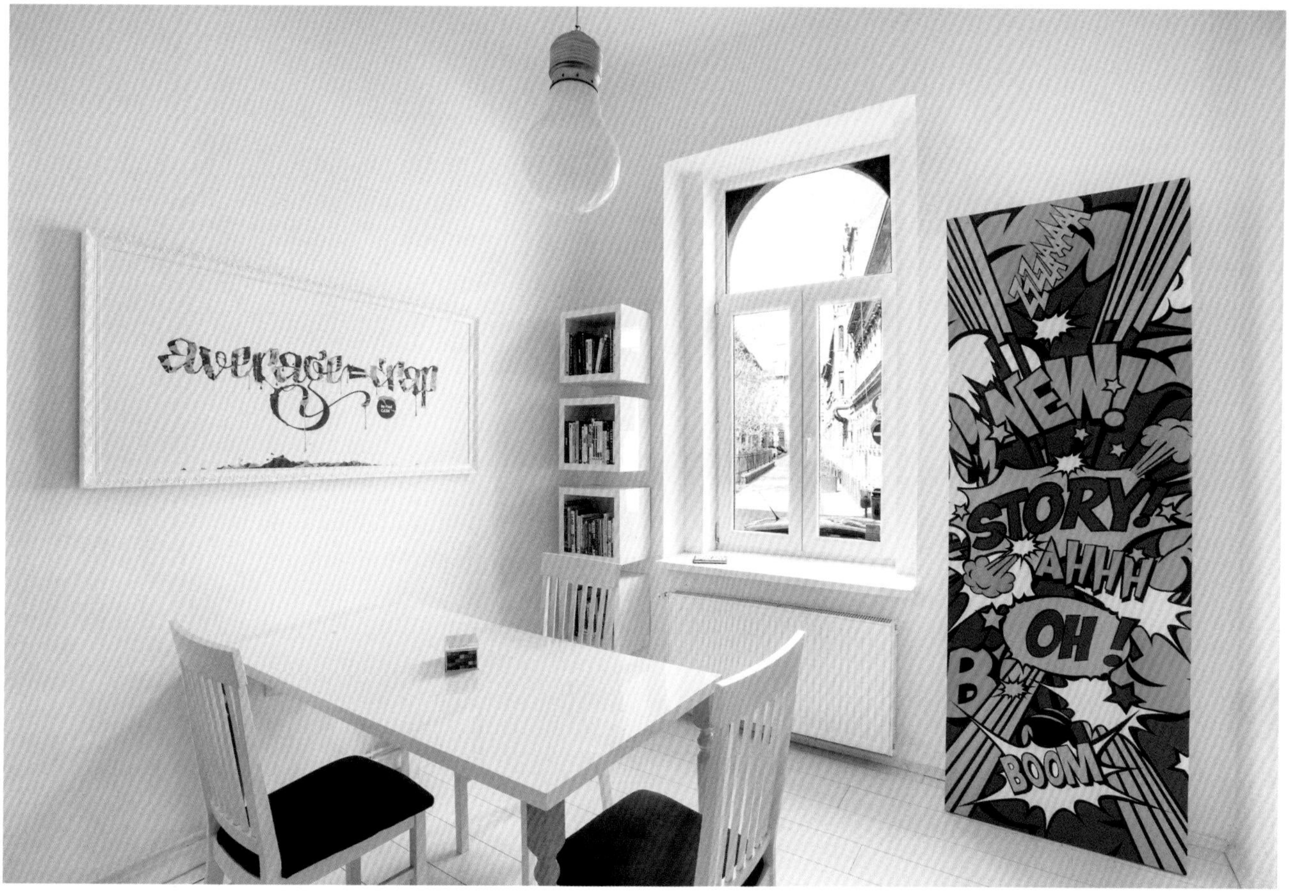

Comics and pop culture

Comics are used throughout the studio as a reference to the role pop culture played in America in the evolution of applied art and advertising. In each room there is a comic illustration that has a connection with the function of the room. The cupboard that serves to hide the boiler is covered with the word BOOM, and in the meeting room, where stories are born, the main word is STORY. The little table on which complimentary chocolates are set has the word POWER on it.

A big personality

In the library-style social room the bookshelf was custom made from the letters of LEARN, which is accompanied by a big "Believe in BETTER" sign that abbreviates to "Believe in BEER" as a sliding door opens across it. Designs with the studio's mottos, strategy, and goals appear around the interior. They form part of the employer's branding effort, but they also give clients and other visitors a feel for the personality and values of the studio.

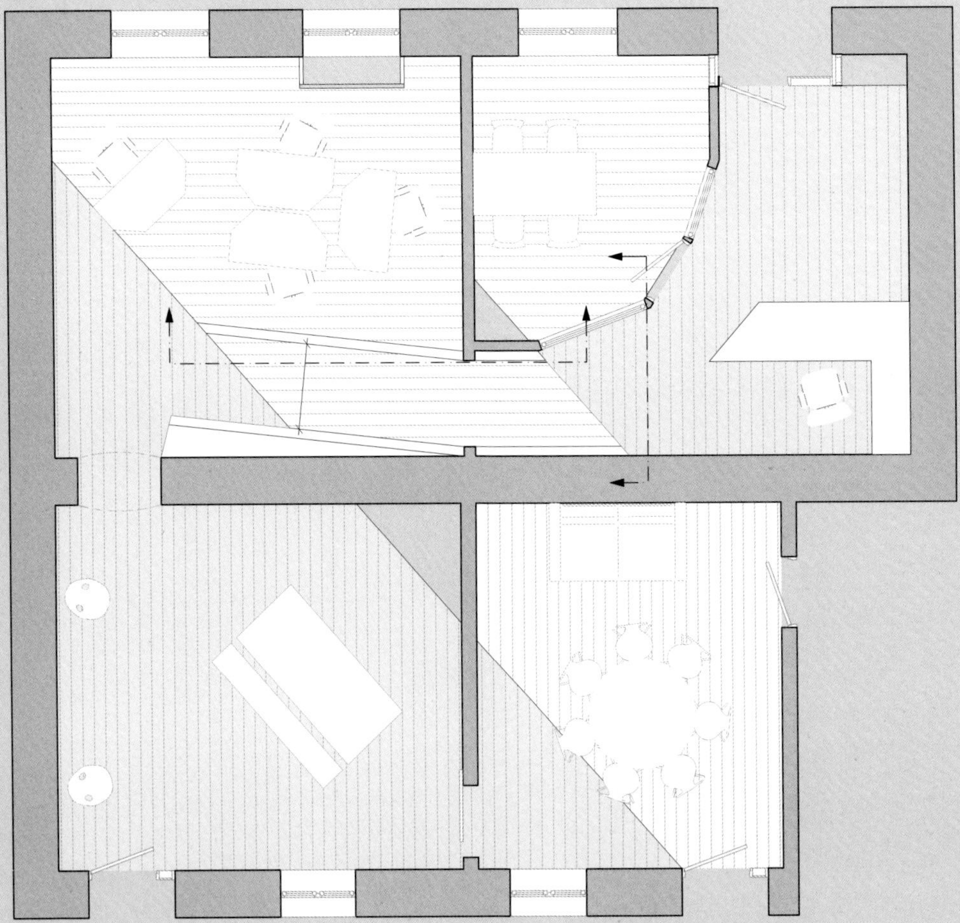

Floor plan

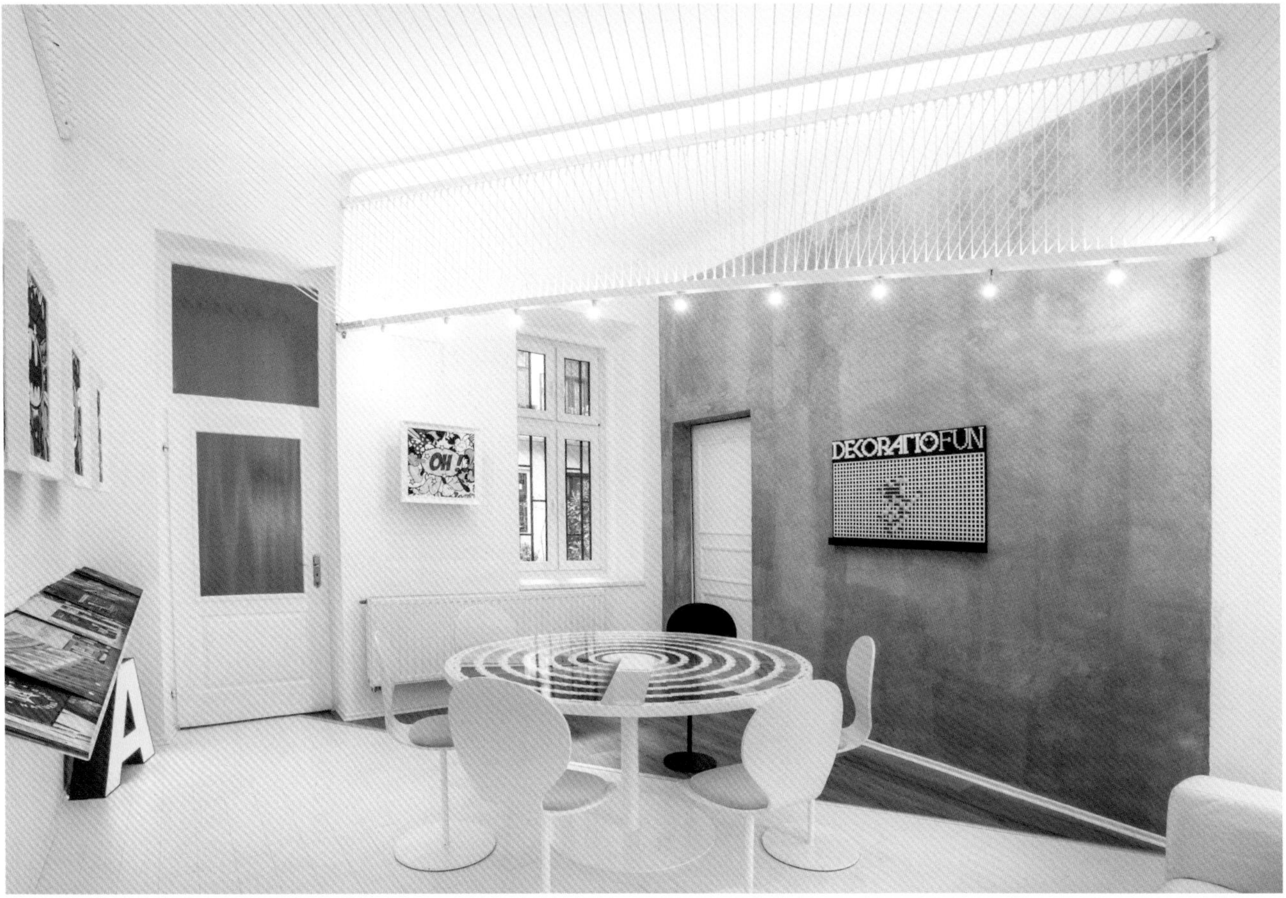
DECORATIOFUN
OH

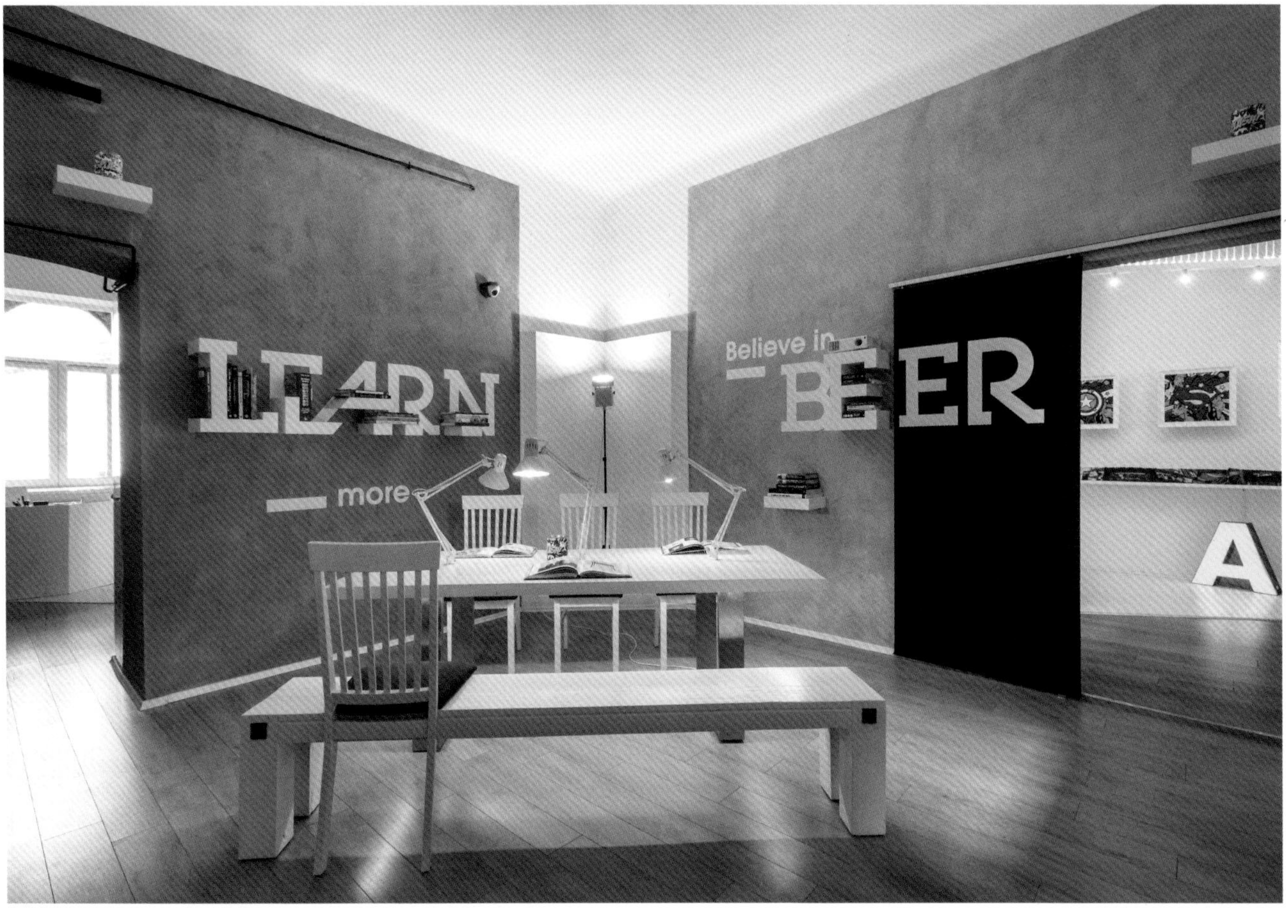
LEARN
more
Believe in
BEER
A

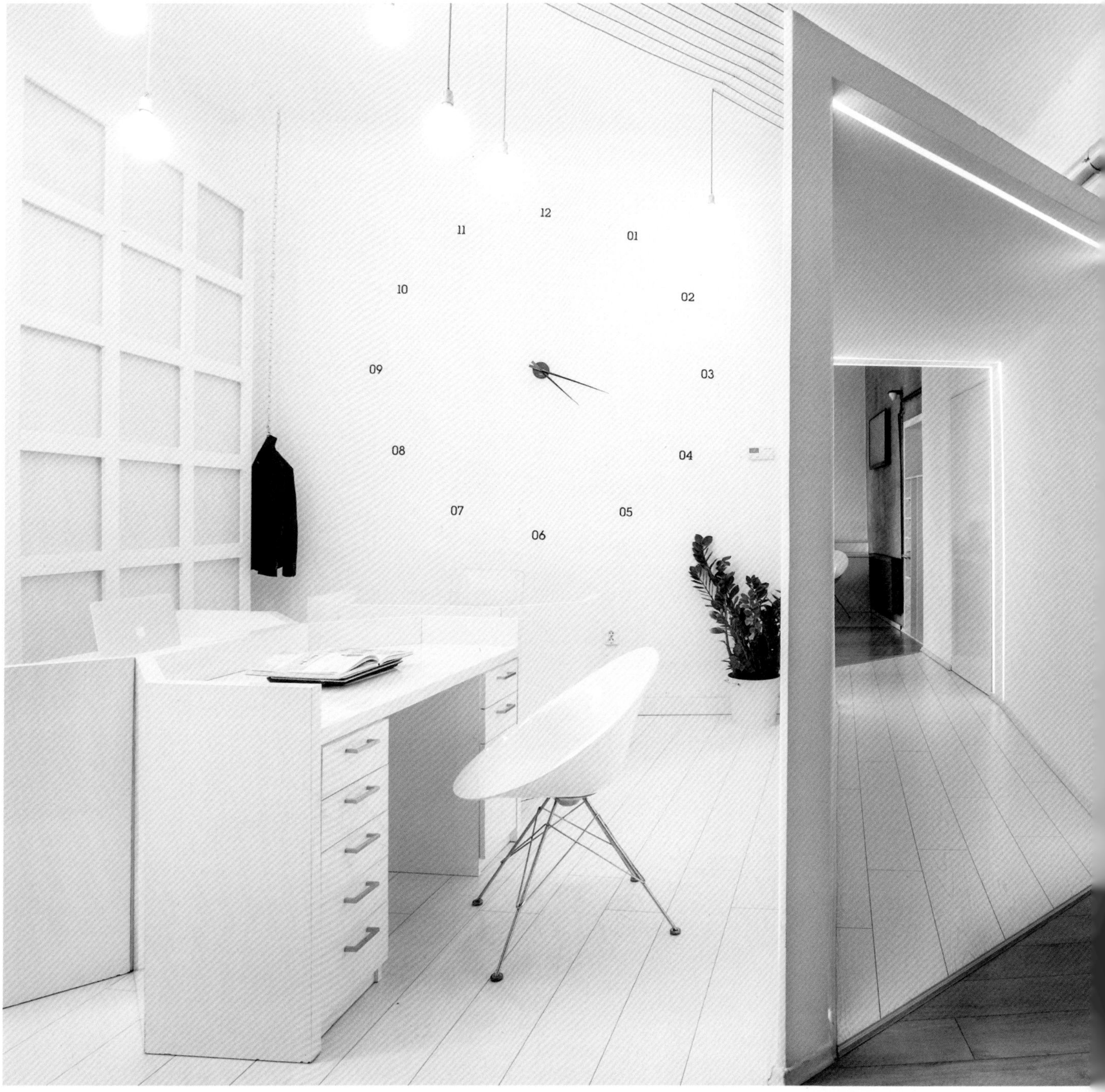
12
11
01
10
02
09
03
08
04
07
05
06

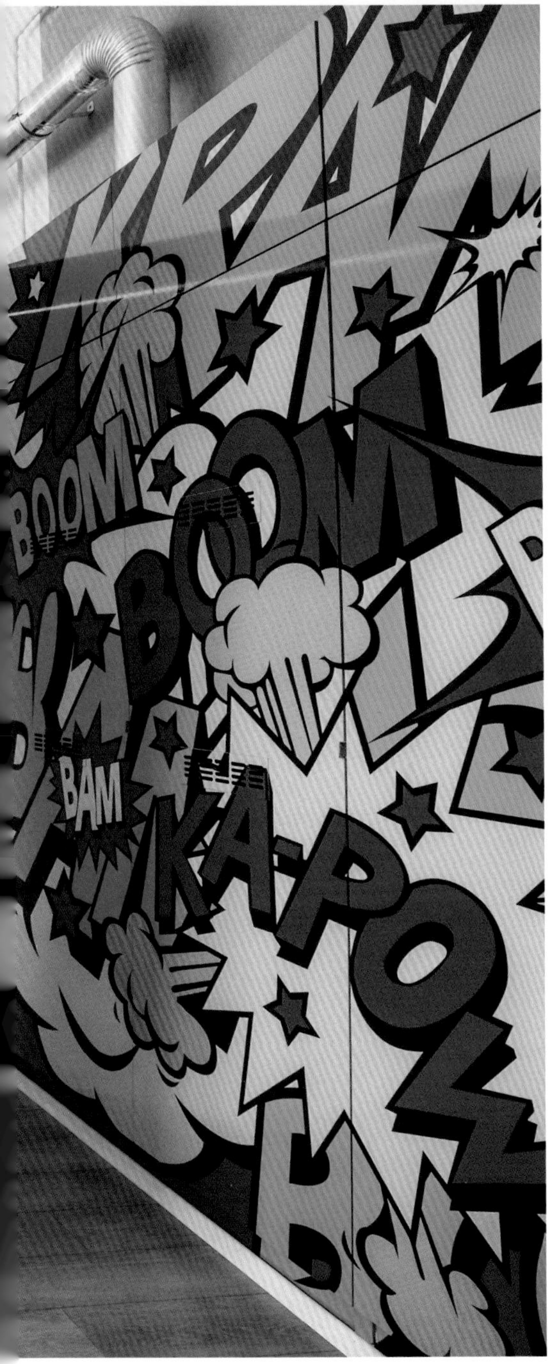
BOOM
BAM
KA-POW

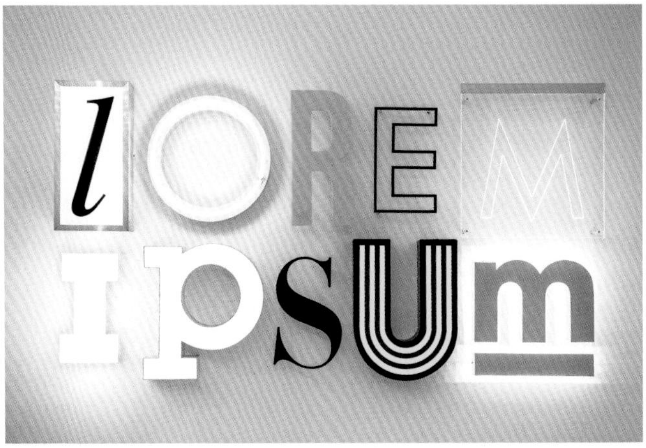
lOREM
IPSUM

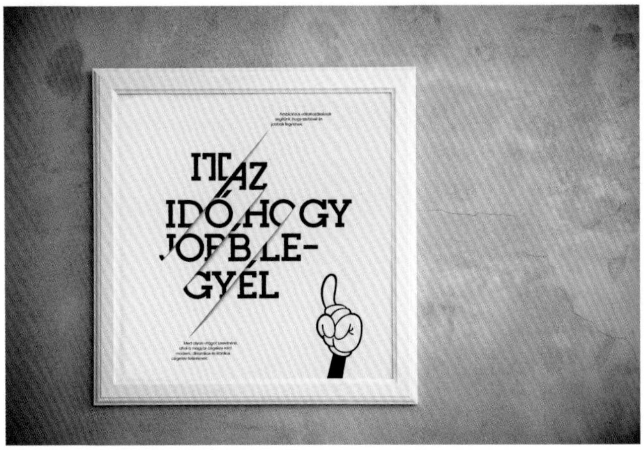
ITT AZ
IDŐ, HOGY
JOBB LE-
GYÉL

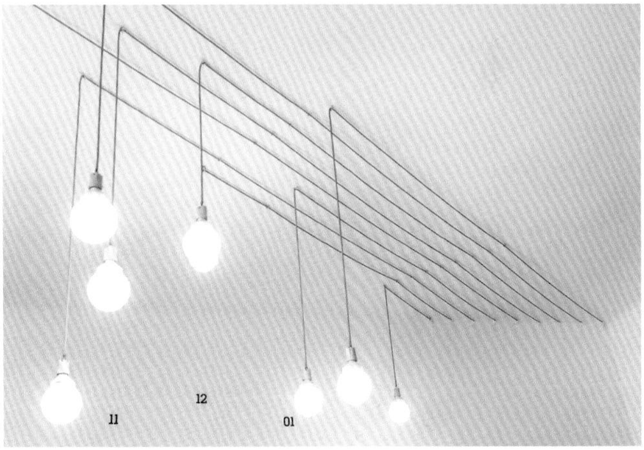
11
12
01

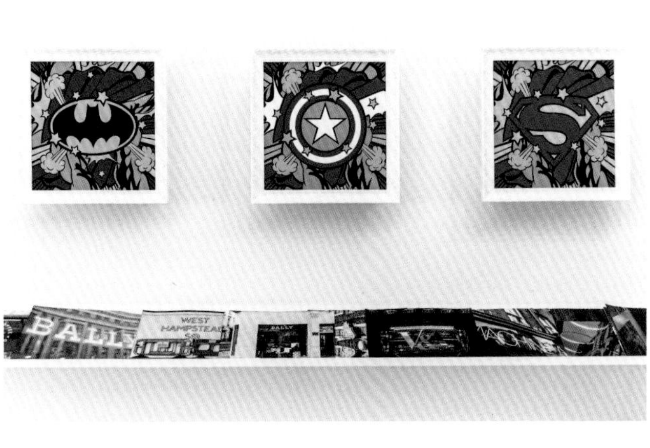

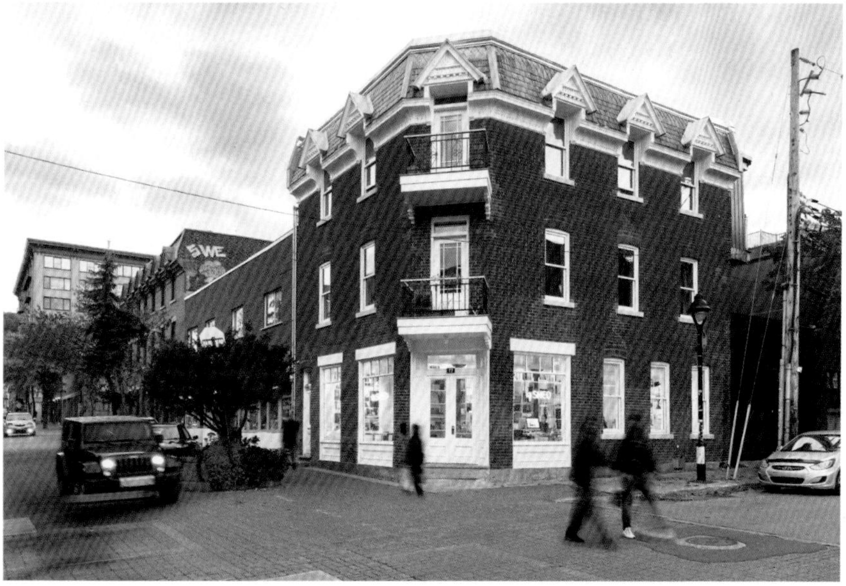

Area:
947 square feet (88 square meters)

Completion:
2015

Design:
la SHED architecture

Photography:
Maxime Brouillet

Montréal, Canada

la SHED

Located in what used to be a Plateau-Mont-Royal general store, la SHED preserves the area's vernacular architecture while adopting a resolutely contemporary appearance that reflects the image of la SHED architecture, a company that performs most of its work in residential sectors and has expertise in the renovation, transformation, and construction of buildings of all types and historical backgrounds.

An open working area

The workshop and adjacent meeting space are completely open and the glass façade allows passersby to observe the architects at work. Halfway between an office and a boutique, the space redefines the traditional architect's office. The original building's structure, at the center of the office, is highlighted by its neon color scheme. On one side of the office is a large white block that contains the meeting room, kitchen, and stationery. The central block on the other side of the office is divided into a materials library that harkens back to the general store's shelving units. These shelves allow light to filter through to the meeting room that is isolated by a frosted glass wall. The wood paneling, table trestles, lighting, and choice of accessories combine to provide the workshop with a casual, collegial, and well-thought-out atmosphere.

Creative spaces

Besides the working space, other areas are also full of creativity. The bathroom, located in the basement at the foot of a black steel staircase, is surprising due to its lack of a partition. The sliding full-height pocket door disappears entirely once open, removing any boundaries within the space. The wall-to-wall mirror at the back of the bathroom conveys an air of mystery while the sink seems to float in the middle of the space. The pitch-black floor and ceiling bounded by the rubble rock foundation wall provide a stark contrast when compared to the white workshop above, which emphasizes the bathroom's enveloping and cozy atmosphere.

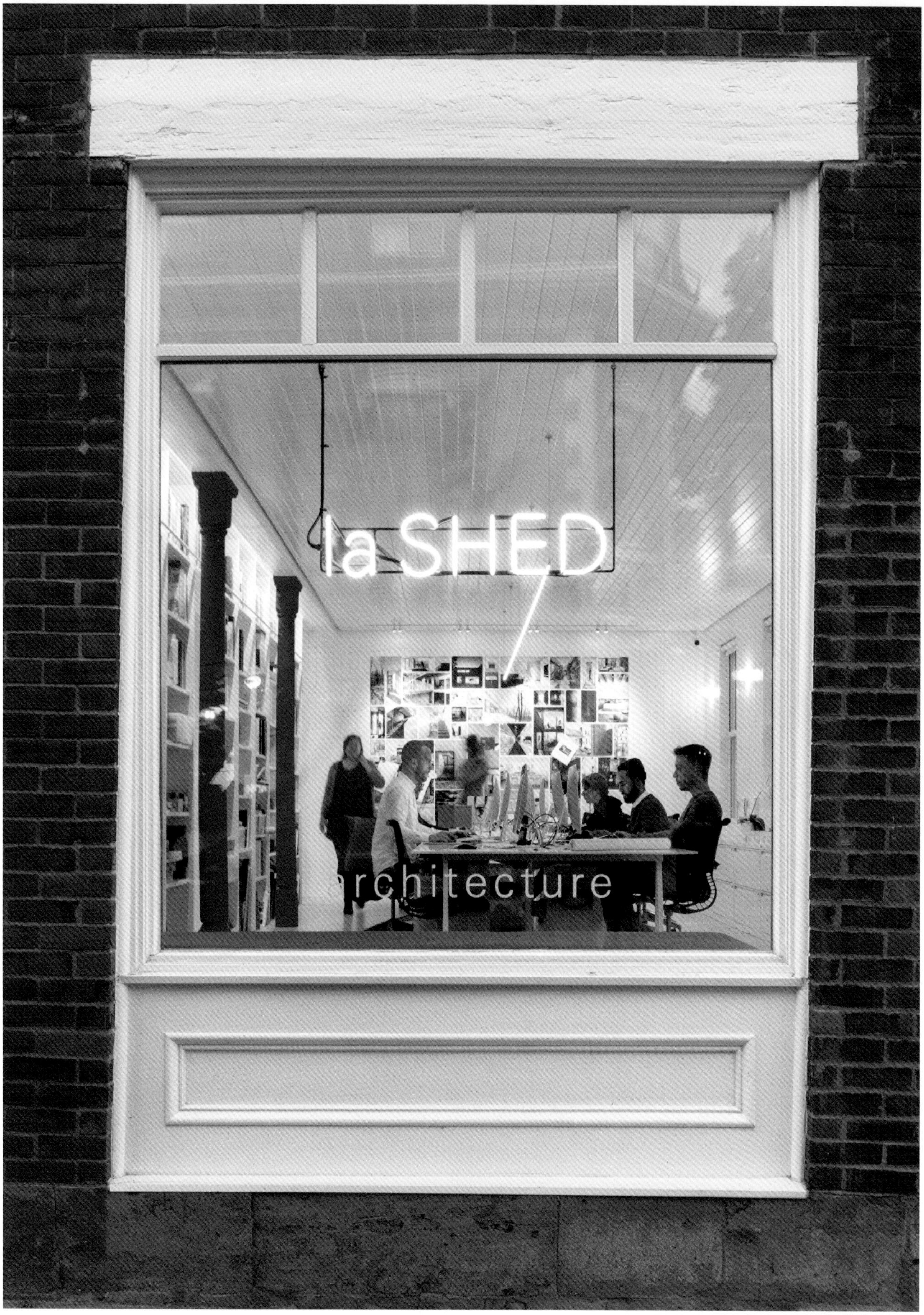
la SHED
architecture

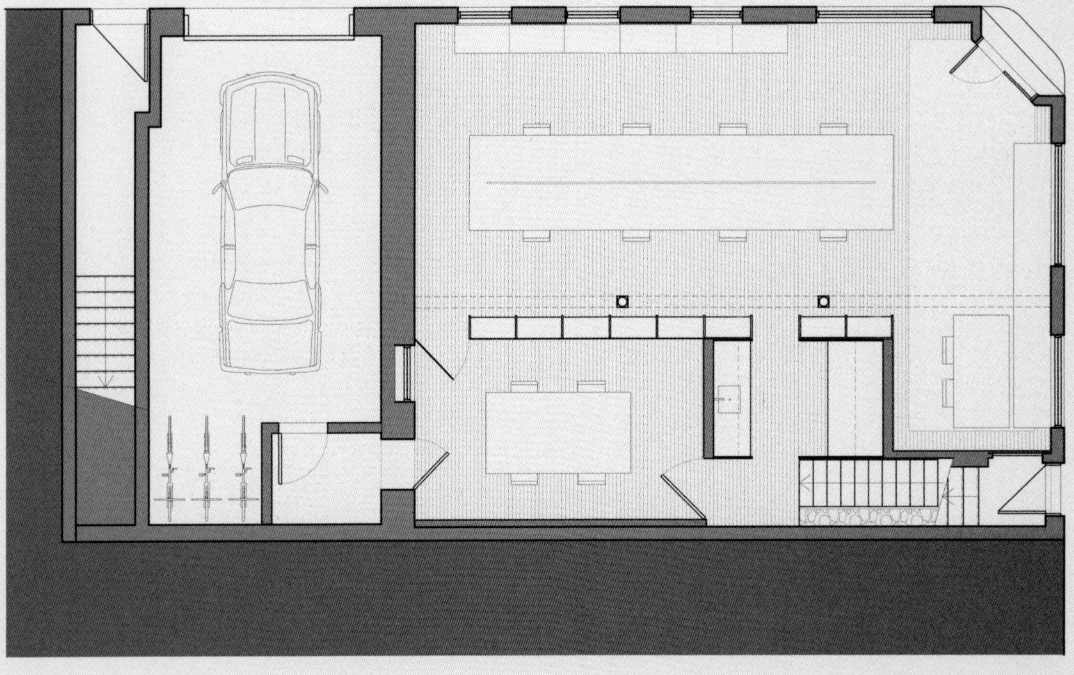

Ground-floor plan

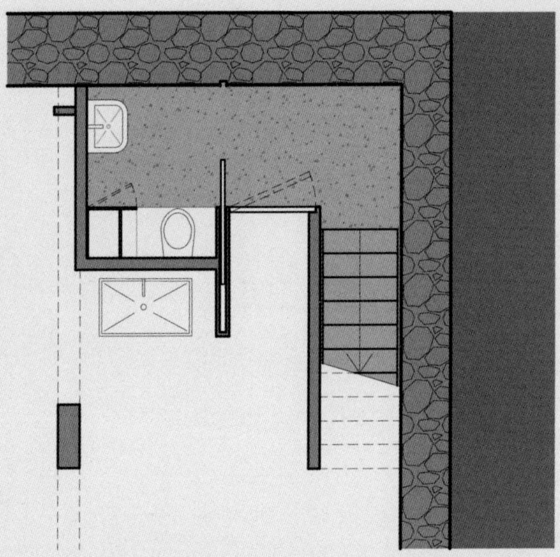

Basement floor plan

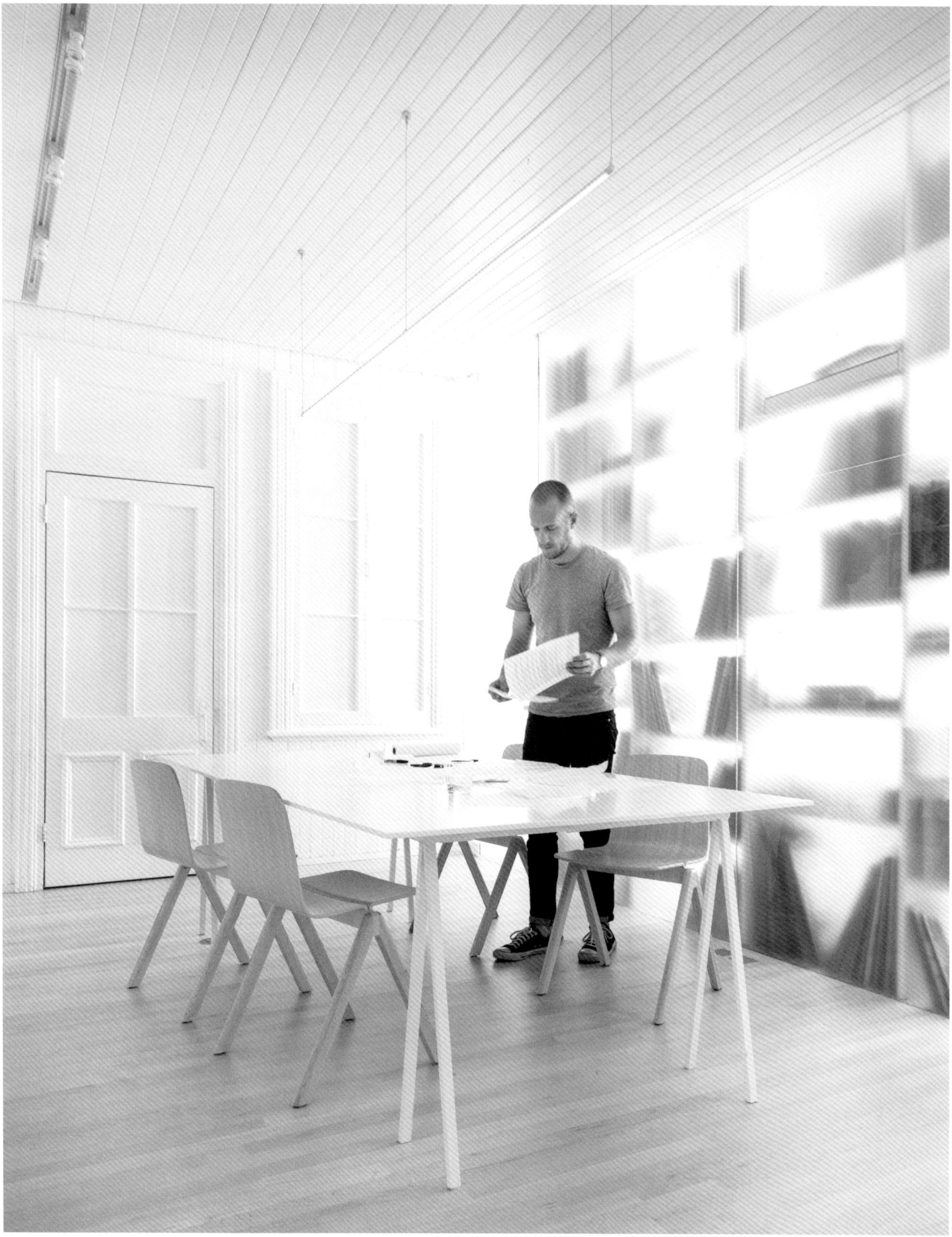

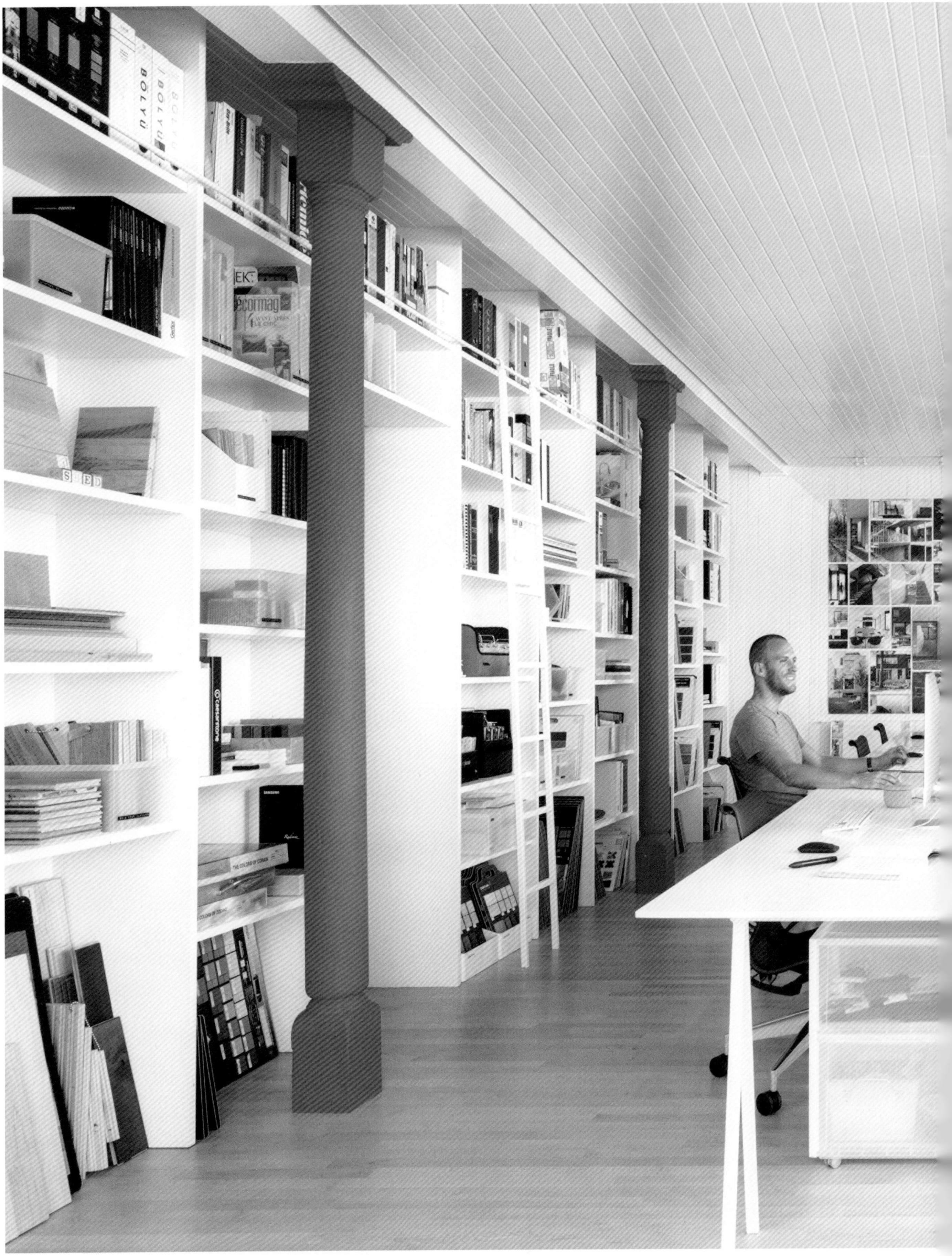

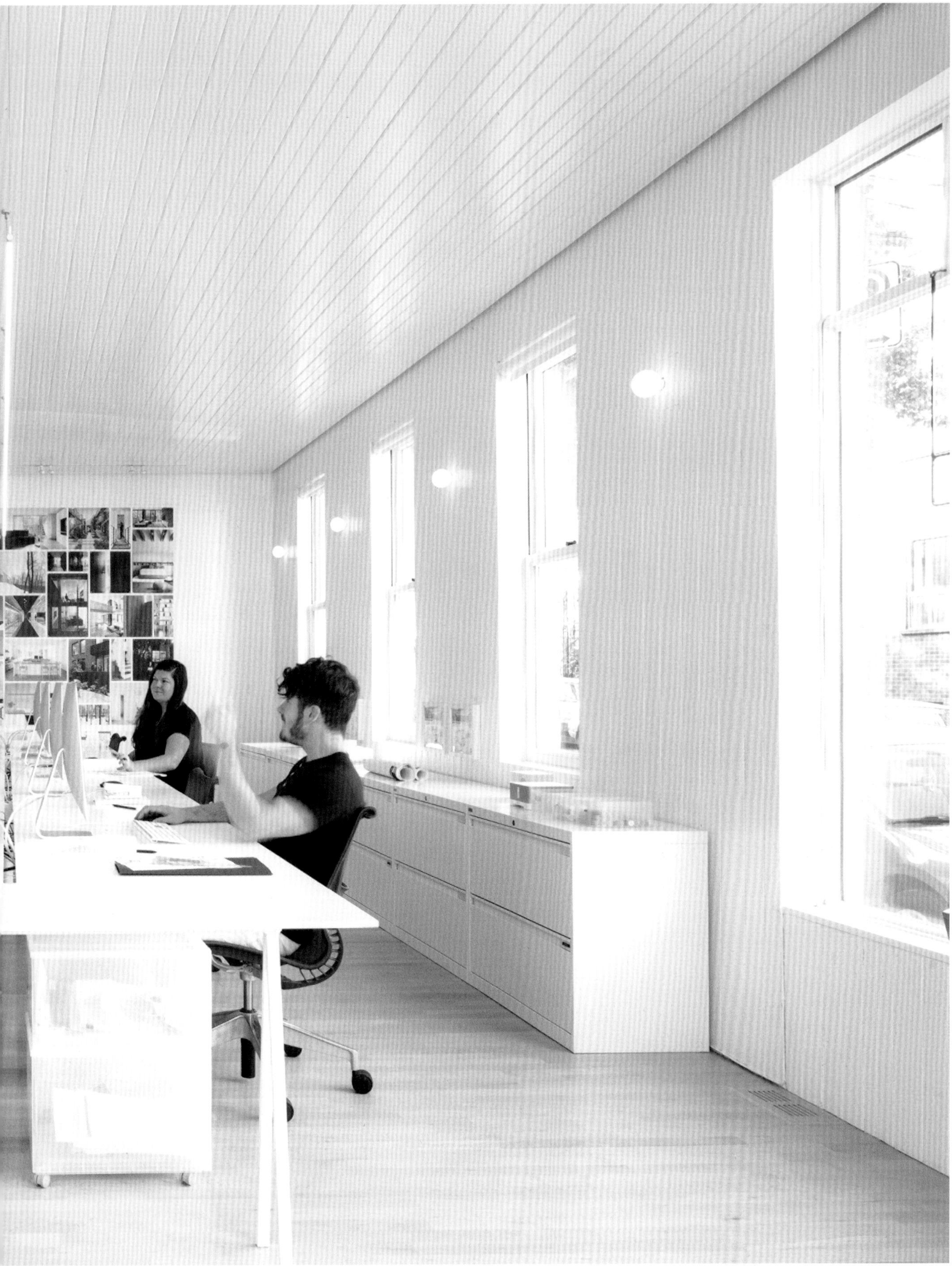

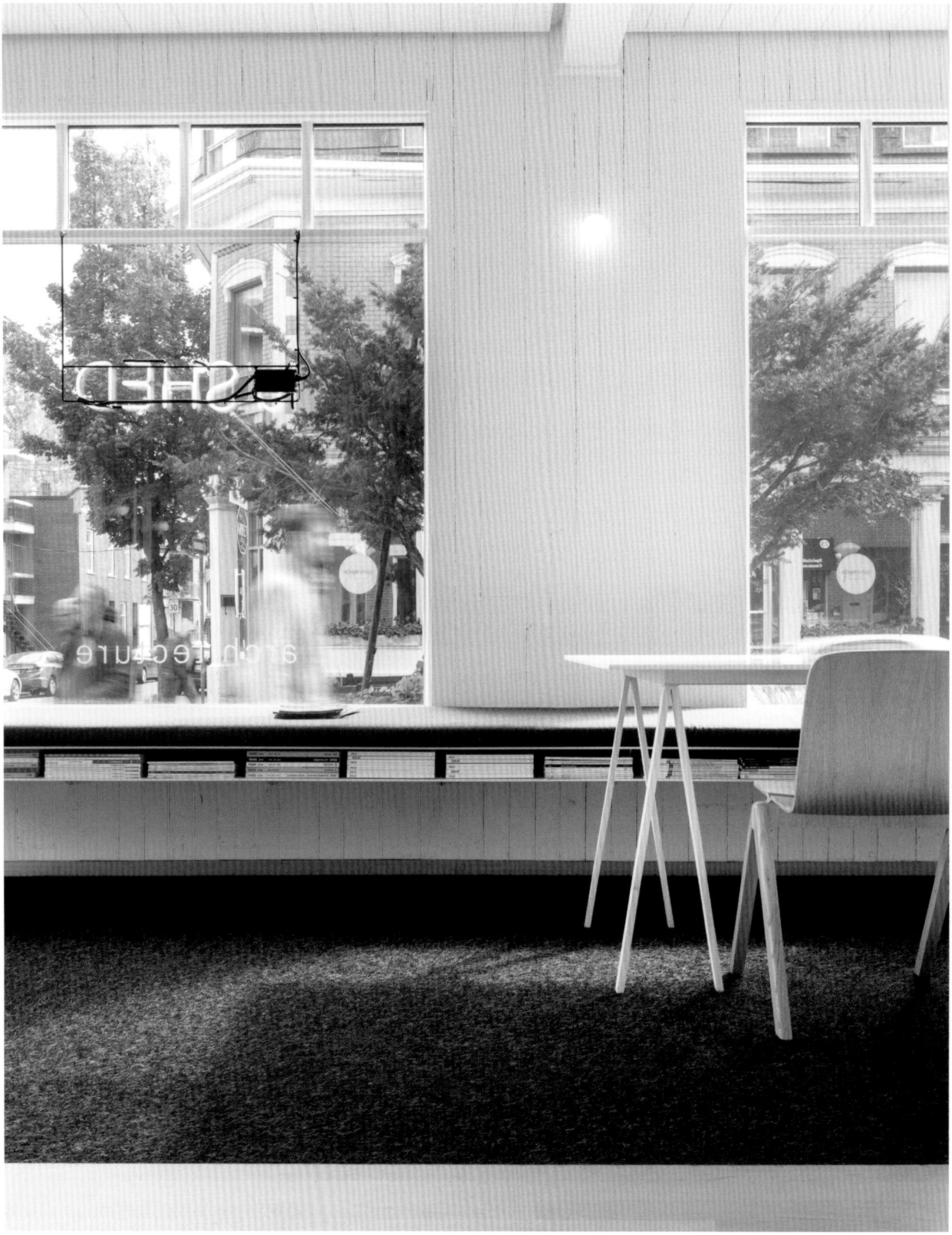

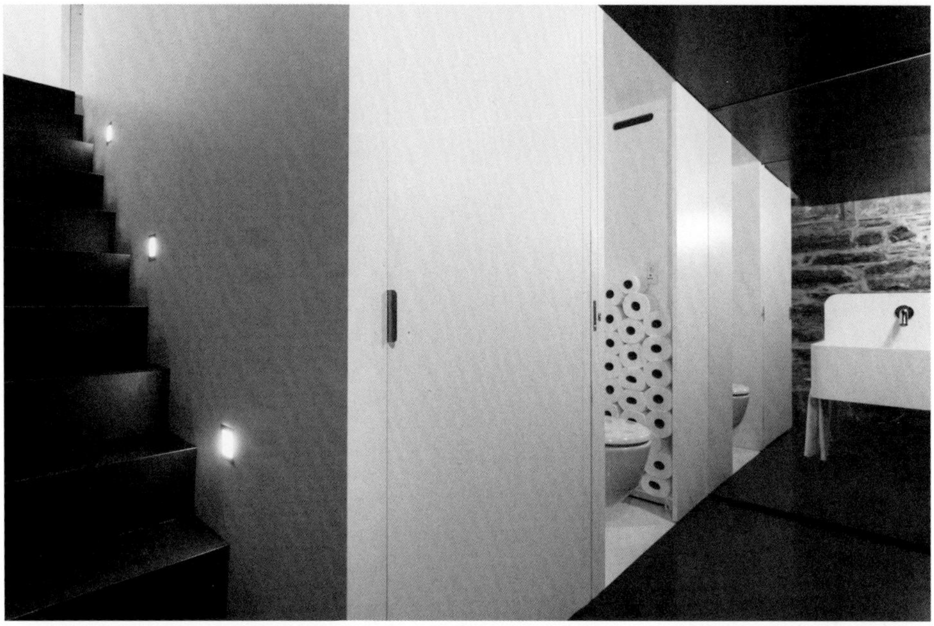

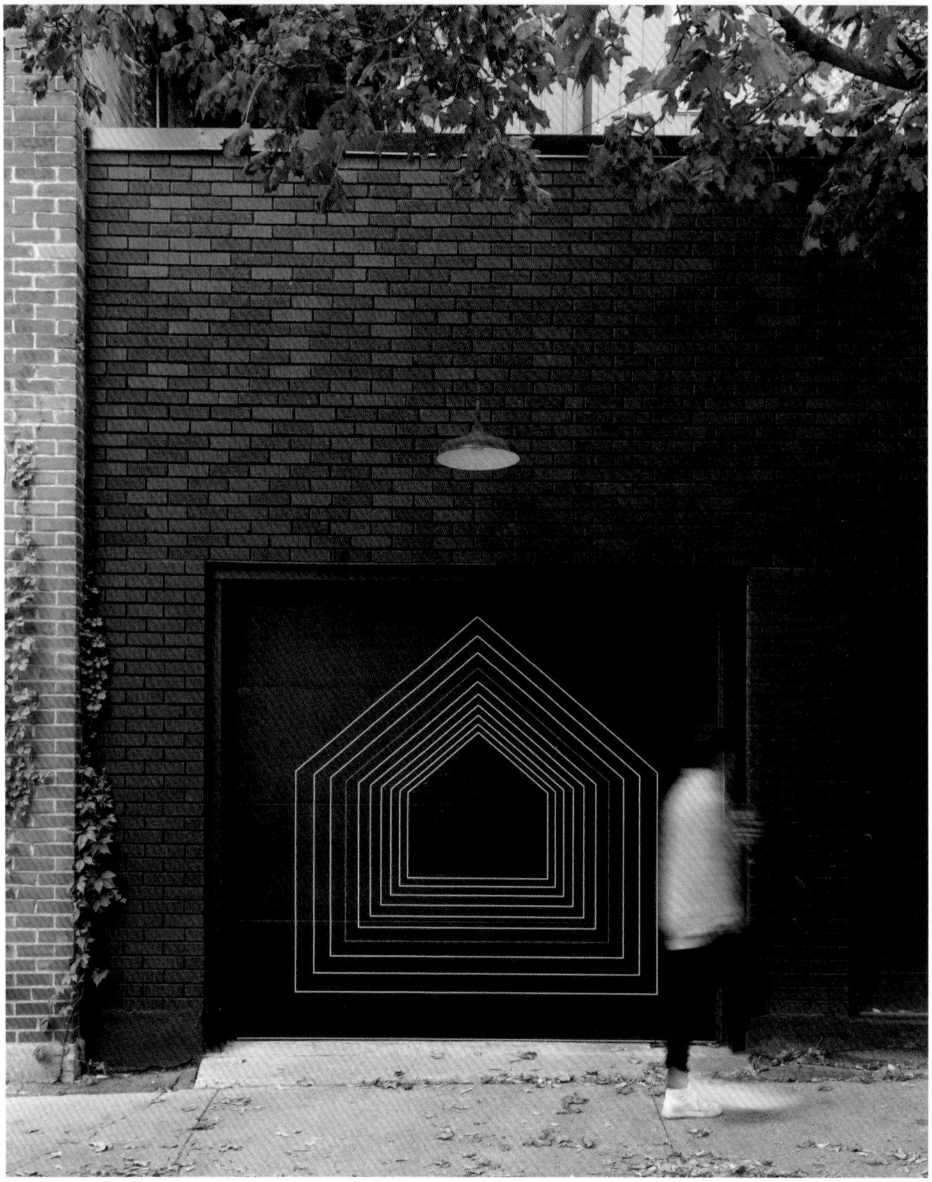

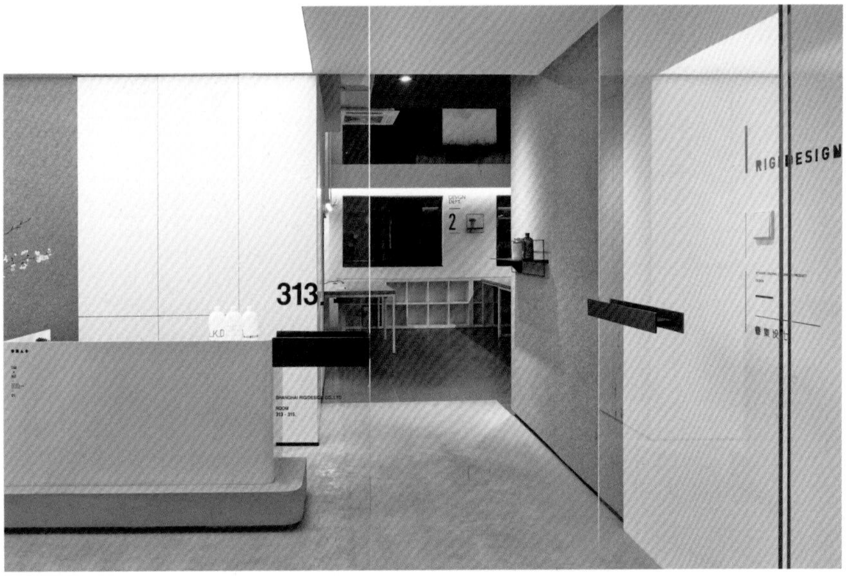

Area:
2,691 square feet (250 square meters)

Completion:
2015

Design:
RIGI Design

Photography:
Jack Wen

Shanghai, China

LK+RIGI Design Office

The site is located in a former factory space with the advantages of natural lighting and high ceilings. The fit-out divided the space into an open office, and independent office, a lab area, a meeting rooms, a materials room, and a small showroom.

To create a spacious office, the high ceilings were retained and exposed by the designers, which created an open and bright space. Above different function zones, colorful boxes were placed to define the areas below, and create a sense of fun. Contrasting colors were used throughout.

A different kind of meeting room

The original space was narrow and tall, which was not ideal for a meeting room. Designers created an internal ceiling shaped as a pitched roof with chamfered edges, while lighting was used to blur the boundaries of the space. The conference table is made of polished wood with its natural colors retained.

Color and intimacy

Creative use of soft dark-gray felts as wall material was used to convey a feeling of intimacy, while at the same time providing a textural contrast to the black and white paint used elsewhere. By using lightweight open bookshelves as partitions, together with plants, the environment was made more friendly and lively.

Throughout the process, designers considered the impact of the design on the staff who would work there, and the stories and designs that would be produced in the office.

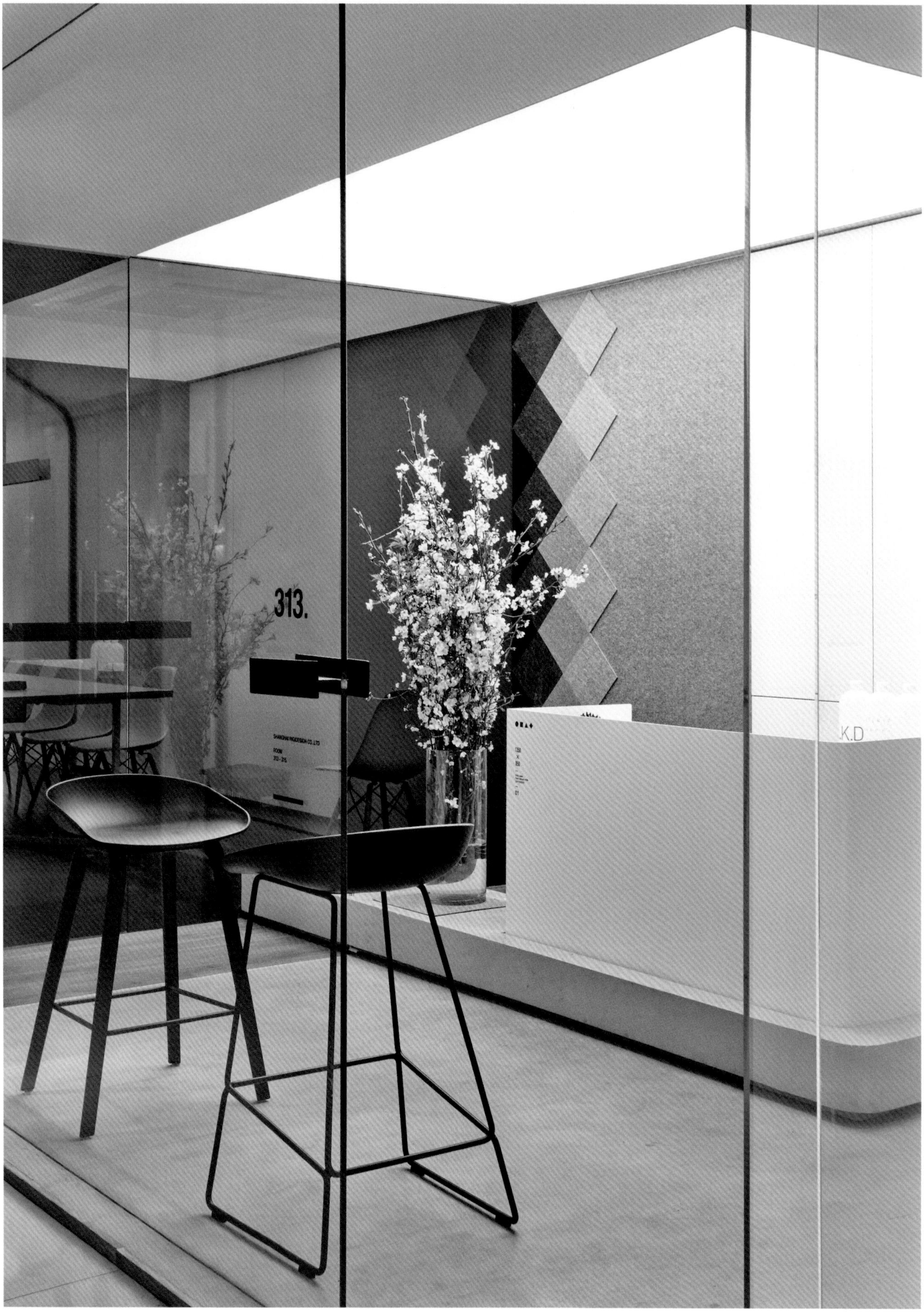
313.
K.D

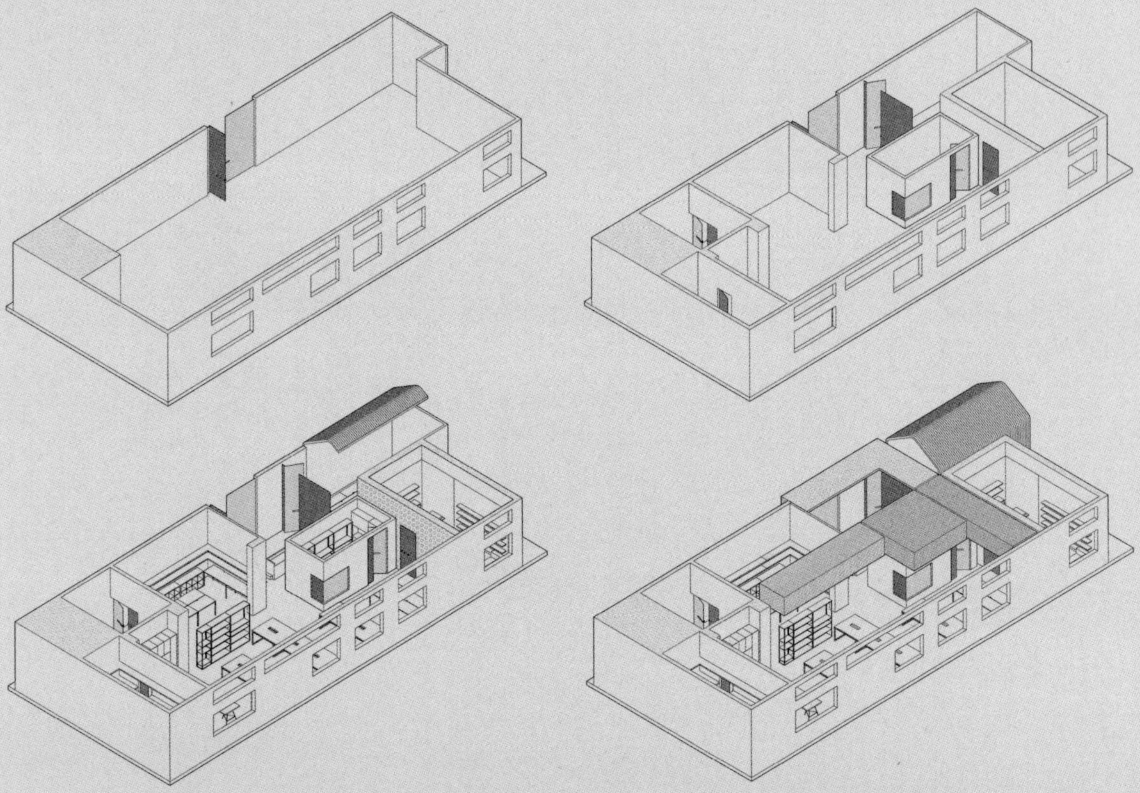

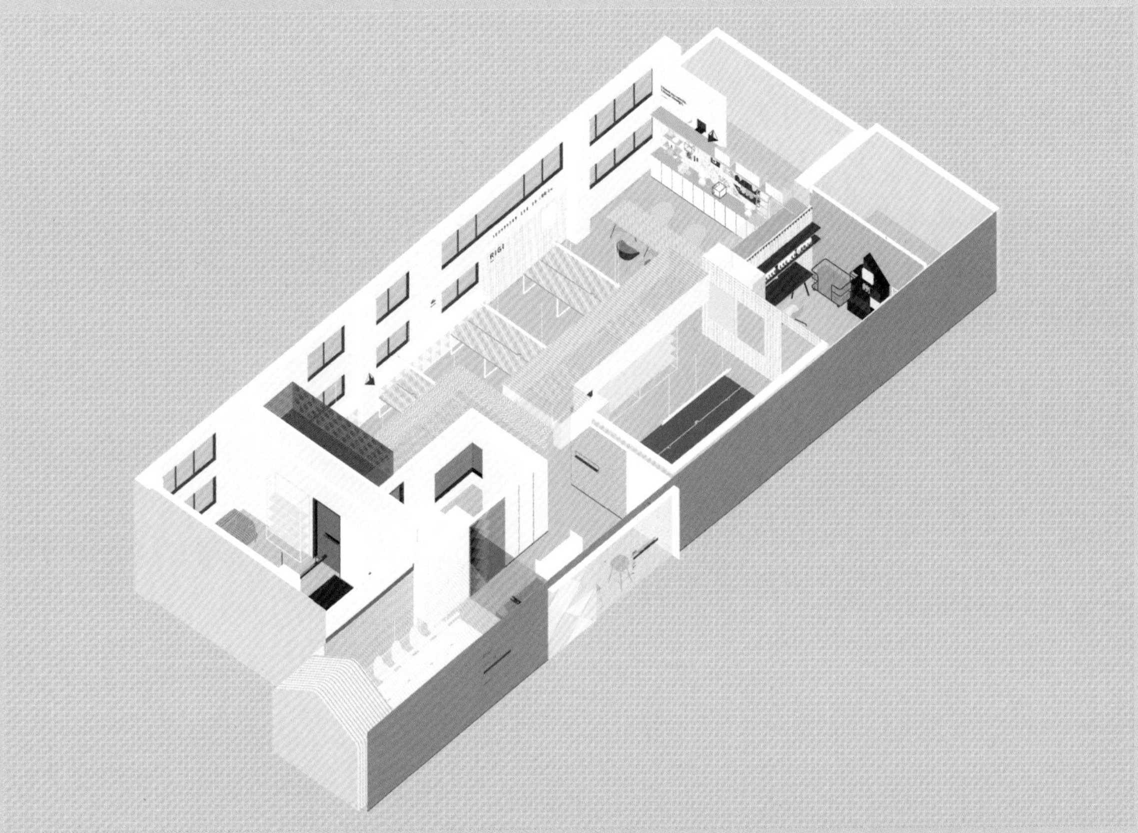

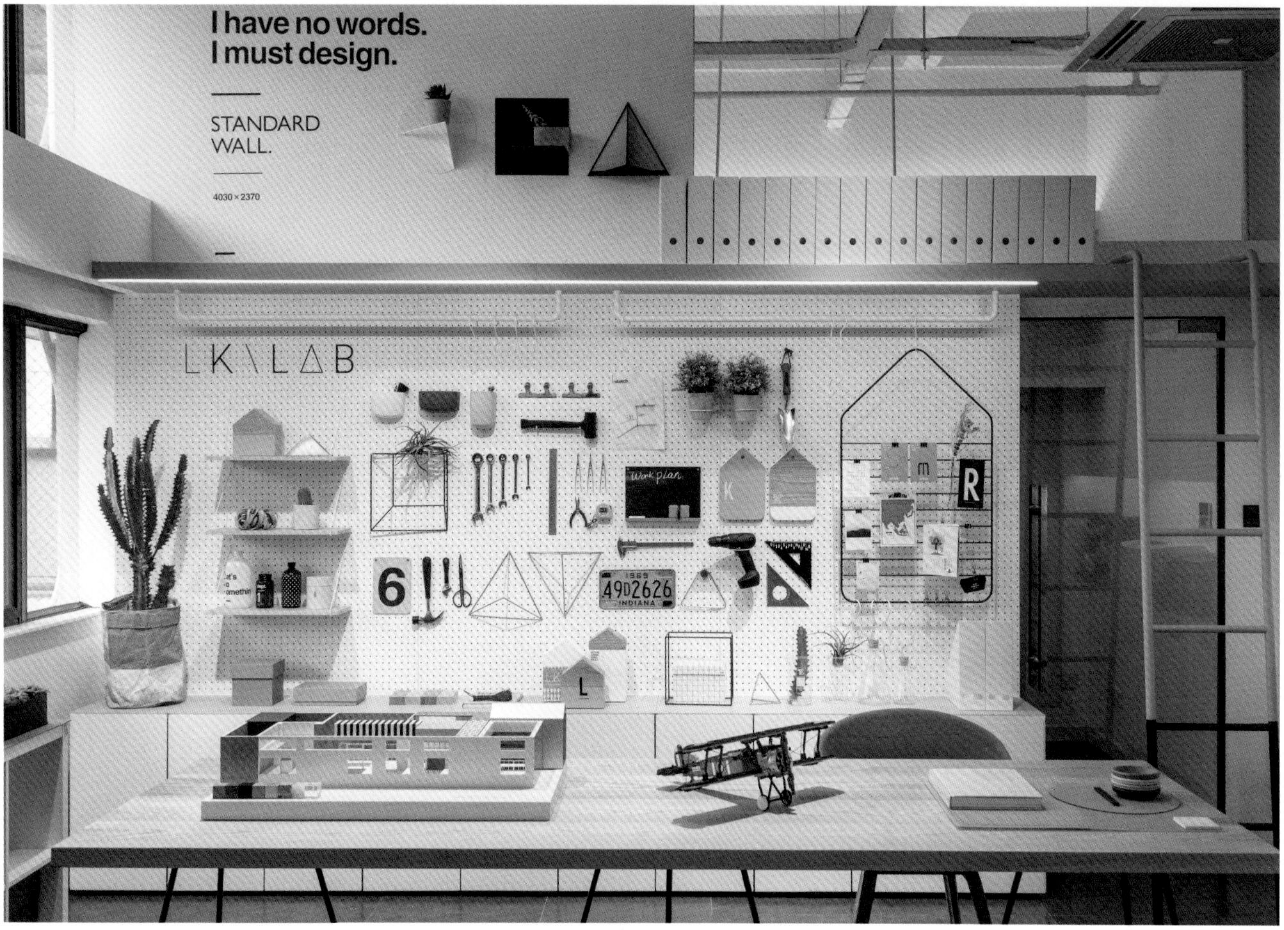
I have no words.
I must design.
STANDARD
WALL.
4030×2370
LK\LAB
Work plan
INDIANA
49D2626

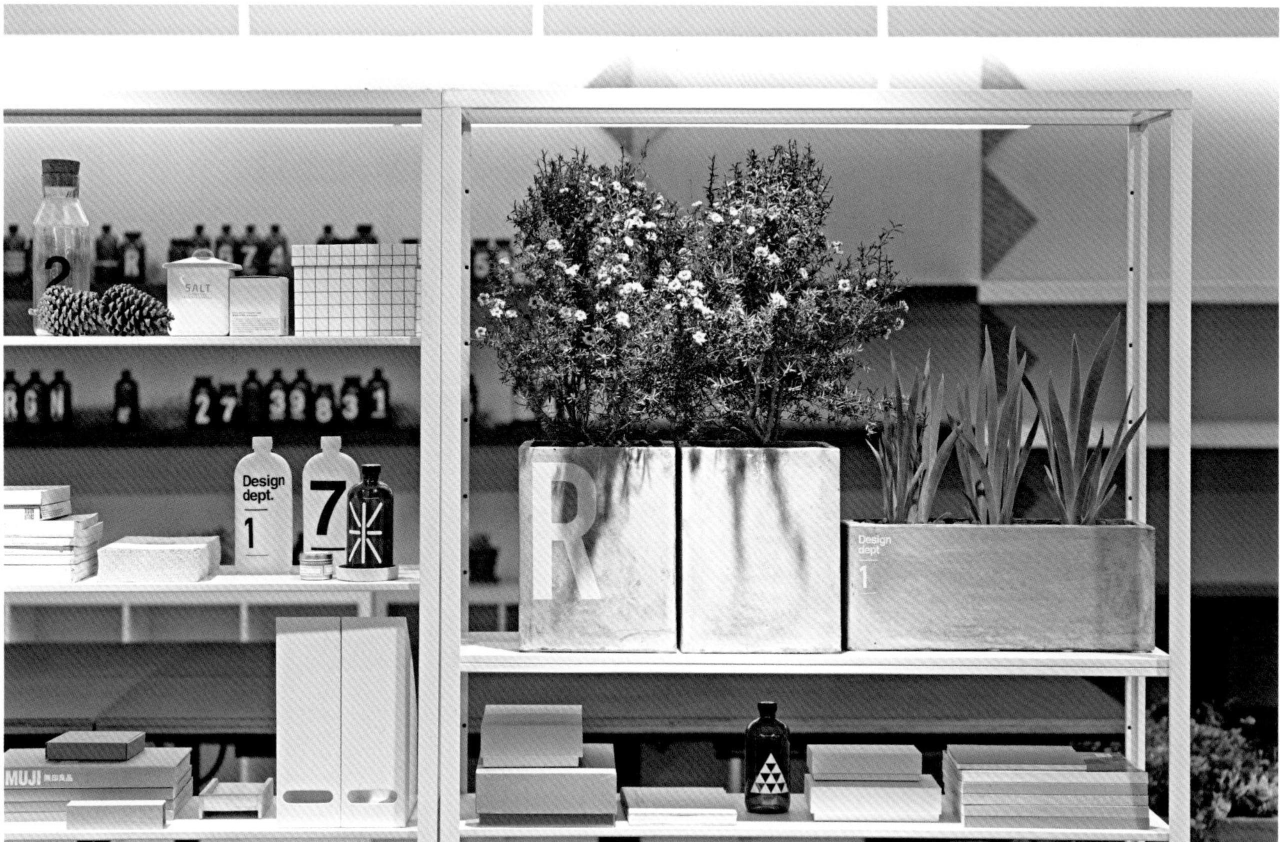
SALT
Design
dept.
1
7
Design
dept
1
MUJI

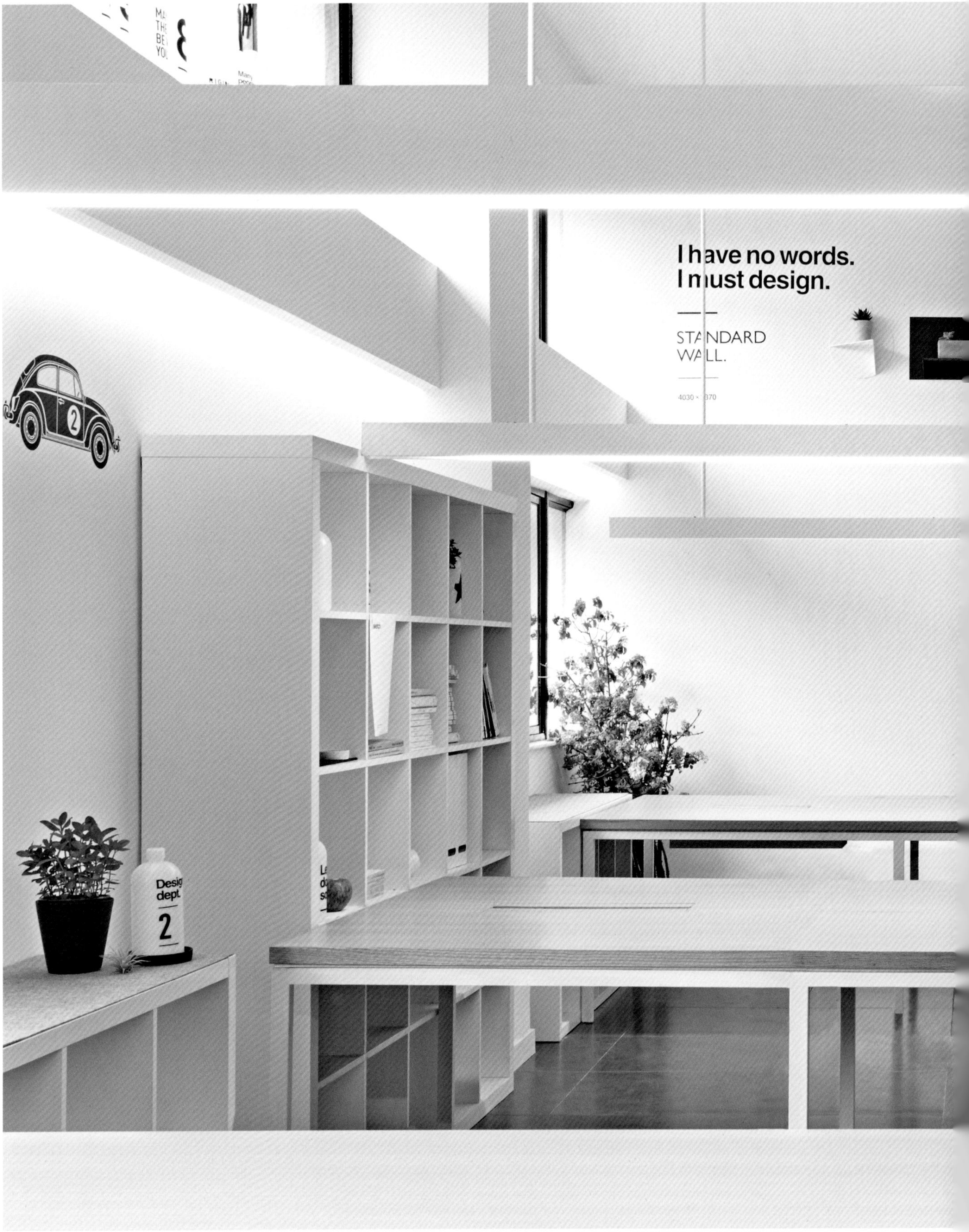
I have no words.
I must design.
STANDARD
WALL.
Design
dept.
2

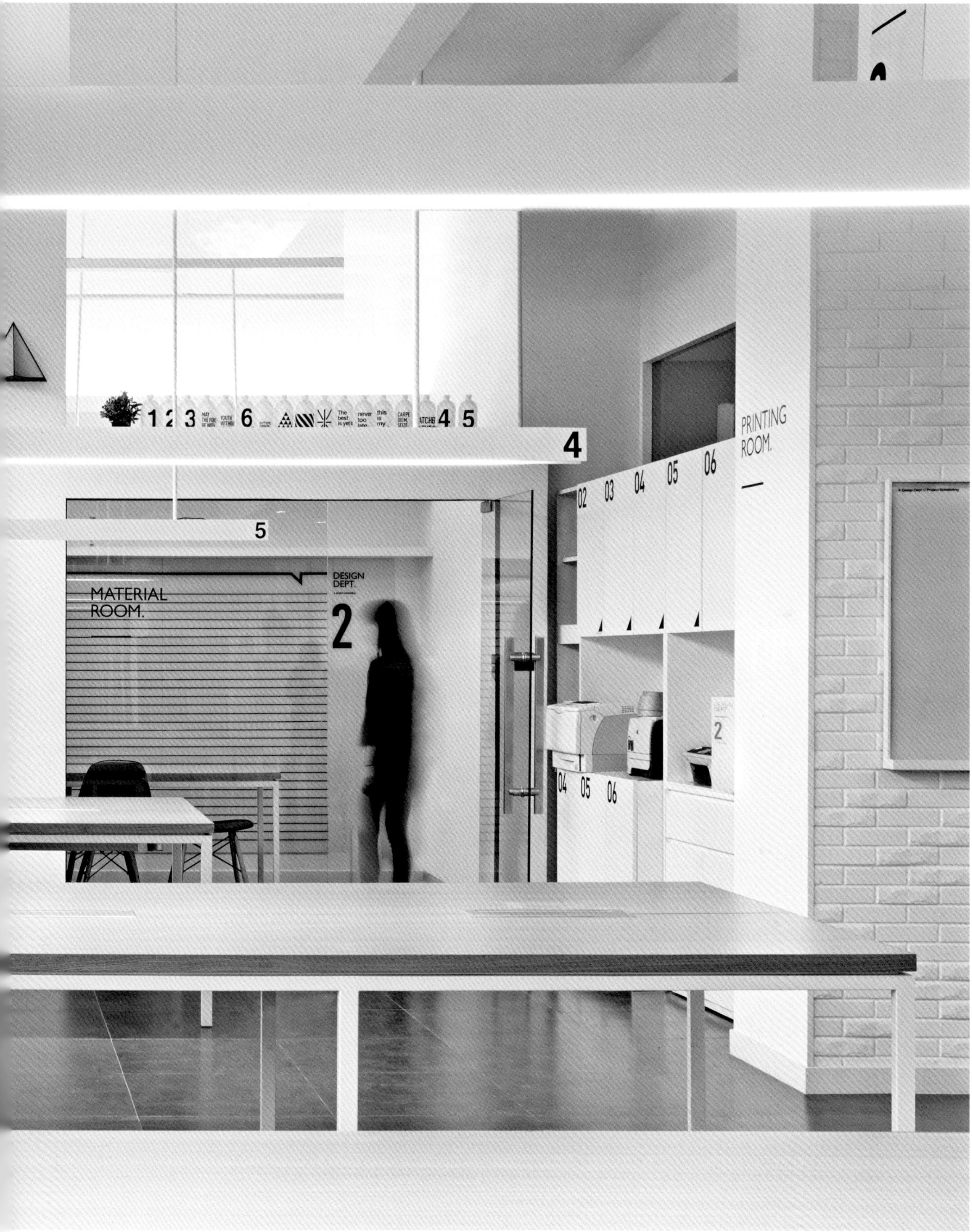
4
5
MATERIAL
ROOM.
DESIGN
DEPT.
2
PRINTING
ROOM.
02 03 04 05 06
04 05 06

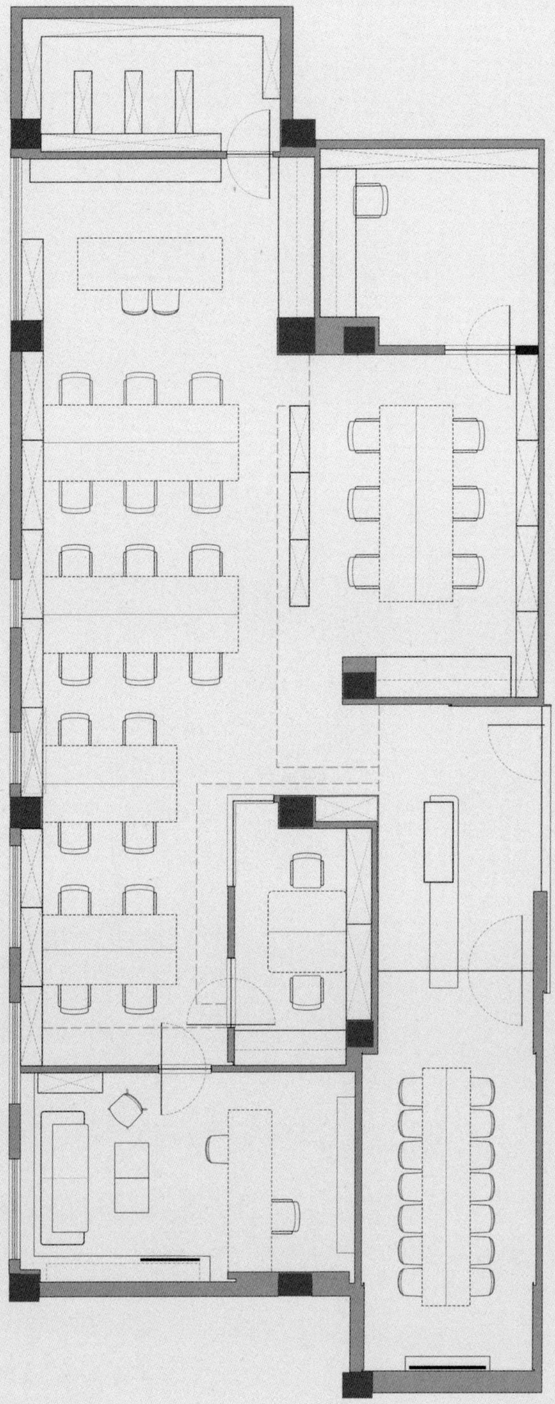

Floor plan

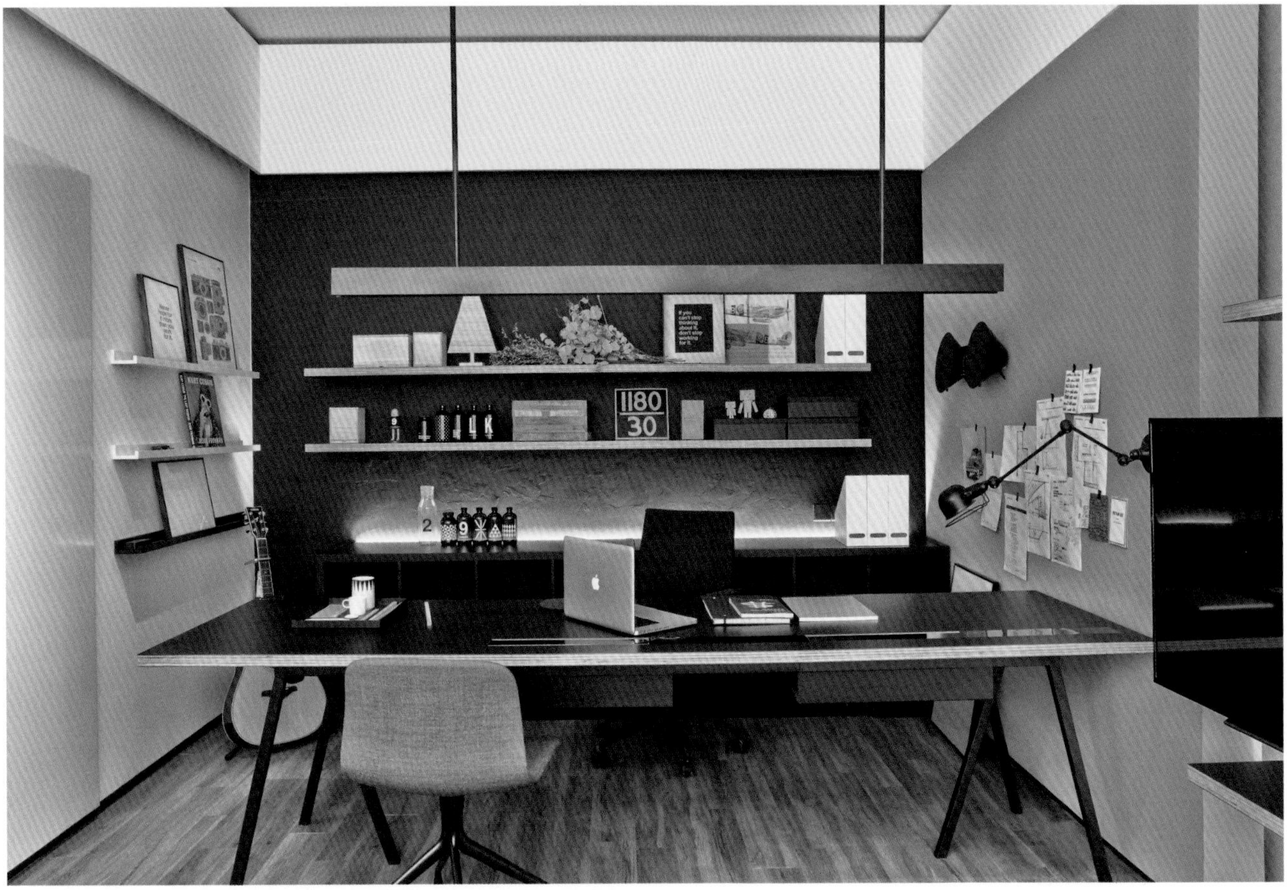
1180
30

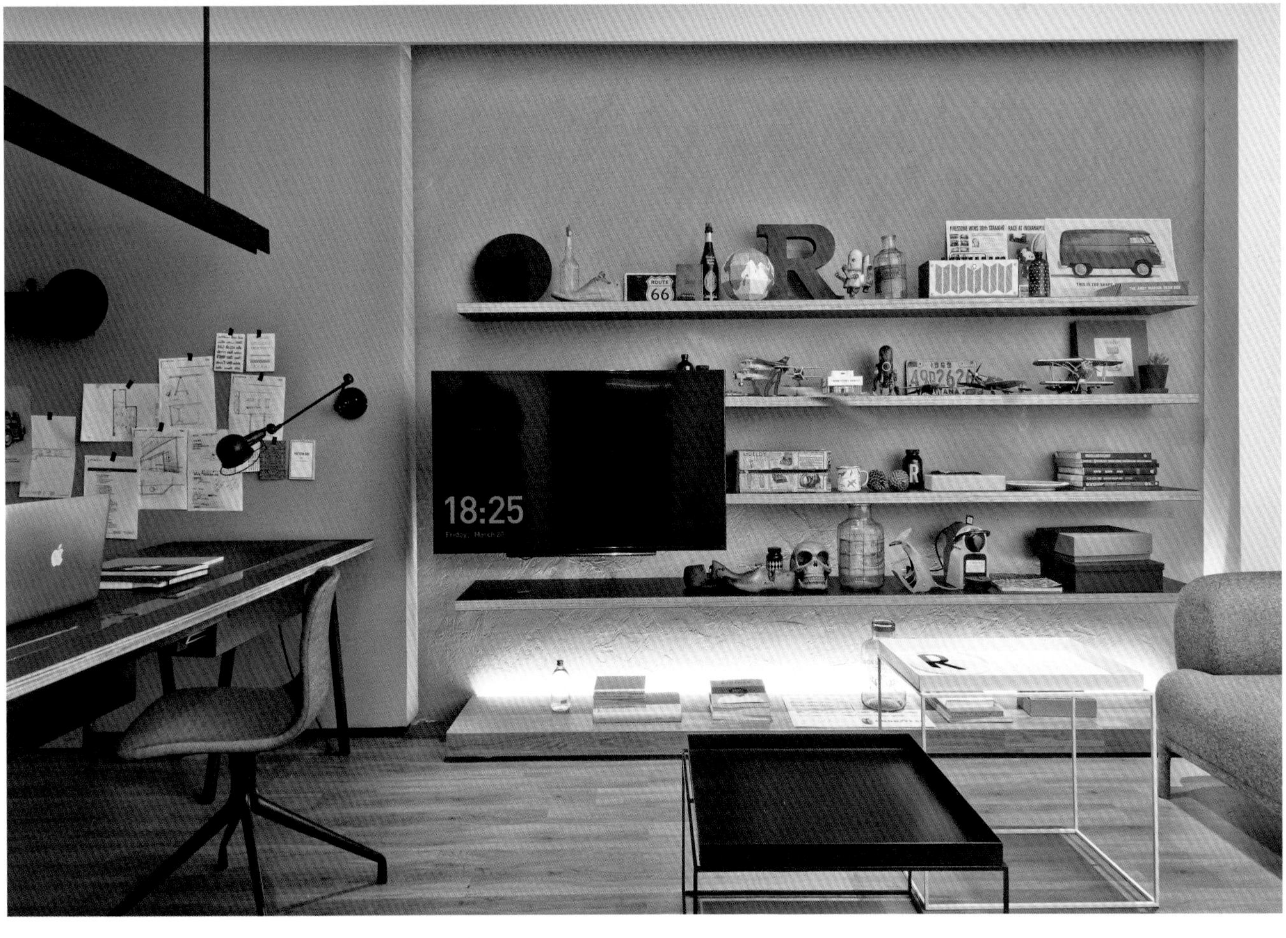
18:25
ROUTE
66

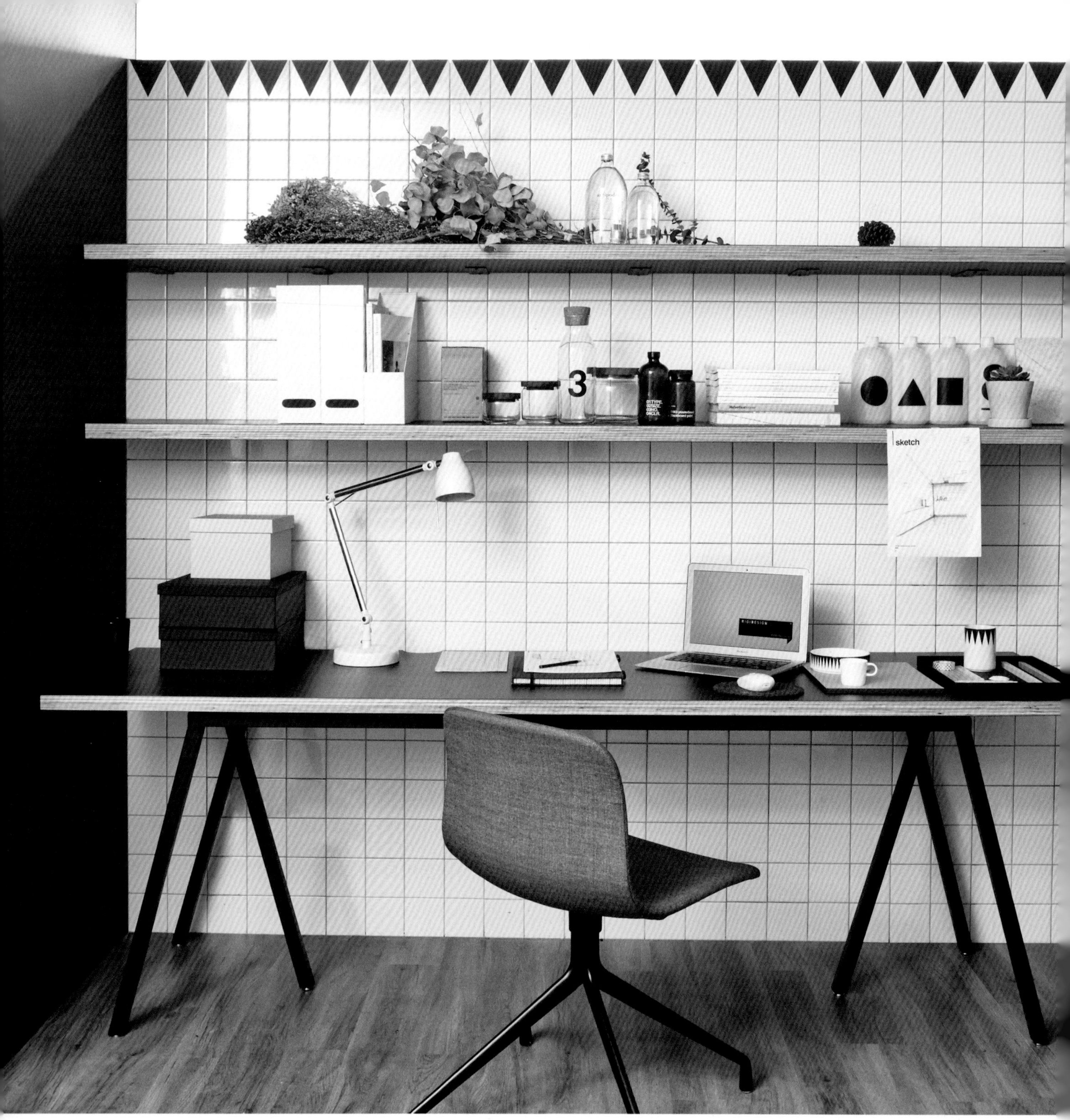
3
sketch

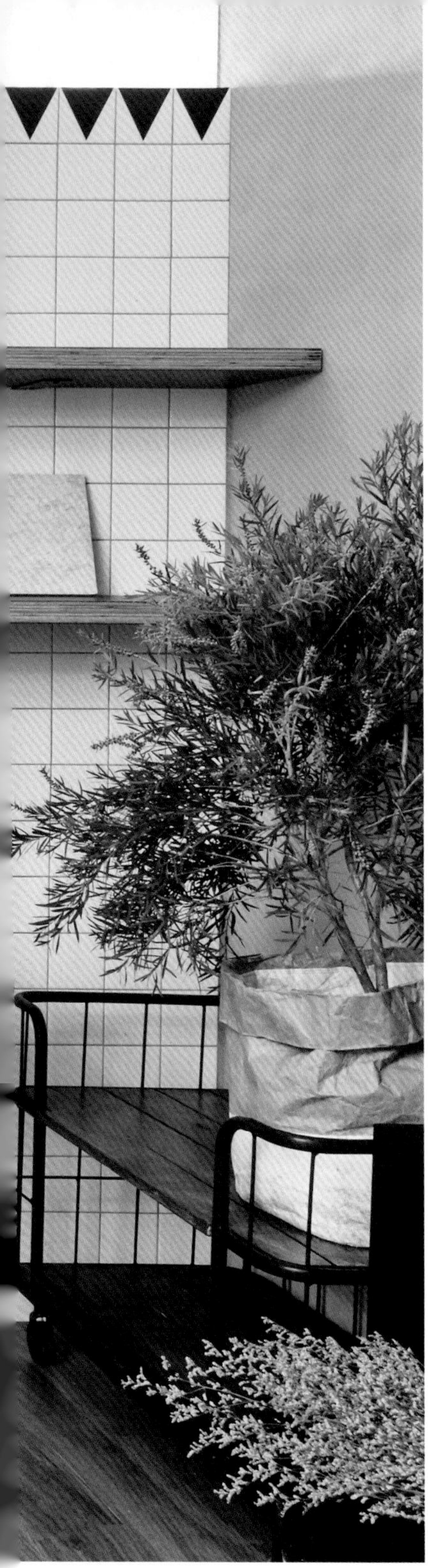

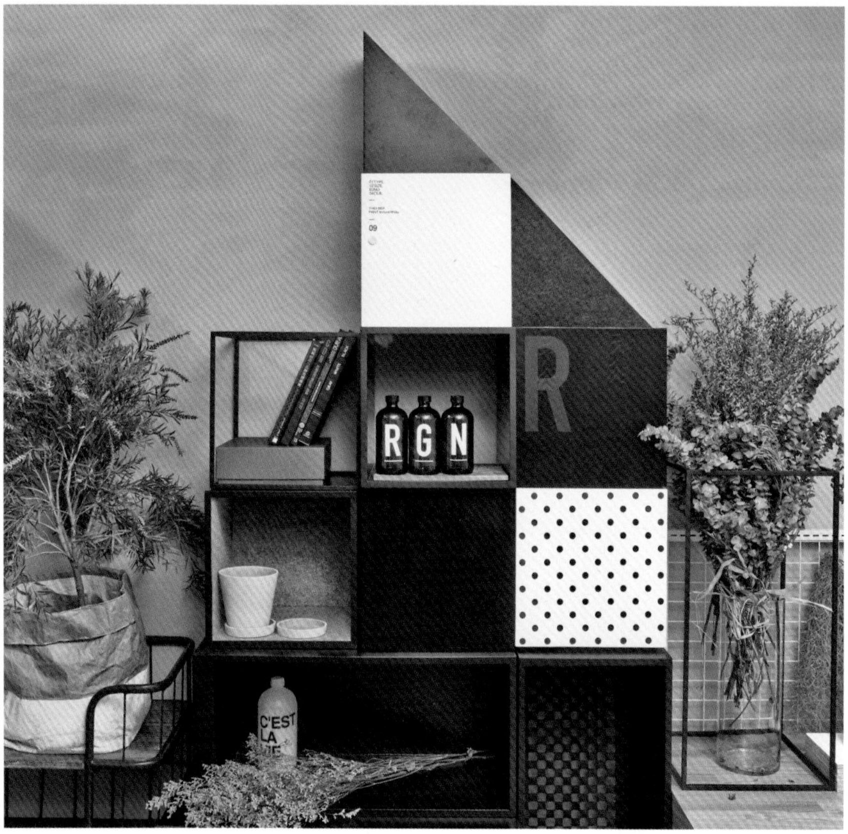
R
RGN
C'EST
LA

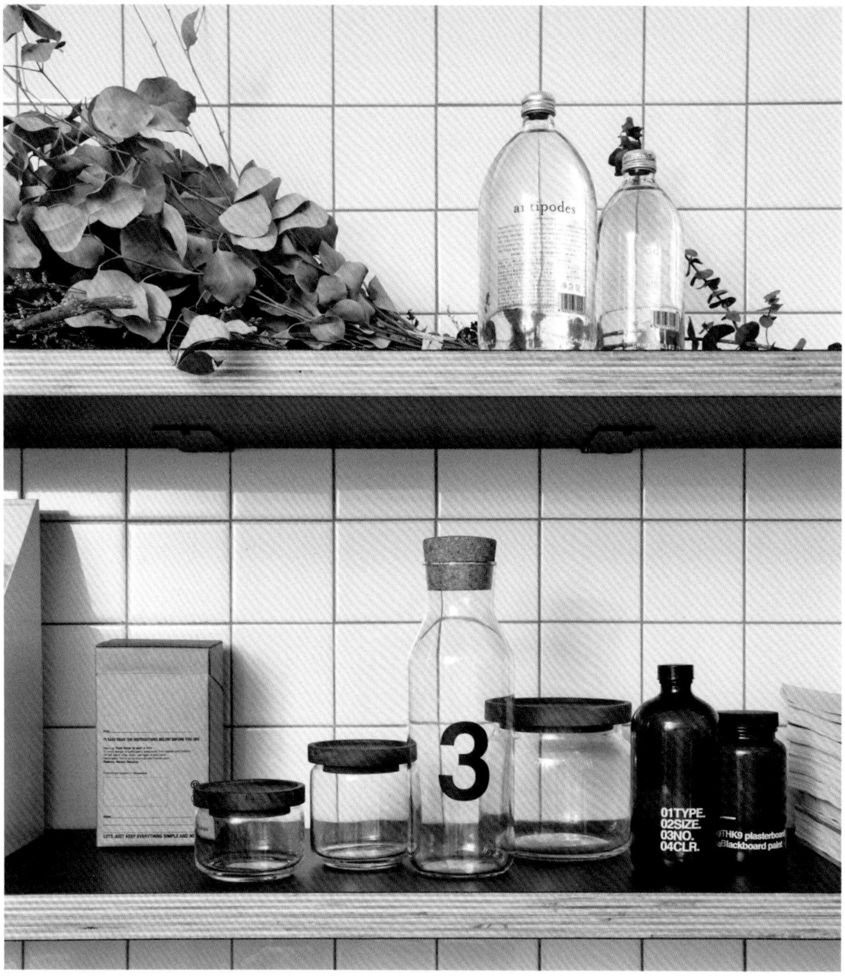
3
01TYPE.
02SIZE.
03NO.
04CLR.

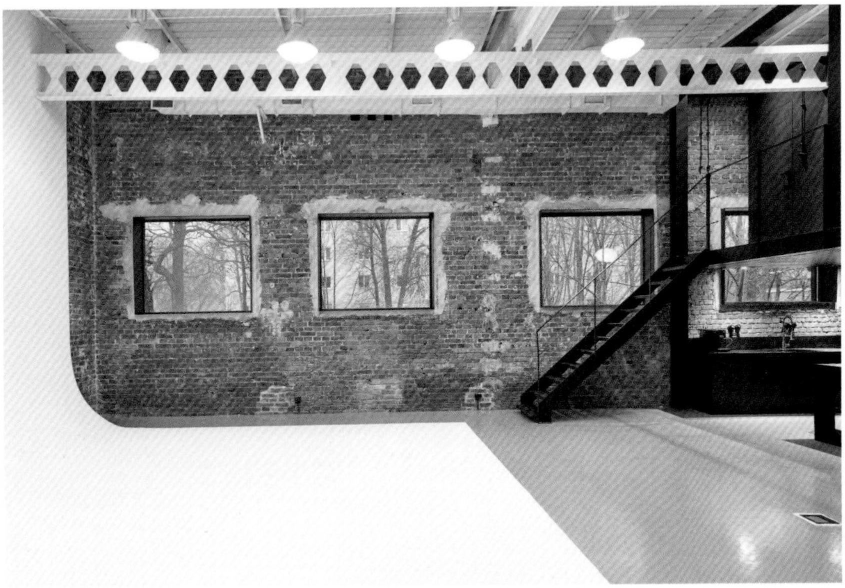

Area:
1,938 square feet (180 square meters)

Completion:
2016

Design:
Mess Architects

Photography:
Studio Flesz

Warsaw, Poland

Photographic Studio in Warsaw

The changing nature of its industrial surroundings was the inspiration for the interior of this photographic studio, situated in a former factory surrounded by similar buildings.

An industrial time capsule

For many years, the building housed a welding workshop. As time went by, its industrial interior required adjustments to make it more suited to the conditions needed for production processes, and welding machinery and metal presses filled up the interior. It became clear to the designers that throughout the years, the interior of the building had undergone many changes from its initial condition, and specific types of industrial processes had contributed to its degradation.

The east-facing wall of the building, which had been stripped of almost all windows, was its most damaged part. When the remaining layers of plaster were removed, clear evidence of intervention into the structure of the original wall appeared around the windows. This had doubtlessly been prompted by the technological requirements for the type of machinery used inside.

Retaining the character

Decisions about materials used for this project were mainly determined by the context of the industrial activity that was once carried out there. Having considered the post-industrial character of the building, the designers decided that steel was an obvious building material. It was not only used for the main parts of the

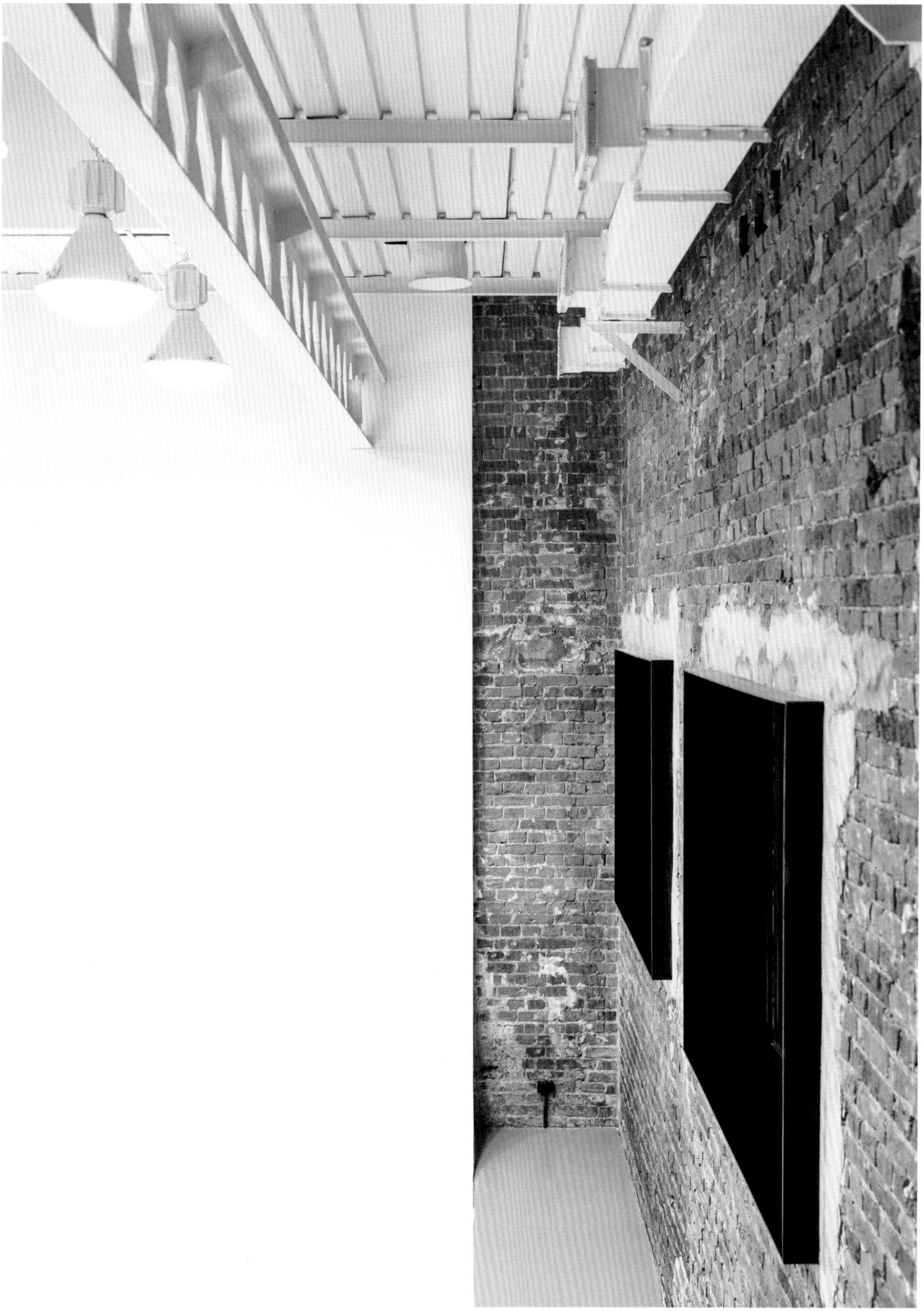

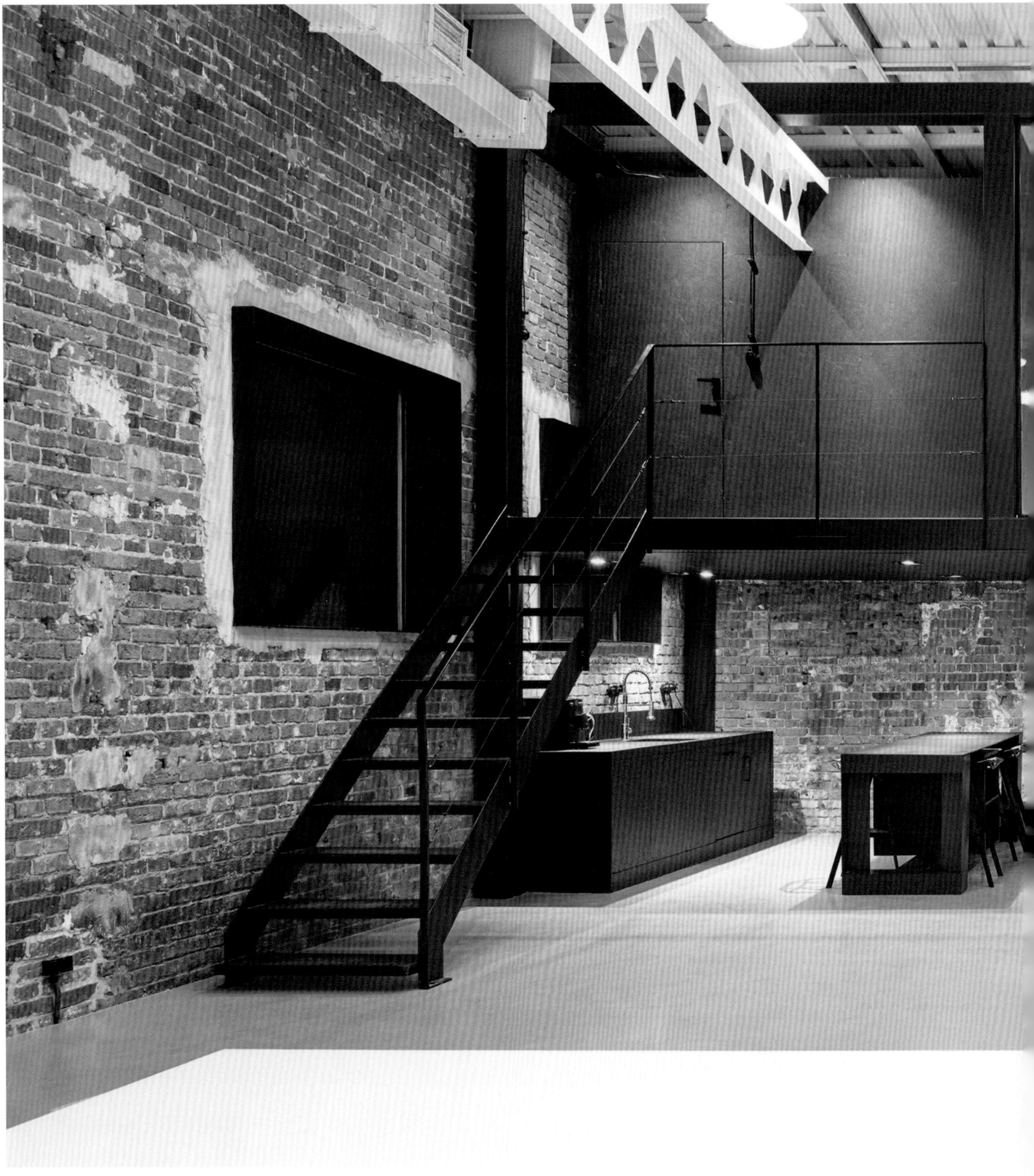

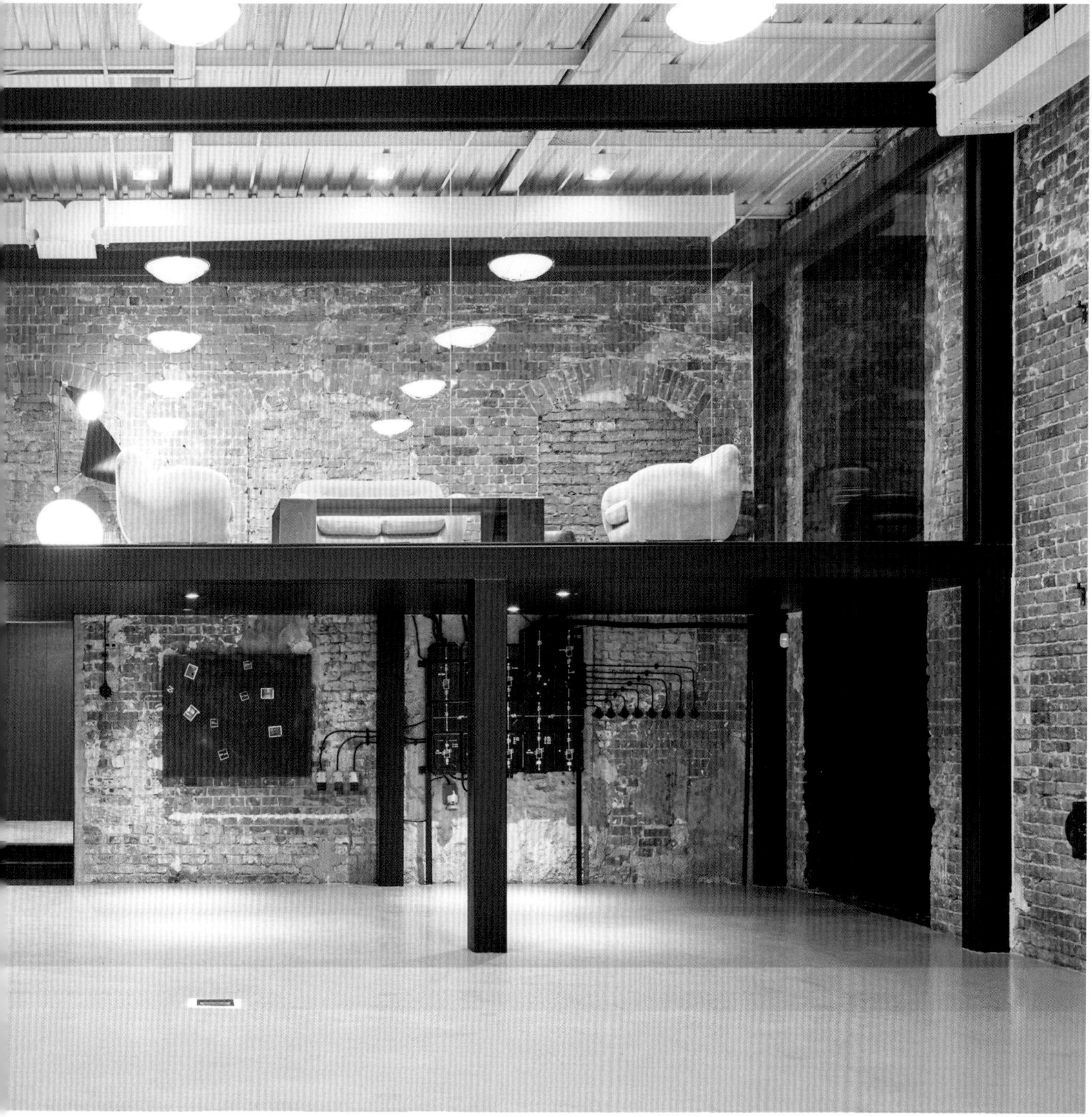

structure that was erected inside, but it also strongly influenced the character of the finishing touches that were used. The distinct passage linking individual areas of the interior, door and window frames, and custom-made furniture, are all based on steel components that are designed to create a time bridge between the modern character of the interior and the industrial soul of this old building. The entire space is full of retro art, bringing inspiration to the photographer.

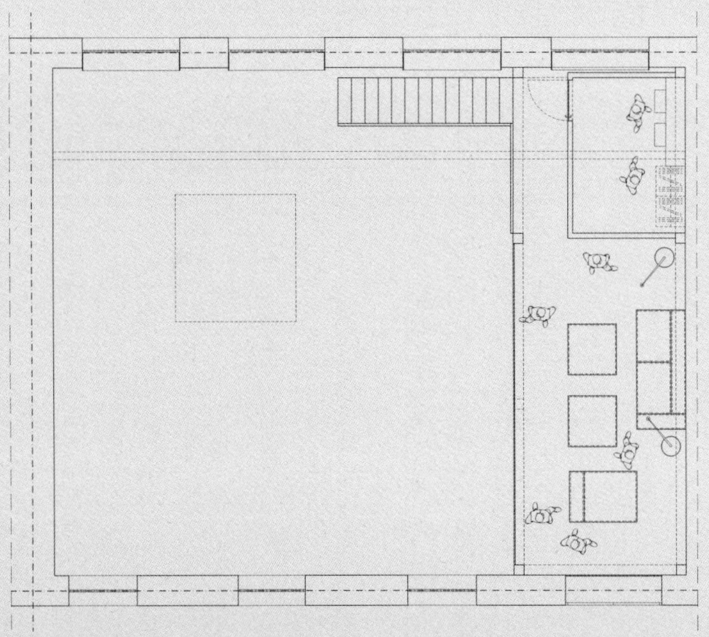

Mezzanine plan

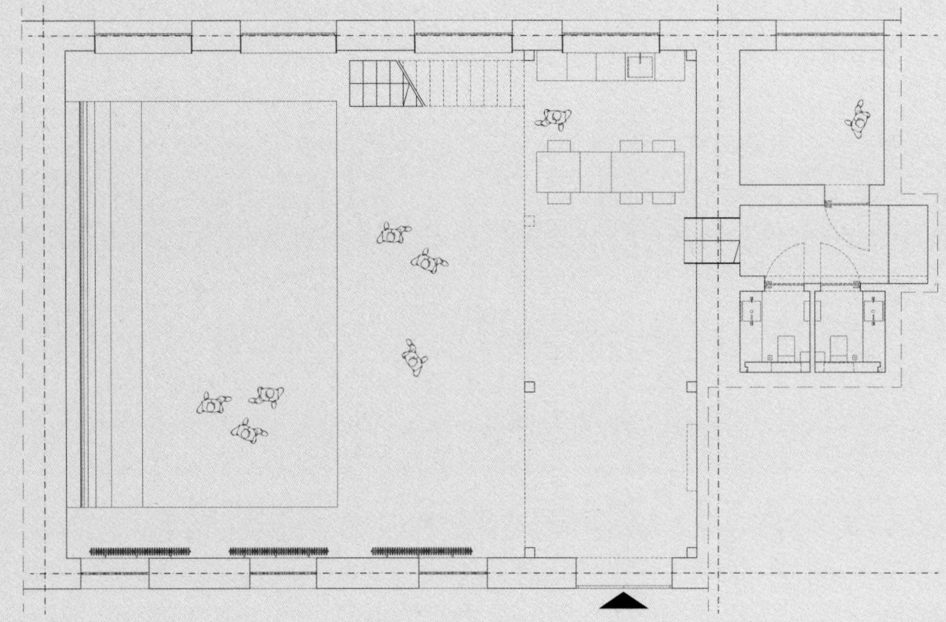

Ground-floor plan

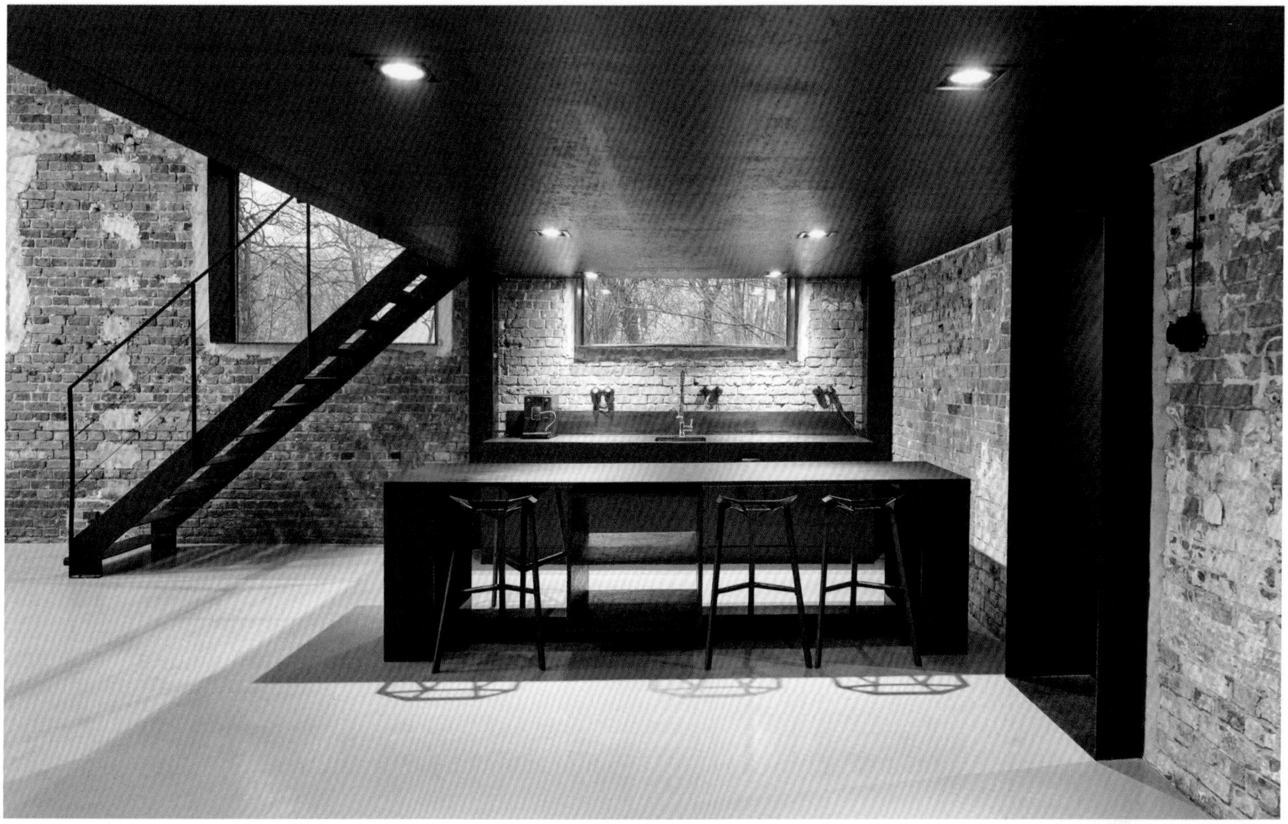

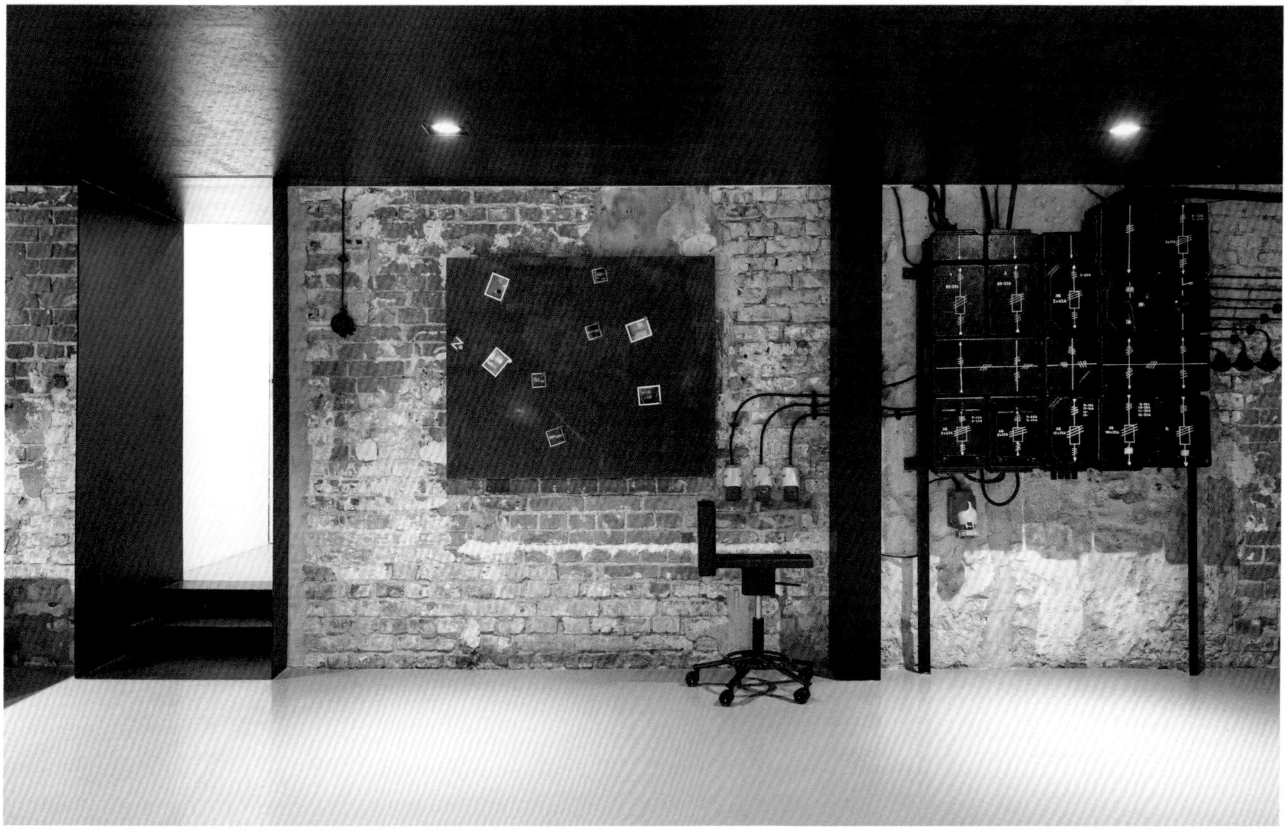

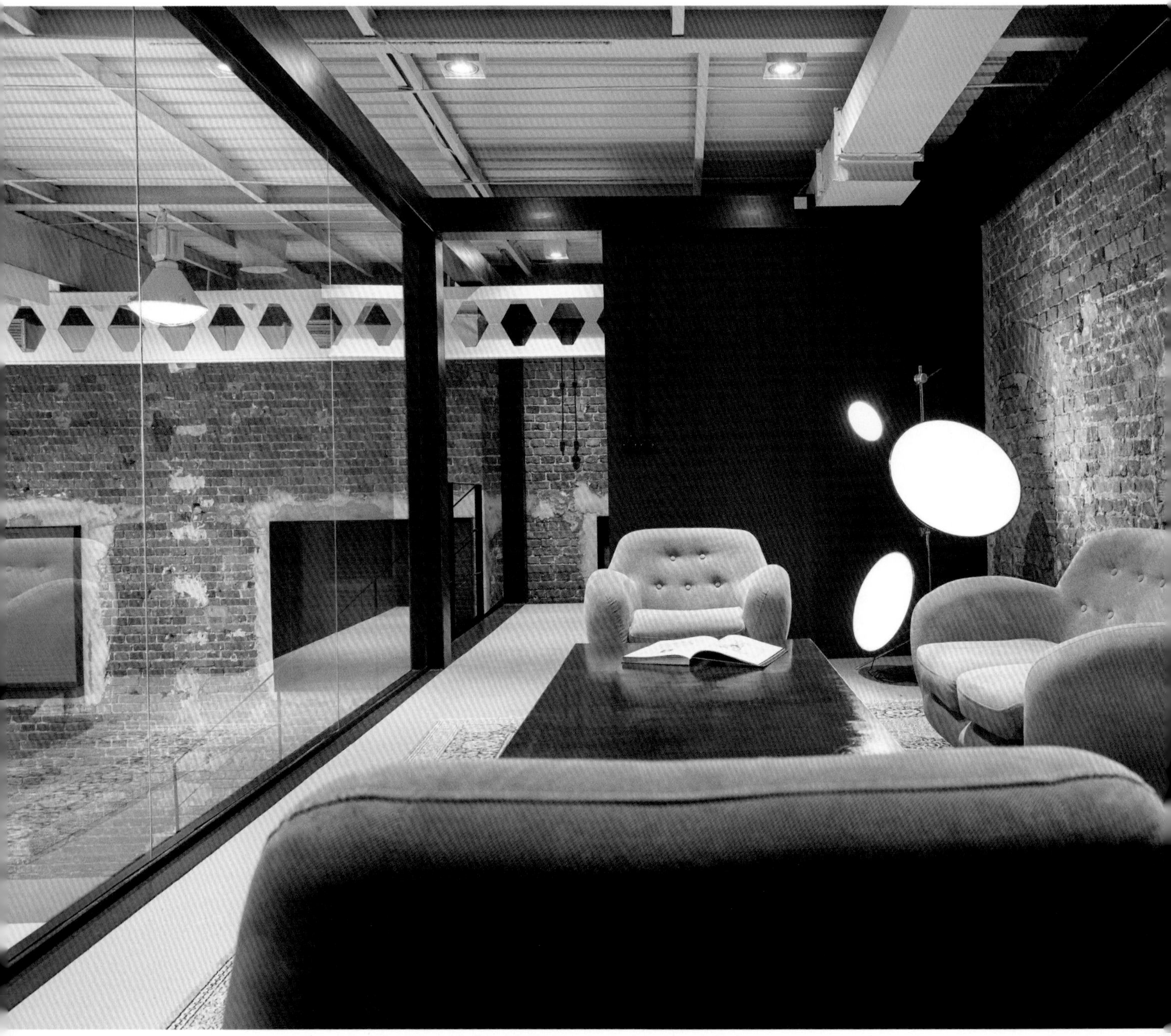

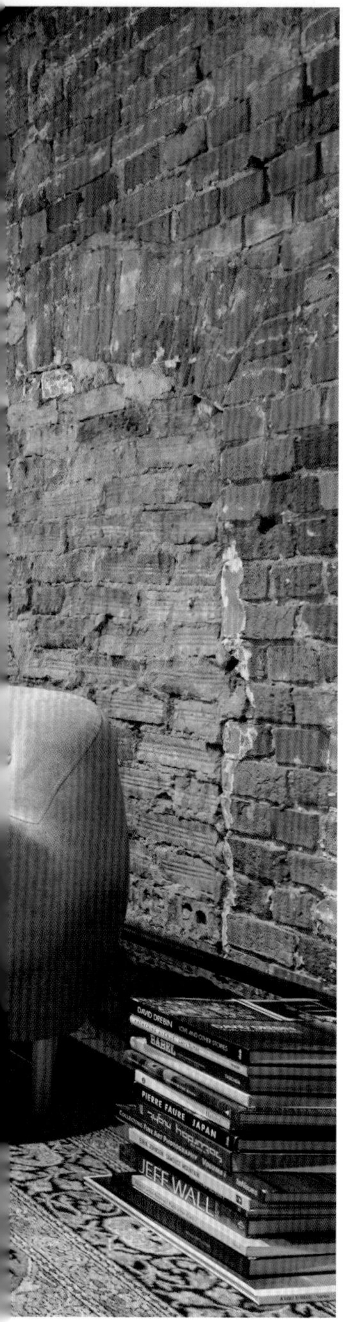
DAVID DREBIN
PIERRE FAURE JAPAN
JEFF WALL

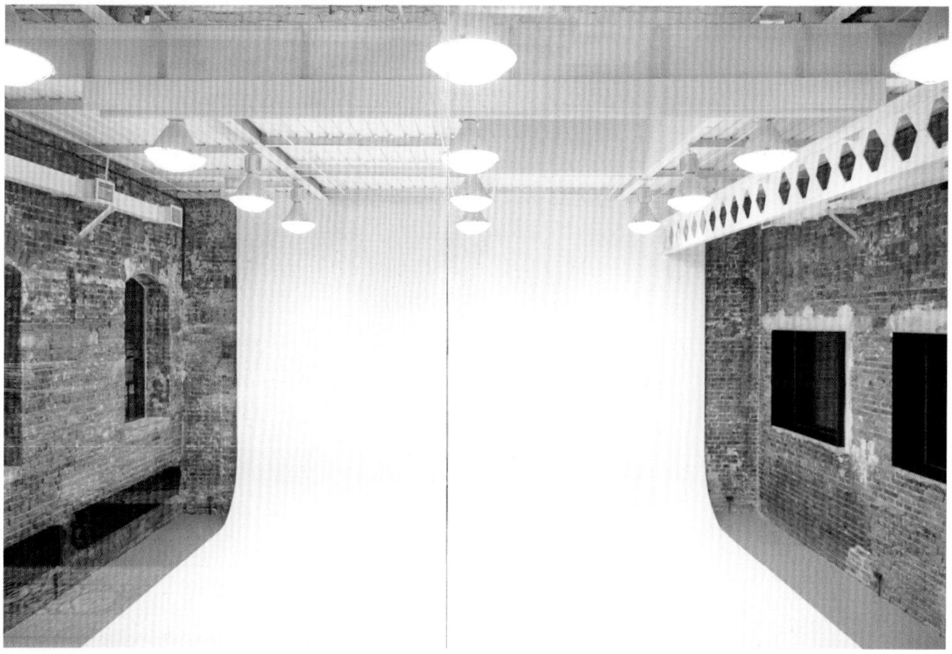

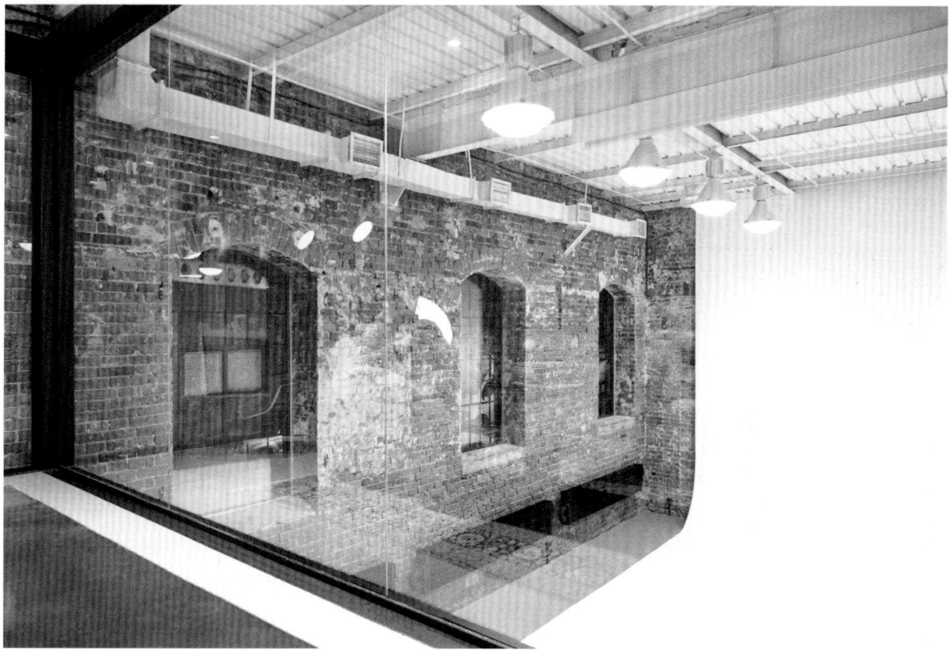

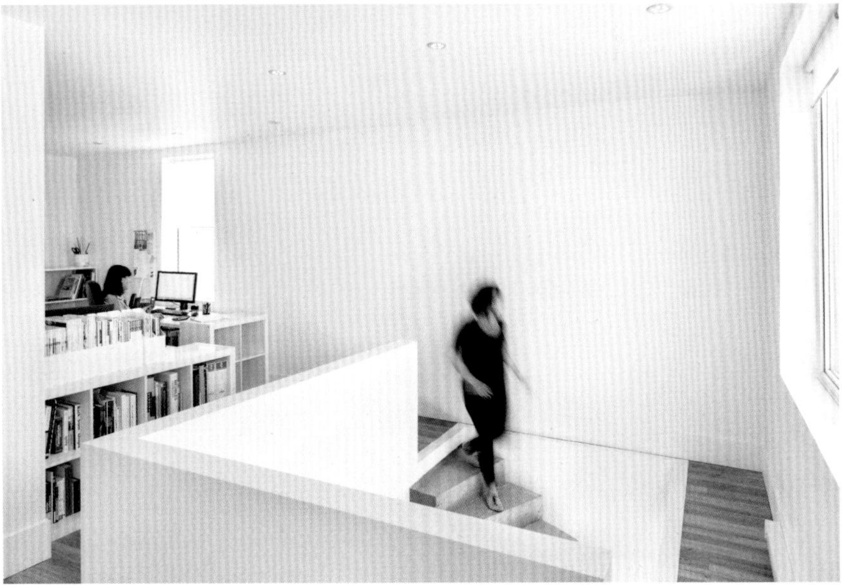

Area:
913 square feet (85 square meters)

Completion:
2015

Design:
Issadesign

Photography:
Adrien Williams

Montréal, Canada

Purity of Concrete

Located in a growing and vibrant neighborhood a step away from downtown Montréal, the headquarters of Issadesign is bright and bold. The building itself has a long history; built in the 1940s, it used to be a fruit store with a wide carriage door for the delivery, and was later owned by a paint manufacturer.

When Issadesign bought the building to transform it into its headquarters, it was imperative to keep a few elements from its past. The concept is a marriage between building technique and contemporary design, the whole tinted with natural light and memories from the past.

Inspiring staff and clients

The space is split vertically between work spaces and the "greet and meet" point. Spread over three floors, the offices offer an inspiring and pleasant space for team members, visitors, and colleagues to create and innovate, with the volume and different floor heights kept from the old fruit shop.

On the first floor, people are welcomed into the offices by a small space painted white; on its right side is a linear cast-in-place concrete staircase. This first staircase brings people to the second floor where they enter in the meeting-room area. This nest of creativity was designed to inspire clients and contributors with a long rallying conference table, surrounded by a selection of samples. The old concrete tiles that composed the ceiling were kept from the old paint shop and painted white.

A canvas for designers

A second cast-in-place concrete staircase, this time with an organic shape, connects the two higher stories with a bold gesture. Bathed in natural light, the workshop on the third floor is used to focus on

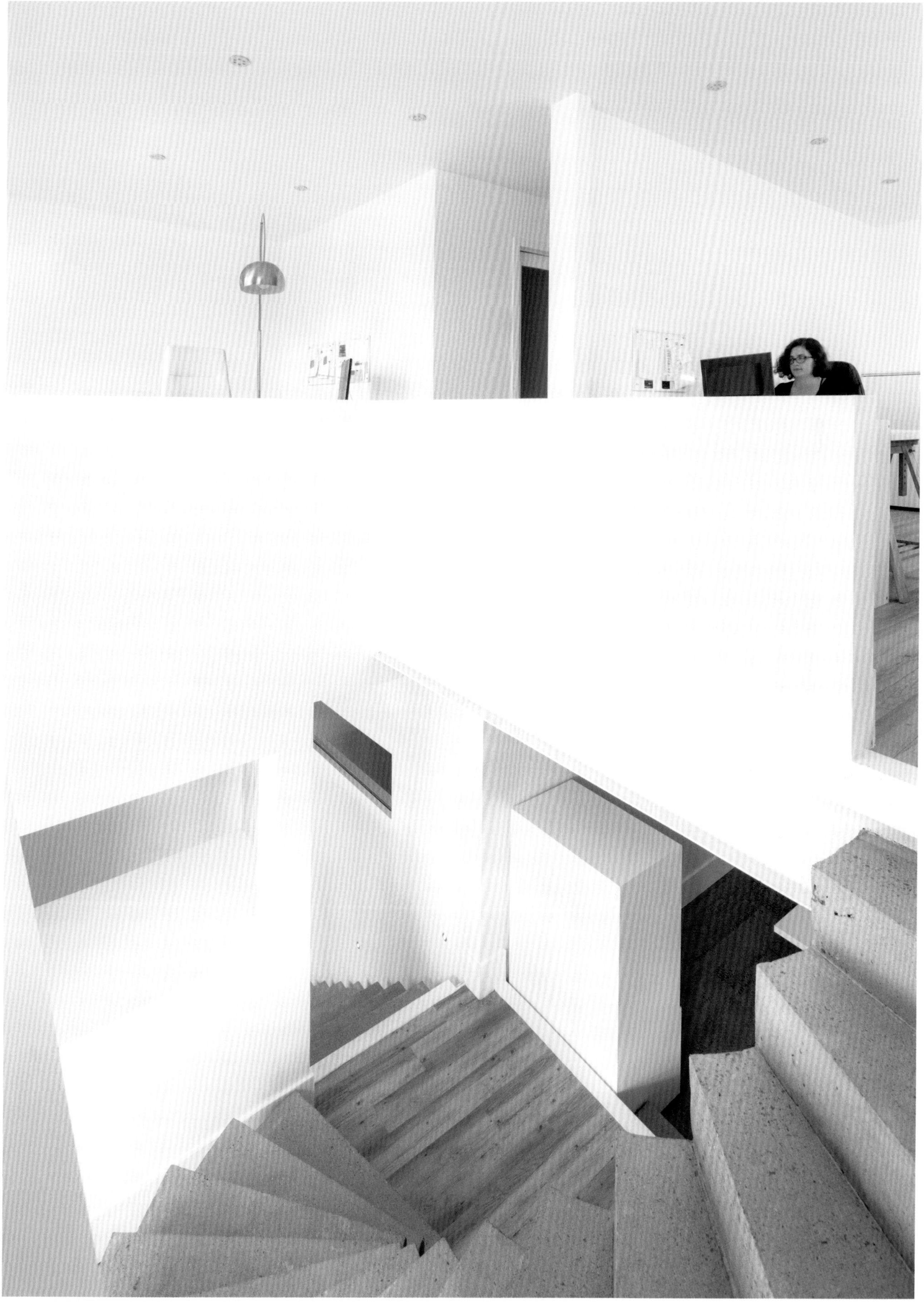

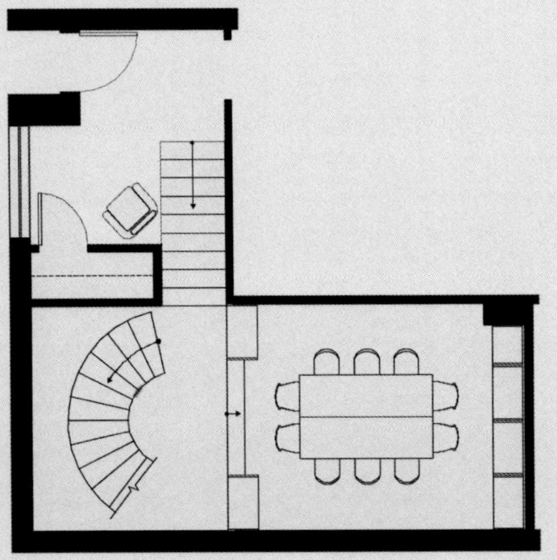

First-floor plan

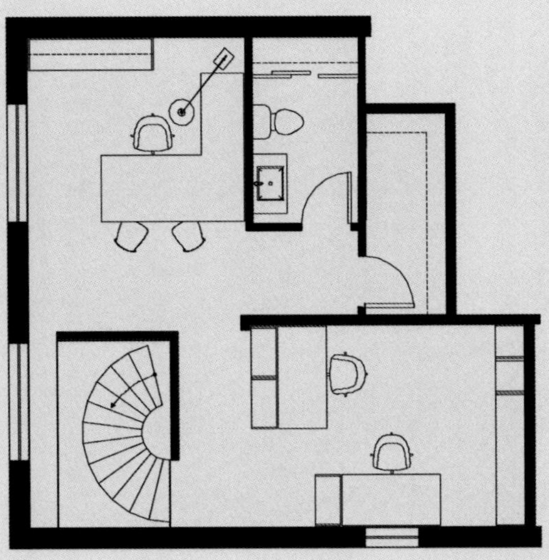

Ground-floor plan

ongoing projects, with plans on the drawing table. All decorated in white, the atelier area places the designers of Issadesign in an open white and bright space for creation, replicating what may seem like an artist's canvas.

The relationship between spaces encourages a fluid circulation between work environments, increasing productivity and creativity on the part of the users, and reflecting the firm's design capabilities and aesthetics.

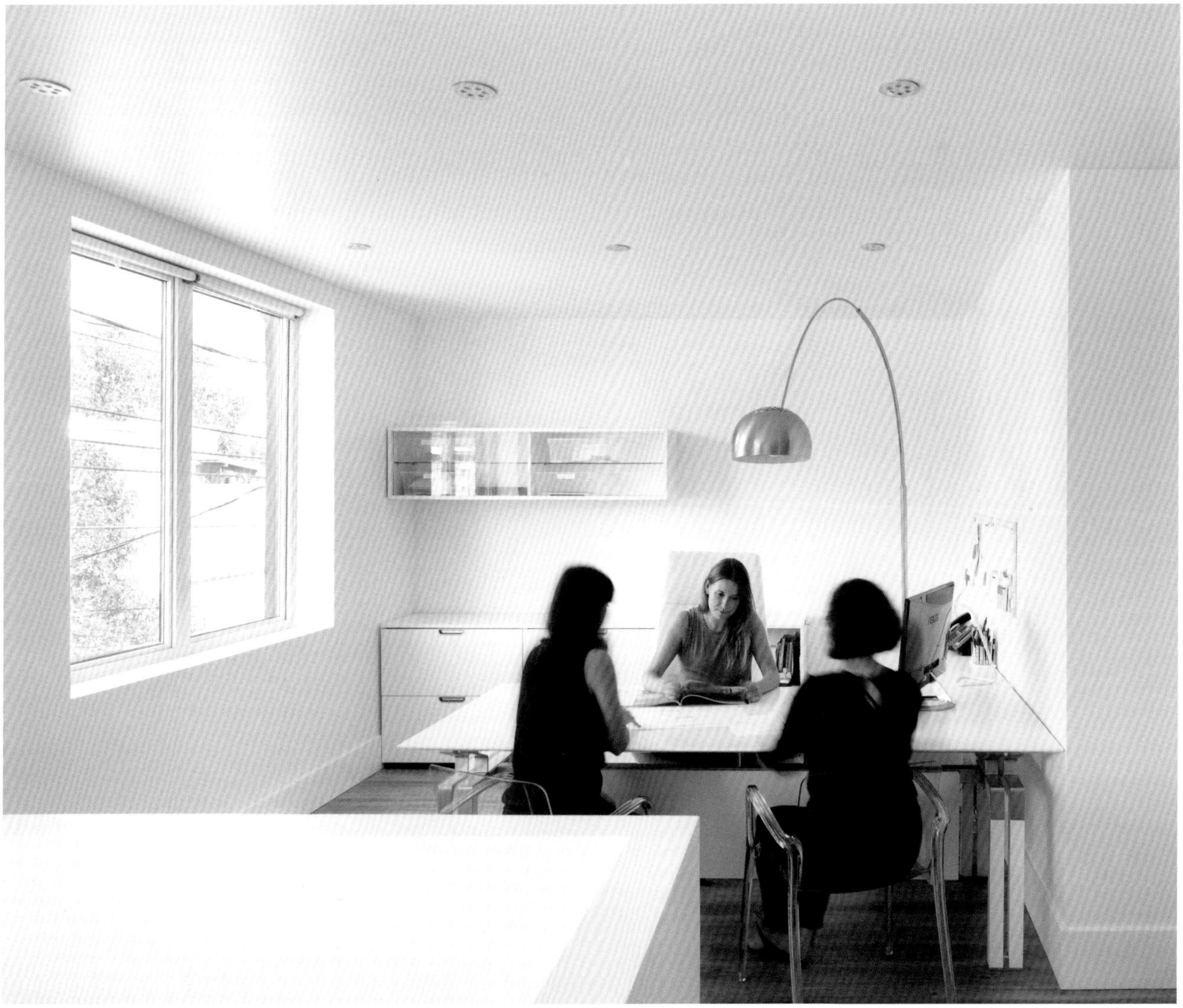

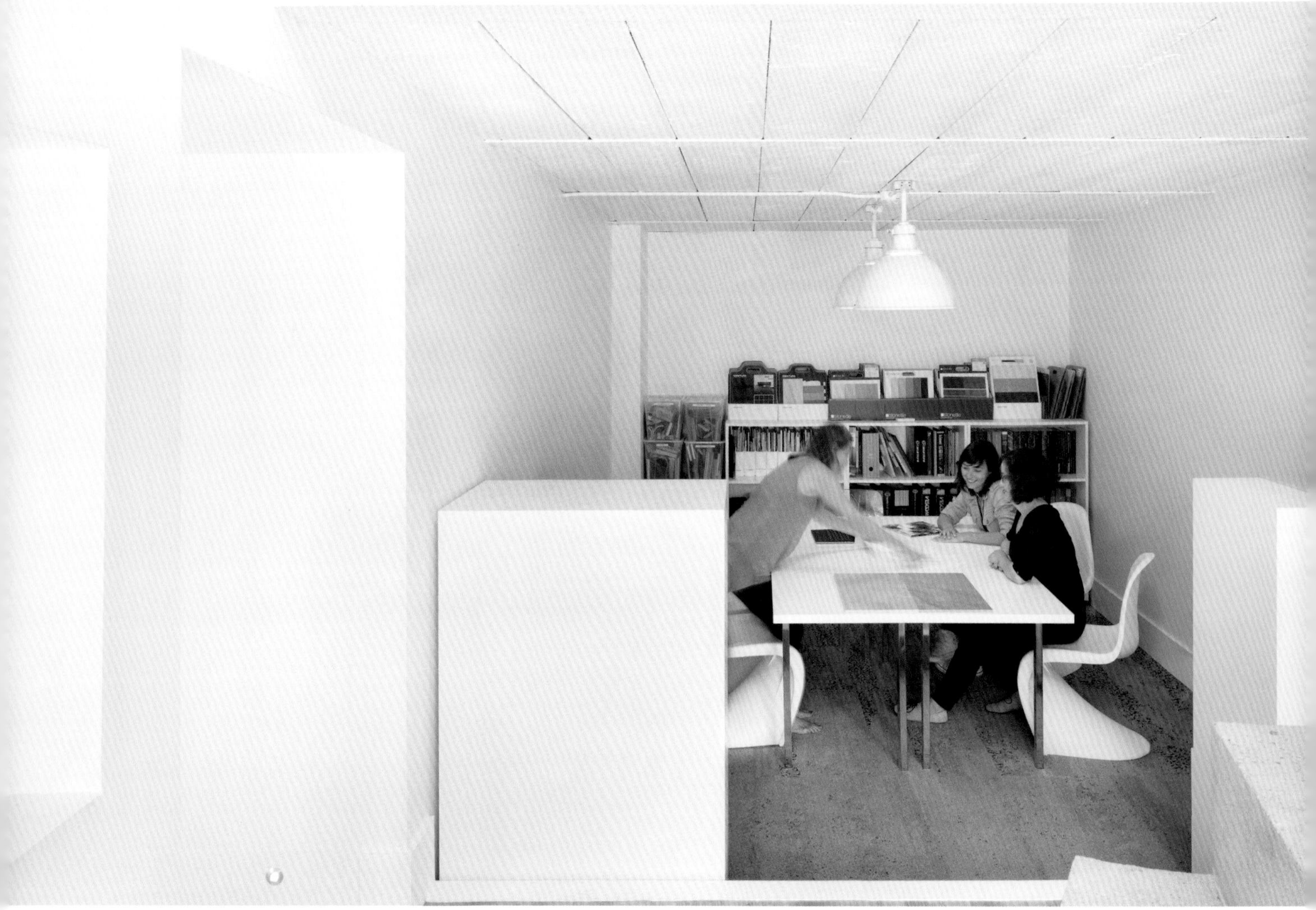

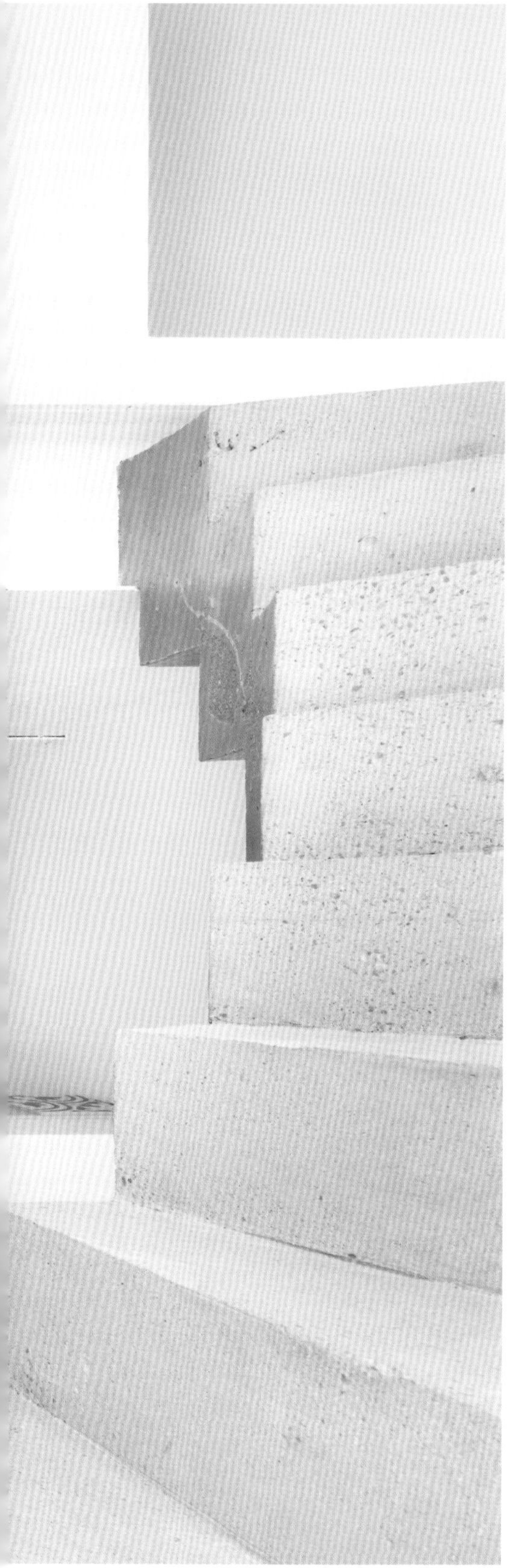

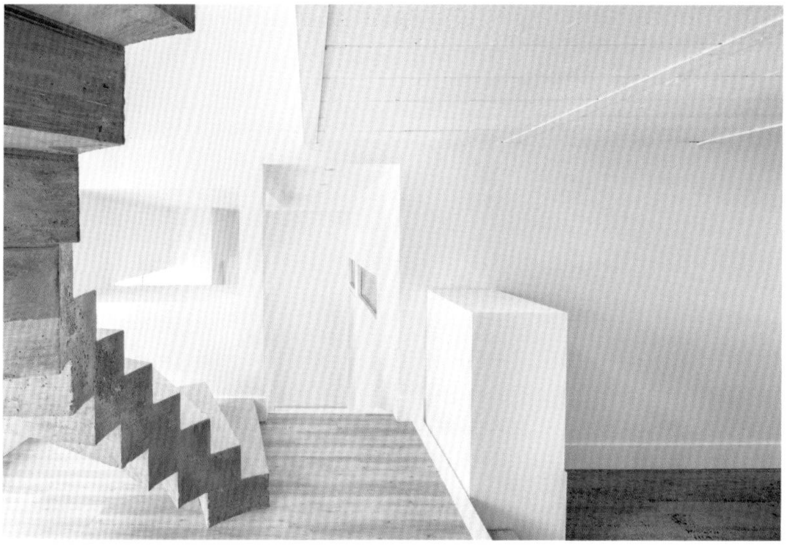

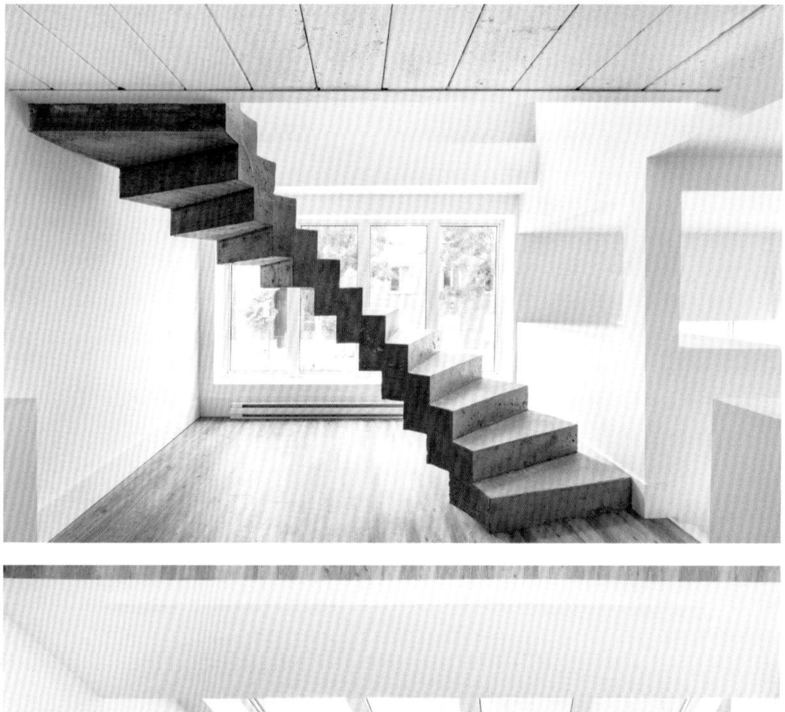

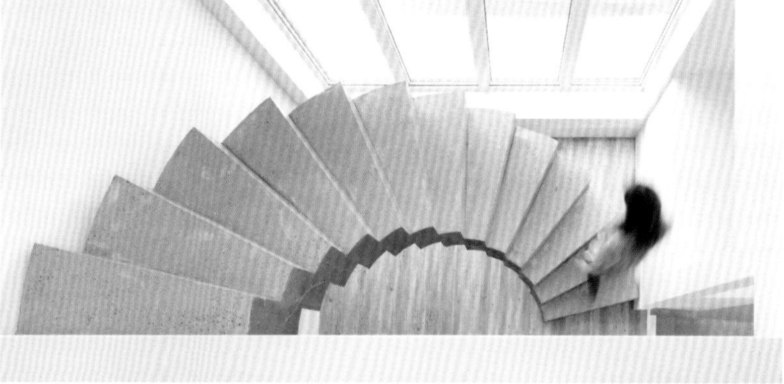

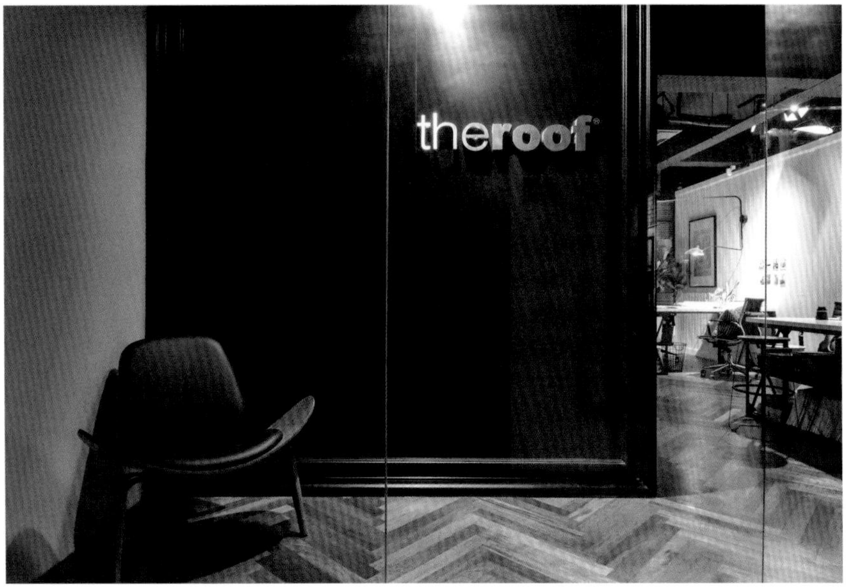

Area:
1,800 square feet (167 square meters)

Completion:
2016

Design:
The Roof Studio

Photography:
Gavin Yam

Subang Jaya, Malaysia

The Roof Lifestyle Concept Studio

The designers have divided this shop lot into two major sections: a showroom that combines industrial and glamorous elements, and the design studio. The rooms are separated by a semi-private area.

Raw and refined

At the main entrance, the front area is a showroom layered with cozy soft furnishings on top of a rustic backdrop, its dark color palette complemented with natural lighting. Raw and unfinished-looking industrial components (cement, exposed bricks, and natural wood) are juxtaposed against a variety of refined materials (quartz, marble, and glossy surfaces) and glamorous décor (crystal chandelier, leather, fur, and mirror fixtures). This dynamic clash between the raw and the refined symbolized the "beauty of imperfection" for the designers.

The showroom adjoins a living area, dining space, and fully functional kitchen. When not in used, the showroom doubles as an extension of the design studio as the dining space can be converted into a meeting area while the kitchen serves as a pantry. The living area is used as a lounge area for the staff. Sectioned off with folding metal and glass panels, the interior design studio adopted a white color palette along with warm wood flooring to offer a more conducive working environment and stimulate the creativity of the designers.

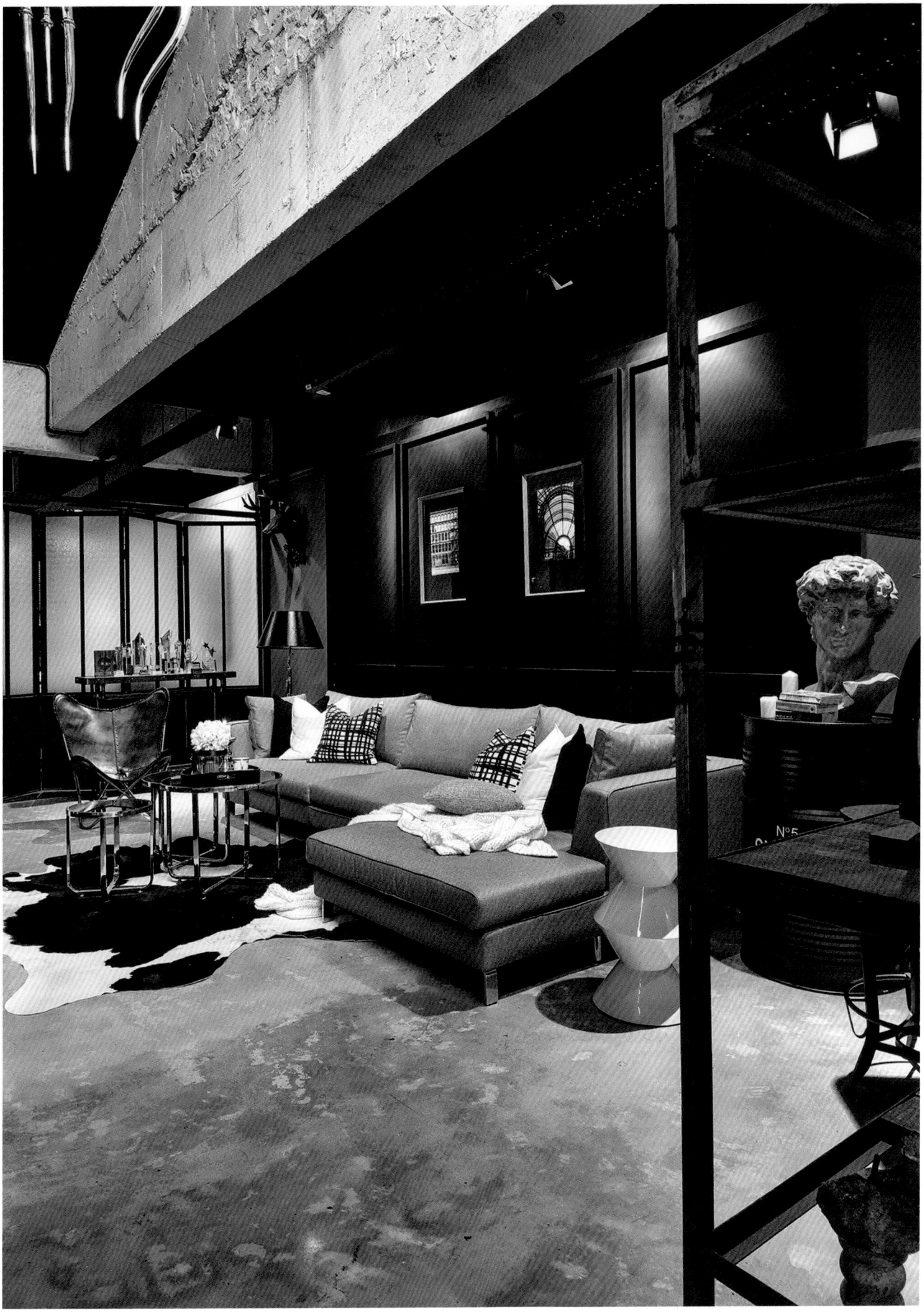

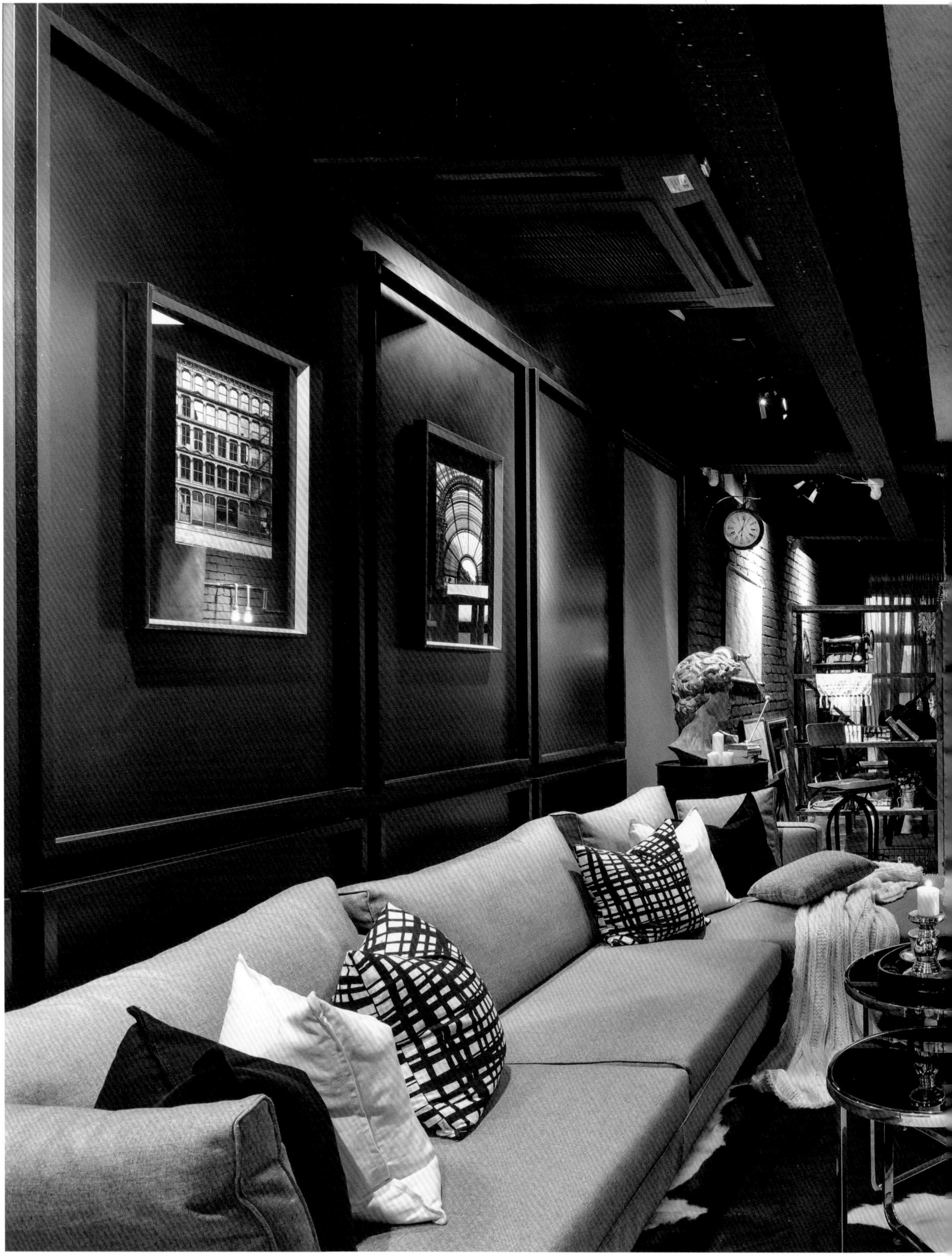

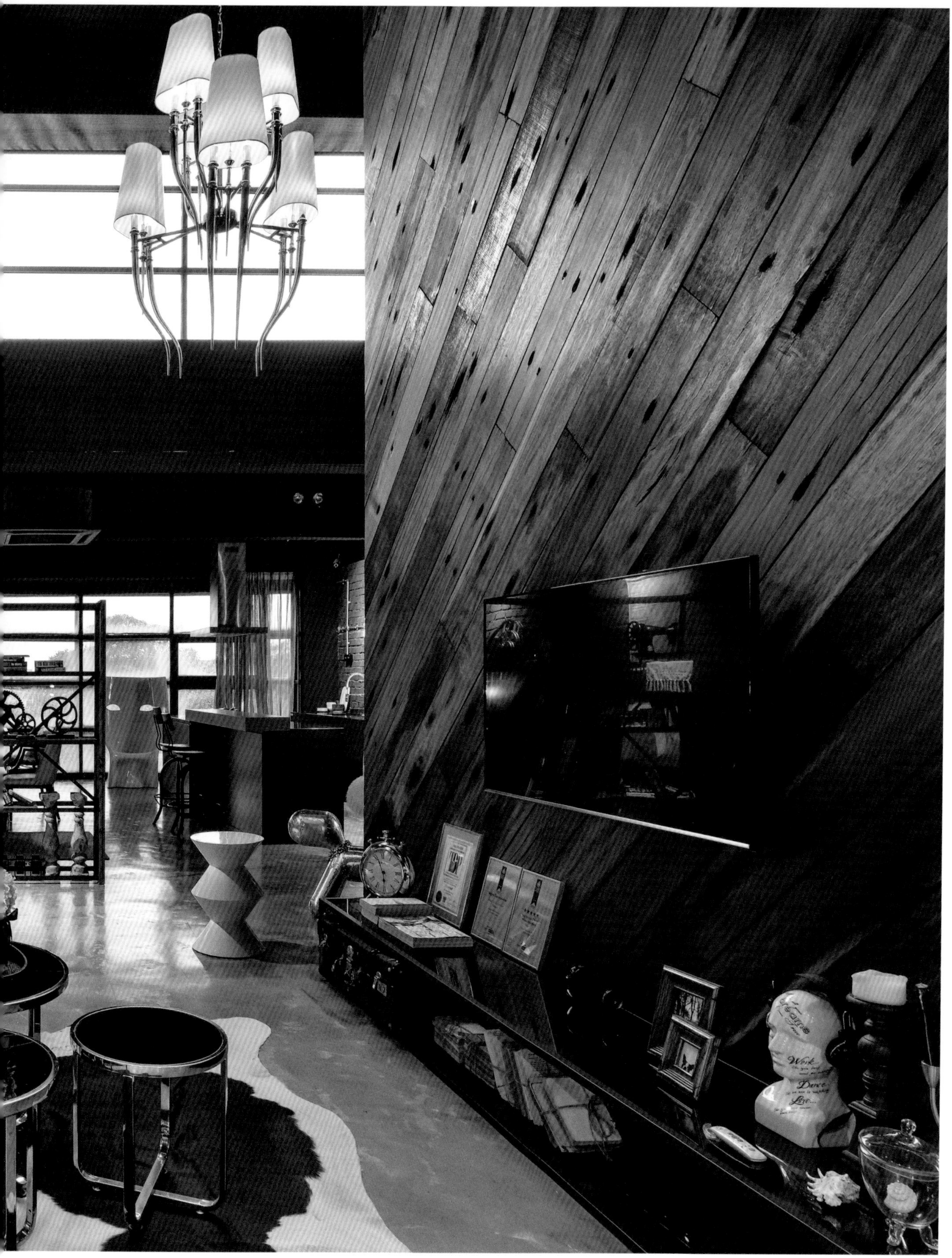

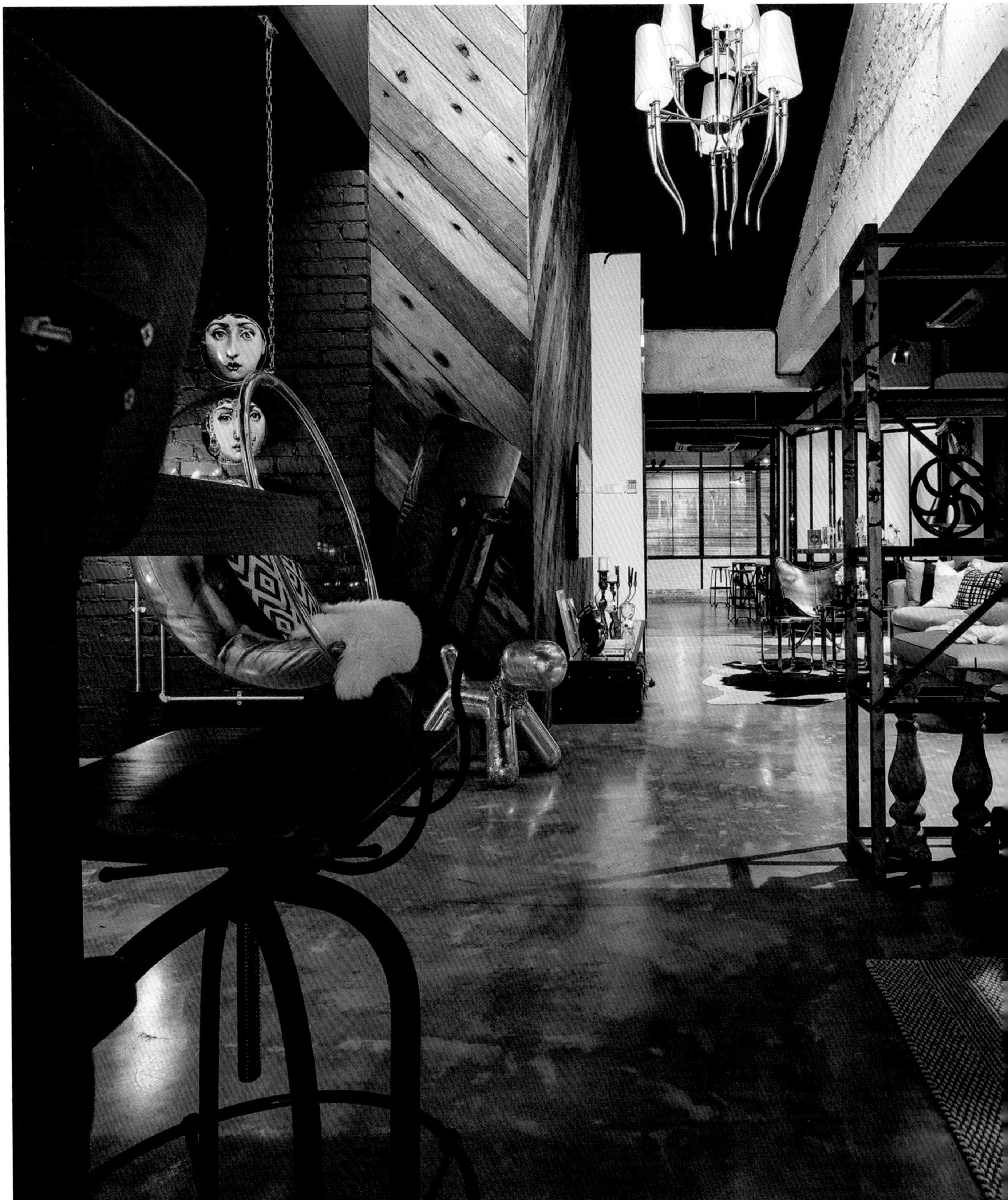

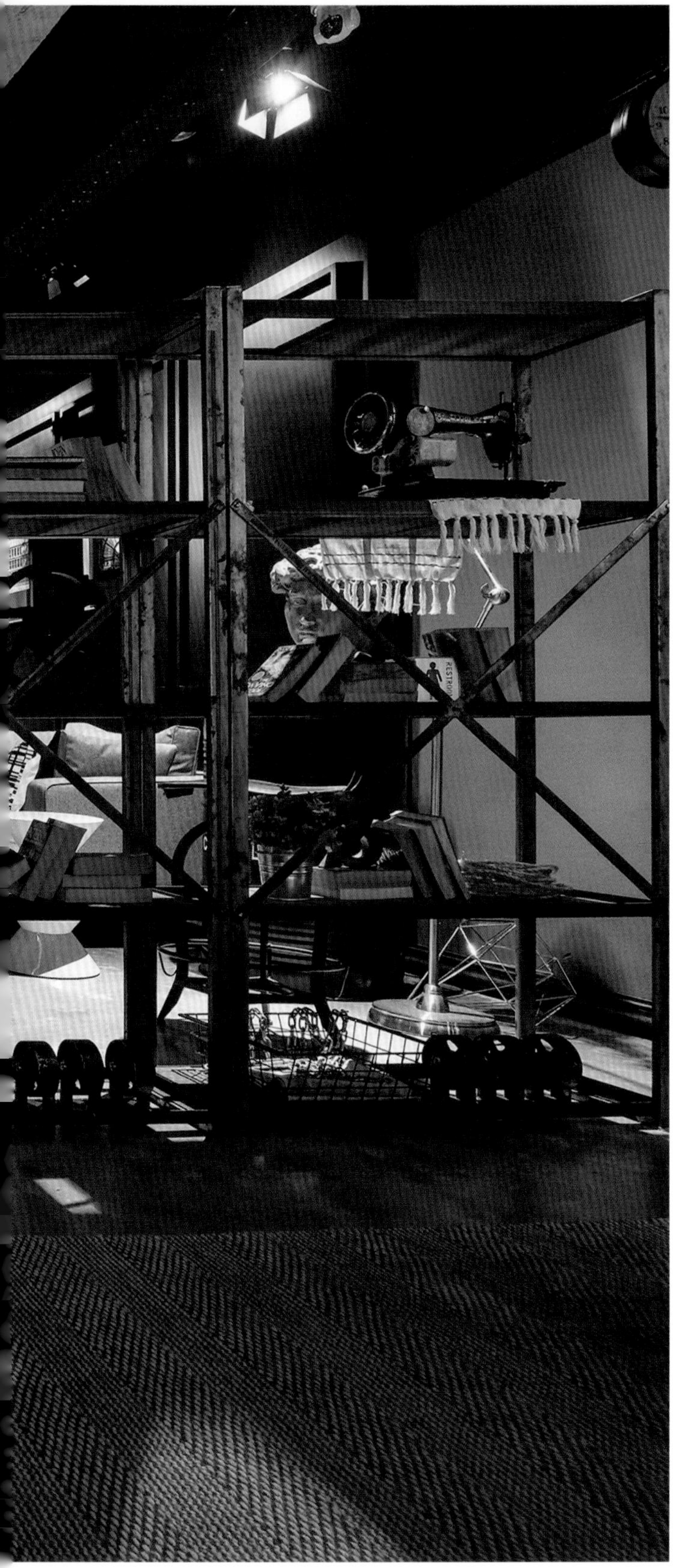

An open plan

The open design encourages the employees to communicate freely with each other. Practicality and cost-efficiency were a major focus in the design process, especially when it came to the open layout, where designers ensured that each space was illuminated with a healthy amount of natural light to reduce energy consumption. At the same time, low-maintenance structures and durable materials such as natural wood and concrete flooring, as well as exposed brick walls, were incorporated into the design; a practical choice for a commercial space while maintaining the authenticity of its design concept.

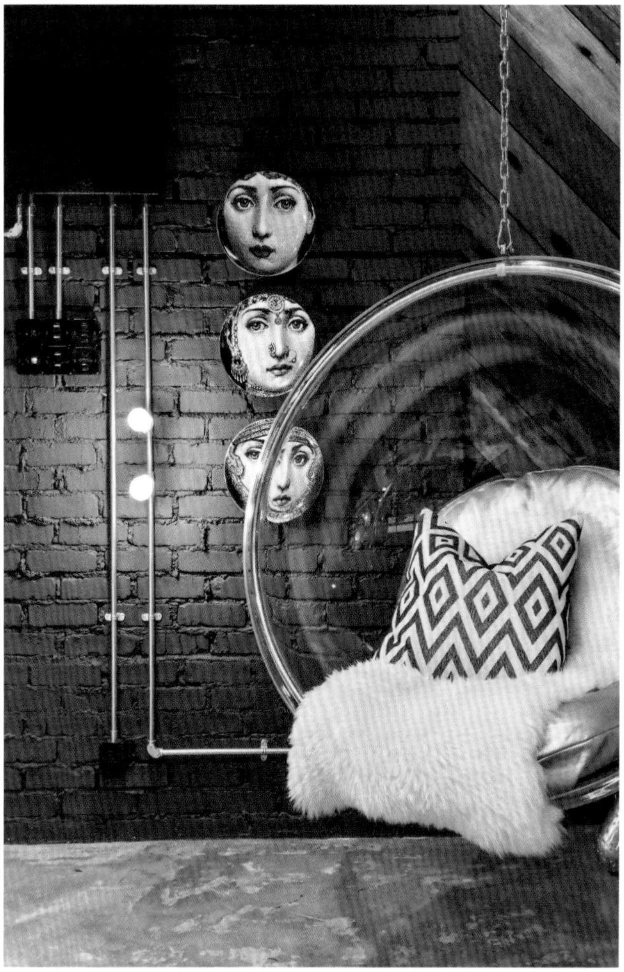

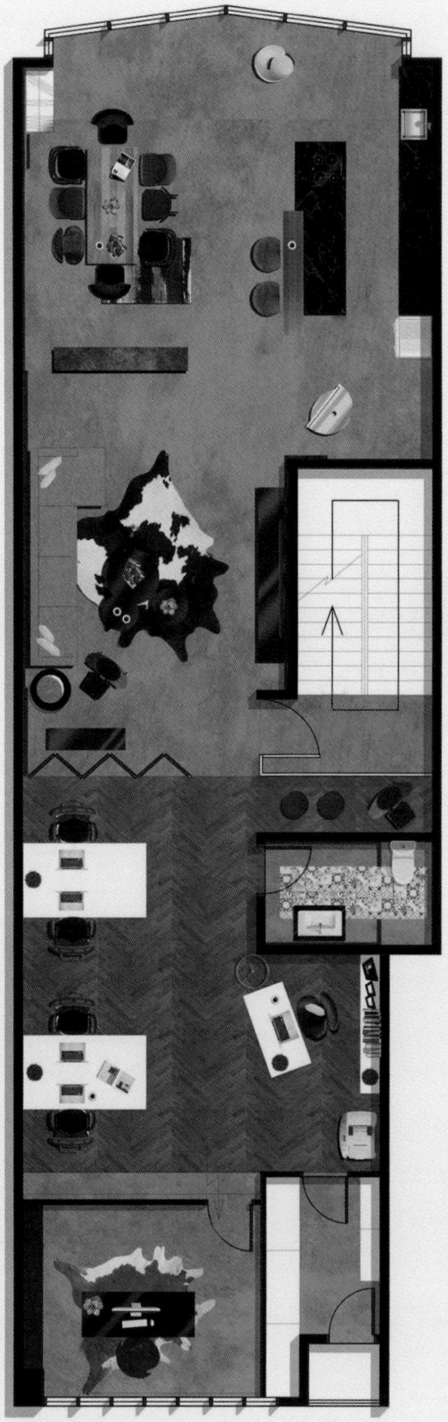

Floor plan

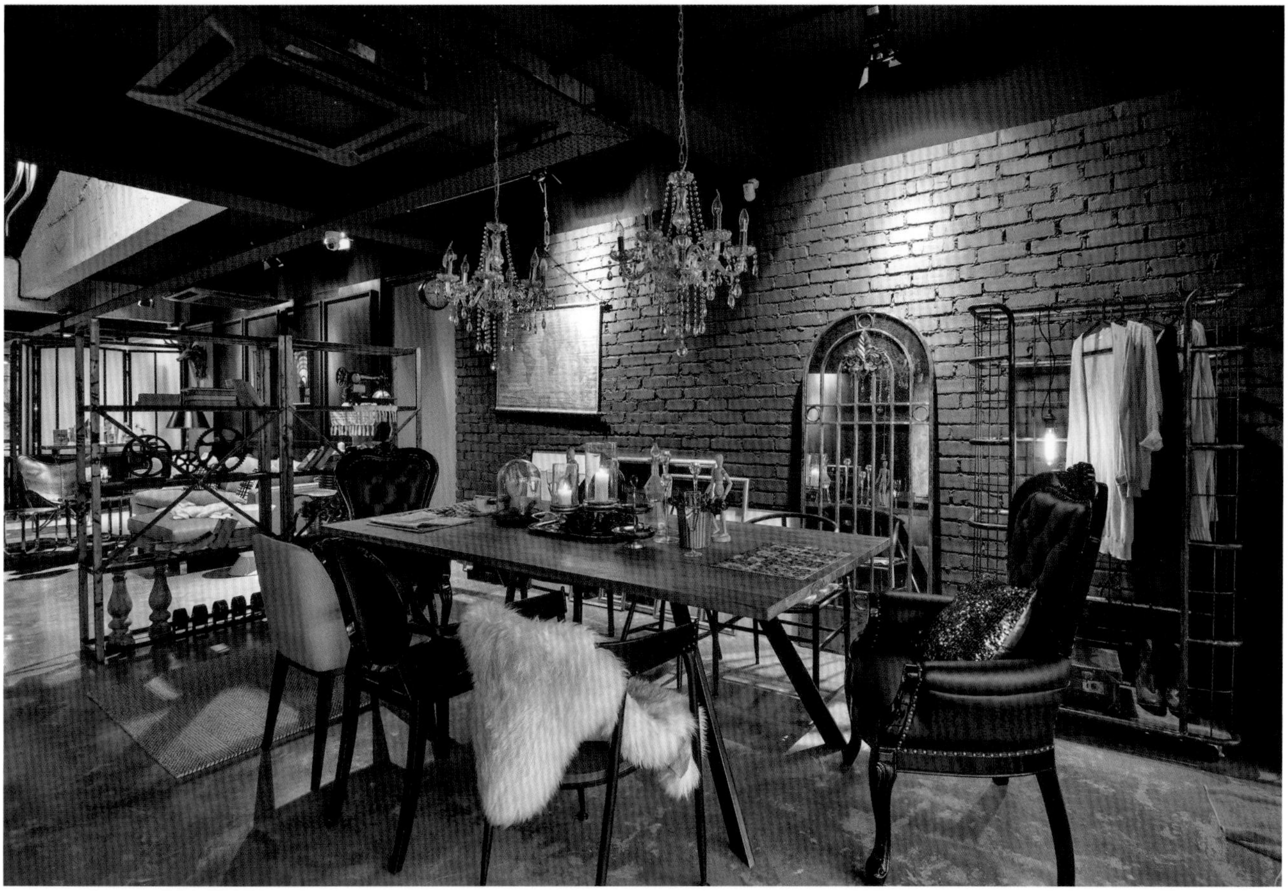

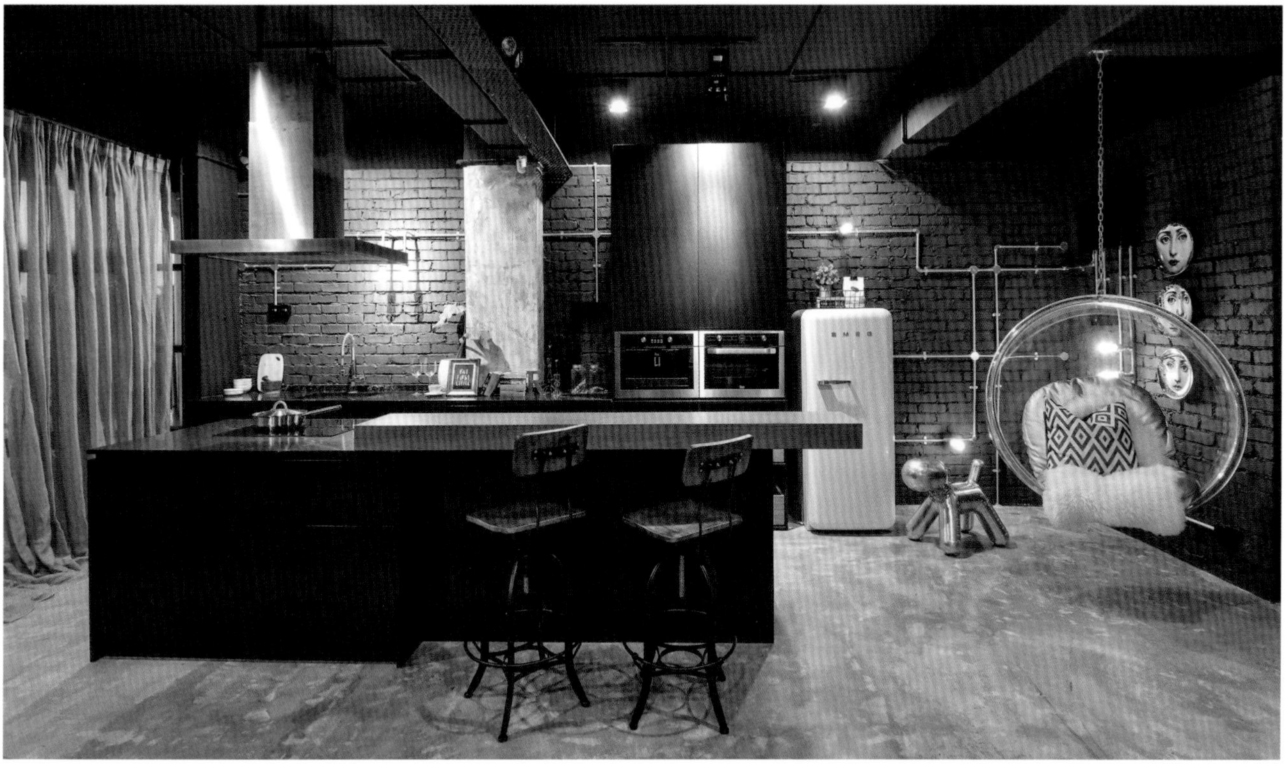

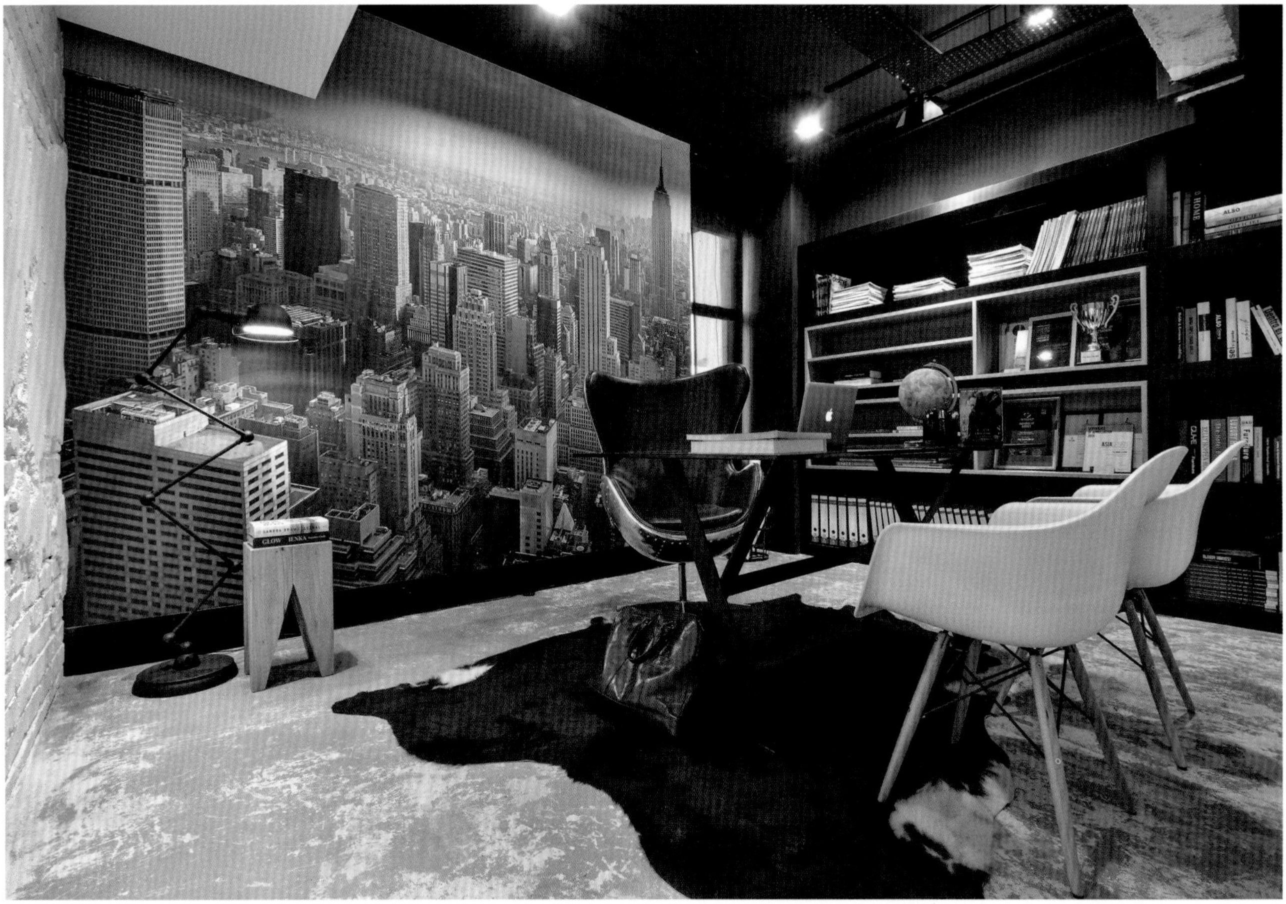

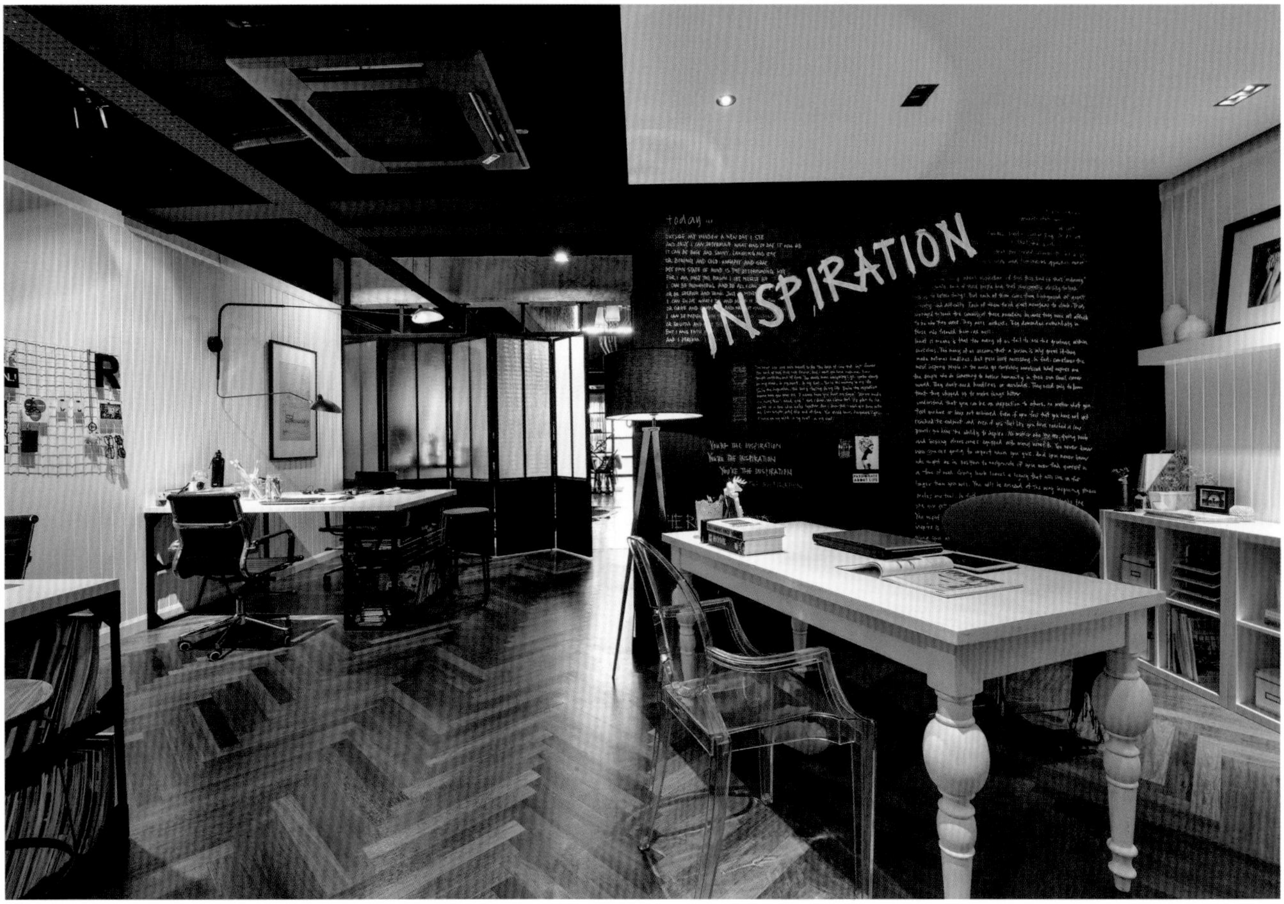
INSPIRATION

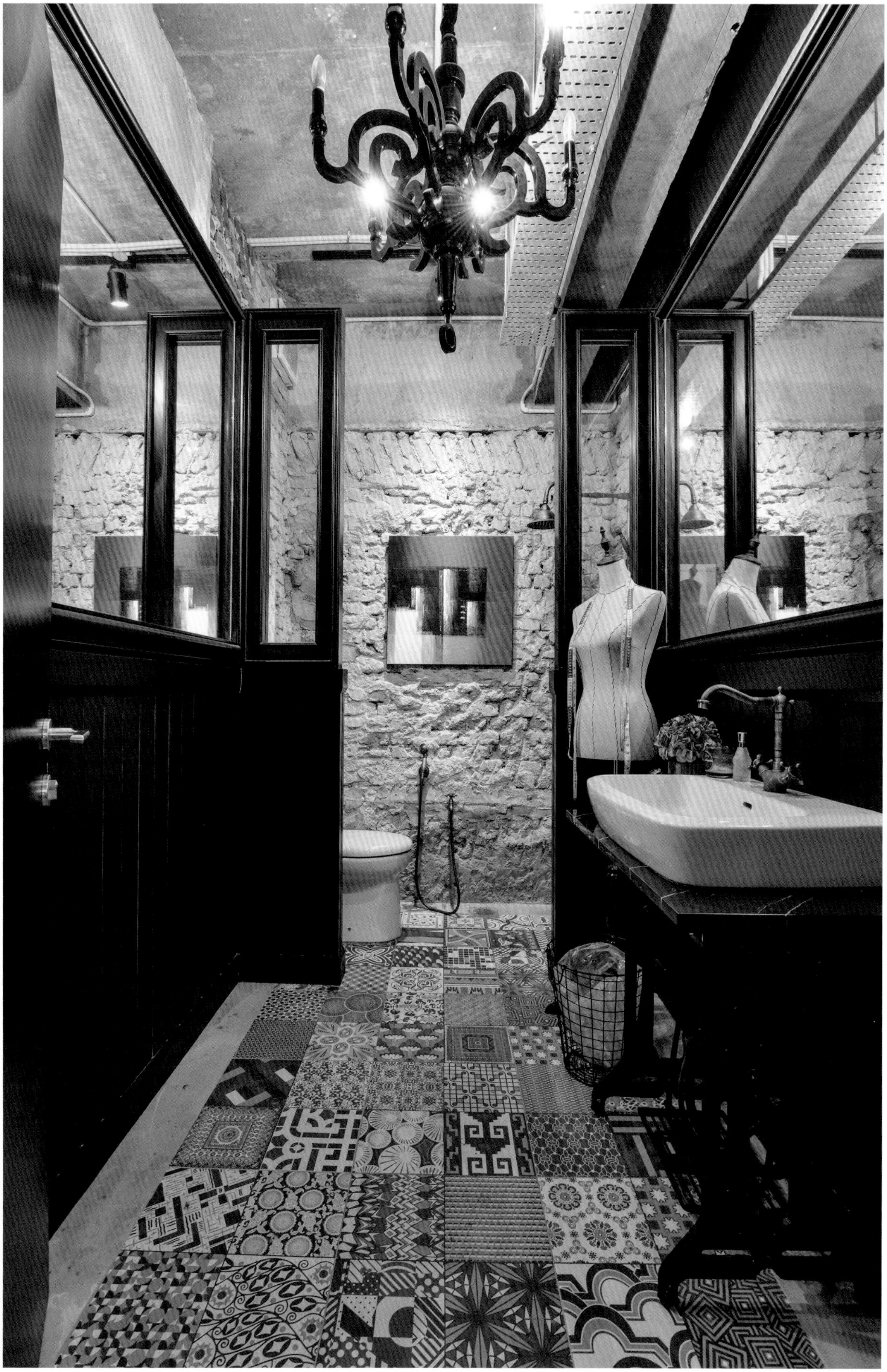

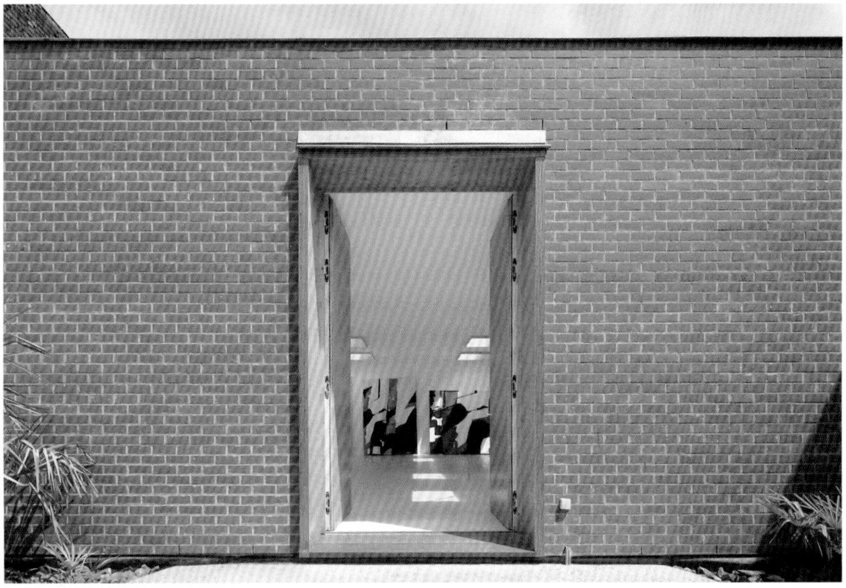

Area:
7,276 square feet (676 square meters)

Completion:
2013

Design:
Tijl Vanmeirhaeghe (Havana architectuur), Carl Bourgeois

Photography:
Filip Dujardin

Antwerp, Belgium

Studio Koen van den Broek

Belgian painter Koen van den Broek bought an old garage in the somewhat inhospitable neighborhood of Merksem along the canal on the east side of Antwerp. He had been receiving international recognition for his work but his paintings were becoming larger and he was fed up with painting in a small studio. He needed air, and space. In search for a literally distant view on his own work, he fell in love with the old garage with its long rectangular spaces and its perspectives.

An architectural road trip

Shortly after, and on the recommendation of his friend the art critic Wouter Davidts, he contacted young Ghent-based architect Tijl Vanmeirhaeghe. There was an immediate connection between their artistic instincts and interests. It was the beginning of a long and fruitful collaboration that ultimately resulted in the birth of the new studio.

The work of Koen van den Broek is based upon Polaroid pictures that document his travels throughout America. As a result, this project was conceived by the architect as a travel through different universes, an architectural road trip with various destinations. The architecture is directed as an endless play dominated by the restlessness of the artist, his everyday search for new inventions and experiences.

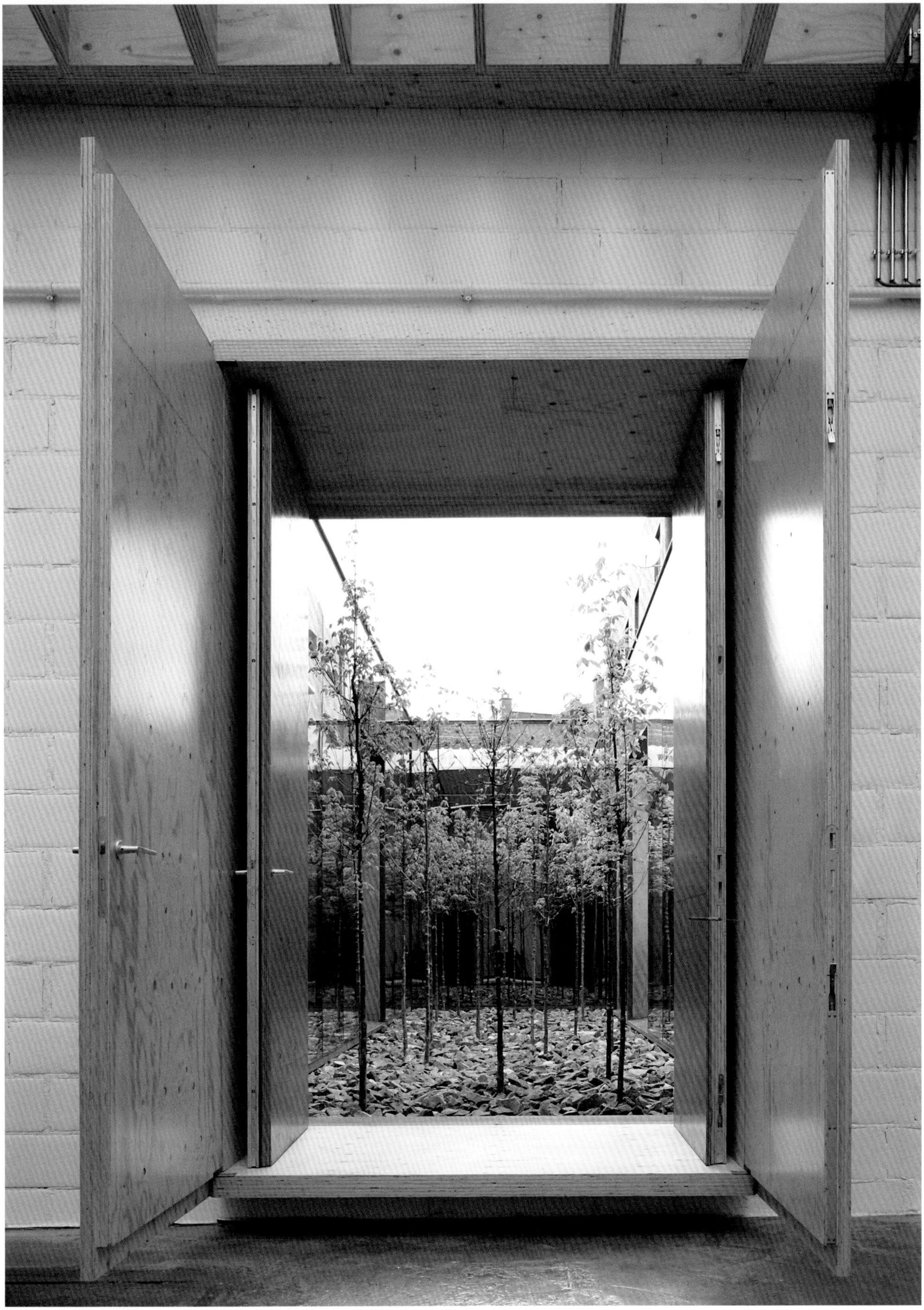

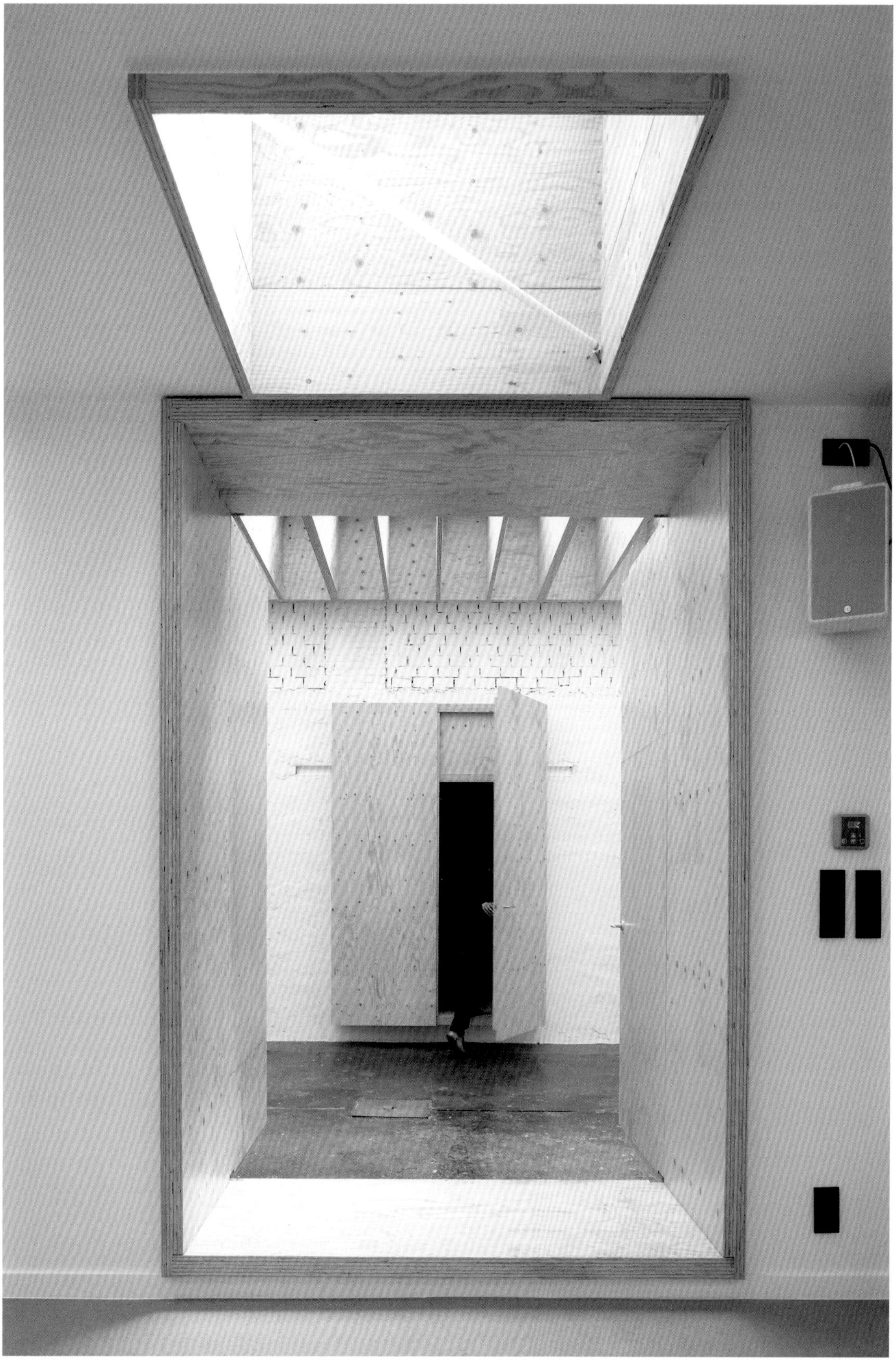

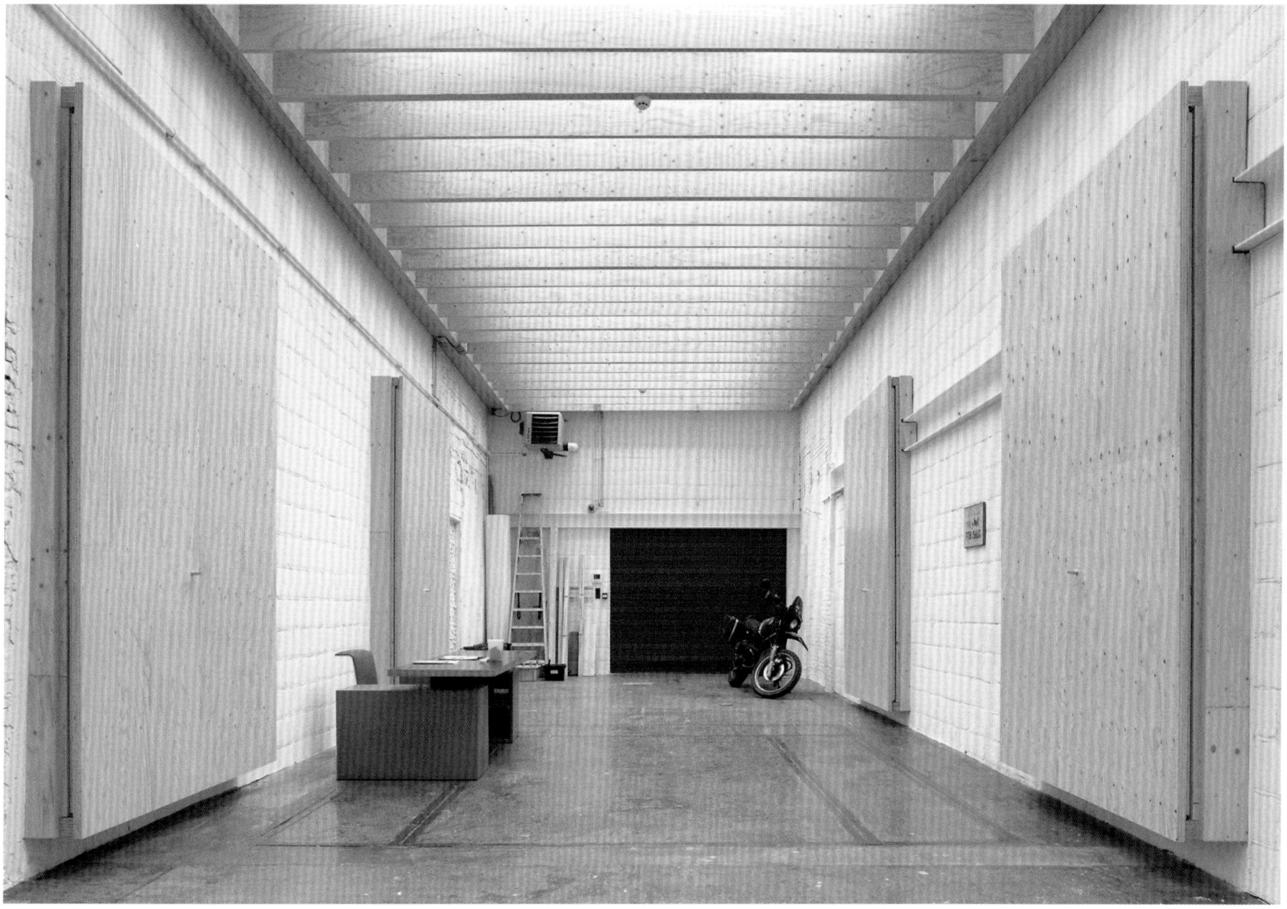

A studio, an exhibition space, and a dwelling

The garage had a single floor embedded in a mingled urban fabric of storages, houses, warehouses, and extensions of all kinds. It had a strong material identity, with its bricks and scars, its concrete pavement, and its blind gates at the street level. However, there was a lack of daylight as the garage had no proper façades.

At the core of the studio there is now a long and rectangular atelier where cars were once run in and out in order to change oil or parts. The space serves as the backbone of the project, with six double doors connecting it to six different spaces. A little rung between the floor level of the central space and the sill of the different doors strengthens the effect of transition when changing rooms. If the studio could be compared to a space station, the doors are its airlocks.

The first couple of doors on the left both serve a big storage space. The third door leads to the library, which is also a projection room. This space is cladded with birch-bark panels that were specially made by John Lindman, a birch-bark canoe builder living and working in Spokane, in the forests of the American east coast. As this room is not a space for drawing or painting, the architect decided to exclude every need for or possibility of hanging up things. The birch bark is wall, cladding, and painting on its own.

The left wing of the studio could not be illuminated naturally because of the upstairs roof terrace of the neighbor. However, the right wing had access to natural light, so all the working spaces are located in this part of the studio. Facing the doors to the library, there's the entrance to a square "white cube" of 32 by 32 feet where most of Koen's painting takes place. The room is also crucial for setups for different exhibitions, which can be tried out here.

The middle doors at the right of the central atelier lead to a drawing studio that can serve as an office space. It has a big north-oriented glass façade facing a patio. This patio has its own doors to the central space, but mostly functions as a gap between working spaces and a small pied-à-terre facing the street side. A small bathroom, kitchen, and bedroom constitute an essential dwelling, cut loose from the artist's studio.

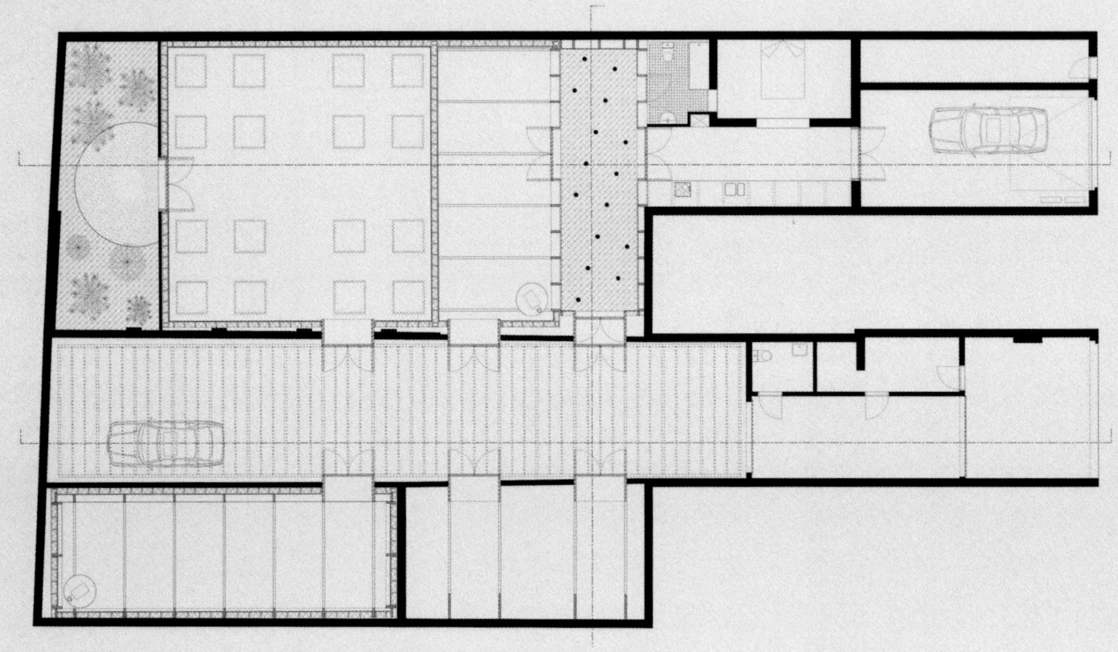

Floor plan

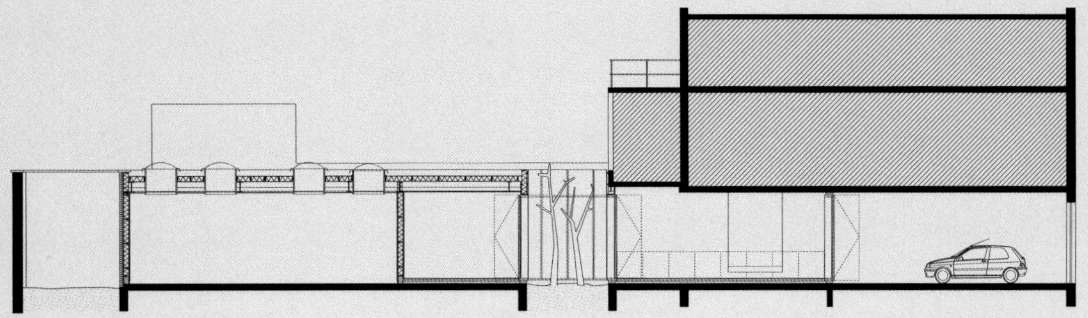

Section

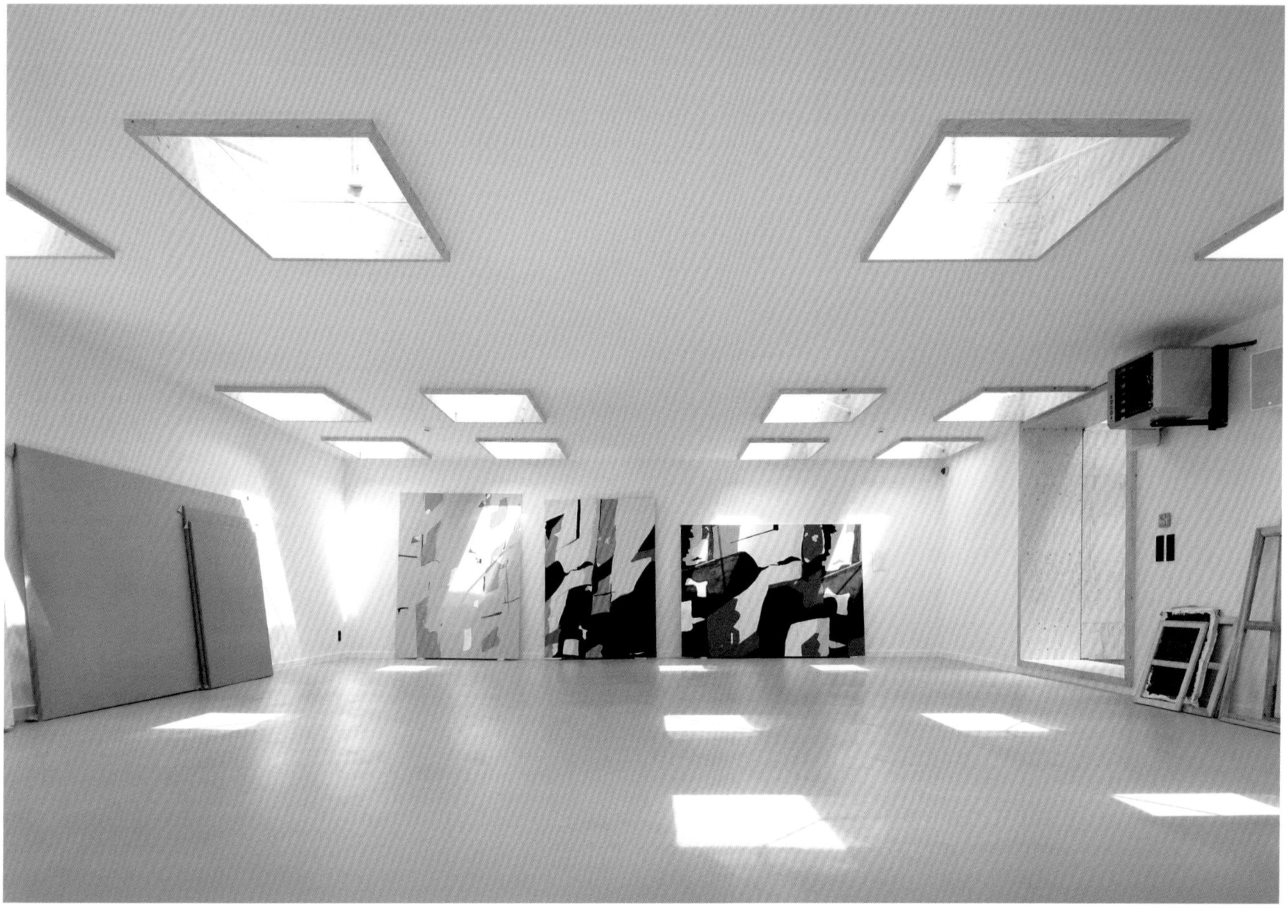

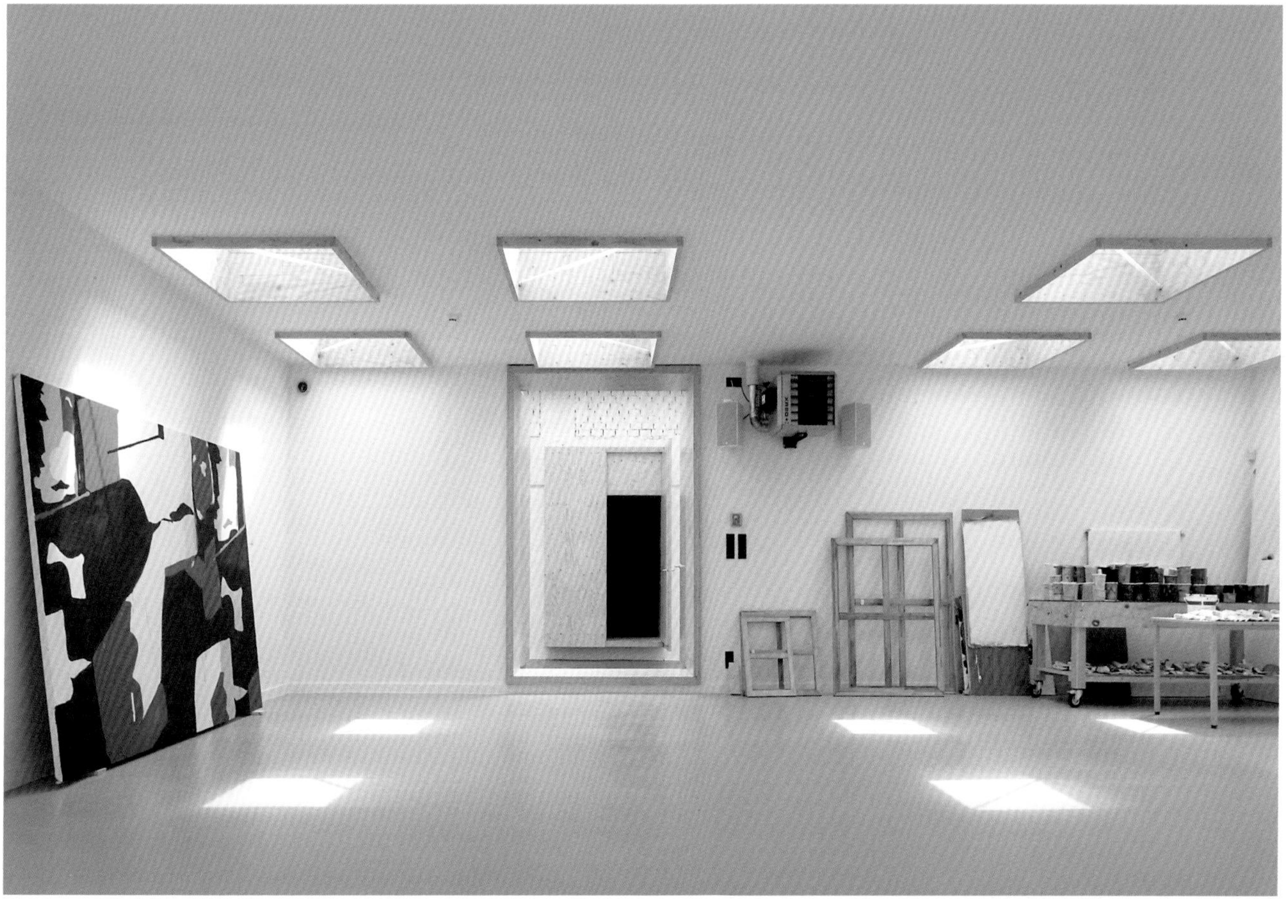

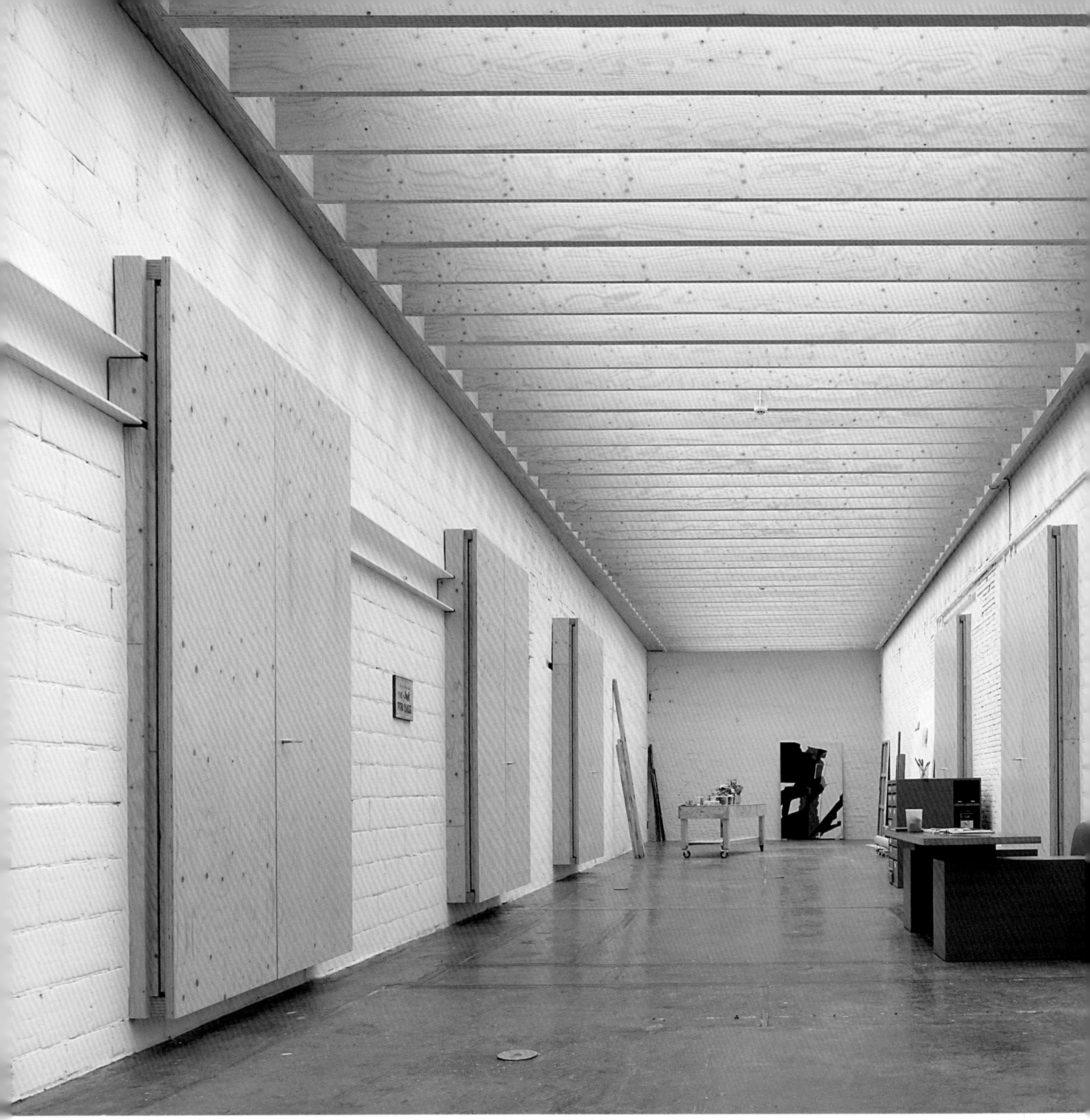

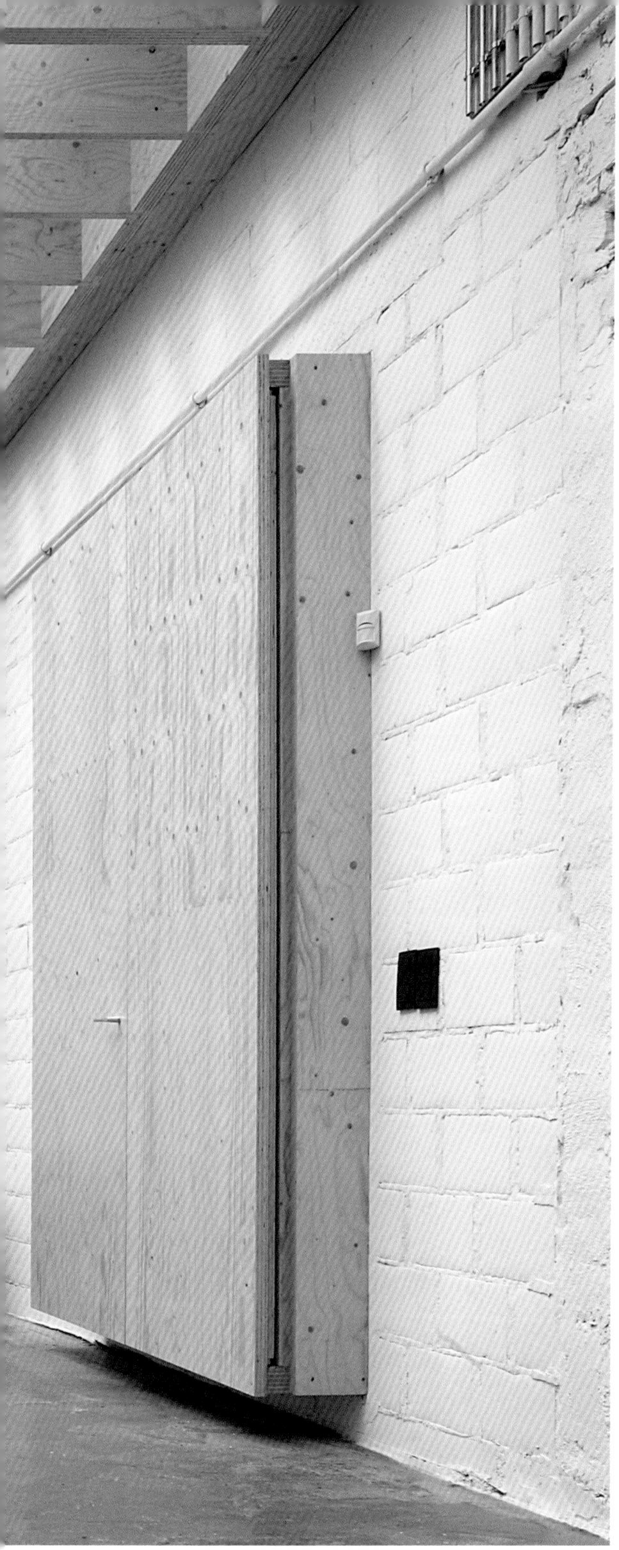

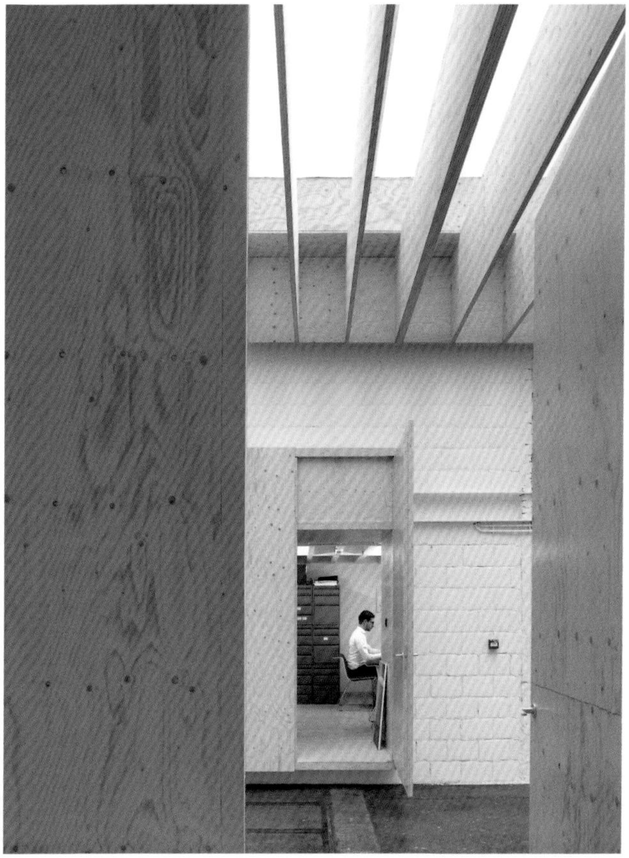

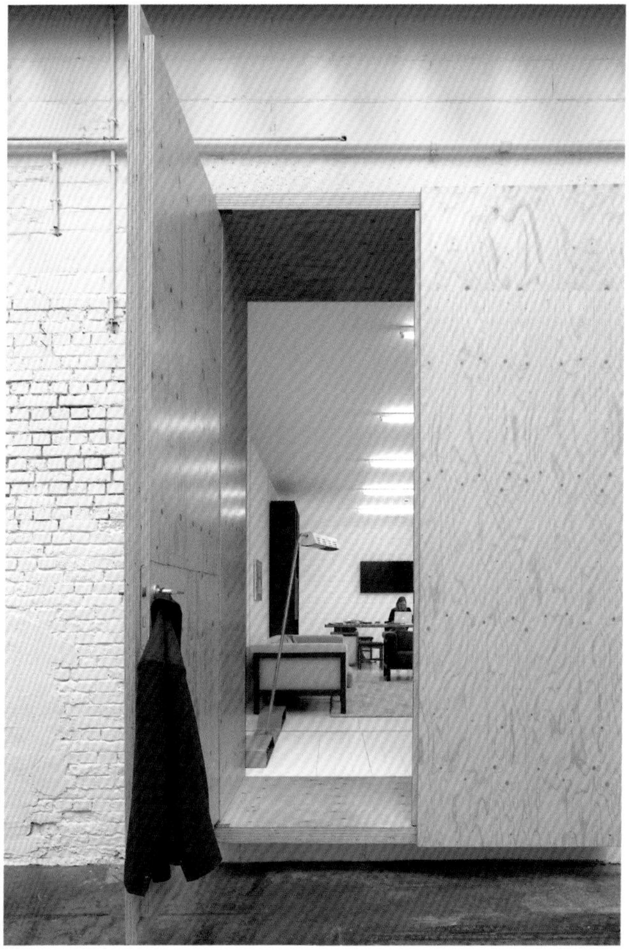

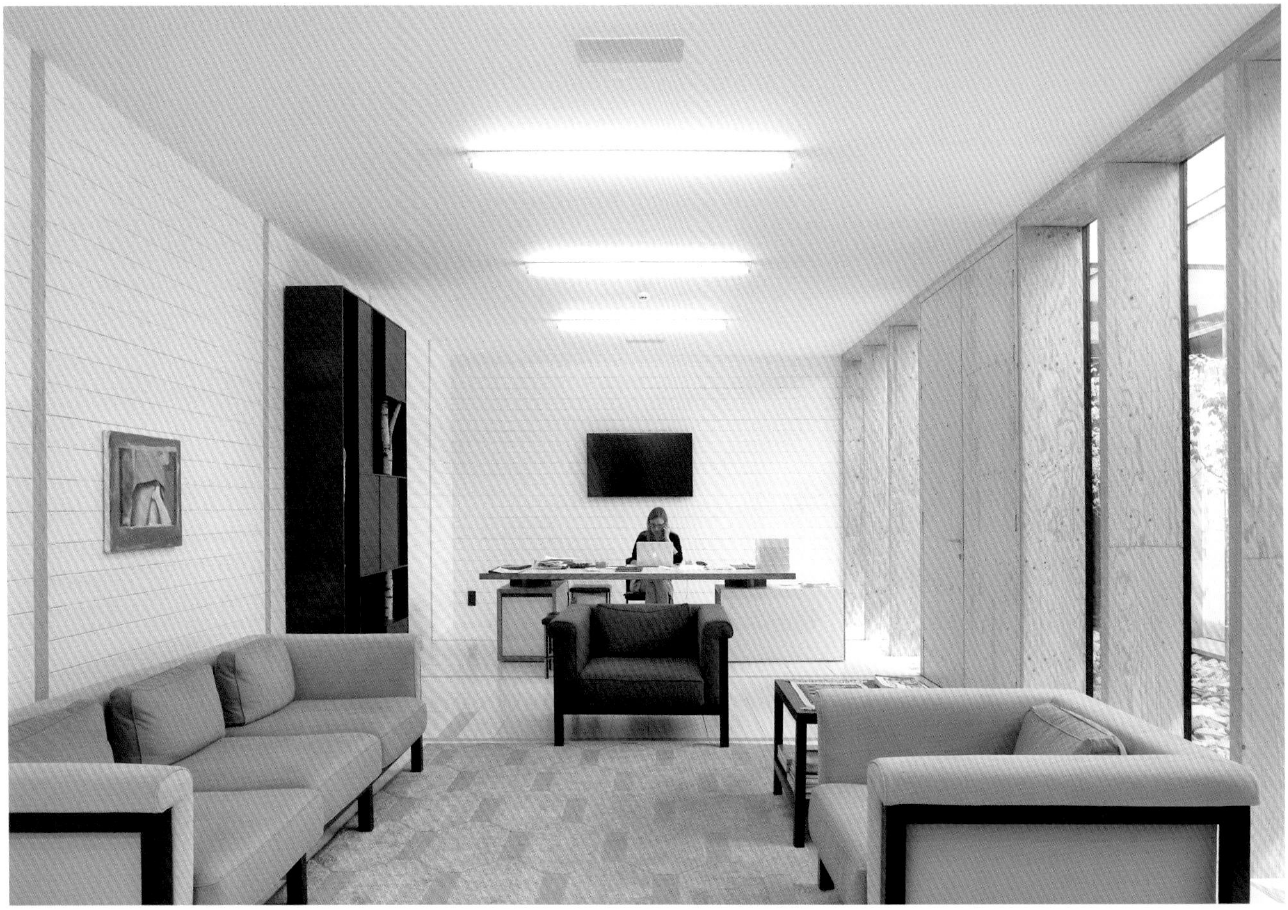

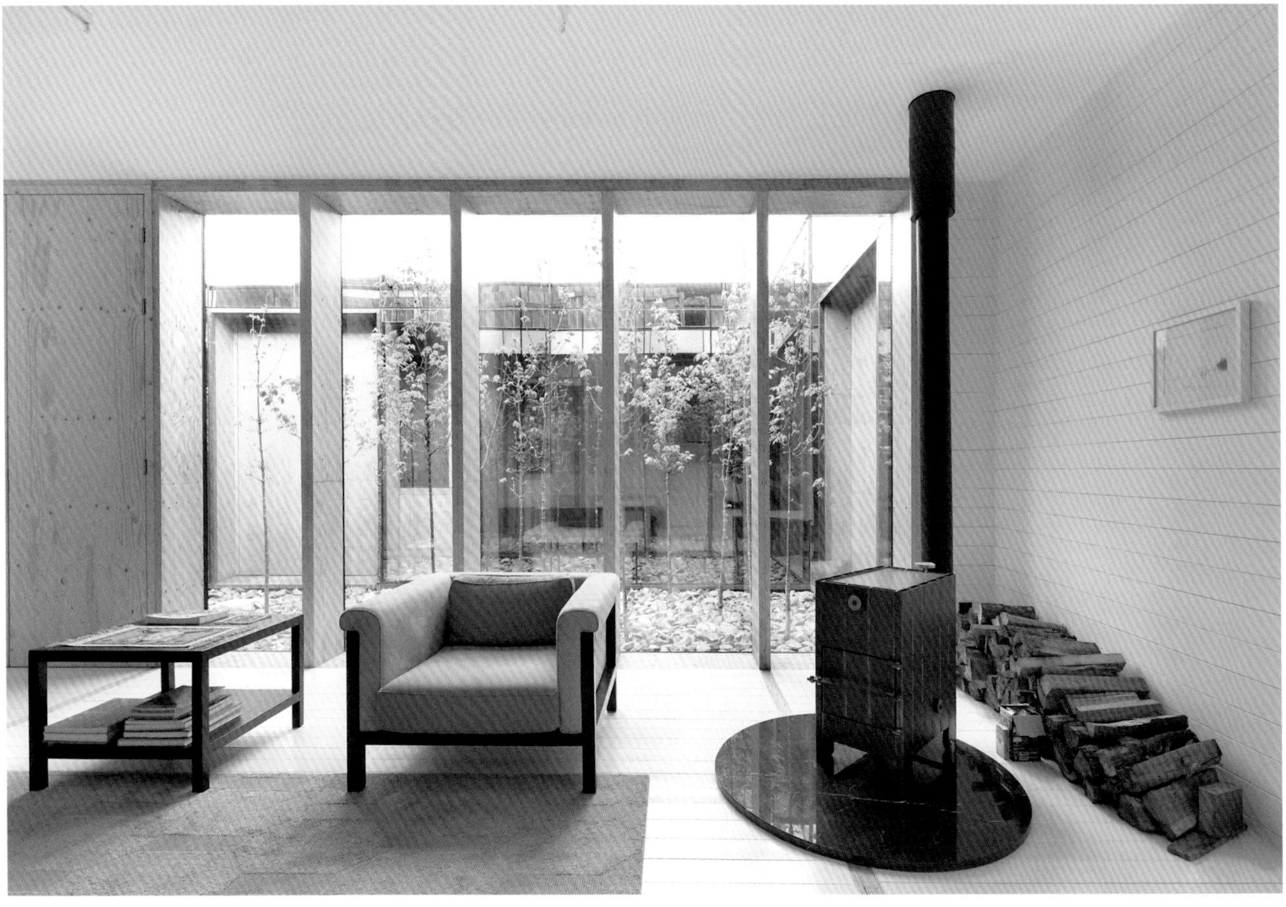

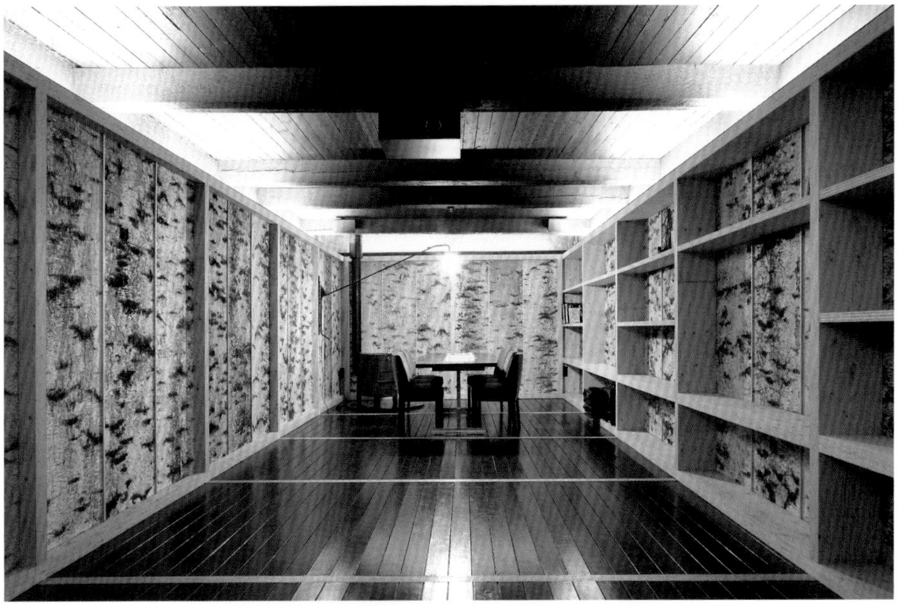

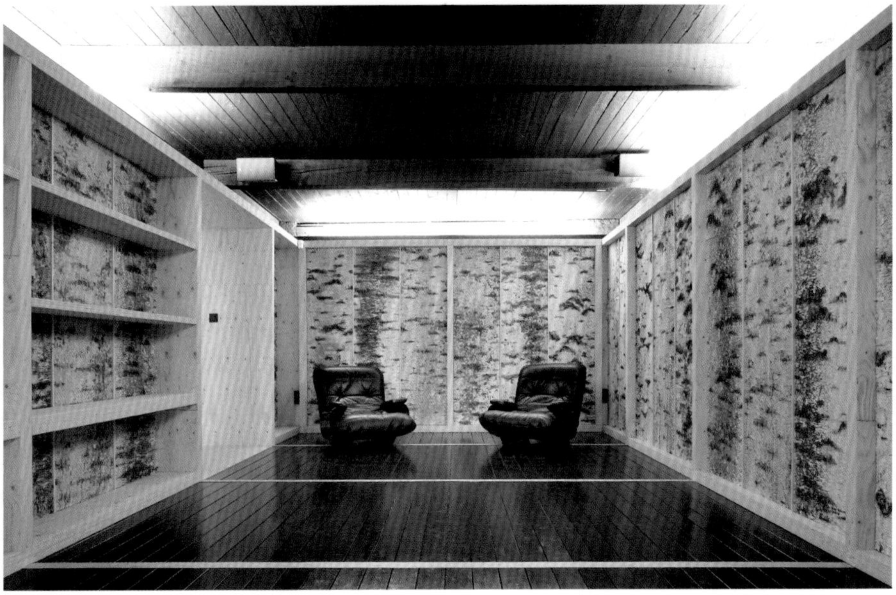

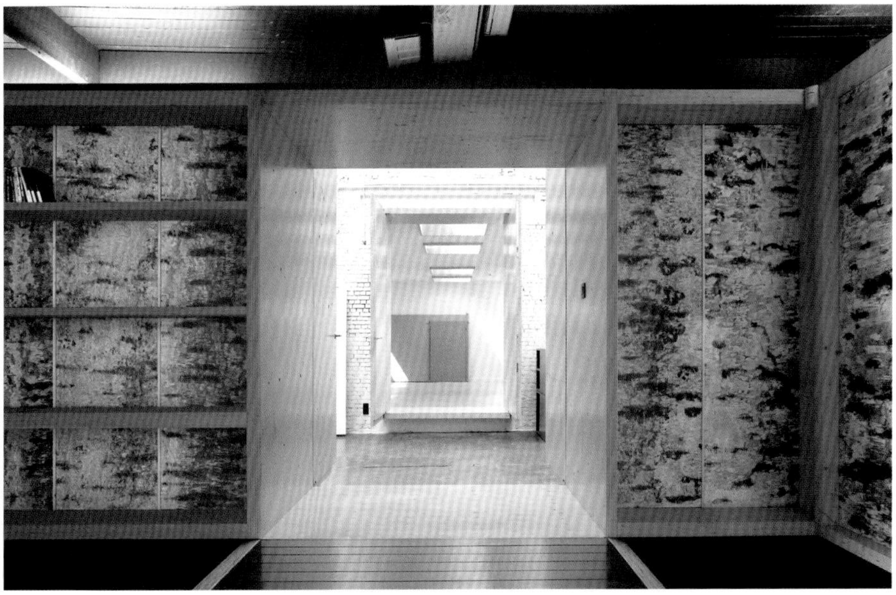

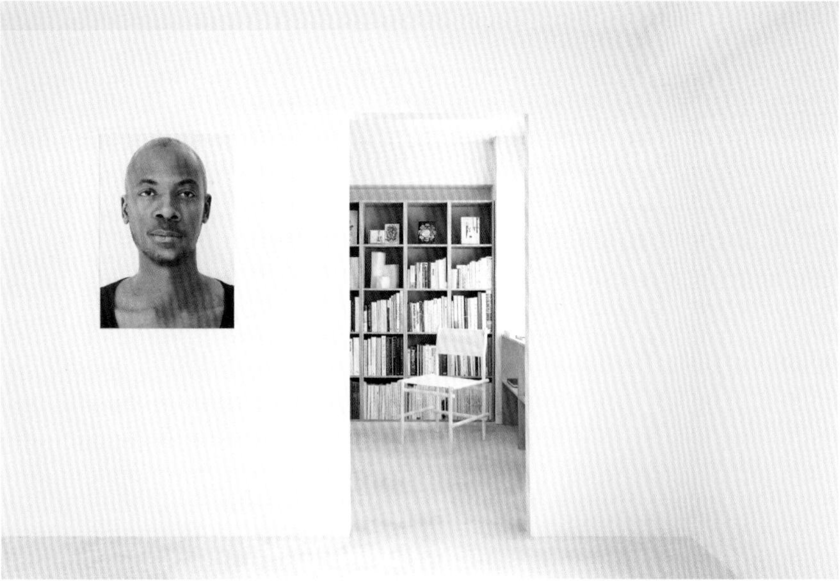

Area:
3,000 square feet (279 square meters)

Completion:
2017

Design:
Seiji Oguri (id inc.)

Photography:
shuntaro (bird and insect)

Tokyo, Japan

Kyodo Office

This creative office space was designed to be used by Japanese design office id inc. and photo and video company bird and insect. It consists of an office, library, workroom, conference room, and photo studio.

A blank sheet

As a place to create various new works, space was created that would function like a blank sheet, without a strong design concept. Walls, standing like drawing extension lines to the old building before its renovation, are used as partition spaces. The architectural structure has several openings that look continuous, making visitors feel a sense of depth.

In the office, there are no complete partitions; instead gently separated spaces let people smoothly move back and forth. A conference room is placed close to the entrance, with a long corridor moving back towards private offices and delineating the space between rooms open to the public and the private areas used only by those who work in the office.

A pure white space

The beauty of this office is that a total project, from product planning and production to final display, can be consistently made. The pure white space has a gallery-like atmosphere so that it also functions as a place for exhibition at any time.

The office furniture is minimalist, continuing the theme of simplicity. By making the space neutral, without any texture, it encourages people to focus on the works created at this office, not on the office itself. The combination of the white walls and mortar floor gives an unfinished impression, focusing the attention of visitors on the creativity born here.

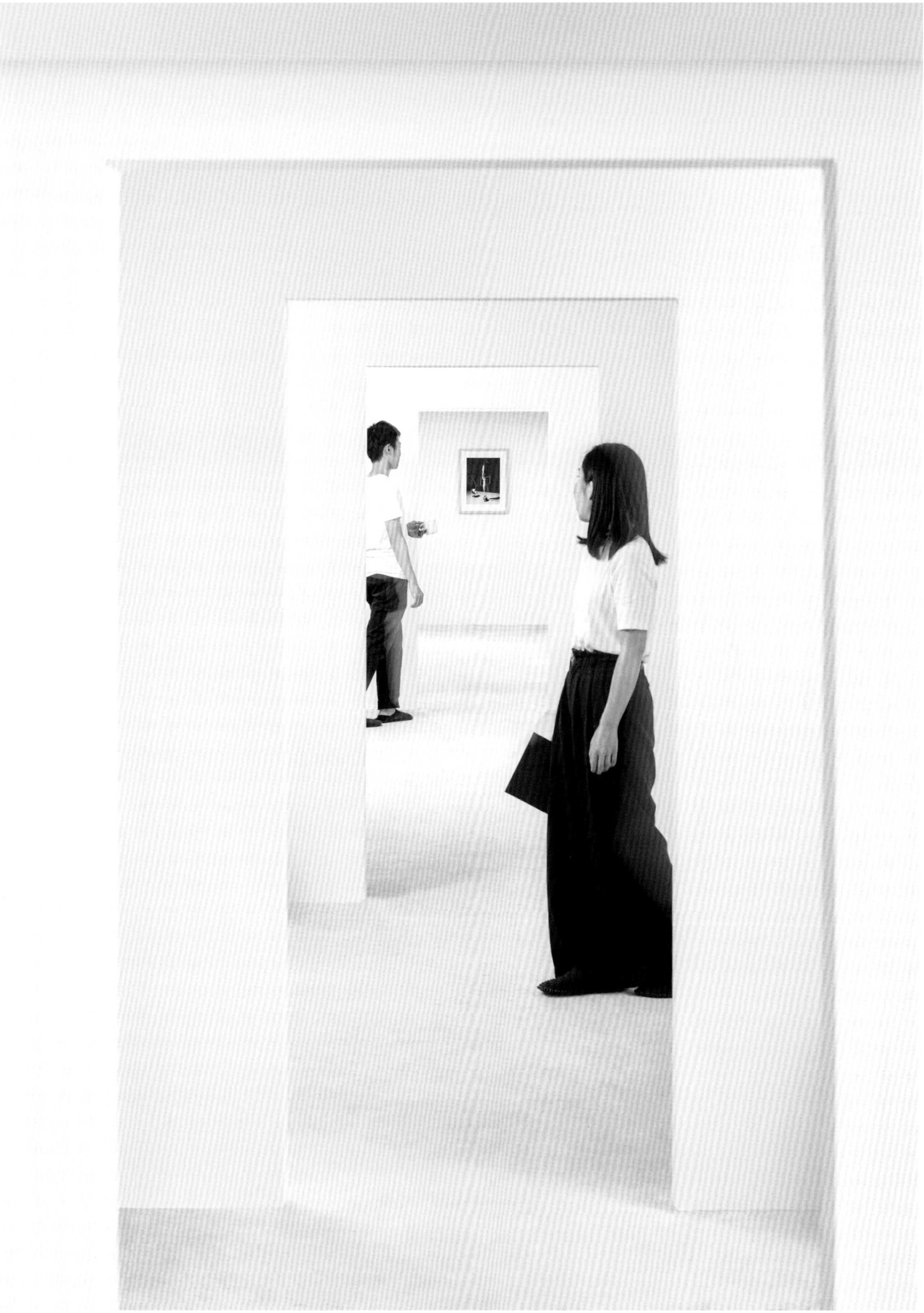

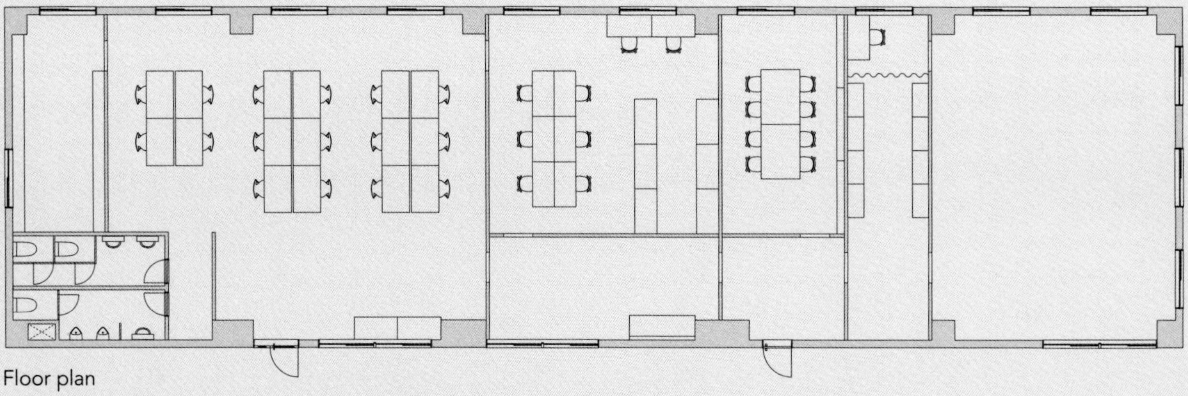
Floor plan

Section

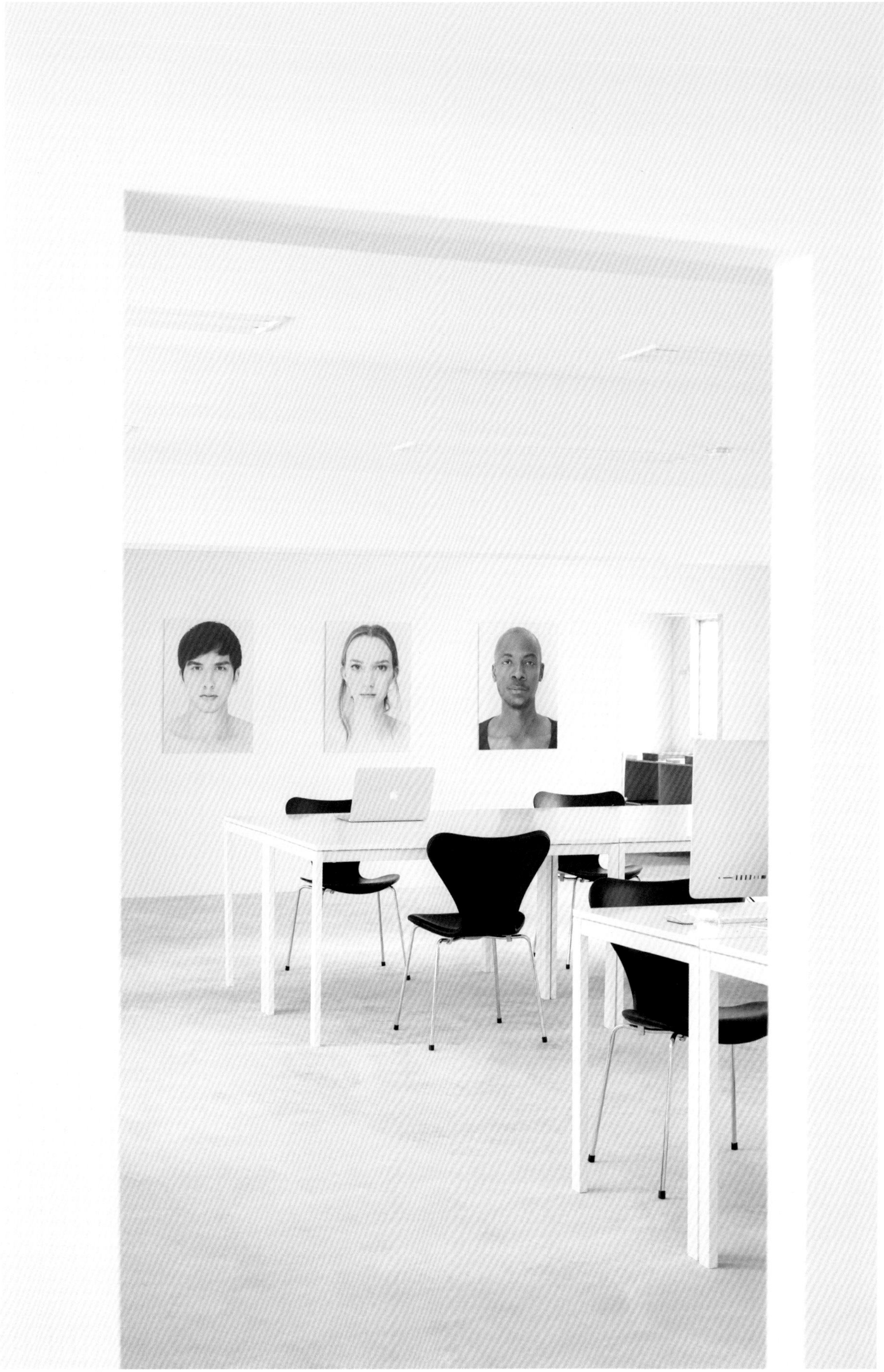

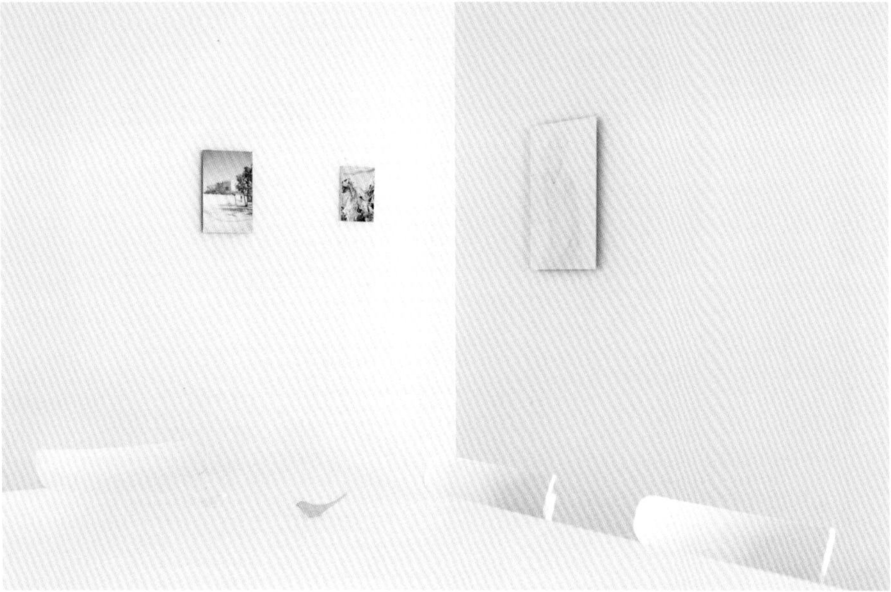

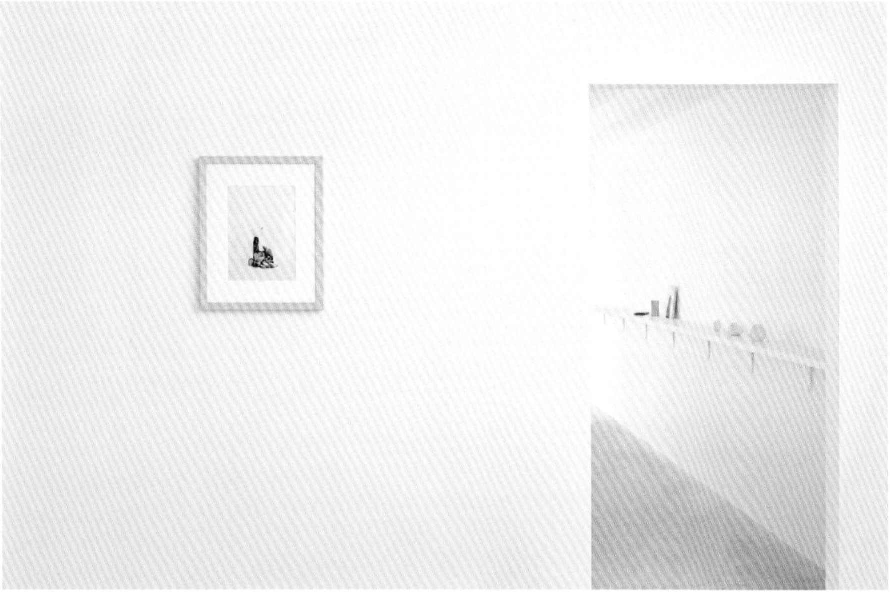

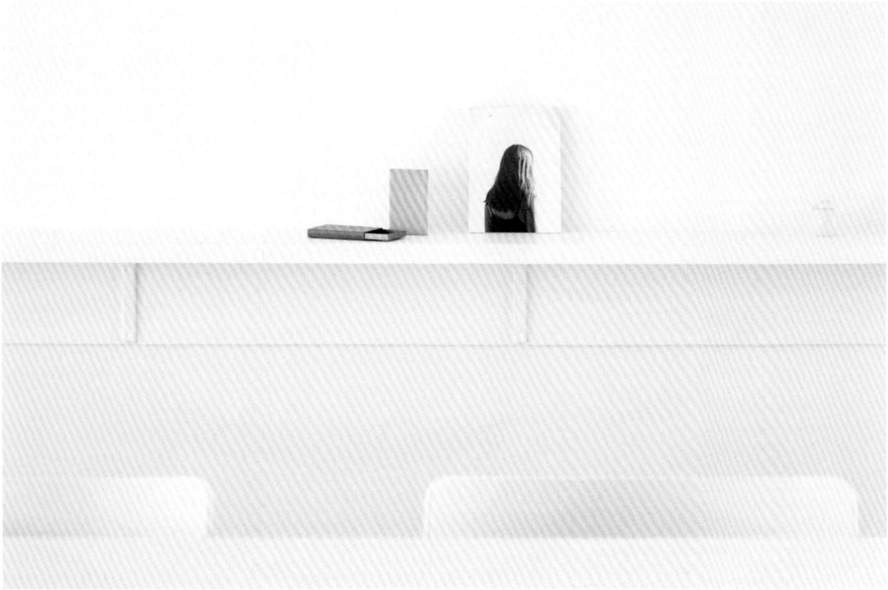

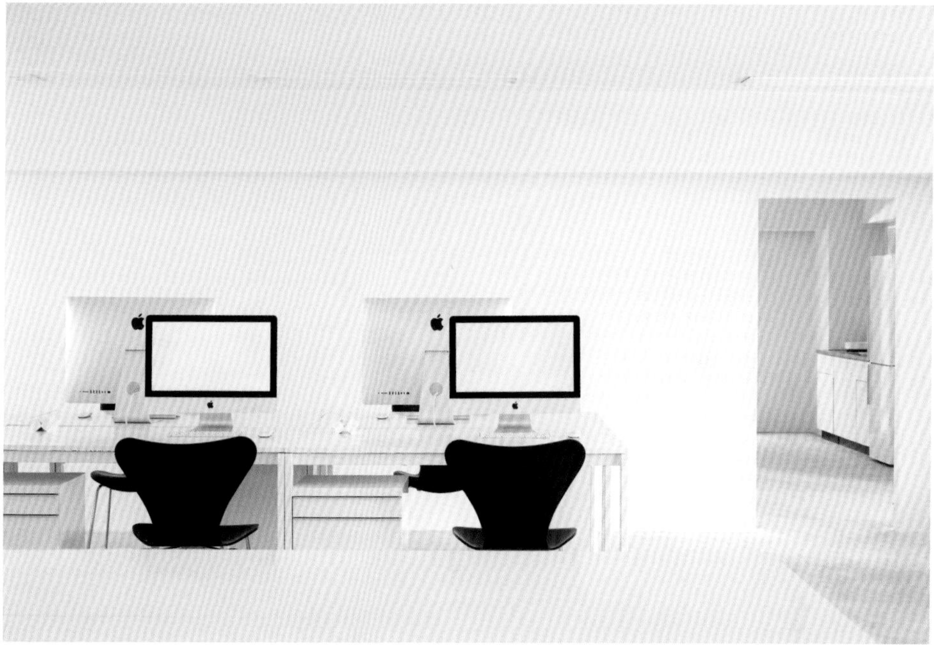

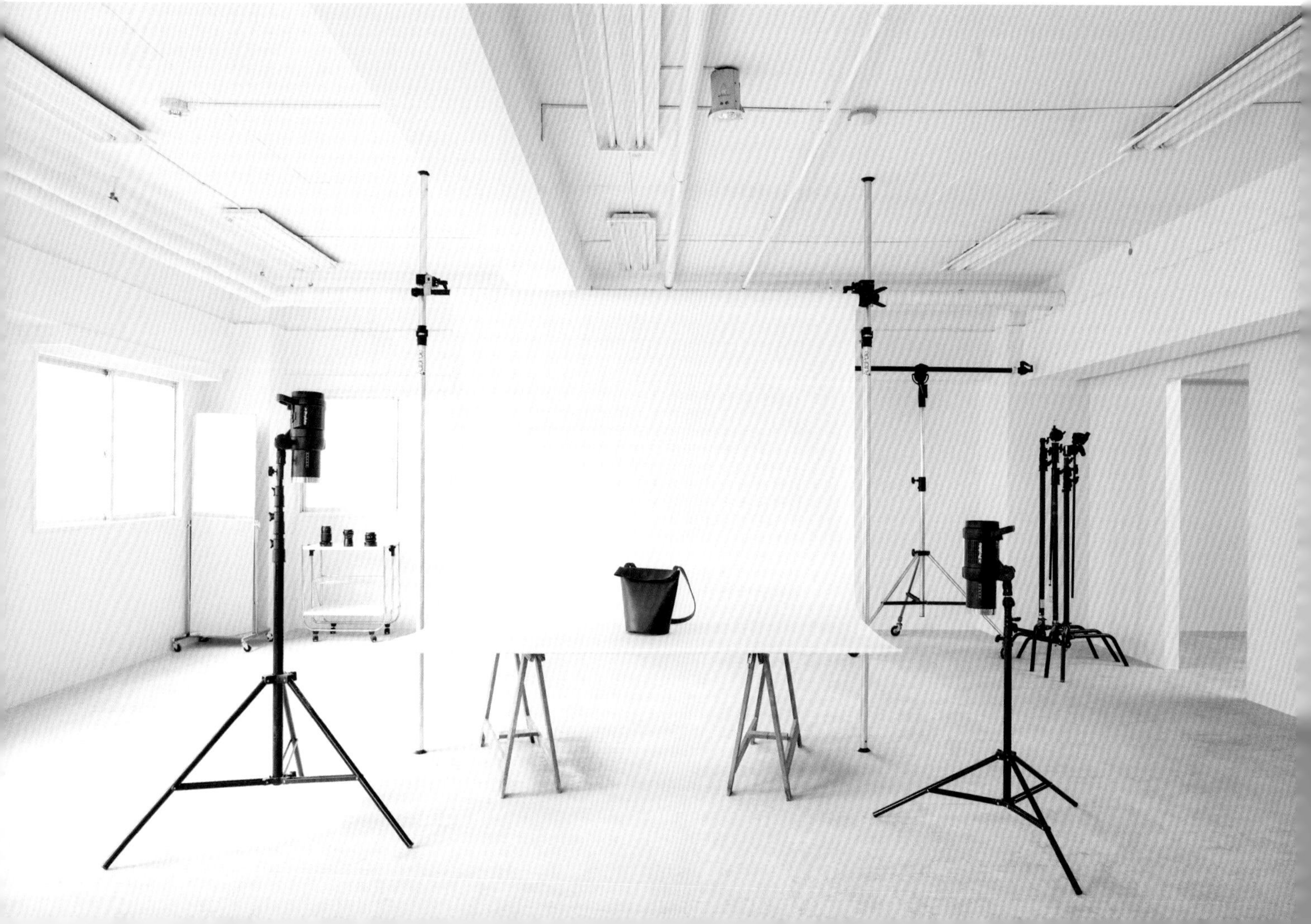

INDEX

Published in Australia in 2020 by
The Images Publishing Group Pty Ltd
ABN 89 059 734 431

Offices

Melbourne
6 Bastow Place
Mulgrave, Victoria 3170
Australia
Tel: +61 3 9561 5544

New York
6 West 18th Street 4B
New York, NY 10011
United States
Tel: +1 212 645 1111

Shanghai
6F, Building C, 838 Guangji Road
Hongkou District, Shanghai 200434
China
Tel: +86 021 31260822

books@imagespublishing.com
www.imagespublishing.com

The Images Publishing Group Reference Number: 1563

NATIONAL LIBRARY OF AUSTRALIA

A catalogue record for this book is available from the National Library of Australia

Title: Creative Spaces for Creative Ideas
Author: Pieter Graaff (Introduction)
ISBN: 9781864708233

Printed by Everbest Printing Investment Limited, in Hong Kong/China